CRIMINAL EVIDENCE IN CONTEXT

Second Edition

Jonathan Doak and Claire McGourlay

Routledge·Cavendish
Taylor & Francis Group
LONDON AND NEW YORK

First edition published by Law Matters Publishing

Second edition published 2009 by Routledge-Cavendish
2 Park Square, Milton Park, Abingdon, Oxon, OX14 4RN

Simultaneously published in the USA and Canada
by Routledge-Cavendish
270 Madison Ave, New York, NY 10016

*Routledge-Cavendish is an imprint of the Taylor & Francis Group,
an Informa business*

Typeset in Palatino by Keyword Group Ltd
Printed and bound in Great Britain by TJ International Ltd., Padstow, Cornwall

British Library Cataloguing-in-Publication Data
A catalogue record for this book is available from the British Library

Library of Congress Cataloging in Publication Data
Doak, Jonathan.
Criminal evidence in context / Jonathan Doak and Claire McGourlay.
p. cm.
1. Evidence, Criminal–Great Britain. I. McGourlay, Claire. II. Title.
KD8371.D63   2008
345.42′06–dc22
2008010023

ISBN 13: 978-0-415-45849-8 (pbk)
ISBN 10: 0-415-45849-8 (pbk)

CONTENTS

PREFACE

This is the second edition of *Criminal Evidence in Context*, which has been considerably expanded and updated since the publication of the previous edition in 2005. The title has now been transferred to Routledge-Cavendish, and we have included three new chapters and undertaken a major re-write of most of the previous chapters. In doing so, we hope we have devised a textbook that students will find accessible and stimulating. As opposed to taking a broad doctrinal sweep of the law of evidence, we have sought to concentrate on those topics that tend to feature commonly on Evidence courses, and in doing so, to take a contextual approach in an effort to rouse the interests of students. Unfortunately, the law of evidence does not readily lend itself to the integration of a contextual perspective, but we have tried, where possible, to discuss how wider policy debates and societal trends have impacted upon the recent evolution of the law.

We have also sought, where relevant, to explore the gap between the 'law of the books' and 'law in practice', which rarely sit together in precise harmony. To this end, we have emphasised the practical significance of evidential rules through integrating examples and fictional case scenarios as the law is explained. We have also endeavoured to integrate examples of the law in action from outside the law reports, and thus draw upon press and media reports, as well as consonant socio-legal and empirical studies. We have also improved the pedagogical value of the book through the addition of 'Key Learning Points' and practice questions at the end of each chapter. Legal updates and further comments will be made available on a regular basis on the Routledge-Cavendish companion website.

Since the publication of the previous edition, we are steadily gaining a clearer insight into how the Criminal Justice Act 2003 is operating in practice. The legislation, which swept aside much of the previous law relating to hearsay, bad character, rules on refreshing memory and those concerning previous consistent and inconsistent statements, is relatively novel in form and has provided the courts with a *tabula rasa* on which to develop an entirely new body of jurisprudence. Only now are we beginning to see the first signs of judicial attitudes towards these changes. Key decisions considered in the text include those of *R v Renda*; *R v Weir and others*; and *R v Campbell* (regarding character evidence); *Maher v DPP*; *R v Singh*; and *R v Xhabri* (regarding hearsay). In other areas, that have been relatively untouched by the 2003 legislation, the appellate courts have delivered significant decisions in *R v Davies* (anonymity); *R v Soroya* (sexual history evidence); *R v Hayter* (confessions) and *R v Keogh* (burden of proof).

It was always going to be unlikely, however, that the Act would change the essential character of the law of evidence as a disparate and unwieldy set of rules, which are not built around any single set of values or rationales. These rules continue to be developed on a largely disordered and haphazard manner, and it is not surprising that students studying the law of criminal evidence often find it difficult to identify any sense of coherency within the subject. In writing this book, we have sought to produce a clear and accessible text, through presenting the relevant law in a comprehensive and systematic way. As such, it is hoped that the book will be of interest not only to law students, including those taking the Legal Practice Course or Bar Vocational Course, but also to non-lawyers who would like to gain some understanding of the evidential rules that operate in the criminal trial.

On a final note, we wish to express our sincere gratitude to Fiona Kinnear and Kate Murphy at Routledge-Cavendish for overseeing the preparation and production of this text. We also thank Ken Lidstone, who provided us with a wealth of material which he gathered over some 30 years in the Department of Law at the University of Sheffield.

Andre Richer and Tony Whittle of QA Law provided useful comments on draft chapters, and Kris Green, Liz Moffat, Abigail Pearce-Dyke and Adam Smith – all students at the University of Sheffield – gave invaluable feedback on the first edition. We are grateful too for the support and advice of all our family and friends. As authors, we accept full responsibility for any errors or omissions in the text. We have attempted to state the law as it stood on 31 January 2008.

Dr Jonathan Doak
Nottingham Law School
Nottingham Trent University

Dr Claire McGourlay
School of Law
University of Sheffield
February 2008

TABLE OF CASES

TABLE OF INTERNATIONAL INSTRUMENTS, STATUTES AND LEGISLATION

CHAPTER 1

KEY CONCEPTS

INTRODUCTION

All material which is produced at court is subject to regulation by the laws of evidence. Decisions on the application of these rules are taken by the trial judge, and will often be concerned with whether or not the evidence should be admitted. The law of evidence is adjectival rather than substantive law. The substantive law is the criminal law – murder, manslaughter, theft, burglary, rape, violence to the person and other crimes – that defines the conduct and mental element that is required for the particular crime. The law of criminal evidence is the law that governs how these criminal offences are to be proved in court.

It should be underlined, however, that the adjectival law is not an entirely separate entity from the substantive law. Often, there will be some degree of overlap between the two. For example, in a murder case the jury have to decide whether the defendant intended to kill or to cause really serious bodily harm. The trial judge will direct them that there has to be a 'virtual certainty of death' and that the defendant(s) had to have an 'appreciation that such was the case'.[1] These aspects of the trial relate to the elements of the offence, and fall within the remit of the substantive criminal law. However, a number of evidential rules will regulate how the case is prosecuted in court. They will dictate where the burden and standard of proof lies; what material may be used by the parties; the form of questioning that can be adopted by the advocates; and the manner in which the jury should assess the evidence. It is therefore unsurprising that, in practice, knowledge of the operation of evidential rules is essential to a full understanding of the criminal legal process. No matter how well versed a lawyer may be in substantive criminal law, he or she will be unable to provide advice to a client, nor prosecute a case, without a firm grasp of the law of evidence.

One of the first principles you are likely to encounter in your study of the law of evidence is that the burden will usually fall on the prosecution to prove beyond reasonable doubt that the defendant committed the prohibited act with the required mental element. However, even in cases where the facts may appear relatively straightforward, in practice evidential rules can complicate the task of proving guilt. Take the following case: Baby James is found dead. The autopsy shows that a blow to the head killed him, probably by coming into contact with a wall or similar hard, flat surface. Marks on his body suggest that the baby was swung against the flat surface while held by the legs. The baby was seen alive the day before he was found dead. Only the mother and her boyfriend had contact with the baby during this period. An open and shut case? By no means, if the mother and the boyfriend maintain their right to refuse to answer questions and refuse to offer any explanation for the child's death. Without evidence that one or the other, or both, committed the act which killed the child, neither can be charged with murder or manslaughter. It is not sufficient simply to charge both and let the jury decide who was responsible. If both parties were charged, each could refuse to give evidence, which would not then be tested through cross-examination. Since the Criminal Justice and Public Order Act 1994, the jury may draw proper inferences from the failure to answer police questions or to give evidence, but these

---

[1] *R v Mathews and Alleyne* [2004] QB 69.

provisions do not replace the requirement for evidence that the defendant intentionally, recklessly or negligently did an act, or failed to do an act, which caused the death of the child. Therefore if there was a prosecution in this case, the lack of evidence would almost certainly result in an acquittal.

If, however, subsequent forensic evidence uncovered some years later tended to implicate the mother and her boyfriend in the child's death, they could then face a retrial.[2] In these circumstances, the prosecution may well find it easier to discharge the burden of proof and convince the jury beyond reasonable doubt that the defendants were responsible for the killing of the child.

THE TRIAL

The function of the judge and jury

The criminal process is designed to culminate in a conclusive confrontation between the parties at trial. The criminal trial involves questions of both law and fact. In trials on indictment, the general rule is that questions of law are to be decided by the trial judge, while questions of fact are to be decided by the jury. Thus matters such as the competence of witnesses, the admissibility of evidence and matters relating to the substantive law are matters of law for the judge, whereas those such as the credibility of a witness, the weight to be attached to the evidence, and the existence or non-existence of the facts in issue are questions of fact, and will be determined by the jury. In the case of trials in the magistrates' courts, the lay justices or stipendiary magistrates will determine questions of both law and fact, and will typically rely heavily on the legally qualified clerk in deciding questions of law.[3]

However, the theoretical distinction that is frequently made between the judge and jury is not always reflected in practice. Jackson has pointed out that 'the traditional view that judges have responsibility merely for the law and juries for the facts is a misleading one, and it is more apt to characterise the factual function as one in which responsibility is shared between the judge and the jury'.[4] There are, for example, occasions when the judge must investigate the preliminary facts in order to decide, for example, whether evidence is admissible, or to determine whether there is sufficient evidence on a particular issue to go before a jury and to evaluate the evidence in order to comment on it when summing up the evidence for the jury.

Furthermore, there are a number of grey areas, where questions of fact may be treated as questions of law, or where questions of law are essentially treated as questions of fact. For example, while the construction of a statute is a matter of law, the construction of ordinary words used in the statute may be a question of fact. The phrase 'insulting behaviour' in section 5 of the Public Order Act 1936 was thought to be a matter of law, but in *Cozens v Brutus*[5] the House of Lords held that where a word in a statute is used in its ordinary sense,

---

[2]Until recently the law was that one cannot thereafter be tried for the same offence. However, Pt 10 of the CJA 2003 provides for the retrial of a person who has been acquitted of a qualifying offence where there is new and compelling evidence that the person was guilty of that offence.

[3]In Northern Ireland, the so-called 'Diplock' courts, which hear trials related to alleged terrorist offences, are presided over by a single judge, who will arbitrate on both law and facts.

[4]Jackson, J 'The Adversary Trial and Trial by Judge Alone' in M. McConville and G. Wilson (eds) *The Oxford Handbook of the Criminal Justice Process* (2002: Oxford, Oxford University Press).

[5][1973] AC 854. The 1936 legislation has now replaced by the Public Order Act 1986.

it is a question of fact for the jury or magistrates to determine whether the proved conduct amounted to insulting behaviour. Similarly, in *R v Feeley*,[6] the word 'dishonestly' as used in the Theft Act 1968 was held to be an ordinary word in common use and therefore a question of fact for the jury.[7] Of particular relevance to the law of evidence is the decision of the Court of Appeal in *R v Fulling*,[8] where the word 'oppression' in section 76(2)(a) of the Police and Criminal Evidence Act 1984 (which governs the admissibility of confessions) was given its ordinary dictionary meaning despite a partial definition in section 76(8).

In practice, however, *Cozens v Brutus* is often ignored, and there is little consistency in approach as to whose function it is to determine the meaning of words. Even the House of Lords disregarded the decision in *R v Caldwell*,[9] where the word 'recklessly', as used in the Criminal Damage Act 1971, was said to be used in its ordinary sense and yet was given a legal definition which differed from that given in the case of *R v Cunningham*.[10] There are countless other examples of ordinary words being legally defined simply because without such definition juries (and judges) are likely to produce different interpretations.

Facts in issue and collateral facts

At the centre of the criminal trial are the facts in issue. In a nutshell, these are the facts which are being contested by the parties. For example, in a case of theft the prosecution must prove that the article alleged to have been stolen was property belonging to another and that the defendant appropriated that property dishonestly with the intention of permanently depriving the owner, or person in possession or control, of that property. If the accused's plea of guilty is based on a lack of dishonesty, the defence may admit that he appropriated property belonging to someone else. The act of taking the goods in question will not, therefore, be a 'fact in issue', since the defence will not attempt to rebut the prosecution's evidence on this point. Instead, the defence will concentrate their efforts on countering the prosecution's case that the defendant acted dishonestly. In this scenario, it is the dishonesty of the accused that is the fact in issue. In many rape cases, the fact that intercourse took place is often admitted, and the trial will thus revolve around the issue of consent. Since the defendant is admitting that the intercourse took place, the only fact in issue here is whether the complainant consented (or the defendant held a reasonable belief that she was consenting).

Those facts which are not directly relevant to the facts in issue are known as collateral facts. In the main, collateral facts are only relevant to the court insofar as they go to the credit of the witness. Cross-examination as to credit is designed to undermine the credibility of the witness in the eyes of the jury and persuade them to give less weight to the evidence of the particular witness. As we shall see in Chapter 4, the law now limits such questioning in relation to collateral facts through the 'Finality Rule', which usually obliges

---

[6][1973] QB 530.
[7]A further example can be found in *DPP v Stonehouse* [1978] AC 854, where it was held that the question whether an act is 'more than merely preparatory to the commission of an offence' for the purposes of section 1 of the Criminal Attempts Act 1981 is one of fact.
[8][1987] QB 426. See discussion in Ch 8, pp 255–57.
[9][1982] AC 341.
[10][1957] QB 396. In *R v G* [2004] 1 AC 1034, the House of Lords reconsidered their decision in *Caldwell* and departed from it, holding that it was just to do so (recklessness is now subjective as in *Cunningham*, as opposed to objective as in *Caldwell*).

the cross-examiner to accept the answer given, and denies the advocate the opportunity to introduce rebutting evidence.

It is often suggested that witnesses are mistaken or, even worse, liars, and many who have given evidence at a criminal trial will say that it felt as if they were on trial and they would think twice before volunteering to give evidence in future. Section 100 of the Criminal Justice Act 2003 restricts the admissibility of the bad character of a witness with the intention of preventing some of the abuses of cross-examination of witnesses. Until recently, the accused was permitted to cross-examine his alleged victim in person. Children and adult victims of rape and other offences were particularly intimidated by this practice. In one case the victim of rape was faced by her alleged attacker who cross-examined her while wearing the same clothes he was alleged to have worn while raping her.[11] The Youth Justice and Criminal Evidence Act 1999 has now changed the law to prevent cross-examination by the defendant in person of children or victims of sexual offences, and judges have discretion to prevent such cross-examination in other appropriate cases. In addition, the Act seeks to control the use of evidence of the sexual behaviour of the complainant in cases of rape and other sexual offences.[12] In the past, it was not unusual for the previous sexual behaviour of the complainant to be used by the defence to suggest that the complainant was of loose moral character and probably consented to the intercourse which took place. This was a factor in the extremely low conviction rate for rape, particularly the form known as acquaintance rape, where the defendant and complainant were known to each other and might well have been intimate in the past. Fortunately, recent years have seen judges exert much closer control over how collateral facts are used by advocates. Not only does this represent an extra degree of protection for victims and witnesses, but it also serves to benefit the criminal justice system as a whole as trials are not unnecessarily bogged down by the use of irrelevant information.

The *voir dire* or 'trial within a trial'

Trial judges also become adjudicators of the facts where a *voir dire* is held. The *voir dire*, or 'trial within a trial', will be held when the admissibility of certain evidence is in dispute. Essentially, the judge will ask the jury to leave the courtroom in order to hear arguments from the prosecution and defence about whether or not a particular piece of evidence should be admitted in evidence. One of the more common scenarios is where the prosecution propose to rely on a confession made by the accused, which the defence argue is inadmissible because it was obtained in breach of section 76 of the Police and Criminal Evidence Act 1984, or in some other way which renders it liable to exclusion under section 78 of that Act. In practice, counsel for the defence will have informed the prosecution that they intend to object to the admissibility of a particular piece of evidence. At the point where the prosecution would have adduced the evidence in question, counsel will intimate to the judge that a point of law has arisen which is to be determined in the absence of the jury. The jury will then be asked to retire and the issue of admissibility will be determined by the judge. Witnesses may be called by both parties in what is essentially a 'mini trial' arising from a contested issue in the case.

It will often be necessary for the defendant to give evidence, particularly if he is alleging some malpractice or illegality in the obtaining of the evidence. If the judge decides the

---

[11] *The Times*, 5 April 2000.
[12] Youth Justice and Criminal Evidence Act 1999, section 41. See Ch 5, pp 150–61.

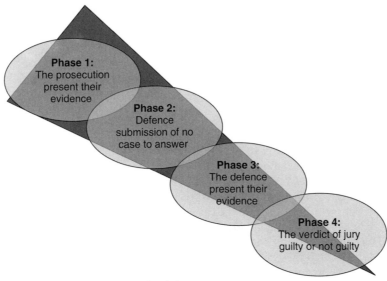

Figure 1.1:   **Phases of the Criminal Trial**

evidence is not admissible, the jury are recalled and the trial continues, but the jury hear nothing of the excluded evidence. If the evidence is deemed admissible, the jury are recalled and the evidence is presented in the normal way.

In magistrates' courts, where the magistrates are adjudicators of both law and fact, there are obvious difficulties in deciding issues such as the admissibility of a confession. There can be no question of a trial within a trial as in the Crown Court, but if the defence make a representation that evidence should not be taken into account, the magistrates must stop the hearing and hold a *voir dire*, as would be done in the Crown Court.

Trial procedure

A brief look at the way in which a typical trial on indictment proceeds (assuming the jury have been selected and the opening address to the jury by prosecution and defence counsel has taken place) may assist in understanding the above. As Figure 1.1 (above) illustrates, there are broadly four phases in the criminal trial.

Phase 1: the prosecution case

The first task of the prosecution (Phase 1) is to adduce sufficient evidence to persuade the judge that there is a case to answer. The prosecution will call their witnesses, who will be led through their evidence by prosecuting counsel (examination-in-chief). The defence will cross-examine those witnesses in an attempt to undermine the evidence given, or, as is too often the case, to discredit the witnesses. After cross-examination, prosecuting counsel will re-examine in order to emphasise the evidence given and to restore the credibility of the witness if damaged in cross-examination. Once the prosecution have presented sufficient evidence to persuade the trial judge that there is a case to answer, that is the end of Phase 1.

It is not permissible for the prosecutor to introduce further evidence after the close of its case.[13] The prosecution case may, however, be strengthened by cross-examination of the defendant and/or any witnesses for the defence. Equally, cross-examination of the victim and any prosecution witnesses, together with evidence from the defendant and/or defence witnesses, may weaken the prosecution case.

Phase 2: a case to answer?

At the end of the prosecution case the defence may submit that there is 'no case to answer' if there appears to be insufficient evidence to persuade a reasonable jury of the defendant's guilt (Phase 2). If the judge agrees, the prosecution will have failed to discharge the evidential burden and the judge will withdraw the case from the jury and direct an acquittal.[14] In most cases which go to trial the prosecution succeed in discharging the evidential burden, which means that the case proceeds and the defence present their case (see Phase 3, below). However, this is not to say that the prosecution have successfully discharged the burden of proof; the jury must be persuaded of the defendant's guilt beyond reasonable doubt.[15] In a case tried on indictment, whether the prosecution have done so or not will not be known until the jury reach their verdict.

Phase 3: the defence case

If the prosecution succeed in producing sufficient evidence to persuade the judge that there is a case to answer, the case proceeds and the defence may then give evidence (Phase 3). The defence must at this stage decide whether the defendant is to give evidence. Counsel for the defence will be aware that section 35 of the Criminal Justice and Public Order Act 1994 provides that inferences may be draw from the failure of the accused to give evidence or if he, without good cause, refuses to answer questions.[16] The section provides for a procedure under which the court must at the end of the prosecution case satisfy itself (in the case of proceedings on indictment) that the accused is aware that the stage has been reached at which evidence can be given for the defence and that he can, if he wishes, give evidence. He will also be told of the effect of his failure to give evidence or without good cause to answer questions (that a proper inference may be drawn). This puts the defendant under some degree of coercion to give evidence, but the strength of the prosecution case will also exert a certain pressure. If the prosecution have presented a strong case which calls for an answer, the failure of the accused to answer it suggests to the jury that he has no answer. The jury may then accept the evidence presented by the prosecution and conclude that he is guilty as charged. If the defendant does give evidence, he may succeed in casting sufficient doubt on the prosecution case to justify an acquittal.

However, it should be underlined that it is also possible that defence evidence may actually serve to strengthen the prosecution case. Where a defendant, or indeed any witness, gives evidence, it is evidence for all purposes, and may be evidence for him also but against his co-accused. For example, a defence witness may admit under cross-examination that he lied to help the defendant, or the defendant himself may under cross-examination make damaging admissions. In cases where more than one defendant is being prosecuted, it is

---

[13] *R v Rice* [1963] 1 QB 857.
[14] *Practice Direction (Submission of No Case)* [1962] 1 WLR 227.
[15] See below, Ch 3.
[16] See below, Ch 4, pp 108–12.

not uncommon for each accused to run a so-called 'cut-throat' defence, where each alleges that the other(s) played a more important role in the offence. Thus the prosecution case against X may receive a substantial boost if Y testifies in defence that X placed him under duress to commit the act in question.

At this point in the trial the defence may have an evidential burden to adduce sufficient evidence of a defence they are relying on. For example, in a murder trial he or she may wish to rely upon self-defence or provocation. If the defence do not adduce sufficient evidence of a particular defence to make it a live issue in the case, and there is no other evidence of that defence, the trial judge will not allow that defence to be put the jury, and the prosecution are not required to adduce evidence rebutting that defence. It thus follows that if the defence are relying on a particular defence, the accused or defence witnesses will usually have to give evidence of that defence. Just as a defence witness may sometimes assist the prosecution case, sometimes a prosecution witness may inadvertently assist the defence. For example, a witness may state that he saw the victim punch the accused who then punched him back – suggesting self-defence. Defence witnesses may also give such evidence, but few juries will accept such a defence if the accused does not testify in person and is not subjected to cross-examination. If there is sufficient evidence to make the particular defence an issue – and this will be for the trial judge to determine – the prosecution must then disprove that defence by persuading the jury beyond reasonable doubt that the particular defence does not apply.

Like prosecuting counsel, defence counsel will lead the witness through his or her evidence and will re-examine defence witnesses after cross-examination. Sometimes the defence will bear the legal or persuasive burden of proving certain defences, eg insanity or diminished responsibility, or they may need to show that defendants have an excuse or justification for their action. Reversing the legal or persuasive burden means that the defence must persuade the jury (on the balance of probabilities) that the defendant was insane or suffering from diminished responsibility, or has the excuse or justification pleaded.[17]

Phase 4: the verdict

After the conclusion of all the evidence and closing speeches, the jury (if present) will be asked to consider their verdict. Before they begin this task however, the trial judge must sum up the case. The judge must direct the jury on the relevant substantive law, remind them of the evidence that has been given and explain a number of evidential matters. A typical direction will begin with an explanation as to which side bears the burden of proof, against what standard those elements will need to be proved. He will normally take the jury through the prosecution evidence and, importantly, point out any defence which that evidence discloses, even if the defence have not relied on that particular defence. For example, on a charge of murder, the defendant may plead self-defence but the evidence may also point towards provocation. In these circumstances, the jury will be directed to consider self-defence first, but, if that fails, they should proceed to consider provocation in the alternative. The particular nature of the evidential directions are given will depend on the nature of each individual case. Thus where the case depends wholly or substantially on identification evidence, a direction on the special need for caution will be required.[18]

---

[17]See below, Ch 3.
[18]See *R v Turnbull* [1977] QB 224, discussed below at pp 18–20.

If there are a number of defendants, but only one of them has confessed, the jury must be directed that the confession is evidence only against that particular defendant.[19]

The judge may also comment on the plausibility and credibility of witnesses, and on the weight which might be attached to particular evidence.[20] He or she may express a fairly strong opinion on such matters, but the jury will be told that ultimately they are the ultimate arbitrators of fact, and may reject any such opinions if they see fit to do so. By the same token however, the judge should be careful not to give an express indication of belief or disbelief in a particular piece of evidence. It would be quite wrong, for example, for a judge to comment that 'it is obvious to everyone in this court that the accused is lying'; though it would be acceptable for him or her to comment thus: 'you may think that the defendant's explanation is not worthy of belief, but that ladies and gentlemen of the jury, is a matter for you'.

Despite the Court of Appeal having stipulated that trial judges should confine themselves to stating matters 'impartially, clearly and logically',[21] some commentators argue that the summing up often unduly influences the jury and could be dispensed with altogether. In the United States, judges are prohibited from giving any indication of how they evaluate the evidence. Apart from interfering with the paradigmatic judicial role as a passive arbiter, any comment on the weight of the evidence also risks usurping the function of the jury by putting pressure on them to arrive at a particular verdict.[22] Referring to one of the most notorious miscarriages of justice of the last century, Lord Bingham made a stinging criticism of the summing up of one of his predecessors in title, Lord Goddard, in the case of Derek Bentley, which was heavily biased in favour of a conviction.[23] Indeed, there are numerous cases where a conviction has been quashed on appeal because of improper comment by the trial judge, but these cases do represent a very small minority.[24] In the great majority of cases, judges tend to be extremely circumspect, and, in any case, it is difficult to ascertain the full extent of their influence over the jury in the absence of any definitive research. Since the law does not permit such research, we may never know the true impact of the summing up upon the deliberations of the jury.[25]

At the end of the trial, the jury will deliver the verdict (Phase 4). One should note that it is commonly supposed that a verdict of 'not guilty' equates with innocence. This is not so. It simply means that the prosecution have failed to satisfy the jury of the defendant's guilt beyond reasonable doubt. The failure to satisfy the jury is often due to a lack of evidence, or to an inability to adduce relevant evidence because it is excluded or inadmissible. Alternatively, the evidence (including any confession by the accused) may be excluded because of some improprieties in how it was obtained.[26]

In law, the term 'not guilty' carries a specific legal meaning and essentially means that the prosecution has failed to discharge the burden of proof. In contrast, media communication frequently represents both acquittals at first instance and successful

---

[19]See below Ch 8, pp 253–54.

[20]See, for example, the judge's comments on the evidence of the witness 'Bromley' in the *Damilola Taylor* case (*The Daily Telegraph*, 22 February 2002).

[21]*R v Berrada* (1989) 91 Cr App R 131.

[22]See generally Wolchover, D. 'Should Judges Sum Up on the Facts?' [1989] Crim LR 781.

[23]*The Times*, 31 July 1998.

[24]See e.g. *R v Berrada* above, where the trial judge described the defendant's allegations that the police had fabricated evidence as 'really monstrous and wicked'.

[25]Section 8 of the Contempt of Court Act 1981 prohibits interviewing jurors in connection with their deliberations.

[26]See discussion in Chs 8 (confessions) and 9 (other forms of improperly obtained evidence) respectively.

appeals as authoritative statements of innocence and full acceptance of the defence cases, thereby both reinforcing and responding to the general public expectation that a verdict of 'not guilty' equates to a declaration of innocence. In a similar vein, one may also note that the fact that an appellate court quashes a conviction does not mean that the convicted person was in fact innocent.[27] Occasionally a higher court will declare that the convicted person is innocent of the crime, but more often the conviction is quashed because it is seen as unsafe. This may be because of a fault in the trial, such as the judge's failure to give a direction to the jury or his having given the wrong direction.

In *R (Mullen) v Secretary of State for the Home Department*,[28] the Home Secretary appealed against a decision of the Court of Appeal where it was held that Mullen, whose conviction for conspiracy to cause explosions was quashed as unsafe, because he had been unlawfully removed from Zimbabwe and brought to the United Kingdom for trial, was entitled to *ex gratia* compensation. It was accepted that Mullen, who had served 10 years of a 30-year sentence, had been properly convicted, and there was no doubt that he was a quartermaster for the IRA. Nonetheless, the manner of his removal from Zimbabwe to UK was seen as blatantly unlawful and therefore an abuse of executive power which justified the quashing of his conviction. The Divisional Court held that the Home Secretary was correct to refuse to pay Mullen *ex gratia* compensation, such payments being intended for persons who were wrongly convicted and shown, by virtue of some new or newly discovered fact, to have been innocent. Although the Court of Appeal took the opposite view, the House of Lords reversed this decision and restored that of the Divisional Court.

The function of the criminal trial

In contrast to the inquisitorial model of justice used in continental Europe, where truth-finding is widely regarded as the overriding goal,[29] its place within the adversarial model has always been open to conjecture. Questions concerning the overriding purpose, or function, of the criminal trial has intrigued commentators and theorists since the inception of the adversarial system in the eighteenth and nineteenth centuries. Some have argued that the adversarial trial provides the best way to determine the truth of what witnesses are saying. Live oral evidence, given under oath, and tested by the parties has been traditionally regarded as the best means of reaching the truth. Although the legal philosopher Jerome Frank disliked the 'fight theory' that underpinned the adversarial model of justice, he nonetheless defended its ability to seek out the truth. In his eyes, parties which have a clear focus on victory will produce the best information for the tribunal of fact to make a determination:

> Many lawyers maintain that the best way for the court to discover the facts in a suit is to have each side strive as hard as it can, in a keenly partisan spirit, to bring to the court's attention the evidence favourable to that side. Macauley said that we obtain the fairest decision 'when two men argue, as unfairly as possible, on opposite sides' for then 'it is certain that no important consideration will altogether escape notice'.[30]

---

[27]See further Nobles, R and Schiff, D *Understanding Miscarriages of Justice* (2000: Oxford, Oxford University Press).
[28][2005] 1 AC 1.
[29]See generally Damaska, M 'Evidentiary Barriers to Conviction and Two Models of Criminal Procedure' (1973) 121 *University of Pennsylvania Law Review* 506.
[30]Frank, J *Courts on Trial* (1949: Princeton, Princeton University Press), p 49.

An alternative justification for the adversarial process is that although adversarial structures do not always lend themselves to accurate truth-finding, it is nonetheless the
dispute-resolution model that is best placed to ensure outcomes are as fair as possible
to parties to the case. Landsman, for example, is quite happy to defend the adversarial
system on the basis that truth is not its primary goal:

> [A] preoccupation with material truth may be not only futile but dangerous to society as
> well. If the objective of the judicial process were the disclosure of facts, then any technique
> that increases the prospect of gathering facts would be permissible.[31]

Landsman proceeds to list examples, such as the use of psychoactive drugs and/or torture
as a means to produce truth. Thus, by necessity, a *truth at all costs* approach to criminal
trials is unworkable given that exclusionary evidential rules,[32] coupled with certain due
process protections, are designed to maintain the integrity of the criminal justice process.
Instead, Landsman defends the adversarial trial on the basis that truth plays second fiddle
to the overriding need for justice. Procedural requirements such as party control, an
impartial decision-maker, and commitment to winning the contest mean that the process
should be broadly equal. Fundamental rights are safeguarded through evidential rules,
which go some way to offsetting the broader range of resources at the disposal of the
prosecution, as well as maintaining integrity and public confidence in the criminal justice
system. In a similar vein, Thibaut and Walker argue that the 'truth-finding' aspect of the
adversarial system is subservient to the overriding goal of 'justice' or 'fairness', since the
outcomes of proceedings will naturally reflect the inputs of the parties.[33] Factual truth
is a prerequisite of justice, as Jeremy Bentham's image of '[i]njustice, and her handmaid
[f]alsehood' underlines.[34]

In practice, however, the underlying structures and processes of the adversarial model
may impede the ability of the trial to uncover the truth. In specific relation to the rules
of evidence, the most obvious evidential constraint in the common law system is that the
court itself cannot undertake a search for relevant evidence; it must rely almost entirely
upon the prosecution and defence to supply it with relevant information.[35] As Landsman
argues, proactively seeking further information outside what the parties were presenting
would heighten the risk of perceived partisanship:

> Adversary theory suggests that if he [the judge] diverges from passivity by attempting to
> develop the evidence at trial, or to arrange the compromise of the case, he runs a serious risk
> of undermining his ability to evaluate neutrally the adversaries' presentations.[36]

Therefore evidence that may be perceived as being neutral, yet may still be relevant, is
often overlooked. McEwan gives the example of the evidence of a key witness whom
neither side wishes to call, since both sides fear what he or she may do to their case.[37]
Evidential rules make no provision for the admissibility of such a witness's testimony, and
thus truth-finding is arguably made more difficult.

---

[31] Landsman, S *The Adversary System, a Description and Defence* (1984: Washington, The American Enterprise
Institute), p 37.
[32] e.g. rules excluding hearsay, character evidence and confession evidence.
[33] Thibaut, J and Walker, L 'A Theory of Procedure' (1978) 66 *California Law Review* 541.
[34] Bentham, J *Rationale of Judicial Evidence* Vol 1 (1827: London, Hunt and Clarke), (1978: New York, Garland).
[35] In theory, judges can widen the scope of the fact-finding process. For example, they may call witnesses
of their own motion (*R v Wallwork* (1958) 42 Cr App R 153). However, this power should be used sparingly
(*R v Roberts* (1984) 80 Cr App R 89).
[36] Landsman (1980), 491, op cit n 31.
[37] McEwan, J *Evidence and the Adversarial Process*, 2nd edn. (1998: Oxford, Hart), p 4.

Furthermore, for the 'fight theory' to work effectively, the prosecution and defence must be relatively equal in terms of resources. The difficulty here is that the potential for the defence to embark on their own evidence-gathering process is significantly hindered in terms of resources. The defence will be highly dependent on the CPS to comply with disclosure obligations in order to sift through the evidence gathered by the police.[38] However, there is a risk that such evidence will already have been selectively filtered by the police or CPS as cases are constructed against suspects, even on a subconscious level.[39] For example, it can be assumed that certain aspects of evidence which sat uneasily alongside the initial 'case theory' of the police or the CPS may have been set to one side; certain lines of enquiry may not have been probed; certain witnesses may not have been interviewed and certain questions may not have been asked. It is thus the case that the truth of past events is routinely deconstructed by criminal investigations, with a new 'truth' being reconstructed within the trial as the parties attempt to persuade the factfinder that their presentation of events represents an historically correct narrative. In this sense, it is arguable that the adversarial model of proof constitutes a poor vehicle for delivering justice that is ultimately based on the 'truth'.[40]

THE CONCEPT OF RELEVANCE

Before a party can adduce any evidence at trial, it must first be shown that the evidence in question is relevant. The legal definition of relevance was laid down by Lord Simon in *R v Kilbourne*.[41] Evidence was considered to be 'relevant' if 'if it is logically probative or disprobative of some matter which requires proof'.[42] This definition is not a decisive indicator as to what evidence should be excluded and what should be included. It does not amount to a legal test for relevance. As Dennis observes, it is frequently referred to as a legal 'concept' as it has no statutory or common law definition or test.[43] The concept of relevance thus remains elusive and open to subjective interpretation. As such, it has also been subject to considerable criticism, particularly from feminist commentators, who have attacked the way in which the concept of relevance has been applied in rape and sexual assault cases. Until the Youth Justice and Criminal Evidence Act 1999 clamped down on the use of previous sexual history evidence, it was commonplace for complainants in rape cases to be cross-examined in detail about their sexual history because trial judges frequently deemed it relevant to the issue of consent.[44]

The House of Lords took relevance to what may be described as its logical extreme in *R v Blastland*.[45] The accused was charged with the murder of a young boy. He claimed

---

[38]The Criminal Procedure and Investigations Act 1996 requires disclosure by the prosecution of previously undisclosed material. This is to be followed by the defence disclosing to the prosecution certain information about the defence case. On receipt of that evidence, the prosecution will be required to disclose any material relevant to the defence case as disclosed. See also Pt 5 of the CJA 2003, which amends this procedure to increase the nature of the disclosure obligations on the defence.

[39]See further McConville, M, Sanders, A and Leng, R *The Case for the Prosecution* (1991: London, Routledge). The authors argue that the police, though normatively neutral, will seek to build a strong case for the prosecution in the investigation of the crime and in the collection of evidence.

[40]See further Doak, J *Victims Rights, Human Rights and Criminal Justice* (2008: Oxford, Hart), Ch 4.

[41][1973] AC 729.

[42]*Ibid.*, 756.

[43]Dennis, I *The Law of Evidence*, 3rd edn (2007: London, Sweet & Maxwell), pp 60–61.

[44]See further below, Ch 5, pp 146–50.

[45][1986] AC 41.

that the murderer was another man, M, who had been in the vicinity while the accused was with the boy. M was investigated by the police, and had made a number of statements in which he admitted the crime, but he later withdrew them. These were inadmissible at Blastland's trial because they were hearsay. However, the defence wished to call a number of witnesses who would say that M had told them of the boy's death at a time when the only way he could have known of it was if he himself had killed him. The House of Lords upheld the trial judge's decision to exclude the evidence of these witnesses on the ground that it was not relevant. The issue at the trial was whether Blastland had committed the crime, and what was relevant to that issue was not the fact of M's knowledge but how he came by it. Since he might have come by it in a number of different ways, there was no rational basis on which the jury could be invited to draw an inference as to how M came by that knowledge or that M, rather than the accused, was the killer.

There are thus various degrees of relevance: a fact may be only slightly relevant; or highly relevant; or somewhere between these two extremes. Until recently, the common law test for the admissibility of evidence of previous convictions or bad character required a high degree of relevance in order to outweigh the prejudicial effect of admitting such evidence. However, in general the degree of relevance does not affect the admissibility of the evidence, though the less relevant the evidence is, the less weight the factfinder will generally be prepared to place upon it. For example, if a witness is someone who has positively identified the defendant as the person seen running away from the scene of a bank robbery, his evidence will probably have very little weight attached to it if he caught only a fleeting glimpse of the offender on a dark night as he ran from the scene. The evidence will still be relevant (and admissible), but will probably carry little weight. On the other hand, if the same witness was in the bank and saw the offender's face for a period of time at close hand, the evidence will probably be seen as being highly relevant, and doubtless the jury will give much greater weight to it. The weight of the evidence will also be affected by the way in which it is given, the character of the witness, and whether or not that witness is discredited in cross-examination. Thus a witness may give what appears to be highly relevant evidence but is then discredited in cross-examination. For example, if the eyewitness in the scenario above claims to recognise the defendant as a person with whom he went to school, and the defence show this witness to have held a longstanding grudge against the defendant, the weight of his evidence may be diminished in the eyes of the jury since he may not be considered a reliable witness.

An example of witnesses who may have been improperly motivated to testify can be found in the infamous trial of Rosemary West, which took place in the Autumn of 1995. It came to light that a number of witnesses had been paid by newspapers, or who had entered into lucrative contracts with newspapers, to publish their stories if West was convicted.[46] Their evidence, though highly relevant, was still admissible, but may have carried relatively little weight in the eyes of the jury since the witnesses may have been motivated to embellish their testimony to ensure a guilty verdict. Indeed, the *West* case is not the only example where money has played a factor in discrediting witnesses. In 1979, the former Liberal Party leader, Jeremy Thorpe, was acquitted of various offences, in part because a central prosecution witness had been promised more money for his story if Thorpe was convicted. Similarly, in the Damilola Taylor murder trial, a 15-year-old witness known as 'Bromley' had been promised a reward of £50,000

---

[46] *The Times*, 4 November 1995.

in return for evidence leading to the conviction of those responsible for the killing. The discussion of the reward with the interviewing police officer, which suggested more interest in the reward than in giving honest evidence, was a factor in the judge's decision to instruct the jury that her evidence was not credible. Although there have been suggestions since that legislation should make payments to witnesses unlawful, these have not been acted upon. It may be noted, however, the Code of Practice which governs the press provides that payments should not be made to witnesses before trial.[47]

FORMS OF EVIDENCE

Direct evidence

Evidence may be received by the court in a variety of different ways. Most commonly, it will take the form of direct oral testimony. This means that the witness will be called on to testify under oath in open court, and everything he or she says will be and tendered as evidence of the truth of the facts asserted. Witnesses can only give evidence of matters that they have themselves perceived with one of their five senses – usually a witness will speak of what he or she directly saw or heard. Such testimony is always admissible, providing it is relevant and the witness is competent to testify.[48] By contrast, witnesses may not give opinions, nor may they relate any hearsay evidence to the court. Hearsay evidence is any statement other than one made by the witness in the course of giving his evidence in the proceedings in question, which is tendered as evidence of the truth of the facts asserted. Such evidence is inadmissible unless subject to a common law or statutory exception. Thus, Philip may testify to the court: 'I saw David strike Alice'. This is direct testimony, since Philip is speaking as an eyewitness. However, should Philip be unable to testify, his friend Gareth would not be able to say 'Philip told me that he had seen David striking Alice'. That would be hearsay, since it would be tendered to prove that the defendant struck victim. There are numerous exceptions to the rule against hearsay, and these are considered further in Chapter 7.

Documentary evidence

Not all evidence, however, needs to be received in oral form. Documentary evidence will also be admissible, and comprises not only written or typed papers, but also maps, plans, graphs, drawings, photographs, tapes (audio and visual), films, negatives and disks, CDs or DVDs. In short, 'documentary evidence' is used to refer to every means of communicating information other than the direct spoken word. The purpose in producing a document varies according to the document and the particular case. Maps may be produced simply to provide the court with a visual picture of the scene of an accident or a crime. For example, in the Rosemary West trial, detailed plans of the house in which a number of bodies were found were produced to provide a visual picture of the location of the various bodies. The formal evidence of the finding of the bodies came from the police and forensic pathologists.

---

[47] *Editors' Code of Practice* (2007), [15.1].
[48] Competency is discussed at Ch 4, pp 85–96.

The situation becomes more complex when we consider the circumstances in which documentary evidence may replace the direct oral evidence of witnesses. Typically, most witnesses in criminal cases will have given a written statement to the police or to a solicitor. However, since these statements have been made out of court and have not been made under oath, the law of evidence places tight constraints on the extent to which they can be used at court. As we shall discuss later, these written statements may be used by the witness to refresh his memory before or while giving evidence if the statement was made fairly soon after the events described.[49] Furthermore, statements in a document, whether made by a witness to the crime or a business document made for the purposes of the business, are admissible in evidence subject to certain conditions and judicial discretion.[50]

Real evidence

In addition to documentary evidence, the court may also receive 'real evidence'. This term is usually taken to mean some material object that is produced to the court for inspection, so that the court may draw its own inference from observation of the particular object. Although real evidence will frequently feature in the cases of either the prosecution or defence, it is usually of little intrinsic value without some accompanying testimony. Thus, a knife may be produced in a murder case as a form of real evidence. However, unless other evidence is available to show that it was the murder weapon and that it is linked to the accused (e.g. it was found in his car and had the victim's blood on it), it proves nothing. Real evidence may also be an original document, a visit to the scene of the crime(s) by the judge and jury, a tape-recording, photograph or video image of the defendant. Real evidence will usually constitute an exception to the hearsay rule. For example, where a computer automatically logs certain forms of information, such evidence will generally be admissible. In *R v Robson, Mitchell and Richards*,[51] the defendants were convicted of armed robbery. The prosecution linked the second defendant with the crime by means of a computer printout of telephone calls made by the second defendant on his mobile phone to that of the first defendant. It was held that the printout was not hearsay but real evidence since the printout was produced by a computer which operated automatically and independently without human intervention.[52]

Circumstantial evidence

Circumstantial evidence is evidence of relevant facts from which the existence, or non-existence, of the facts in issue may be inferred. Such evidence may include any of the above forms of evidence except, of course, direct testimony relating to the facts in issue. It is with direct oral testimony that circumstantial evidence is contrasted. Popular fiction and televised legal dramas often portray circumstantial evidence in rather derogatory terms; phrases such as 'the case against the accused is only circumstantial' are relatively commonplace. However, in practice, circumstantial evidence is relied upon by the parties just as much as direct oral testimony. This is, perhaps, unsurprising, since it is in the

---

[49]See Ch 5, pp 121–25.
[50]See below, Ch 7.
[51][1991] Crim LR 362.
[52]See further discussion in Ch 7, pp 216–17.

nature of most crimes that they are not committed in the presence of eyewitnesses, and thus circumstantial evidence may be the only available evidence. However, as the Court of Appeal recently acknowledged in *R v Pinnock*,[53] contrary to popular perception, circumstantial evidence may be highly cogent:

> [I]t is our experience that appeals against conviction are all too often launched on the basis that where the Crown has little or no direct evidence upon which it can rely, but invites the court to draw inferences from circumstantial evidence, that this is in itself a good indicator of the weakness of the prosecution case. In our combined experience this is simply not the case. Circumstantial evidence can provide and often does provide a very strong case against an accused person. Provided the inferences the Crown invite the jury to draw from the circumstances are safe and proper inferences, then defence counsel will have a difficult job in persuading this court that a conviction secured upon them is unsafe.[54]

This is a view apparently shared by Cross and Tapper who, citing Pollock CB in *R v Exall* (1866) F & F 922, liken such evidence to a multi-stranded rope:

> One strand of the cord might be insufficient to sustain the weight, but three stranded together might be of sufficient strength. Thus ... there may be a combination of circumstances, not one of which would raise a reasonable conviction or more than mere suspicion: but the three taken together may create a conclusion of guilt with as much certainty as human affairs can require.[55]

Take the following example. Emma is charged with the murder of Julia by stabbing her in an alleyway behind a club they both frequented. On the night of Julia's death, Emma and Julia had an argument in the club, which resulted in Julia being thrown out at around 9.30 pm. Around 30 minutes later, Emma was seen leaving the club in an agitated state through the back door, which led unto the alleyway where Julia's body was later found. At about 10.15pm, a woman fitting Emma's description was seen running away from the alleyway, a few minutes after witnesses heard loud voices followed by a scream. Emma's jacket was stained with lime wash, which was identical to that used on a wall in the alley where Julia was found, and a button from her jacket was found at the scene of the murder. The murder weapon, a carving knife, was of the same brand as those contained in a knife block in Emma's kitchen. One knife is missing from the block. While no witnesses may have seen Emma stab Julia, there is plenty of circumstantial evidence to suggest she was involved. When we tie the various strands of it together, there appears to be a very strong case against Emma.

Evidence of motive

Those familiar with substantive criminal law will be aware of the distinction between motive and mental element. The fact that the defendant holds a grudge against a victim, or stood to benefit from the death of a particular person contributes nothing to the question whether the defendant intended to kill the victim when he struck him. However, it may still be regarded as a useful piece of evidence, insofar as it makes it more probable that the defendant was responsible for a particular act. By itself, evidence of motive is not sufficient to convict the defendant, but when considered alongside the other pieces of evidence, it

---

[53][2006] EWCA Crim 3119.
[54]*Ibid.*, [68].
[55]Tapper, C *Cross & Tapper on Evidence*, 11th edn, (2007: Oxford, Oxford University Press), p 32.

will strengthen the prosecution case. Equally, the absence of a motive might weaken the prosecution case.

CORROBORATION AND IDENTIFICATION

'Corroboration' is the term used to describe evidence that supports the truth of facts asserted by another witness. At its simplest, it could mean no more than another independent witness giving similar testimony, so that each witness supports the other. More often, corroboration may be more complex and comprise a considerable amount of detail. Forensic evidence often provides corroboration, although DNA evidence is now seen as direct, and often conclusive, evidence. In appropriate cases where it is alleged that the defendant committed the same offence against a number of victims, such as a multiple rape, the jury may take the evidence of other victims into account when considering the count against a particular victim, so that each victim supports the evidence of the other victims, thus providing mutual corroboration.

Unlike many civil law systems, corroboration is not generally required to establish guilt in English law. In practice however, the lack of any corroboration may mean that the case is too weak to prosecute or, if prosecuted, it may be difficult to persuade the jury of the defendant's guilt. Until recently, the common law had created mandatory requirements that the jury be warned of the danger of convicting on the uncorroborated evidence of certain categories of witnesses: accomplices giving evidence for the prosecution; complainants in sexual cases; and child witnesses.

The growth of the corroboration requirements during the nineteenth and twentieth centuries illustrates how many of our evidential rules developed as a form of protection for the accused based on what may have been a mistaken belief that such rules were essential to a fair trial. The mistrust of evidence given by an accomplice was understandable, but the mistrust of victims of sexual offences and children was less so. The requirement that a specific warning be given can be traced back to the writings of Hale in the seventeenth century, who warned of the danger of false accusation in rape cases, observing that the charge was 'an accusation easy to be made and hard to be proved, and harder to be defended by the party accused, tho' never so innocent'.[56] Hale went on to state that if the complainant was of good character and reported the crime promptly, the greater her credibility; though if she were of ill-repute and slow to complain, the less credible her testimony. Hale's observations became the stock-in-trade of defence lawyers, and some judges included them in their summing up.

The Criminal Law Amendment Act 1885 created several new sexual offences, including one intended to stop what became known as the 'white slave trade', (the abduction of young girls for sexual purposes), and, in line with Hale's strictures, this offence was subject to a requirement of corroboration.[57] However, rape remained a common law offence, and it was not until 1910 that the Court of Appeal laid down a requirement that the judge should warn the jury that it is dangerous to act on the unsupported evidence of the complainant in sexual cases.[58] The requirement soon became mandatory and developed a life of its own.

The 'mandatory warning', as it became known, developed over the years into an excessively technical requirement that contributed greatly to the difficulties experienced

---

[56] Hale, Sir Matthew *The History of the Pleas of the Crown* (1736), 635–36.
[57] Criminal Law Amendment Act 1885, section 3.
[58] *R v Graham* (1910) 4 Cr App R 218.

in prosecuting alleged rapists and child abusers. The 'full' warning comprised four requirements:

(a) the warning to the jury that it was dangerous to convict on the uncorroborated evidence of the particular witness, though they might convict despite the absence of any corroboration;

(b) an explanation of corroboration, which had developed a technical meaning;

(c) a direction as to what evidence was, or was not, capable of amounting to corroboration; and

(d) a direction that it was for them (the jury) to decide whether that evidence did in fact constitute corroboration.

Sometimes the warning was accompanied by a justification for it. In respect of accomplices, this was usually that they might have a purpose of their own to serve in giving evidence for the prosecution; they might exaggerate the role of others, while minimising their own role in the hope of a lighter sentence. In respect of victims of sexual offences, the justification was usually based on the likelihood of false accusation based on sexual neurosis, spite or shame at having consented to intercourse, which the victim now regretted. So far as children were concerned, it was assumed, without supporting evidence, that a child's evidence was less trustworthy than that of an adult. The failure to give the warning led to a quashing of the conviction, and there were numerous unjustified acquittals resulting from this or from a failure correctly to identify the evidence that was capable of being corroborated. Precisely what the effect of this warning was on the jury can, however, only be a matter of speculation.

Towards the end of the twentieth century, the mandatory corroboration warnings were perceived as being outdated and ill-founded. As policy–makers became increasingly aware of the plight of victims of sexual offences and child witnesses, they were gradually dismantled. The corroboration requirement in respect of children was the first to be abolished. Section 34 of the Criminal Justice Act 1988 abrogated the requirement of a warning in respect of children giving sworn evidence and the requirement of actual corroboration in respect of children giving unsworn evidence. An attempt to require judges to give a cautionary warning, and in effect continue the old law, notwithstanding the statutory intervention, was rejected by the Court of Appeal in R v Pryce.[59]

The other two requirements (in respect of sexual complainants and accomplices) were abolished by section 32 of the Criminal Justice and Public Order Act 1994. Inevitably, that was not the end of the matter. Whilst the statute abolished the need for 'obligatory' warnings, it remained possible for a judge to warn a jury in a particular case that it might be dangerous to convict on the uncorroborated evidence of a particular witness where there was a particular reason to do so. In R v Makanjuola,[60] counsel for the defendant tried unsuccessfully to re-impose the common law rule when he argued on appeal that where a judge does exercise his discretion to warn the jury, he had to give the full warning ((a) to (d) above). Lord Taylor CJ, speaking for the Court of Appeal, rejected this submission and stated that section 32(1) abrogated entirely the requirement to give a corroborative direction in respect of an alleged accomplice or a complainant of a sexual offence simply because the witness falls into one of those categories. It was to be for the judge alone to determine what, if any, warning was necessary in such cases, taking into account the circumstances of

---

[59][1991] Crim LR 379.
[60][1995] 3 All ER 730.

the case, the issues raised and the content and quality of the witness's evidence. Where the judge did decide to issue a warning, this should not be done solely because the witness is a complainant of a sexual offence or an accomplice. There would need to be an evidential basis for suggesting that the evidence of the witness may be unreliable, which would not include mere suggestions by cross-examining counsel.

It is now clear that the common law rules have finally been laid to rest. The judge retains a discretion to warn the jury in terms appropriate to the facts of a particular case. Where a witness has been shown to be unreliable, the judge may consider it necessary to urge caution. In a more extreme case, if the witness is shown to have lied, to have made previous false complaints or to bear the defendant a grudge, a stronger warning may be appropriate and the judge may suggest that it would be wise to look for supporting material before acting on the impugned witness's evidence.[61]

Identification evidence

Eyewitness identification evidence implicating the accused is often highly cogent, and consequently a high degree of weight may be placed upon it by the factfinder. Where it serves merely to corroborate other evidence, it is not generally problematic. However, there is greater cause for concern where it is used as the sole or primary basis for the prosecution's case.

Eighteenth and nineteenth-century lawyers were well aware of the fallibility of identification evidence, but the fact that such evidence was a frequent source of false convictions failed to lead to any formal safeguards. However, many judges, perhaps personally aware of the risk of false conviction, took to warning the jury of the possible dangers of convicting on identification evidence alone, or even went so far as to direct an acquittal where they thought the identification was too poor to sustain a conviction. Indeed, it was the false conviction of one Adolf Beck, who had been mistakenly identified by a number of victims of theft and fraud,[62] which led to the creation of the Court of Appeal in 1907.

Despite the clear miscarriage of justice in Beck's case, it was not until 1977 that the Court of Appeal laid down guidelines relating to possible mistaken identification. The Court of Appeal was responding to the Devlin Report,[63] which recommended that there should be no conviction in a case in which the prosecution relied wholly or mainly on the evidence of visual identification by one or more witnesses. The guidelines laid down by the Court of Appeal in *R v Turnbull*[64] did not go so far, but instead required the lower courts to instruct the jury to bear in mind the possible dangers of identification evidence and take a number of factors into account. Key questions jurors ought to consider include:

- How long was the suspect under observation?
- At what distance?
- In what light?

---

[61] For a reaffirmation of the principles set out in *Makanjuola*, see *R v Muncaster* [1999] Crim LR 409 and *R v Causeley* [1999] Crim LR 572.
[62] See generally Coates, T *The Strange Case of Adolph Beck* (2001: London, Stationery Office Books).
[63] Lord Devlin, *The Report of the Committee on Evidence of Identification in Criminal Cases*, Cmnd 338 (1976: London, HMSO).
[64] [1977] QB 224.

- Was the observation impeded?
- Had the witness seen the suspect before? (is the identification one of pure recognition rather than the identification of a stranger?)
- How often? If only occasionally, had he any special reason for remembering the accused?
- How long elapsed between the original observation and the subsequent identification to police?
- Were there any particular reasons for noting the suspect?

It was added by the Court that a failure to follow these guidelines is likely to result in a conviction being quashed.

Since the decision in *Turnbull*, a number of cases have come before the Court of Appeal whereby the judge did not give the jury the *Turnbull* direction in full. In *R v Curry; Keeble*,[65] the judge had instructed the jury that they should bear in mind that there was a risk of mistaken identification. They should thus evaluate the extent of that risk, taking into account the fact that it would be much higher where the identification had been based upon a fleeting glance. The defence appealed, contending that a full *Turnbull* warning should have been given. Dismissing the case, the Court of Appeal stated that the warning in *Turnbull* was not intended to deal with every case involving a minor identification problem, but was only intended to deal with cases of fleeting encounters. Since the identification evidence in this case was not based on a fleeting glance, the full warning was not necessary.

By contrast, the appellant in *Andrews*[66] was successful in arguing that a full form of the *Turnbull* warning should have been given. Here, the victim was violently attacked by three men, who ran off on being approached by the police. A short time later, the defendant was discovered in a nearby street, and was aggressive and confrontational towards the police. One of the police officers identified him as one of those involved in the attack a short time earlier. The judge had declined to give a full *Turnbull* warning, and had even told the jury that the officer's description 'quite plainly' identified the accused. Allowing the appeal, the Court of Appeal stated the judge had effectively usurped the function of the jury in determining whether the identification was accurate. Furthermore, since the issue of identity was central to the case, a full *Turnbull* warning should have been given.

Likewise, a direction should be given even where the eyewitness believes he or she recognises the accused from a previous encounter. In *R v Ryan*,[67] for example, such a direction was deemed to be appropriate even though the eyewitness recognised the accused as being the brother of a school friend. Although the Court of Appeal conceded in *Turnbull* that 'recognition may be more reliable than identification of a stranger', it proceeded to stress the jury should always be reminded that mistakes in recognition of close relatives and friends are sometimes made.[68]

In *R v Slater*,[69] the Court of Appeal made a fine distinction between identification evidence that places the accused at the scene of the offence, and identification evidence that relates to his or her particular actions. The case concerned an assault which took place in a nightclub. The defendant had admitted that he had been present, and had witnessed the

---

[65][1983] Crim LR 737.
[66][1993] Crim.LR 590. See also *R v Thornton* (1995) 1 Cr App R 578.
[67][1990] Crim LR 50.
[68]See also *Beckford v R* (1993) 97 Cr App R 405.
[69][1995] Crim LR 244.

disturbance, but denied any involvement. The victim had, however, described his assailant as a 'very big man' – a description that matched the defendant, who was 'a man of unusually large size'. The accused was convicted and appealed on the ground, *inter alia*, that the judge should have given a full *Turnbull* direction. Dismissing the appeal, the Court held that the need for such a direction arose where there was a possibility of mistaken identification. This possibility would generally arise when the issue was whether the defendant was present and a witness claimed to identify him on the basis of a previous sighting. Where, however, there was no issue as to the defendant's presence at or near the scene of the offence, but the issue was as to what he was doing, it did not automatically follow that such a direction had to be given. Whether such a direction was necessary would ultimately turn on the individual facts of a particular case. In instant case, the appellant was of wholly unusual size and there was no evidence to suggest that any one else in the nightclub was remotely similar in height to him. The issue was not really one of identification, but instead concerned what the appellant had done, and it would be 'contrary to common sense' to require the direction in all cases where presence is admitted but conduct disputed. Accordingly, the judge was not required to give a full *Turnbull* direction.

It is therefore apparent that a Turnbull warning need not be given in every case that involves identification evidence.[70] However, if a warning was not given where it ought to have been, the conviction will normally be quashed.[71] It should also be noted that, as expert evidence relating to voice identification and facial mapping becomes more commonplace, the Court of Appeal has stipulated that an even more stringent warning than the Turnbull direction will normally be necessary.[72]

THE FUTURE OF CRIMINAL EVIDENCE

A number of well-publicised miscarriages of justice, such as the Birmingham Six, Judith Ward and the Guildford Four, were instrumental in bringing about a crisis of confidence in the criminal justice system in the early 1990s. In response to these concerns, the government established the Royal Commission on Criminal Justice,[73] which recommended a number of key changes to evidential and procedural rules relating to disclosure and other safeguards for the defence. Yet, as the decade progressed, specific components of the criminal justice system continued to be placed under scrutiny. These included the treatment of victims and witnesses in court;[74] problems arising from adjournments and delays;[75] and the role of the Crown Prosecution Service.[76]

Sir Robin Auld's *Review of the Criminal Courts in England and Wales*[77] contained a number of radical proposals designed to streamline criminal procedure and radically overhaul the law of evidence. The Review recommended the adoption of a number of inquisitorial-style features into the English system. For example, it was conceded that adversarial combat in the pre-trial phase was inappropriate and a more co-operative regime

---

[70]There is no need, for example, to give it where a witness identifies a vehicle – *R v Browning* (1991) 94 Cr App R 109.

[71]See e.g. *R v Hunjan* (1979) 68 Cr App R 99; *Reid v R*(1990) 90 Cr App R 121.

[72]*R v Roberts* [2000] Crim LR 183. See further discussion below in Ch 10.

[73]Royal Commission on Criminal Justice, *Report*, Cmnd 2263 (1993: London, HMSO).

[74]Home Office, *Speaking Up for Justice* (1998: London, Home Office).

[75]Audit Commission, *The Route to Justice* (2002: London, HMSO).

[76]Glidewell, I *Review of the Crown Prosecution Service*, Cmnd 3960 (1998: London, Home Office).

[77]Auld, Sir Robin *Review of the Criminal Courts of England and Wales*, Cmnd 9376 (2002: London, HMSO).

of disclosure was recommended. Other features were somewhat reminiscent of practices in continental jurisdictions and were aimed at tempering the very partisan nature of the adversarial justice system. These included the recommendation to codify the criminal law and law of evidence; a greater managerial role for trial judges; and further pre-trial co-operation between the parties. Sir Robin's observation that the adversarial system should 'move away from technical rules of inadmissibility to trusting judicial and lay factfinders to give relevant evidence the weight it deserves'[78] also reflects the approach followed in most inquisitorial trials. As such, judges would play a much more pro-active role in the trial, and have a much broader discretion in relation to the admissibility of evidence.

It is also worth noting that Lord Justice Auld acknowledged some of the drawbacks of oral evidence, including the effects of stress and delay upon witnesses. He appears to have used this observation as a springboard for a number of his recommendations, which included the relaxation of the rules on admissibility of previous witness statements, the relaxation of the hearsay rule, and the extension of the use of televised evidence. He seemed to accept that indirect testimony can, in certain circumstances, be as reliable and cogent as direct oral evidence.

The Criminal Justice Act 2003 and the Criminal Procedure Rules of 2005 gave legislative effect to most of these reforms, signifying a shift away from a rigid regime of exclusionary evidential rules towards a broader freedom of proof. While the full impact of these reforms will be discussed in subsequent chapters, it is worth noting at this juncture that the hearsay rule has undergone substantial erosion,[79] as have rules relating to the automatic exclusion of bad character evidence. Furthermore, the Criminal Procedure Rules 2005 lay down a new 'overriding objective', that courts and everyone involved in a criminal case must pursue: to deal with the case justly.[80] The priority afforded to a particular principle or value in this way is something that is very much alien to the common law tradition. The following years will no doubt provide some interesting insights as to how the courts intend to apply such principles in practice.

Technology is also set to change the ways in which evidence is given. Already evidence can be given via satellite link, so that witnesses overseas are able to give evidence without appearing in person.[81] Similarly, the Crime (International Co-operation) Act 2003 allows evidence requested by foreign countries to be taken by telephone. Technology has also brought benefits to lawyers, judges and jurors: instead of pouring over mountains of documents, it is now possible in many cases for evidence to be called up on a computer screen. In fraud cases, this is particularly valuable where juries may be asked to consider a range of complex financial documents.

Perhaps the most important advances for technology have been the benefits reaped for vulnerable witnesses. As we shall see in the next chapter, the Youth Justice and Criminal Evidence Act 1999 provides that children and other vulnerable witnesses can give their evidence-in-chief by means of a pre-recorded video, and also may be cross-examined and re-examined on video, so that they need never be present in court. Doubtless the rules of evidence will continue to be amended and modified for the new age. It is not improbable that in the future we will be able to give evidence via a mobile phone with a video picture being transmitted.

---

[78] At [2.17].
[79] See further Ch 7.
[80] Criminal Procedure Rules 2005, r. 1.1.
[81] CJA 2003, Pt VIII.

Some commentators have argued that tinkering with evidential and procedural rules and introducing new technology are unlikely to tackle many of the system's current problems in an effective manner.[82] Whilst a number of law reform and working groups throughout the common law world have mooted the idea of replacing our adversarial system with a more continental style of process, they have proceeded to defend staunchly the retention of the adversarial system with what has been described by Van Kessel as 'self-righteous adoration'.[83] While many of these groups do recognise certain inherent weaknesses in the system, none has gone so far so as to recommend its outright abolition, and most display a strong aversion to any prospect of transplanting inquisitorial procedures.

In England, the reports of various reform bodies have failed to address the idea of introducing an inquisitorial system in any real depth. The notion was considered summarily before being promptly dismissed in the Philips Royal Commission of 1981 and the Runciman Royal Commission of 1993. The latter Commission suggested that it would be content to see the system move in a more inquisitorial direction, while the more recent *Auld Review of the Criminal Courts* was happy to recommend the 'grafting' of certain elements of inquisitorial procedure onto the adversarial framework. However, not all commentators are agreed that such an approach can work effectively: Edwards comments that cherry-picking and transplanting individual components of inquisitorial systems risks diffusing 'the worst tendencies of combativeness in the Anglo-American system, while retaining some of the salutary features of the continental inquisitorial system'.[84]

The prospect of transplanting an inquisitorial model into the legal system of England and Wales has few supporters within the legal profession, law reform bodies or political parties. It thus remains highly unlikely that such radical reform would occur in the short to medium term, although it does appear that criminal justice policy is currently in a process of transformation, with policy-makers seemingly more ready to acknowledge the shortcomings of the adversarial trial system and look for solutions outside the adversarial framework. There appears to be an increasing tendency to borrow the facets of other systems which are believed to work effectively. Pizzi notes that among the judiciary, legislature and legal profession there is 'less attachment to failed doctrinal structures of the past and a willingness to look for what will work'.[85] A need to temper adversarial processes has been broadly acknowledged, and both the Auld Review and the latest Criminal Justice Act have laid down a pathway for a more radical rethink of the perceived merits of the adversarial model of justice. The restriction of the right to trial by jury; the dismantling of a number of exclusionary rules of evidence; and the expansion of opportunities for witnesses to give evidence by alternative means are all recent developments in modern criminal justice policy which sit uneasily alongside traditional perceptions of the adversarial paradigm.

New international criminal trial systems, such as the International Criminal Court and the International Criminal Tribunal for the Former Yugoslavia, have been instrumental in developing something approaching an international consensus on best trial practice, and the emphasis placed on the rights of victims and witnesses within these

---

[82]See e.g. Ellison, L *The Adversarial Process and the Vulnerable Witness* (2001: Oxford, Oxford University Press); Doak, op cit n 40; Pizzi, W *Trials without Truth* (1999: New York, New York University Press).

[83]Van Kessel, G 'Adversary Excesses in the American Criminal Trial' (1992) 67 *Notre Dame LR* 403, 409.

[84]Edwards, H 'Comments on Mirjan Damaska's "Of Evidentiary Transplants"' 45 American J of Comp Law 853, 855; see also Corker, D 'The Worst of Both Worlds' (2002) 152 (1997) NLJ 1741.

[85]Pizzi, op cit n 82 at 231.

institutions probably acted as a catalyst in the improved protections now available to vulnerable witnesses and the erosion of exclusionary rules of evidence. We should also not underestimate the impact of the European Court of Human Rights. Over the past decade, there is an increased willingness of the Court to venture into areas concerning the law of evidence, around which it has traditionally steered a wide berth. Indeed, Jackson has observed a discernible shift in the way we have tended in the past to categorise systems of evidence according to the adversarial or inquisitorial spectrum, and argues that the Court is in the process of developing a new model of proof that might more accurately be characterised as 'participatory'.[86] While it may be some time before the full impact of this shift upon the parameters of the adversarial system can be fully ascertained, it seems certain that international harmonisation and the expansion of human rights norms will continue to inform the operation of the rules of evidence for the foreseeable future.

KEY LEARNING POINTS

- In criminal trials, the general rule is that judges determine issues of law and juries determine the facts.
- Questions of admissibility are decided within a *voir dire*, otherwise known as a 'trial within a trial'.
- Once both sides have presented their case, the judge should direct the jury on the law. He or she may also wish to comment on the weight of the evidence.
- All evidence adduced at the trial must be relevant.
- Corroboration and care warnings are no longer mandatory, but are discretionary.
- In cases where the prosecution case rests substantially on eyewitness identification, a special warning to the jury, known as the *Turnbull* Direction, is required.

? *QUESTIONS*

(1) Billy and Michael are convicted of attempted burglary, primarily on the basis of the identification evidence provided by Helen. Helen gives evidence to the effect that she was leaving her office one evening around 8pm. It was twilight, and there was a light mist in the air. Across the street, she saw two bald men of heavy build and wearing black leather jackets using a crowbar to prise open a door on a building directly opposite her. She tells the police that she thinks the men in question are Billy and Michael Coleman, with whom she went to school. The police arrest Billy and Michael, both of whom match Helen's description.

In summing up, the judge says the following:

'Ladies and gentlemen of the jury, you are reminded that identification evidence is fraught with many difficulties. In particular, you must bear in

Continued

---

[86]Jackson, J 'The Effect of Human Rights on Criminal Evidentiary Processes: Towards Convergence, Divergence or Realignment?' 68 MLR 737.

?   *QUESTIONS (Continued)*

mind that a witness may be very certain in her own mind as to the identity of the person in question, but it is worth noting that an honest and convincing witness may also be mistaken. However, in a case such as this, where the eyewitness has known both the accused from her schooldays, the evidence is likely to be highly cogent and you may decide to convict on that basis'.

Assess Billy and Michael's prospects for appeal.

(2) 'The supposed safeguards relating to the use of identification evidence in criminal trials are woefully inadequate'.

Discuss the issues raised in the above quotation.

(3) 'The concept of relevance is simply too vague to be of any real use in contemporary criminal trials'.

To what extent do you agree with the above statement?

(4) Harriet has alleged that she was raped by George two years ago on the night of her sixteenth birthday. George has admitted they had intercourse but alleges it was consensual. Since Harriet has only recently come forward with the allegations, the prosecution are unable to rely on any forensic evidence. Is it possible that George may be convicted on the basis of Harriet's testimony alone and, if so, should the judge issue any particular warning to the jury?

SUGGESTED FURTHER READING

Jackson, J 'Insufficiency of identification evidence based on personal impression'. [1986] Crim LR 203.

Hartshorne, J. 'Corroboration and care warnings after Makanjuola' [1998] 2 E & P 1.

McConville, M *Corroboration and Confessions: The Impact of a Rule Requiring that no Conviction be sustained on the Basis of Confession Evidence Alone*, RCCJ Research Study No 13 (1993: London, HMSO).

Ormerod, D 'Sounds familiar? Voice identification evidence'. [2001] Crim LR 595.

Wolchover, D 'Should judges sum up on the facts?' [1989] Crim LR 781.

CHAPTER 2

THE PRINCIPLE OF ORALITY

INTRODUCTION

Lord Devlin once remarked that 'the centrepiece of the adversary system is the oral trial'.[87] The principle of orality states that evidence should normally be received through the live oral testimony of witnesses in court, speaking from their own direct knowledge. As noted in the previous chapter, although the use of documentary and real evidence does play a role in criminal proceedings, the adversarial trial is primarily geared to receiving evidence in oral form before an open court. The view that oral evidence is an intrinsically superior form of evidence is widely accepted within the courts and the legal profession. Its perceived advantages were outlined by the High Court of Australia in *Butera v DPP*:[88]

> A witness who gives evidence orally demonstrates, for good or ill, more about his or her credibility than a witness whose evidence is given in documentary form. Oral evidence is public; written evidence may not be. Oral evidence gives to the trial the atmosphere which, though intangible, is often critical to the jury's consideration of the witnesses. By generally restricting the jury to consideration of testimonial evidence in its oral form, it is thought that the jury's discussion of the case in the jury's room will be more open, the exchange of views among jurors will more easily occur than if the evidence were given in writing or the jurors were each armed with a written transcript of the evidence.[89]

The principle of orality not only reflects the desirability of receiving testimony in person, but consists of a number of different limbs, as Dennis explains:

> There is firstly the general rule that a witness may give testimony only about matters of which the witness has personal knowledge. Secondly, testimony must be given on oath or affirmation … Thirdly, a requirement for oral testimony enables the factfinder to observe the demeanour of the witness when giving evidence, and to take this into account in deciding the weight to be attached to the testimony. Fourthly, witnesses who give oral testimony can be cross-examined in person at the time, thereby enabling the cross-examiner to maximise the impact and efficiency of the questioning. Fifthly, collateral evidence of the witness's credibility can sometimes be adduced in the form of evidence of the witness's bias, previous convictions, discreditable conduct… and reputation for veracity.[90]

Yet, in spite of these purported advantages, the alleged superiority attached to oral evidence is something which is to be found uniquely in the Anglo-American common law tradition. In the view of McEwan:

> Alleged superiority of oral testimony is not universally accepted. Like historians, continental jurisdictions prefer documentary sources. A French treatise speaks of 'the primacy of written proof and the mistrust which is prima facie inspired by oral testimony', which is seen as highly subjective.[91]

---

[87] Devlin, P *The Judge* (1979: Oxford, Oxford University Press), p 54.
[88] (1987) 167 CLR 180.
[89] *Ibid.*, 189, as cited by Dennis, I *The Law of Evidence*, 3rd edn (2007: London, Sweet & Maxwell), p 491.
[90] *Ibid.*
[91] McEwan, J 'Documentary Hearsay Evidence – Refuge for the Vulnerable Witness?' [1989] Crim LR 629, 631.

Similarly, Spencer and Flin have argued that 'our preference for oral evidence seems to be a purely cultural one. This preference is not shared by lawyers outside the English-speaking world'.[92] The authors proceed to discuss a body of research which casts doubt on the assumption that oral testimony is more likely to produce reliable evidence. The authors' concerns about oral evidence may be attributed to two major factors:

> First, it [oral testimony] is nearly always given a long time after the event in question. Secondly, when giving evidence live at trial a witness is normally suffering from stress. If there are two scientific facts about the psychology of the human memory which are clear beyond any doubt, one is that memory for an event fades gradually with time, and the other is that stress beyond a certain level can impair the power of recall.[93]

In addition to stress, psychologists have observed that memories are susceptible to changes over time, and become conflated with other real or imaginary events.[94] Events are interpreted and re-interpreted over time, and the time gap between the events in question, giving a statement to the police, and then testifying at trial will often run into many months or even years. This is particularly true where the event in question was of a traumatic nature. Haward has illustrated how psychologists have acknowledged that the brain actively represses information about stressful past events, and will thus be engaged in a constant process of selecting, highlighting and deleting memories.[95] Even though the vast majority of witnesses who testify in court may be giving a bona fide account according to their memory, they may still be mistaken about all the facts or certain facts. Some, for one reason or another, may be subconsciously prejudiced or biased in the way they perceive past events,[96] and some may actively choose to be dishonest. Other witnesses will be limited in their ability to articulate clearly what they recall, perhaps because of age, disability, or illness.[97] The accounts of others may be adversely affected by a sense of 'extreme eagerness' to assist the police with their inquiries.[98] Taking all of these factors into account, it is highly questionable whether oral testimony is really the most reliable method of accessing the truth about past events.

THE OATH

At one time, the principle of orality required that all witnesses testify under oath on the Bible. The courts appeared to regard it as a form of acknowledgement by the witness of a belief that, if he or she did not keep to it, the consequences would suffer 'some kind

---

[92]Spencer, J and Flin, R *The Evidence of Children*, 2nd edn (1993: London, Blackstone), p 267.

[93]*Ibid.*, p 268.

[94]For an overview of the psychological literature, see Loftus, E, Wolchover, D, and Page, D. 'General Review of the Psychology of Witness Testimony' in A Heaton-Armstrong, E Shepherd, G Gudjonsson, and D Wolchover (eds) *Witness Testimony Psychological, Investigative and Evidential Perspectives* (2006: Oxford, Oxford University Press).

[95]*Ibid.*

[96]See Greer, D S 'Anything But The Truth? The Reliability of Testimony in Criminal Trials' (1971) 11 *Brit J Crim* 147.

[97]Most commonly (though not exclusively) this affects child witnesses and witnesses with learning disabilities. For a general overview, see respectively Murphy, G and Clare, I 'The Effect of Learning Disabilities on Witness Testimony' in A Heaton-Armstrong *et al.* op cit n 94. 'Investigative Interviewing with Children: Progress and Pitfalls' in A Heaton-Armstrong *et al.* op cit n 94.

[98]Gudjonsson, G (2006), 'The Psychological Vulnerabilies of Witnesses and the Risk of False Assusations and False Confessions' in A Heaton-Armstrong *et al.* op cit n 94, p 66.

of divine punishment, although it need not be as bad as hell-fire'.[99] In practice, this rule served to exclude all non-Christians and atheists, who were considered incompetent to testify. The modern law is to be found in the Oaths Act 1978. Section 1 provides for the manner of the administration of the oath to Christians and those of the Jewish faith. The oath is administered routinely unless the witness objects. In the case of witnesses of a religion other than Christian or Jewish, the Act provides that the oath shall be administered in any lawful manner.[100] Such witnesses will usually take the oath upon whichever holy book is appropriate to their religion.[101] In *R v Kemble*,[102] it was decided that whether an oath was lawful depended not on the intricacies of the particular religion, but on whether the oath appears to the court to be binding on the conscience of the witness and, if so, whether the witness in question considers the oath to be binding on his conscience.

If the witness objects to the taking of an oath, he or she may instead make a solemn affirmation.[103] Such affirmation may replace the oath if the court is not equipped to administer the oath in accordance with the religion of the witness.[104] To avoid the possibility that a non-religious witness might claim that his evidence given on oath is invalid, section 4(2) provides that the fact that a person had at the time of taking the oath no religious belief 'shall not for any purpose affect the validity of the oath'. If a witness wilfully makes a material statement on oath or affirmation that he or she knows is false or does not believe to be true, he or she will have committed the offence of perjury.[105]

There have been a number of proposals to abolish the religious oath on the basis that perhaps a majority of witnesses have no particular religion. Nothing has come of these proposals, though there are now categories of witnesses who may give evidence unsworn. The most important of these are children under 14 years, who are not permitted to be sworn for the purposes of giving evidence in court, since it is assumed that they do not have sufficient appreciation of the solemnity of the occasion and the particular responsibility to tell the truth.[106] Adult witnesses who are able to give intelligible testimony are presumed to have such an appreciation. However, section 56 of the YJCEA 1999 also provides the court with a power to receive the unsworn evidence of a person who is over 14, provided they are competent but for some reason do not have sufficient appreciation of the solemnity of the occasion and the particular responsibility to tell the truth which is involved in taking the oath. Thus, for the first time in the history of the English criminal justice system, certain adult witnesses are now able to give evidence unsworn.

THE EXPERIENCE OF VULNERABLE WITNESSES

One of the most lamentable effects of the principle of orality relates to its impact upon witnesses. For the vast majority of those called to give evidence, the courtroom will be an unfamiliar and austere environment, dominated by lawyers and court officials. It is perhaps unsurprising that research has uncovered that many witnesses may find the

---

[99]Spencer, J and Flin, R *The Evidence Of Children* (1993: Oxford, Blackstone), p 51, citing Brett MR in *Attorney General v Bradlaugh* (1885) 14 QBD 667.
[100]Oaths Act 1978 section 1(3).
[101]See for example: http://www.wynnechambers.co.uk/pdf/Swearing_an_Oath.pdf.
[102][1990] 1 WLR 1111.
[103]Oaths Act 1978, section 5(1).
[104]Oaths Act 1978, section 5(2).
[105]Perjury Act 1911, section 1(1).
[106]Youth Justice and Criminal Evidence Act 1999, section 55(2).

process of giving evidence alienating and stressful.[107] The formality of procedure, the forbidding atmosphere, and the presence of wigs and gowns are likely to contribute to this general sense of unease which results in many witnesses feeling as outsiders to a highly ritualised and professionalised process.[108] While feelings of stress, anxiety or consternation are commonplace among many witnesses with diverse characteristics testifying in very different types of cases, it is well established that such emotions are likely to be exacerbated among certain classes of witnesses. There is a considerable body of research charting the plight of child witnesses, complainants in sexual cases, witnesses suffering from learning disabilities, and witnesses in fear of intimidation. Not only may their sense of despondency cause them undue distress before, during and after giving testimony, but from the point of view of the legal system, as suggested above, it may also negatively impact upon their ability to recall accurately past events.[109]

Child witnesses

It is, perhaps, overly obvious to state that many children find the experience extremely daunting and confusing. Research has shown that children experience considerable anxiety in the lead-up to a court appearance, as well as experiencing so-called 'secondary victimisation' whilst giving evidence. In their study of 218 children in 1992, Goodman *et al.* compared the behavioural disturbances of those who testified with those who did not.[110] Of those who testified, the researchers reported that confronting the defendant in court brought back traumatic memories, caused sleep disturbance and exacerbated feelings of pain, hurt and helplessness. More specifically, the more frightened a child was of confronting the accused, the fewer questions the child would answer.[111]

In particular, stress levels are exacerbated by the unfamiliar language used in court by barristers. Davies and Noon's study of child witnesses in England found that 25 per cent of all questions were inappropriate to the witness's age.[112] Brennan and Brennan's survey of child witnesses in Australia identified thirteen different linguistic devices which were used regularly to confuse child witnesses. The use of complex sentence structures and advanced vocabulary served to exacerbate the unfamiliar situation in which children found themselves, and the researchers found that questions were frequently highly stylised (e.g. 'I put it to you ...;' 'I suggest to you') or employed complex grammatical structures involving negatives (e.g. 'Now you did have a bruise, did you not, near one of your breasts?'; 'Now this happened on a Friday, did it not?'). In the words of the researchers:

> Cross-examination is that part of court proceedings where the interests and rights of the
> child are most likely to be ignored and sacrificed ... The techniques used are all created

---

[107]See Angle, H, Malam, S, and Carey, C. *Witness Satisfaction: findings from the Witness Satisfaction Survey 2002* (2003: London, Home Office). The researchers reported that 21% of all witnesses surveyed felt intimidated either by the process of giving evidence or by the courtroom environment. See also Shapland,J, Willmore, J and Duff, P *et al., Victims in the Criminal Justice System* (1985: Aldershot, Gower); Whitehead, E. *Witness Satisfaction: Findings from the Witness Satisfaction Survey 2000* (2001: London, Home Office).

[108]See generally Rock, P *The Social World of the English Crown Court* (1993: Oxford, Clarendon).

[109]For an overview of the literature on this point, see Ellison, L *The Adversarial Process and the Vulnerable Witness* (2001: Oxford, Oxford University Press), pp 19-23.

[110]Goodman, G, Taub, EP, Jones, D, England, P, Port, L, Rudy, L, and Rado, L *Testifying in Criminal Court: Emotional Effects on Child Sexual Assault Victims* (1992: Chicago, University of Chicago Press).

[111]*Ibid.*, 121.

[112]Davies, G and Noon, E (1991). Only 36% of barristers made extensive efforts to adapt their language so as to make it suitable for the child.

with words, since they are the only currency of the court ... Under conditions of cross-examination the child is placed in an adversarial and stressful situation which tests the resilience of even the most confident of adults ... The right of the lawyer to directly oppose the evidence given by the child witness, the implicit hostility which surrounds cross-examination, alien language forms, and the sheer volume of questions asked, all conspire to confuse the child. It is a quick and easy step to destroy the credibility of the child witness.[113]

A recent survey of 50 child witnesses carried out on behalf of the NSPCC by Plotnikoff and Woolfson found that over half the children interviewed said that they did not understand some words or found some questions confusing.[114] Just five of the child witnesses interviewed described defence lawyers as 'polite', but nineteen said the lawyers were not polite. Defence counsel were described as 'aggressive', 'sarcastic', 'cross', 'shouting', 'rude', 'harassing', 'disrespectful', 'arrogant', 'overpowering', 'badgering', 'scary' and 'pushy'. Cordon *et al.* cite a number of other studies which arrived at similar findings.[115] They describe how advocates will frequently try to lure child witnesses into a false sense of security, by asking non-substantive questions about the child's background and interests, before subtly moving on to elicit substantive information which contradicts the child's original testimony. They also present evidence which suggests that cross-examiners typically capitalise on children's tendencies to be suggestible and to fantasise. The goal in many cross-examinations, they argue, is to 'keep the child off balance to increase the chance of inconsistencies'.[116]

Complainants in rape and sexual cases

Trials for sexual offences differ from other criminal hearings in a number of respects. Often, the fact that intercourse actually took place is not a contested issue. Most rape cases usually turn upon the issue of consent, which can give rise to a number of evidential difficulties, particularly where the complainant and the accused have previously engaged in a consensual sexual relationship. Since the complainant and the accused will usually be the only witnesses to the incident in question, rape trials frequently boil down to a battle of credibility between the accused and the alleged victim. One of the main methods used by defence counsel to attack the character of the rape complainant is to suggest that she is sexually disreputable, alluding to loose moral values and a decadent lifestyle. By their very nature, sexual offences are notoriously invasive, and many victims will struggle with emotional and psychological consequences of victimisation for years to come.[117] Sex crimes carry a notoriously high attrition rate,[118] and it is thus particularly unfortunate that those who find the courage to testify about their ordeal in open court will be subjected to character assassination.

---

[113]*Ibid.*, p 91.

[114]Plotnikoff, J and Woolfson, R *In Their Own Words: The Experiences of 50 Young Witnesses in Criminal Proceedings* (2004: London, NSPCC).

[115]Cordon, I, Goodman, G, and Anderson, S 'Children in Court' in P J Van Koppen and S D Penrod (eds). *Adversarial versus Inquisitorial Justice* (2003: New York, Kluwer).

[116]*Ibid.*, pp 175–177.

[117]See e.g. Santiago, J, McCall-Perez, F, Gorcey, M, and Beigel, A 'Long-term psychological effects of rape in 35 rape victims' (1985) 142 *American Journal of Psychiatry* 1338.

[118]See Kelly, L, Lovett, J and Regan, L *A Gap or Chasm? Attrition in Reported Rape Cases*, Home Office Research Study No 293 (2005: London, Home Office).

It is only in relatively recent times that the plight of rape and sexual assault complainants at court has been uncovered. In 1978, Holmstrom and Burgess were among the first to conduct research into the issue, and concluded that 'overwhelmingly, both adult and young [rape] victims found court an extremely stressful experience'.[119] Since then, a substantial body of literature has rapidly grown to support this view. The most stressful aspect of the court appearance is cross-examination, which is often particularly humiliating for complainants. It is not uncommon for them to be questioned in relation to intimate details of their private lives, as well as being asked to recount to a public courtroom intricate details of an invasive and traumatising attack. As Grohovsky describes, the victim's body becomes something of a crime scene in itself 'from which evidence must be collected and analysed'.[120]

The most distressing type of questions are likely to be those that relate to the complainant's lifestyle and sexual history. In a survey of 116 rape complainants, Lees records complainants being asked details about their underwear, make-up, social lifestyle, menstrual cycle and drug habits:[121]

> Questions addressed to the women in the trials I monitored included whether she had had previous sex with men other than the defendant, whether she was a single mother, whether the man she was living with was the father of her children; the colour of her present and past boyfriends ... who looked after her children while she was at work; whether she was in the habit of going to nightclubs on her own late at night; whether she smoked cannabis and drank alcohol ... what underwear she had on; whether she wore false eyelashes and red lipstick; whether the defendant had 'used her previously'.[122]

The vast majority of complainants interviewed by Lees (83 per cent) said that they felt as though they were on trial, rather than the defendant. Similarly, a 1996 survey of rape complainants by Victim Support found that 12 per cent of women said their experience in court was actually worse than the rape itself.[123] Furthermore, 41 per cent of women felt anger or they had been re-victimised in court.[124]

As noted below, while steps have been taken in recent years to limit the potential for attacks on the complainant, there are concerns that these are inadequate and are unlikely to address the fundamental difficulties faced by rape complainants.

Witnesses with learning disabilities

Since the adversarial system relies heavily on oral testimony, there is a presumption that all witnesses are able to communicate effectively. As we have discovered in relation to young children, this will not necessarily be the case. Witnesses with learning disabilities are also likely to find the task of understanding questions and articulating their answers extremely difficult under adversarial conditions. In a study carried out in the mid-1990s,

---

[119]Holstrom, L and Burgess, A W (1974) 'Rape Trauma Syndrome' 131 *American Journal of Psychiatry* pp 981, 986.

[120]Grohovsky, J (2000) 'Giving Voice to Victims: Why the Criminal Justice System in England and Wales Should Allow Victims to Speak Up for Themselves' 64 *Journal of Criminal Law* pp 416, 417.

[121]Lees, S (1996) *Carnal Knowledge: Rape on Trial* (London, Hamish Hamilton), pp 139–149.

[122]*Ibid.*, p 134.

[123]Victim Support, *Women, Rape and the Criminal Justice System* (1996: London, Victim Support)

[124]*Ibid.*

Sanders *et al.* identified three key areas which are likely to make learning-disabled witnesses at risk of heightened vulnerability in court.[125] First, such witnesses are often impaired in terms of their memory: their ability to absorb, memorise and then recall events is often lessened. Secondly, such witnesses often encounter difficulties in communicating. Many possess a restricted vocabulary and have therefore a limited means of articulating themselves. Finally, these witnesses often respond to aggressive questioning by attempting to pacify the questioner by offering the response he/she thinks they are looking for.

The researchers concluded that witnesses with learning difficulties suffer from enhanced levels of stress and many such witnesses were reported as feeling bullied or pressurized when testifying, which, in turn, impacted negatively upon their testimony. In addition, and in a similar fashion to the treatment of child witnesses, counsel frequently used convoluted language as a device to confuse witnesses or make them contradict themselves.[126] In spite of their powers to do so, judges rarely intervened to prevent inappropriate questioning and failed to adapt their own language to make allowances for the witness.[127] Other studies have arrived at similar findings, both Kebbell *et al.* and O'Kelly *et al.* have reported that lawyers had done little to adjust their questioning style and that there were no significant differences in the readiness of the judiciary to intervene to clarify questioning among witnesses with learning difficulties and those without.[128]

Witnesses in fear of intimidation

A further group of witnesses who may be particularly vulnerable are those at risk of intimidation or reprisals as a result of giving evidence. Witness intimidation is a particular problem, especially where the alleged offenders are part of the community in which the witness lives, or where the community is hostile to the police. One intimidation incident, reported in the national press, concerned the trial of four men for causing grievous bodily harm to a witness to a murder. One prospective witness was sitting in a crowded pub, when he was suddenly set upon by four masked men. His punishment for testifying was the loss of his hand, which was hacked off with a butcher's knife.[129] The Home Office publication, *Working with Intimidated Witnesses*,[130] envisages that the problem of witness intimidation is on the increase: the number of cases for perverting the course of justice (which includes witness intimidation) rose by over 30 per cent between 2000 and 2005. Working from the 1998 British Crime Survey, Tarling *et al.* concluded that intimidation occurs in almost 10 per cent of reported crime and in 20 per cent of unreported crime.[131] Intimidation of victims may take various forms, from verbal taunts or threats, to physical jousting or to serious physical violence. It may range from a relatively low-key, one-off

---

[125]Sanders, A, Creation, J, Bird, S, and Weber, L *Victims with Learning Disabilities: Negotiating the Criminal Justice System*, Home Office Research Findings No 44 (1996: London, Home Office).

[126]*Ibid.*, p 76.

[127]*Ibid.*

[128]O'Kelly, C, Kebbell, M, Hatton, C, and Johnson, S 'Judicial intervention in court cases involving witnesses with and without learning disabilities' (2003) 8 *Legal and Criminological Psychology* 229; Kebbell, M, Hatton, C, and Johnson, S 'Witnesses with intellectual disabilities in court: What questions are asked and what influence do they have?' (2004) 9 *Legal and Criminological Psychology* 23.

[129]*The Times*, 5 April 1997.

[130]Home Office, *Working with Intimidated Witnesses* (2006: London, Home Office).

[131]Tarling, R, *et al.*, *Victim and Witness Intimidation: Key Findings from the British Crime Survey* (2000: London, Home Office).

incident, to a chain of events amounting to ongoing harassment and persistent threatening behaviour.[132]

Recent studies suggest that certain groups of people, or witnesses who testify in particular types of cases, are at heightened risk of intimidation. Levels of intimidation appear to be greater amongst poorer socio-economic groups,[133] victims of crime (particularly victims of violence),[134] racial and sexual minorities,[135] and women – particularly in cases involving domestic violence,[136] or those involving sexual offences.[137] Where a case concerns organised crime or terrorist activity, it is quite possible that the associates of those on trial may seek to coerce witnesses from giving evidence through duress or physical violence.

Even if witness intimidation only occurs in a relatively small proportion of cases, there is nonetheless a risk that the *fear* of intimidation may act to prevent many victims reporting crime or giving evidence in court. Although intimidation is more often seen as a pre-trial problem, Hamlyn *et al.* noted that those who were intimidated were more likely to suffer secondary victimisation at court,[138] and victims were more likely to suffer than other witnesses.[139] Despite national initiatives to ensure separate waiting facilities for victims and defendants, meetings in the court precinct still seem to be commonplace.[140] One troubling finding from recent observational research conducted by Fielding was that many of the court-based professionals seemed unsure how to react and viewed it as someone else's problem.[141]

Other witnesses

The problems experienced by these various classes of 'vulnerable' classes of witnesses are particularly well documented, but they should not detract from the fact that most lay witnesses will find the prospecting of giving evidence somewhat daunting and stressful.[142] In his study of proceedings at Wood Green Crown Court, Rock found that

---

[132]Tarling, R, *et al.* (*ibid*) found that almost over two thirds of incidents featured verbal abuse, 16% physical assaults and 9% damage to property. However, the reasons underlying intimidation are unclear. In only a small minority of cases (8%) did the victim believe that the reason behind the intimidation was to prevent them giving evidence. In nearly 50% of cases victims thought it was simply that the offender wanted to 'annoy' or 'upset' them. For a further quarter the intimidation was viewed as part of an ongoing series of offences against them, for example in cases of domestic violence. See also Maynard *Witness intimidation, strategies for prevention* (1994); Fyfe, NR and McKay, H *Making it safe to speak? A study of witness intimidation and protection in Strathclyde* (1999).

[133]Tarling *et al.*, op cit n 131.

[134]Elliott, R "Vulnerable and Intimidated Witnesses:. A Review of the Literature" (1998: London, Home Office). See also Angle *et al.*, op cit n 107.

[135]Elliott, *ibid*.

[136]Elliott, *ibid*.; Tarling *et al.*, op cit n 131.

[137]Lees, op cit n 121, p 108.

[138]Hamlyn, B, Phelps, A, Turtle, J, and Sattar, G *Are Special Measures Working? Evidence from Surveys of Vulnerable and Intimidated Witnesses*, Home Office Research Study 283 (2004: London, Home Office), p xi.

[139]*Ibid.*, p 19.

[140]*Ibid.*

[141]Fielding, N *Courting Violence* (2006: Oxford, Oxford University Press), p 215.

[142]Of course, proceedings will be inevitably less stressful for those who regularly appear in court as part of their professional duties. Police officers, customs officials, and expert witnesses are much less likely to be unnerved by the process of giving evidence.

'as a matter of course, and in most ordinary trials, gravely wounding allegations would be put to witnesses'.[143] Witnesses, he reported, were frequently bullied, harassed and felt as though they were on trial in 'the most charged of all secular rituals'.[144] Often, witnesses were not permitted to give their evidence at a greater rate than the desired pace of the transcriber, and on occasions were told to slow down their evidence.[145] Rock also observed that 'nothing was allowed to remain tacit, elided, discreet or *sotto voce*',[146] with witnesses being asked to 'speak up' if they failed to make themselves audible to the entire court.[147] Evidently, if witnesses are relaying to the court intimate details of their private lives, including past indiscretions, or even something as mundane as their addresses and occupations, they may be reluctant or embarrassed to make certain facts public knowledge.[148] Rock noted that this can cause particular awkwardness in witnesses where they are required to flout the taboos of language, with the Court hearing details of 'all the violent doings and language of the bedroom, street and public house, witnesses having to cite the heedless and profane speech of angry relationships'.[149] For most judges and legal professions, distress was a perfectly natural aspect of criminal trials.[150]

Similar findings were uncovered by Fielding, who examined the conduct of trials involving violent offences.[151] Many witnesses experienced feelings of stress and alienation, but, like Rock, Fielding found that these emotions were perceived by lawyers and judges as unfortunate, but essential, aspects of the court hearing.[152] On occasions, judges would attempt to mitigate the experience by 'pacing' proceedings, offering tissues or water, or sympathetic words,[153] but Fielding describes how the 'fear factor' seemed to enhance credibility, with advocates engaging in a range of well-established techniques, including 'rapid fire questioning', with witnesses being visibly upset by public interrogation about very intimate or private matters.

As research into the experience of witnesses continues to be disseminated on a regular basis, it is becoming increasingly apparent that the underlying adversarial paradigm itself renders the experience of testifying so distressful for so many witnesses. We shall return to this theme later in this chapter.

SPECIAL MEASURES: A PANACEA FOR VULNERABLE WITNESSES?

The past two decades have witnessed considerable efforts to address some of the problems highlighted above, with successive governments introducing a range of measures to help reduce secondary victimisation in the courtroom. The first statutory measures were contained in the Criminal Justice Act 1988, which made provision for children, with the leave of the court, to give all their evidence by live television link in cases involving

---

[143] Rock, P *The Social World of an English Crown Court* (1993: Oxford, Clarendon Press), p 88.
[144] *Ibid.*, p 267.
[145] *Ibid.*
[146] *Ibid.*
[147] *Ibid.*
[148] Compare Fielding, op cit n 141, who found that having one's address made public caused many victims anxiety (at p 214).
[149] Rock, op cit n 143, p 50.
[150] *Ibid.*, 151–153.
[151] Fielding, op cit n 141.
[152] *Ibid.*, 38; 45–46.
[153] *Ibid.*, 45–50.

offences of a sexual or violent nature.[154] In practice, this would mean that, subject to the discretion of the court, the child could avoid having to give evidence in the austerity of the courtroom and would not have to face to prospect of being confronted by the accused.

Shortly after the enactment of the legislation, the government established an advisory group in 1989, chaired by Judge Thomas Pigot QC, to consider its full implications.[155] The terms of reference of the advisory group were to examine the 'growing body of support for a change in the law, so that video recordings of interviews with victims could be readily used as evidence in trials for child abuse'. However, the Home Secretary also made clear that the Government could not contemplate the effacement of the defendant's right to cross-examination, thus effectively rejecting the possibility of pre-recorded cross-examination before the group had even commenced its enquiry. The group based its work around two 'rudimentary principles':

- that child witnesses' involvement in criminal proceedings should be concluded as rapidly as possible without compromising the interests of justice; and
- that children should give evidence in surroundings and circumstances which do not intimidate or overawe them, and the number of people present should be kept to a minimum.

The Pigot Committee recognised that the TV link was only a partial solution and recommended that:

- no child under 14 (17 in sexual offences) should have to give evidence in open court where the offence involved is one of violence or of a sexual nature, or cruelty or neglect;
- children's evidence-in-chief should be replaced by a video-taped interview;
- cross-examination of the child should take place at an out-of-court preliminary hearing when the judge and counsel would be present, the videoed evidence and cross-examination being shown to the jury at the appropriate point in the trial when the child would have given evidence.

Had they been implemented, these proposals would have meant that child witnesses need never appear in court. Instead, all questioning would be pre-recorded outside the court in an informal atmosphere shortly after the charges had been brought against the accused. This radical proposal was, however, met with stiff opposition, and the Criminal Justice Act 1991 which followed stopped well short of implementing the recommendations of the Pigot Committee. Instead, the Act made provision for the child's evidence-in-chief to be recorded in advance of the trial,[156] but made no equivalent provision for cross-examination or re-examination. Thus section 54 of the Act required, as a condition of the admissibility of the video evidence, that the child be available for cross-examination – undoubtedly the most gruelling aspect of the questioning process.[157] Nonetheless, the reform was given a broad welcome. For the first time, the Government had accepted that courts had duties to safeguard the interests of certain witnesses, and acknowledged their status as victims, as

---

[154]CJA 1988, section 32. This provision was subsequently extended by the subsequent CJA 1991 to include children under 17, where a sexual offence was concerned.

[155]Pigot, Judge T *Report of the Advisory Group on Video Evidence* (1989: London, HMSO).

[156]Note, however, that only children under 15 (physical abuse) or under 17 (sexual abuse) could take advantage of the provision.

[157]Such cross-examination could, however, be carried out via the television link under the 1988 Act providing the relevant criteria were met.

opposed to mere servants of the criminal justice system. However, the legislation still fell well short of offering a fully comprehensive set of procedural protections for vulnerable witnesses, and was severely limited in a number of respects.

First, the legislation applied only to a limited class of persons for a limited range of specified offences in criminal cases only. The reforms failed to deal with other vulnerable witnesses, such as adult complainants in sexual cases, or the physically disabled and mentally ill. Secondly, even where child witnesses were deemed eligible to make use of such measures, the range of measures open to them remained very limited. Only the child's evidence-in-chief was to be pre-recorded, and the key recommendation of the Pigot Committee, that children should not be forced into giving any evidence in court against their will, was ignored. Thirdly, the nature of legislation created an overly complex and piecemeal framework of rules on children's evidence, contained in three separate statutes: the Children and Young Persons Act 1933; the Criminal Justice Act 1988; and the Criminal Justice Act 1991. The government failed to seize the opportunity to consolidate the law in the 1991 Act, and its scope thus remained uncertain and confusing.

The provisions of the 1988–91 Acts were overly complex, poorly drafted, and they also gave rise to numerous legal lacunae. For example, whereas the live link and the use of video-recorded evidence were limited to trial on indictment and in youth courts, no provision was made for children who had to testify in magistrates' courts. Another major omission was the lack of any comprehensive guidance or criteria, other than the rather ambiguous 'interests of justice' test.[158] Likewise, no mechanisms were in place for ascertaining the child witness's expectations or desires; there was no guidance as to whether the views of the child should be taken into account, or indeed how such views were to be ascertained. Such omissions and complexities resulted in an uncertain regime where judicial discretion had a key role to play. In the absence of comprehensive guidelines, the prevailing climate of uncertainty and inconsistent practice was bound to be perpetuated.

The YJCEA 1999

Following the election of the Labour Government in May 1997, the new Home Secretary, Jack Straw, announced the setting up of a Home Office Interdepartmental Working Group, to examine and make recommendations on the treatment of vulnerable and intimidated witnesses within the criminal justice system. Its terms of reference included the identification of measures at all stages of the criminal justice process which would improve the treatment of vulnerable witnesses, and further measures that might encourage witnesses to give evidence in court. Members of the Group were drawn from a range of government departments, and included representatives of Victim Support and the Association of Chief Police Officers. Special conferences were held to facilitate discussion with the judiciary and legal profession, and in drawing up their recommendations the Group drew heavily on the findings of a number of academic studies. The Group published its report, *Speaking Up for Justice*, in June 1998.[159]

The Report made a total of 78 recommendations, 26 of which required legislation. It highlighted the need for training for all those involved in the criminal justice system to assist them in responding to the needs of vulnerable witnesses, including children.

---

[158] CJA 1988, section 32A(3)(c).
[159] Home Office, *Speaking Up for Justice*, Report of the Interdepartmental Working Group on the Treatment of Vulnerable or Intimidated Witnesses in the Criminal Justice System (1998: London, Home Office).

A plethora of recommendations dealt with a variety of victims' issues, including measures to combat witness intimidation and a wide range of measures to protect vulnerable and intimidated witnesses within the trial itself. The Group identified two categories of witness who should receive assistance at the discretion of the court. First, the Report concluded that those witnesses whose vulnerability related to the effects of age, disability or illness (category 'a' witnesses) would automatically be entitled to some form of special protection. However, in the case of witnesses who may be vulnerable or intimidated for reasons relating to their particular situation or the circumstances of the case (category 'b' witnesses), it was recommended that the trial judge retain discretion in determining whether or not the granting of such measures would be appropriate. In contrast to the half-hearted attempt to implement the Pigot Report in 1991, most of the *Speaking Up for Justice* recommendations were implemented in Part II of the Youth Justice and Criminal Evidence Act 1999 .

Like the previous regime contained in the Criminal Justice Acts 1988–91, the current provisions that seek to protect vulnerable witnesses in court are something of a statutory minefield. Applications for special measures directions will usually be made before the trial begins during the Plea and Case Management Hearing. In determining whether or not to issue a special measures direction, the court has to concern itself with three issues:

- the eligibility of the witness;
- the availability of the range of special measures; and
- the desirability of making a special measures direction in the circumstances of the case.

In keeping with the recommendations of the Working Group, the eligibility of a witness for a special measures direction will depend upon the characteristics of an individual witness, rather than hinging on whether or not the witness falls within a list of closed categories, as was the case under the previous legislative regime.

Eligibility – child witnesses

Under section 16(1)(a) of the 1999 Act, a child witness is eligible for special measures if he or she is less than 17 years old at the time of the hearing. However, once it has been established that a child is eligible, the court must then consider which special measure(s) should be made available. The apparent simplicity of section 16 then gives way to an extremely complex framework of presumptions and rules, contained in sections 21 and 22, and which John Greenwood MP described as resembling 'linguistic linguini ... best digested in a darkened room with two aspirins'.[160]

Section 21 sets out a three-tiered hierarchy for child witnesses. At the top of this hierarchy are children testifying in sexual offences.[161] Next, provisions are made concerning the eligibility of children testifying in offences involving physical assault, neglect, kidnapping, false imprisonment or abduction under the Child Abduction Act 1984,[162] and they are

---

[160]*Hansard*, Standing Ctte E, 22 June 1999, as cited by Hoyano, L. 'Variations on a theme by Pigot: Special measures directions for child witnesses' [2000] Crim LR 250 260. This rather complex series of rules seems to have been the culmination of a long, drawn out parliamentary debate over the scope of the rules, which resulted in a number of late amendments to the Bill being tabled.
[161]YJCEA 1999, section 21(1)(b)(i).
[162]YJCEA 1999, section 21(1)(b)(ii).

followed at the bottom of the hierarchy by child witnesses who fall outside these categories and who are therefore assumed not to be "in need of special protection".[163] No distinction is made between children who are alleged victims and those who are eyewitnesses to offences against others, although the measures are not available to child defendants.[164]

Section 21(2)–(5) sets out a series of presumptions as to how these three categories of witnesses should give their evidence. For witnesses at the top of the hierarchy (children testifying in sex cases), the primary rule provides that their evidence be video-recorded under section 27, and, in addition, that cross-examination be pre-recorded under section 28. Children in cases of abduction, cruelty or neglect have the benefit of a presumption in favour of video-taped interview and live link, though not video-taped cross-examination. As with children in cases of sexual offences, it is not necessary to show that the quality of their evidence would be improved. For all other children who are deemed not to be in need of special protection, there is a presumption that they give all their evidence by way of live link, which the defence may rebut.

The distinction in section 21 between sexual and non-sexual offences is extremely arbitrary, and contravenes the Working Group's recommendation that the availability of special measures should relate to the age of the child and not the nature of the offence.[165] Indeed, the government now appears to have accepted the need to review this part of the legislation, so that all applications for special measures would be based on the 'assessed need' of the witness.[166] However, similar criticisms can be levied at the imposition of a rather arbitrary straightjacket concerning the operation of the primary rule in relation to age limits. Where a witness has turned 17 before he or she begins to give evidence, and he or she is not eligible for special measures for any other reason, section 21(8) stipulates that the direction should be revoked. However, if the witness turns 17 after he has begun to give evidence, the special measures direction will continue to apply.[167] Although these provisions were designed to reduce confusion for the witness and the court by providing a clear set of rules, it does seem questionable whether it is right to place such a high degree of emphasis on a particular date. If, for example, a child who is 16½-years old, and is witness to a heinous crime, the need for special measures may be just as necessary six months later, when he or she turns 17.[168]

---

[163]YJCEA 1999, section 21(1)(b).

[164]Neither are adult defendants eligible under section 17. See further discussion below at pp 39–40.

[165]Home Office, op cit n 159, [10.8].

[166]Office for Criminal Justice Reform, *Improving the Criminal Trial Process for Young Witnesses: A Consultation Paper* (2007: London, Ministry of Justice), [4.11].

[167]This subsection is made subject to section 21(9), which provides that where the witness is eligible only because he is under 17 and the special measures direction provides for the examination-in-chief and cross-examination to be conducted by video-recording under sections 27 and 28, then the direction may still apply if the witness is over 17 by the time the trial proper commences, provided he was under 17 when the video recording was made. Section 22 of the Act purports to deal with the rather unusual situation in which a person under 17 is a witness to or victim of a crime, and who was under that age when a video recording of his evidence-in-chief was made, but over 17 when the court had to determine whether any special measures should apply. He or she will then be deemed a 'qualifying witness' as defined by section 22(1). If he or she was a witness to or victim of a sexual offence, or an offence of assault or kidnapping, then he or she will count as a qualifying witness in need of special protection. Section 21(2)–(7) apply to such witnesses, so that they too are to be treated as child witnesses under section 21. They must therefore be allowed to give their evidence-in-chief by means of a video recording and, if victims of or witnesses to sexual offences, be cross-examined on video as well. Other special measures that might improve the quality of their evidence can also be made available, as they can to child witnesses within section 21.

[168]See above, p 33.

If this scenario were to arise in practice however, other provisions contained in the Act may assist. For example, a child who is eligible under section 16(1)(a) may also be eligible under section 17 if he is in fear or distress; and if the witness is a victim of a sexual offence, section 17(4) creates a presumption that the witness is eligible for special measures. Furthermore, if the child witness is eligible under both sections, then section 21(8) will carry not effect, since it solely applies to child witnesses only eligible under section 16(1)(a). Child witnesses in need of special protection who get the benefit of special measures under sections 27 and 28 will get the benefit of these special measures after they are 17, so long as they were under that age when the cross-examination was recorded. It follows that section 21(8) will only apply to a witness to a non-sexual offence who obtains the special measures simply on age and for no other reason. Such witnesses may well be able to cope without them.

Eligibility – adult witnesses

If the court considers that the quality of the evidence given by a witness is likely to be diminished by reason of any circumstances falling within section 16(2) or 17(2), adult witnesses may also be eligible for a special measures direction under sections 16 or 17. Section 16(2) of the 1999 Act implements the recommendations of the Working Group that, like children, those suffering from mental or physical disability should automatically be entitled to special measures. Such witnesses are basically those affected by mental disorder or impairment of intelligence and social functioning, and those affected by a physical disability or disorder. The court should consult witnesses prior to trial in relation to their wishes,[169] and the opinions of expert witnesses or carers may also be taken into account. Ultimately, the appropriateness of any special measure will effectively depend on the nature of the disability.

Section 17 provides that a witness is eligible for special measures if the quality of his evidence 'is likely to be diminished by reason of fear or distress'. Nevertheless, unless the witness is a complainant in a sexual case (section 17(4) see below), the fact that a witness produces evidence that he suffers from fear or distress about the prospect of testifying does not give rise to automatic eligibility. Section 17(2) requires the court to consider a range of factors in arriving at its determination. These are:

(a) the nature and alleged circumstances of the offence to which the proceedings relate;

(b) the age of the witness;

(c) such of the following matters as appear to the court to be relevant, namely –

   (i) the social and cultural background and ethnic origins of the witness,

   (ii) the domestic and employment circumstances of the witness, and

   (iii) any religious beliefs or political opinions of the witness;

(d) any behaviour towards the witness on the part of –

   (i) the accused,

   (ii) members of the family or associates of the accused, or

   (iii) any other person who is likely to be an accused or a witness in the proceedings.

---

[169]YJCEA 1999, section 16(4).

In addition, section 17(3) provides that the court must also consider any views expressed by the witness.

Under section 17(4), the court must presume that a sexual complainant is an 'eligible witness', unless the witness expresses the wish not to be treated as one, although the defence may attempt to rebut the presumption. Nevertheless, this provision is particularly welcome, in that police can now guarantee complainants in rape and sexual assault cases that, if they have to go to court, they should normally be eligible at least for one or more of the special measures.

The defendant

Since one of the most commonly cited reasons for introducing the legislation was to enable children to give the best evidence in court, it was something of an anomaly that child defendants (or indeed vulnerable accused persons of any age) were not be permitted to rely on this mechanism. From the outset, there were fears that this stipulation could constitute a potential breach of the principle of equality of arms under the European Convention. This concept states that when the prosecution and defence are in court, there must be a level playing field between them. In *Delcourt v Belgium*,[170] it was held that the accused should not be placed in a position where he is at a substantial disadvantage in presenting his case compared with the prosecution. This was evidently a particular concern of one former barrister who told the House of Commons:

> In one trial ... 58 people were in court when my client, aged 15, who was charged, with a school friend, with murdering an old lady, should have gone into the witness box to give evidence to try to save herself from a life sentence. The voyeurism in the public gallery was palpable and unavoidable, because people wanted to see the horror of young children who were said to have done horrible things. Compare her situation with that of the prosecution witnesses, also children of about 15, who had witnessed pretty small events of no great importance to them. They came to court, went straight to a room with their parents, chatted to a nice usher and watched their video on TV. They were then questioned in a quiet room by people grinning at them from the TV, just like being interviewed on a Saturday morning breakfast show. One lad had his lunch pail with him in the room. How does that amount to equality of arms between a child defendant and the prosecution?[171]

In the joined cases of *T v United Kingdom; V v United Kingdom*,[172] the European Court of Human Rights found no breach of Article 6 in relation to the well-publicised trial of two 10-year-olds convicted for the murder of toddler Jamie Bulger. However, the Court went on to stress the need for special provisions to be made available for child defendants in order that they could fully participate in the proceedings against them.

In light of this judgment, the Attorney General issued guidance to the Crown Courts dealing with young defendants tried on indictment that encouraged them to consider using their common law powers to alter procedures in cases involving juveniles.[173] It was suggested, for example, that young defendants be allowed to sit with family or friends, and that counsel remove wigs and gowns by counsel. However, the exclusion of the defendant

---

[170] (1970) 1 EHRR 355.
[171] *Hansard*, H.C. Deb, 24 October 2002, Col 159.
[172] (2000) 30 EHRR 121.
[173] *Practice Direction (Crown Court: Trial of Children and Young Persons)* [2000] 1 WLR 659.

from the regime of special measures continued with no sign of any statutory amendment coming to the aid of vulnerable accused persons.

This was a concern with which Baroness Hale seemed to identify in *R v Camberwell Green Youth Court*,[174] in commenting that the problems facing child defendants were 'very real'. However, she proceeded to note that were the regime to be applied to the accused, a number of awkward questions would have to be addressed concerning the conduct of any video-recorded examination-in-chief or the nature of binding evidential presumption.[175] As such, the House of Lords concluded that the fact such measures were not available to child defendants did not interfere with their fair trial rights under the European Convention.

The dictum of Baroness Hale was considered by the Court of Appeal in *R v Ukpabio*.[176] Again, the Court underlined that there was no power within the 1999 Act under which provision could be made for a fearful or vulnerable defendant to give evidence via a video link. However, Latham LJ proceeded to state that, in line with Convention requirements, 'there might be exceptional circumstances where it was appropriate for a defendant to be absent from the courtroom, but to ensure that he was able to participate in proceedings by video link where the relevant technological equipment was available'.[177] In other words, use of a video link to alleviate fear or counteract vulnerability was not permissible under the YJCE Act, but it was permissible (and arguably mandatory) for the court to make such an order using its inherent common law powers that would enable a defendant to participate effectively in the trial.

In recognition of the fact that the law as it stood sat awkwardly alongside the Convention requirements of equality of arms and effective participation, section 47 of the Police and Justice Act 2006 inserted section 33A into the 1999 legislation which largely reflects the Court of Appeal's decision in *Ukpabio*. The amendment to the YJCE Act introduces provisions whereby defendants under the age of 18 or those with mental disorders, whose ability to participate effectively as a witness is compromised by reason of mental disorder, impaired intellectual ability or social functioning, may be able give evidence by video link. This provision is subject to two stipulations. First, the mechanism must actually be capable of improving the ability of the witness to participate, and, secondly, the court must be satisfied that it is in the interests of justice for the youth to give evidence through a live link. It should be stressed, however, that the new provisions are entirely self-contained within section 33A, and do not alter the fact that the accused is not classed as an 'eligible' witness for the purposes of sections 16 of 17. Thus, the court is only entitled to give a live link direction in favour of a vulnerable defendant by virtue of this section; the other special measures contained in Part II of the legislation continue to be limited to non-defendant witnesses.

Types of special measures

Once the court determines that the adult witness is eligible for a special measures direction, the decision must be made as to which measure(s) would be likely to optimise the quality of that witness's evidence under section 19. In doing so, it should have regard to all the

---

[174] [2005] 1 WLR 393.
[175] *Ibid.*, at [57].
[176] [2008] 1 Cr App R 6.
[177] Ibid., [17].

circumstances of the case, including in particular any views expressed by the witness and whether the measure or measures might tend to inhibit such evidence being effectively tested by a party to the proceedings.[178] A variety of measures are provided for in sections 23–29 of the Act. These are:

- Screening the witness from the accused;
- Giving evidence by live link;
- Giving evidence in private;
- Removing wigs and gowns;
- Video-recording the evidence in chief;
- Video-recording the cross-examination or re-examination;
- Examining the witness through an intermediary;
- Providing aids to communication.

Screens

The use of screens is the first of the special measures to be outlined in section 23 of the 1999 Act. The provision reflects a pre-existing practice at common law, which was sanctioned by the Court of Appeal in *R v X, Y and Z*.[179] Although not formally provided for by statute, the use of screens became increasingly common for child witnesses during the 1980s and early 1990s. However, some teething troubles began to surface. Spencer and Flin pointed out that there was a considerable degree of uncertainty about when the trial judge should give leave to order their use. It therefore seemed to rest largely on chance whether or not the use of screens would be permitted.[180] There were also unanswered administrative questions over whose job it was to supply the screens. The placing of the measure on a statutory footing should now resolve these questions, and the measure is one of the least contentious, in so far as the witness is still seated in the actual courtroom. He or she will then sit behind an erected screen while giving evidence. Screens are also easy to use and require few resources. Furthermore, since both the defendant and the victim will remain in the actual courtroom, so the disruptive effect on proceedings will be minimal.

Live link

Originally provided for by section 32 of the Criminal Justice Act 1988, section 24 of the 1999 Act provides for witnesses to give evidence by live link. In most cases where the live link is used, the jury will have sight of a large television monitor enabling them to see and hear the witness, and there will usually be at least one other monitor positioned so that the defendant, advocates and judge can see and hear the witness's evidence. The witness will typically be seated in another room in the court precinct, facing another workstation, but seen and heard only by the person speaking (i.e. counsel or the judge). Importantly, the witness would be spared the ordeal of seeing the accused. Where the witness who gives evidence-in-chief by live link, there is a presumption that he or she will continue to give evidence in same way throughout the proceedings.[181]

---

[178] YJCEA 1999, section 19(2)–(3).
[179] (1989) 91 Cr App R 36.
[180] Spencer and Flin, op cit n 99, p 101.
[181] YJCEA 1999, section 24(3)–(4).

Evaluations of the live link under previous statutory regimes have been carried out in England and Wales by Davies and Noon[182] and in Scotland by Murray.[183]In both studies, findings indicate that the facility carries a range of benefits for child witnesses. Davies and Noon found that the mechanism had reduced levels of stress suffered by child witnesses, who had, as a consequence, been more forthcoming in their evidence, and Murray noted that they were more likely to say that they were fairly treated. The Australian Law Reform Commission's evaluation of the live link in the Australian Capital Territory revealed that children who knew they could use the facility when they wanted to do so were less anxious than those who were unable to use it, despite expressing a desire to do so.[184] These findings also indicated that emotional outbreaks from the child would be less likely to occur when giving evidence over the link. The professionals and parents of children in that study all said that a live link reduced stress on children as they gave evidence and some believed that the use of the live link permitted some cases to be prosecuted that may not have proceeded without it.[185]

One particularly welcome finding is that there seems to be a solid base of support for the use of the link among practitioners. Davies and Noon found that 42 per cent of judges reported a 'very favourable' impression of the link whilst a third reported a 'favourable' impression with only some reservations. Just 16 per cent believed the use of a screen to be a superior mechanism.[186] Overall, it would seem that the advent of the live link has been something which seems to have been broadly accepted by most stakeholders in the criminal justice system. It undoubtedly enables children to give clearer and better quality evidence, while significantly reducing the level of stress they feel in doing so. If the emotional impact of the evidence is diminished in this process, it would seem to be a price worth paying if it enables children to feel more comfortable about coming to court.

Evidence given in private

Section 25 of the 1999 Act empowers the judge to order the courtroom to be cleared of people who do not need to be present while a witness gives evidence. The direction will apply to individuals or groups of people, rather than areas of the court, and will mostly affect those in the public gallery. The court must allow at least one member of the press to remain if one has been nominated by the press. The measure will only be available in a case involving a sexual offence, or when the court is persuaded that someone has tried to intimidate, or is likely to try to intimidate, the witness. These are relatively narrow grounds, which mean that many child witnesses and those with learning difficulties will not be able to benefit from such a direction.

Removal of Wigs and Gowns

Section 26 of the 1999 Act stipulates that a special measures direction may provide for the wearing of wigs or gowns to be dispensed with during the giving of the witness's evidence.

---

[182]Davies, G and Noon, E *An Evaluation of the Live Link for Child Witnesses* (1991: London, Home Office).
[183]Murray, K (1995) *Live Television Link – An Evaluation of its Use by Child Witnesses* (1995: Edinburgh, Scottish Office Central Research Unit).
[184]Australian Law Reform Commission, (1992) *Children's Evidence: Closed Circuit Television*, Report 63 (1992: Canberra, Australian Law Reform Commission) , p 3.
[185]*Ibid.*, p 4.
[186]Davies and Noon, op cit n 182, pp 103–115.

As with the power to clear the public gallery, such a procedure has always remained within the power of the court at common law. The potential benefits of this measure are obvious, in that witnesses may feel less daunted by the formality of the proceedings. It would particularly aid young witnesses, who may feel overawed by the austere atmosphere of the trial setting. Unlike some of the other special measures, this has not proved to be particularly contentious. However, the research conducted by Sanders *et al.* into the experiences of witnesses with learning disabilities, found that the power was used in a haphazard fashion. Witnesses who gave evidence whilst counsel wore their full regalia described the proceedings as 'scarier'.[187]

It has also been suggested that some witnesses may feel that they prefer the judge and counsel to wear their wigs and gowns so that the trial is a formal rather than a casual procedure and gives them a sense that the process is being taken seriously.[188] Ellison has also suggested that some witnesses may expect wigs to be worn from their knowledge of the legal system and may thus be thrown by their absence.[189] Obviously if a child indicates that he or she does not want this sort of special treatment, no such application should be made, and he or she should be able to give evidence in the normal setting.

Video-recorded evidence-in-chief

As a matter of course, video-recorded interviews are conducted by the police in accordance with a Home Office Memorandum that takes account of the rules of evidence. Despite this, video-recorded interviews often contain inadmissible statements, and occasionally the interviewer will allow his prejudices to show and render the video interview inadmissible because it assumed the defendant's guilt. Section 27 of the Youth Justice and Criminal Evidence Act 1999 created a new exception to the hearsay rule in providing for the admissibility of a video-recorded interview with an eligible witness to be substituted for that witness's examination-in-chief.[190]

As pre-recorded evidence is somewhat more contentious than some of the other measures provided for in the legislation, certain specific protections are in place for the accused. Foremost amongst these is the stipulation that such a direction may not be given if the court considers that it would be against the interests of justice to do so.[191] Furthermore, the court must balance any prejudice to the accused with the desirability of showing the whole of the recorded interview;[192] and the court may direct that the recording should not be admitted if it appears that the witness will not be available for cross-examination, or that rules of disclosure have not been followed.[193] A witness giving evidence in this way must be called by the party tendering the evidence, and may not give evidence-in-chief through means other than the recording without the permission of the court.[194]

---

[187] Sanders *et al.*, op cit n 125 at pp 64–65.

[188] *The Guardian*, 17 January 2003.

[189] Ellison, op cit n 109, p 34.

[190] As with evidence given by live link (see pp 41–42 above), the CJA 2003 adopted the recommendation of Lord Justice Auld in his *Review of the Criminal Courts* by extending the use of video-recorded evidence beyond the rather narrow confines of the 1999 Act. Section 137 of the 2003 Act gives a judge the power to issue a direction that a video recording of the evidence-in-chief of a witness should be admitted in trials of offences triable on indictment and prescribed offences triable either way, if it enables the witness to give better evidence and it is in the interest of justice to do so.

[191] YJCEA 1999, section 27(2).

[192] YJCEA 1999, section 27(3).

[193] YJCEA 1999, section 27(4).

[194] YJCEA 1999, section 27(5)(a).

Such protections reflect the fact that, although research has shown that pre-recorded interviews considerably reduce stress levels among users, the attitudes of practitioners are mixed. A Home Office Study, carried out by Davies *et al.* found that 93 per cent of judges and 41 per cent of barristers were in favour of the principle of videotaped interviews.[195] Just over one-third of barristers (37 per cent), and just over one-half of judges (53 per cent) in England and Wales considered the admissibility of the video would serve the interests of justice or the interests of the child, while 20 per cent of judges and 50 per cent of barristers thought that it might make it more difficult to detect false allegations. The judiciary were particularly concerned about the possibility of poor interview techniques,[196] with only a handful of defence barristers agreeing that the interviewers had followed the rules of evidence.

While Pigot unanimously endorsed the value of video-taped evidence, the Report also stressed the importance of making clear to the court the nature of the original allegations, as well as the demeanour and behaviour of the child. It was also emphasised that since such interviews were both evidential and investigatory in their nature, they would need to be guided by some form of code in order to ensure that they would not be used at trial. The Home Office and the courts have been active in formulating a number of controls in relation to the manner of questioning used in the pre-recorded interviews and on how the video recording ought to be used in evidence. Foremost amongst these controls was the publication of the Memorandum of Good Practice, which was issued jointly by the Home Office and the Department of Health in 1992.[197] The aim of the Memorandum was to assist interviewers from the Child Protection Units who would normally be responsible for producing these tapes. Although it was not intended to operate as a legally binding code, it does summarise various evidential rules, in order to discourage the use of leading or hypothetical questions.[198]

The Memorandum, which was revised and updated by the Home Office in 2001,[199] also outlines a number of points about the technical aspects of the production. It states that the child's voice should be of clear and consistent audible quality. The video should also give a clear picture of the head and face of the witness, and if possible, the rest of the body. A recommended procedure is also set out for all interviews to follow, and it is suggested that they do not last for longer than one hour. Interviewers are encouraged to follow a four-phase structure to the interview, which should begin with a 'free-narrative' phase, where the interviewer poses a series of open-ended, general questions. From there, the interview should increasingly move on to the use of more specific questions, but without any pressure being applied to the child. Furthermore, interviewers should avoid the use of suggestion and leading questions as far as possible, and the child should not be placed under pressure to recollect.

---

[195]Davies, G, Wilson, C, Mitchell, R, and Milsom, J *Videotaping Children's Evidence: An Evaluation* (1995: London, Home Office). p 11.

[196]*Ibid.*, p 12. 41% of judges anticipated that this may constitute a major disadvantage.

[197]Home Office, *Memorandum of Good Practice on Videorecorded Interview with Child Witnesses for Criminal Proceedings* (1992: London, Home Office). Such guidelines were recommended by the Pigot Report at [4.8].

[198]See *Re E (a minor) (Child Abuse: Evidence)* [1987] 1 FLR 269, where the High Court disapproved of the use of a number of videos which had been based on questioning techniques used in therapy of children who were suspected of having being abused.

[199]Home Office, *Achieving the Best Evidence in Criminal Proceedings: Guidance for Vulnerable and Intimidated Witnesses, Including Children* (2001: London, Home Office).

Video-recorded cross-examination and re-examination

One of the most radical measures is contained in section 28 of the Youth Justice and Criminal Evidence Act, which provides for the cross-examination and re-examination of a witness in advance of the trial. The video-recorded cross-examination may, but need not, take place in the physical presence of the judge or magistrates and the defence and legal representatives. However, a judge or magistrate will have to be able to control the proceedings. It is intended that the judge or magistrate in charge of this procedure will normally be the trial judge. All the people mentioned in this paragraph will have to be able to see and hear the witness being cross-examined and communicate with anyone who is in the room with the witness, such as an intermediary acting under section 29 below.

The provision was aimed at preventing the sort of disparaging cross-examination directed at the 15-year-old witness known as 'Bromley' in the Damilola Taylor murder trial. That case showed the need for proper testing of the evidence of a witness by cross-examination, but can also be seen as an example of the abuse of cross-examination, the 15-year-old having being exposed to 15 hours of cross-examination by four experienced Oxbridge graduates. The defence claim that she was an ill-prepared witness who, by sensitive but probing techniques of skilled criminal advocacy, was shown to be inconsistent and unreliable. Had the section 28 procedure been available to her, she still would have been subject to proper cross-examination and testing of her evidence, but under more controlled conditions.

Receipt of the entire testimony of a child outside the formal courtroom environment in advance of the trial clearly holds the potential to significantly reduce fear and apprehension and allow the child to achieve some sense of closure within a relatively short timeframe after the offence. However, the government declined to implement this provision when most of the other special measures came into force in July 2002, and announced in December 2004 that its implementation would be postponed indefinitely, pending a wider inquiry into Children's Evidence. In a subsequent consultation paper,[200] the government proposed to retain section 28, but in an amended form, that would cover only 'a small group of the most vulnerable witnesses' which would include 'very young children, those with a terminal or degenerative illness and those suffering from some form of mental incapacity'.[201] As Hoyano argues, the Review Group seemed to overlook two crucial facts: first, that most vulnerable witnesses actually *desire* pre-recorded examination; and, secondly, that such schemes have operated with relative success in other jurisdictions.[202] The question as to how precisely the modified version of section 28 might operate in practice has been left open to consultation, but it is not clear how restricting the categories of witness eligible to make use of it would overcome the envisaged procedural complications.

Examination of a witness through an intermediary

The most innovative measure contained in the 1999 legislation is to be found in section 29, which provides that an intermediary may not only communicate questions and answers to and from a witness, but may also explain the questions and answers to

---

[200] Office for Criminal Justice Reform, op cit n 166.

[201] *Ibid.*, at [3.5].

[202] Hoyano, L 'The Child Witness Review: Much Ado about Too Little' [2007] Crim LR 849.

enable them to be understood. Only child witnesses and those who are eligible under section 16 of the Act can apply to be examined through an intermediary.[203] The judge, jury and legal representatives must be able to see and hear the proceedings, and to communicate with the intermediary.[204] The procedure cannot be used in relation to a recorded interview with a witness, unless the court issues a further special measures direction.[205]

The idea of an intermediary was first proposed by the Pigot Committee in 1989. It was the only proposal of the Committee that was not unanimous. The rationale for the introduction of the mechanism would appear to have been that it would reduce the stress levels for child witnesses, and as such would enhance the quality of their evidence. Whilst the use of screens, television links and pre-recorded evidence-in-chief have now been in place for some years with relatively few opponents, the use of intermediaries is particularly contentious as it is viewed as being so alien to the nature of the adversarial process. A major perceived risk is that the traditional role of counsel would be significantly undermined, since questions would be put to the child by the intermediary, who would be free to use very different voice tones and interrogative techniques than those which defence counsel might believe to be in the interests of his client. As Hoyano points out, there is obviously the potential for a particular meaning or emphasis to be lost, which in turn could lead to disputes between the questioner and the intermediary on which the trial judge would have to adjudicate.[206]

It is easy to imagine situations in which it might be necessary to call upon the services of an intermediary at an early stage in an investigation or proceedings involving a witness who has a particular problem in communicating. Where intermediaries are used at an early stage of the investigation or proceedings, and subsequently an application is made for a video recording of an interview in which they were involved to be admitted as evidence, that direction can be given despite the judge, magistrate or legal representative not having been present. However, the intermediary who was involved must still gain the court's approval retrospectively before the recording can be admitted. Intermediaries will have to declare that they will perform their functions faithfully, and will have the same obligation as foreign language interpreters not to make a wilfully false or misleading statement to the witness or the court. If they do make such statements they will commit an offence under the Perjury Act 1911.

As shown above, the use of the intermediary procedure is particularly alien to the adversarial process, which explains why they were not rolled out nationally for some eight years after the legislation received its royal assent. However, following a relatively positive evaluation of pilot schemes,[207] the government finally gave the go-ahead for nationwide implementation of section 29 in September 2007. In time, this facility should serve to spare young child witnesses from some of the techniques commonly used to confuse and bewilder witnesses through complex sentence structures and the conniving manipulation of language.[208]

---

[203] Witnesses who are vulnerable only by reason of fear or distress may not benefit (YJCEA 1999, section 18(2)).

[204] YJCEA 1999, section 29(3).

[205] YJCEA 1999, section 29(6).

[206] Hoyano, L 'Variations on a Theme by Pigot: Special Measures Directions for Child Witnesses' [2000] Crim LR 250, 272.

[207] See Plotnikoff, J and Woolfson, R 'Making Best Use of the Intermediary Special Measure at Trial' [2008] Crim LR 91.

[208] See above, pp 28–29.

Aids to communication

The eighth special measure, contained in section 30 of the Act, stipulates that witnesses eligible for special measures by virtue of section 16 s may be provided with such aids as the court considers appropriate. Such aids may be used to enable questions or answers to be communicated to, or by, the witness and are designed to counteract any disability or disorder that impedes effective communication. Such devices might include sign boards, communications aids for the disabled, and other aids that may allow deaf or dumb witnesses to communicate more effectively. It is not intended to include devices for disguising speech, sometimes used to preserve anonymity. Suffice to say that it is one of the least contentious measures contained within the Act.

A new era for vulnerable witnesses?

Early research findings into the operation of special measures have been broadly positive. Hamlyn *et al.* have found that high proportions of witnesses who used special measures found them helpful,[209] and that they were significantly more confident that the criminal justice system was effective in delivering justice and meeting the needs of victims.[210] Moreover, one third of interviewees said they would not have been willing and able to give evidence without them, and this figure rose to 44 per cent when the same question was posed to victims of sexual offences. Similar positive findings have been reported by Burton *et al.*[211] These researchers reported that whilst, overall, special measures were having a positive impact, the mechanisms used to identify vulnerable witnesses and assess their individual needs had to be improved.

It would thus appear that, on the basis of research conducted to date, special measures mark a positive step forward for vulnerable witnesses. Many witnesses will no longer have to give live oral evidence and undergo detailed questioning about their private lives in open court. In this sense, the legislation can be said to strike a better balance between the interests of the various parties involved in the criminal action. It is also indicative that certain key principles of the adversarial trial, such as orality, confrontation and live cross-examination, may no longer be viewed as principles so sacrosanct that they ought to operate in a way that causes undue distress to victims and witnesses.

While the Youth Justice and Criminal Evidence Act 1999 has marked a great leap forward for vulnerable witnesses, the legislation is by no means perfectly formulated. In addition to some of the concerns outlined previously, it has also been argued that the legislation does not go far enough in addressing secondary victimisation. The Act will only come to the aid of witnesses who are legally eligible for assistance under the statute. The vast majority of witnesses, including victims of crime, will continue to give live, oral evidence. Even for those witnesses who do fall under the ambit of the legislation, the excesses of the adversarial trial are only partially reduced, rather than removed. Even if witnesses give evidence via a television link, for example, they will still be then subjected to the same techniques and devices commonly used to disorientate or intimidate witnesses

---

[209] Hamlyn, B, Phelps, A, Turtle, J, and Sattar, G *Are Special Measures Working? Evidence from surveys of vulnerable and intimidated witnesses*, Home Office Research Study No 283 (2004, London: Home Office).

[210] One third of all witnesses using special measures said they would not have been willing to give evidence without this help; this figure stood at 44 per cent where the witnesses were victims of sexual offences.

[211] Burton, M, Evans, R, and Sanders, A *Are Special Measures for Vulnerable and Intimidated Witnesses Working? Evidence from the criminal justice agencies*, Home Office Online Report 01/06 (2006: London, Home Office).

during cross-examination. It would appear that the root of the problem lies in the 'fight theory' that underpins the criminal trial. At the end of the day, it is the prospect of a heated courtroom duel that will drive counsel to pursue victory at all costs, notwithstanding the impact upon victims and witnesses.

As long as policy-makers continue to view orality and cross-examination as requisite features of our mode of trial, witnesses in court are unlikely to be relieved of secondary victimisation. As Louise Ellison has argued, effective solutions to the problems facing vulnerable witnesses can be found only by looking *beyond* the adversarial system, since there is an inherent 'basic conflict between the needs and interests of vulnerable witnesses and the resultant evidentiary safeguards of the adversarial trial process'.[212] In this, the inquisitorial jurisdictions may hold valuable lessons for policy-makers, since there is a relatively wide consensus that witnesses are spared much of the trauma associated with testifying.[213] However, in the short term at least, a radical overhaul of the adversarial system remains unlikely, given that many practitioners would seem to be concerned with the loss of effect of evidence upon the jury, and view televised testimony as being 'artificial, remote and less compelling'.[214]

Other concerns with special measures stem from the idea that the accused has a 'right of confrontation', that is, a right to be physically present to view the opposing witnesses when they are giving evidence against him. While this is a constitutional right in the United States of America,[215] such a right does not have any grounding either in English common law, or under the European Convention on Human Rights. Instead, both parties to the trial are said to have the right to put forward and challenge effectively the evidence adduced by the opposition. While the common law has traditionally recognised the right of the accused to be present during his trial,[216] there is no authority to suggest that this right should entail physical confrontation.[217]

Similarly, the right of confrontation does not appear to form part of the fair trial requirements of the European Convention. While Article 6(3)(d) gives the accused the right 'to examine or have examined witnesses against him and to obtain the attendance and examination of witnesses on his behalf under the same conditions as witnesses against him', the wording of the Convention itself gives little guidance as to whether physical confrontation is an element of Article 6(3)(d). While the case law would appear to place an emphasis on the need for witnesses at least to attend the trial proper and be available to have their evidence challenged, it does not bear out the argument that confrontation is an essential ingredient to meaningful cross-examination. It is clear from the Convention case law that special measures to shield vulnerable witnesses from the accused will not contravene the Convention, provided they are strictly necessary.[218]

---

[212]Ellison, op cit n 109, p 7.

[213]For an overview of the treatment of vulnerable witnesses in the inquisitorial systems of Europe, see Doak, J, *Victims Rights, Human Rights and Criminal Justice* (2008: Hart, Oxford), pp 265–284.

[214]Ellison, op cit n 109, p 60.

[215]In the US, the Sixth Amendment states that 'the accused shall enjoy the right . . . to be confronted with the witness against him'. This right has been described by the Supreme Court as 'one of the fundamental guarantees of life and liberty ... long deemed so essential for the due protection of life and liberty that it is guarded against legislative and judicial action by provisions in the constitution of the United States' (*Kirby v United States* (1899) 174 US 47, 55).

[216]*R v Lee Kun* [1916] 1 KB 337.

[217]See further Doak, J 'Shielding Vulnerable Witnesses from Adversarial Showdown: A Bridge Too Far?' (2000) 16 J Civ Lib 216.

[218]See *Kostovski v Netherlands* (1989) 12 EHRR 434; *Doorson v Netherlands* (1996) 22 EHRR 330; *Van Mechelen v Netherlands* (1998) 25 EHRR 657.

Indeed, the compatibility of special measures with the Convention was recently considered by the House of Lords in the case of *R (D) v Camberwell Green Youth Court*.[219] Here, the applicants challenged the requirement for the court, under section 21(5) of the Youth Justice and Criminal Evidence Act 1999, to give a special measures direction in favour of video-recording their evidence-in-chief where child witnesses were 'in need of special assistance' (i.e., they were victims of sexual abuse). It was alleged that this requirement deprived the court of any power to consider whether the restriction on the rights of the defence was necessary or in the interests of justice. The House of Lords rejected the appeal, holding that just because some of the evidence was produced by contemporaneous television transmission, the fair trial rights of the accused were not compromised since he could see and hear the evidence, and had every opportunity to challenge and question the witnesses against him at the trial itself. Counsel for the appellants suggested that the case law should be read in the light of the adversarial tradition, whereby the core principle was that all evidence was received orally in front of the accused, but this argument was dismissed by the court which stated that Parliament had determined that there were sound policy grounds to depart from the 'norm' of oral testimony in the accused's presence.[220]

OTHER PROTECTIONS FOR WITNESSES IN FEAR

Outside the regime of special measures, it is worth highlighting some further mechanisms that may be of particular value for those witnesses who fear intimidation by a third party. Although the Criminal Justice and Public Order Act 1994 sought to deal with the problem by creating a new offence of witness intimidation, in practice this has done little to reduce the amount or the effect of the practice.

Witness protection programmes, which are widely used in the United States, are becoming increasingly common in this country. The Metropolitan Police and Greater Manchester Police have had such a programme for some years. *In extremis*, what is known as 'first tier protection', can involve moving the witness and his family from the area and changing identities. More often a lesser degree of protection is required, which might involve supplying the witness with a 'panic button', a device that alerts the police to the need for assistance in the event of a threat.

In terms of testifying at the trial itself, two further arrangements are worth noting. These involve the concealment of identity of a particular witness; and the use of a written hearsay statement in place of oral testimony.

The concealment of identity

The concept of concealing the identity of a witness sits uneasily alongside the principle of open justice. This is a corollary of the principle of orality, and lies alongside it at the heart of the adversarial trial. As Lord Steyn noted in *Re S*:[221]

> A criminal trial is a public event. The principle of open justice puts, as has often been said, the judge and all who participate in the trial under intense scrutiny. The glare of

---

[219] [2005] 1 WLR 393.
[220] *Ibid.*, [52]–[53].
[221] [2005] 1 AC 593.

contemporaneous publicity ensures that trials are properly conducted. It is a valuable check on the criminal process. Moreover, the public interest may be as much involved in the circumstances of a remarkable acquittal as in a surprising conviction. Informed public debate is necessary about all such matters. Full contemporaneous reporting of criminal trials in progress promotes public confidence in the administration of justice. It promotes the values of the rule of law.[222]

However, as public awareness of witness intimidation has increased, both the courts and Parliament have recognised specific circumstances that will justify a departure from the principle of open justice. The most obvious means of doing this is through the issue of an anonymity order. This will withhold the witness's name, address and personal details from all parties in the trial, as well as the general public. Such a step, however, has never been undertaken lightly by the courts. It has always been accepted by the common law that accused persons have a fundamental right to know the identity of their accusers, including witnesses for the prosecution. This right can be denied only in rare and exceptional circumstances, and whether such circumstances exist is a matter for the trial judge to determine in the exercise of his discretion. These circumstances are considered in further depth below.

However, it is worth noting that there are some practical steps, short of outright anonymity, that are considerably less contentious and are thus more common within criminal trials. For example, the witness can be protected from undue publicity where to publicise his name and other details might endanger his safety, or where it is necessary to the fair and proper administration of justice. Thus such witnesses may be permitted to write down his name and other details rather than identify themselves in open court. In such a scenario, the identity of the witness will only be withheld from the public record, but his or her identity will be known to the parties to the trial.[223]

The particular problems facing complainants in sex cases, and in cases involving child witnesses, are also recognised in statute. It is a criminal offence under the Sexual Offences (Amendment) Act 1992 for any organisation to publish the victim's name, photograph or other details which may be used to identify an individual throughout their lifetime.[224] Child witnesses, including victims and defendants, are subject to similar protections.[225] Section 44 of the 1999 Act automatically prohibits the reporting of any matter which might lead the public to identify a person under the age of 18 as a potential defendant, victim or witness as soon as a criminal investigation has begun.[226] Furthermore, legislators have now acknowledged that other adult witnesses may also desire some measure of privacy when testifying. Section 46 of the Youth Justice and Criminal Evidence Act gives the court power to restrict reporting about certain adult witnesses (other than the accused) in criminal proceedings. Such a witness will be eligible for protection if the

---

[222] *Ibid.*, [30].

[223] *R v Socialist Worker, ex p Attorney-General* [1975] 1 All ER 142.

[224] Although originally limited to offences of rape, the prohibition was extended to other sexual offences by the Criminal Justice and Public Order Act 1994, sch 9, para 52. The Act now applies to the vast majority of offences under the Sexual Offences Acts of 1956 and 2003 and includes participatory and inchoate offences.

[225] See further *R (Gazette Media Company Ltd) v Teesside Crown Court* [2006] Crim LR 157 and discussion in Gillespie, A, and Bettinson, V 'Preventing Secondary Victimisation Through Anonymity' (2007) 70 MLR 114.

[226] This provision replaces section 39 of the Children and Young Persons Act 1933, which granted a court the power to prohibit the reporting of the name, address, school or other particulars identifying children and young persons under the age of 17 who are involved in proceedings.

quality of his evidence or his co-operation with the preparation of the case is likely to be diminished by reason of fear or distress in connection with identification by the public as a witness.[227] Victims of blackmail are also permitted to give evidence incognito, a practice confirmed by the House of Lords in *Attorney-General v Leveller Magazine*.[228] Section 11 of the Contempt of Court Act 1981 permits the court to prohibit the publication of the name of a witness or other matters in connection with proceedings. This will be justified only where publication would frustrate or render impracticable the administration of justice.[229]

Where a witness wishes that his or her identity is withheld entirely, this is rightly subject to a relatively stringent legal test. In *R v DJX*,[230] Lord Lane CJ emphasised the overriding duty of the trial judge to see that justice is done by ensuring that the system operates fairly to all those concerned. This included fairness to both parties, and their witnesses. If a court is satisfied that there is a real risk to the administration of justice, because witnesses for the prosecution have reasonable grounds for fearing for their safety if their identities are disclosed, then the court has the power to take reasonable steps to protect the witnesses. However, in considering what steps to take, the court must bear in mind any possible prejudice to the rights of the defence and the interests of justice generally. Ultimately, justice requires that the court balance any prejudice to the accused with the interests of justice generally.

These principles were applied in *R v Watford Magistrates' Court, ex p Lenman*.[231] Here, a number of prosecution witnesses gave evidence in a case which involved a number of youths who had rampaged through the town, violently attacking a number of people, one of whom was seriously wounded by stabbing. By order of the court, the identities of the witnesses were withheld because of fears for their own safety. In their statements to the police, the witnesses had been permitted to use pseudonyms; and the prosecution applied for them to be allowed to give evidence from behind screens, using voice-distortion equipment to disguise their voices. The magistrates granted the application, subject to the defence solicitors being able to see the witnesses. The defendant's application for a judicial review was dismissed.

This decision was followed in *R v Taylor (Gary)*.[232] Here, the prosecution sought leave to allow Miss A, whose evidence was central to the case, to testify from behind a screen. Although counsel and the jury could still see her, it was also requested that she be allowed to remain anonymous. The defendants, who were charged with disposing of the body of a murdered man by dismembering, could not see her directly but only through a TV monitor. The trial judge granted the application. The question raised on appeal was whether he was correct in doing so. In holding that he was, the Court of Appeal confirmed that the decision to grant witnesses protection by these means was pre-eminently one for the

---

[227] Quality of evidence relates to its quality in terms of completeness, coherence and accuracy (sections 12(b)). The court may make a reporting restriction direction in respect of such a person if the making of such an order is likely to improve the quality of the evidence of the witness or his co-operation in the preparation (sections 3), having regard to a number of factors contained in sections 4. The court must also consider whether the making of a reporting direction would be in the interests of justice and consider the public interest in avoiding the imposition of a substantial and unreasonable restriction on the reporting of proceedings (sections 8).

[228] [1979] AC 440.

[229] *R v Malvern JJ, ex p Evans; R v Evesham JJ, ex p McDonagh* [1988] QB 540.

[230] (1988) 91 Cr App R 36.

[231] [1993] Crim LR 388.

[232] (1994) *The Times*, 17 August.

discretion of the trial judge. The Court further recognised that the possible grounds for anonymity might include the witness's fear for his/her family or other persons. The Court offered the following guidelines to which a trial judge should have regard in exercising his discretion:

(a) There must be real grounds for fear of the consequences if evidence was given. In practical terms it might be sufficient to draw a parallel with section 23(3)(b) of the Criminal Justice Act 1988,[233] which is concerned with the admissibility of statements where the witness does not give oral evidence through fear, but in principle it might not be necessary for the witness to be concerned for himself alone, the concern could be for other persons or for his family.

(b) The evidence must be sufficiently relevant and important to make it unfair to make the Crown proceed without it.

(c) The Crown must satisfy the court that the creditworthiness of the witness had been fully investigated and disclosed.

(d) The court must be satisfied that there is no undue prejudice to the accused, although some prejudice is inevitable, even if it is only the qualification placed on the right of the accused to confront a witness. There might also be factors pointing the other way, for example, where the defendant could see the witness on a TV screen.

(e) The court could balance the need for protection of the witness, including the extent of that protection, against the unfairness or the appearance of unfairness.

(f) There is no reason in principle why the same considerations should not apply to defence witnesses.

In *R v Lord Saville of Newdigate and others, ex p A and others*,[234] the Divisional Court allowed an application for judicial review of a decision by a tribunal appointed under the Tribunal of Inquiry (Evidence) Act 1921 to inquire into the events of Bloody Sunday on 30 January 1972, which led to the killing of 13 civilians in Londonderry, Northern Ireland by paratroopers. The tribunal had originally decided that the soldiers involved should not be permitted to remain anonymous, despite them having argued that their lives may have been endangered by dissident republicans. The Divisional Court's decision was based largely on the fact that the tribunal was significantly different from ordinary adversarial proceedings. Since proceedings were generally inquisitorial in nature, its ability to discover the truth should not be impeded by granting anonymity. On those grounds, the Court stated that the additional degree of openness gained by disclosure of names was so compelling for the public interest as to warrant subjecting the soldiers to a significant danger to their lives. For that reason, in a later application to the tribunal, soldiers required to give evidence were permitted to do so by means of a video link rather than travelling to Londonderry and giving evidence in person.

　　The most recent authority on the use of anonymity orders is the Court of Appeal decision in *R v Davis; R v Ellis*.[235] These two murder cases were both widely reported in the media at the time of the events in question. In *R v Davis*, two men were shot dead at a New Year's Eve Party. Their deaths resulted from a surge of violence by an individual who discharged a loaded gun, who killed one of his intended victims, along with an innocent bystander.

---

[233]See now CJA 2003, section 117.
[234][1999] 4 All ER 860.
[235][2006] 1 WLR 3130.

A single bullet killed both men. Ellis's case concerned the shooting of a man believed to be a member of a Birmingham gang known as the Johnson Crew. The appellants were members of the rival Burger Bar Crew.

A number of witnesses at both trials had their anonymity protected by voice modulation and screens. The appellants contended that, since their conviction was based solely or substantially on the evidence of anonymous witnesses, the practice was incompatible with Article 6 of the Convention. Dismissing their appeal, the Court held that the use of anonymity in trials was an acceptable practice where witnesses were in a state of 'justifiable and genuine fear' and whose testimony could be tested in the adversarial process.[236] Providing appropriate safeguards were in place, the trial would not be considered to be unfair. While the Court acknowledged that witness protection programmes could provide a useful alternative to anonymity in some cases, it stressed that they were best suited for professional criminals giving evidence against former associates. If prosecutions in difficult cases such as these are to have a chance of being successful, then it is obviously vital the courts are prepared to recognise the legitimate need for anonymity in the most exceptional circumstances.

Admission of a written statement

Witnesses who are fearful of intimidation or reprisals may also avoid coming to court altogether in certain circumstances. Section 116(2)(e) of the Criminal Justice Act 2003 creates an exception to the hearsay rule, whereby a written statement of a frightened witness may be read out in court in place of oral evidence. The difficulty with this mechanism is that the defence will be unable to cross-examine the witness, so counsel may attempt to persuade the jury that little weight should be attached to it. Counsel will also be free to attack the credibility of the witness, and may actively suggest that they disbelieve its contents. For those reasons, the courts will generally prefer that the witness attends court and relies on one or more of the special measures contained in the Youth Justice and Criminal Evidence Act. This provision is considered in greater depth in Chapter 7.[237]

KEY LEARNING POINTS

- Research has shown that vulnerable witnesses have found the experience of testifying in adversarial proceedings extremely stressful.
- All child witnesses will be entitled to at least one special measure at court.
- All complainants in sexual cases will be presumed to be entitled to at least one special measure at court.
- Other witnesses may be entitled to special measures, depending on the court's assessment of their needs.
- Victims of sexual offences and child witnesses will ordinarily have their identity withheld from the public and press.
- Witnesses may only testify anonymously in exceptional circumstances.

---

[236] *Ibid.*, 3148.
[237] See below, Ch 7, pp 223–227.

(1) Consider what measures, if any, the court may put in place to assist the following witnesses:

a) Alec, who was subject to a series of sexual assaults when he was eight years old in a local care home. He is now 16, and has just reported the incident to the police. He is likely to be 17 by the time the case comes to trial.

b) Sally, who was recently physically assaulted by a leader at her youth club. She is 12 years old.

c) Yvonne, who was raped by her step father at the age of 14. She is now 26 years old.

d) Danny, who was the victim of a hit-and-run incident. He is 84 years old, and is very frail

e) Paul, 15, who witnessed his girlfriend, aged 17, suffer a violent sexual assault.

f) Mandy, 32, who witnessed a local gang commit a robbery at a filling station. She is fearful that she may be subject to retaliation if she gives evidence for the prosecution.

(2) 'The courts should only resort to anonymity orders for fearful witnesses in the most exceptional of cases. If a lesser measure would suffice, then that measure should be implemented'.

Does the above quotation reflect the rules relating to witness anonymity in English law?

(3) 'While the government may well have had honourable intentions in introducing a wide range of special measures for vulnerable witnesses, ultimately such measures are unlikely to change the experience of testifying for many. Not only is the legislative framework which created the special measures unduly complex, but also the entire culture of the adversarial form of trial means that special measures can never provide an effective means of protecting vulnerable witnesses'.

Evaluate the issues raised in the above quotation.

SUGGESTED FURTHER READING

Birch, D 'A Better Deal for Vulnerable Witnesses?' [2000] Crim LR 223.

Cooper, D 'Pigot Unfulfilled: Video-Recorded Cross-Examination Under Section 28 of the Youth Justice and Criminal Evidence Act 1999' [2005] Crim LR 456.

Costigan, R, and Thomas, P 'Anonymous Witnesses' (2000) 51 *Northern Ireland Legal Quarterly* 326.

Ellison, L *The Adversarial Process and the Vulnerable Witness* (2001: Oxford, Oxford University Press).

Gillespie, A, and Bettinson, V 'Preventing secondary victimisation through anonymity' (2007) 70 *Modern Law Review* 114.

Hoyano, L 'The Child Witness Review: Much Ado about too Little' [2007] Crim LR 849.

CHAPTER 3

THE BURDEN OF PROOF

INTRODUCTION

A central feature of most common law jurisdictions is that the prosecution have the burden of proving the guilt of the accused person beyond reasonable doubt. In *Woolmington v DPP*,[238] the House of Lords held that it was for the prosecution to prove all the elements of the crime, including the mental element. In *Woolmington*, the accused was charged with murdering his estranged wife. He admitted shooting her, but claimed he had shot her by accident. The trial judge directed the jury that once it was established that the victim had died as a result of the accused's act, the defence bore the burden of proving that it was an accident rather than an intentional killing. The House of Lords held this to be a misdirection. In the words of Viscount Sankey:

> While the prosecution must prove the guilt of the prisoner, there is no ... burden laid on the prisoner to prove his innocence and it is sufficient for him to raise a doubt as to his guilt. Throughout the web of English criminal law one golden thread is always to be seen, that it is the duty of the prosecution to prove the prisoner's guilt subject to the defence of insanity and subject also to any statutory exception ... No matter what the charge or where the trial, the principle that the prosecution must prove the guilt of the prisoner is part of the common law of England (and Wales) and no attempt to whittle it down can be entertained.[239]

It was this decision in 1935 which first clearly established the so-called 'golden thread' of English criminal law: the principle that it is for the prosecution to prove the defendant's guilt. As the House of Lords proceeded to state, this rule was subject only to the common law exception of insanity and any statutory exception created by Parliament.

LEGAL AND EVIDENTIAL BURDENS

The expression 'burden of proof' properly describes the 'legal' or 'persuasive' burden, that being the obligation on the prosecution to prove all the facts necessary to establish the defendant's guilt. However, the term is also (incorrectly) used to describe the 'evidential' burden – the obligation upon either the prosecution or the defence to produce sufficient evidence to establish the facts. It is more accurate to describe this duty as the 'burden of adducing evidence'.

The importance of distinguishing between the two forms of burden cannot be overestimated.[240] So far as the prosecution are concerned, the persuasive and evidential burdens are two sides of the same coin – without adducing sufficient evidence of the facts of the offence, they would not be able to discharge their legal burden. If the prosecution adduce sufficient evidence to establish a prima facie case, the defence may then respond by calling its own witnesses. Nevertheless, it should be noted that the defence do not have to *disprove* the prosecution case (though they may seek to do so). It is sufficient for counsel

---

[238] [1935] AC 462.
[239] At 481.
[240] See Lord Hope's comments in *R v DPP, ex p Kebilene* [2000] 2 AC 326.

to raise a reasonable doubt in the minds of the factfinder. The defence may, if counsel so chooses, take the chance that the prosecution case will not satisfy the jury beyond reasonable doubt and decide not to call any evidence. However, it will be apparent that such a strategy is replete with risk, so in the majority of cases, the defence will challenge the evidence of the prosecution by calling its own witnesses as well as the accused in person. On occasions, the evidence which the defence propose to rely on to discharge the evidential burden may emanate from the prosecution's case. Such a scenario could, for example, arise where a prosecution witness had given evidence of the victim attacking the defendant and the defendant then retaliating. This would generally be considered good grounds on which to put the issue of self-defence to the court. The prosecution will then bear the legal burden of disproving the defence beyond reasonable doubt.[241]

Self-defence is just one example of a defence which will impose an evidential burden on the defence to adduce sufficient evidence for the defence to be put to the trier of fact. Others include non-insane automatism,[242] intoxication,[243] duress,[244] and provocation.[245] In practical terms, this will usually mean that the defendant must give evidence himself, or call witnesses to substantiate any defence. A failure to do so will result in the prosecution's case being uncontested. Indeed, if the prosecution have presented strong arguments and there is no good reason why the accused should not give evidence, the jury will probably draw a common sense inference that the defence has no answer to the prosecution's case. Thus, a practical consequence of an evidential burden is that the defendant is compelled to go into the witness box and give evidence of the defence, since the jury may be more likely to convict in the absence of such testimony.[246]

It should be noted that there are circumstances in which the defence may raise a particular defence which is potentially inconsistent with another. For example, assume that Kim is charged with the murder of her boyfriend, Rodney. She claims Rodney verbally abused her for a period of hours, before physically attacking her. She then admits having stabbed him with a kitchen knife. The best defence for Kim may be self-defence, which, if it succeeds, will result in an acquittal. Alternatively, she may be able to argue provocation. In either case, she will bear an evidential burden and the prosecution will bear a legal burden to disprove the defences. However, a key difference is that provocation essentially amounts to a guilty plea to manslaughter, and would also potentially undermine her argument of self-defence. If, however, there is sufficient evidence of provocation, the judge is under a duty to put that defence to the jury alongside any other defence – even where defence counsel has not raised it.[247] Since the defence must disclose their defence(s) to the prosecution before trial,[248] the prosecution will be aware of the possibility of potentially contradictory defences being put to the jury, and may use this information to highlight potential inconsistencies in an effort to show that neither defence will apply.

---

[241] *R v Lobell* [1957] 1 QB 547.

[242] *Bratty v Attorney-General for Northern Ireland* [1963] AC 386.

[243] *R v Foote* [1964] Crim LR 405.

[244] *R v Gill* (1963) 47 Cr App R 166.

[245] *Mancini v DPP* [1942] AC 1.

[246] As noted in Chapter 4, under section 35 of the Criminal Justice and Public Order Act 1994, the trial judge may direct the jury that they may draw 'such inferences as appear proper' from the failure of the accused to give evidence.

[247] See Doran, S, 'Alternative defences: The "Invisible Burden" on the Trial Judge' [1991] Crim LR 878; and *R v Watson* [1992] Crim LR 434.

[248] Disclosure obligations for both parties are contained in the Criminal Procedure and Investigations Act 1996 (as amended by the Criminal Justice Act 2003).

As we shall see later in this chapter, there is one common law provision (insanity), as well as many statutory provisions, which place the legal or persuasive burden of proof of a defence on the accused. In such cases, the accused stands to be convicted if the defence fails to convince the jury on the balance of probabilities. Previously, when faced with a statutory provision which placed a reverse legal burden on the accused, the courts had to accept that this was the will of Parliament and apply the law no matter how unfair it may have seemed. However, the position has changed since the Human Rights Act 1998 took effect in October 2000. Where the court finds that a reverse burden is incompatible with the European Convention on Human Rights, it may declare a statutory provision incompatible or, relying on section 3, interpret the statutory provision so as to avoid any incompatibility. As we shall see later, this provision has been relied on in the appellate courts to 'read down' legislation which imposes a reverse legal burden of proof on the defendant. Thus the word 'prove' is interpreted as requiring the defendant to adduce sufficient evidence to make it an issue which the prosecution must disprove (i.e. an evidential burden) rather than imposing a requirement on the defendant to prove the issue on the balance of probabilities (i.e. a legal burden). Following the readiness of the courts to adopt this strategy, Parliament seems to be increasingly accepting the fact that reverse legal burdens are not always necessary. For example, section 118 of the Terrorism Act 2000 expressly converts a number of reverse burdens contained in various provisions of the Act to evidential burdens.

The standard of proof

The 'standard of proof' refers to the level or degree of proof which must be established. There are only two standards: the criminal standard of proof, which is 'proof beyond reasonable doubt'; and the civil standard, which is proof 'on the balance of probabilities'.

Proof beyond reasonable doubt

Where the prosecution bear the legal or persuasive burden, they must establish a defendant's guilt beyond reasonable doubt. This standard applies in all criminal trials, whether before magistrates or on indictment before a jury. If there is a reasonable doubt created by the evidence adduced either by the prosecution or by the defence, the prosecution have not made out their case and the defendant must be acquitted.[249] Many judicial attempts have been made to define what is, or is not, 'reasonable doubt'. For the most part, these efforts have generally shed little light on the term. One of the better definitions, however, was that given by Lord Denning in *Miller v Minister of Pensions*:[250]

> It need not reach certainty, but it must carry a high degree of probability. Proof beyond reasonable doubt does not mean proof beyond a shadow of a doubt. The law would fail to protect the community if it admitted of fanciful possibilities to deflect the course of justice. If the evidence is so strong against a man as to leave only a remote possibility in his favour which can be dismissed with the sentence, 'of course it is possible but not in the least probable', the case is proved beyond reasonable doubt but nothing short of that will suffice.[251]

---

[249] *Woolmington v DPP* [1935] AC 462.
[250] [1947] 2 All ER 372.
[251] At 373.

Even this relatively clear definition has been subject to criticism, and there have been no shortage of attempts in the intervening period to define 'reasonable doubt' in terms which a jury might better understand. Thus in *Walters v The Queen*,[252] the Privy Council approved the definition as 'that quality of doubt which when you are dealing with matters of importance in your own affairs, you allow to influence you one way or another'.[253] However, this was disapproved of in *R v Gray*[254] because it pitched the standard too low. The reference to 'important affairs', however, was deemed acceptable, since decisions regarding such important matters invoke a more reflective thought process, and thus one where a higher standard is likely to be applied. In *R v Ching*,[255] the analogy between buying a house and taking out a mortgage was approved; the jury would have to be as sure as they would be in taking out a residential mortgage before they had proof beyond reasonable doubt. All such definitions, however, merely highlight the fact that the jury are making an important decision and do little to indicate what degree of doubt justifies an acquittal. Their decision is also highly subjective and relative to individual jurors' experiences. The Court of Appeal in *Ching* advised that judges would be well advised not to attempt any gloss on what is meant by 'sure' or 'reasonable doubt'; while in *R v Adey*,[256] the Court of Appeal displayed a marked reluctance to extend further the definition of 'being sure' or 'beyond reasonable doubt'.[257]

The higher standard of proof in criminal cases may explain why a defendant in a criminal case who is found not guilty can nevertheless be found liable for damages in a civil claim. In civil cases, the standard of proof is based on the balance of probabilities.[258] Thus, while a jury in a criminal trial can return a 'not guilty' verdict, a civil court can find the same person liable under the law of tort on identical evidence. To some extent, this differentiation may be explicable by the absence of the jury in civil cases (with the exception of defamation). When someone is sued in a claim which suggests dishonesty or serious criminality, the civil standard of proof is in reality little different from the criminal standard – the consequences of finding against the defendant being so serious as to require something close to the criminal standard. The real difference may be that the trial judge considers the evidence, and is (perhaps incorrectly) assumed to be less likely to be prejudiced by irrelevant issues than the lay jury.

Proof on the balance of probabilities

On those relatively rare occasions where the defence bear the legal burden on an issue at trial, they must prove it on the balance of probabilities. Again, Lord Denning in *Miller v Minister of Pensions*[259] summarised the nature of this standard effectively in stating:

> If the evidence is such that the tribunal may say 'we think it is more probable than not' the burden is discharged, but if the probabilities are equal it is not.[260]

---

[252][1969] 2 AC 26.
[253]At 28.
[254](1973) 58 Cr App R 177.
[255](1976) 63 Cr App R 7.
[256][1998] EWCA Crim 781.
[257]See also *R v Stephens* (2002) *The Times*, 27 June.
[258]See below, pp 58–59.
[259][1947] 2 All ER 372.
[260]At 374.

The Judicial Studies Board suggested the following direction be conveyed to the jury:

> If the prosecution has not made you sure that the defendant has (set out what the prosecution must prove), that is an end of the matter and you must find the defendant 'Not Guilty'. However, if and only if, you are sure of those matters, you must consider whether the defendant [e.g. had a reasonable excuse etc for doing what he did]. The law is that that is a matter for him to prove on all the evidence; but whenever the law requires a defendant to prove something, he does not have to make you sure of it. He has to show that it is probable, which means it is more likely than not, that [e.g. he had reasonable excuse etc for doing it]. If you decide that probably he did [e.g. have a reasonable excuse etc for doing it], you must find him 'Not Guilty'. If you decide that he did not, then providing that the prosecution has made you sure of what it has to prove, you must find him 'Guilty'.[261]

TARNISHING THE THREAD – EXCEPTIONS TO *WOOLMINGTON*

Despite their Lordships proclamation in *Woolmington v DPP*[262] that no whittling down of the principle should be entertained, there has been a significant tarnishing of the 'golden thread' in the years since this decision. For the most part, this has been brought about by an increasing number of express statutory provisions reversing the burden of proof or creating presumptions against the defence. While the House of Lords accepted Parliament had the power to reverse the burden of proof, their Lordships cannot have anticipated that departures from the 'golden thread' would be so commonplace in the early years of the 21st century. Where Parliament intends that the accused will bear the full legal burden, this will normally be stipulated clearly in the relevant legislation. Problems tend to arise on those occasions where the intended construction of the statute is less clear, thereby charging the courts with the task to ascertain the legislature's intention. Certainly, it would have been open to the courts to uphold the fundamental nature of the principle in *Woolmington* by refusing to accept any displacement of it without a clearly expressed statutory provision. However, in *R v Hunt*,[263] the House of Lords accepted that the fundamental principle can also be displaced by implication, as well as by an express statutory provision.

Before examining the reversal of the burden of proof by statute in detail, we first turn to those circumstances where the common law places the burden on the defence.

Common law exceptions

During the 18th and 19th centuries, it was generally accepted that, in trials on indictment, it was for the prosecution to prove guilt beyond reasonable doubt. However, in practice juries were often offered vastly different judicial directions on this point. For example, Chitty's *Practical Treatise on Criminal Law*, first published in 1816,[264] stated that the direction ought to be that the jury should convict if guilt was proved (or clearly proved) to their (complete) satisfaction, or if they believed the prosecution witnesses. Despite this straightforward indication that the burden of proof fell on the prosecution, there was a growing body of opinion that such a burden did not include a duty to disprove defences raised by the accused

---

[261] Specimen Direction 1C, available online at the Judicial Studies Board website: http://www.jsboard.co.uk/criminal_law/cbb/index.htm [accessed 27 Feb. 08].

[262] [1935] AC 462.

[263] [1987] AC 352.

[264] Chitty, J *A Practical Treatise on Criminal Law*, Vol 1 (1816: London, Valpy).

at trial. Both jurists and judges appeared open to the suggestion that the burden of proving defences was on the accused. A body of case law developed in which the persuasive burden of disproving defences fell on the accused in relation to defences such as duress or self-defence. In cases of murder, it was accepted that once the prosecution had proved that the accused had killed the victim, the burden was then on him to establish that the case was not one of murder by proving that the killing was an accident or was in self-defence (or was manslaughter due to provocation or lack of an intent to kill). It followed that throughout the greater part of the nineteenth century, the rule that the prosecution bore the burden of proof referred only to the prosecution's duty to prove that the act alleged to be criminal had been committed by the accused – what in modern times is described as the *actus reus*. The law on proving the mental element (*mens rea*) required in major crimes such as murder had yet to be clarified. In murder cases the law presumed malice aforethought from the fact of killing, but it is clear that the prosecution were not required to prove an intention to kill; rather it was for the accused to prove a lack of such an intention.

Over time, the common law gradually modified its position, and by the time *Woolmington* came before the House of Lords, insanity was the only defence that the accused was required to prove at common law. This had been clear law since *Arnold's Case*,[265] and was confirmed by the decision in *M'Naghten's Case*,[266] which remains the leading authority on insanity in English criminal law. Today, the defence of insanity remains the sole common law exception to the principle that the prosecution shoulder the legal burden of proof. As with the other circumstances where the burden is reversed, the defence must prove insantiy on the balance of probabilities, as opposed to 'beyond reasonable doubt'.

Express statutory reversal

With the exception of insanity, the 'golden thread' established in *Woolmington* thus remains intact at common law. However, constitutionally, the courts must accept the will of Parliament, so where the legislature clearly places the burden of proof on the defence, the courts cannot override the sovereignty of Parliament by disapplying a statute. There is generally less concern about the placing of burdens on the defendant when the offence is only triable as a summary offence.[267] It follows that Parliament is more ready to reverse the burden of proof in such cases.[268] Such offences are often regulatory offences, and generally the courts have had little difficulty in determining the reverse legal burden to be justifiable in these circumstances.[269]

Parliamentary draughtsmen use a number of different mechanisms to reverse the burden of proof. In most cases, the legislation will stipulate quite clearly that the defence must prove certain circumstances to be in existence in order to make use of an available defence.[270] Another common device is to include a presumption of fact or law which the

---

[265](1724) 16 St Tr 694, 764.

[266](1840) 10 Cl & Fin 200.

[267]i.e. where the offence is considered to be minor and punishable by a fine and no more than 12 months' imprisonment.

[268]See Prevention of Crime Act 1953, section 1; Criminal Justice Act 1988, sections 139 and 141; Criminal Justice and Public Order Act 1994, section 69; Health and Safety at Work Act 1974, section 40; and Insolvency Act 1986, section 206(1).

[269]*L v DPP* [2002] Crim LR 320; *R v Alleyne* [2004] QB 69.

[270]For example, section 139(4) of the Criminal Justice Act 1988 provides a defence for an accused charged with possession of a bladed weapon in a public place if he can establish some 'lawful authority or reasonable excuse' for being in possession of the offensive article.

court must accept as proved unless the defence rebut that presumption. By way of example, we may consider how the burden of proof is framed in relation to driving with excess alcohol. The proportion of alcohol in a person's body will depend on a number of factors, most importantly, when he or she last consumed alcohol. If a driver has recently consumed alcohol, the amount in the bloodstream will be rising steadily as the body absorbs it. On occasions, this can work in the driver's favour since a breath sample or blood sample may not show excess amounts before all the alcohol has been absorbed. There will also come a point when the body ceases to absorb the alcohol and starts to destroy it. Some drivers, when they fail a breath test and are later required to provide a specimen of blood or urine at the police station, seek to take advantage of this process by delaying the taking of a sample until a time when they believe their body has destroyed enough alcohol to return a legal sample. Alternatively, the driver may claim that the sample (which shows an illegal amount of alcohol) taken an hour or more after he had ceased to drive, did not reflect the lower, legal amount which it was when he was driving. In order to counteract these possibilities (and suggestions of post-offence consumption of alcohol), the statute provides for back-calculation to establish the blood alcohol level at the time of the offence. Section 15(2) of the Road Traffic Offenders Act 1988, as amended by the Road Traffic Act 1991, provides:

> Evidence of the proportion of alcohol or any drug in a specimen of breath, blood, or urine provided by the accused shall, in all cases ... be taken into account and ... it shall be assumed that the proportion of alcohol in the accused's breath, blood or urine at the time of the alleged offence was not less than the specimen.

This section goes further than simply placing the legal burden of proof on the defendant. It is, in effect, an irrebuttable presumption that the proportion of alcohol in the defendant's blood at the time of the offence was not less than that shown in the specimen. The presumption will not apply if the accused proves that he or she consumed alcohol before the specimen was provided and after he ceased to drive, attempted to drive or was in charge of the vehicle.[271] However, there is no opportunity to rebut the presumption by proving that the proportion of alcohol in the blood was less than that shown by the analysis.

The absence of such an opportunity to prove that the blood alcohol level at the time of the offence was in fact less than shown by the specimen was subject to challenge under the Human Rights Act 1998 in *Parker v DPP*.[272] The defendant failed a roadside breath test, and roughly one hour later provided a specimen of blood that exceeded the prescribed proportion of alcohol. He was convicted of driving with excess alcohol, and appealed arguing that the presumption contained in section 15(2) section was incompatible with Article 6(2) of the European Convention. Dismissing the appeal, Lord Justice Waller rejected the contention that the only way the provision could be valid would be if words were read into the section to the effect that the assumption would not be made 'unless proved to the contrary'. In the view of the Court, since it was the alcohol consumption prior to driving at which the offence was aimed, it did not tarnish the presumption of innocence to assume that the quantity of alcohol in the sample taken at the police station was the quantity which the motorist had in his blood at the time that at the material time. Even if that were taking it too far, having regard to the importance of what is at stake – pedestrians' and other motorists' lives – the presumption was reasonable one,

---

[271] Road Traffic Offenders Act 1988, section 15(3).
[272] [2001] RTR 240.

and in the view of the Court, this did not amount to an infringement of Convention rights.

Section 15(3) of the Road Traffic Offenders Act 1988 prevents the presumption in subsection (2) from operating if the accused proves that he consumed alcohol before he gave the specimen and after he had ceased to drive, attempted to drive, or was in charge of a motor vehicle. This was the subject of the appeal in *R v Drummond*.[273] D had driven into a scooter, killing the passenger and seriously injuring the driver. D admitted that he had been aware that his car had struck something on the road, but that, seeing nothing else around, he had driven on. In his defence, D stated that he was in a state of shock when he arrived home and saw the extent of the damage to his car. He claimed his wife had given him two measures of gin to calm him down, which explained why he provided two positive samples of breath shortly after his arrest. He was convicted of causing death by careless driving, and appealed arguing that the stipulation in section 15(2) that he should prove that he had consumed the alcohol after the alleged incident constituted a violation of the presumption of innocence under the Human Rights Act 1998. In the view of the Court of Appeal, the statutory reversal of the presumption of innocence was wholly justifiable, and was no greater than necessary to minimise the social evil of drink driving.

Similar facts were present in *Sheldrake v DPP*.[274] Here, the defendant was found to be over the alcohol limit in his car in a public place, but later claimed he had been trying to get a lift from a friend. Section 5(2) of the 1988 Act affords a potential defence if it can be proved that, at the time of the alleged offence, the circumstances were such that there was no likelihood of the motorist driving the vehicle while he remained above the prescribed limit. It was held that this placed the legal or persuasive burden of proof on the defendant. In this case, having failed to persuade the court on the balance of probabilities that there was no likelihood of him driving while over the limit, the defendant was convicted. The Divisional Court allowed the appellant's appeal by a majority of 2:1. Lord Justice Clarke stated two clear points. First, the prosecution had failed to show that it was necessary to impose a legal burden on the accused; and second the prosecution had been unsuccessful in showing that there was no likelihood of the defendant driving while over the limit. To do so would be disproportionate. Thus, the Court held that section 5(2) of the 1988 Act should be read down under the Human Rights Act 1998 so as to impose an evidential burden only. However, a different view was taken by the House of Lords. Assuming that the section infringed the presumption of innocence and that it was directed to a legitimate object – the prevention of death, injury and damage caused by unfit drivers – Lord Bingham asked whether the provision met the test of acceptability identified in the Strasbourg jurisprudence.[275] Accepting that it plainly did, he went on to state that he did 'not regard the burden placed on the defendant as beyond reasonable limits or in any way arbitrary'. He also concluded that it was not 'objectionable to criminalise a defendant's conduct in the circumstances without requiring a prosecutor to prove a criminal intent'. This was on the basis that:

> [T]he defendant has a full opportunity to show that there was no likelihood of his driving, a matter so closely conditioned by his own knowledge and state of mind at the material time as to make it more appropriate for him to prove on the balance of probabilities that he would

---

[273] [2002] RTR 21.
[274] [2005] 1 AC 246.
[275] See discussion below, pp 77–78.

not have been likely to drive than for the prosecutor to prove, beyond reasonable doubt, that he would.[276]

In their Lordships' opinion, the imposition of a legal burden did not go beyond what was necessary and it was not unfair to the defendant, given the legitimate object of the legislation of protecting society from the very real dangers of driving with excess alcohol.

Unfortunately, not all statutes are clearly expressed, and it may be unclear in some cases as to who should shoulder the burden. Some statutes contain provisions in which the burden of proof is clearly placed on either the prosecution or defence, while others are silent on the matter. For example, *Polychronakis v Richards and Jerrom Ltd*[277] highlighted an apparent ambiguity in section 80(1) of the Environmental Protection Act 1990. The legislation contained two subsections which clearly imposed the legal burden of proving a specified defence on the accused. However, a third subsection provided for a defence of reasonable excuse, without specifying whether the prosecution should prove the absence, or the defence the presence, of that excuse. The magistrates' court imposed the burden upon the accused. The Queen's Bench Division held that they had been wrong to do so, and stated that, in such circumstances, the court must interpret the statute or section and endeavour to determine whether Parliament intended to place the legal burden of proof on the prosecution or the defence.[278] In this particular instance, it was held that once the defendant had laid the proper evidential basis for the contention of a reasonable excuse, it was for the prosecution to satisfy the court to the criminal standard of proof that the excuse was not a reasonable one.

Implied statutory exceptions

It might be expected that, for a statutory displacement of the fundamental presumption of innocence to arise, there would be an express provision within the legislation stipulating that the prosecution must prove all aspects of the offence. However, this has rarely been the case, meaning that it is left to the courts to ascertain Parliament's intentions.

Summary offences

As Parliament grew in strength during the eighteenth and nineteenth centuries, it began to create a new range of statutory offences. Many of these were comparatively minor in nature and were triable as summary offences in magistrates' courts. In the middle of the nineteenth century, Parliament sought to bring the trial of summary offences into line with the trial of indictable offences by passing the Summary Jurisdiction Act 1848. This Act required that where the defendant relied in his defence upon any exemption, proviso, excuse or qualification, then it was for him to prove that he came within any such exception. After the statute took effect, the common law and statute law proceeded on a parallel course, with both modes of trial placing the burden on the defendant to prove any defence relied upon in the nature of an excuse (such as accident or self-defence) in relation to indictable offences, or

---

[276] At [41].

[277] [1998] Env LR 346.

[278] However, as we shall see below, parliamentary intention is no longer sufficient in itself to justify a reverse legal burden. Under the Strasbourg jurisprudence, any such reverse burden must be justifiable and proportionate to the particular mischief which the statute seeks to counter.

that the defendant fell within any exception, exemption etc. in relation to summary offences. The 1848 legislation has been re-enacted over the years, and the equivalent provision is today contained within section 101 of the Magistrates' Courts Act 1980. As the title of the legislation suggests, the provision applies only to magistrates' courts, meaning it only covers summary offences or 'either way' offences which are tried summarily. Section 101 states:

> Where the defendant to an information or complaint relies for his defence on an exception, exemption, proviso, excuse or qualification whether or not it accompanies the description of the offence or matter of complaint in the enactment creating the offence or on which the complaint is founded, the burden of proving the exception, exemption, proviso, excuse or qualification shall be on him and this notwithstanding that the information or complaint contains an allegation negativing the exception, etc.

There are numerous examples of statutes expressly worded so as to render a certain act as an offence unless done by someone licensed or qualified to do the act, or if done without lawful authority or excuse. For example, driving a motor vehicle without being the holder of a licence to drive; keeping a vehicle without an excise licence (tax disc); selling intoxicating liquor without a licence; possessing a firearm without a licence; possessing certain drugs without a doctor's certificate; delivering a child while not being a qualified midwife; practising medicine when not qualified; obstructing the highway without lawful authority or excuse; possessing forged currency without lawful authority or excuse; and many more besides. These are all offences that fall within the scope of section 101 and will thereby place the burden of proof on the accused.

In *Gatland v Metropolitan Police Commissioner*[279] and *Nimmo v Alexander Cowan Ltd*,[280] it was held that the defendant in cases to which section 101 applies bears the legal or persuasive burden of proving that he comes within the exception, proviso, excuse or qualification upon which he relies, and not simply the evidential burden to the same effect. Thus, it is not sufficient to produce some evidence of a defence and leave it to the prosecution to rebut it, as may be done with specific defences such as self-defence, duress, or an alibi. Instead, the defence counsel must prove that the relevant exception applies, but need only do so on the balance of probabilities. It was argued in *Nimmo* that such a reversal of the burden appears logical since the defendant would be in a better position to discharge it. From the outset, this consideration blatantly contradicts Viscount Sankey's 'golden thread'; it will be recalled that in *Woolmington* the House of Lords referred specifically to the fact that the fundamental principle would apply 'no matter what the charge or where the trial'. However, since Parliament is supreme, the fundamental principle must give way to any statutory reversal.

When this type of case comes to court, the magistrates must first analyse the statute in question in order to determine whether section 101 applies. Naturally, the defence will frequently deny that it does and claim that the prosecution bears the entire legal burden. Section 101 distinguishes between 'the description of the offence' and 'any exception'. Any matter which is part of the description of the offence must be proved by the prosecution; it is only with regard to exceptions, provisos, excuses or qualifications that the onus of proof is on the defendant.

While there is no doubt that such provisions significantly whittle down the presumption of innocence, it is unlikely that they will be found to be in automatic breach of Article 6(2)

---

[279][1968] 2 QB 279.
[280][1968] AC 107.

of the European Convention on Human Rights. In *Salabiaku v France*[281] the European Court of Human Rights accepted that all the Convention States make use of reverse burdens and presumptions. Such burdens were not contrary to the Convention per se, providing they confined within 'reasonable limits', and were framed in such a way so as to take into account the importance of what is at stake, while maintaining the rights of the defendant. Given that a summary conviction is punishable by a fine or a sentence of imprisonment not exceeding 12 months, the offence is not usually seen as so serious as to prevent the burden being reversed. On the one hand, many such reversals are regulatory offences passed for the protection of society, which tends to justify the imposition of a reverse burden.[282] Yet, on the other hand, some commentators view such offences as stretching beyond the traditional remit of the criminal law, and have called for them to be decriminalised. As Padfield suggests:

> The time has come for a category of administrative regulations which would carry little stigma and no possibility of imprisonment. Only for such 'non-crimes' should strict liability or reverse burdens be acceptable.[283]

Indictable offences

Although section 101 of the Magistrates' Courts Act 1980 only applies to summary proceedings, the Court of Appeal enunciated an almost identical principle which applies to trials on indictment in *R v Edwards*.[284] In the view of the Court of Appeal, the forerunner to section 101 was simply a codification of an older common law rule. This was deduced from the fact that the origins of the provision are to be found in section 14 of the Summary Jurisdiction Act 1848, which stated that:

> it shall not be necessary for the prosecutor or complainant in that behalf to prove a negative, but the defendant may prove the affirmative thereof in his defence, if he would have advantage of the same.

In passing this legislation, Parliament was doing no more than putting into statutory form an old common law rule which, as we have seen, was applied by the court of trial and the Court of Appeal in *Woolmington* (though later reversed by the House of Lords). Since the majority of offences were statutory in nature, the Court of Appeal saw no reason why the rule in what is now section 101 of the Magistrates' Court Act 1980 should not be applied by the common law so that indictable and summary offences would be treated alike. After all, there appeared to be no sound rationale as to why an 'either way' offence should be tried according to different rules depending on whether it was tried summarily or on indictment.

In *Edwards* itself, the defendant was convicted of selling alcohol without a justice's licence under section 160 of the Licensing Act 1964.[285] The prosecution called no evidence that the appellant did not hold a justice's licence, leaving him to show, if he could, that he did possess one. The conviction was upheld by the Divisional Court and by the Court of Appeal. In the words of Lawton LJ:

> In our judgment this line of authority establishes that over the centuries the common law, as a result of experience and the need to ensure that justice is done both to the community and

---

[281] (1991) 13 EHRR 379.
[282] See e.g. the discussion of Road Traffic Offenders Act 1988, ss15(2)–(3), above at pp 61–62.
[283] Padfield, N. 'The Burden of Proof Unresolved' 64 CLJ 17.
[284] [1975] QB 27.
[285] Now a summary offence, but when *Edwards* was heard it was triable on indictment.

to defendants, has evolved an exception to the fundamental rule of our criminal law that the prosecution must prove every element of the offence charged. This exception, like so much else in the common law, was hammered out on the anvil of pleading. It is limited to offences arising under enactments which prohibit the doing of an act save in specified circumstances or by persons of specified classes or specified qualifications or with the licence or permission of specified authorities. Whenever the prosecution seeks to rely on this exception, the court must construe the enactment under which the charge is laid. If the true construction is that the enactment prohibits the doing of acts, subject to provisos, exemptions and the like, then the prosecution can rely upon the exception.[286]

Clearly, the Court of Appeal had taken into account the fact that it would have been just as easy for the defendant to produce evidence of the possession of a licence (if he had one), as for the prosecution to prove he did not. Such records are kept by clerks to the justices, and are readily available to anyone on request. However, the decision in *Edwards* is not limited to cases when the defendant has peculiar knowledge, or where one party can more easily prove the particular defence. Instead, it is based on the particular linguistic structure adopted within a piece of legislation. Where words or a phrase within a statute prohibit certain acts subject to provisos, exemptions and the like, the defendant bears the legal burden of proving that proviso, exemption, etc. It follows from this that the Court of Appeal confined the decision of the House of Lords in *Woolmington* to common law offences, such as murder, and statutory offences which are not framed to prohibit the doing of acts subject to some form of exception. Those statutory offences which are framed to prohibit the doing of acts subject to a proviso or exemption are placed outside the fundamental principle expressed in that case.

The decision in *R v Edwards* received qualified approval by the House of Lords in *R v Hunt*.[287] The House of Lords in *Hunt* stated that Lawson LJ's statement was better regarded as merely a guide to a statute's construction rather than as an exception to the rule that the prosecution bear the burden of proof. Their Lordships laid down a subjective approach, stating that the question of whether the defendant bears a legal burden of proof should not always be determined by the wording of the particular statute. The words 'any statutory exception' in *Woolmington* were not confined to statutory exceptions in which the burden of proof was expressly placed on the defendant. A statute can do so expressly or impliedly on its true construction. Therefore, when the statute was not clear it was a matter of construction, and a number of considerations then applied. Amongst the factors to be taken into account were whether Parliament intended to place a heavy burden on the defendant; the nature of the mischief the legislation sought to resolve; and whether that mischief was serious in its nature. Most importantly, their Lordships in *Hunt* declared that any ambiguities within the legislation should be resolved in favour of the accused.

The defendant in *Hunt* was charged with possession of a controlled drug, morphine, contrary to section 5(2) of the Misuse of Drugs Act 1971. A search of his house revealed a fold of paper containing morphine, which was mixed with caffeine and atropine (which were not controlled drugs). The prosecution called no evidence as to the proportion of morphine in the mixture. The defence submitted that there was no case to answer because schedule 1 to the Misuse of Drugs Regulations 1973, provided that a preparation containing not more than 0.2% morphine which was not readily recoverable did not fall within section 5.[288] Since the

---

[286] At 39–40.

[287] [1987] AC 352.

[288] SI 1973/797, as amended by the Misuse of Drugs (Amendment) Regulations 1983 (SI 1983/788).

prosecution had failed to prove that the amount of morphine in the mixture exceeded this volume, the defence argued that they had not proved that the mixture constituted a controlled drug for the purposes of the Act. The trial judge rejected this submission, and the accused was convicted.

On appeal, the court upheld this ruling on the ground that the defendant bore the burden of proving that the mixture fell within the exception provided by schedule 1 to the 1973 Regulations. The House of Lords, however, overturned this decision, holding that the prosecution bore the burden of proving that the mixture did not come within the exception. Properly analysed, the offence consisted not of being in possession of morphine itself, but of being in possession of morphine other than a preparation specified in schedule 1. The percentage of morphine was part of the description of the offence, not an exception to it. It followed that the prosecution had to prove that the levels of morphine within the mixture were above 0.2%.

It is arguable that the courts, applying the common law, significantly failed to protect their own fundamental principle of the presumption of innocence by allowing its displacement by implication, rather than insisting on an express provision as the House of Lords did in *Hunt*. If the courts had seized the opportunity to insist on express provisions to reverse the burden, such a declaration would have had the effect of placing the responsibility of undermining such a fundamental right of its citizens squarely on the shoulders of Parliament. In turn, Parliament would then be under a duty to give reasons for imposing a reverse burden of proof on defendants in particular statutes. Instead, the courts conspired – wittingly or unwittingly – in the undermining of fundamental rights by using the smokescreen of an unspoken intention of Parliament to justify a reversal. This led to a loss of respect in the legislature for the presumption of innocence and meant that a potential buffer between the practical power of the state and the comparative weakness of the individual was considerably diminished.

However, in contemporary practice, it is suggested that the decisions in Edwards and Hunt are now primarily of historical interest for three main reasons. First, as Lord Griffiths himself stated in *Hunt*:

> the principle is limited …. I have little doubt that the occasions on which the statute will be construed as imposing a burden of proof on a defendant which do not fall within this formulation are likely to be exceedingly rare.[289]

Secondly, in the years since *Hunt*, the implied statutory reversals of indictable offences have become extremely rare, if not extinct. Almost all implied statutory reversals now concern comparatively minor offences, triable only in magistrates' courts. Even the offence of which Edwards was convicted today lies within the exclusive jurisdiction of the magistrates' court.

Thirdly, the Human Rights Act 1998 (discussed in greater depth below) has significantly altered the way in which such reversals should be handled by the courts. If there is a serious indictable offence which prohibits the doing of an act in specified circumstances – this covers, for example, persons of a specified class; those without specified qualifications; persons without a licence or permission from specified authorities – the court would be obliged to take into account an array of new factors, including the concept of proportionality under Article 6(2) of the Convention, and the post-HRA case law. Such factors are likely to operate in favour of the accused, and courts may be prepared to 'read down' any implied reverse burden so that the defence will bear only an evidential burden.

---

[289] At 375.

THE IMPACT OF THE HUMAN RIGHTS ACT

Article 6(2) of the Convention

Article 6(2) of the European Convention on Human Rights protects the right of a defendant to be presumed innocent until proven guilty and in doing so, enshrines the fundamental principle of criminal law enunciated in *Woolmington*. Although there have been relatively few cases in which the Strasbourg organs have considered the principle, it did arise in *X v United Kingdom*.[290] Here, the Commission upheld the reverse burden contained in section 30(2) of the Sexual Offences Act 1956. Under this provision, any man who lives habitually with a prostitute, or who exercises control or influence over her movements in a way which shows he is aiding and abetting or compelling her prostitution, shall be presumed to be knowingly living on the earnings of prostitution unless he proves the contrary. The Commission held that, provided the presumption was rebuttable and reasonable, it would not violate Article 6(2). It proceeded to emphasise, however, that where such a provision was widely or unreasonably worded, it could have the same effect as a presumption of guilt and would contravene the Convention.

The leading Strasbourg case is that of *Salabiaku v France*,[291] which concerned a provision of the French Criminal Code which placed the burden of proof squarely on the defendant to prove that he was not guilty of smuggling where he was found to be in possession of prohibited goods. In rejecting the complaint, the Court stated that:

> Presumptions of fact or law operate in every legal system. Clearly the Convention does not prohibit such presumptions in principle. It does, however, require the Contracting State to remain within certain limits in this respect as regards criminal law … Article 6(2) does not, therefore, regard presumptions of law or fact with indifference. It requires States to confine them within the reasonable limits which take into account the importance of what is at stake and maintains the rights of the defence.[292]

The guidance in *Salabiaku* was applied in *H v United Kingdom*,[293] where the Commission rejected the applicant's contention that the burden on the accused to prove insanity on the balance of probabilities in criminal proceedings was contrary to the presumption of innocence and therefore in violation of Article 6. Similarly, in *Bates v United Kingdom*,[294] the Court dismissed the applicant's argument that section 5(5) of the Dangerous Dogs Act 1991 contravened the Convention standards. This provision creates a presumption that the dog is one to which the Act applies unless the contrary is shown by the defence.

The Prevention of Terrorism (Temporary Provisions) Act 1989

Even before the Human Rights Act took effect, the Convention standards had begun to infiltrate decision-making processes in the domestic courts. In *R v DPP, ex p Kebilene and others*,[295] three Algerians were prosecuted for offences under sections 16A and 16B of

---

[290] App No 5124/71, 23 March 1972.
[291] (1991) 13 EHRR 379.
[292] At [28].
[293] App No 15023/89, 4 April 1990.
[294] App No 26280/95, 16 January 1996.
[295] [2000] 2 AC 326.

the Prevention of Terrorism (Temporary Provisions) Act 1989. These provisions created the offences of 'possession of articles for the purposes of terrorism' and of 'collecting or recording information for such a purpose'. In both cases, the burden of proof was placed clearly and unequivocally on the defendant. Section 16A stipulated that the accused would have to prove that the possession of the articles was not for the purposes of terrorism, or else that he was not in possession of those articles; and similarly, in relation to the offence under section 16B, the defendant had to prove that he had a reasonable excuse for collecting or recording the information.

At the close of the prosecution case, the defence obtained a ruling that the sections were incompatible with Article 6(2) of the European Convention on Human Rights. The Director of Public Prosecutions, whose consent was required before a prosecution could be undertaken, appeared before the trial judge to argue that the judge's ruling was wrong. The trial judge maintained his position and the case went to the Divisional Court, which agreed with him. At the time, the Human Rights Act 1998 was not in force, its implementation having been delayed until October 2000. The Divisional Court, however, decided that the sections undermined the presumption of innocence protected by Article 6(2) in a 'blatant and obvious way'. It proceeded to point out that the prosecution would be a waste of time and money since the defendants would, if convicted, appeal. In addition, if the appeal were to go ahead at a time when the Human Rights Act 1998 Act were in force, it would almost certainly be allowed. The Divisional Court thus held that the Director of Public Prosecutions had acted unlawfully, and granted a declaration to this effect.

The Director of Public Prosecutions appealed to the House of Lords, which held that the courts had no power to review a decision of the Director of Public Prosecutions. That was sufficient to dispose of the appeal, and unfortunately the majority expressed no concluded views on the compatibility of the sections with Article 6(2). Lord Hobhouse, however, noted that the provisions were arguable, but emphasised that that presumptions and reverse burdens were not uncommon within European states, and nor were they necessarily incompatible with the Convention. Lord Hope, meanwhile, adopted the suggestion of counsel for the Director of Public Prosecutions that three questions should be considered in determining whether a reverse burden strikes a balance between the rights of the individual and those of the State:[296]

- What does the prosecution have to prove in order to transfer the onus to the defence?
- What is the burden of the accused? Does it relate to something which is likely to be difficult for him to prove, or does it relate to something which is likely to be within his knowledge or to which he readily has access?
- What is the nature of the threat faced by society which the provision is designed to combat?

However, despite posing these questions, Lord Hope stated that no definitive view could be expressed as to question of compatibility in the instant case since the trial itself had not yet been concluded. Nonetheless, in suggesting that the matter was open to argument he appeared to disagree with the Divisional Court's view that they were incompatible.[297]

---

[296] As will be seen, these questions have been applied in later cases.
[297] The case then proceeded to trial, but was abandoned after a witness, said to be an agent working for MI5, refused to give evidence because he feared for his life. Unfortunately the compatibility of the sections therefore remained untested.

The Terrorism Act 2000

In 2000, Parliament decided to repeal the Prevention of Terrorism (Temporary Provisions) Act 1989, which required annual renewal by Parliament, and to replace it with a permanent statute. Parliament responded to the comments in *Kebilene*[298] by re-enacting sections 16A and 16B of the 1989 Act as sections 57 and 58 of the Terrorism Act 2000, but added section 118, which converts these reverse legal burdens into evidential burdens. Section 58 makes it an offence, punishable to the same extent as section 57, to collect or make a record of information likely to be useful to a person committing or preparing an act of terrorism, or to possess a document or record containing information of that kind. Section 58(3) also provides that it is a defence for a person charged with an offence under this section to prove that he had a reasonable excuse for his action or possession. Sections 12(4), 39(5)(a), 54, 77 and 103 also contain provisions making it a defence for the accused to prove certain facts or for presumptions to be made. For example, the court may assume that the accused possessed the article or object in question, unless he proves that he did not know of its presence on the premises or that he had no control over it.

At first sight, it appeared that the government was ignoring the opinion of the House of Lords in *Kebilene*. However, section 118 contains provisions which make it clear that the defendant charged with offences under the relevant sections bears only an evidential burden. This means that the matter must be taken as proved against the accused unless the accused adduces sufficient evidence to raise an issue on the matter in court. Thereafter, if the evidential burden is discharged, the prosecution face the burden of satisfying the legal burden beyond reasonable doubt.[299] In addition, the use of the phrase 'a live issue'[300] within the statute means that it is not enough merely to allege a potentially relevant fact; the accused must raise *sufficient* evidence to make it an issue which can be put to the court or jury. In jury trials, this will be a matter for the judge to determine. If he or she is satisfied that the matter is 'an issue', the jury will be directed to consider whether, in the light of that evidence, the prosecution have disproved that evidence beyond reasonable doubt. If, however, the judge decides there is insufficient evidence to raise the issue, he or she will direct the jury to consider the matter proved in accordance with the provisions of the particular statutory provision.

In years to come, we shall almost certainly see new challenges brought in respect of this legislation. Consider, for example, section 57 of the Act which provides:

(1) A person commits an offence if he possesses an article in circumstances which give rise to a reasonable suspicion that his possession is for a purpose connected with the commission, preparation or instigation of an act of terrorism.

(2) It is a defence for a person charged with an offence under this section to prove that his possession of the article was not for a purpose connected with the commission, preparation or instigation of an act of terrorism.

(3) In proceedings for an offence under this section, if it is proved that an article—
    (a) was on any premises at the same time as the accused, or
    (b) was on premises of which the accused was the occupier or which he habitually used otherwise than as a member of the public,

---

[298][2000] 2 AC 326.
[299]See the rule as to evidential burdens stated in *R v Gill* (1963) 47 Cr App R 166, 172, set out at p 56 above.
[300]Or, as in sections 118(2) and (4), simply 'an issue'.

> the court may assume that the accused possessed the article, unless he proves that he did not know of its presence on the premises or that he had no control over it …

Here, the legal or persuasive burden on the prosecution has been softened by the fact that there need only be 'reasonable suspicion' that the article is possessed for the purposes of terrorism. 'Reasonable suspicion' is normally sufficient to ground an arrest, but is not proof that an offence has been committed. The need to prove possession arises only if the accused adduces evidence that the article, though in his possession, was not possessed for the purposes of terrorism. Only then need the prosecution prove beyond reasonable doubt that it was possessed for that purpose. Similarly, where the article is on the premises occupied or habitually used by the accused, possession is assumed unless the accused adduces evidence that he did not know of its presence, or, if he did, that he had no control over it. Only if such evidence is adduced are the prosecution required to prove that he knew or had control over it. It follows that if the accused decides not to give evidence, he might be convicted by virtue of presumptions against him and on reasonable suspicion falling short of proof.

This is one of the reasons why the Divisional Court in *Kebilene*[301] believed that the predecessor of section 57 was in breach of the European Convention on Human Rights. Ironically, long before the Human Rights Act was conceived, the Criminal Law Revision Committee recommended that whenever a statute places a burden on the accused, it should be treated as an evidential rather than persuasive burden.[302] Section 118 of the Terrorism Act 2000 accomplishes this in respect of most of the provisions within that Act, and is to be welcomed. However, it should not be assumed that a serious offence cannot be the subject of a reverse legal burden. Not all reverse legal burdens in the Terrorism Act 2000 are covered by section 118. Parliament expressly intended that, for some offences, the legal burden of proof should fall squarely on the defendant. Traditionally, that would have meant that the courts were bound by such an intention.[303] However, in *Attorney-General's Reference (No 4 of 2002); Sheldrake v DPP (Conjoined Appeals)*,[304] the House of Lords held that section 11(2) of the Terrorism Act 2000 did not impose a reverse burden of proof on the defence and did not infringe the presumption of innocence so as to breach Article 6(2) of the Convention:

> The task of the court is never to decide whether a reverse burden should be imposed on a defendant, but always to assess whether a burden enacted by Parliament unjustifiably infringes the presumption of innocence. It may nonetheless be questioned whether … 'the assumption should be that Parliament would not have made an exception without good reason'. Such an approach may lead the court to give too much weight to the enactment under review and too little to the presumption of innocence and the obligation imposed on it by section 3 [of the Human Rights Act 1999].[305]

This statement underlines the impact of the Human Rights Act 1998 in altering the orthodox role of the courts in statutory interpretation: the express intention of Parliament to impose a reverse burden is no longer conclusive – it must be shown that a reverse onus is both necessary and proportionate in relation to the particular statute.

---

[301] [2000] 2 AC 326.
[302] Criminal Law Revision Committee, *Eleventh Report: Evidence (General)*, Cmnd 4991 (1972: London, HMSO).
[303] *Attorney-General's Reference (No 4 of 2002)* [2003] 3 WLR 1153.
[304] [2005] 1 AC 264.
[305] per Lord Bingham, at [31].

Misuse of Drugs Act 1971/Homicide Act 1957

In *R v Lambert, Ali and Jordan*,[306] the first appellant, Lambert, had been convicted of possession of a Class A drug with intent to supply, contrary to section 5 of the Misuse of Drugs Act 1971. The section makes it clear that it is for the accused to prove, inter alia, that he neither knew nor suspected the existence of some fact alleged by the prosecution if he is to be acquitted of the offence charged. Ali and Jordan had both been convicted of murder, but had pleaded the defence of diminished responsibility under section 2 of the Homicide Act 1957. Like the common law exception of insanity, the defence of diminished responsibility must be proved by the accused. All three appellants complained that the respective statutory provisions under which they had been convicted were in breach of Article 6 of the European Convention on Human Rights, but their arguments were rejected by the Court of Appeal.

So far as the defence of diminished responsibility was concerned, the Court had no difficulty in finding no breach of Article 6. The fact that the prosecution had no power to compel a defendant to testify meant that it would be exceedingly difficult for the prosecution to prove a negative. Likewise, the Court also took account of the fact that the prosecution were required to prove all the ingredients of the offence. Section 2 of the Homicide Act 1957 was of benefit to defendants who were in a position to take advantage of it. In the view of the Court, it did not matter whether it was treated as creating a defence to a charge of murder or an exception – section 2 did not contravene Article 6.

Lambert, who was found in possession of a controlled drug, argued that he did not know the bag he carried contained such drugs. However, section 28(3) of the Misuse of Drugs Act 1971 provides that the accused:

> shall not be acquitted of the offence charged by reason only of proving that he neither knew or suspected nor had reason to suspect that the substance or product in question was the particular controlled drug alleged; but

> shall be acquitted ... if he proves that he neither believed nor suspected nor had reason to suspect that the substance or product in question was a controlled drug ...

In relation to section 28, the Court emphasised the fact that for the defendant to be guilty of possession of drugs, the prosecution must prove an identifiable *actus reus* and *mens rea*. However, it was not necessary to prove that the defendant knew that the box contained drugs, only that he knew it contained something which proved to be drugs. This was a deliberate policy of Parliament, and the substance of the offence was reflected in the language of statute. Sections 5(4) and 28 did not impose additional ingredients which had to be proved to complete the offence, but rather provided a way of avoiding liability for what would otherwise be an offence. Noting that it was commonplace for a defendant to seek to avoid guilt by saying he thought he had pornography or gold and not drugs in a box or package, the Court stated that such defence was difficult for the prosecution to rebut. In essence, the formulation of this statutory provision was designed to make the defendant responsible for making sure he did not take into his possession containers which, in fact, contained drugs.

In addition, the Court held that there was a clear social objective in discouraging trading in drugs, and that the level of sentence would reflect the extent to which the defendant was responsible for the drugs in his possession. In the opinion of the Court, there was

---

[306] [2001] 1 All ER 1014.

an objective justification for the choice in the case of drugs, and the justification was not disproportionate. This particular part of the decision, in respect of the defendant Lambert and section 28 of the Misuse of Drugs Act 1971, was the subject of an appeal to the House of Lords.[307]

By a majority of 4:1, with Lord Hutton dissenting, their Lordships dismissed Lambert's appeal on the somewhat technical ground that the Human Rights Act 1998 could not be applied retrospectively. However, in respect of section 28 itself, their Lordships accepted that the prosecution only had to prove that the accused had a bag with something in it in his custody and control, and that the something in it was a controlled drug. It was not necessary for the prosecution to prove that the accused had known that the contents constituted a controlled drug, let alone a particular controlled drug.[308] The accused might then seek to establish one of the defences in section 5(4) or section 28. Lord Steyn, giving judgment for the majority stated:

> It follows that a legislative interference with the presumption of innocence requires justification and must not be greater than necessary. The principle of proportionality must be observed.[309]

While accepting that there was an objective basis for the justification, he went on to stress that any such justification must be proportionate. The burden, he noted, was on the state to show that the legislative means were not greater than necessary. Where there is an objective justification for some inroad into unsettling the presumption of innocence, the legislature had to choose whether it was more appropriate to impose a legal burden or an evidential burden on the accused. A transfer of a legal burden amounted to a far more drastic interference with the presumption of innocence than the creation of an evidential burden. A reverse legal burden involved the risk that the jury might convict where the accused had not discharged the legal burden resting on him. However, such a risk was not present if the nature of the burden was evidential only.

In respect of section 28, his Lordship observed that the prosecution must establish that the prohibited drugs were in the possession of the defendant and that he knew the package contained something. The accused must then prove, on a balance of probabilities, that he did not know the package contained controlled drugs. If the jury were in doubt on this issue, they must convict. This might occur where the accused adduced sufficient evidence to raise a doubt about his guilt, but the jury were not convinced on a balance of probabilities that his account was true. Indeed, it obliged the court to convict if the version of the accused was as likely to be true as not.

This particular aspect of the decision has a far-reaching consequence insofar as a guilty verdict may be returned in respect of an offence punishable by life imprisonment, even though the jury might consider that it is reasonably possible that the accused has been duped. Moreover, there may be real difficulties in determining the real facts upon which the sentencer must act in such cases. In any event, the burden of showing that only a reverse legal burden can overcome the difficulties of the prosecution in drugs cases is a heavy one. Lord Steyn pointed out that some of the difficulties faced by the prosecution are already dealt with by the practicalities of procedure and the rules of evidence. Thus, the relevant facts are peculiarly within the knowledge of the possessor of the container. This presumptively suggests, in the absence of evidence to the contrary, that the person

---

[307] *R v Lambert* [2002] AC 545.
[308] See *R v McNamara* (1988) 87 Cr App R 246.
[309] At [34].

in possession of the container knew what was in it. This would be a complete answer to a submission of no case to answer, and it would also be a factor which the trial judge would put before the jury. After all, it is common sense that possession of a package containing drugs demands a full and adequate explanation.

Lord Steyn concluded that he was satisfied that the transfer of the legal burden in section 28 was a disproportionate reaction to difficulties faced by the prosecution in drug cases. It was therefore sufficient to impose an evidential burden on the accused. It followed that section 28 should be 'read down' in a way which is compatible with Convention rights by reading the words 'prove' and 'proves' as meaning giving sufficient evidence. Reading these words in such a way had the effect of imposing only an evidential-only burden on the accused.

The Insolvency Act 1986

The decision in Lambert[310] was applied in R v Carass.[311] The defendant was charged with concealing debts in anticipation of a winding up, contrary to section 206(1)(a) of the Insolvency Act 1986. Section 206(4) provides that it is a defence for the accused to prove that he had no intent to defraud. On an interlocutory appeal against a finding by the trial judge that section 206(4) of the 1986 Act imposed a legal burden of proof on the accused, the Court of Appeal held that the word 'prove' in section 206(4) must be read as 'adduce sufficient evidence', thereby imposing an evidential rather than a persuasive burden. Waller LJ, giving the judgment of the court, stated that if a reverse legal burden were to be imposed on an accused, it had to be justified and demonstrated why a legal or persuasive burden (rather than an evidential burden) was necessary. Their Lordships did not believe that a legal burden was justifiable or necessary. Common sense dictated that if concealment of the debt was proved, the evidential burden itself would be quite difficult for the defendant to satisfy. Even if the accused did satisfy it, it would be less than satisfactory if he could still be convicted if the jury were not sure that he had intended to defraud. Nothing their Lordships had seen demonstrated a justification for that being a possible result under section 206 because of some 'threat faced by society'.[312] It was therefore held that the judge was wrong in so far as he felt obliged to direct the jury that section 206(4) imposed a legal burden on the defendant. The burden was evidential only and it was appropriate to read the word 'prove' in section 206(4) as 'adduce sufficient evidence'. On this point however, it should be noted that the House of Lords in Attorney-General's Reference (No 4 of 2002); Sheldrake v DPP (Conjoined Appeals)[313] concluded that Carass had been wrongly decided.

Discussion

The above decisions clearly indicate that, at least in relation to the most serious offences, statutory reversals of the burden of proof will be frequently 'read down' by the courts as imposing only an evidential burden on the accused under the Human Rights Act. It will be recalled that section 118 of the Terrorism Act 2000 makes almost all reversals of the

---

[310] [2001] 1 All ER 1014.
[311] [2002] Crim LR 316.
[312] R v DPP, ex p Kebilene [2000] 2 AC 326.
[313] [2005] 1 AC 264. See p 77 for further discussion.

burden of proof within that Act evidential burdens. This Act, together with the decision of the House of Lords in *Lambert*, suggests that Parliament and the courts have been coming around to the idea that placing the legal burden of proof on the accused can rarely be justified under the European Convention on Human Rights. There are few more serious offences than those contained in the Terrorism Act, and few offences which are so serious a threat to society as the abuse of drugs; and if these offences do not justify the imposition of a legal burden of proof on the accused, it is difficult to envisage offences that might. There may, however, be a difference of approach in relation to offences which, though serious in their effect on society and in terms of the punishment imposed on conviction, are essentially regulatory and are not seen as truly criminal.[314]

This was a point that was probed further by the House of Lords in *R v Johnstone*.[315] Here their Lordships recognised that the law still lacked some measure of clarity and sought to outline a fresh set of principles for determining when a reverse burden would be justifiable under the Human Rights Act. Johnstone was convicted of an offence under section 92(1)(b) of the Copyright Act 1994 by illegally copying CDs by Bon Jovi and others. He had sought to rely, inter alia, on a defence provided in section 92(5), which stipulates that:

> It is a defence for a person charged with an offence under this section to show that he believed on reasonable grounds that the use of the sign in the manner in which it was used, or was to be used, was not an infringement of the registered trademark.

The defendant's appeal was allowed on other grounds, although the Court of Appeal had read section 92(5) as imposing no more than an evidential burden on the defendant. It was on this point (which was not in the end determinative of the appeal), that the House of Lords disagreed. Lord Nicholls, giving judgment with which the majority agreed, came to the conclusion that section 92(5) imposed a legal burden on the accused. The court took a variety of factors into account in reaching this decision:

> A sound starting point is to remember that if an accused is required to prove a fact on the balance of probabilities to avoid conviction, this permits a conviction in spite of the fact-finding tribunal having a reasonable doubt as to the guilt of the accused ... This consequence of a reverse burden of proof should colour one's approach when evaluating the reasons why it is said that, in the absence of a persuasive burden on the accused, the public interest will be prejudiced to an extent which justifies placing a persuasive burden on the accused. The more serious the punishment which may flow from conviction, the more compelling must be the reasons. The extent and nature of the factual matters required to be proved by the accused, and their importance relative to the matters required to be proved by the prosecution, have to be taken into account. So also does the extent to which the burden on the accused relates to facts which, if they exist, are readily provable by him as matters within his own knowledge or to which he has ready access. In evaluating these factors the court's role is one of review. Parliament, not the court, is charged with the primary responsibility for deciding, as a matter of policy, what should be the constituent elements of a criminal offence.[316]

In the instant case, his Lordship found a number of compelling reasons why the burden should be legal rather than evidential in nature, including the urgent international pressure to restrain fraudulent trading in counterfeit goods; the framing of offences against section 92 as offences of 'near absolute liability'; and the dependence of the section 92(5) defence

---

[314] See *R v S (Trademark Defence)* [2003] 1 Cr App R 602 and *Davies v HSE* (2002) *The Times*, 27 December.
[315] [2003] 1 WLR 1736.
[316] At [50].

on facts within the defendant's own knowledge. There were, in particular, clear policy reasons for imposing the burden on the accused, including that fewer investigations and prosecutions into counterfeit goods would occur where the burden of proving dishonesty fell upon the prosecution.

It was recognised in *Attorney-General's Reference (No 1 of 2004)*[317] that there appeared to be a significant difference in emphasis between the approach of Lord Steyn in *Lambert*[318] and that of Lord Nicholls in *Johnstone*.[319] Evidently, the former had a much more robust approach to the question of compatibility, one which, if followed, would mean that a great number of legal burdens should in future be read down so as to constitute an evidential burden only. In expressing a clear preference for the approach of Lord Nicholls, the Lord Chief Justice noted that his angle was considerably more flexible and reflective of the intention behind the Human Rights Act 1998, which aimed to strike a balance between the role of Parliament and that of the courts. It was also more up-to-date and, unlike Lord Steyn's speech, was endorsed by all the other members of the House. Thus the decision in *Carass* was impliedly overruled.

The Court of Appeal proceeded to note that, where courts were confronted with a reverse burden, three pertinent questions should be addressed:

- whether the particular provision placed an evidential or a legal burden on the defendant;
- if it did impose a legal burden, deciding whether the legal burden could be justified; and
- if it could not be justified, whether it could be read down so that it was an evidential burden.

In determining whether the imposition of the burden was justifiable, the Court stated that ten general factors could be borne in mind (though it recognised that these might not be appropriate in all situations):

(a) Courts should strongly discourage the citation of authority to them other than Johnstone's case and this guidance. *Johnstone* is at present the latest word on the subject.

(b) The common law and the language of Article 6(2) had the same effect. Both permitted legal reverse burdens of proof or presumptions in appropriate circumstances.

(c) Reverse legal burdens were probably justified if the overall burden of proof was on the prosecution – that is the prosecution had to prove the essential ingredients of the offence. There were, however, situations where significant reasons present themselves as to why it is fair and reasonable to deny the accused the general protection normally guaranteed by the presumption of innocence.

(d) Where the exception went no further than was reasonably necessary to achieve the objective of the reverse burden – and was proportionate – it was sufficient if the exception was reasonably necessary in all the circumstances. The assumption should be that Parliament would not have made an exception without good reason. While the judge must make his own decision as to whether there was a contravention of Article 6, the task of a judge was to review Parliament's approach, as Lord Nicholls indicated in *Johnstone*.

(e) If only an evidential burden was placed on the defendant there would be no risk of contravention of Article 6(2).

---

[317] [2004] 1 WLR 2111.
[318] [2001] 1 All ER 1014.
[319] [2003] 1 WLR 1736.

(f) When ascertaining whether an exception was justified, the courts must construe the provision to ascertain what would be the realistic effects of the reverse burden. In doing so, the courts should be more concerned with substance than form. If the proper interpretation was that the statutory provision created an offence plus an exception, that would in itself be a strong indication that there was no contravention of Article 6(2).

(g) The easier it was for the accused to discharge the burden, the more likely it was that the reverse burden was justified. That would be the case where the facts were within the defendant's own knowledge. How difficult it would be for the prosecution to establish the facts was also indicative of whether a reverse legal burden was justified.

(h) The ultimate question was: would the exception prevent a fair trial? If it would, it must either be 'read down', if that was possible, or declared incompatible.

(i) Caution must be exercised when considering the seriousness of the offence and the power of punishment. The need for a reverse burden was not necessarily reflected by the gravity of the offence; though from a defendant's point of view the more serious the offence, the more important it was that there was no interference with the presumption of innocence.

(j) If guidance was needed as to the approach of the European Court of Human Rights, that was provided by *Salabiaku v France* at para 28: 'Article 6(2) does not regard presumptions of fact or of law with indifference. It requires states to confine them within reasonable limits which takes into account the importance of what is at stake and maintains the rights of the defence'.[320]

As the law stood in the light of the decisions in *Johnstone* and *Attorney-General's Reference (No 1 of 2004)*, it was considerably easier to persuade the court that Parliament knew what it was doing in enacting a reversal of the burden of proof and that imposing a reverse legal burden was necessary, reasonable and proportionate in the particular circumstances. However, the decision of the House of Lords in *Attorney-General's Reference (No 4 of 2002); Sheldrake v DPP (Conjoined Appeals)*[321] has further modified the position. Lord Bingham of Cornhill made it clear that both *Lambert* and *Johnstone* were recent decisions of the House of Lords, binding on all lower courts for what they decided:

> Nothing said in *R v Johnstone* suggests an intention to depart from or modify the earlier decision, which should not be treated as superseded or implicitly overruled. Differences of emphasis ... were explicable by the difference in the subject matter of the two cases. Section 5 of the Misuse of Drugs Act 1971 and section 92 of the Trade Marks Act 1994 were directed to serious social and economic problems. But the justifiability and fairness of the respective exoneration provisions had to be judged in the particular context of each case.[322]

In light of this decision, the guidelines laid down in *Attorney-General's Reference (No 1 of 2004)* were modified. *Lambert* or *Johnstone* can now be cited according to the particular context in which the provision under consideration operates. *Johnstone* is the latest word on economic offences which, though serious, may not be considered 'truly criminal'; *Lambert* is the latest word on 'truly criminal offences', and the court agreed with Lord Bingham's comments in *Attorney-General's Reference (No 1 of 2004)* that *Carass* had been wrongly decided. The assumption contained in guideline (d) above, that Parliament would not have made an

---

[320] At [52].
[321] [2005] 1 AC 264.
[322] At [30].

exception without good reason, was also erroneous, since it might lead a court to give too much weight to the enactment under review and too little to the presumption of innocence and the obligation imposed on it by section 3 of the Human Rights Act 1998.

The combined effect of the Terrorism Act 2000 Act and the decisions in *Lambert* and *Carrass* appeared to be moving toward an endorsement of the recommendation of the Criminal Law Revision Committee's Eleventh Report,[323] which suggested that whenever a statute placed a burden of proof on the accused, it should be treated as evidential rather than legal in nature. However, *Johnstone* and in *Attorney-General's Reference (No 1 of 2004)* clearly put a brake on the movement towards the replacement of legal burdens with evidential-only burdens and the restoration of the fundamental nature of the presumption of innocence. The latest decision of the House of Lords in *Attorney General's Reference (No 4 of 2002); Sheldrake v DPP* suggests not so much a brake on the movement, but an acceptance that there can be different approaches in relation to what may be termed 'real crime' and what may be termed 'regulatory offences' which are not truly criminal.

It can thus be confidently forecast that many statutes, including the Official Secrets Act 1989 and the Terrorism Act 2000, which concern serious criminal offences and place a reverse burden on the defence, will be the subject of a challenge in the future. The essential question for the courts will be whether the provisions are necessary, justifiable and proportionate, but despite two recent House of Lords decisions (*Lambert* and *Sheldrake*), and numerous recent Court of Appeal decisions, there remains no definitive test that can be applied by the lower courts to determine whether a particular provision is Convention-compliant. The Courts have rejected the formulation of any generic rule or test, preferring instead to treat each case on its own merits.[324] The closest the Courts have come to offering any general guidance is the Court of Appeal's formulation of a list of factors to take into account in *Attorney General's Reference (No 1 of 2004)*. However, even these have had to be modified in light of the House of Lords decision in *Attorney-General's Reference (No 4 of 2002); Sheldrake v DPP*, and there is no guarantee that those aspects of the guidance that remain good law will remain so indefinitely.

However, on the basis of recent trends, the likelihood is that in future years we shall see many more statutes being 'read down' and interpreted in such a way so as to impose an evidential burden only. Indeed, this is precisely what happened to certain provisions of the Official Secrets Act 1989 in the recent case of *R v Keogh*.[325] The defendant, civil servant David Keogh, was charged with allegedly leaking a document containing what was purported to be a discussion between the then Prime Minister Tony Blair and US President George Bush concerning policy in Iraq to his co-defendant Leo O'Connor, a political researcher for Parliament. The trial judge ruled that sections 2(3) and 3(4) of the 1989 Act created strict liability offences which imposed a reverse legal burden on the defendant and that they were justifiable. On appeal, Keogh contended that the burden to be shouldered under these provisions was arduous and unjustifiable.

Allowing the appeal, the Court of Appeal mooted whether the reverse burden contained within the challenged sections was necessary for the effective operation of the 1989 Act. They concluded that procedurally, the trial would be 'completely unbalanced' if – according to the reverse burden – the prosecution were to wait until the defendant gave evidence as to his *mens rea* before advancing with their case. It was established that the trial would better (and more effectively) proceed if the burden of proving the defendant's *mens rea* lies with

---

[323]Criminal Law Revision Committee, op cit n 302.
[324]See *Lambert*, [34]; *Sheldrake*, [21].
[325][2007] 1 WLR 1500.

prosecution from the outset. Therefore, the reverse burdens contained within sections 2(3) and 3(4) of the Official Secrets Act 1989 were, by their natural meanings, 'disproportionate and unjustifiable' and should be 'read down' to form evidential burdens only.[326]

While some statutory reversals of the burden of proof can be justified as being confined within reasonable limits given the importance of what is at stake, it is clear, nonetheless, that placing an evidential burden on the accused achieves the same purpose, while better maintaining the rights of the defence. Placing an evidential burden on the accused requires him to raise issue(s) that the prosecution must then rebut. This process still assists the prosecution by clarifying the issue(s) with which they must deal and, given the disclosure provisions which now apply to the defence, the prosecution can be made aware of those issues before trial, thus enabling them to handle such matters more efficiently. This, it could be contended, is fair to the accused since he or she as an individual is arguably best place to know what those issues are, and how to access relevant evidence to prove them. However, by the same token, it should be borne in mind that placing a legal burden of proof on the defence may lead to an unfair trial and result in the conviction of a defendant in circumstances where the jury continues to harbour some degree of doubt as to the accused's guilt.

In *R v Brook*,[327] the appellant alleged, somewhat unusually, that being asked questions in cross-examination by the prosecution was tantamount to a reversal of the burden of proof. The defendant was charged with, and convicted of, seven counts of rape, three of attempted rape and six of indecent assault. During cross-examination, counsel for the prosecution applied to the judge to be allowed to ask the defendant whether he could think of any grounds why the complainants should lie. The judge gave permission and the question was put to the defendant. Following his conviction and sentence of 11 years' imprisonment, the defendant appealed. The grounds for appeal were, inter alia, that it was unfair and tantamount to a shifting of the (legal) burden of proof for the prosecution to have been permitted to ask that question.

Lord Justice Rose, giving the judgment of the court, said that the question under scrutiny was one which had been widely, if not invariably, put in such cases for at least 40 years without any recorded expression of disapproval from the courts. Indeed, in this jurisdiction there was no authority on the point. Having considered authorities from other jurisdictions, it was held that the question put at trial was not unfair and did not shift the burden of proof. It was an admissible question because it was relevant. For example, if something were known to the defendant which provided a reason for the complainant to lie, that would tend to undermine the complainant's credibility – and if a defendant unexpectedly gave a positive answer, that might be relevant to his own credibility.

In the recent case of *R v BD*,[328] the Court of Appeal was faced with another atypical challenge in another case involving an alleged sexual assault. At first instance, the defendant was convicted on five specimen counts of indecent assault on a female who, at the time, was between 13 and 14 years old. During the trial, the defendant sought to cross-examine the defendant and her over an earlier complaint of indecent assault she made against another man, X, who was subsequently acquitted. The defendant also sought to call X as a witness in a bid to prove that the complainant's allegation against him was, like her complaint against X, based on collusion and fabrication. Applying the finality rule,[329] the judge allowed the

---

[326] At [33].
[327] (2003) *The Times*, 3 March.
[328] [2007] EWCA Crim 4.
[329] See Ch 5, pp 134–42.

defence counsel to ask each witness about their previous complains and whether they had concocted them.[330] However, the court refused to allow the defence to call X, since it was apparent that the purpose of calling him had more to do with discrediting the complainants, rather than adducing evidence surrounding the matters in issue.

It was held, dismissing the appeal, that if X were called and his evidence submitted, the situation would be tantamount to the reversal of the burden of proof onto the complainants. Essentially, the defence had been attempting to equate the previous acquittal of X with an automatic presumption of innocence in favour of the defendant in the immediate case. In addition, to cross-examine X, if he were called, would have effectively resulted in a re-trial of his guilt for an offence which took place nearly nine years earlier.

RESTORING THE FUNDAMENTAL NATURE OF THE RIGHT?

The advent of the Human Rights Act 1998 and the incorporation of the European Convention on Human Rights into our domestic law have provided means by which the fundamental nature of the right to be presumed innocent can be restored. However, as the cases considered above make clear, the provisions of Article 6 are not absolute and can be displaced for good reason.[331] It must be borne in mind that the European Convention on Human Rights is a document prepared by European nations with diverse legal cultures, backgrounds and criminal processes. In order to obtain agreement, those who drafted the Convention tended to agree on the lowest common denominator and almost all rights are qualified and can be displaced in the public interest when it is necessary and reasonable to do so. It follows that the Convention can provide only limited protection by requiring States to show that displacement of the fundamental right is necessary, justified and proportionate. It is, for example, unlikely that reverse burdens and presumptions in a majority of summary offences will be found to be in breach of Article 6 as some of the decisions already made under the Human Rights Act 1998 make clear.[332]

As the law currently stands, it is only the reverse burdens and presumptions which apply to serious indictable offences that are likely to contravene Article 6[333] and, as the guidance in *Attorney-General's Reference (No 1 of 2004)* makes clear, the seriousness of the offence and the punishment to be imposed are not the sole criteria. Courts are required to look to the realistic effect of imposing a reverse burden. Where the offence is regulatory in nature and intended to protect the public, reverse legal burdens are unlikely to be seen as incompatible with Article 6(2) if the effect of reading them down to evidential burdens is to make the investigation and prosecution of such offences more difficult. In the years to come, it may be that serious offences such as terrorism and dealing in prohibited drugs, will be seen as truly criminal and thus more deserving of the protection provided by the presumption of innocence.

The incorporation of the Convention provisions has obliged the courts to consider whether provisions which prima facie contravene Article 6 can be justified. In future, Parliament will itself have to justify any new statutory provision which is incompatible with

---

[330]If they had admitted making up their previous accusations, further questioning would have been permitted.
[331]See earlier discussion above at p 75 of regulatory offences having reverse burdens.
[332]See e.g. *L v DPP* [2003] QB 137, *Parker v DPP* [2001] RTR 240 and *Sheldrake* (above).
[333]See, for example, the decisions in *Lambert* and *Kebilene* (above).

Article 6 and the courts must decide whether existing reverse burdens which place a legal burden of proof on the defence can also be justified. The early promise of the Terrorism Act 2000 and the decisions in *Lambert*[334] and *Carass*[335] – that few such provisions in relation to the more serious offences can or will be justified – is now less likely to be realised. Instead, the more pragmatic approaches the Court of Appeal in *Johnstone* and *Attorney-General's Reference (No 1 of 2004)*, and the House of Lords in *Sheldrake* will hold sway. This approach is likely to lead to an acceptance of reverse burdens in relation to a majority of regulatory offences where reverse burdens are prevalent despite the seriousness of the offence and punishment. There are few truly criminal offences containing reverse burdens and it is in relation to such offences that one might expect the courts to 'read down' legal burdens. Therefore, it is likely that future researchers asking how many indictable or either way offences contain reverse burdens will find no significant reduction from the 40 per cent found by researchers prior to the Human Rights Act 1998 and no great advance for the cause of the rights of the defence.[336]

Interestingly, the Criminal Law Revision Committee, which contended that reverse burdens should be evidential only, also advocated the effective abolition of the right to silence along the lines of what are now sections 34 to 38 of the Criminal Justice and Public Order Act 1994.[337] A consequence of placing an evidential burden on the accused is that the accused must adduce evidence of the particular defence or risk being found guilty. The right to remain silent, to decline to give evidence and require the prosecution to prove one's guilt, is no longer available to the accused where the offence-creating statute includes a reverse burden which requires the accused to adduce sufficient evidence. The accused is not required to prove his innocence, but is required to adduce sufficient evidence of a particular defence which will create a reasonable doubt – unless the prosecution disprove the defence beyond reasonable doubt. In adducing the required evidence, the defendant, in theory, does not have to give evidence himself, but in practice he or she must almost always go into the witness box as most of the evidence he wishes to adduce will be within his or her own exclusive knowledge. If the accused does decide to appear in the dock, he or she will then be exposed to cross-examination, which is likely to assist the prosecution in proving his guilt.

As was indicated by Lord Justice Waller in *Carass*,[338] the evidential burden can be difficult for the defence to satisfy where, as in a case under section 206(1)(a) of the Insolvency Act 1986, the prosecution prove a concealment of the debt. At first sight, it may appear to be unimportant whether the burden on the accused is legal or evidential, since in both instances the accused will be placed under pressure to give evidence and be exposed to cross-examination. There is, however, one very significant difference. As was made clear by Lord Steyn in *Lambert*,[339] placing a legal burden on the accused can result in a conviction where the jury have a reasonable doubt that the defence have not made out their case sufficiently, while placing an evidential burden does not carry that risk – it is a much lower threshold for the defence to overcome. The other key difference is that imposing a legal burden may be incompatible with Article 6 of the European Convention on Human Rights, while imposing an evidential burden will not.

---

[334] [2001] 1 All ER 1014.
[335] [2002] Crim LR 316.
[336] Ashworth, A and Blake, M 'Presumption of Innocence in English Criminal Law' [1996] Crim LR 306.
[337] Criminal Law Revision Committee, op cit n 302, [140].
[338] [2002] Crim LR 316.
[339] [2001] 1 All ER 1014.

Some will argue that the imposition of the evidential burden is only the lesser of two evils, since it will still require the accused to give evidence and, in that sense, may be seen as another attack on the accused's right to silence alongside that imposed by section 35 of the Criminal Justice and Public Order Act 1994.[340] Others will argue that, like section 35, the imposition of an evidential burden does little to change the position of the accused, particularly where he or she is confronted with overwhelming evidence. In practice, the pressure of the prosecution case is in itself usually enough to require most defendants to give evidence or risk conviction by not doing so. Whichever position is preferred, the fact remains that the 'golden thread' of English criminal law is qualified by the imposition of a reverse burden of proof, and one might legitimately argue that 'a qualified fundamental principle' is something of a contradiction in terms.

Thus the Human Rights Act 1998 ensures that the responsibility for maintaining such fundamental freedoms as the presumption of innocence will be placed on Parliament, using the circuitous route of a challenge to a statutory provision under the Human Rights Act 1998. Parliament will then be forced to take the burden of proof, and other fundamental freedoms, more seriously than it has in the past, but there remains much room for what the European Court of Human Rights describes as 'a margin of appreciation'. This means that fundamental freedoms can be whittled down, but only 'within the reasonable limits', taking into account the importance of what is at stake and ensuring to maintain the rights of the defence. Fine words, some may say, to justify the qualification of a fundamental right.

KEY LEARNING POINTS

- The 'golden thread' of English criminal law encapsulates the general principle that the burden of proof falls on the prosecution.
- Burdens may be either legal or evidential in nature.
- There is one established common law exception to the principle (insanity), as well as numerous express and implied statutory exceptions.
- Providing reverse burdens are confined within 'reasonable limits', and were framed in such a way so as to take into account the importance of what is at stake, they will not violate Article 6(2) ECHR.
- There is no universal 'test' that can be applied to determine whether a reverse burden is justifiable.

?   QUESTIONS

1. The Terrorism (Further Measures) Bill 2008 [fictional] contains the following provisions:

   Clause 1

   (1) It shall be an offence for any person to assist another in any way whatsoever whether by act or omission in the commission, preparation or instigation of an act of terrorism.

   Continued

---

[340]See below, Ch 4 pp 99–112.

(2) Where the prosecution have proved assistance in the commission, preparation or instigation of an act of terrorism by an act or omission it is a defence for the accused to prove that he either did not know or had no reason to suspect that the assistance given was in the commission, preparation or instigation of an act of terrorism.

(3) This offence is punishable on indictment by a maximum of ten years imprisonment.

Clause 25(1) of the Bill further provides that where, in accordance with a provision mentioned in clause 25(2), it is a defence for a person charged with an offence to prove a particular matter, if the person adduces sufficient evidence to raise an issue with respect to the matter the court or jury shall assume that the defence is satisfied unless the prosecution proves beyond reasonable doubt that it is not. Clause 25(2) lists a number of clauses but not clause 1.

Consider whether the above provision, if enacted in the above terms, would be compatible with Article 6(2) of the European Convention on Human Rights and if not, how it may be amended so as to be compatible.

2. 'No matter what the charge or where the trial, the principle that the prosecution must prove the guilt of the prisoner is part of the common law of England and no attempt to whittle it down can be entertained' per Viscount Sankey LC in *Woolmington v Director of Public Prosecutions* (1935) AC 462, 481.
   Is the 'golden thread' of English criminal law still valid today?

3. 'The presumption of innocence, one of the central tenets of a fair trial as enshrined in Article 6 of the European Convention on Human Rights, is epitomised by the requirement that the prosecution prove the guilt of the accused beyond all reasonable doubt. In practice, however, the principle has been whittled down by parliamentary intervention and judicial interpretation. It is hoped that reliance on the Human Rights Act 1998 will serve to restore the principle to its fundamental status'.

Discuss the issues raised in the above statement.

SUGGESTED FURTHER READING

Ashworth, A. and Blake, M 'The presumption of innocence in English criminal law' [1998] Crim LR 306.

Dennis, I 'Reverse onuses and the presumption of innocence: in search of principle' [2005] Crim LR 901.

Dingwall, G 'Statutory exceptions, burdens of proof and the Human Rights Act 1998' (2002) 65 MLR 450.

Hamer, D 'The presumption of innocence and reverse burdens: a balancing act' (2007) 66 CLJ 142.

Padfield, N 'The burden of proof unresolved' (2005) 64 CLJ 17.

Roberts, P 'The resumption of innocence brought home? *Kebilene* deconstructed' (2002) 118 LQR 41.

CHAPTER 4

COMPETENCE, COMPELLABILITY AND THE PRIVILEGE AGAINST SELF-INCRIMINATION

INTRODUCTION

This chapter deals with the rules relating to those circumstances when a witness is reluctant to divulge information or to testify in court at all. As a starting point, we consider the rules relating to competence and compellability of witnesses. The term 'competency' is concerned with who *may* lawfully testify as a witness, whereas the term 'compellability' is concerned with who may be lawfully *obliged* to testify. The chapter then proceeds to examine the closely related issue of the privilege against self-incrimination, which concerns the extent to which suspects and accused persons can be made to produce evidence against themselves. Finally, we consider the effects of remaining silent in response to questioning.

COMPETENT AND COMPELLABLE WITNESSES

Section 53 of the Youth Justice and Criminal Evidence Act 1999 stipulates a general rule that all witnesses are competent, and all competent witnesses are compellable. In other words, all witnesses are under a legal obligation to give evidence if called upon to do so and may be subject to a legal penalty for failure to carry out that duty. A competent witness may be compelled to give evidence by the threat of being held in contempt (punishable by imprisonment) for failing to do so.[341]

Although it is usually the case that competence will automatically give rise to compellability, there are three major exceptions to this rule. First, the spouse of an accused is now a competent witness by virtue of section 53(1) of the Youth Justice and Criminal Evidence Act 1999. However, as we shall see below, he or she is only compellable for the prosecution against the accused,[342] or a co-accused, in the very limited circumstances provided for in section 80(3) of the Police and Criminal Evidence Act 1984.[343] Secondly, the accused was made a competent witness in his own defence by the Criminal Evidence Act 1898, but is not a competent witness for the prosecution in any proceedings so long as he remains charged with an offence in the proceedings. An accused person is not compellable, but, as noted below, if he or she chooses to give evidence there is no privilege against self-incrimination in respect of the offences with which he is charged.[344] Lastly, diplomats, foreign heads of state and the sovereign are competent, but not compellable witnesses.

All witnesses who are compellable have a privilege against self-incrimination that permits them to refuse to answer questions if the answer would incriminate them (sometimes referred to as the right to silence). Lawyers may refuse to answer questions about advice given to clients on the grounds of legal professional privilege,[345] and

---

[341]See e.g. *R v Renshaw* [1989] Crim LR 811; *R v Holt and Bird* (1996) *The Times*, 31 October.

[342]Unless the spouse is jointly tried with the defendant, in which case he/she will not be competent for the prosecution.

[343]See below, pp 90–94.

[344]Section 1(2) of the Criminal Evidence Act 1898.

[345]The scope of legal professional privilege at common law is contained in section 10 of the Police and Criminal Evidence Act 1984. See also *R v Central Criminal Court ex p Francis and Francis* [1989] AC 346.

government officials and quasi-government bodies may be able to rely on public interest immunity to refuse to answer certain questions.[346] Otherwise, a witness can be punished for contempt of court if he or she refuses to answer questions. This rule will apply to the clergy, doctors, counsellors and others professionals who are in a confidential or fiduciary relationship with their clients. Such persons have no legal right to refuse to answer questions, though in practice most prosecutors would be reluctant to put such a person in the position of having to breach the moral duty of confidentiality unless absolutely necessary. Journalists cannot normally be required to disclose their source of information, but there is a procedure under section 10 of the Contempt of Court Act 1981 by which they can be required to do so.

Problematic witnesses

Child witnesses

Historically, all witnesses were treated in a similar fashion in court, irrespective of age. Children who were deemed capable of distinguishing between good and evil were expected to take the oath and give evidence orally from the witness box in open court.[347] However, in time this rule came to be considered unsatisfactory and led to the enactment of section 38 of the Children and Young Persons Act 1933 (now repealed), which permitted a child of tender years (under 14) to give evidence unsworn, providing the child understood the duty to speak the truth, and was of sufficient intelligence to justify the reception of his evidence.

However, it was not until the mid-1970s that the old common law rules governing evidence on oath were subject to reform. In *R v Hayes*,[348] the Court of Appeal formulated a more secular test. Thereafter, the key question for the trial judge was 'whether the child has a sufficient appreciation of the solemnity of the occasion and the added responsibility to tell the truth which is involved in taking an oath, over and above the duty to tell the truth which is an ordinary duty of normal social contact'.[349] In practice, there was little difference between this test for giving sworn evidence and that in section 38 of the Children and Young Persons Act 1933 for unsworn evidence. However, mistrust of children's evidence continued in the common law requirement that children giving sworn evidence had to be the subject of a warning to the jury of the danger of acting on their uncorroborated evidence, though they could still choose to act on it even if uncorroborated.[350] Additionally, a child giving unsworn evidence under section 38 of the Children and Young Persons Act 1933 required actual corroboration in the form of other independent evidence supporting his evidence, otherwise there could be no conviction.

These corroboration rules, together with the reluctance to treat young children as competent witnesses, created difficulties for prosecutors and were arguably a key factor underlying the relatively high attrition rates for child abuse which prevailed until the last decade of the twentieth century. Both requirements were removed by section 34 of the

---

[346]The beginning of the modern approach to public interest immunity can be seen in *Conway v Rimmer* [1968] AC 910, in which the House of Lords reversed its earlier ruling in *Duncan v Cammell Laird* [1942] AC 624 and held that, in such cases, it was for the court to decide where the balance of public interest lay: in protecting a government claim for secrecy or in upholding a litigant's right to have all relevant materials available for the proper adjudication of his claim.

[347]*R v Brasier* (1779) 1 Leach 199.

[348]64 Cr App R 194.

[349]At 196.

[350]See Ch 1, pp 16–18.

Criminal Justice Act 1988, which then meant that there were two just two issues for the trial judge to consider in determining the competence of a child to give evidence:

- whether the child was capable of giving evidence at all; and
- if so, whether that evidence should be sworn or unsworn.

The first raised issues beyond the obvious question of whether the child was capable of giving coherent and intelligible evidence. There is a degree of trauma involved in attending and giving evidence in public in open court, and being faced by the alleged assailant.[351] The common law made no concession to children of whatever age. If they gave evidence they did so as if they were adults, apart from giving their evidence unsworn. However, historically judges had adopted a protective approach which ignored the question of whether the child was capable of giving evidence. This involved treating the very young child witness as incompetent, even though the child might very well have been able to understand questions and give intelligible answers.

Sections 53 to 57 of the Youth Justice and Criminal Evidence Act 1999 now provide for a much more straightforward approach. There is a presumption that all witnesses are competent regardless of age, unless they are unable to understand the questions and give answers that can be understood.[352] It is of course conceivable that this could exclude a very young child; if doubts are raised as to the competence of a witness, it is for the party calling the witness to prove that he is able to communicate intelligibly on the balance of probabilities.[353] The Act also provides that no witness under the age of 14 is to be sworn, and that witnesses over 14 are eligible to be sworn only if they understand the solemnity of a criminal trial and that taking an oath places a particular responsibility on them to tell the truth.[354] Such witnesses may, however, give evidence unsworn.[355]

In *R v MacPherson*,[356] the appellant was charged with having committed indecent assault upon a four-year-old girl. The trial judge, having watched the memorandum interview, rejected the defence's contention that the witness was incompetent and allowed her evidence. The appellant was convicted, and appealed on the grounds that the judge erred in determining S's competence on the basis of her memorandum video alone; that he had no, or insufficient, regard to the requirement that he assess the child's ability to understand and answer questions within the forensic forum as a witness as required by section 53 of the Act; and that, in reaching his decision, he had no, or insufficient regard, to the girl's ability to participate meaningfully in cross-examination. These arguments were, however, dismissed by the Court of Appeal. It was held that the judge had properly assessed the child's ability to 'understand questions put to him as a witness and give answers to them which could be understood'. In particular, the Court noted that the words 'put to him as a witness' within section 53(3)(a) meant the equivalent of 'being asked of him in court',

---

[351] See Ch 2, pp 28–29.

[352] Youth Justice and Criminal Evidence Act 1999, section 53(3).

[353] Youth Justice and Criminal Evidence Act 1999, section 54(2).

[354] Youth Justice and Criminal Evidence Act 1999, section 55(2)(a).

[355] Youth Justice and Criminal Evidence Act 1999, section 56. In *R v Day* [1997] 1 Cr App R 181, it was held that where a child was aged under 14 when the video was made but over 14 when the video is presented as evidence in cross-examined in court or via a TV link, the child should be sworn. This is likely to be the position under the 1999 Act. It follows that fewer children will appear in court; but if the situation in *Day* is repeated and the child witness is then over 14 years of age when the video is tendered in evidence then, consistent with section 55(2), he can only give sworn evidence. It is the practice when video-taping an interview with a child close to 14, who might well be over that age when appearing in court, for the child to affirm at the beginning of the interview.

[356] [2006] 1 Cr App R 459.

so that a child who could only communicate in baby-language with his mother would not ordinarily be competent, but a young child like the girl in the instant case, who could speak and understand basic English with strangers, would be competent. Moreover, the Act laid down no requirement that the child should be aware of his or her status as a witness: questions of credibility and reliability were matters for the jury and were not relevant to the issue of competence.

As John Spencer has observed, the rules introduced by the 1999 Act governing the competency of child witnesses are of symbolic, as well as practical, importance. He notes that the rules 'mark the final transition from a system where the courts refused to hear all sorts of persons for fear they might not tell the truth, to one where the courts listen to everybody, and try to decide whether they are truthful or not on the basis of what they have said'.[357] Combined with the range of special measures that have been made available to assist such witnesses,[358] it is hoped that the rights of children coming to court will be respected and protected in a much more comprehensive fashion than has traditionally been the case in criminal trials in England and Wales.

Witnesses with physical and learning disabilities

Witnesses who suffer from physical or mental disabilities that impact upon their ability to communicate have traditionally presented problems for the courts. At common law, 'persons of unsound mind' who were not capable of understanding the nature of the oath and of giving rational evidence were not competent witnesses. The test was whether the witness understood the nature of the oath and the divine sanction. Thus in *R v Hill*,[359] the witness was an inmate of a lunatic asylum who suffered from the delusion that he was possessed by spirits who talked to him. Medical evidence was given that the witness was capable of giving an account of any transaction that he witnessed. The Court of Appeal held that the judge had correctly ruled that the witness was competent. In any such case, it was for the trial judge to examine the witness and determine, on the basis of the responses to his questions, whether the witness understands the nature of the oath.

Surprisingly, the requirement of belief in some form of divine sanction if one failed to tell the truth continued to underpin the test of competency for adults with learning disabilities until the decision of the Court of Appeal in *R v Bellamy*.[360] The case concerned the testimony of a rape complainant, aged 33 but with a mental age of 10. At trial, the judge heard evidence from the complainant's social worker and questioned the complainant both about her belief in God and about her understanding of the importance of telling the truth. He decided that she was a competent witness, but lacked a sufficient belief in the existence of God to take a binding oath. The Court of Appeal held her appreciation of the theological intricacies of the oath should have been discarded as irrelevant. The answers the complainant had given to initial questioning indicated that she satisfied the *Hayes* test. Although *Hayes* had only been regarded as an authority in respect of child witnesses, the Court of Appeal held that the same test should be applied for adult witnesses under the modern law. Thus, applying *Hayes*, the trial judge would have to ascertain whether the witness had a sufficient appreciation of the solemnity of

---

[357]Spencer J, 'The Youth Justice and Criminal Evidence Act 1999: The Evidence Provisions', *Archbold News*, January 2000, 5–8.

[358]See Ch 2, pp 35–47.

[359](1851) 2 Den 254.

[360](1985) 82 Cr App R 222.

the occasion and the added responsibility to tell the truth which is involved in taking an oath.

In those cases where the witness was competent but unable to communicate, perhaps through some form of physical disability impairing their speech, the provisions of section 23 of the Criminal Justice Act 1988 allowed the statement of the witness to be admitted in evidence without the need for the witness to give oral evidence, providing certain conditions were satisfied. One such condition, contained in section 23(2)(a),[361] was that the person who made the statement was, by reason of his bodily or mental condition, unfit to give evidence. The provision was applied in *R v Duffy*,[362] where the accused was convicted of the manslaughter of V. V's son had witnessed the killing, but was physically handicapped with very poor power of speech, and the only person capable of understanding him was a social worker. The social worker attended a police interview with the deceased's son which was video recorded. The social worker asked the questions and confirmed the answers for the benefit of the camera, and compiled a transcript of the interview. The trial judge refused to admit the video under that provision on the grounds that the video was of poor quality and the fact that it needed translation by the interviewer meant that it was effectively the evidence of the interviewer, not that of the deceased's son. However, the Court of Appeal ruled that the trial judge had erred in reaching this decision. Essentially, the social worker was in a position akin to a translator who could give admissible evidence of his interpretation of what the witness was saying in the interview.

Following the reforms contained in Part II of the Youth Justice and Criminal Evidence Act 1999, witnesses suffering from a learning disability or a physical disability are subject to the same test of competence as children.[363] Thus, under section 53 of the Act, all witnesses are presumed to be competent unless it is shown that they are unable to understand the questions and give answers that can be understood. In practice, this presumption will rarely be called into question, but where the issue is raised it is for the parties to satisfy the court on the balance of probabilities that the witness is competent to give evidence. In the event that a witness is deemed incompetent, it is still possible for the court to receive his or her evidence. As we shall see in Chapter 7,[364] the successor of section 23 of the 1988 Act, section 116(2)(b) of the Criminal Justice Act 2003, may be used in under certain circumstances to admit an out of court statement where the relevant person is unfit to be a witness because of his or her mental condition. However, this provision can only be relied upon where the person who made the statement was competent to make it at the material time.[365]

In *R v Sed*,[366] the trial judge admitted the video statement of an 81-year-old woman suffering from Alzheimer's disease, under section 23 of the Criminal Justice Act 1988. Although the woman's answers on the video were somewhat confused, she stated that a man had had sexual intercourse with her without her consent. Expert medical evidence indicated that at the time of her interview she was not fit to give evidence in court

---

[361] Now section 116(2)(b) of the Criminal Justice Act 2003.

[362] [1999] QB 919.

[363] It should also be borne in mind that the Act provides for a range of special measures which could be used in court to assist such witnesses in giving evidence in open court – see Ch 2, pp 40–47.

[364] See Ch 7, p 220.

[365] Criminal Justice Act 2003, section 116(1)(a). Section 116(3) effectively applies section 53(3) of the Youth Justice and Criminal Evidence Act 1999 in relation to an out of court statement, while section 116(4) provides for the same means of determining competency as is set out in section 54 of the 1999 Act. See also section 123 of the Criminal Justice Act 2003.

[366] [2004] 1 WLR 3218.

owing to her dementia. Applying the test of competence set out in section 53 of the 1999 Act, the judge ruled that the witness was competent, and admitted the video statement.

The accused was convicted, and his appeal was dismissed. The question for the Court of Appeal centred on which test of competence ought to be applied for the purposes of a documentary statement admissible under section 23 of the 1988 Act. Even though the trial had taken place before section 53 of the 1999 Act came into force, Lord Justice Auld said that its formulation of a new notion of competence was a reasonable, though not obligatory, approach for the judge to adopt when considering whether to admit the hearsay evidence. Ultimately, it was concerned with assessing the extent and impact of any mental or psychiatric illness at the time the statement was made. To this end, section 123(3) of the Criminal Justice Act 2003 now makes it clear that consideration of section 53 of the 1999 Act is now obligatory when considering the admissibility of a hearsay statement contained in any document.

The spouse of the accused

The common law rules relating to the competence and compellability of the accused's spouse were complex and confused. The wife or husband of a person charged in the proceedings was generally considered to be incompetent, except in respect of a small number of serious offences. The House of Lords' decision in *Hoskyn v Metropolitan Police Commissioner*[367] changed this view, and thereafter, the common law rule was that the wife or husband of a defendant could not give evidence for the prosecution no matter how serious the charge.

The Criminal Law Revision Committee accepted that a wife ought not to be compelled to testify against her husband.[368] The Committee felt that compulsion could unnecessarily disrupt marital harmony, and place one partner in the invidious position of having to incriminate the other. It concluded, however, that wives should be compellable to testify for certain offences against the person of the wife or children (aged under 16) of the same household as the accused; otherwise these offences might go undetected – or, if detected, unpunished – given that there are rarely any other witnesses to domestic crimes of this nature. It was further felt that in relation to crimes against children of the household, the wife might be guilty of some complicity and for that reason reluctant to testify without the compulsion of law. These two factors, combined with the serious nature of the offences, justified compellability. However, the Committee emphasised that the seriousness of the offence was not in itself sufficient to justify compelling a spouse to testify against the other spouse.[369]

Nevertheless, some 12 years later, when the Police and Criminal Evidence Bill was going through Parliament, a number of high profile cases of child sex abuse persuaded the government to extend compellability to include sexual offences against, or assaults upon, any child under 16. Section 80 of the 1984 Act, as amended by the Youth Justice and Criminal Evidence Act 1999, forms the basis of the current legal framework.

Section 80(2A) makes a wife compellable for the prosecution or a co-defendant (unless she is jointly charged with her husband) if, and only if, the offence constitutes

---

[367][1979] AC 474.
[368]Criminal Law Revision Committee *11th Report, Evidence (General)*, Cmnd 4991 (1972: London, HMSO).
[369]*Ibid.*, at [143]–[157].

a 'specified offence'. Under section 80(3), an offence is defined as a 'specified offence' for the purposes of section 80(2A) if:

(a) it involves an assault on, or injury or threat of injury to, the wife or husband or a person who was at the material time under the age of 16;

(b) it is a sexual offence alleged to have been committed in respect of a person who was at the material time under that age; or

(c) it consists of attempting or conspiring to commit, or of aiding, abetting, counselling, procuring or inciting the commission of, an offence falling within para (a) or (b) above.

A spouse is now competent in all cases (unless also charged in the proceedings) and can give evidence in any case, but can only be compelled to do so in the limited circumstances provided for in section 80(3)(a), (b) and (c) (a specified offence).[370] This provision does, however, create anomalies. For example, a wife cannot be compelled to give evidence against her husband charged with the rape and murder of a girl aged 16 years and 1 month, but can be compelled to give evidence against her husband if he is charged with indecent assault on a 15-year-old girl by pinching her bottom. This position is consistent with the Criminal Law Revision Committee's refusal to be swayed simply by the seriousness of the offence. A recent high profile example of this aberration can be found in the case of Fred West. He and his wife were jointly charged with more than 10 murders of young girls. If the wife had not been charged with West, she would have been compellable for the prosecution on charges of rape and murder of girls aged under 16, but not in respect of the same charges where the victims were 16 or over.

West's case highlights a further peculiarity. Where multiple victims are involved, a spouse may be compellable in respect of one offence, but not the other. Suppose Keith and Jane are married with two children, Hilda (16) and Tammy (15). Keith is charged with the rape of both his daughters. In practice however, were such a case to come to court, the accused would almost certainly be tried for the two different counts of rape at the same trial. Since rape is a specified offence for the purposes of section 80(3)(b), Jane will be compellable by the prosecution in respect of the alleged offence committed against Tammy, but not in relation to the alleged rape of Hilda. In respect of this latter offence, Jane will be entitled to refuse to give evidence. This is likely to create problems for the prosecution and court, who must determine what evidence is relevant to which offence, and what evidence the wife can be compelled to give and what evidence she can refuse to give. Evidence may very well be intermingled, so although technically the jury should only consider Jane's evidence in respect of Tammy, it may be difficult for them to draw a clear line of division to separate the evidence in respect of the two different offences.

When the government took the opportunity to revise section 80 as part of the reforms introduced by the Youth Justice and Criminal Evidence Act 1999, it would have been logical to provide that where the accused is charged with a specified offence in respect of which his spouse is compellable, and with other offences in respect of which she is not compellable, she should be compellable in respect of all offences charged.

In effect the spouse has been given a privilege against being compelled to give evidence against the other spouse unless the offence falls within section 80(3). He or she can waive the privilege and give evidence if he or she wishes to do so in those cases to which section 80(3) does not apply. However, any such decision must be made in full knowledge of his

---

[370]Section 84(1) of the Civil Partnership Act 2004 provides that: 'Any enactment or rule of law relating to the giving of evidence by a spouse applies in relation to a civil partner as it applies to the spouse'.

or her right not to give evidence. Thus, where a spouse who is not compellable chooses to give evidence, the trial judge must ensure that the decision to give evidence is made in the knowledge that he or she is not compelled to do so.[371] Given the fact that one of the core functions of the criminal justice system ought to be protection of the public at large, it seems highly questionable, particularly in serious cases, that a spouse should effectively hold a form of veto on a conviction.

It is also debatable as to whether the scope of section 80(3)(a) includes a sexual offence against the spouse. Could it be the case, for example, that the wife of the accused could be compellable to give evidence against her husband accused of raping her? This question was not considered by the Criminal Law Revision Committee in 1972, nor by the framers of the Police and Criminal Evidence Act 1984, because at that time there was no offence of marital rape. When the husband's immunity at common law for marital rape was abolished by the decision of the House of Lords in *RvR*,[372] the question is thus raised as to whether, in such cases, the wife may be compellable by the prosecution. Given that rape usually involves an assault or threat of an assault, the answer would appear to be 'yes'. However, in their report *Rape Within Marriage*,[373] the Law Commission drew attention to the presumably intended contrast between section 80(3)(a), which refers to assault, and section 80(3)(b), which refers to 'sexual' offences committed against persons under 16. If rape is considered to be a sexual offence, it follows that a wife is not compellable on a charge against her husband of raping her. This view is supported by the redefinition of 'rape' in section 1 of the Sexual Offences Act 2003, which, while including lack of consent, speaks of 'intentional penetration' of the vagina, anus or mouth. It is likely that the courts will interpret rape as including an assault for the purposes of section 80(3)(a), given that any touching without consent constitutes an assault. Such an interpretation is supported by section 2 of the 2003 Act, which creates the offence of assault by penetration by parts of the body or by any object other than the penis. Since the offences are almost identically worded, it would seem that rape of a spouse would now fall within the ambit of section 80(3)(a) of the 1984 Act.

When section 80(3) was first formulated, it was hoped that the provision might assist in the prosecution of domestic violence cases, which, like child abuse, have a notoriously high attrition rate. It is often the case that a wife withdraws her complaint before a file is passed to the Crown Prosecution Service, and in these circumstances the CPS will tend not to bring charges (or will later drop charges) on the grounds that there is little prospect of a conviction.[374] In such cases it would be open to the prosecution to use section 80(3) and threaten the wife with punishment for contempt if she refuses to testify. This course of action would, however, be extremely undesirable, in that it could result in the absurd situation where the victim is imprisoned and the alleged perpetrator would go unpunished. There is also some evidence from other jurisdictions that a policy of pursuing prosecutions regardless of the witness's reluctance to testify can serve to discourage victims from reporting of domestic violence.[375] If the victim is in fear because of threats of intimidation, she is eligible for such measures which may assist her to give evidence.[376] There is also the possibility that her statement of evidence can be admitted in documentary form under

---

[371] *R v Pitt* [1983] QB 25.

[372] [1992] 1 AC 599.

[373] Law Commission, *Rape Within Marriage*, Law Com No 205 (1990: London, HMSO).

[374] See further Her Majesty's Chief Inspector of Constabulary and Her Majesty's Chief Inspector of the Crown Prosecution Service, *Violence at Home* (2004: London, HMSO).

[375] See generally Buzawa, E and Buzawa, C *Domestic Violence: The Criminal Justice Response*, 3rd ed (2003: Thousand Oaks CA, Sage).

[376] See Ch 2, pp 38–39.

section 116(2)(e) of the Criminal Justice Act 2003.[377] While such provisions may relieve to some extent the victim's fear of testifying, they will not ultimately affect the privilege provided by section 80(3), or the refusal to testify based on the emotional tie between victim and offender.

Even where a reluctant spouse does testify, she may refuse to give the expected testimony. In these circumstances, she can be treated as a hostile witness, and previous statements made to the police that are inconsistent with what the witness says in the witness box can be put to the witness and, if accepted as correct, be put in evidence.[378] However, the weight given to such evidence is much reduced by the process, and the jury may not give much credence to a witness who has said one thing to the police and something else in court.

It should be noted that it is only the wife, husband or civil partner, who has the right to refuse to give evidence in those cases not covered by section 80(3). Co-habitees, no matter how long they have lived together, are competent and compellable in all cases, as are all children, parents, siblings and other close relatives. This is somewhat anomalous given the increasing tendency to put partners in the same position as spouses (note the recent passage of the Civil Partnership Act 2004) and the fact that the blood relationship can be as strong as, if not stronger than, the marital bond. Compelling a partner, son or daughter to give evidence against the other partner or parent, or compelling the partner or parent to give evidence against their children, is likely to have as great an impact on the family and relationship as compelling the legal spouse. Seemingly, the law is not concerned with what compelling a spouse to give evidence does to the family, only with what it might do to the marriage. In *R v Pearce*,[379] the Court of Appeal confirmed that co-habitees and children were not within section 80(3). In that case, it was argued on behalf of the appellant that compelling partners and children of the marriage to give evidence constituted a breach of Article 8(1) of the European Convention on Human Rights. However, the Court of Appeal rejected the argument, holding that such compulsion was necessary in a democratic society to prevent crime.

The institution of marriage has, of course, undergone radical transformation in the decades since section 80 came into force. Originally the wife was not a competent witness because of the unity principle that the common law recognised. However, with around 40 per cent of marriages now ending in divorce, and with two-thirds of people believing that there is little difference between marriage and cohabitation,[380] it might be asked whether a more modern approach should be enacted which would place on the spouse the same social responsibility to give evidence as non-spouses. This would involve repealing section 80 and putting spouses under the same moral and legal obligation as any other witness who can choose not to testify, but on pain of punishment. Thus a priest has no legal privilege and cannot lawfully refuse to disclose matters confided to him, even under the seal of the confessional. Journalists have gone to prison rather than testify as to the source of information obtained. It is increasingly difficult to justify a more privileged position for the spouse.

Alternatively, it may be argued that the emphasis should be on preserving family relationships, so that the privilege should be extended to include partners, children and close relatives. However, given the increase in abuse within families, the exceptions

---

[377] Replacing section 23 of the Criminal Justice Act 1988. See Ch 7, pp 223–27.
[378] Criminal Procedure Act 1865, section 3. See further Ch 5, pp 130–31.
[379] [2002] 1 Cr App R 551.
[380] National Centre for Social Research, *British Social Attitudes Survey 2008* (2008: London, NCSR).

contained in section 80(3) must remain if the family members are to be protected from criminal abuse. A number of Australian states, including Victoria, New South Wales and South Australia, have adopted a discretionary approach in various forms, whereby the spouse is compellable in all cases, but the trial judge has a discretion to exempt the spouse from giving evidence where the public interest in obtaining the spouse's evidence is outweighed by private interests, such as the likely damage to the marital relationship or the harshness of compelling the spouse to testify. Factors to be considered in exercising that discretion include the nature of the offence charged, the likely significance of the spouse's evidence in the case, the state of the relationship between the spouses and the likely effect upon it of compelling the spouse to testify. Under such a discretionary system a wife is unlikely to be compelled to testify against her husband who is charged with a minor offence, but is likely to be compelled when she has evidence of some significance and the offence is a serious one.

In 1972, the Criminal Law Revision Committee refused to recommend reform based on the seriousness of the crime, stating that 'the law has never ... made the seriousness of an offence by itself a ground for compellability, and we do not do so now'.[381] Instead the Committee sought a balance between 'the desirability that all available evidence which might conduce to the right verdict should be before the court', against:

- the objection on social grounds to disturbing marital harmony more than is absolutely necessary, and
- what many regard as the harshness of compelling a wife to give evidence against her husband.

However, suppose Paul is charged with the abduction, rape and murder of several teenage girls, all over 16. All the crimes were allegedly committed in the family home, but the bodies of the victims were found in various locations some distance from the home. There is forensic evidence of the presence of some of the victims in the home, but no witnesses other than Madge, his wife. A psychologist states that Madge is under the influence of the husband, but if compelled to give evidence, she may be able to overcome that influence. Where should the balance lie in such a case?

It is worth noting that the failure of the wife or husband of the accused to give evidence shall not be made the subject of any comment by the prosecution. The judge may comment on the failure of the spouse to testify, but there is little that can be said about the wife whose loyalty to her husband causes her to decline to give evidence against him.

Former spouses, future spouses and polygamous 'spouses'

Under section 80(5) of the Police and Criminal Evidence Act 1984, former spouses shall be competent and compellable to give evidence as if that person and the accused had never been married. Only those who have had the divorce decree made absolute are compellable.[382] The position regarding future spouses was considered in *R (Crown Prosecution Service) v Registrar-General of Births, Deaths and Marriages*,[383] where the accused, charged with murder and held on remand, sought permission to marry his long-term

---

[381]Criminal Law Revision Committee, op cit n 26, [152].
[382]*R v Cruttenden* [1991] Crim LR 537.
[383][2003] 1 QB 1222.

partner. Since she was a witness for the prosecution, and would by virtue of section 80 of the 1984 Act cease to be a compellable witness at his trial, the CPS attempted to persuade the Registrar-General and the director of the prison not to allow the marriage to take place until after the trial. When both declined to do so, their decision was challenged by way of judicial review. The Court of Appeal held that there was no power to prevent, on the grounds of public policy, the marriage between a prisoner on remand and his long-term partner, despite the fact that the marriage would make her a non-compellable witness at his forthcoming trial for murder. It was accepted that the duty of the Registrar-General under section 31 of the Marriage Act 1949 was absolute. There were, however, circumstances in which that absolute duty would be subject to implied limitations on public policy grounds. Authorities were cited to show that no person should profit from his own serious crime, and that statutes should be interpreted to prevent a grave crime being committed or the course of justice perverted. However, entering into a lawful marriage, despite the consequences that followed from the provisions of section 80 of the 1984 Act, did not amount to perverting the course of justice.

The application of section 80 to a polygamous marriage was considered by the Court of Appeal in *R v Khan*.[384] Khan, who was already married under English law, underwent a Muslim marriage taking a second 'wife'. The marriage was not recognised in England, and it was thus held that his second 'wife' was competent and compellable for the prosecution on the charges against Khan. Although this case was decided before section 80 came into force, the decision would be the same under section 80 either because the woman is not married to a person charged in the proceedings and must therefore be treated as any other witness, or because section 80(5) operates to treat her as not married.

The accused

Prior to 1898, accused persons were incompetent to give evidence in their own defence. Instead, a defendant could make an unsworn statement from the dock, which could be taken into account by the trier of fact, but was not technically regarded as evidence.[385] Section 1 of the Criminal Evidence Act 1898 provided that accused persons were competent to give evidence in their own defence. However, it remained the case that they could not be compelled to do so. Thus, where the accused decides to give evidence, he or she will be treated as any other witness and be exposed to cross-examination. He or she can be questioned in relation to any matter as to the offence charged,[386] although no questions may be asked in relation to previous bad character or previous convictions, except in the circumstances provided for in the Criminal Justice Act 2003.[387]

The accused is also a competent witness for a co-accused,[388] but is not compellable.[389] However, a defendant is not competent to testify for the prosecution so long as he or she is a person charged in the proceedings, that is named in the indictment, whether alone or with others.[390] There are, nonetheless, four ways in which an accused can be removed from

---

[384](1987) 84 Cr App R 44.

[385]The right to make an unsworn statement from the dock as an alternative to testifying was abolished by section 72 of the Criminal Justice Act 1982.

[386]Section 1(2) of the Criminal Evidence Act 1898 makes it clear that the accused has no privilege against self-incrimination in respect of the offence charged.

[387]See further Ch 6.

[388]Youth Justice and Criminal Evidence Act 1999, section 53(1).

[389]Criminal Evidence Act 1898, section 1(1).

[390]Youth Justice and Criminal Evidence Act 1999, section 53(4).

the indictment, thus making him a competent and compellable witness for the prosecution. These arise where:

- D is acquitted, with the prosecution offering no evidence;
- D pleads guilty and is subsequently removed from the indictment;[391]
- The Attorney-General enters a *nolle prosequi*;[392]
- D is removed from the indictment and is tried separately.

In each of these circumstances, the defendant is then a competent and a compellable witness for the prosecution against a co-accused.

THE PRIVILEGE AGAINST SELF-INCRIMINATION

Of course, in many cases, the defendant may have no desire to testify at all in court – even in his own defence. Section 1(b) of the Criminal Evidence Act 1898 originally forbade comment by the prosecution on the failure of the defendant to give evidence.[393] This broadly reflected what is commonly termed 'the privilege against self-incrimination'. In very broad terms, the principle prohibits any form of compulsion on a suspect to provide evidence against himself, and nor should he or she be placed under any obligation to help the police with their inquiries.[394]

A further aspect of the privilege against self-incrimination is a suspect's right not to have adverse inferences drawn from his failure to answer questions, or, once accused, his failure to testify at trial (the so-called 'right to silence'). Without this protection there is an element of indirect compulsion to answer questions or give evidence, to avoid the drawing of such inferences. The protections afforded by a 'right to silence' have been severely curtailed by sections 34–37 Criminal Justice and Public Order Act 1994, so that now 'proper inferences' may be drawn from an accused's failure to respond to questioning. We will return to these provisions later in the chapter.

The 'Even Terms' rule

At common law, where the parties are on even terms, an accusation by X that is unanswered by Y can be said to provide evidence that Y accepted the truth of the allegation.[395] This constitutes the 'even terms' rule, and is grounded on the basis that it is a natural and intuitive response to deny a false allegation made by another lay person who does not occupy any position of authority.[396] Thus, at trial, an accused's conduct or demeanour in response to such allegations may be used as evidence of guilt by the

---

[391] If those who were his co-accused plead not guilty, they go to trial.

[392] A *nolle prosequi* is essentially a writ which stays the prosecution against the person named on it. Thus if the accused is the subject of such a writ, he cannot be prosecuted in respect of the offence(s) with which he is charged and is removed from the indictment. The trial will then proceed against anyone else named in the indictment.

[393] This provision was later abolished by section 168 of and sch 11 of the Criminal Justice and Public Order Act 1994.

[394] *Rice v Connolly* [1966] 2 QB 414.

[395] This principle is preserved pursuant to section 34(5) of the Criminal Justice and Public Order Act 1994.

[396] See *R v Hall* [1971] 1 WLR 298; *R v Parkes* [1976] 1 WLR 1251.

prosecution. The rule was summarised by Cave J in *R v Mitchell* [397] in the following terms:

> Undoubtedly, when persons are speaking on even terms and a charge is made, and the person charged says nothing, and expresses no indignation, and does nothing to repel the charge, that is some evidence to show that he admits the charge to be true.

The principle was applied in *Parkes v The Queen*.[398] Parkes was charged with murder by the stabbing of a young woman. The victim's mother found her bleeding from her wounds and saw the defendant nearby holding a knife. She twice accused him of stabbing her daughter. He did not reply. She then took hold of him saying she was going to hold him until the police arrived. He made to strike her with the knife, cutting her finger. The Privy Council upheld the judge's direction to the jury that they could take the defendant's reaction and his silence into account when determining whether he was or was not guilty of murder.

A more modern, and widely reported, example is to be found in the evidence given by a witness in the trial of Barry George for the murder of Jill Dando, the television presenter.[399] Lenita Bailey was a customer at a hairdresser's near the accused's flat. She knew him and recalled a conversation with him. George came into the salon and claimed police were harassing him over the death of Jill Dando. He complained that they had searched his home and his mother's house. Ms Bailey said to him, 'Did you do it?'. George remained silent and stared at the floor. She repeated the question twice more and asked him to look at her. At trial, she said, 'His lips moved as if he was thinking of an answer but none was forthcoming'. Her evidence of the discussion, or lack of it, was admitted, and George was convicted.[400]

The defendant and the mother in *Parkes*, and the witness and defendant in the Dando trial, were clearly on equal terms and it was reasonable to expect a denial of the accusation if that was the position. By contrast, a suspect arrested by the police will not usually be seen as being on equal terms with the police, although in *R v Chandler*[401] it was held that a suspect interviewed by police in the presence of his solicitor was on even terms, and therefore a failure to respond to an accusation before caution could be taken into account by the jury. That decision has now been overtaken by events, and in particular the requirement under PACE that a suspect be cautioned when he or she is suspected of involvement in a crime before the actual arrest.[402] Whatever the position might be at common law in relation to the above, it does not apply in situations where a defendant refuses to leave his prison cell to be interviewed by police and thus remains silent.[403] This is a very different situation from one where, for example, the defendant fails to offer an explanation for the fact that he was in possession of stolen goods.[404] If the accused's silence is deemed admissible, it may then be inferred from that silence that he or she has accepted the truth of what is being said.[405]

---

[397] (1892) 17 Cox CC 503, at 508.

[398] (1977) 64 Cr App R 25.

[399] *The Times*, 5 May 2001.

[400] On 15 November 2007, the Court of Appeal quashed the conviction and ordered a re-trial following fresh evidence that had come to light (see *The Times*, 16 November 2007).

[401] [1976] 1 WLR 585. However, as a general rule the accused will never be on even terms with a police officer. The Court in *Chandler* suggested *obiter* that a suspect may be on even terms with the police if a solicitor was present. This has never been followed.

[402] Code C, [10.1].

[403] *R v Gilbert* (1977) 66 Cr App R 237; *R v Johnson and R v Hind* (2005) *The Times*, 3 May.

[404] *R v Raviraj* (1986) 85 Cr App R 93.

[405] See *R v Christie* [1914] AC 545.

The judicial direction

In addition to the 'even terms' rule, the common law originally prohibited both the prosecution counsel and the judge from making any comment where the accused chose to remain silent,[406] failed to answer any specific questions,[407] or failed to reveal the nature of his defence in advance of trial.[408] In *R v Martinez-Tobon*,[409] the Court of Appeal held that judges should abide by the following principles in summing up to the jury:

- The judge should give a direction along the lines of the Judicial Studies Board specimen direction based on *R v Bathurst*.[410] That is:

    o The defendant does not have to give evidence. He is entitled to sit in the dock and require the prosecution to prove its case. You must not assume that he is guilty because he has not given evidence. The fact that he has not given evidence proves nothing one way or the other. It does not establish his guilt. On the other hand, it means that there is no evidence from the defendant to undermine, contradict or explain the evidence put before you by the prosecution.

- The essentials of that direction are that the defendant is under no obligation to testify, and the jury should not assume he is guilty because he has not given evidence.

- Provided those essentials are complied with, the judge may think it appropriate to make a stronger comment where the defence case involves alleged facts which are at variance with the prosecution evidence, or additional to it and exculpatory, and must, if true, be within the knowledge of the defendant.

- The nature and strength of such comment must be a matter for the discretion of the judge and will depend on the circumstances of the individual case. However, it must not be such as to contradict or nullify the essentials of the conventional direction.

These stipulations have, however, been qualified by changes introduced by the Criminal Justice and Public Order Act 1994 and the Criminal Procedure and Investigations Act 1996. The principal aim behind these two pieces of legislation was to prevent the use of 'ambush' defences at trial, whereby the defendant would remain silent until trial, in the hope that the prosecution would not have time to rebut the defence. Part I of the Criminal Procedure and Investigations Act 1996[411] provides for primary disclosure of prosecution material to the defence that is to be followed by disclosure by the defence of a statement containing the outline of their defence. Such a statement should outline the general nature of the defence, and must include reference to any specific defences to be relied upon. In addition, the statement should give details of any matters about which it takes issue with the prosecution, and the reasons for doing so (including any relevant points of law). Moreover, where the accused proposes to rely on an alibi defence, the statement should give the name, address and date of birth of any witness the accused believes is able to give evidence in support of the alibi, or as many of those details as possible. Once the defence have complied with these obligations, the prosecution will undertake secondary disclosure of any further material that is relevant in the light of the defence disclosed or issues raised.

---

[406] *R v Lecky* [1944] KB 80.

[407] *R v Gilbert* (1977) 66 Cr App R 237.

[408] *R v Lewis* (1973) 57 Cr App R 860.

[409] [1994] 1 WLR 388. See also *R v Jackson* [1953] 1 WLR 591; *R v Sparrow* (1973) 57 Cr App R 352; *R v Hook* [1994] TLR 375.

[410] [1968] 2 QB 99.

[411] As amended by Pt 5 of the Criminal Justice Act 2003.

Section 11 of the Act provides that, where the defence are required to disclose their defence, and the accused:

- fails to give the prosecutor a defence statement under section 5;

- gives the prosecutor a defence statement but does so only after the expiry of the specified period;

- sets out inconsistent defences in the defence statement given under section 5;

- puts forward a defence which is different from that disclosed in the defence statement;

- at his trial adduces evidence in support of an alibi without having given particulars of the alibi in the defence statement; or

- at his trial calls a witness to give evidence in support of an alibi without having provided the prosecution with the name of that witness and any information necessary to trace him;

then the court or any other party (with the leave of the court) may make such comment as appears appropriate, and the court or jury may draw such inferences as appear proper in deciding whether the accused is guilty of the offence concerned.

The right to silence

In addition to the provisions of the 1996 Act concerning disclosure, the Criminal Justice and Public Order Act 1994 effected radical changes in respect of the suspect's rights to silence. Despite widespread questions about the wisdom of abrogating such a longstanding component of the common law, the government was persuaded that some amendment to the law was necessary in order to restore the balance following the raft of safeguards for the accused contained in the Police and Criminal Evidence Act 1984.[412] In amending the law to allow inferences to be drawn from the accused's silence, the government had not only ignored advice of the Bar Council, Criminal Bar Association and Law Society, but had also rejected the majority recommendation of the Royal Commission on Criminal Justice that the status quo be retained.[413] The decision can, perhaps, be attributed to the political agenda of the day, and the prevailing crime control ethos that prevailed in criminal justice policy-making under the then Home Secretary, Michael Howard.[414] The government were also keen to draw parallels with the fact that an identical provision had been introduced in Northern Ireland some six years earlier and appeared to have been operating successfully.[415]

---

[412]For further discussion see Birch, D, 'Suffering in Silence: A Cost-Benefit Analysis of section 34 of the Criminal Justice and Public Order Act 1994' [1999] Crim LR 769.

[413]Royal Commission on Criminal Justice, *Report*, Cmnd 2263 (1993: London, HMSO), [4.13]. The Commission noted that not only are the circumstances of police interrogation disorientating and intimidating in themselves, but there can be no justification for requiring a suspect to answer questions when he or she may be unclear both about the nature of the offence which he or she is alleged to have committed and about the legal definitions of intent, dishonesty and so forth on which the indictment may turn. See also Royal Commission on Criminal Procedure, *Report*, Cmnd 8092 (1981: London, HMSO); Zander, M 'Abolition of the Right to Silence, 1972–1994' in D Morgan and G Stephenson (eds) *Suspicion and Silence: The Right to Silence in Criminal Investigations* (1994: London, Blackstone).

[414]Criminal Law Revision Committee, op cit n 368. See also Home Office, *Report of the Working Group on the Right to Silence* (1989: London, Home Office).

[415]See Criminal Evidence (Northern Ireland) Order 1988 (SI 1988/1987), arts 3-6. See further Jackson, J D 'Recent Developments in Criminal Evidence' (1989) 40 NILQ 105; 'Curtailing the Right of Silence: Lessons from Northern Ireland' [1991] Crim LR 404; Justice, *The Right of Silence Debate: The Northern Ireland Experience*

The trier of fact may now draw 'such inferences as appear proper' in four situations:

- where an accused fails to mention any facts when being questioned under caution before charge that he later relies upon in his defence at trial;[416]
- where he fails to give evidence at his trial.[417]
- where he fails to account for the presence of any object, substance or mark on his person, clothing or footwear, or otherwise in his possession or at any place in which he is at the time of arrest;[418] or
- where he fails to account for his presence at a place at or about the time of the commission of an offence.[419]

Section 34: A failure to mention facts when questioned...

Section 34 affects the defendant's right to silence prior to trial, and has been the source of considerable debate both in the appellate courts as well as in academic journals. The provision stipulates:

(1) Where, in any proceedings against a person for an offence, evidence is given that the accused –
   (a) at any time before he was charged with the offence, on being questioned under caution by a constable trying to discover whether or by whom the offence has been committed, failed to mention any fact relied on in his defence in those proceedings; or
   (b) on being charged with the offence or officially informed that he might be prosecuted for it, failed to mention any such fact, being a fact which in the circumstances existing at the time the accused could reasonably have been expected to mention when so questioned, charged or informed, as the case may be, subsection (2) below applies.

(2) Where this subsection applies –
   (d) the court or jury, in determining whether the accused is guilty of the offence charged, may draw such inferences from the failure as appear proper.

(2A) Where the accused was at an authorised place of detention at the time of the failure, subsections (1) and (2) above do not apply if he had not been allowed an opportunity to consult a solicitor prior to being questioned, charged or informed as mentioned in subsection (1) above.

(3) Subject to any directions by the court, evidence tending to establish the failure may be given before or after evidence tending to establish the fact which the accused is alleged to have failed to mention.

The provision thus places an onus on the suspect to provide explanations in response to police questioning. It should be noted, however, that the nature of this obligation

---

(1994: London, Justice). Later research would, however, suggest that the legislation had little impact upon conviction rates in the province – see See Jackson, J, Quinn, K and Wolfe, M, *Legislating Against Silence: The Northern Ireland Experience* (1995); Jackson, J (1993) 'Inferences from Silence: From Common Law to Common Sense' 44 NILQ 103.

[416]Criminal Justice and Public Order Act 1994, section 34.

[417]Criminal Justice and Public Order Act 1994, section 35.

[418]Criminal Justice and Public Order Act 1994, section 36.

[419]Criminal Justice and Public Order Act 1994, section 37. Section 38 of the Act allows for interpretation and savings for sections 34, 35, 36 and 37.

is not absolute. A failure to respond to police questioning cannot of itself prove the defendant's guilt.[420] The section merely allows the trier of fact to consider what, if any, inferences should be drawn; and no inferences should be drawn if the fact in question has been shown to be true.[421] In that respect, there is no automatic sanction if the accused opts to remain silent.

In the years after the provision took effect, the appellate courts were quick to formulate a range of additional protections for the suspect. In *R v Argent*,[422] the accused was convicted of manslaughter, and appealed, contending that the trial judge had been wrong to direct the jury that they were free to draw 'such inferences as appear proper' from his failure to answer questions in a police interview. Dismissing the appeal, the Court of Appeal highlighted that the fact that the section could only apply in very specific circumstances, was ultimately dependent on a range of safeguards:

- Proceedings must be underway against a person for an offence;
- The failure to mention facts must occur before the defendant is charged or on being charged;
- The failure must occur during questioning under caution;[423]
- The questioning must be directed to trying to discover whether or by whom the alleged offence has been committed;
- The defence must actively seek to rely on the omitted facts in the proceedings;
- The fact which the accused fails to mention must be one which, in the circumstances existing at the time, he or she could reasonably be expected to mention when questioned.

A number of these issues merit further consideration.

The need for a caution

For an inference to be drawn there must have been questioning under caution.[424] The standard police caution, which had to be amended in response to the legislation, reads as follows:

> You do not have to say anything. But it may harm your defence if you do not mention when questioned something which you later rely on in court. Anything you do say may be given in evidence.[425]

Although we may be accustomed to hearing these words frequently in police television dramas, it is a matter of some concern that there is evidence to suggest that not all suspects will understand its full implications. A study by Buckle *et al* suggested that

---

[420] A conviction should not be 'wholly or mainly' based on the inference from the defendant's silence: Criminal Justice and Public Order Act 1994, section 38(3). See further *R v Dolbur* [2000] Crim LR 178; *Practice Direction* [1995] 2 Cr App R 192; Specimen Direction at http://www.jsboard.co.uk/criminal_law/cbb/mf_05.htm.

[421] *R v Webber* [2004] 1 All ER 770.

[422] [1997] 2 Cr App R 27.

[423] See *R v Johnson* [2005] EWCA Crim 971. The questioning can be conducted by constables or persons who are either charged with the duty to investigate offences or charge offenders. This, for example, will include store detectives (depending on their contract of employment), customs officers, and RSPCA officials.

[424] As to what constitutes 'questioning', see also (*ibid*). Here, the Court of Appeal concluded no question was in fact put to the accused and therefore his failure to respond did not come within the ambit of the phrase 'on being questioned'.

[425] PACE, Code C, [10.4].

both police officers and legal advisors doubted the extent to which suspects understood the caution, even where it was explained in lay terms.[426] The researchers also suggested that the new caution is harder to understand than the old one, which simply read:

> 'You do not have to say anything unless you wish to do so, but what you say may be given in evidence'

Failure to mention facts

In order to prevent adverse inferences being drawn, a suspect's solicitor will sometimes prepare a written statement, which is simply read out to the police or handed to an officer irrespective of whether or not the suspect answers police questions. There is a risk, of course, with such a strategy, in that the defence must take care to ensure that the statement sets out in full the facts of the defence case. If a material fact is omitted and subsequently relied on in court, inferences may be drawn.[427] This will occur regardless of whether the suspect has refused to answer police questions.[428] Thus in *R v Knight*,[429] K, who had been arrested on suspicion of indecent assault, presented a written statement to the police, and subsequently declined (on the advice of his solicitor) to answer any questions about his version of events. The trial judge directed the jury that they were still at liberty to draw inferences from K's failure to respond to questioning. However, allowing the appeal, the Court of Appeal noted that since K's statement had contained all the facts that K later relied on in court, no adverse inferences could be drawn. The objective of section 34(1)(a) was to prevent a suspect from relying on facts in court that should properly have been disclosed to the police during questioning. There was no requirement that a suspect submit to police cross-examination, and, indeed, such a requirement could constitute an even greater intrusion into a suspect's general right of silence than a requirement on the suspect to disclose his factual defence. Had Parliament intended that section 34 should include such a requirement, the legislation would have expressly stated so. Despite the resolution of the case in favour of the appellant, the Court of Appeal was still keen to sound a note of caution in respect of pre-prepared statements:

> The making of a pre-prepared statement is not in itself an inevitable antidote to later adverse inferences. The pre-prepared statement may be incomplete in comparison with the defendant's later account at trial, or it may be, to whatever degree, inconsistent with that account...We wish to make it crystal clear that of itself the making of a pre-prepared statement gives no automatic immunity against adverse inferences under section 34.[430]

It is thus clear that, in advising this course of action, the legal representative must be very cautious about taking this approach as the practical line of attack taken by the Court of Appeal in *Knight* could backfire on the defendant if not used correctly.

---

[426] Buckle, T, Street, R and Brown D *The Right of Silence: The Impact of the Criminal Justice and Public Order Act 1994*, Home Office Research Study No 199 (2000: London, Home Office).

[427] See *R v Turner* [2004] 1 Cr App R 24, [25]. Here the Court of Appeal observed the 'dangerous course for an innocent person who subsequently discovers at trial that something significant was omitted' from the pre-prepared statement.

[428] See also Choo, A, 'Prepared Statements, Legal Advice and the Right to Silence: R v Knight' (2004) 8 E & P 62.

[429] [2004] 1 WLR 340.

[430] At [13]. See also *R v Ali (Sarfraz)* [2001] EWCA Crim 863; *T v DPP* [2007] EWHC 1793.

The objective of the questioning

The questioning must be directed to trying to discover whether or by whom the alleged offence had been committed. If the questioning officer already has sufficient evidence to charge the suspect, any subsequent questions will not be directed to discovering whether or by whom the offence has been committed, and the section will not apply in such circumstances.[431] However, inferences may still be drawn if, in such circumstances, the officer maintains an open mind and is allowing the suspect an opportunity to relate his or her version of events.[432] Code C of PACE has recently been amended to this effect.[433]

Reliance in court

Inferences can only be drawn by the factfinder if the defence later relies on a fact at trial. For example, an accused may submit an alibi defence, or suggest that he acted in self-defence, having failed to mention any such fact in response to direct questioning by the police. However, a fact must be distinguished from a theory, or speculation, as to what might have happened, as illustrated by the case of *Nickolson*.[434] Here the defendant was asked in cross-examination if he could explain the existence of semen on the complainant's nightdress. He speculated that perhaps the complainant had picked up the semen from his bathroom. The court held that the accused was not relying on this as a fact, but merely offering a possible explanation, and the failure to mention this explanation at earlier interview was not caught by section 34. Likewise, a failure to mention a trivial fact or small detail will fall outside the scope of the provision.[435]

The fact also need not be established by the defendant's testimony for it to be relied upon in defence. It can be established by other defence evidence, or in cross-examination of a prosecution witness.[436] In *Webber*, the House of Lords went further, holding that a positive suggestion put to a witness by counsel could amount to a fact relied on in the accused's defence for the purpose of section 34, even if the suggestion was not adopted by the witness:

> 'Fact' should be given a broad and not a narrow or pedantic meaning. The word covers any alleged fact which is in issue and is put forward as part of the defence case: if the defendant advances at trial any pure fact or exculpatory explanation or account which, if it were true, he could reasonably have been expected to advance earlier, section 34 is potentially applicable. When directing the jury in this case the trial judge made repeated reference to 'fact or matter', which is consistent with the reference to 'something' in the caution and in our view expresses the meaning of the subsection There would be a similar reliance, the House held, where counsel adopts on behalf of his client in closing submissions evidence by a co-defendant.[437]

---

[431]See *R v Pointer* [1997] Crim LR 676; *R v Gayle* [1999] Crim LR 502.

[432]See *R v McGuinness* [1999] Crim LR 318; *R v Ioannou* [1999] Crim LR 586; *R v Odeyemi* [1999] Crim LR 828.

[433]See Code C, [11.6]. See Further Cape, E 'Detention Without Charge: What Does "Sufficient Evidence to Charge" Mean?' [1999] Crim LR 874, 'The Revised PACE Codes of Practice: A Further Step Towards Inquisitorialism' [2003] Crim LR 355.

[434]*R v Nickolson* [1999] Crim LR 61. cf. *Esimu* [2007] EWCA Crim 1380. In *Nickolson* the Court of Appeal allowed the appeal as when the defendant was interviewed by police, neither the police nor the defendant were aware of the semen stain, and he could not reasonably be expected to give an explanation for it. See also *R v B (MT)* [2000] Crim LR 181.

[435]*R v Brizzalari* [2004] EWCA Crim 310. Ultimately this will be a question for the trial judge to determine.

[436]See *R v Bowers* [1998] Crim LR 817.

[437]At [37]. *Webber* was followed in *Esimu*, in which inferences were properly drawn from a failure to explain to police as to how his fingerprints came to be found on false number plates attached to a stolen car, but advanced an explanation at his trial that he might have removed them whilst working as a valet business.

However, the defendant will be deemed to have relied upon a fact if he does no more than admit a fact asserted by the prosecution (i.e. a bare admission), although it seems that denial of the prosecution's alleged fact may be construed as automatic reliance upon any contradictory fact.[438] Thus, it seems that admissions and denials appear to be treated differently by the courts. Furthermore, where the defendant does not testify and does not advance other evidence (i.e. merely tests the prosecution case), then section 34 cannot apply since no evidence will be relied upon in their defence.[439]

Reasonably be expected to mention… in the circumstances existing at the time

Section 34 was not intended to capture all failures by the accused to mention relevant facts; only those which he or she could have been reasonably expected to mention in the circumstances existing at the time. On many occasions, the defence will wish to explain the defendant's silence to the jury and explain why he or she did not respond to the relevant question(s). Indeed, in *Turner*, the Court of Appeal stated that it was incumbent upon the prosecution to charge defendants as to why they chose to remain silent, and give them an opportunity to provide an explanation.

In *Argent*, the Court of Appeal made it clear that the question as to what could be considered reasonable at the time was solely a matter for the jury, and each case was to be decided on its own individual facts. Ultimately, what might be considered reasonable for X in a particular circumstance, might not be considerable reasonable for Y in a similar situation. The question of reasonableness is thus subjective, and to this end:

> matters such as time of day, the defendant's age, experience, mental capacity, state of health, sobriety, tiredness, knowledge, personality and legal advice are all part of the relevant circumstances; but these are only examples of what may be relevant.[440]

The Judicial Studies Board Specimen Direction breaks the issue of reasonableness down into three distinct issues:[441]

- when interviewed could the defendant reasonably have been expected to mention the facts on which he now relies;
- that the only sensible explanation for his failure to reasonably mention the fact is that he had no answer at the time or none that would stand up to scrutiny;
- that apart from his failure to mention those facts, the prosecution's case against him is so strong that it clearly calls for an answer by him.[442]

In addition if the trial judge concludes that the requirements of section 34 are not fulfilled and he cannot leave it to the jury to draw inferences, then the judge must positively direct the jury that they must not hold the accused's failure to answer questions against him.[443]

---

[438] *R v Betts and Hall* [2001] 2 Cr App R 257.
[439] *R v Moshaid* [1998] Crim LR 420.
[440] At [33].
[441] The Judical Studies Board Specimen Direction: *Practice Direction* [1995] 2 Cr App R 192; http://www.jsboard.co.uk/criminal_law/cbb/mf_05.htm.
[442] This has been clarified by the Court of Appeal. See *R v Gill* [2001] 1 Cr App R 11; *R v Bromfield* [2002] EWCA Crim 195; *R v Chenia* [2002] EWCA 2345; *R v Paton* [2007] EWCA Crim 1572.
[443] This is called a 'McGarry Direction': *R v McGarry* [1999] 1 Cr App R 377.

Section 34 and legal advice

One of the most contentious aspects of the 1994 legislation was the fact that inferences could be drawn from the suspect's silence even where he or she had not received legal advice. In *Murray v United Kingdom*,[444] the applicant alleged that the failure to allow him access to a lawyer, coupled with the drawing of inferences from his silence, constituted a violation of Article 6 of the European Convention on Human Rights.[445] Significantly, the Court found the UK government to be in breach of Article 6 in denying the accused access to a solicitor, but found no violation in permitting inferences to be drawn from the failure of the accused to explain his presence at the scene of the crime, or his failure to give evidence at his trial. Whilst the Court recognised that the right to remain silent under police questioning and the privilege against self-incrimination lie at the heart of the notion of a fair trial, the right to silence was not absolute. Providing certain safeguards were in place, inferences could be drawn where a defendant had failed to provide an explanation in circumstances where the facts called for such an explanation. However, the Court did find a breach of Article 6(1) in relation to the separate issue of the 48 hour delay in accessing legal advice,[446] and held that adverse inferences should never be drawn where a suspect did not have access to legal advice. In response to the decision in Murray, the government introduced section 58 of the Youth Justice and Criminal Evidence Act 1999, which provides that no inferences can now be drawn if the accused was in police detention and did not have prior access to a solicitor.

A related problem occurs where the suspect is given access to a solicitor, who subsequently advises him or her to remain silent. In *R v Condron and Condron*,[447] both suspects were heroin users and their solicitor considered that they were unfit to be interviewed. However, the police doctor determined that they were fit to answer questions, and the suspects subsequently remained silent on the advice of their solicitor. At trial, the defendants rebutted the prosecution evidence with various explanations, all of which could have been given in response to police questions. The trial judge rejected a submission that, since their solicitor had given bona fide advice to the defendants to remain silent, no adverse inference could be drawn. The judge directed the jury that it was a matter for them to decide whether any adverse inferences could be drawn against the defendants. The jury convicted, and the Court of Appeal affirmed the convictions stating that the application of section 34 could not ultimately depend upon the nature of the legal advice given to a client. Delivering the judgment of the court, Stuart-Smith LJ stated:

> It is not so much the advice given by the solicitor, as the reason why the defendant chose not to answer questions that is important. That is a question of fact which may be very much in issue.[448]

---

[444] (1996) 22 EHRR 29.

[445] In Murray's case, inferences were drawn by under the Criminal Evidence (Northern Ireland) Order 1989, arts 3–6 of which are broadly equivalent to sections 34–38 Criminal Justice and Public Order Act 1994.

[446] This was permissible under section 15 of the Northern Ireland (Emergency Provisions) Act 1987.

[447] [1997] 1 WLR 827.

[448] At 833. A similar view was taken by Lord Bingham in *Argent*: 'The jury is not concerned with the correctness of the solicitor's advice, nor with whether it complies with the Law Society Guidelines, but with the reasonableness of the defendant's conduct in all the circumstances which the jury have found to exist. A highly relevant circumstance is the advice given to a defendant. The advice given to the defendant is a matter for the jury to consider' (at [35] and [36]).

Following this decision, the appellants took their case to the European Court of Human Rights.[449] The Strasbourg Court held that the applicants had not received a fair trial under Article 6(1). It was held that the judge at first instance had not taken into account the fact that the accused was advised by his lawyer to maintain his silence, and that there may have been good reason why such advice may be given. Thus the direction of the trial judge had failed to reflect the balance which the Court, in its *Murray* judgment, sought to strike between the right to silence and the circumstances in which an adverse inference may be drawn from silence. The Court here reiterated the fact that, provided appropriate safeguards were in place, an accused's silence could be taken into account in assessing the persuasiveness of the evidence adduced by the prosecution against him. While the trial judge drew the jury's attention to this explanation, he had done so in terms which left the jury at liberty to draw an adverse inference notwithstanding that it may have been satisfied as to the plausibility of the explanation. In the Court's opinion, as a matter of fairness, the jury should have been directed that it could only draw an adverse inference if satisfied that the applicant's silence at the police interview could *only* sensibly be attributed to their having no answer or none that would stand up to cross-examination.

Ultimately, therefore, the jury should consider the context of any legal advice and take this into account in assessing the overall reasonableness of the suspect's decision to remain silent. For example, it might be suggested that the solicitor advised the client not to answer questions since he or she had been given little or no details of the nature of the case against the defendant. Arguably, if the solicitor is not in a position to usefully advise his client, the best course of action is to advise silence until the full nature of the material in the hands of the police is made known. Furthermore, if this material is so highly complex so as to require specialist advice or forensic analysis, or relates to matters so long ago, then no immediate response may be feasible.[450] In *R v Betts and Hall*,[451] Kay LJ stated that the key issue was whether the decision to remain silent was motivated by advice that was important, as opposed to the actual content of that advice:

> It is not the quality of the decision but the genuineness of the decision that matters. If it is a plausible explanation that the reason for not mentioning facts is that the particular appellant acted on the advice of his solicitor and not because he had no, or no satisfactory, answer to give then no inference can be drawn.

> That conclusion does not give a licence to a guilty person to shield behind the advice of his solicitor. The adequacy of the explanation advanced may well be relevant as to whether or not the advice was truly the reason for not mentioning the facts. A person, who is anxious not to answer questions because he has no or no adequate explanation to offer, gains no protection from his lawyer's advice because that advice is no more than a convenient way of disguising his true motivation for not mentioning facts.[452]

At first sight, it appears that there was scope for this dictum in *Betts and Hall* to be interpreted as meaning that once it has been shown that the advice has genuinely been relied on, adverse

---

[449]*Condron v United Kingdom* (2001) 31 EHRR 1. See also *Averill v United Kingdom* (2001) 31 EHRR 839 and *Beckles v. United Kingdom* (2003) 36 EHRR 162.
[450]See further comments of Rose LJ in *R v Roble* [1997] Crim LR 449.
[451][2001] 2 Cr App R 257.
[452]At [53]–[54].

comment is thereby disallowed. However, this is not quite correct. Further clarification on this point was provided by the Court of Appeal in *R v Howell*:[453]

> The premise of such a position is that in such circumstances if it is in principle not reasonable to expect the suspect to mention the facts in question. We do not believe that is so. What is reasonable depends on all the circumstances ... The kind of circumstance which may most likely justify silence will be such matters as the suspect's condition (ill-health, in particular mental disability; confusion; intoxication; shock, and so forth – of course we are not laying down an authoritative list), or his inability genuinely to recollect events without reference to documents which are not to hand, or communication with other persons who may be able to assist his recollection. There must always be soundly based objective reasons for silence, sufficiently cogent and telling to weigh in the balance against the clear public interest in an account being given by the suspect to the police. Solicitors bearing the important responsibility of giving advice to suspects at police stations must always have that in mind.[454]

In *R v Hoare and Pierce*,[455] the Court of Appeal held that there was no inconsistency between *Betts and Hall* on the one hand, and the cases of *Howell* and *Knight* on the other. The Court commented:

> The section 34 inference is concerned with flushing out innocence at an early stage or supporting other evidence of guilt at a later stage, not simply with whether a guilty defendant is entitled, or genuinely or reasonably believes that he is entitled, to rely on legal rights of which his solicitor has advised him. Legal entitlement is one thing. An accused's reason for exercising it is another. His belief in his entitlement may be genuine, but it does not follow that his reason for exercising it is.[456]

A further attempt to clarify the position was made in *R v Beckles*:[457]

> In our judgment, in a case where a solicitor's advice is relied upon by the defendant, the ultimate question for the jury remains under section 34 whether the facts relied on at the trial were facts which the defendant could reasonably have been expected to mention at interview. If they were not, that is the end of the matter. If the jury consider that the defendant genuinely relied on the advice, that is not necessarily the end of the matter. It may still not have been reasonable for him to rely on the advice, or the advice may not have been the true explanation for his silence.[458]

In *Betts and Hall*, Lord Justice Kay was particularly concerned with 'whether or not the advice was truly the reason for not mentioning the facts'.[459] In the same paragraph, he also notes that:

> A person, who is anxious not to answer questions because he has no or no adequate explanation to offer, gains no protection from his lawyer's advice because that advice is no more than a convenient way of disguising his true motivation for not mentioning facts.

If, in the last situation, it is possible to say that the defendant genuinely acted upon the advice, the fact that he did so because it suited his purpose may then mean he was not acting

---

[453] [2003] Crim LR 404. See further Choo, A, and Jennings, A 'Silence on Legal Advice Revisited: R v Howell' (2003) 7 E & P 185; Cape E 'Police Station Advice: Defence Strategies after Condron' (1997) 17 (Oct) *Legal Action* 19.

[454] At [23].

[455] [2005] 1 WLR 1804.

[456] At [54].

[457] [2005] 1 WLR 2829.

[458] 'At [46]'.

[459] At [54].

reasonably in failure to mention the relevant facts. Ultimately, however, any question of reasonableness remains to be determined by the jury. If they conclude the accused was acting unreasonably, they are free to draw an adverse inference from his silence.

As Dennis suggests, one problem with the attempts to clarify this line of case law has been that the courts do not appear to recognise the inconsistency between asking the jury to decide as a question of fact why the defendant had remained silent, and then assessing the quality of that decision.[460] Logically, it would appear to follow that if a defendant kept silent on legal advice, and not because he had no story to give or none that would stand up to scrutiny, then it does not matter whether the advice was well-grounded or not. From a due process perspective, where defendants genuinely rely on the advice of their legal representatives, they should not be penalised for doing so. If this were the case, what would be given by way of concession with one hand would effectively be taken away by the other.

Police disclosure and section 34

There is no requirement for the police to disclose any information to the suspect or his/her legal advise at the police station.[461] However, in practice, most officers are prepared to give solicitors some information about the offence. If this were not the case, police interviews would grind to a halt routinely so that the lawyer can take instructions from his client when further information is disclosed.[462] Also, it might be suggested that a small minority of officers may be tempted to lie about information that they have or have not disclosed. Defence solicitors are thus taught to routinely assess the integrity of the police case, in case the police infer that the evidence is stronger than it later turns out to be.[463] If the police do relay false information to the legal advisor, then any evidence obtained is likely to be excluded.[464] Lack of disclosure, however, may become an issue at trial and provide circumstances from which a jury might conclude that a defendant's silence during questioning by the police was reasonable.[465]

Section 35 – The effect of not giving evidence

It will be recalled from the discussion above that, while accused persons have been competent to testify in their own defence since the end of the nineteenth century, they cannot be compelled to give evidence. One of the reasons why the provisions of the 1994 Act proved so contentious was the fact that section 35 of the legislation effectively means

---

[460]Dennis, I 'Silence in the Police Station the Marginalisation of Section 34' [2002] Crim LR 25, at p 34.

[461]*Imran and Hussain* [1997] Crim LR 754. See also *R v Thirwell* [2002] EWCA Crim 2703, where there was no duty to disclose provisional medical evidence of how the victim had died. There was limited disclosure in *DPP v Ara* [2001] 4 All ER 559, but only to the extent of imposing a duty on the police to disclose the contents of a previous interview so the lawyer could advise his client on whether to accept a caution. PACE does however exempt from this the custody record. Legal representatives have a right to see the custody record (Code of Practice C, [2.4]) which they should read and make careful notes from. They are entitled to a copy. The exemption also applies to the initial description of a witness if identification is an issue (Code of Practice C, [3.1a].

[462]The PEACE method of interviewing used by the police encourages information giving but not full disclosure.

[463]See generally, Cape, E and Luqmani, J *Defending Suspects at Police Stations*, 5th ed (2007: London, LAG).

[464]*R v Mason* [1987] 3 All ER.

[465]*R v Roble* [1997] Crim LR 449.

that adverse consequences may well result from a defendant's failure to testify. Section 35(2) provides that the court or jury 'may draw such inferences as appear proper from the failure of the accused to give evidence or his refusal, without good cause, to answer any question'.

In spite of the outcry among the legal profession and various civil liberties pressure groups that arose in the immediate aftermath of the legislation, it is arguable that the only significant change to the pre-existing common law is that the prosecution were now able to comment on the failure of the accused to give evidence. It is questionable whether section 35 of the Criminal Justice and Public Order Act 1994 has any real effect on the common law as set out in *Martinez-Tobon*. The government clearly *intended* to change the law, but whether they actually succeeded in doing remains doubtful.

Two points ought to be emphasised. First, the silence of the accused is not of itself evidence, and, as such, a refusal to answer questions adds nothing to the prosecution case. If the defendant is to be convicted, the conviction must be based on all the evidence presented to the jury. Inferences are drawn from the evidence and the silence of the accused serves only to leave the prosecution evidence unchanged. If it remains essentially the same the jury may then infer that it is true and, if they are satisfied beyond reasonable doubt, they may convict. Arguably, it is therefore incorrect to allude to 'inferences from silence'; it may be more accurate (albeit more verbose) to speak of 'inferences from the prosecution evidence and lack of rebutting evidence from the accused'. This accords with the one of the core principles laid down in *Martinez-Tobon*, namely that the silence of the accused adds nothing to the prosecution case, nor does it take anything away.

Secondly, section 38(3) makes it clear that, *inter alia*, no conviction can be made solely on the inferences drawn under section 35. The inferences, if any, will be drawn from the evidence. It may be that, in certain cases, the only *proper* inference is that the accused is guilty, but that conclusion stems from the fact that the prosecution have presented a strong case that persuades the jury that the accused is guilty beyond any reasonable doubt.[466] In *Murray v DPP*,[467] the trial judge had told the jury that it was remarkable that the accused, in the light of the cumulative strength of circumstantial and forensic evidence against him, had not given evidence, and that it was only common sense to infer 'that he was not prepared to assert his innocence on oath because that was not the case'. The House of Lords appeared to reject the suggestion that the silence provisions were merely declaratory of the common law, and upheld the conviction for murder. It stated that, in appropriate circumstances, the inference that the person was guilty of the offence with which he was charged is permissible. Put in such stark terms, the decision can be seen as suggesting that the silence of the accused can be used as direct evidence of guilt. However, silence is never direct evidence of anything; rather, it is negative evidence in the sense suggested by the Court of Appeal in *Martinez-Tobon*. If, therefore, the prosecution have produced an overwhelming case against the accused who does not give evidence, it may well be common sense to infer that he is guilty as charged, but the inference is drawn from the fact that the prosecution case is unchanged and uncontradicted, not from the fact that D has refused to answer questions. The jury then convict on the prosecution evidence, not on the silence of the accused.

---

[466]See *R v Hawkins* [1997] 1 Cr App R 234; *R v Petkar and Farquar* [2003] EWCA Crim 2668; *R v Adetoro* [2006] EWCA Crim 1716; *Steele, Whomes and Corry* [2006] EWCA Crim 194; *R v Boyle and Ford* EWCA Crim 2101

[467][1994] 1 WLR 1 (a decision based on the Northern Ireland legislation). See also *R v Ackinlose* [1996] Crim LR 747; *R v Friend* [1997] Crim LR 817 and *R v Kavanagh* [2005] EWHC 820.

In summary, prosecuting counsel is now permitted to comment on the failure of the accused to give evidence, and will doubtless emphasise that the prosecution case is unchallenged and uncontradicted. The trial judge may direct the jury that they may draw proper inferences and indicate what those proper inferences are in the particular case, drawing attention to the fact that the prosecution case has not been changed in any way. To this end, the judge may also point out that if the accused had been able to contradict, undermine or explain the prosecution evidence, they may conclude that the reason why he has not chosen to do so is that he is unable to do so.

Safeguards under section 35

No inferences may be drawn under section 35 'if it appears to the court that the physical or mental condition of the accused makes it undesirable for him to give evidence'.[468] It is, however, incumbent on the defence to adduce evidence of such a condition: the court is not free to make inquiries of its own motion.[469] The scope of the provision was considered by the Court of Appeal in *R v Friend*.[470] The accused, a 15-year-old boy, was on trial for murder and did not wish to give evidence. The trial judge rejected a defence submission that no inferences should be drawn on the grounds that he had a mental age of nine. In the judge's view, the fact that D had been able to give a clear account of events in his statements to the police suggested that he was capable of testifying in court. The accused was subsequently convicted, and argued that since the legislation had (at that point) provided for no inferences to be drawn in cases involving a person under the age of 14,[471] the Court of Appeal had 'applied the wrong test'.

Dismissing the appeal, the Court stated that it was inappropriate to speak of a 'test' to be applied in this type of situation. Instead, it was for the judge to determine whether or not it was undesirable for a defendant to give evidence. Even though the defendant had a mental age of nine, it did not follow that he had, or should have had, the same immunity from adverse inference as a person under the age of 14. Instead, it was open to the defence to introduce medical evidence concerning the mental age of the defendant, which could then be taken into account by the jury in determining 'such inferences as appear proper'.

The significance of this particular phrase was considered by the Court of Appeal in *R v Cowan, Gayle and Ricciardi*,[472] where it was argued by defence counsel that section 35 was so at variance with established common law principles that its operation should be reduced and marginalised as far as possible. Therefore, it was contended that defence counsel ought to be allowed to present reasons or excuses for not drawing inferences from the failure of the accused to testify without the need for evidence. It was proposed, for example, that one reason for not drawing inferences might be the fact that the accused wished to attack the character of a prosecution witness, and then avoid the risk of being cross-examined on his own record by declining to testify.[473] The Court rejected this argument, pointing out that this would lead to the bizarre result that a defendant with previous convictions would be in a more privileged position than one with a clean record. The Court accepted that, apart

---

[468] Criminal Justice and Public Order Act 1994, section 35(1)(b).
[469] *R v A* [1997] Crim LR 883.
[470] [1997] 1 WLR 1433.
[471] Criminal Justice and Public Order Act, section 35(1). These words were subsequently removed from the legislation by Crime and Disorder Act 1998, sch 10.
[472] [1996] QB 373.
[473] See Ch 6, pp 194–96.

from the mandatory provisions of section 35, it would be open to a court to decline to draw an adverse inference from silence at trial and for a judge to direct or advise a jury against drawing such inference if the circumstances of the case justified such a course. However, in order for this scenario to arise, there would need to be some evidential basis for doing so, or some exceptional factors in the case.[474]

The Court of Appeal then proceeded to stress that the inferences permitted by section 35 were only such 'as appear proper'. The inclusion of that phrase within the legislation was, in the Court's view, intended to confer a broad discretion to a trial judge to decide in all the circumstances whether any proper inferences were capable of being drawn by the jury. If no such inferences could be drawn, the jury should be instructed not to draw any. Otherwise, it was for the jury to decide what, if any, inferences might be drawn. The Court then proposed a number of elements that judicial directions to the jury should contain by way of safeguards to the accused:

- the jury may choose to draw inferences or may choose not to draw inferences as they see fit;
- the burden of proof still lies with the prosecution;
- the defendant is still entitled to remain silent if he so chooses;
- the defendant's guilt cannot be inferred on the basis of silence alone;
- the prosecution must first establish that the accused has a case to answer.

Taking this guidance into account, the Specimen Direction provided by the Judicial Studies Board reads as follows:

> The defendant has not given evidence. That is his right. He is entitled to remain silent and to require the prosecution to make you sure of his guilt. You must not assume he is guilty because he has not given evidence. But two matters arise from his silence.
>
> In the first place, you try this case according to the evidence, and you will appreciate that the defendant has not given evidence at this trial to undermine, contradict or explain the evidence put before you by the prosecution.
>
> In the second place, his silence at this trial may count against him. This is because you may draw the conclusion that he has not given evidence because he has no answer to the prosecution's case, or none that would bear examination. If you do draw that conclusion, you must not convict him wholly or mainly on the strength of it, but you may treat it as some additional support for the prosecution's case.
>
> However, you may draw such a conclusion against him only if you think it is a fair and proper conclusion, and you are satisfied about two things: first, that the prosecution's case is so strong that it clearly calls for an answer by him; and second, that the only sensible explanation for his silence is that he has no answer, or none that would bear examination.[475]

It is, of course, impossible to anticipate all the circumstances in which a judge might think it right to direct or advise a jury against drawing adverse inferences, and it may not even be

---

[474]For example, in *R v McManus* [2001] EWCA Crim 2455, the Court of Appeal conceded that section 35 did not come into play where there was no factual dispute between the parties. The issue in that case was whether particular premises were a 'disorderly house', and the facts were largely agreed upon between the prosecution and defence.

[475]*Practice Direction* [1995] 2 Cr App R 192. In *R v Becouarn* [2005] 1 WLR 2589, Lord Carswell regarded the specimen direction as 'sufficiently fair to defendants... [and that] the direction had been used for some years and appears to have stood the test of time' (at [25]).

wise to give examples, as each case must turn on its own facts.[476] In *Cowan*, it was underlined that the Court of Appeal would not lightly interfere with a judge's exercise of discretion to direct or advise the jury as to the drawing of inferences from silence, nor would it offer any guidance as to the nature, extent and degree of such inferences. On the one hand, it can be contended that this position merely serves to consolidate the common law (and, perhaps, common sense?) approach that juries had been applying for many years before the 1994 legislation was conceived. Fundamentally, it does not affect the burden of proof, nor does it detract from the accused's right to remain silent and to refuse to give evidence. On the other, it may be argued that it is undesirable to leave such a broad measure of discretion in the hands of judges. Perhaps, as far as the drawing of inferences from silence is concerned, the interests of justice are best served through a consistent and certain approach, rather than through the allure of a flexible discretion.

Section 36 and section 37

The final two circumstances which allow inferences to be drawn from silence are outlined in sections 36 and 37 of the 1994 Act. Section 36 permits inferences to be drawn at trial if the accused fails to account for the presence of objects, substances or marks on his person providing the following conditions are satisfied:

- the suspect is under arrest;
- the object, mark or substance is found on his person; clothing; footwear; or is 'otherwise in his possession';
- that the arresting officer or constable investigating the case reasonably believes that the presence of the object, substance or mark may be attributable to the participation of the person arrested in the commission of a specified offence;
- the constable informs the person arrested that he so believes, and requests him to account for the presence of the object, substance or mark using 'ordinary language';[477]
- the suspect is allowed an opportunity to consult a solicitor prior to the request for an explanation being made.

This is clearly narrower than section 34 or 35, focusing solely on the failure to account for objects, substances or marks at the point of arrest. It can also be noted that inferences may be drawn irrespective of whether the accused proposes to rely on an explanation at trial on a fact which was not mentioned at the time of arrest. Of greater significance still is the fact that no requirement of reasonableness applies. While the defence may well put forward an explanation at trial as to why the accused failed to account for the object, substance or mark, the trier of fact is under no obligation to find that the accused could reasonably have been expected to account for the object, substance or mark prior to drawing any inferences.

Neither is there any requirement that the defendant be told the specific offence of which he has been suspected of having committed. In *R v Compton*,[478] two brothers were convicted of conspiracy to supply both cannabis and heroin. Police had recovered substantial amounts of used bank notes, heavily contaminated with heroin, at each of the brothers' houses.

---

[476] *R v McLernon* (1990) 10 NIJB 91, 102.
[477] For this purpose, the special caution contained in Code of Practice C, [10.11] should be used.
[478] [2002] EWCA Crime 2825.

When asked to account for this at interview, both suspects remained silent. The judge accordingly directed the jury that they could draw 'such inferences as appeared to be proper', and the defendants were convicted. On appeal, it was alleged that section 36 should not apply since the officer had told one of the brothers, when delivering the caution, that he was being investigated for 'drug trafficking'. When charges were brought, they were unrelated to trafficking, and were confined to conspiracy to supply. The Court of Appeal rejected the appellant's contention that this was an inadequately specific description of the offence of conspiracy as required by section 36(1)(b). In the view of the Court, it was sufficient that the suspect had been made aware of the general context of the investigation.

Section 37 of the 1994 Act is formulated in very similar terms to section 36, but is concerned with inferences drawn where the accused fails to account for his presence at the scene of the crime. The following conditions must be satisfied:

- the suspect is under arrest;
- the suspect was found at a place at or about the time the offence is alleged to have been committed;
- the arresting officer or constable investigating the case reasonably believes that his presence at the scene at the time of arrest may be attributable to the participation of the person arrested in the commission of a specified offence;
- the constable informs the person arrested that he so believes, and requests him to account for the presence of the object, substance or mark using 'ordinary language';[479]
- the suspect is allowed an opportunity to consult a solicitor prior to the request for an explanation being made.

The case of *R v Martin*[480] provides a useful example of the equivalent Northern Ireland provision in operation. Here, a leading member of Sinn Féin had been arrested next door to a property where a police informer was allegedly being interrogated by the IRA. When asked to account for his presence, the accused remained silent. At trial, the accused admitted that he had been in the house where the alleged informer was being held, but claimed he had run off to the house next door when he heard the police coming. He told the court that he had no idea that the person in question was being held against his will, and said he had gone to the house to arrange a press conference to publicise the informer's claim that he had been forced to turn informer by the police. When asked why he had refused to provide this explanation at the outset, the defendant replied that he had refused to do so 'out of principle'. In these circumstances, the court was satisfied that it was proper to draw an inference that the accused was actually present in the house for the purpose of keeping the informer captive against his will.

Concluding comment

In the law of evidence, there are few issues that arouse such impassioned debate as frequently as the right to silence. For some, permitting adverse inferences to be drawn

---

[479] For this purpose, the special caution contained in Code of Practice C, [10.11] should be used.
[480] Unreported, 8 May 1991, as cited by Jackson, J 'Interpreting the Silence Provisions: The Northern Ireland Cases' [1995] Crim LR 587, pp 592–93.

should not be seen as a step that contradicts the privilege against self-incrimination, as it simply permits the trier of fact to make a commonsense assessment of all the relevant evidence in the case. Ultimately, it may be seen as somewhat foolhardy, if not manifestly unjust, to ignore the fact that most reasonable people who are innocent of allegations will attempt to rebut them at every given opportunity. However, for many human rights and civil liberties commentators, the fear is that any inferences from silence operate as a backdoor means of coercion. Curtailing the right in any form will effectively amount to shifting the burden of proof from the prosecution to the defence. In simple terms, it could be said that it is nonsensical for the law to guarantee a fundamental right in the form of the privilege against incrimination, and then penalise a person who chooses to exercise it.[481]

However one views the merits of such arguments, it is clear that the 1994 legislation undoubtedly constitutes a significant inroad to the right, at least as regards pre-trial silence. Certainly, in the common law world, few jurisdictions have sought to mirror the English approach, which arguably constitutes the thin end of the wedge. In the United States, the right to silence is enshrined in the Fifth Amendment, and it is similarly entrenched in the legal systems of Canada, South Africa and India.[482] This is, perhaps, unsurprising given that the legislation has not affected the conviction rate,[483] although it has resulted in a slightly higher level of response to police questions. In contrast to 77 per cent of suspects attempting all questions posed to them in the interview before the measures took effect, 84 per cent attempted to answer all questions once the provisions were in force.[484] To some extent, this small rise may be attributed to the fact that solicitors are now wary of advising clients to remain silent,[485] knowing that they could be blamed for any adverse inference that might be drawn when the case comes to court.

Although there is no shortage of opposition from both academic and civil liberties groups to the 1994 provisions,[486] there is currently no significant pressure on the political platform for either repeal or amendment. However, as Dennis points out, the case law that has emanated from Strasbourg and the consequential statutory amendments that have followed have already resulted in a significant change to the practical operation of the provisions.[487] Nonetheless, as Dennis himself acknowledges, the legislation has survived the advent of the Human Rights Act 1998, and it has not to date been declared incompatible with Article 6 of the European Convention on Human Rights.[488] For the time being, at

---

[481]See further Michael, J and Emmerson, B 'Current Topic: The Right to Silence' (1995) 1 EHRLR 4.

[482]See section 11(c) of the Canadian Charter of Rights; section 35 Constitution of the Republic of South Africa; and Art 20(3) of the Constitution of India respectively. Section 89(1) of the Uniform Evidence Acts in Australia also prohibits the drawing of any inferences from an accused's failure to respond to questioning.

[483]Jackson *et al.*, op cit n 415.

[484]Bucke, T, Street, R and Brown, D *The Right of Silence: The Impact of the Criminal Justice and Public Order Act 1994*, Home Office Research Study No 199 (2000: London, Home Office).

[485]*Ibid.*

[486]See e.g. Leng, R 'Silence pre-trial, reasonable expectations and the normative distortion of fact-finding' (2001) 5 E & P 240; Birch, op cit n 412; Justice, op cit n 415; Easton, S *The Right to Silence*, 2nd ed (1998: Aldershot, Ashgate).

[487]Dennis, op cit n 460.

[488]The 'right to silence' is not mentioned expressly in Article 6. However, it is well established that it is a standard that lies at the heart of the generic provision laid down in Article 6(1). See further *Delcourt v Belgium* (1970) 1 EHRR 355; *Moreiva de Azvedo v Portugal* (1992) 13 EHRR 731; *Funke v France* (1993) 16 EHRR 297; *Murray v United Kingdom* (above); *Saunders v United Kingdom* (1997) 23 EHRR 313; *Heaney and McGuinness v Ireland* App No. 34720/97, 21 Dec 2000; *Averill v United Kingdom* (above); *Condron v United Kingdom* (above); *Beckles v United Kingdom* (above).

least, we can be fairly confident that the current regime permitting adverse inferences is here to stay.

KEY LEARNING POINTS

- The general rule is that all competent witnesses are compellable.
- Exceptions to the rule apply with respect to child witnesses, witnesses with physical and mental disabilities, the spouse of the accused, and the accused.
- Juries may draw 'such inferences as appear proper' where the defence have failed to comply with disclosure requirements or where one of the circumstances contained sections 34–37 of the Criminal justice and Public Order Act 1994 applies.
- The drawing of inferences from silence dose not *per se* contravene ECHR rights
- Inferences may not be drown if the suspect did not have access to legal advice.

? QUESTIONS

1. 'The danger is that the less responsive an accused is, the more difficult it will be for the court or jury to make any inference which it can be satisfied is correct. They are left to speculate about what people in the accused's position might be expected to do if guilty or innocent'.

   Consider the issues raised in the above statement. Does authorising the drawing of inferences encourage a court or jury to be less cautious than it otherwise might be in such situations?

2. Pauline, aged 18, has an IQ of 75 and a reading age of 8. She is stopped outside a local clothes shop by Tansey, a fellow shopper, who accuses her of placing a T-shirt in her bag without paying for it. Pauline shrugs her shoulders, and walks on. Later that evening, the police arrest Pauline on suspicion of theft. At the police station, Pauline's solicitor advises her not to answer any questions since she 'will just end up in more trouble'.

   (1) Advise the prosecution of what use it may make of Tansey's evidence at the trial.

   (2) Advise counsel for the defence whether the jury may draw inferences from Pauline's failure to answer questions, and what the significance may of be the solicitor's advice to remain silent.

3. Roger is charged with (i) causing grievous bodily harm to his wife Mary Jane, and (ii) with raping of his stepdaughter Betty on the same date. The Prosecution wish to call the following witnesses:

On Count 1 - Mary - wife of the accused

On Count 2 - Mary

        Betty – stepdaughter of the accused, aged 17

        Kate – daughter of the accused, aged 7

        Martha - mother of the accused, aged 85.

Continued

Summary of the facts

In the early hours of the 30th September, Mary was awakened by the cries of her daughter, Betty, aged 17 years. She went into her daughter's bedroom and found her lying on her bed naked and crying. She was holding her nightdress, which was torn. Mary asked her daughter why she was crying and Betty complained that her stepfather, Roger, had raped her.

Mary then confronted her husband who was asleep on the couch in the lounge. She states that she asked him whether he had intercourse with Betty. His response was simply to glare at her. Later that evening, she states that her husband punched her in the face and knocked her unconscious. When she came around, she had received what appeared to be a knife wound across her face.

Witness statements were subsequently taken from everyone who was in the property on the evening in question.

Betty has given the police an account of what happened on the evening in question, but does not wish to appear in court and claims she is fearful of her stepfather.

Mary's statement also implicates the accused both in relation to the alleged rape as well as the alleged attack upon herself. However, since the incident the couple have been reconciled and Mary is refusing to give evidence against her husband.

Kate, aged 7 years, was asleep in the bedroom she shared with Betty. She told police that she was woken by Betty's screams and saw her father 'on top of Betty' and her sister telling him to stop.

Martha, mother to the accused and the grandmother of the complainant, made a statement in which she said that she had got up to go to the toilet in the middle of the night and heard screams coming from Betty's bedroom and the voice of her granddaughter telling someone to get out. She then saw her son leaving Betty's bedroom. Martha is aged 85, and in frail health. She appears to be mentally sound, but Roger has told his defence team that she is in the early stages of Alzheimer's disease and is getting confused. She has stated that the prospect of giving evidence against her son causes her distress and she is very reluctant to do so.

Roger denies the rape of his stepdaughter, but admits having struck her in the heat of an argument they had had on the night in question. He claims that she has never liked him since he married her mother, and has accused him out of spite. In relation to the attack on his wife, he claims that when his wife woke him she had the knife in her hand and threatened him with it. The cut on his wife's arm was caused, he claims, either accidentally or in self-defence.

(a) Consider whether the various witnesses competent and compellable for the prosecution or the defence and whether their evidence will be given sworn or unsworn.

(b) What is the evidential significance of Roger's failure to respond to Mary's question as to whether he raped Betty?

SUGGESTED FURTHER READING

Bucke, T, Street, R and Brown, D *The Right of Silence: The Impact of the Criminal Justice and Public Order Act 1994*, Home Office Research Study No. 199 (2000).

Dennis, I 'Silence in the Police Station: The Marginalisation of Section 34', [2002] Crim LR 25.

Jackson, J 'Silence and Proof: Extending the Boundaries of Criminal Procedure in the UK' (2001) 5 E & P 145.

Jennings, A, Ashworth, A and Emmerson, B 'Silence and Safety: The Impact of Human Rights Law' [2000] Crim LR 879.

Penny, S 'What's Wrong with Self Incrimination? The Wayward Path of Self Incrimination Law in the Post-Charter Era. Part 1: Justifications for Rules Preventing Self-Incrimination' (2003) 48 *Criminal Law Quarterly* 249.

CHAPTER 5

EXAMINATION AND CROSS-EXAMINATION

INTRODUCTION

Traditionally, the adversarial paradigm has granted criminal advocates a considerable freedom in how they present their cases at court, and the manner in which they question witnesses. This freedom is not, however, unfettered. The conduct of the advocates, and the way in which evidence is elicited from witnesses, is subject to the oversight of the trial judge. However, judicial intervention is not regarded as a feature of the adversarial system, since control of the trial and evidence rests with the parties. Whilst the judge has a role in ensuring that proceedings are conducted in accordance with the rules of evidence and procedure, he or she will generally refrain from intervening when witnesses are being questioned by counsel. As Lord Denning famously stated in *Jones v National Coal Board*:[489]

> The judge's part in all this is to hearken to the evidence, only himself asking questions of witnesses when it is necessary to clear up any point that has been overlooked or left obscure; to see that the advocates behave themselves seemly and keep to the rules laid down by law; to exclude irrelevancies and discourage repetition; to make sure by wise intervention that he follows the points the advocates are making and can assess their worth and at the end to make up his mind where the truth lies.[490]

The adversarial model of justice dictates that the decision-maker, whether judge or jury, must rely on the parties exclusively for all the material facts.[491] Proactively seeking further information outside what the parties were presenting would heighten the risk of perceived partisanship. Indeed, an overly interventionist judge thus runs the risk of not just appearing to be partial to one side, but also of having a conviction overturned on appeal.[492] This danger was recognised by the Court of Appeal in *Sharp*:[493]

> The judge may be in danger of seeming to enter the arena in the sense that he may appear partial to one side or the other. This may arise from the hostile tone of questioning or implied criticism of counsel who is conducting the examination or cross-examination, or if the judge is impressed by a witness, perhaps suggesting excuses or explanations for a witness's conduct which is open to attack by counsel from the opposite party.[494]

While the role of the trial judge as an impartial and neutral umpire is often regarded as fundamental to the adversarial process, questions remain as the degree to which practice reflects theory.[495] For example, judges occasionally exercise common law powers to question witnesses themselves,[496] and may even call witnesses of their own motion.[497]

---

[489] *Jones v National Coal Board* [1957] 2 QB 55.
[490] At 64.
[491] Damaska, M *The Faces of Justice and State Authority* (1986: New Haven, CT, Yale University Press), p 136.
[492] See, for example, the Court of Appeal decision in *R v Gunning* [1980] Crim LR 592.
[493] [1993] 3 All ER 225.
[494] At 231.
[495] McEwan, J *Evidence and the Adversarial Process: The Modern Law* (1998: Oxford, Hart), p 13.
[496] *R v Hopper* [1915] 2 KB 431; *R v Cain* (1936) 25 Cr App R 204.
[497] *R v Wallwork* (1958) 42 Cr App R 153.

They are also under a duty to intervene in order to prevent over-zealous or protracted cross-examination of an offensive or oppressive nature.[498] However, in contemporary criminal practice, the primary role of the judge lies in overseeing the enforcement of evidential and procedural rules. By contrast, the parties in the trial hold a near-complete autonomy to gather, select and present evidence before the tribunal of fact. The commencement, conduct and termination of proceedings rest largely in their hands. They will decide which facts are in issue and which are not, which proofs to generate and which witnesses will be called to aid them in the pursuit of victory. The high level of party control is not really surprising, given that the opportunity to present one's arguments and then confront those of the opposing party lies at the heart of the adversarial process.[499]

The only legal controls on the parties are the rules of evidence, and the extent to which the trial judge enforces them or exercises discretion to place limits on the parameters of the questioning process. In recent years, however, concerns over the manner in which witnesses are treated in court have been instrumental in focusing the attention of academics and policy-makers on the need for more effective rules to govern the questioning of witnesses. This chapter sets out to analyse and evaluate these rules, which are mostly located within the Youth Justice and Criminal Evidence Act 1999 and the Criminal Justice Act 2003.

EXAMINATION-IN-CHIEF

All witnesses called to testify in the criminal trial will be questioned first by the party calling them. This process is known as the examination-in-chief, and usually the questioner will aim to portray the witness in a favourable light, since the testimony he or she gives should bolster the overall strength of that party's case. Counsel will try to elicit only those facts which he or she feels should be included, and will do everything to avoid the witness speaking about anything that the questioner feels should be omitted from the testimony. Arguably, the principal goal is to manipulate witness testimony in such a way that victory is made more likely. The responses of witnesses are closely controlled through a series of carefully crafted questions and answers. Stone offers the following advice to counsel on how to conduct a successful examination-in-chief:

> It should be noted that controlled questioning does dictate the subject of enquiry and how it progresses, it does not involve leading. It does not suggest any answers, although the evidence is controlled by selection and editing. The witness is taken through his evidence by tightly framed questions, in small steps, and in an orderly and deliberate way, to ensure that all material facts are covered, and to avoid inadmissible, irrelevant, harmful or prejudicial evidence.[500]

Witnesses are thus confined to answering questions within the parameters set down by the questioner. In this way, testimony is shaped to bring out its maximum adversarial effect,[501] and witnesses and victims are thereby denied the opportunity to tell their story to the court using their own words.

---

[498] *Mechanical and General Inventions Co Ltd and Lehwess v Austin and Austin Motor Co Ltd* [1935] AC 346; *Wong Kam-ming v R* [1980] AC 247.
[499] Stone, M *Cross-Examination in Criminal Trials*, 2nd ed (1995: London, Butterworths), p 114.
[500] *Ibid.*, 94.
[501] Pizzi, W *Trials without Truth* (1999: New York, New York University Press), p 197.

Leading questions

Prior to coming to court, witnesses will usually have made a statement to the police (if a prosecution witness), or to the defence solicitor (if a defence witness); at trial counsel will take the witness through that statement. In examination-in-chief, leading questions, which suggest the answer required or which suggest the existence of disputed facts to which the witness has not yet testified, are only allowed where the evidence being elicited is purely formal and undisputed.[502] Assume, for example, that John has witnessed a fatal shooting, and is called to give evidence by the prosecution. It is permissible for counsel to set the scene by asking the witness questions such as 'Your name is ...?', 'And you work at ...?', to which the answers are 'Yes', but not a question such as, 'You saw the accused running from the house, just after you heard a shot?'.

The dangers of such questions are obvious; John may have seen someone run from the house; he may be sure it was the accused, or merely thinks that it probably was. However, a simple 'yes' will serve to obscure any degree of doubt. The law of evidence thus requires that such questions be put in a form which allows the witness to say what he or she saw without suggesting the answer required. Thus, having placed John outside the house, counsel should then ask whether he heard anything. If John responds by saying that he heard a noise like a gunshot, counsel can then elicit more information by asking 'What happened next?'; the answer may be, 'I saw a man running from the house'. The next question might be, 'Can you identify this man?', and so on. Questions should then follow about how he was so sure it was the accused and the circumstances of the identification. Obviously, this type of question takes considerably longer than one particular leading question, but is regarded as better evidence. If this rule is contravened, evidence elicited in consequence is still admissible, although the court will generally attach less weight to it.[503]

Refreshing memory

Out of court

All witnesses may refresh their memories from statements or other documents made reasonably close to the events about which they are to give evidence. Both prosecution and defence witnesses are entitled to a copy of their statements and to refresh their memory from them at any time up to the point where they go into the witness box. The leading case in this area is *R v Richardson*,[504] where the defendant was charged with two counts of burglary. Shortly before giving evidence all five prosecution witnesses refreshed their memories from statements made to the police approximately one year beforehand. The Court of Appeal held that there was nothing improper in this:

> There can be no absolute rule that witnesses may not before trial see the statements they made at some period reasonably close to the event which is the subject of the trial. Indeed one can imagine many cases, particularly those of a complex nature, when such a rule would militate very greatly against the interests of justice.[505]

---

[502] Leading questions are, however, permitted on those rare occasions when a witness is declared to be hostile. See below pp 130–31.

[503] *Moor v Moor* [1954] 1 WLR 927.

[504] [1971] 2 QB 484.

[505] per Sachs LJ, at 490.

The Court in *Richardson* quoted with approval the comments of the Supreme Court of Hong Kong in *Lau Pak Ngam v R*,[506] where it was stated that if a witness is deprived of the opportunity to refresh his memory, his testimony becomes more a test of memory than truthfulness. In the view of the court, to deprive witnesses of such an opportunity would create genuine difficulties for the honest witnesses, while doing little to hamper dishonest witnesses. Such a rule would also make life impossible for those police officers who deal daily with many cases and are then expected to give evidence at subsequent trials on a regular basis. In *Lau Pak Ngam* itself, a police officer met with the main prosecution witnesses on the day before the trial and read aloud statements which been taken from them shortly after the incidents occurred. All the witnesses concerned were present at the time, so that each heard what the others intended to say. Although the Court of Appeal in *Richardson* expressed the view that it would be wrong to hand witnesses their statements in circumstances which enabled or encouraged them to compare testimony, in the case at hand such circumstances did not arise.

In *R v Westwell*,[507] the Court of Appeal said it was desirable, though not essential, that the defence be informed when Crown witnesses had seen their statements, so that the defence might, when appropriate, draw attention to this in cross-examination. The Court clearly felt that the fact that a witness has been able to refresh his memory is a matter which may then allow the jury to draw an inference that the witness who gives evidence without first refreshing his memory may be a better witness. This observation comes close to endorsing the view that testimony is more a test of memory, rather than a record of historical accuracy. The reality is that the witness who refreshes his memory is likely to be more truthful than one who does not. Since the memory may fade or be distorted by the passage of time, there is a clear benefit to the justice system as a whole in enabling witnesses to refer to previous statements before giving evidence.

In court

The rules are more stringent where witnesses wish to refresh their memory once they have begun to give evidence. The principle of orality, coupled with the desire of advocates to catch witnesses 'on the hoof', has meant access to previous statements for the purposes of refreshing memory has been greatly restricted. At common law, a witness was only allowed to refresh his or her memory while giving evidence by reference to any written statement made or verified by that witness, whilst the facts were still fresh in his or her mind. For the most part, such statements tended to be contained in police documents or notebooks, but it was not uncommon for witnesses to refer to diaries, order/receipt books, or any other record that was relevant. However, even an old scrap of paper, or the back of a cigarette packet, might have contained the relevant information that is required. No matter where the information was recorded, providing that note was made or verified by the witness in question, the common law permitted it to be used as a basis for refreshing memory.[508] Although such an approach was often scorned by the defence, prosecution counsel would generally take the witness through his or her original statement as part of the examination-in-chief. It thus made little sense to preclude witnesses from seeing these

---

[506] [1966] Crim LR 443.

[507] [1976] 2 All ER 812.

[508] It was quite common for one police officer to make a note of what was being said, and for the other to read it aloud and verify it as accurate. This was accepted as good practice by the Court of Appeal in *R v Bass* [1953] 1 QB 680, where officers referred to the same notebook in order to refresh their memories.

statements where they could serve to remind them of facts which they might otherwise have forgotten in the passage of time.

The common law also required that the statement in question must have been made or verified by the witness while the facts were still fresh in his or her mind. While the Court of Appeal in *Richardson* emphasised that this requirement should provide for some elasticity and should not confine witnesses to an overly short period of time, the distinction between statements which were considered to be sufficiently contemporaneous and those which were not continued to vex the courts in subsequent years. The approach of the courts was inconsistent and unpredictable, which is reflected in the fact that there was no obvious basis for imposing a contemporaneity requirement on those witnesses who refreshed their memories whilst giving evidence, but not on those who refreshed their memories before coming to court.[509]

In *R v Da Silva*,[510] the Court of Appeal held that the trial judge had properly exercised his discretion to allow the witness, who had started to give evidence, to refresh his memory from a statement made one month after the events to which it related. This was in spite of the fact that the statement did not concern contemporaneous events, and neither was it made while the facts were fresh in the mind of the witness. Recognising that it would have been open to the witness to have read the statement before coming into court, the Court said it was equally proper to allow the witness to refresh his memory from that statement in court, subject to four conditions:

(a) the witness must indicate that he cannot recall the details of events because of the lapse of time since they took place;

(b) he must have made a statement much nearer the time of the events so that the contents of his statement represented his recollection at the time he made it;

(c) he has not read the statement before coming into the witness box; and

(d) he wished to have an opportunity to read the statement before he continued to give evidence.

An even broader approach was adopted in *R v South Ribble Stipendiary Magistrate, ex p Cochrane*.[511] Here, the witness had made three statements to the police. The first of these statements was made some two weeks after the events to which they referred. At committal proceedings, some 18 months later, the magistrate permitted the witness to refresh his memory from these statements, even though the witness had already spent 10 to 15 minutes reading them before he went into the witness box. The Queen's Bench Divisional Court dismissed a judicial review application to quash the decision to commit the defendant for trial in spite of the fact that the third condition laid down in *Da Silva* had not been satisfied:

> It seems to me that a judge has a real discretion as to whether to permit a witness to refresh his memory from a non-contemporaneous document. By a real discretion, I mean a strong discretion, a choice of alternatives of free binding criteria. I do not mean the so-called weak discretion which is not a true judicial discretion at all, but simply a binding rule of law to be followed by the judge.[512]

As Dennis notes, it would seem that this decision means that 'there appears to be nothing to stop a judge allowing a witness to refer repeatedly to a non-contemporaneous document

---

[509]See comments of McNeill J in *Owen v Edwards* (1983) 77 Cr App R 191, 195.

[510](1990) 90 Cr App R 233.

[511][1996] 2 Cr App R 544.

[512]*Ibid.*, per Henry LJ, at 551.

in the course of testifying' and the appeal courts should be prepared 'to give the judge a generous margin of appreciation in applying the discretion'.[513]

At common law, the document used to refresh the memory was not evidence of the truth of its contents; the oral testimony was the evidence to be considered by the trier of fact, not the note or record to which the witness made reference. Thus if a witness used a diary or other record to recall dates or entries, the other party could require the production of that diary or record and could cross-examine on it without making it evidence in the case. If the cross-examiner sought to probe other aspects of the document not referred to by the witness, the other party could then insist on treating the document as evidence in the case. In such an event, the document would then become an exhibit and the jury would have a right to inspect it. However, in these circumstances, the evidential value of the exhibit was limited to showing that the witness's testimony as given in the witness box was consistent with those earlier entries. However, this rule, like those other aspects of the common law discussed above, has been subject to legislative change in the Criminal Justice Act 2003.

Reform – the Criminal Justice Act 2003

The common law rules on the use of documents to refresh the memory while giving oral evidence have now been replaced by section 139 of the Criminal Justice Act 2003. Subsection (1) creates a presumption that a witness in criminal proceedings may refresh his memory from a document subject to two conditions:

(a) that he indicates that the document represents his recollection at the time he made it; and

(b) that his recollection was likely to be significantly better at the time the document was made (or verified).

These requirements reflect the common law position as finally arrived at in *R v South Ribble Stipendiary Magistrate, ex p Cochrane*, and it is to be hoped that the courts will construe the phrase 'at an earlier time' both more broadly and more consistently than the manner in which the contemporaneity requirement was previously handled at common law.

One of the reasons why the courts have traditionally regarded witness statements, in particular, with some measure of suspicion is that the police may, advertently or inadvertently, bias the statement towards a particular version of events. One method of counteracting these fears is to make audio or video recordings of witness statements. Although this option is resource-intensive and logistically difficult, section 139(2) recognises the possibility that the transcripts of sound recordings might be used in some instances as memory-refreshing documents. Whilst the section only refers the use of such a document in court while giving oral evidence, the fact that the witness might have had the opportunity to refresh his memory before giving evidence will not affect the presumption created by section 139.

Section 120(3) of the 2003 Act is also relevant to documents used in this way. This provision preserves the common law rule that the document used to refresh the memory is not evidence unless the cross-examination probed other issues within the document beyond the specific entries to which the witness referred. As noted above, in these types of cases the refreshing document was only evidence of the consistency of the witness.

---

[513] Dennis, I, *The Law of Evidence*, 3rd ed (2007, London: Sweet and Maxwell), p 576.

The new statutory provision stipulates that it is admissible as evidence of the truth of the matter stated, and thus constitutes an exception to the hearsay rule.[514] However, it only applies to statements made by the witness on a previous occasion, and does not extend to those documents verified by him or her. Thus, if a witness uses a diary or other record to recall dates or entries, the other party can require the production of that diary or record and cross-examine on it without making it evidence in the case. However, if the cross-examiner goes further and introduces other dates or entries not referred to by the witness, the other party can insist on treating the document as evidence of the truth of the matters stated if the witness could have given oral evidence of those matters. As under the common law, the document thus becomes an exhibit in the case and the jury have a right to inspect it.

Previous consistent statements

At common law, the general rule was that a witness might not seek to bolster his evidence by reference to the fact that he said the same thing out of court on an earlier occasion. Counsel should avoid making any reference to any such statement. Thus in *R v Roberts*,[515] the accused, charged with murder, claimed that the gun had gone off accidentally. He was not allowed to call evidence that two days after the shooting he had told his father that it was an accident. Such statements were excluded because they were hearsay, that is, they were made to a third party out of court. As such, they could not be used to prove the truth of the facts asserted therein.

This rule is largely maintained under section 120 of the Criminal Justice Act 2003, but is subject to a number of exceptions. These cover (a) statements to rebut allegations of fabrication; (b) previous statements identifying persons, places or objects; (c) evidence of recent complaint; (d) previous statements by the accused in response to accusations; and (e) statements forming part of the *res gestae*. Each of these categories is now considered in turn.

Statements to rebut evidence of fabrication

The courts have long accepted that counsel may introduce evidence of previous statements in order to rebut a charge that a witness had fabricated evidence. For example, in *R v Benjamin*,[516] a police officer was allowed to produce his notebook in evidence in order to rebut a charge of fabrication. The fact that the notes were in chronological order demonstrated that they were not fabricated as alleged. Likewise, in *R v Oyesiku*,[517] counsel for the prosecution alleged that the defendant's wife was inventing evidence. Under re-examination by the defence, counsel adduced evidence of a previous statement the witness had given to her husband's solicitor shortly after his arrest. The Court of Appeal held that the trial judge had been correct to do so, since it rebutted the allegation that she had concocted evidence in court. At common law, however, such statements could not be used as evidence of the truth of the contents of a previous statement. This position has now been altered under section 120(2) CJA 2003, which provides that where a previous statement

---

[514] See further Ch 7.
[515] [1942] 1 All ER 187.
[516] (1913) 8 Cr App R 146.
[517] (1971) 56 Cr App R 240.

is admitted to rebut a suggestion that a witness has fabricated his or her testimony, that statement is admissible as evidence of 'any matter stated of which oral evidence by the witness would be admissible'.

Previous statements identifying persons, places or objects

Section 120(4) to (7) of the 2003 Act deals with the not uncommon situation where the witness has, in the past, made a statement to another person identifying a person, place or thing but cannot remember the detail when called to give evidence (such as a car registration number). Under the previous law, the witness would have been unable to rely on any document containing the relevant information if he had not verified it; and the person to whom any oral statement had been made could not give evidence in person unless it fell within an established exception to the hearsay rule. Section 120(4) of the 2003 Act now stipulates that any such statement will be admissible as evidence of the facts contained within it, provided the witness states that he made the statement and believes it to be true, and one of the conditions laid out in subsections (5)–(7) is met:

> (5) The first condition is that the statement identifies or describes a person, object or place.
>
> (6) The second condition is that the statement was made by a witness when the matters stated were fresh in his memory but he does not remember them, and cannot reasonably be expected to remember them, well enough to give oral evidence of them in the proceedings.
>
> (7) The third condition is that—
>> (a) the witness claims to be a person against whom an offence has been committed,
>>
>> (b) the offence is one to which the proceedings relate,
>>
>> (c) the statement consists of a complaint made by the witness (whether to a person in authority or not) about conduct which would, if proved, constitute the offence or part of the offence,
>>
>> (d) the complaint was made as soon as could reasonably be expected after the alleged conduct,
>>
>> (e) the complaint was not made as a result of a threat or a promise, and
>>
>> (f) before the statement is adduced the witness gives oral evidence in connection with its subject matter.
>
> (8) For the purposes of subsection (7) the fact that the complaint was elicited (for example, by a leading question) is irrelevant unless a threat or a promise was involved.

Section 120(4) thus permits the person to whom the statement was made to give evidence, or for the document containing the relevant information to be admitted, providing the above conditions are satisfied. Thus, where a witness has picked out a suspect in an identity parade, but cannot remember the 'number' of that person in the line-up, a police officer present may give evidence to this effect.[518] Similarly, suppose Kim witnesses a bank robbery and gives the registration number of the getaway car to Mike, a traffic warden. Mike makes a note of the number, but fails to ask Kim to verify it. Kim cannot remember the registration number when called to give evidence, but she tells counsel that she made the statement and to the best of her belief it was true. Although Kim will be unable to refresh her memory since the conditions under section 139 are not met, Mike can now

---

[518] *R v Osborne and Virtue* [1973] QB 678.

testify that Kim gave him the registration number and he can relate that number to the court directly.[519]

Evidence of recent complaint

A complaint made by the victim of an alleged sexual offence was one of the longest-standing exceptions to the common rule against admitting previous consistent statements. Indeed, before the advent of professional policing, there was a general presumption that all victims of crime should raise a 'hue and cry' within the neighbourhood. An early complaint that one had been robbed, raped or was otherwise the victim of a crime was essential if there was to be any likelihood of catching the alleged offender. In *R v Wink*,[520] a police officer was allowed to prove that the witness had complained to him of robbery. This was only a few years after the creation of the Metropolitan Police in 1829, and there is no later case of a complaint being admitted in these circumstances, other than in relation to sexual offences. In such cases, particularly those involving rape, the rule continued to survive. Whilst an early complaint was said to be consistent with lack of consent; a late complaint was considered to be inconsistent with the allegation that the act was not consensual. Neither assumption had any basis in fact, and the practice was described by a US court as a 'perverted survival of [an] ancient requirement' which ought to be abolished.[521] It is therefore somewhat surprising that rather than abolish the requirement of an early complaint altogether, section 120(7)(d) extends it to any and all offences.

Section 120(4) makes it clear that a complaint is now admissible as evidence as evidence of the truth of the matters stated. Section 120(8) removes a former restriction that the complaint must be voluntary and should not have been made as the result of leading questions, while section 120(7)(e) requires that the complaint was not made as a result of a threat or promise. Thus if a mother sees her daughter in a distressed and dishevelled state and says, 'He raped you, didn't he?', a positive reply would be admissible. Questions such as 'Why are you crying?' or, as in *Osbourne*,[522] 'Why are you going home?', will not affect the admissibility of the complaint. However, if a father threatened his daughter with violence unless she told him what had happened, the subsequent complaint would not be admissible.

At common law, it was the case that the complaint should be made at the first opportunity which reasonably offered itself after the alleged offence. This rule is largely preserved by the 2003 Act, section 120(7)(d) of which requires that, 'the complaint was made as soon as could reasonably be expected after the alleged conduct'. In *R v Valentine*,[523] the complainant was walking home at 11.30 pm, when she met the defendant, a complete stranger to her. She was persuaded to join him for a meal at a nearby restaurant. They left the restaurant together at 12.30 am, and began to walk towards her home. The defendant suggested that they cut across a playing field and she agreed. When they got to the middle of the field he threatened her with a table knife, and then raped her. The complainant arrived home at 2.30 am. Her parents and elder brother were at home but were asleep. The next morning she went into her brother's room and told him she had been attacked with

---

[519]See the discussion of section 117(5) Criminal Justice Act 2003 in Chapter 6, pp 228–231, for an alternative, if more cumbersome, means of introducing the registration number.

[520](1834) 6 Car & P 397.

[521]*Commonwealth v Cleary* 172 Mass 175, 176 (1898).

[522][1905] 1 KB 551.

[523][1996] 2 Cr App R 213.

a knife, but said she did not want to tell her parents. She went to work during the afternoon, and in the evening told a friend she had been raped.

The defence had contended that the complaint made to the friend during the evening was inadmissible because it was not made at the first opportunity that reasonably presented itself. However, both the trial judge and the Court of Appeal rejected this argument, and in doing so displayed a more understanding attitude to a rape victim than has often been present in the criminal courts.[524] The trial judge remarked:

> I do not think the law requires me to say that the evidence [of the second complaint] should be excluded in those circumstances [the circumstances being that the complainant had bottled up the matter for some 24 hours] if the first opportunity could be said to be that opportunity where she felt herself able to say [that she had been raped]. Not every woman can bring herself to say that a man has raped her, even if she has been most cruelly raped. I think we understand that in these courts these days, even if it was not appreciated by Victorian judges, who started laying down this principle toward the end of the last century.[525]

Roch L J, giving the judgement of the Court of Appeal, expressed similar sentiments when he observed:

> We now have a greater understanding that those who are the victims of sexual offences, be they male or female, often need time before they can bring themselves to tell what has been done to them; that some victims will find it quite impossible to complain to anyone other than a parent or member of their family whereas others may feel it quite impossible to tell their parents or members of their family.[526]

In the view of the Court of Appeal, it was not necessary that a complaint had to be made at the first opportunity which presented itself. It was sufficient if it was made at the first *reasonable* opportunity. The question as to when such an opportunity arose depended upon the particular circumstances, including the character of the complainant and the relationship between her and the person she complained to, and the person to whom she might have complained, but did not. It was also held that a complaint will not be inadmissible merely because there has been an earlier complaint, provided that the complaint was made as speedily as could reasonably be expected.[527] However, it is not permissible for the prosecution to lead evidence that the complaint had been in substantially the same terms on several occasions soon after the alleged offence. Such evidence may be prejudicial in that it might induce the jury to regard the reports of individual complaints as evidence of the truth of what was asserted.

In *R v S*,[528] questions arose as to whether evidence of recent complaint ought to be admitted where there were inconsistencies between the complainant's evidence and that of the person to whom she complained. The prosecution case was that the defendant started sexually abusing the complainant, S, when she was 9- or 10-years-old. The abuse took the form of indecent touching, which continued until she left home at the age of 19. In her evidence-in-chief, S stated that from the age of 10 or 11 she was also subjected to more serious sexual abuse, which included sexual intercourse. The prosecution applied to adduce evidence of her complaint to a former school friend, C, in whom she had confided when she was 13- or 14-years-old. C's evidence was that S had told her about the defendant touching

---

[524]See below, pp 146–50; Ch 2, pp 29–30.
[525]At 219.
[526]At 224.
[527]Cf. *R v Birks* [2003] 2 Cr App R 7.
[528][2004] 3 All ER 689.

her. However, at trial, S testified that she had told C not just about the indecent assaults, but also about the more serious penetrative assaults. The defendant objected to C's evidence of the sexual conduct of which S complained, but the trial judge permitted the evidence to be given.

The Court of Appeal rejected the appellant's contention that the complaint to her friend was wrongly admitted given the inconsistency between the details of her earlier complainants and her evidence. In the view of the Court, the decision in each case as to whether such evidence was sufficiently consistent for it to be admissible must depend on the facts. It was not necessary that the recent complaint disclosed the ingredients of the offence; it would, however, usually be necessary that the complainant disclosed evidence of material and relevant unlawful sexual conduct by the defendant which would support the credibility of the complainant. It would not, therefore, usually be necessary for the complainant to have described the full extent of the unlawful sexual conduct alleged by the complainant in the witness box, provided that it was capable of supporting the credibility of the complainant's evidence given at trial. It was for the jury to assess the significance of any differences between the two accounts. Although the Court found that the testimony was properly admitted, the conviction itself was rendered unsafe because the judge's direction to the jury regarding the evidence was insufficient in that he failed to draw attention to the inconsistencies between the evidence of C and that of S. The appeal was therefore allowed.

Even when the common law required that a jury be warned of the danger of relying on the uncorroborated evidence of the complainant in a case of rape,[529] it was made absolutely clear that a recent complaint could not be independent corroboration since it came from the victim herself.[530] This remains the case under the 2003 Act, even though the evidence of a recent complaint is now admissible as evidence of the truth of the matters asserted. The failure to make this clear to the jury has been, and doubtless will continue to be, a common ground for appeal.

It should be emphasised, however, that evidence of recent complaint may only be introduced where the complainant gives evidence in person. Thus in *R v Wallwork*,[531] the accused was charged with incest with his daughter, aged 5. The child was called to give evidence but said nothing. Her grandmother then gave evidence that the child complained to her about the accused's conduct. The Court of Appeal held that this evidence had been wrongly admitted because there was no evidence from the child with which it could be consistent. Section 120 does not change this common law rule. Section 120(1) stipulates that the provision applies only where the witness is called to give evidence in criminal proceedings, and section 120(4)(b) makes it clear that the previous statement is admissible only if the witness indicates that to the best of his belief he made the statement, and that to the best of his belief it contains the truth.

All of the case law discussed above is likely to be followed in applying the requirement of section 120(7)(d) of the 2003 Act, not only in respect of rape complainants, but also complainants in relation to many other offences. This is despite noises made by the Court of Appeal in *R v O*,[532] to the effect that the provisions within the new legislation were free-standing, and courts were not bound by preceding case law. Nonetheless, in that particular case the Court still seemed to echo the general tenor of the common law in the run-up to

---

[529] See Ch 1, pp 161–18.
[530] *R v Lillyman* [1896] 2 QB 167.
[531] (1958) 42 Cr App R 153.
[532] [2006] 2 Cr App R 27.

the introduction of the act, and placed a considerable degree of emphasis upon the need to consider the context of each particular complaint and the circumstances in which it was made. Thus the guidance laid down in *Valentine* and *S* is still likely to be valid in contemporary practice.

Previous statements by the accused in response to accusations

Statements made by the accused to the police or other investigatory authority are commonly adduced by the prosecution whether they contain admissions or denials. Where such a statement contains an admission, it will generally constitute a confession, and will be admissible as an exception to the hearsay rule. Where such previous statements are adduced as confession evidence, they will be regarded as evidence of the facts stated and not merely as evidence of consistency. The rules relating to the admissibility of confessions are considered in detail in Chapter 8.

Statements forming part of the res gestae

A previous consistent statement was admissible at common law if it was part of the *res gestae*, that is, part of the transaction, story or event to which it related. This exception to the rule against hearsay is preserved by section 118 of the 2003 Act. Thus in *R v Fowkes*,[533] the accused, also known as 'Butcher', was charged with murder. A witness gave evidence that he was in a room with a police officer and his father, when the latter was killed by a shot fired through the window. Immediately beforehand, a face had appeared at the window, and the witness was permitted to testify that he had shouted, 'There's Butcher' (the name by which the accused was known). The scope of the *res gestae* doctrine is examined in Chapter 7.[534]

Unfavourable and hostile witnesses

Sometimes witnesses will fail to give the evidence expected by the party that calls them. For a variety of reasons, sometimes the testimony given under oath at trial conflicts with, or substantially differs from, a previous statement. In these circumstances, the witness cannot be cross-examined as to the inconsistency between what he is saying, or not saying, in the witness box and what he or she said in an earlier statement. However, it is important to draw a distinction between a witness who is merely *unfavourable* to the party calling him or her, and one whose answers are positively hostile to the questioner.

A witness is considered to be unfavourable where he or she is simply confused about the facts or cannot remember the details. Such witnesses will not be motivated by malice or dishonesty, but their testimony is likely to undermine the examining party's case to some extent. Where this happens, counsel cannot cross-examine the witness, or attack his or her credibility.[535] In modern times, this problem may be resolved by allowing the witness to refresh his memory from the statement made nearer to the event to which he testifies.[536]

---

[533] (1856) *The Times*, 8 March.
[534] See Ch 7, pp 232–38.
[535] *Ewer v Ambrose* (1825) 3 B & C 746.
[536] *R v South Ribble Stipendiary Magistrate, ex p Cochrane* (see p 124 above). See also *R v Maw* [1994] Crim LR 841.

If that is not possible or does not resolve the problem, other witnesses can be called to give the evidence which the unfavourable witness was expected to give, or to rebut any aspects of the testimony.

Occasionally, a witness will be 'hostile', and will not give the evidence expected out of malice or dishonesty. Possibly, he or she may be fearful of giving evidence or may have formed their own view as to the overall merits of the case. An application for leave to treat any witness as hostile must be made by the examining party. Ultimately, this is a matter for the court to determine. Where the judge grants leaves, the party may then cross-examine the witness. This will enable counsel to ask leading questions,[537] and put any previous inconsistent statements to the witness.[538]

PRINCIPLES OF CROSS-EXAMINATION

At an earlier period all questioning in criminal trials was initiated by the judge, which usually led to a 'freewheeling discussion' between the witnesses, the defendant and the judge.[539] The practice of witnesses being cross-examined by defence counsel appears to have emerged in the 1730s, with the purpose being to 'supplement rather than supplant questioning by the court'.[540] The practice became more commonplace during the late eighteenth century,[541] although during the nineteenth century however, the nature of cross-examination underwent a sea change. As the number of lawyers increased and litigation grew, the function of the judge as active inquirer was gradually usurped.[542] Lawyers began to assume ownership of the trial, which underlined the need for closer control of a system that was increasingly characterised by partisan advocacy.

By the first half of the nineteenth century, Landsman notes that 'flamboyant courtroom advocacy was the main avenue to success'.[543] He also observes that cross-examination took on an increasingly aggressive tone, with fierce attacks being launched on the motives and character of the witnesses:

> Accompanying the increase in counsel's participation in litigation, and especially the intensification of cross-examination, came an amplified acerbity by the advocates. Where once it was the judges who made caustic remarks, it was now the cross-examining lawyers who were sarcastic interrogators.[544]

The primacy of cross-examination as an indispensable feature of the adversarial process was established in the early nineteenth century.[545] In subsequent years, the fervent and aggressive nature of the process became deeply rooted in trial advocacy. Practitioners came to view it as having superseded the oath as an indispensable method of uncovering the truth by rooting out unreliable witnesses.[546] Indeed, since the limitations placed on

---

[537] *R v Thompson* (1976) 64 Cr App R 96.

[538] s 3 Criminal Procedure Act 1865. See discussion below, pp 141–42.

[539] Landsman, S 'A Brief Survey of the Development of the Adversary System' (1983) 44 *Ohio State Law Journal* 713, 727.

[540] Langbein, J H *The Origins of the Adversary Criminal Trial* (2003: Oxford, Oxford University Press), p 291.

[541] *Ibid*.

[542] *Ibid.*, pp 242–244.

[543] Landsman, op cit n 539, p 733.

[544] Landsman, S 'The Rise of the Contentious Spirit: Adversary Procedure in Eighteenth Century England' (1990) 75 Cornell Law Review 497, 536.

[545] Langbein, op cit n 540, p 246.

[546] *Ibid*.

defence counsel at that time forbade barristers from addressing the jury directly,[547] cross-examination was viewed as the most effective means of undermining the prosecution case.[548] Langbein cites one anonymous commentator who wrote that it was 'the most perfect and effectual system for unravelling of falsehood ever devised by the ingenuity of mortals',[549] and Bentham labelled it as a 'grand security… against erroneous or mendacious testimony'.[550]

Towards the end of the nineteenth century, the courts came to recognise cross-examination as a fundamental right of the defence counsel. Any sworn witness was expected to undergo cross-examination as a matter of course. In conducting cross-examination, it was accepted that advocates themselves had a very broad leeway in determining their style and lines of questioning.[551] The role of defence counsel became much more proactive, where eloquent advocacy and zealous questioning were highly desirable skills.[552] The role of the prosecutor also changed. Professional advocates came to prosecute cases much more frequently, and assumed a more adversarial stance in the presentation of their cases to match the increased zeal of defence counsel. [553] As the trial moved increasingly towards the form of a dual between two parties, it became clear that this new-found fervour in the criminal courtrooms had to be 'tempered' by responsibility.[554] The conduct of advocates had to be regulated more closely, and this was primarily effected through the formulation of new rules of evidence and fresh understandings about the role of these rules within the overall context of the criminal trial.

The indispensable nature of cross-examination to the criminal trial is still accepted today.[555] In its modern context, the purpose of cross-examination is said to be twofold: (1) to weaken the case for the other side; and (2) to establish facts that are favourable to the case for the cross-examiner.[556] However, it might be added that, in modern times, the first of these objectives is achieved not by discrediting the *evidence* by demonstrating that it does not fit with other evidence before the jury, but by seeking to discredit the *witness* so that the jury will not believe, or give little credence to his or her testimony. Parties have a right to cross-examine all witnesses on any relevant issue, or on any matter concerning a witness's credibility. In contrast to examination-in-chief, leading questions may be put to witnesses. Strictly speaking, the cross-examiner should not 'suggest' matters to witnesses, but in practice there are few advocates who do not, at least occasionally, adopt the phrase 'I put it to you that…' or 'Isn't it the case that …'. Witnesses can easily be upset by suggestions that they are mistaken or, even worse, lying. Of course, counsel will often stop short of calling the witness a liar, but phrases such as 'I suggest that what you have described never happened' have but one interpretation.

The centrality of cross-examination to the adversarial trial is underlined by the consequences of failing to cross-examine a witness. In such an event, counsel may be

---

[547]The prohibition on defence counsel to addressing the jury was lifted by the Prisoner's Counsel Act 1836.

[548]Langbein, op cit n 540, p 296.

[549]*Ibid.*

[550]Bentham, J *The Rationale of Judicial Evidence Specially Applied to English Trials* (1827: London, Hunt & Clark), as cited by Langbein op cit n 540, p 246.

[551]Landsman, op cit n 51, p 539.

[552]*Ibid.*, p 594.

[553]Langbein, J 'The Historical Origins of the Privilege Against Self-Incrimination at Common Law' (1994) 92 *Michigan Law Review* 1047, p 1069.

[554]Cairns, D *Advocacy and the Making of the Adversarial Trial 1800–1865* (Oxford: Clarendon (1998), p 165.

[555]See e.g. *R v Paraskeva* (1982) 76 Cr App R 162.

[556]Du Cann, R *The Art of the Advocate* (1993: London, Penguin), p 11.

deemed to have accepted the witness's version of events if the testimony has gone unchallenged.[557] If a party has been prevented from cross-examining a witness, that witness's testimony may be regarded as inadmissible, or may be afforded little weight. For example, in *R v Doolin*,[558] where the witness died before cross-examination, the testimony was still deemed to be admissible since the judge had given an appropriate warning to the jury. By contrast, in *R v Lawless*,[559] it was stated that where the testimony formed a central plank of the prosecution case, a judicial warning was not sufficient to prevent any prejudice to the accused. The Court of Appeal held that the entire testimony should have been excluded.

The question of admissibility will thus depend upon the nature of the evidence in question and its importance to the case as a whole. On occasions, the courts have been confronted with cases where only a partial cross-examination has taken place. For example, in *R v Stretton*,[560] the victim of an alleged rape and indecent assault was epileptic, and fell ill whilst testifying. When it became clear she was unable to continue, the trial judge directed the jury that if they felt the defence had been deprived of the opportunity properly to test her evidence, they should acquit the defendant. However, the defendant was convicted, and his appeal was dismissed on the ground that the trial judge had properly exercised his discretion to allow the trial to continue in such circumstances. The Court placed considerable emphasis on the fact that cross-examination had proceeded for some time before the witness became ill, and the trial judge gave a clear warning to the jury and urged them to consider carefully the impact of the complainant's failure to complete her testimony. Similarly, in *R v Wyatt*,[561] a 7-year-old child, the alleged victim of an indecent assault, gave her evidence-in-chief via a TV link and was cross-examined for some 20 minutes before becoming too distressed to continue. Although there was no lengthy warning to the jury as there had been in *Stretton*, the Court of Appeal was satisfied that the jury had been fairly directed on the girl's evidence and upheld the conviction. If little or no cross-examination takes place, an adjournment of the trial to enable the witness to recover might assist, or a new trial might be possible. However, in cases like those above, the witness is unlikely to be helped by an adjournment, and even less likely to be able to withstand the ordeal of another trial; the choice for the trial judge is then between continuing with the trial (with an appropriate direction to the jury), or directing an outright acquittal.

The nature of cross-examination

Traditionally, many commentators, and indeed the legal profession, have maintained that the purpose of cross-examination is to investigate the truth of the witness's evidence. It was Wigmore who famously remarked that cross-examination was 'beyond any doubt the greatest legal engine ever invented for the discovery of truth'.[562] Similarly, Buckner argued that the primary purpose of cross-examination should be 'to catch truth, ever an elusive fugitive'.[563] However, such arguments have been increasingly questioned in recent

---

[557]*R v Wood Green Court, ex p Taylor* [1995] Crim LR 879.

[558](1832) 1 Jebb CC 123.

[559](1993) 98 Cr App R 342.

[560](1988) 86 Cr App R 7.

[561][1990] Crim LR 343.

[562]Wigmore, J H *A Treatise on the Anglo-American System of Evidence in Trials at Common Law*, 3rd ed (1940: Boston, Brown & Co), [1367].

[563]Buckner, E R 'Comments on the Uses and Abuses of Cross-Examination' in F L Wellman (ed), *The Art of Cross-Examination* (1936: New York: Simon & Schuster), p 216.

years. The Australian Law Reform Commission has stated that 'so far as obtaining accurate testimony is concerned, [cross-examination] is arguably the poorest of the techniques employed at present in the common law courts',[564] and John Langbein has described it as a 'flawed theory of truth-seeking'.[565] Cross-examination does not necessarily aim to elicit the truth, but to challenge or correct what has just been heard. Counsel will only desire that the witness testifies about those events which will lend credence to the particular case theory being advanced.

To this end, advocacy is naturally aggressive and confrontational, and advocates have a vast range of tactics at their disposal to unsettle witnesses. This in itself means that the witness will be 'in the worst possible frame of mind to be examined – he will be agitated, confused and bewildered'.[566] As shown in Chapter 2, witnesses are often required to answer insulting and invasive questions about aspects of their lives that they would much rather were kept private. Moreover, by implication, the jury is invited to draw assumptions about the confused and distraught state of the witness, which opens the doorway to potentially inaccurate fact-finding since there is no evidence to suggest that the witness's demeanour is a reliable indicator to determine the veracity of the evidence.[567]

Recollections of past events, along with associated evidence, are routinely manipulated, decontextualised and re-categorised by the parties at trial, before any attempt is made to re-organise them so that they correspond with abstract legal principles. In particular, advocates will often resort to the use of suggestion by putting scenarios to witnesses and then asking them to comment. This maximises the likelihood that the witness will only give relay those facts to the court which counsel desires. Some witnesses are more susceptible to suggestion than others. Research has indicated that suggestion is a particularly effective technique for the advocate to establish control in cases involving children[568] or those with learning disabilities,[569] particularly where such a witness views the questioner as an authority figure.[570] In this way, the testimony of individual witnesses is filtered and recast it in a favourable light. There is no doubt that cross-examination, when properly conducted, can lead to better evidence by disclosing deliberate lies or unintended errors and misconceptions. However, the reality is that, far from acting as an effective tool for recovery of the truth, cross-examination is all too often used to hide or obfuscate it.

The finality rule

Whilst counsel retains a broad leeway in the forms of questions that are put to witnesses, cross-examination is not designed to be a 'fishing expedition'.[571] One of the most important

---

[564] Australian Law Reform Commission, *The Manner of Giving Evidence* Research Paper No 8 (1982), [10.5].
[565] Landbein, op cit n 52, p 247.
[566] Harris, R *Hints on Advocacy* (1892: Boston, MA, Little Brown), cited by Fielding, N. *Courting Violence* (2006: Oxford, Oxford University Press), p 219.
[567] See generally Wellborn, O 'Demeanour' 76 *Cornell Law Review* 1075.
[568] See Hedderman, C *Children's Evidence: the Need for Corroboration*, Research and Planning Unit Paper 41 (1987: London, Home Office), p 28; Spencer J R, and Flin, R *The Evidence of Children*, 2nd edn (1993: London, Blackstone).
[569] Sanders Creation, J, Bird, S and Weber, L *Victims with Learning Disabilities: Negotiating the Criminal Justice System*, Home Office Research Findings No 44 (1996: London, Home Office), pp 75–76.
[570] Milne, R, and Bull, R. *Investigating Interviewing: Psychology and Practice* (1999: Chichester, Wiley).
[571] McEwan, op cit n 495, p 103.

restrictions upon counsel is the operation of the finality rule. The rule is a natural corollary of the concept of relevance,[572] and states that questions which are not directly relevant to the issue(s) in the proceedings must be regarded as final. For example, in *R v Burke*,[573] the cross-examiner alleged the witness, who was testifying through an interpreter in Irish, had been heard talking to two other people in the court precinct in English. The witness denied this ever happened, and since it was irrelevant to the facts in issue, counsel could not adduce any evidence in rebuttal. Whilst neither counsel nor the jury is required to believe the answer to a collateral question,[574] counsel is prevented from calling further evidence to demonstrate that the answer is not true. Matters concerning the credit of a witness or the credibility of evidence given are generally regarded as collateral matters because they do not bear directly on the issue(s) before the jury.

In *Attorney-General v Hitchcock*,[575] the witness had been asked whether he had said in an out-of-court statement that he had been offered money to give evidence by excise officers. He denied having said this, and it was held that counsel could not call evidence to prove that he had because it was a collateral matter. A less than helpful test of what constitutes a collateral matter was proposed by Pollock CB:

> If the answer of a witness is a matter which you would be allowed on your own part to prove in evidence – if it has such a connection with the issues that you would be allowed to give it in evidence – then it is a matter on which you may contradict [the witness].[576]

This test is, of course, something of a tautology, and is tantamount to saying that a matter is 'in issue' if it is 'in issue'. More accurately, it might be said that a fact constitutes a 'matter in issue' if it must be established by either party in order to discharge the burden of proof. Only in these circumstances will counsel be able to adduce rebutting evidence to disprove the answer of the witness. If the answer relates to collateral issues, and is thereby not relevant to any material issue in dispute, the finality rule applies and no rebutting evidence is admissible.

The distinction between facts in issue and collateral issues can be a difficult one to draw at times, especially in some sexual cases. In *R v Funderburk*,[577] the defendant alleged that the complainant, who described in graphic detail losing her virginity to him, was lying as she was already sexually experienced. He wished to adduce evidence that the girl had told him, and others, on a number of occasions that she was sexually experienced. If such evidence was relevant to the credibility of the witness alone, it could not be adduced, although if it was relevant to the facts in issue, then it could be heard. The trial judge refused permission, although his refusal was overturned by the Court of Appeal. As they saw it, these facts were intimately connected with the facts in issue. Similarly, in the subsequent case of *R v Nagrecha*,[578] the complainant had alleged that she had been indecently assaulted by her employer. The trial judge had ruled that the defence could not adduce evidence of similar allegations made by the complainant against other men, although the complainant denied ever having made such a complaint before. The Court of Appeal allowed the appeal and stated that such questioning should have been allowed since it went to the

---

[572] See Ch 1, pp 11–13.
[573] (1858) 8 Cox CC 44.
[574] *Hobbs v Tinling* [1929] 2 KB 1.
[575] (1847) 1 Ex 91.
[576] *Ibid.*, at 99.
[577] [1990] 2 All ER 482.
[578] [1997] 2 Cr App R 401.

issue of whether an assault had actually occurred at all, and not merely to the witness's credibility.

The ultimate decision as to whether or not a matter is regarded as collateral rests with the trial judge, and will not lightly be subject to interference by the Court of Appeal.[579] Thus much will depend upon the trial judge's own perception of what is or is not logically probative of the facts in issue. In this sense, the judge's beliefs, experiences, social mores, prejudices and values will all come into play, which underlines the fact that concept of relevance and the operation of the finality rule are both fundamentally elusive and open to subjective interpretation.

In addition to some measure of uncertainty surrounding the scope of the rule, it should also be underlined that there are five established exceptions that may apply. These concern evidence of previous convictions; evidence of bias or prejudice; evidence of physical or mental disability affecting reliability; evidence of a reputation for untruthfulness; and previous inconsistent statements. Each of these categories is now considered in turn.

Previous convictions

Section 6 of the Criminal Procedure Act 1865 provides that a 'witness may be questioned as to whether he has been convicted of an [offence] and upon being so questioned, if he either denies or does not admit the fact, or refuses to answer, it shall be lawful for the cross-examining party to prove such conviction'.

Prior to the Criminal Justice Act 2003, a witness, other than the defendant, could be asked about his previous convictions in accordance with the above provision on the basis that previous convictions were always relevant to the credibility of the witness. However, previous convictions will now fall clearly within the definition of 'bad character' in section 98 of the 2003 Act. Thus, to cross-examine a non-defendant witness, the requirements of section 100 must be met.[580] In the case of the accused, the evidence must be admitted under one of the eight gateways set out in section 101.[581] Where such evidence is admitted, it will fall outside the scope of the finality rule, even if counsel has introduced the evidence solely to attack the credibility of the witness.

The Rehabilitation of Offenders Act 1974 does not apply to criminal trials, but in practice it is exceedingly rare for advocates to challenge the credibility of a witness through adducing evidence of spent convictions. *Practice Direction (Criminal Proceedings: Consolidation)*[582] recommends that judges and advocates avoid making reference to spent convictions insofar as it is possible. In the case of non-defendant witnesses, section 100(3) of the 2003 Act additionally requires that the trial judge have regard to a number of factors, including the relevant timeframe. Similarly, section 108 lays down a general principle that convictions obtained whilst the defendant was a juvenile are not normally relevant (and neither would they be relevant for a non-defendant witness). In the vast majority of cases, convictions obtained by any witness as a child, or those spent convictions under the Rehabilitation Act 1974 are likely to be seen as being so marginal as to be excluded, as appropriate, under either section 100 or section 101 of the Criminal Justice Act 2003.

---

[579] *R v Somers* [1999] Crim LR 744.
[580] See below, pp 142–45.
[581] See below, Ch 6.
[582] [2002] 1 WLR 2870.

Bias or partiality

A witness may be questioned about matters that suggest bias or partiality and, if denied, the necessary facts may be proved in rebuttal. Such bias or partiality, though collateral in the sense that it goes to credibility, can also impact upon the material issues in the sense that it may tend to suggest that evidence was manufactured, or that there is no case to answer. In *R v Mendy*,[583] the husband of the accused, who was to be called as a witness for her, was waiting to give evidence outside the courtroom. He was seen talking to a man who had been in court taking notes. The implication was that, knowing what evidence had been given, he could tailor his testimony to assist his wife's defence. Under cross-examination he denied this, and the prosecution were allowed to bring evidence to rebut his denial. The Court of Appeal held that the rule of finality was not absolute and should not prevent the jury hearing evidence that suggested an attempt to pervert the course of justice. Similarly, in *R v Phillips*,[584] the defendant was charged with incest and the defence wanted to pursue a line of questioning which suggested that his two daughters, the alleged victims, had admitted to others that the allegations against their father were untrue. The children denied having made these statements, and the judge refused leave to allow the defence to bring evidence in rebuttal. However, here the Court of Appeal held that the judge was wrong to do so; the questions and the evidence went to the heart of the issue in the case and were not collateral.

More recent cases involving police evidence have given a new twist to this line of authority. In *R v Busby*,[585] it was alleged that police officers had threatened a defence witness in order to prevent him giving evidence. This allegation was denied by the officers. The court, however, found that this was not a collateral matter, but went to the material issues since, if true, it would show an attempt to influence the outcome of the trial. Referring to *Mendy* and *Phillips*, the Court of Appeal held that the evidence in rebuttal of the denial was clearly admissible. At the time it was reported, there was some suggestion that this case was something of a novel departure from precedent, but it is now broadly accepted that it is in line with the earlier cases, being concerned simply with a different way of seeking to pervert the course of justice.

However, the decision in *R v Edwards*[586] sits less comfortably with earlier authorities. Here, defence counsel alleged a confession had been fabricated, and wished to cross-examine the police officers about evidence they had given in previous cases which was, allegedly, tainted. The juries in these earlier cases had returned verdicts of not guilty, which tended to imply that the police officers had fabricated parts of their evidence. The Court of Appeal found that, since it could be demonstrated that the jury had disbelieved the evidence of the officers in a previous trial, the jury in the present case was entitled to be made aware of this fact. The officers could therefore be asked about their evidence in these earlier trials. Somewhat surprisingly, the Court then proceeded to state that in the event of the officers giving answers that were unfavourable to the defence, the finality rule would apply and the defence would not be able to call evidence in rebuttal. This appears to contradict the Court's contention that the jury should be aware of facts which suggest that the officer is not the truthful witness he purports to be. There may be evidence to suggest that the police officer is dishonest, but we must rely on the honesty of the officer to ensure that the jury become aware of that evidence. Of course, a police officer will rarely deny

[583](1976) 64 Cr App R 4.
[584](1936) 26 Cr App R 17.
[585](1982) 75 Cr App R 79.
[586][1991] 1 WLR 207.

facts that are in the public domain, or answer falsely and expose himself to a charge of perjury. Nonetheless, it seems strange that on the rare occasion when this might happen, the defence will be unable to expose the truth unless counsel is able to bring it within one of the other exceptions to the finality rule.

The *Edwards* case concerned the activities of the West Midland Serious Crime Squad in the 1980s. In the latter part of the decade it became apparent that some officers had either manufactured confessions or used threats of violence to obtain them. The police and prosecution feared that the opening up of the role of the police officers in other trials would lead to an overall loss of credibility and unjust acquittals. Where an officer's background is open to an attack on his credibility, the prosecutor's natural reaction is, where possible, not to call that officer as a witness. In these circumstances, the proper course would be to call the witness and ask at the outset of the examination-in-chief whether he had been suspended or subject to other disciplinary action, otherwise the court would assume he is a serving officer.

Furthermore, the officer should be required to give evidence in accordance with his statement and not merely tendered for cross-examination, which is the practice when more than one officer is to give the same evidence. In *R v Haringey Justices, ex p DPP*,[587] Stuart-Smith L J held that a witness's credibility should be determined in relation to the content of his evidence and not in relation to his credit generally. This was the correct position unless counsel argued that the evidence might be untrue because the witness had previously been found guilty of perjury, perverting the course of justice, or for some other verifiable reason. Some purely collateral act of dishonesty, whether proved or merely suspected, did not mean that a witness's evidence on a wholly unrelated matter was not credible. Such a view may well appear rational in theory, but in practice prosecution and defence counsel will seek to expose a witness's bad character and any previous convictions with a view to suggesting to the jury that he is not worthy of belief. Convictions for dishonesty are used to suggest that a person who is dishonest in one respect is probably dishonest in another respect. Other convictions will be used to suggest that the witness is of poor moral character and for that reason less worthy of belief. As noted below, the adduction of bad character evidence of non-defendant witnesses is now subject to the enhanced relevance test set out in section 100 of the 2003 Act. If counsel believes that this test will be satisfied in relation to a particular witness, he or she might put the character of that witness before the jury themselves, rather than allowing the other side to expose it, which might suggest an attempt to hide it from the jury and deceive them.

In *R v Edwards (Maxine)*,[588] the Stoke Newington Drugs Squad, (whose members had been the subject of an inquiry into planting of evidence and perjury known as Operation Jackpot), arrested Edwards on suspicion of possessing crack cocaine with intent to supply. The police alleged that when they searched her they discovered eight foil wraps, later found to contain crack cocaine, and £175 cash. They said that she had admitted that the wraps contained cocaine while in the car on the way to the police station. She refused to sign a note of this admission and at her trial said she had never been in possession of the foil wraps. The police, she alleged, had found them in a parked car that she was standing beside. She was convicted and her initial application for leave to appeal was refused. However, following the inquiry into the Drug Squad's activities, and the acquittal of a number of persons arrested and charged by the Squad, the Home Secretary referred the case back to the Court of Appeal.

---

[587] [1996] QB 351.
[588] [1996] 2 Cr App R 345.

Allowing the appeal, the Court held that the appellant was one of a number of persons convicted on very similar evidence from officers of the Stoke Newington Drug Squad and who had complained that the evidence was fabricated. Despite the fact that no charges or disciplinary proceedings had been brought against the officers who had arrested the appellant, the conviction was still regarded as unsafe:

> Once the suspicion of perjury starts to infect the evidence and permeate cases in which the witnesses have been involved, and which are closely similar, the evidence on which such convictions are based becomes as questionable as it was in the cases in which the appeals have already been allowed. It is impossible to be confident that had the jury which convicted this appellant known the facts and circumstances in the other cases in which [the witness] had been involved, that they would have been bound to convict this appellant.[589]

The above test was applied in *R v Whelan*,[590] where the accused had been convicted of possessing cannabis. The arresting officers in the case were arrested and suspended from duty after an investigation into their conduct in other cases of alleged possession of drugs. This had led the prosecution to offer no evidence in other cases in which the arrested officers were involved. On appeal, the prosecution conceded that they had known at the time of trial that the officers were under investigation. However, it was contended that they had not actively relied upon their evidence. The Court of Appeal allowed the appeal and held that the prosecution were right to make the concession.

As a final point in relation to the bias exception, it should be added that its scope is likely to be considerably narrower than has previously been the case following the enactment of the Criminal Justice Act 2003. This is because the type of evidence traditionally encapsulated under this head, particularly regarding allegations of corruption within the police, is likely to fall within the ambit of section 98 of the Act. As such, this evidence will only be admissible if the requirements of section 100 (in the case of non-defendants) or section 101 (in the case of defendants) are satisfied. The bias exception at common law is therefore only likely to come into play where the conduct in question falls short of the commission of a criminal offence or 'other reprehensible behaviour' as defined by the 2003 Act.

Evidence of physical or mental disability affecting reliability

Almost all witnesses who give identification evidence will be cross-examined about their eyesight and whether they wear glasses. American trial dramas are replete with examples of the trial lawyer testing the eyesight of a witness in court and dramatically showing that he or she is unable to see how many fingers are being held up. The effect is to totally destroy the credibility of the witness. While such theatrics are seldom seen in English courts, the effect of proving that the witness, who claims to have positively identified the accused from a distance of 20 metres, has defective vision and cannot see clearly beyond five metres, is the same. Such an example was given in the leading case on this area of law, *Toohey v The Metropolitan Police Commissioner*.[591] Here, the accused was convicted of assault with intent to rob. The defence was that the alleged victim had been drinking and, while the accused and his friends were trying to help him by taking him home, he became hysterical and accused them of attempting to rob him. The trial judge allowed evidence from a doctor that the victim had been drinking and appeared agitated when examined, but refused to

---

[589]*Ibid.*, per Beldam LJ, at 350.
[590][1997] Crim LR 353.
[591][1965] AC 595.

allow the witness to state his opinion that the drink exacerbated the hysteria, and that the victim was more prone to hysteria than the average person. The House of Lords allowed the appeal, and held that the doctor should have been allowed to give his opinion on these matters.[592] Such evidence was admissible to show that the witness was unreliable, irrespective of whether it affected his credibility:

> Medical evidence is admissible to show that the witness suffers from some disease or defect or abnormality of mind that affects the reliability of his evidence. Such evidence is not confined to a general opinion of the unreliability of the witness but may give all matters necessary to show, not only the foundation of and the reasons for the diagnosis, but also the extent to which the credibility of the witness is affected.[593]

The opposing party may call expert evidence in rebuttal, but such evidence should be confined to the issues raised by the medical evidence and should not usurp the role of the jury in determining whether the particular witness is credible:

> Human evidence … is subject to many cross-currents such as partiality, prejudice, self-interest and above all, imagination and accuracy. These are matters with which the jury, helped by cross-examination and common sense, must do their best. But when a witness through physical (in which I include mental) disease or abnormality is not capable of giving a true or reliable account to the jury, it must surely be allowable for medical science to reveal this vital hidden fact to them.[594]

The point is further illustrated by the decision of May J in *R v Mackenney*,[595] where a psychologist was refused permission to testify that the witness was a psychopath who was likely to be lying. A distinction was drawn between the witness who suffers from a mental disability that makes him incapable of giving evidence, and the witness who is capable of giving reliable evidence but may not be doing so. The jury may need help with the former, but it is for them, assisted by cross-examination and common sense, to determine whether a witness who is *capable* of giving reliable evidence is, in fact, doing so.

Evidence of a reputation for untruthfulness

It has long been the case that a witness may give evidence that another witness, called by the opposing party, has a reputation for untruthfulness and should not be believed on his oath. This rule was restated in *R v Richardson* in the following terms:[596]

1. A witness may be asked whether he has knowledge of the impugned witness's general reputation for veracity and whether (from such knowledge) he would believe the witness's sworn testimony.

2. The witness called to impeach the credibility of another witness may also express his individual opinion (based upon his personal knowledge) as to whether the latter is to be believed on his oath, and is not confined to giving an opinion based merely on general reputation.

3. But whether his opinion as to the impugned witness's credibility be based simply upon the latter's general reputation for veracity or upon his personal knowledge, the

---

[592] See further Ch 10.
[593] per Pearce LJ, at 609.
[594] *Ibid.*, at 608.
[595] (1981) 72 Cr App R 78.
[596] [1969] 1 QB 299.

witness cannot be permitted to indicate during his examination-in-chief the particular facts, circumstances or incidents that formed the basis of his opinion, although he may be cross-examined as to them.[597]

Although such evidence is likely to constitute hearsay, section 118(1) of the Criminal Justice Act 2003 preserves this common law exception to the rule.[598] While the law of evidence should rightfully formulate rules to protect the integrity of the criminal trial, the danger with evidence concerning poor reputations is that such disparaging charges may be entirely unearned and nothing more than the product of malicious gossip. As we shall see in Chapter 10, the general rule in relation to opinion evidence is that witnesses give evidence of facts, and only experts are permitted to express opinions to the courts. If the witness is not allowed to give evidence of particular facts on which his opinion is based, how are the jury to determine what weight to attach to such an opinion? If a witness is called for this purpose, it is open to the other side to call witnesses as to that witness's reputation and so on, thus unnecessarily prolonging trial.[599] Although, in practice, this particular exception to the finality rule is exercised infrequently, any evidence that is adduced to this end may also have to meet the test laid down in section 100 of the 2003 Act if the alleged degree of 'untruthfulness' should cross the threshold of 'misconduct' under section 98.

Previous inconsistent statements

On occasions, the cross-examiner will aim to discredit a witness by revealing to the jury that he or she made a previous oral or written statement that is inconsistent with his or her testimony. If the witness denies having made such a statement, the finality rule will not apply and section 4 of the Criminal Procedure Act 1865 allows counsel to adduce that statement in rebuttal. The provision refers to statements which 'are relative to the subject matter of the indictment or proceedings', and whether the statement is or is not 'relative' (i.e. relevant) is a matter for the trial judge. Under section 5 of the 1865 Act, where counsel intends to use contents of a written statement to contradict the witness, the document must be shown to the witness, and his or her attention must be drawn to the contradictory aspects. The witness should be requested to read those parts and then asked whether he or she still wishes to stand by what was said in court. If the witness accepts the contents of the statement, the document then becomes part of the evidence, replacing any earlier testimony. If the witness sticks to the oral testimony given in court, the cross-examiner may wish to use the document to contradict what the witness said. If so, counsel must prove the document and put it in evidence. The court and jury may then inspect the whole document, though the trial judge may direct that the jury see only those parts referred to in cross-examination.[600]

When a previous inconsistent statement was adduced into evidence in these circumstances, it was not evidence of the truth of its contents but went only to the consistency and credit of the witness. The judge had to make this clear to the jury. However, following a recommendation by the Law Commission,[601] that rule has now been changed by section 119(1) of the Criminal Justice Act 2003. Under this provision, any previous inconsistent statement is now regarded as evidence of any matter stated therein, of which

---

[597] *Ibid.*, per Edmund-Davies LJ at 304–5.
[598] See Ch 7, p 231.
[599] See e.g. *R v Bogie* [1992] Crim LR 302.
[600] *R v Beattie* (1989) 89 Cr App R 302.
[601] Law Commission, *Hearsay and Related Topics*, Law Comm No 245 (1997: London, HMSO), [10.92].

oral evidence by that person would be admissible. Section 119(2) makes a similar provision when a previous inconsistent statement is admitted to attack the credibility of a witness who does not give oral evidence but whose statement is admitted under one of the exceptions to the hearsay rule created or preserved by the 2003 Act.[602]

Character attacks on non-defendant witnesses

Since the enactment of the Criminal Justice Act 2003, evidence adduced under any of the exceptions to the finality rule that tends to attack the credibility of the witness will also have to pass the test laid down in section 100 of the legislation. In recognition of increased concern about the plight of victims and other vulnerable witnesses at court, section 100 was introduced with the aim of preventing counsel from making unfounded or irrelevant allegations of misconduct against non-defendant witnesses.

Under the new scheme, permission must be sought from the court where counsel wishes to adduce evidence of the bad character of a non-defendant.[603] As we shall see in Chapter 6, 'bad character' is defined by section 98 of the 2003 Act as 'evidence of, or a disposition towards, misconduct on his part, other than evidence which has to do with the alleged facts of the offence with which the defendant is charged, or ... evidence of misconduct in connection with the investigation or prosecution of the offence'. Under section 112, it is clear that 'misconduct' is intended to be defined broadly and to cover evidence that shows that a person has committed an offence, or has acted in a reprehensible way (or is disposed to do so), as well as evidence from which this might be inferred. This might include previous convictions, as well as evidence on charges being tried concurrently and evidence relating to offences for which a person has been charged, where the charge is not prosecuted, or for which the person was subsequently acquitted.[604]

The court may only grant leave for such evidence to be adduced if one of three circumstances applies:

(a) it is important explanatory evidence,

(b) it has substantial probative value in relation to a matter which—

    (i) is a matter in issue in the proceedings, and

    (ii) is of substantial importance in the context of the case as a whole,

or

(c) all parties to the proceedings agree to the evidence being admissible.

Important explanatory evidence

The term 'explanatory evidence' is used to describe evidence that, while not going to the question of whether the defendant is guilty, is necessary for the jury to have a proper

---

[602]See Ch 7, pp 239–40.

[603]Criminal Justice Act 2003, section 100(4).

[604]In *R v Hall-Chung* (2007) EWCA Crim 3429, the Court of Appeal held that evidence that a witness had taken an overdose did not amount to evidence of bad character under section 98, and thus the witness could be cross-examined about the matter without counsel having to apply for leave under section 100. This is the only reported case at the time of writing, but as the definitions contained in sections 98 and 112 apply to both defendants and non-defendants, the case law that has developed under section 101 is also relevant for the purposes of section 100. See discussion in Ch 6, pp 173–76.

understanding of other evidence being given in the case by putting it in its proper context. The concept is explored in greater depth in Chapter 6,[605] but for the purposes of this chapter it is sufficient to note that such evidence can only be admitted where, without it, the magistrates or jury would find it impossible or difficult to understand other evidence in the case.[606] If, therefore, the facts or account to which the bad character relates are largely understandable without this additional explanation, the evidence will not be admitted. The explanation must also give the court some substantial assistance in understanding the case as a whole. In other words, it will not be enough for the evidence to assist the court to understand some trivial piece of evidence. An example is provided by the case of *R v M (T)*.[607] Here, the Court of Appeal held that where daughters and sons had been raped and buggered by their father, and the sons were obliged to watch him abuse his daughters and later to abuse them themselves, evidence of 'introductory incidents' was correctly admitted as essential background or 'explanatory evidence'. This included evidence that the accused son was obliged to watch the abuse of his sisters by his father and that, when aged 16, he had gone on seriously to abuse his 10-year-old sister. The court said that such evidence was admissible not as evidence of propensity going to guilt, but as necessary background to enable the jury to understand what would otherwise be an incomplete and incomprehensible account. Similarly, in *R v Sawoniuk*,[608] where the defendant was charged with war crimes in Belorussia during the Second World War, evidence of his role as a police officer under the occupying Germans was admitted as explanatory evidence.

Substantial probative value...

Evidence is of probative value, or relevant, to a matter in issue where it helps to prove that issue one way or the other. In respect of non-defendants, such evidence is most likely to be relevant where a question is raised about the credibility of the victim or witness as this is likely to affect the court's assessment of the issue on which the witness is giving evidence. It might also cover attempts by the defence to engage in so-called 'victim-blaming' tactics, which are particularly well-documented in cases involving rape and domestic violence.[609] In order for such evidence to be admitted, it must satisfy the 'enhanced relevance' test set out in section 100(1)(b). This basically means that the evidence must be of substantial probative value and the matter to which it relates must be of substantial importance in the context of the case. Thus evidence that goes only to a trivial or minor issue in the case will be inadmissible.

Section 100(3) directs the court to take into account a number of factors when assessing the probative value of evidence of a non-defendant's bad character. These include the nature and number of the events to which it relates and when those events occurred. When considering evidence that is probative because of its similarity with evidence in the case (e.g. where the defence suggests that another person was more likely to have committed the offence), the court should take into account the nature and extent of the similarities and dissimilarities.[610] Similarly, where the evidence is being tendered to suggest a particular

---

[605]See Ch 6, pp 180–81.
[606]Criminal Justice Act 2003, section 100(2).
[607][2000] 1 WLR 421.
[608][2000] 2 Cr App R 220.
[609]See e.g. Adler, Z *Rape on Trial* (1987: London, Kegan Paul); Abrahms, D, Viky, G, Masser, B and Gerd, B 'Perceptions of stranger and acquaintance rape: The role of benevolent and hostile sexism in victim blame and rape proclivity' (2003) 84 *Journal of Personality and Social Psychology* 111.
[610]Criminal Justice Act 2003, section 100(3)(c).

person was responsible, the court must consider the extent to which the evidence shows or tends to show that the same person was responsible on each occasion.[611]

Under the previous law, evidence of the victim's or witness's past would be routinely adduced in order to challenge their credibility as a witness, particularly where the defendant did not himself have any previous convictions. The defence is now required to enunciate precisely how the evidence meets the required threshold as part of the 'enhanced relevance' test. Under this scheme, attacks on the character of a witness must be justified in terms of substantial relevance to credibility. In its 2001 report on character evidence, the Law Commission provided examples of how such a scheme might operate in practice:[612]

> D is charged with theft. W, who was D's employee at the time of the alleged offence, is a witness who will give incriminating evidence which a jury could hardly accept without convicting D. The bad character evidence in question is the fact (not disputed by the prosecution) that, in her previous job, W was dishonest in her expenses claims. D says that the witness is incompetent and therefore mistaken. It is hard to conceive that the evidence would be admissible under our enhanced test.

> Alternatively, D is charged with theft, and wishes to ask W about an allegation that she was dishonest in her previous job. In this example, D's case is that W is lying not incompetent. The fact that in the relatively recent past she has been guilty of dishonesty at the workplace might well surmount the test of enhanced relevance.

> A third variation: D is charged with theft and wishes to ask W about an allegation of dishonesty 10 years previously, or in a non-work context. The court might well take the view that it did not pass the enhanced relevance test (applying section 100(3)(b)).[613]

As the Law Commission proceeded to note, before the 2003 Act, the evidence of the victim's or witness's past might well be put in or allowed in all three of the above scenarios, or at least under the last two. The basis for this was that since there was a general dispute about the reliability of a witness's evidence, any evidence which might reflect on his credibility as a witness should be admitted, especially if the defendant did not have any previous convictions. Under the 'enhanced relevance' test, the court would force the advocate to consider and articulate why it is that the evidence ought to be admitted as satisfying that test. The outcome might be that a witness will be saved a public humiliation for a cause which could not sensibly have been thought to advance the defendant's case. At the very least the defence will be forced to sharpen up the focus of their attack.

The enhanced relevance test would also assist in a case featured on the Channel 4 *Dispatches* programme, *Getting Away with Rape*, which re-enacted a number of actual rape trials. In one particular case, the young complainant was cross-examined about a shoplifting conviction that took place after the alleged rape. The defence was consent. Under the proposed scheme, that conviction should not be adduced since it would not substantially advance the defence case, though it could nonetheless serve to damage the credibility of the complainant.

This distinction between evidence of substantial relevance and that of marginal relevance has not always been made in the past. It is noted below that, in the cross-examination of victims of rape, one reason for the failure of a statutory attempt to limit

---

[611]Criminal Justice Act 2003, section 100(3)(d).

[612]Law Commission, *Evidence of Character in Criminal Proceedings*, Report No 273 (2001: London, HMSO).

[613]*Ibid.*, [9.32].

cross-examination on previous sexual history was the inability (or reluctance) of the judiciary to distinguish between evidence of substantial relevance to the issue, usually consent, and evidence of only marginal relevance.[614] In *R v A (No 2)*,[615] discussed below, the House of Lords held that the exclusion of evidence of marginal relevance to the defence does not necessarily involve a breach of Art 6(2) of the European Convention. Such a decision must turn on the facts of each individual case. Similarly, the exclusion of evidence of marginal relevance to the credibility of a witness will not affect the fairness of the trial.

However, where the 'bad character' in question is regarded as a central issue in the case, section 100 is unlikely to prevent its admissibility. As the Court of Appeal stated in *R v S (Andrew)*,[616] a 'matter in issue' may include not only a disputed fact, but also whether or not a particular witness is telling the truth. Here, the accused was charged with indecent assault. He alleged that the complainant, a prostitute, had informed him that she would accuse him of rape if he did not give her an additional payment on top of the £10 they had agreed upon for sexual services. She denied having made such a demand, but the court held that defence counsel should have been allowed to cross-examine her in relation to previous convictions related to theft and burglary since they showed a propensity to act dishonestly. Such a propensity had substantial probative value in relation to whether the complainant had tried to blackmail the defendant. In *R v Yaxley-Lennon*, one of the conjoined appeals in *R v Weir and others*,[617] the appellant was convicted of assault occasioning actual bodily harm and assault with intent to resist apprehension. He appealed against conviction on two grounds. The first ground was that evidence that a defence witness had been cautioned by the police for the possession of cocaine should have been inadmissible since it went to credibility alone and therefore fell outside the scope of section 100. In the alternative, the appellant argued that even if credibility was encompassed by the provision, the evidence did not pass the test of admissibility since it was not of substantial importance in the context of the case as a whole.

The first ground of appeal was rejected: the Court stated that it was clear that section 100 was capable of applying to matters pertaining solely to the credibility of a witness. However, the Court accepted the appellant's submissions in respect of the second ground of appeal. Accepting that the caution did not relate to an offence of dishonesty nor did it constitute evidence of untruthfulness, the Court also noted that it related to an incident after the events in issue; that the witness, by agreeing to be cautioned, had accepted her guilt; that the witness was frank about her caution in evidence; and that there was no suggestion that she was under the influence of drugs during the incident itself. For these reasons, the evidence should not have been admitted and the jury should have been discharged.[618]

Whilst, overall, the introduction of section 100 seems to offer some degree of additional protection for victims and other non-defendant witnesses, its long-term impact is still difficult to ascertain. The decision in *S* has already provided us with some evidence that the courts may veer towards admissibility where the line between material issues and credibility is blurred, and this may continue to be the predominant approach in cases of sexual and domestic violence where it is commonly alleged that the defendant's behaviour is often precipitated by the victim's conduct.[619]

---

[614]See below, pp 150–51.

[615][2002] 1 AC 45.

[616]See e.g. [2006] 2 Cr App R 31.

[617][2006] 1 WLR 1885.

[618]However, the Court of Appeal declined to quash the conviction having reviewed the evidence as a whole.

[619]See e.g. Fielding, op cit n 566, pp 104–105, where a number of such instances are recorded.

The cross-examination of rape complainants

Despite the enactment of section 100, it is in the inherent nature of all contested criminal cases that witnesses of all descriptions and backgrounds will often find their accounts of events and their character called into question. This section examines the experiences of victims of rape and sexual assault under cross-examination.

In Chapter 2, it was noted how advocates will routinely attempt to exploit the weaknesses in the complainant's evidence, by embarking upon character assassination. During the 1980s and 1990s, research revealed astounding levels of distress caused to complainants by the manner in which questioning was conducted in court.[620] In a small minority of these cases, the complainants' distress was hugely exacerbated where defendants opted to conduct their own defence.[621] While self-representation in cases involving violence against children or child sex abuse was prohibited by the Criminal Justice Act 1988,[622] two high profile cases in the 1990s highlighted the potentially gruelling nature of cross-examinations conducted by the accused in person.[623] In *R v Edwards (Ralston)*,[624] the defendant came to court wearing the same clothes it was alleged he had worn while committing the alleged rape, and proceeded to subject the complainant to a lengthy and deeply intrusive cross-examination about aspects of her private life and their relationship together. In *Brown (Milton)*,[625] the defendant had been convicted of raping two women at knifepoint, and had dispensed with the services of counsel and solicitors at an early stage of the trial. Like Edwards, he subjected the complainants to a lengthy and vicious cross-examination, prompting the trial judge to express alarm that the law permitted such cross-examination to occur in the first place:

> It is a highly regrettable and extremely sad aspect of this case that despite my repeated efforts during the first two days of your trial you insisted on dispensing with the services of highly competent leading and junior counsel and solicitors, the third set you had been allocated at public expense, thereafter subjecting your victims to merciless cross-examination clearly designed to intimidate and humiliate them. In the course of your questioning you made outrageous and repulsive suggestions to both witnesses ... Although I took what steps I could to minimise that ordeal by repeated efforts to prevent repetitious and irrelevant questioning, nevertheless the whole experience must for those women have been horrifying and it is highly regrettable in my view, and a matter of understandable public concern, that the law as it stands permits a situation where an unrepresented defendant in a sexual assault case has a virtually unfettered right to personally question his victim in such needlessly extended and agonising detail for the obvious purpose of intimidation and humiliation.[626]

---

[620]See Ch 2, pp 29–30.

[621]As a general rule, any person charged in criminal proceedings is entitled to conduct his own defence under section 2 Criminal Procedure Act 1865.

[622]S 34A, inserted by Criminal Justice Act 1991, section 55(7).

[623]Where a defendant is unrepresented, the court has an inherent common law power to prevent the process being abused by the defendant, but in *R v Morley* [1988] QB 601 the Court of Appeal held that that power is to be exercised exceedingly sparingly. In consequence, where a defendant was unrepresented, trial judges tended to allow more latitude in cross-examination to avoid providing grounds for a successful appeal on the basis that the defendant was not permitted to defend himself effectively.

[624](1996) *The Times*, 23 August 1996.

[625][1998] 2 Cr App R 364.

[626]*Ibid.*, 368–369.

In refusing leave to appeal, the Court of Appeal approved the decision of the trial judge and offered further guidance to judges in cases involving unrepresented defendants:

> The trial judge is, however, obliged to have regard not only to the need to ensure a fair trial for the defendant but also to the reasonable interests of the other parties to the court process, in particular witnesses, and among witnesses particularly those who are obliged to relive by describing in the witness box an ordeal to which they say they have been subject. It is the clear duty of the trial judge to do everything he can, consistently with giving the defendant a fair trial, to minimise the trauma suffered by other participants. Furthermore, a trial is not fair if a defendant, by choosing to represent himself, gains the advantage he would not have had if represented of abusing the rules in relation to relevance and repetition which apply when witnesses are questioned".[627]

Prompted by the publicity afforded to these cases, and recommendations contained within *Speaking Up for Justice*, the Youth Justice and Criminal Evidence Act 1999 restricted the right of the accused to self-representation. Unrepresented defendants are now not permitted to cross-examine child witnesses at all, nor can they cross-examine adult witness in certain types of cases. Furthermore, a broad discretion has been created to prohibit cross-examination by unrepresented defendants in other circumstances as the judge sees fit. Under section 34 of the Act, no person charged with a sexual offence may cross-examine a witness who is the complainant in that offence.[628] This section also replaces and extends the scope of Section 34A of the Criminal Justice Act 1988, which had originally prohibited self-representation in cases concerning child violence or child sex abuse. Section 35 replaces and extends this provision to cover a much broader range of offences against children.[629]

The discretion contained in section 35 of the Act permits courts to issue directions prohibiting unrepresented defendants from cross-examining complainants in circumstances other than those covered in section 34. Such a direction may be given following the application by the prosecution or of the court's own motion, providing the court is satisfied that the test contained in section 36(2) is satisfied. This stipulates that the court may prohibit the accused from cross-examining any witness where it appears that the quality of evidence given by the witness on cross-examination is (a) likely to be diminished if the cross-examination is conducted by the accused in person, and would be likely to be improved if a direction were given under this section, and (b) that it would not be contrary to the interests of justice to give such a direction. Section 36(3) sets out a list of criteria for the court to take into account in determining this last question. [630] Sections 37 to 40 of the Act deal with practical matters relating to these directions, and include the power of the court to appoint a representative for an accused in these circumstances where he declines to do so himself.[631]

The provisions of the Act contain a number of safeguards for the accused, including the duty imposed on the trial judge under section 39 to give such a warning as he considers necessary to prevent prejudicial inferences being drawn against the accused by the jury in such circumstances. There have nonetheless been suggestions that this provision may

---

[627] *Ibid.*, 371, per Bingham CJ.

[628] Or in relation to any other offence with which that person is charged in the proceedings.

[629] These are extended to include kidnapping, false imprisonment and abduction.

[630] In arriving at its determination, the court should have regard, *inter alia*, to a range of factors set out in section 36(3) (a)–(d), those being: (a) whether the witness has expressed any opinion as to whether or not he or she is content to be cross-examined by the accused in person; (b) the nature of the questions likely to be asked; (c) any behaviour on the part of the accused at any stage of the proceedings, both generally and in relation to the witness; and (d) any relationship between the witness and the accused.

[631] YJCEA 1999, section 38.

contravene Article 6 of the European Convention.[632] However, the case law, most notably the decision of the European Court of Human Rights in *Croissant v Germany* does not seem to support such a view.[633] Here, the Court held that restricting the choice of counsel for the accused did not affect his ability to challenge the evidence against him.

Of course, even where defendants are represented, the questions put to the complainant by counsel may seem just as distressing. While judges must remain impartial, the common law does permit them to exercise a discretion to take over the cross-examination of a particular witness. In *R v Cameron*,[634] a 14-year-old rape complainant broke down after 15 minutes of cross-examination, and refused to answer any more questions put to her by defence counsel. In the absence of the witness the judge discussed the matter with counsel, and asked the defence to provide him with the material and questions that the advocate had intended put to the witness. The judge then told counsel that he would question the witness himself, but would not use questions that were nothing more than mere comments, or would serve no purpose other than to inflame the witness. In the interests of fairness, the judge then told prosecuting counsel that she would have to forgo re-examination. Although the Court of Appeal found the judge was not wrong in principle to take over the questioning, the particular solution adopted here would not ordinarily be appropriate to the situation of an adult witness who, without good excuse, refused to answer questions put in cross-examination.

Previous sexual history evidence

Research has consistently underlined that the most difficult aspect of cross-examination for complainants in rape and sexual assault cases was the elicitation of previous sexual history evidence. On a regular basis, defence counsel would seek to elicit information concerning the previous sexual experiences of the complainant with the accused, as well as with other men. It might be assumed that since questions concerning previous sexual history were not directed to proving a fact in issue, these should be regarded as being collateral, and therefore subject to the finality rule. This, however, is not the case. The common law has traditionally accepted that in crimes of rape, attempted rape and assault with intent to commit rape, acts of intercourse between the victim and the accused were relevant to the issue and could thus be the subject of cross-examination and rebuttal of any denials.[635] The common law also permitted the complainant to be cross-examined about acts of intercourse with men other than the accused, but, because this was a collateral matter, her denial of such acts could not be contradicted by calling evidence of such acts of intercourse.[636] However, the fact that the finality rule applied in this situation did not prevent counsel asking the questions that, regardless of the answer, were designed to cast doubt on the complainant's moral character and her credibility by suggesting that she was a 'loose' woman.

In *R v Bashir and Manzur*,[637] it was held that evidence that the complainant in a case of rape was a prostitute was admissible to contradict a denial, because it went to the issue

---

[632] *The Daily Telegraph*, 21 May 1998, as cited by Ellison, L 'Cross-examination of Rape Complainants' [1998] Crim LR 606, 611. Ellison also notes that the proposal was condemned by the Criminal Bar Association and Bar Council.

[633] (1993) 16 EHRR 135. There would seem to be no absolute right for an accused to access a lawyer of his own choosing. See also *Philis v Greece* (1991) 13 EHRR 741.

[634] (2001) *The Times*, 3 May.

[635] *R v Riley* (1887) 18 QBD 481.

[636] *R v Holmes* (1871) LR 1 CCR 334.

[637] [1969] 1 WLR 1303.

of consent. Similarly, in *R v Krausz*,[638] the accused, charged with rape, alleged that he met the complainant in a pub for the first time and she had agreed to sleep with him. After intercourse she demanded money, and complained of rape after he refused to pay. The Court of Appeal held the judge was wrong to refuse to allow the defence to call evidence of previous similar conduct by the complainant to rebut her denial.

Yet even in the early 1970s, it was questionable whether the fact that a woman was promiscuous was of any relevance to the question whether she consented to intercourse on a particular occasion. The Report of the Heilbron Commission in 1975 recognised that the common law rules proved to be unsatisfactory in a number of ways.[639] The Advisory Group expressed concerned that, in many cases, the complainant's actions and character became the overriding issue at the trial rather than the culpability of the defendant's actions. The common law also failed to reflect society's changing views about sexual morality, and the Group concluded that restrictions on cross-examination were needed in order to prevent questioning which 'does not advance the cause of justice but in effect puts the woman on trial'.[640] In conclusion, the Report recommended that no evidence of the previous sexual history of the complainant with persons other than the accused should be admitted unless (i) the judge is satisfied that the evidence relates to behaviour on the part of the complainant which was strikingly similar to her alleged behaviour on the occasion of, or in relation to, events immediately preceding the alleged offence; and (ii) the degree of relevance of that evidence to issues arising in the trial is such that it would be unfair to the accused to exclude it.

Section 2 of the Sexual Offences (Amendment) Act 1976 placed restrictions on the cross-examination of a complainant in cases of rape and other sexual offences, but not in the way the Heilbron Report recommended. The new statutory test under section 2(2) of the 1976 Act was whether 'it would be unfair to that defendant to refuse to allow the evidence to be adduced or the question to be asked'.

The principal problems with section 2 of the 1976 Act were twofold. First, the emphasis on fairness to the accused to the exclusion of any detriment to the complainant, and the failure to require a high degree of relevance to an issue in the trial before the evidence could be admitted, allowed evidence of past sexual history to be adduced or question(s) to be asked about such history. Ultimately, the decision whether or not to grant leave to allow the defence to cross-examine the witness about previous sexual history was a matter for the trial judge. The Court of Appeal made clear in *R v Viola*[641] that this was not a matter of judicial discretion. The judge had to determine, first, whether the evidence was relevant to the issue of consent, then whether or not it would be unfair to the accused to disallow such questioning. The second problem was the failure of the provision to control cross-examination about previous sexual history between the accused and the complainant, since the section applied only to 'persons other than the defendant'. Given that a majority of alleged rapes involve an acquaintance, and many of these involve previous acts of intercourse between the parties, the section failed to make any impact in relation to sexual history evidence in the vast majority of cases.

Any prospect that the new provision might herald the end of complainants being questioned about their previous sexual history quickly disappeared as section 2 was emasculated by the courts. The distinction between questions going to credit and questions

---

[638](1973) 57 Cr App R 466.
[639]Heilbron, R *Report of the Advisory Group on the Law of Rape*, Cmnd 6352 (1975: London, HMSO).
[640]*Ibid.*, p 15.
[641][1982] 3 All ER 73.

going to the issue had effectively disappeared in rape trials. The previous behaviour of the complainant was almost always seen to be relevant to the issue, usually consent, with the result that the finality rule was overridden. By the late 1980s, it had become apparent that the questioning of rape complainants in court had been largely unaffected by the 1976 Act. Research by Zsuzsanna Adler found that an application to admit sexual history evidence was made under section 2 in 40 per cent of the cases studied, and was admitted in 75 per cent of such applications.[642] The research further suggested that, contrary to the intention behind section 2, such evidence was routinely used with little reference to the concept of relevance. Instead, previous sexual history evidence was used to discredit her character in the eyes of the jury. A more recent study by Lees confirmed these findings: over half of all female acquaintances of rape complainants had been cross-examined about their sexual history with men other than the defendant.[643]

Reform: the Youth Justice and Criminal Evidence Act 1999

In 1998, *Speaking Up for Justice* paved the way for a major overhaul of the law regulating sexual history evidence. The subsequent Youth Justice and Criminal Evidence Act 1999 repealed section 2 of the 1976 legislation. The new provision, contained in section 41 of the 1999 Act, is not the easiest to interpret, but it basically prescribes a blanket rule prohibiting the admissibility of any evidence concerning the previous 'sexual behaviour' of the complainant in any trials involving a sexual offence.[644] This rule is, however, subject to four somewhat narrow exceptions in subsections (3) and (5). Before considering these provisions in detail, it is worth considering what precisely is meant by the term 'sexual behaviour'.

This issue has confronted the Court of Appeal on a surprisingly frequent basis in the short time the provision has been in force. The leading case is that of *R v T; R v H*.[645] In two separate cases T was charged with rape on his niece, and H with indecent assault on his stepdaughter. The trial judge had refused to allow cross-examination directed by the defence to one of the complainants alleging past fabrication of such an assault, and the other complainant's failure to mention the alleged assault when complaining of other such assaults. In T's case it was submitted that the proposed questions were about the failure to mention the allegations and not about 'sexual behaviour'. In H's case it was argued that the questions were about lies, albeit about sexual matters.

Adopting a purposive approach in interpreting the statute, the Court noted that the mischief, at which section 41 was aimed, was to prevent evidence of the complainant's sexual behaviour being admitted and presented to the jury with the invitation to infer from it that a person with a colourful sexual history is more likely to tell lies, or to have consented to the sexual intercourse subject of the charge. However, in these circumstances, the questions were clearly relevant to the issues in the trial and did not constitute 'evidence of sexual behaviour' for the purposes of section 42(1)(c). The Court noted that, as in the past, a distinction had to be drawn between questions about sexual behaviour itself, and questions concerning *statements* about such behaviour by the complainant. While it would be profoundly improper to elicit details of a complainant's previous sexual experience under the guise of previous false complaints, this danger could be counteracted by the

---

[642] Adler, op cit n 120.
[643] Lees, S *Carnal Knowledge: Rape on Trial* (1996: London, Hamish Hamilton).
[644] YJCEA 1999, section 41(1).
[645] [2002] 1 WLR 632.

intervention of the trial judge to prevent abuse of questioning where there was not an evidential basis for the defence asserting that a previous statement had been made and that it was untrue. The appeal was thus allowed.

Similar reasoning was adopted in *R v Mukadi*,[646] where the complainant approached a supermarket security officer wearing a short skirt and a vest top. They went to a park where they drank a bottle of wine, before a sexual encounter took place at the defendant's flat. While the complainant admitted oral sex and kissing was consensual, she claimed intercourse was not. In support of his defence that the complainant had consented, the defence attempted to adduce evidence that before the woman had entered the store that day she was standing on the pavement when a large and expensive car drew up, driven by a sole male much older than she. The complainant got in, and they drove to a filling station.

At first instance, the judge refused to admit this evidence since it was not relevant to the issue of consent. The Court of Appeal, however, concluded that he had been wrong to do so since it would have been possible for the jury to infer that when the complainant got into the car, she had anticipated some sexual activity with the occupant. This evidence could serve to rebut her claim that she went to the defendant's flat merely to get to know him with a view to becoming friends. If the jury had heard about the previous incident, that would have been relevant when assessing that part of her evidence.[647] Subsequent decisions have confirmed that false allegations are not 'evidence about sexual behaviour' but refer instead to a general propensity to be untruthful.[648] Providing the defence merely use such evidence to show that a particular statement was likely to be false, section 41 will not prohibit its use in this way.

It now appears to be firmly established that section 41 does not cover those cases where the defence has a proper evidential basis for alleging that the complainant has made an untruthful statement in relation to alleged act. However, even where there is such a basis, the Court of Appeal held in *R v V*[649] that leave must also be obtained under section 100, since allegations of false complaints would constitute evidence of a non-defendant's bad character.

The exceptions to the rule

Providing the conduct in question constitutes 'sexual behaviour', an application must be made to the court to show that the anticipated line of questioning falls within one of the four exceptions of the blanket rule laid down in section 41(1). These will come into play if the evidence is relevant to (a) an issue in the case other than consent; (b) sexual behaviour 'at or about' the time of the incident in question; (c) previous behaviour which is 'so similar ... so that similarity cannot be explained by coincidence'; and (d) the need to rebut prosecution evidence. Each of these heads is now considered below.

---

[646][2004] Crim LR 373.

[647]If this act constituted sexual behaviour, it was admissible under section 41(3)(b) and a refusal of leave under section 41(2)(b) would have had the effect of rendering unsafe a conclusion of the jury on the issue of consent. If it was not sexual behaviour it was not within section 41 and was relevant and admissible. The Court of Appeal took the view that, in the circumstances, C's behaviour shortly before 'picking up' M probably was 'sexual behaviour' coming close to acting as a prostitute picking up clients for sex and was clearly relevant to the issue of whether C consented to intercourse with M.

[648]See also *R v Garaxo* [2005] Crim LR 883; *R v W* [2005] Crim LR 965.

[649][2006] EWCA Crim 1901.

Section 41(3)(a) – an issue other than an issue of consent

Under section 41(3)(a) of the 1999 Act, the court may grant leave if the evidence or
questioning relates to any issue that has to be proved other than an issue as to whether
the complainant consented. Section 42(1)(b) defines 'issue of consent' as meaning any
issue whether the complainant in fact consented to the conduct constituting the offence
with which the accused is charged. Thus, the defendant's *belief* that the complainant was
consenting falls within the scope of section 41(3)(a) as relevant to an issue other than consent.

In *R v Y*,[650] one of the first cases heard under the new provision, the defendant alleged
that the complainant had consented to intercourse or, if not, that he believed that she
had consented. At a preparatory hearing, the judge refused leave for the defence to cross-
examine the complainant about a recent sexual relationship with the accused. This ruling
was challenged by the defendant, and the Court of Appeal took the view that such evidence
was relevant to any *belief* in consent that the defendant may have had. It was thus admissible
pursuant to section 41(3)(a), but could not be used to establish *actual* consent on the part
of the complainant. In the view of the Court, the previous sexual relationship between the
complainant and the accused was clearly relevant to *belief* in consent as a matter of common
sense, although this was restricted to sexual behaviour in the recent past, prior to events
giving rise to the charge. The court did not accept that such an approach stemmed from a
sexist view of women; rather, it was said to reflect human nature:

> The trial process would be unduly distorted if the jury were precluded from knowing, if
> it were the case, that the complainant and the defendant had recently taken part in sexual
> activity with each other and it might be that a fair trial would not be possible if there could not
> be adduced in support of the defence of consent, evidence as to the complainant's previous
> consensual recent sexual activity with the defendant.[651]

One may respectfully disagree with Lord Justice Rose's view of human nature expressed
above, and with a similar view expressed by Lord Steyn on appeal to the House of Lords.[652]
The entire purpose of the restriction on the use of sexual history is to deny the relevance
of the complainant's previous sexual history except in the circumstances indicated in
section 41(3). It may well be necessary for the jury to know of the previous relationship,
but not for the purpose of inferring that, because the complainant consented to intercourse
on previous occasions, she might well have consented on the specific occasion in question.
For example, if a wife complains of rape within marriage, it would be nonsensical to hide
from the jury the fact that the defendant and complainant are married and have engaged
in sexual activity within that marriage.

As in *R v Y*, the fact that the accused had recently had a sexual relationship with the
complainant may give rise to a belief that she will consent to sexual intercourse and may
explain why he approached her in the first place, but the previous relationship will not
by itself provide grounds for a belief that she was consenting to the intercourse that is the
subject of the charge. It is therefore submitted that the sexual behaviour of the complainant
with the defendant can be relevant to support a belief in consent if, and only if, it is
sufficiently proximate to the act of intercourse.

Additional circumstances may make previous sexual activity between the defendant
and the complainant relevant to, and provide reasonable grounds for, belief that the woman

---

[650] (2001) *The Times*, 13 February.
[651] per Rose LJ, [31].
[652] See p 56 below.

was consenting. For example, suppose the defendant and the complainant had consensual sexual intercourse in the past as part of a simulated rape fantasy. As part of this simulation, assume that D pretended to force himself upon C, who pretended to resist through vocal protests and physical resistance. If the alleged rape took place in similar circumstances, the accused might well have believed that she was consenting when in fact she was not. The basis for this belief would be the fact that D had consensual intercourse with C in the past, and that she had displayed a similar reaction in such circumstances. As section 1(2) of the Sexual Offences Act 2003 makes clear, the jury must determine whether the belief was reasonable having regard to all the circumstances, including any steps taken by the defendant to ascertain whether the complainant was consenting. The fact that she was behaving exactly as she had behaved in the past when the intercourse was consensual, is a circumstance providing a reasonable basis for the defendant's belief that she was consenting on this occasion. However, had the previous sexual relationship between D and C not involved simulated rape or any other extraordinary circumstances, that relationship would be unlikely to be relevant to the defence of belief in consent.

There are other scenarios that could arise where the issue is not consent. For example, in *R v Elahee*,[653] a decision was based on section 2 of the 1976 legislation, a 13-year-old girl alleged that she was walking past a takeaway restaurant when the accused, a 43-year-old man, led her into a lobby and raped her. The accused claimed that the complainant had introduced herself and, without invitation on his part, had touched his genital area. He said he had pushed her away and no sexual intercourse took place, the allegations being a complete fabrication. Medical evidence was that the complainant displayed no injury and that her hymen was not intact. She had told the doctor that she had full sexual intercourse some 12 months previously with her boyfriend, but that had been edited out of the doctor's statement and the jury were not made aware of what the complainant had said. Counsel for the accused sought leave under section 2 of the 1976 Act to elicit that evidence from the complainant, arguing that it was relevant to show that, contrary to her outward appearance, the complainant was a person capable of the conduct alleged by the accused. The trial judge refused leave and the accused was convicted.

Somewhat predictably, the appeal was allowed. It was held that the issue in this case was not one of consent, but concern about who had made the first approach. The evidence of the complainant's previous sexual experience was a matter that was relevant to an issue in the trial insofar as it enabled the jury to assess the plausibility of the defendant's account. Disallowing such cross-examination gave rise to the clear risk that the jury would have regarded the medical evidence as confirmation of the complainant's evidence, and thus posed a real danger that the jurors may have taken a different view of the evidence had the statement not been edited. The defendant's conviction was found to be unsafe, and a retrial was ordered.

This is a good example of how section 2 routinely failed to protect the complainant. The doctor's evidence was that the complainant's hymen was already broken. The prosecution, after discussion with the judge, put that information on the record lest the jury assume that the accused was responsible. The defence were not satisfied with that and made application under section 2 to allow the complainant to be questioned about the previous act of intercourse because, without that evidence, the jury might think it unlikely that a 13-year-old would approach and touch a 43-year-old man as alleged. It was also alleged that it would also have been unfair, once the jury had been told that the complainant's

---

[653] [1999] Crim LR 399.

hymen was already broken, for them not to be told the details. This, it was contended, may have led them to speculate about other ways in which it might have been broken.

This is a spurious argument. In truth, the evidence of one act of intercourse with a boyfriend 12 months earlier is of no relevance to the issue of who made the initial advance. It may very well be the case that virgins in their early teens do not generally approach middle-aged men and initiate sexual contact, but then neither do the vast majority of women. Recent studies suggest that many teenagers have some sexual experience, and some have a great deal,[654] but sexual experience in itself does not suggest a tendency to approach middle-aged men in the manner suggested. As for the suggested speculation, given that the jury had been told that the hymen was already broken it would have been clear to them that the accused was not responsible. If they did speculate as to the cause, it would not have been prejudicial or unfair to the accused. Arguably, it would have been better to tell the jury not to speculate, rather than to introduce C's previous sexual history. It is possibly true, as the Court of Appeal suggests, that 'if the jury knew about the complainant's sexual activity on a previous occasion they might take a different view of the case'; but why would they do so? Simply because she was not a virgin? If so, this is precisely the sort of prejudicial reasoning which section 2 of the 1976 Act sought to prevent. Had *Elahee* been heard under the new regime, it is doubtful whether the application of section 41 would have made any difference. Assuming the court viewed the complainant's previous sexual behaviour as relevant to the issue of who made the first approach, then the refusal of leave to allow C to be questioned about the previous act of intercourse might have the result of rendering unsafe a conclusion of the jury on a relevant issue. It follows that the same result would have been reached under section 41 and the supposed reform will have made no difference.

Section 41(3)(b) – sexual behaviour 'at or about' the same time

This provision places a severe constraint on the adduction of evidence or questions about any sexual behaviour. In the first draft of the Bill, it was expressed as 24 hours either side of the offence. The 1999 Act itself adopts the phrase 'at or about the same time', which certainly provides a greater degree of flexibility, but is intended generally to be interpreted no more widely than 24 hours before or after the offence. It would permit evidence such as that in *Viola*, where the complainant was seen to be drinking and flirting with men before the alleged rape, and afterwards a man, naked but for his socks, was seen sleeping on her couch. The obvious inference the court was invited to draw was that she was drunk and looking for sex, and therefore was likely to have consented to the intercourse that took place some little time later. Many would argue that this is the kind of character assassination that, though permitted under the 1976 Act, ought to be prevented. However, it would seem that such questioning would still be permissible under section 41(3)(b) of the 1999 Act.

In *R v A (No 2)*, the House of Lords declined to assign a specific temporal limit to the phrase 'at or about the same time', but were unanimous in holding that a sexual relationship between the defendant and the complainant some three weeks before the alleged rape fell outside the scope of section 41(3)(b). While holding that the test was a flexible one to be

---

[654]See generally Brook, *Teenage Sexual Activity, online report at* http://www.brook.org.uk/contentplain/ Fact1_TeenageSexualActivity.pdf [accessed 24/02/08]; Wellings K, Field J, Johnson AM, *et al. Sexual behaviour in Britain* (1994: London, Penguin); Wellings K, Nanchahal K, Macdowall W, *et al* 'Sexual behaviour in Britain: early heterosexual experience' (2001) 358 *Lancet* 1843–1850; Erens B, McManus S, Field J, *et al, National Survey of Sexual Attitudes and Lifestyles II: Technical Report.* (2001: London, National Centre for Social Research).

determined in the light of the particular circumstances of a case, their Lordships offered confusing guidance. Lord Slynn thought the words should be given a narrow meaning, which would restrict evidence and questions to sexual behaviour of the complainant that was 'really contemporaneous' with the event subject of the charge. By contrast, Lord Steyn thought that the complainant's invitation to the defendant to have sex with her made earlier in the evening would be within the subsection, but he thought the temporal restriction would not extend to days, weeks or months. Lord Hope of Craighead referred to the statutory *Notes of Guidance*, which expected that the phrase should not be interpreted more widely than 24 hours before or after the offence. In the view of Lord Hutton, it was clear that an act one week before the offence was outside the subsection, and Lord Clyde thought it would be difficult to extend the provision to include a period of several days.

Section 41(3)(c) – previous behaviour which is 'so similar ... that the similarity cannot be explained by coincidence'

Until a very late stage in the passage of the Bill that is now the 1999 Act, section 41(3) contained only two exceptions to the blanket rule of exclusion – those outlined in paragraphs (a) and (b). It was feared, however, that to confine the relevant evidence to a 24-hour period either side of the alleged rape would be unfair to the accused. The potential for such an injustice to arise is demonstrated by the facts of *R v Cox*.[655] Here, the complainant alleged that the defendant had raped her while her boyfriend was in police custody. The defence was granted permission to cross-examine her about alleged intercourse she had on a previous occasion with another man, whilst her boyfriend was away. On that occasion, C also complained that she had been raped. The defence contended that she did so, as in the instant case, in order to hide her infidelity. Had the Bill been enacted in its original form, the previous sexual behaviour in this case would fall well outside the period required under section 41(3)(b). In turn, the accused would have been effectively denied the right to adduce relevant evidence to the court.

To this end, it seems that policy-makers took into account the concerns expressed by, among others, Judge Andrew Geddes. Geddes argued that there was little evidence that section 2 of the 1976 Act was not working and that the radical change effected by section 41 was unjustified.[656] He described 'a not uncommon case' in which a former co-habitee of the accused alleges that he came to the house where the complainant lived (often the former matrimonial home) and raped her, whereas the accused claims that the intercourse was consensual. In these circumstances, the defence may often try to allege that, in spite of the fact that the relationship had broken down, the complainant had nonetheless frequently allowed the accused back in the house, and that sexual intercourse had taken place on virtually every occasion with her consent. If the jury are unaware that there has been a long history of the complainant consenting to sexual intercourse with the accused after they had separated, there must be a real danger that they would convict where otherwise they would acquit.

In response to these criticisms, section 41(3)(c) was added to the Bill, which applies when the issue is one of consent. The purpose of the subsection is to allow the defence to cross-examine the complainant about his or her previous sexual behaviour where such conduct is so similar to that in the instant case that the similarity cannot reasonably be explained

---

[655] (1986) 84 Cr App R 132.
[656] Geddes, A 'The exclusion of evidence relating to a complainant's sexual behaviour in sexual offence trials' (1999) 149 NLJ 1084.

as a coincidence. Such a similarity may tend to lend credence to any suggestion defence may make that the complainant was disposed to having consensual sexual intercourse in a particular or distinctive way. For example, in *R v Tahed*,[657] the Court of Appeal quashed a conviction where the complainant had claimed she was raped on a climbing frame in a public park. It was held that the defence had been improperly denied the opportunity to cross-examine her about a similar sexual encounter than took place at the same climbing frame three weeks beforehand.

The leading case on the scope of section 41(3)(c) is now *R v A (No 2)*, which is how the case of *R v Y* was reported when the Director of Public Prosecutions was given leave to take the Court of Appeal's decision to the House of Lords. It will be recalled that the accused wanted to cross-examine the complainant on the sexual relationship that he claimed they had been having up until three weeks prior to the alleged rape. The respondent argued that, in restricting cross-examination on the prior consensual sexual relationship between the complainant and the defendant, section 41 of the 1999 Act effectively denied the defendant the means to present an effective defence. It was contended that the legislation thus contravened the defendant's right to a fair trial under Article 6 of the European Convention on Human Rights. The House of Lords dismissed the Crown's appeal and concurred with the view that the absence of evidential material relevant to the issue of consent could infringe the accused's Article 6 rights.

As Lord Steyn recognised, the crux of the conundrum facing the courts was the fact that section 41 imposed the same exclusionary provisions in respect of the complainant's sexual history with the accused as with other men:

> The statute did not achieve its object of preventing the illegitimate use of prior sexual experience in rape trials. In retrospect one can now see that the structure of this legislation was flawed. In respect of sexual experience between a complainant and other men, which can only in the rarest cases have any relevance, it created too broad an inclusionary discretion. Moreover, it left wholly unregulated questioning or evidence about previous sexual experience between the complainant and the defendant, even if remote in time and context. There was a serious mischief to be corrected.[658]

It might be contended that the logic underpinning Lord Steyn's analysis seems sound. It is arguably more likely that a woman will consent to intercourse with a person whom she knows well and has had a previous sexual relationship with, than to intercourse with a total stranger. Therefore, this type of previous sexual history between the complainant and the defendant will, on some occasions, be relevant to the issue of consent insofar as it might throw light on the complainant's state of mind. By the same token however, Lord Steyn was keen to stress that such evidence would not constitute proof that the complainant consented on the occasion in question: relevance and sufficiency of proof were entirely different matters.

However, the difficulty for the court was that a literal interpretation of the Act would lead to the exclusion of this relevant evidence: none of the relevant exceptions to the blanket rule of exclusion applied. Since this effectively amounted to a violation of the accused's fair trial rights under the European Convention, the House of Lords construed section 41(3)(c) of the Act somewhat creatively, through exercising its interpretive obligation under section 3 of the Human Rights Act 1998. This provision requires courts to interpret legislation in a way that is compatible with Convention rights, insofar as it is possible to do. Thus it was

---

[657][2004] All ER (D) 346.
[658]*Ibid.*, [12].

held that section 41(3)(c) should be read subject to the proviso that the previous sexual history evidence should nonetheless be admitted where it 'is nevertheless so relevant to the issue of consent that to exclude it would endanger the fairness of the trial under Article 6 of the Convention'.[659]

Thus, in future cases where the defence seeks to admit sexual history evidence that falls outside the literal scope of the exceptions contained within section 41, the court must then apply a further test. Essentially, the trial judge must ask whether the evidence should nonetheless be admitted where the evidence was so relevant to the issue of consent that to exclude it could violate the fairness of the trial. In this sense, the House of Lords has effectively made the legislation subject to the common law concept of relevance.

The House of Lords held that, while the statute pursued desirable goals, the methods adopted amounted to legislative overkill. It was realistic to proceed on the basis that the legislature would not, if alerted to the problem, have wished to deny the right to an accused to put forward a full and complete defence by advancing truly probative material, and that was the basis on which section 3 of the Human Rights Act came into play. However, the effect of the decision in *A* was to restore to the trial judge some degree of control over the ambit of cross-examination in relation to previous sexual history evidence. The test of admissibility was whether the evidence, and questioning in relation to it, was nevertheless so relevant to the issue of consent that to exclude it would endanger the fairness of the trial under Article 6. If that test was satisfied, the evidence should not be excluded. Lord Slynn, Lord Hope, Lord Clyde and Lord Hutton delivered speeches concurring in the result.

However, since their Lordships gave little guidance as to when such questions would be relevant and when they might not, problems could arise in future years since the question of relevance is placed back in the hands of trial judges. In effect, the House of Lords has removed a bar on the exercise of discretion imposed by Parliament. While the logic behind the decision in *R v A* seems sound enough on the basis of those particular facts, the door is now left slightly ajar for future interpretations of the legislation which may stretch well beyond what Parliament had originally intended. As Grohovsky remarked, section 41(3)(c) is 'both vague enough and broad enough to permit almost limitless irrelevant and prejudicial evidence'.[660] Although it seems very unlikely that *R v A* could ever be used as a basis on which to admit previous sexual history evidence in respect of third parties, it remains to be seen whether judicial attitudes have changed sufficiently to sustain this approach in the years to come.

Rebutting prosecution evidence – section 41(1)(5)

The other occasion when the judge can give leave for sexual behaviour evidence to be admitted is when the defence wish to dispute evidence that the prosecution has introduced about the complainant's sexual behaviour. This is based on the principle that there should be equality of arms between the parties. Any evidence called in rebuttal must go no further than directly to contradict or explain claims made by or on behalf of the complainant. Thus if the prosecution evidence states or suggests that the complainant was a virgin before the alleged rape, evidence that she previously had had intercourse with another or others could be adduced. However, section 41(6) provides that any evidence or questioning about

---

[659] *Ibid.*, 15, *per* Lord Steyn.
[660] Grohovsky, J 'Giving Voice to Victims: Why the Criminal Justice System in England and Wales Should Allow Victims to Speak Up for Themselves' (2000) *J Crim L* 421.

sexual behaviour must relate to a specific instance, or instances, of such behaviour. Intrusive interrogations concerning the complainant's general lifestyle will not be permitted.

The provision was subject to challenge before the Court of Appeal in *R v Soroya*.[661] The appellant had been convicted of raping the 19-year-old complainant. She had claimed that she had tried to put him off having sex with her by telling him she was a virgin. At trial, the complainant admitted that she had intercourse on one previous occasion with a boyfriend. The defence wish to contest this fact by claiming she was much more sexually experienced, but the judge refused leave for them to adduce any previous sexual history evidence. Section 41(5) could not be relied upon in these particular circumstances since they were unable to adduce any relevant evidence to rebut the claims of the prosecution.

In summing up, the judge highlighted to the jury that the defence was not permitted to ask any questions about sexual history, but indicated that the defence did not accept the complainant's account that she had only had intercourse on one previous occasion. Following his conviction, the appellant contended that section 41 had interfered with the principle of equality of arms and thereby had violated his Convention right to a fair trial. While the prosecution had been allowed to introduce evidence of previous sexual history, the defence had been refused leave. In effect, this meant that section 41 was fundamentally unbalanced in that operated adversely to the defendant.

Dismissing the appeal, the Court held that the object of the legislation was to prevent anyone, prosecution or defence, from asking questions that might cause embarrassment or difficulty to a complainant. In the instant case, the prosecution had not relied, directly or indirectly, on the complainant's previous sexual history. The issue of C's sexual experience had only arisen in the first place, as an integral part of the incident, and to avoid the rape, she had made what was admittedly an untruthful claim that she was a virgin. From the prosecution's point of view it had been important evidence bearing on the issue of consent. No justified complaint could be directed at the admission of that evidence, and, as such, the conviction was safe.

Yet even if the defence had been allowed to introduce evidence it rebuttal under section 41(5), there would still be an arguable case that the additional hurdles placed in their path could interfere with the principle of equality of arms. As David Ormerod states in his note on the case:

> Even where the defence are able to rebut the evidence of the Crown, it might still be argued that section 41(5) does not provide a complete solution because the defence are not as free to adduce rebuttal evidence as the Crown are to lead it. First, the prosecution are not subject to the notice requirements as are the defence. Second, the defence must satisfy the judge as to the requirements of section 41(5) and 41(2). Third, the defence must point to specific allegations within section 41(6). The defence position under section 41(5) is clearly restricted even though such rebuttal is not hedged in by section 41(4) and the defence may be allowed to impugn the complainant's credibility ... Bearing in mind the restrictions on the defence, is the potential inequality compatible with the Strasbourg jurisprudence recognising that some measures are necessary in sexual cases to protect the private life of the complainant and that equality of arms demands only that a party is not placed at a substantial disadvantage vis-à-vis the opposing party?[662]

No doubt the courts will be confronted again with this issue in the not too distant future.

---

[661] [2007] Crim LR 181.
[662] Ormerod, D 'Case Comment: Sexual History Evidence' [2007] Crim LR 181.

The additional protection: section 41(4)

Section 41(4) also provides a further safeguard for the complainant in providing that evidence will not be regarded as relating to a relevant issue in the case 'if it appears to the court to be reasonable to assume that the purpose … for which it would be adduced or asked is to establish or elicit material for impugning the credibility of the complainant as a witness'. The judge must also be satisfied under section 41(2) 'that a refusal of leave might have the result of rendering unsafe a conclusion of the jury … on any relevant issue in the case'. This is an improvement on the test under the 1976 Act and the interpretation of that test in *R v Lawrence*,[663] where May J stated that questioning about the complainant's relationships with other men should only be allowed when the jury might tend to take a different view had the evidence been adduced or the questions asked. The problem with this stipulation was that juries, on hearing about the complainant's sexual history, often would take a different view based on bias or prejudice resulting from the debasement of the complainant's character.

In respect of section 41, the question whether the conclusion of a jury might be unsafe is inevitably based on guesswork, given that we cannot ask the jury why they came to a particular conclusion. However, the judgment as to whether a conclusion of the jury might be unsafe if the evidence is not adduced or the questions not asked, will again be based on the relevance of the evidence or question to the relevant issue(s) in the case. The difficulty is that once again there is no requirement of a substantial degree of relevance to the issue. The phrase in section 41(2)(b), 'the refusal of leave *might* have the result', suggests a low degree of relevance, allowing sexual history evidence more readily than if the section said 'refusal of leave *would* have the result'.

However, section 41(4) attempts to restore the distinction between credit and the issue, in providing that:

> [N]o evidence or question shall be regarded as relating to a relevant issue in the case if it appears to the court to be reasonable to assume that the purpose (or main purpose) for which it would be adduced or asked is to establish or elicit material for impugning the credibility of the complainant as a witness.

Much will depend on whether the courts are prepared to accept this distinction. The fact that the evidence may be of marginal relevance, but nonetheless may be very damaging to the complainant makes it reasonable to assume that the purpose (or main purpose) is to impugn credibility, rather than assist in proving or disproving the relevant issue. On the other hand, if the evidence is highly relevant and highly prejudicial, it cannot be reasonable to assume that the purpose (or main purpose) of adducing the evidence is to impugn credibility, though that is an inevitable consequence of allowing the evidence to be adduced.

In *R v Martin (Durwayne)*,[664] the Court of Appeal emphasised the distinction between the *main* purpose of adducing the evidence and *one* of the purposes. The defendant alleged that the complainant had pestered him for sex and that it was his rejection of her advances which led to her making a false allegation against him. The trial judge refused to permit cross-examination of the complainant as to the alleged sexual acts on the basis that the main purpose of the cross-examination was to impugn the credibility of the complainant. The Court of Appeal took the view that the judge's ruling was wrong. Although one

---

[663][1977] Crim LR 492.
[664][2004] 2 Cr App R 22.

purpose of the proposed questions was to impugn the credibility of C, this was not the main purpose. The primary reason why the defence had sought to adduce the evidence was to strengthen their case, not to impugn the credibility of the complainant. Accordingly the judge's ruling was wrong.[665] This briefly reported case suggests that section 41(4) may not provide the intended safeguard against attempts by defence counsel to blacken the complainant's character.

Section 41: procedure and practice

It may be useful briefly to note the procedure that is used where a party wishes to apply to the court to admit evidence under section 41. Section 43 provides that any application will be heard in the absence of the jury, any witnesses (other than the defendant), the public and the press. Rules of court will require the applicant to specify, in relation to each item of evidence or question to which they relate, particulars of the grounds on which it is asserted that leave should be granted. The court will be able to require from the parties to the proceedings any information it considers will assist in making the decision whether or not to grant leave. Reasons for giving or refusing leave must be stated in open court (but in the absence of the jury), and if leave is granted the court must indicate the extent to which evidence may be adduced or questions asked in pursuance of the leave. This will give the trial judge more time to consider the application (under the previous law such applications were made orally during the course of trial) and will require a reasoned argument, in writing from the defence, to which counsel for the prosecution can respond. It may also put an end to the improper practice of asking questions about the complainant's sexual behaviour that should not be asked, unless and until leave has been given. As noted above, research conducted in relation to the old law suggested that questions about the complainant's previous sexual history were asked without application to the trial judge either because judge and counsel were unaware of the requirement for leave, or perhaps deliberately to avoid the restriction on such questions. The fact that there is new law and new procedures in place should ensure that counsel in rape trials are aware of the restrictions on questions about the complainant's sexual behaviour, and of the need to support any application for leave with reasoned argument.

However, despite this safeguard, recently published empirical research suggests that the new legislation is not operating as well as might be expected. Indeed, sexual history evidence is still being used by defence counsel on a routine basis. In a recent study by Kelly *et al.*,[666] applications to admit sexual history evidence were made in a third of all rape trials, and two-thirds of these were successful. Moreover, interviews with 17 judges revealed that many had very little knowledge of the legislation prohibiting or allowing the use of sexual history evidence. This explains another disconcerting finding, namely that counsel frequently conducted cross-examinations about the complainant's sexual history without seeking permission from the judge at all. In three-quarters of these cases, the judge failed to intervene to prevent such questioning.

It therefore seems that some elements of the judiciary are reluctant to enforce the new rules as Parliament intended. Kibble has observed how judges he interviewed 'were highly

---

[665]However, the Court of Appeal declined to overturn the conviction on the grounds that the defendant did not give evidence and the judge would have directed the jury that the question, if allowed, did not result in any evidence on which the jury could act.
[666]Kelly, L, Lovett, J and Regan, L *A Gap or Chasm? Attrition in Reported Rape Cases*, Home Office Research Study No 293 (2005: London, Home Office).

sceptical of the argument that sexual history evidence was overwhelmingly prejudicial and should therefore generally be excluded'.[667] The legislation was described by judges as 'an impenetrable maze', 'a dog's breakfast' and a 'nightmare'.[668] As a result, irrelevant evidence relating to previous sexual behaviour was still commonly used in rape trials. This suggests that even if Parliament had succeeded in formulating a perfectly balanced rule on paper that did not give rise to need to 'read down' the legislation, the ultimate success of such a provision could be severely hampered by attitudinal resistance on the part of the judiciary. Regrettably, it seems that some judicial attitudes continue to undermine efforts to protect effectively rape complainants in court.

KEY LEARNING POINTS

- Before giving evidence, all witnesses may refresh their memories from statements or other documents made reasonably close to the events about which they are to give evidence.

- Whilst giving evidence, section 139 CJA 2003 creates a presumption that a witness in criminal proceedings may refresh his or her memory from a document subject to certain conditions.

- A witness might not seek to bolster his evidence by reference to a previous consistent statement, except in one of the circumstances provided for in section 120 CJA 2003.

- Counsel can only ask leading questions in cross-examination or where the court determines that the witness is hostile.

- The finality rule dictates that a witness's answer to a collateral question is final, unless one of the exceptions of the rule applies.

- Section 100 CJA 2003 aims to protect all non-defendant witnesses from character attacks.

- Evidence of a complainant's previous sexual history is not generally admissible unless one of the four exceptions in section 41 YJCEA applies or the judge feels it ought to be admitted to ensure a fair trial.

?   *QUESTIONS*

1. Dan is charged with robbery. It is alleged that he snatched a handbag belonging to Martha, after knocking her to the ground. You are asked to address a number of questions in respect of the following witnesses who will testify at trial:
   (a) Martha, aged 62, is the alleged victim. She identified Dan as the assailant, and told police that he lives in her tenement block. Police are aware that there has been an ongoing feud between Martha's family and Dan's family for some years. In particular, Martha has made some twenty complaints to the police and the local council about noise emanating

Continued

---

[667] Kibble, N *Judicial Perspectives on Section 41 of the Youth Justice and Criminal Evidence Act 1999* (2004: London, Criminal Bar Association).
[668] *Ibid.*

from the flat occupied by Dan, and has told the police that it was 'time he was locked up once and for all'.

Can the defence cross-examine Martha about this animosity and bring evidence in rebuttal if she denies it?

(b) William lives in the same estate as the victim and the defendant. He will say that he saw the defendant, whom he knows by sight, knock Martha to the ground, snatch the handbag and run off. The defence has evidence that William has recently been diagnosed as a diabetic but is refusing to stick to the diet given him. He insists on eating foods with a high sugar content which, while not putting him into a hyperglycaemic coma, can affect his eyesight and balance.

Can the defence cross-examine William about his condition and bring medical evidence as to the effect of his condition on him and his ability to identify the accused?

(c) Dan confessed to DC Lyons in the course of a police interview. However, the defence allege that he only did so because DC Lyons threatened to charge his brother with possession of heroin if he did not do so. DC Lyons was recently demoted after the acquittal on appeal of a man convicted of robbery, when it became apparent that the confession had been fabricated.

On the assumption that the confession is admitted, can the defence cross-examine DC Lyons about this acquittal and the subsequent disciplinary proceedings and demotion?

(d) Benjamin, a traffic warden, was on duty on the day of the robbery. He made a statement to the police later that day in which he said that he had chased the assailant, who fitted the description of the defendant. Benjamin says the assailant managed to outrun him, but claims he saw the man enter Flat 222 on the second floor, which is occupied by the defendant's family. The trial took place nearly ten months after the offence and the prosecution permitted Benjamin to read his statement before going into the witness box. Despite having done so, once Ben starts to give evidence he states that he is unable to recall the details of his statement. The prosecution now apply for leave to allow Benjamin to refresh his memory from the statement made to the police. The defence object.

Assuming you are the trial judge, would you permit the witness to refresh his memory?

2. Elliott was engaged to be married to Christine for several months in 2001, during which time full intercourse regularly took place between them consensually. Christine broke off the relationship when she discovered Elliott was sleeping with another woman. In June 2006 they met again at a party given by a mutual friend. Christine told guests that she felt unwell, said she was going upstairs to lie down. She then alleges that

Continued

? *QUESTIONS (Continued)*

Elliott entered the bedroom and raped her, despite her struggling and asking him to stop. In defence, Elliott states that Christine had asked him to resume their relationship earlier in the evening, and invited him to the bedroom where intercourse then took place with her consent.

Elliott pleads not guilty to rape. Can defence counsel adduce evidence of his previous relationship with Christine?

(b) Would your answer be any different if the following information came to light? It transpires that, during their relationship, the intercourse that took place did so in the circumstances of simulated rape. That is, Christine pretended to resist Elliott by screaming, protesting and struggling, and Elliott pretended to overcome her resistance using force.

3. 'Section 41 has clearly failed in obtaining its legislative goal; the time has come to overhaul the provision so as to ensure that previous sexual history can never be adduced against a complainant in a rape trial'.
Do you agree with the above statement?

SUGGESTED FURTHER READING

Birch, D, 'Untangling sexual history evidence: a rejoinder to Professor Temkin' [2003] Crim LR 370.

Durston, G, 'Previous (in)consistent statements after the Criminal Justice Act 2003' [2005] Crim LR 206.

Kelly, L, Temkin, J, Griffiths, S, (2006) *Section 41: An Evaluation of New Legislation Limiting Sexual History in Rape Trials*, Home Office Online Report 20/06 (London, Home Office).

Kibble, N, 'Judicial perspectives on the operation of section 41 and the relevance and admissibility of prior sexual history evidence: four scenarios: Part 1' [2005] Crim LR 190.

Kibble, N, 'Judicial discretion and the admissibility of prior sexual history evidence under section 41 of the Youth Justice and Criminal Evidence Act 1999: sometimes sticking to your guns means shooting yourself in the foot: Part 2' [2005] Crim LR 263.

Temkin, J, 'Sexual history evidence – beware the backlash' [2003] Crim LR 217.

CHAPTER 6

EVIDENCE OF CHARACTER

INTRODUCTION

This chapter examines the admissibility of the accused's previous good or bad character in evidence. As a starting point, it is worth underlining that the rules relating to this topic are clouded by a number of definitional issues. For the most part, as far as its usage within the law of evidence is concerned, 'character' refers to the tendency of a person to act, think or feel in a particular way. 'Disposition' and 'propensity' are alternative terms with the same meaning, and you will find that they are widely used in case law and academic commentary on the subject. Thus, a person with previous convictions for violence may be described as being of a 'violent disposition' or having a 'propensity towards violence', whereas someone of good character may be described as 'a person of integrity'.

There are many ways in which a person's character may be made known to a court, although it is most commonly revealed through reference to any previous convictions. However, not all convictions carry the same stigma: a minor motoring offence, for example, is unlikely to influence a jury in the same way as a serious sexual offence. As we shall see, bad character can also be acquired by the commission of criminal acts for which a person has been acquitted, or where a prosecution does not proceed for lack of evidence. Similarly, good character can be shown by the absence of convictions, or by association with good people or causes, such as being a churchgoer or member of voluntary or charitable organisations. Yet, by the same token, it is worth bearing in mind that much of the evidence of good or bad character stems from a reputation that may or may not be a true reflection of the person's character. For example, the parish priest may enjoy a very upstanding position in the community, but may be abusing choirboys. The bank employee may appear to be the epitome of respectability, but may be stealing from his bank. A national sporting hero may be widely admired in the national press, but may be abusing and battering his wife. Nevertheless, in law all persons are treated as being of good character until the contrary is proved.

Traditionally, evidence of the accused's previous misconduct has been inadmissible in criminal proceedings on grounds that it was both irrelevant and overly prejudicial. However, from the late nineteenth century, the courts and legislature came to accept the fact that there were certain circumstances where it would be in the interests of justice for this evidence to be made known to the trier of fact. From that point in time, until the early part of this century, the law developed in something of a haphazard fashion, owing to the fact that the use of such evidence against a defendant would often be highly contentious. Whilst some commentators argued in favour of a system of free proof that would allow all incidents of previous misconduct to be admitted in every case, others were highly sceptical of the true value of such evidence and argued for the retention of a wide-reaching exclusionary rule. As we shall see, the framers of the CJA 2003 clearly favoured a shift towards the former approach.

THE RATIONALE FOR EXCLUSION

The primary rationale for excluding character evidence stems from the fear that evidence of bad character might have a disproportionately prejudicial affect on the jury. It is, perhaps, something of an irony that, despite the supposedly revered status of the jury as an institution of English criminal justice, we are seemingly not quite prepared to place faith in them to properly assess the impact of previous convictions. The primary fear has always been that the jury may attach too much weight to such evidence, and thereby embark on 'the forbidden chain of reasoning' by inferring guilt from general disposition or propensity.

In spite of this mistrust, there is no hard evidence of such prejudice amongst jurors, as section 8 of the Contempt of Court Act 1981 prevents research into the deliberations of juries. However, research conducted with 'shadow' or 'mock' juries has tended to show that the admission of previous convictions increased the chance of a guilty verdict only in those cases where the offence was similar to that charged.[669] It has also been suggested that juries may be more likely to convict if told the defendant had previous convictions of indecent assault on a child, regardless of the nature of the offence with which he was charged. Such convictions are understandably viewed with a greater degree of revulsion than most, and it is probably dangerous to draw wider conclusions about the ability of juries to deal with potentially prejudicial evidence. Importantly, Lloyd Bostock's research also suggests that juries do give real weight to an instruction to disregard relevant previous convictions wrongly admitted.[670] If it is indeed the case that juries are able to follow judicial directions carefully, perhaps the apparent decline in the exclusionary rules relating to character evidence is to be welcomed as a sign of a greater degree of trust now being placed in the jury to evaluate the evidence fairly.

The second reason for the exclusion of bad character evidence was that it is broadly considered irrelevant. There is no reason why a defendant who committed a criminal act in the past will be guilty of the offence with he is charged in a future case. However, the law of evidence has long accepted that an exception to this principle arises where the accused has a conviction of a very similar nature. In such instances, his past behaviour might provide evidence of a particular character trait that would make it more probable that he committed the offence charged. This is what is commonly referred to as 'evidence of disposition'. As the Criminal Law Revision Committee explained:

> Evidence of other misconduct of the accused tending to show that he has a disposition to commit the kind of offence charged may clearly be highly relevant in the sense of making it more probable that he committed the offence charged; and this is the sense in which relevance must be understood for the purpose of the law of evidence. Obviously if there is no other evidence at all to connect the accused with the offence charged, the fact that he has a disposition to commit this kind of offence, then evidence of disposition must be of greater or lesser value according to the circumstances.[671]

As the Committee emphasises, there must be evidence linking the defendant to the crime with which he or she is charged, and the previous conviction should only comprise part

---

[669]Cornish, W and Sealey, A ('Juries and the Rules of Evidence, The LSE Jury Project [1973] Crim LR 208; Lloyd Bostock, S. 'The Effect on Juries of Hearing about the Defendant's Previous Criminal Record' [2000] Crim LR 734. For an overview of further research conducted into juries, see generally Sanders, A. and Young, R. *Criminal Justice* (2007: Oxford, Oxford University Press), pp 535–542.

[670]Lloyd-Bostock, *ibid*.

[671]Criminal Law Revision Committee, Eleventh Report, *Evidence (General)*, Cmnd 4999) (1972: London, HMSO), [72].

of the prosecution case. It is therefore suggested it is fundamentally misguided to speak of juries being 'prejudiced'. Arguably, it is correct that previous convictions *should* make the jury more likely to convict since it adds something of value to the prosecution case. In this sense, the prospect of conviction will then be increased, not because the jury are prejudiced by hearing of the previous conviction(s), but because of the increased weight of the evidence which supports the defendant's guilt.

The common law recognised this fact, but looked for a high degree of relevance in the previous convictions, which in turn outweighed any possible prejudice resulting from the admission of the convictions. Arguably, the use of the term 'prejudice' in relation to evidence that is potentially highly relevant is somewhat inappropriate. The fact that its use may serve to increase the likelihood of the defendant being found guilty ought not really to be termed 'prejudicial', since all prosecution evidence is directed to this end.

Indeed, it can be added that 'disposition evidence' normally forms part of the investigating judge's dossier in most inquisitorial systems, where there is a considerably higher degree of faith placed in the factfinder. Although continental factfinders are likely to consist partly, or entirely, of professional judges, there is no reason per se that a legally qualified judge should be less open to prejudice than a member of the general public. Until recently, the scandal of jury service in England and Wales was that so many professional people were exempt from it, meaning that juries were often extremely unrepresentative of society at large. However, the Criminal Justice Act 2003 removes most of the previous exemptions, making jury service compulsory for a wide range of professionals, including those connected with the legal system such as judges, barristers, solicitors and police officers. Whether this broadening of representation will lead to a greater trust in the ability of future juries to handle potentially prejudicial material remains to be seen.

THE EVOLUTION OF THE LAW

Until very recently, the admissibility of evidence of bad character was governed both by the 'similar fact rule' at common law, and by the rules laid down in the Criminal Evidence Act 1898. As much the case law continues to have a bearing on the contemporary regime, contained in the Criminal Justice Act 2003, it is worth recounting some of the main features of the law as it stood.

The 'similar fact' rule

The main exception to the rule excluding bad character evidence was known (somewhat misleadingly) as the 'similar fact' rule. It was laid down in *Makin v The Attorney-General for New South Wales*,[672] where a husband and wife were convicted of murdering a foster child, whose body was found buried in their garden. During their trial, the Crown had introduced evidence of 12 further bodies of babies and young children that had been discovered at their previous residences. The question for the Privy Council was whether this evidence had been rightly admitted. In the words of Lord Hershell:

> It is undoubtedly not competent for the prosecution to adduce evidence tending to show that the accused has been guilty of criminal acts other than those covered by the indictment, for

---

[672][1894] AC 57.

the purpose of leading to the conclusion that the accused is a person likely from his criminal conduct or character to have committed the offence for which he was being tried.

On the other hand, the mere fact that the evidence tends to show the commission of other crimes does not render it inadmissible if it be relevant to an issue before the jury, and it may be so relevant if it bears upon the question whether the acts alleged to constitute the crime charged in the indictment were designed or accidental, or to rebut a defence which would otherwise be open to the accused.[673]

The first paragraph of this excerpt sets out the general rule that one cannot adduce evidence of previous criminal conduct in order to show that the defendant is a person likely from his criminal conduct or character to have committed the offence charged. In the second paragraph, Lord Hershell explains the exception to that rule, in stating that such evidence is admissible if it is relevant to an issue in the case, such as rebutting a defence of accident or any other defence open to the accused.

Over the years the rule was refined so that the basis of the admissibility of evidence of bad character was that it had to be not merely relevant to an issue in the case, but *so* relevant that its probative value outweighed any prejudice that might arise. One of the most straightforward ways of establishing relevance was to show a similarity between the manner and circumstances in which the previous offences were committed and the manner and circumstances in which the offence charged had been committed. It was this comparative exercise that led to the description of such evidence as 'similar fact evidence'. Perhaps the most infamous example of its application came in *R v Smith*,[674] popularly known as the 'Brides in the Bath' case, where the defendant was accused of drowning his wife in the bath. Having run the defence of death by accident, the prosecution adduced evidence that two previous wives had arrived at an unfortunate end in a remarkably similar fashion. In all three cases, the accused stood to gain financially from their deaths, and all three women had drowned in the bath shortly after having wed him.

In *Boardman v DPP*,[675] there was a shift in emphasis from adducing the similar fact evidence to the amount of relevance it bore to the matter in issue. In this case, the House of Lords developed the idea that, in order to be admissible, the similar fact evidence should have 'striking similarity' with the facts of the instant case. In the years that followed, this was interpreted as imposing a mandatory requirement upon the prosecution to show how any evidence they sought to adduce under this head bore a 'striking similarity' to the manner and circumstances in which the offence charged was committed. Merely committing the same offence in a manner which was the 'stock-in-trade' of persons committing such an offence was not sufficient to make evidence of the previous offences admissible. Instead, there had to be some 'unique and striking similarity' in the manner in which the previous offences had been committed. Consequently, the courts began to refuse to admit such evidence unless it was strikingly similar to the way in which the offence charged had been committed. Inevitably, this rendered the task of the prosecution considerably more difficult. Increasingly, similar fact evidence was ruled inadmissible, and the Court of Appeal seemed ever more willing to quash convictions were the extent of similarity could not be described as 'striking'.[676]

---

[673] *Ibid.*, 65.
[674] (1915) 11 Cr App R 229.
[675] [1975] AC 42.
[676] See eg *Inder* (1977) 67 Cr App R 143; *Clarke* (1977) 67 Cr App R 398; *Scarrott* [1978] QB 1016; *Brooks* (1990) 92 Cr App R 36.

The House of Lords sought to remedy this problem in *DPP v P*.[677] In this case, a father was accused of rape and incest with his two daughters. As in *Boardman*, the question was whether the evidence in relation to each daughter was cross-admissible. The common features were that in each case there was evidence to indicate that the father had exercised dictatorial power over each girl, and that in each case he had paid for an abortion. The Court of Appeal had held that although the cases bore similarities, they could not be said to be striking. On that basis, the evidence should not have been admitted. However, this decision was reversed by the House of Lords, which concluded that striking similarities ought not to be the determining criteria of admissibility. Their Lordships stated that striking similarities were merely one method of establishing the probative force of the evidence, particularly in cases where the identity of the accused was at issue. In the instant case, the issue was not identity, but whether an offence had actually been committed. There were therefore other ways of deriving probative force:

> When a question of the kind raised in this case arises I consider that the judge must first decide whether there is material upon which the jury would be entitled to conclude that the evidence of one victim, about what occurred to that victim, is so related to the evidence given by another victim, about what happened to that other victim, that the evidence of the first victim provides strong enough support for the evidence of the second victim to make it just to admit it notwithstanding the prejudicial effect of admitting the evidence. This relationship, from which the support is derived, may take many forms and while these forms may include 'striking similarity' in the manner in which the crime was committed, consisting of unusual characteristics in its execution the necessary relationship is by no means confined to such circumstances. Relationships in time and circumstances other than those may well be important relationships in this connection. Where the identity of the perpetrator is in issue, and evidence of this kind is important in that connection, obviously something in the nature of what has been called in argument a signature or other special feature will be necessary. To transpose this requirement to other situations where the question is whether a crime has been committed, rather than who did commit it, is to impose an unnecessary and improper restriction on the principle.[678]

As a result of this decision, the rule in *Boardman* concerning 'striking similarity' was subject to a broader interpretation. In practice, this meant that similar fact evidence became more frequently admissible, particularly in cases involving sexual abuse of children by carers or parents. However, overall the rule will be remembered by many as a device that was overly narrow in scope, and served to impede the flow of information to the jury. This paternalism led to much relevant evidence being excluded, and, arguably, many travesties of justice followed.

In August 1992, the jury at the Old Bailey acquitted Simon Berkowitz of the burglary of a solicitor's office and the theft of personal documents belonging to Paddy Ashdown, the then leader of the Liberal Democrats.[679] Berkowitz was caught in possession of the stolen documents, which he was trying to sell to the media. He admitted possession of them, but claimed they had been given to him by a man in a pub. The jury was not, however, told that Berkowitz had 240 previous convictions, 230 of them for burglary and a majority of these for burglary of solicitors' offices and the theft of documents. The prosecution had applied to the trial judge to allow these convictions to go before the jury as evidence of guilt, but the judge refused on the ground that it would be too prejudicial to do so. It is, at

---

[677] [1991] 2 AC 447.

[678] *Ibid.*, 462.

[679] *The Times*, 13 August 1992.

the very least, arguable that a man found in possession of goods stolen in the burglary of a solicitor's office, who has some 200 convictions for burglary of a solicitor's office, committed the burglary in question. That is not to say that one merely jumps from the fact of previous convictions to conviction on the present charge – there must be other evidence linking the defendant to the present burglary. However, this was indeed the case with Berkowitz (the stolen documents were found in his possession), and it seems odd that the evidence of his previous convictions for burglaries were somehow found to be insufficiently relevant to be placed before a jury.

Another more serious case arose in 1987 when one William Beggs was convicted of murder at Teeside Crown Court. At the trial, Beggs admitted the killing, but claimed he did so in self-defence. However, the Court of Appeal found that evidence was incorrectly introduced by the prosecution to rebut his defence,[680] which concerned his past tendencies to attack sleeping young men and inflict grievous wounds with sharp instruments. In the view of the Court, these incidences were insufficiently similar, and the conviction was quashed. In 2001, Beggs was back at court in Edinburgh, and found guilty of sexually assaulting and murdering a young man whose body had been dismembered and decapitated, and the police began further investigations after traces of blood belonging to 17 other men were uncovered at his flat.[681] We may never know how many deaths or serious assaults could have been prevented had the Court of Appeal taken a less restrictive view of the evidence of his disposition towards violence 12 years earlier.

There is no doubt that the fact that a person has a disposition to commit particular offences can be highly relevant evidence in certain cases.[682] In view of the ongoing difficulties surrounding the uneven application of the similar fact rule, it is perhaps unsurprising that the government took the decision to abolish it in the Criminal Justice Act 2003.[683] However, as we shall see later, section 101(1)(d) of the legislation provides for the admissibility of 'bad character' evidence if it is relevant to an important matter in issue between the defendant and the prosecution. Such an issue may include a propensity to commit the kind of offence charged or to be untruthful, and such a propensity may be established by evidence that the defendant has been convicted of offences of the same description as, or in the same category as, the offence with which he is charged. Thus, although the formulation of the rule has entirely changed, the new statutory provision should envelop those types of cases to which the similar fact rule would previously have been applied.

The Criminal Evidence Act 1898

Alongside the similar fact rule at common law, the Criminal Evidence Act 1898 also permitted evidence of bad character to be adduced in certain circumstances. It should be underlined, however, that evidence admitted under this legislation went to the question of credibility only; juries would be instructed not to use it as evidence of guilt. Prior to enactment of the 1898 Act, defendants were not permitted to give evidence in their own defence; thereafter they were able to do so upon application to the court. This meant that accused persons could choose to give evidence, but could not be compelled to do so.

---

[680](1989) 90 Cr App R 430.
[681]*The Times*, 15 October 2001.
[682]See further the remarks of the Criminal Law Revision Committee, op cit n 671, at p 149.
[683]Criminal Justice Act 2003, section 99.

The framers of the Act were faced with two problems resulting from the decision to make the accused a competent witness in his own defence:

- whether the accused should be entitled to claim the privilege against self-incrimination in respect of the offence charged; and

- whether, and to what extent, defendants should be open to cross-examination about their previous bad character for the purpose of either proving their guilt on the offence charged or attacking their credibility as witnesses.

The Act represented a compromise by providing that while the defendant could be cross-examined as to any matter concerning the offences with which he was charged,[684] he was also given a 'shield against cross-examination as to his bad character' which prevented such cross-examination unless one of the circumstances set out in section 1(3) of the Act applied.

Section 1(3) provided for three circumstances where the shield could be lost. The first, contained in section 1(3)(a), was resorted to least often, and provided for the admissibility of 'proof that he has committed or been convicted of such other offence is admissible evidence to show that he is guilty of an offence with which he is then charged'. In effect, this provision allowed the accused to be cross-examined about his previous bad character when it was exceptionally admissible at common law (as similar fact evidence) or by statute to prove his guilt on the offence charged (e.g. on charges of driving whilst disqualified).

Secondly, the shield would be lost where the accused 'has personally or by his advocate asked questions of the witnesses for the prosecution with a view to establish his own good character, or has given evidence of his own good character, or the nature or conduct of his defence is such as to involve imputations on the character of the prosecutor or the witnesses for the prosecution, or the deceased victim of the alleged crime'.[685] This provision thus protected the accused from cross-examination about previous bad character unless the accused asserted his own good character by giving or calling character evidence,[686] or attacked the character of prosecution witnesses or the deceased victim of the offence charged.[687] The subsection was essentially founded on the 'tit-for-tat' principle, in that it was intended to be an automatic response so that the jury, who had to decide whom they were going to believe, knew the character of the person casting the imputations. One exception to the rule arose in rape cases, where the defendant alleged consent.[688] This was regarded as an attack on the character of the complainant, thus defence counsel was at liberty to probe issues relating to the complainant's lifestyle and sexual history without the shield being lost.[689]

The result was that comparatively minor imputations resulted in a long history of previous convictions being admitted, even when the imputation was seen as necessary to the defence. For example, in *R v Bishop*,[690] the defendant, charged with burglary,

---

[684]Criminal Evidence Act 1898, section 1(2).

[685]Criminal Evidence Act 1898, section 1(3)(b).

[686]See eg *Samuel* (1956) 40 Cr App R 8, where the accused was charged with stealing a camera. In his defence, he alleged that he was going to return it to the police as lost property, and proceeded to give evidence of two other occasions on which he had returned lost property. In these circumstances, his shield was lost, and cross-examination was permitted about previous thefts.

[687]See eg *Rappolt* (1911) 6 Cr App R 156, where the defendant said that a prosecution witness was such an awful liar that his own brother would never believe him.

[688]*R v Turner* [1944] KB 463.

[689]See also Ch 5, pp 148–49.

[690][1975] QB 274.

sought to explain the presence of his fingerprints in the burgled premises by alleging a homosexual relationship between himself and the occupier. As the occupier was a witness for the prosecution, this was seen as an imputation on his character, thereby entitling the prosecution to cross-examine the defendant on his previous convictions. In the lower courts, some judges felt this was unfair and had been exercising their discretion for some years to exclude attacks on the accused's character where it they felt such cross-examination would unfairly prejudice the jury. However, this was outside the remit of the statute, and in *Selvey v DPP*,[691] the House of Lords rejected what it described as a 'fetter' on the exercise of the discretion and held that the discretion should only be used to disallow cross-examination on bad character in the most exceptional of cases.

A final circumstance where the defendant's shield could be lost was provided by section 1(3)(c) of the Act. This applied where a co-accused ran a 'cut-throat' defence, and attacked the character of another co-accused to suggest that he or she was more likely to have committed the offence in question.[692] In these circumstances, the co-accused was permitted to cross-examine another co-accused as to his previous convictions. The trial judge had no discretion to prevent such cross-examination, but he was obliged to direct the jury that the cross-examination went only to the credibility of the co-accused and was not to be used in order to determine his guilt.[693]

The road to reform

A range of practical and conceptual difficulties plagued the application of both the similar fact rule at common law and the 1898 Act. In particular, there were concerns that the rules were open to abuse by corrupt police officers, who invented confessions or planted evidence which they knew the defendant could not dispute without being seen to cast imputations on them. In such circumstances, the defendant's often lengthy list of convictions would be put before the jury. In a 2001 Report, the Law Commission recommended that the law be entirely overhauled.[694] It recommended that a radically different regime be introduced which would cover the use of character evidence relating to both defendants and non-defendants. Accepting that bad character evidence did have the potential to be prejudicial, it recommended that a general rule of exclusion be put in place, but made subject to a number of statutory exceptions that would partially reflect, though would also serve to clarify, aspects of the law as it stood. In relation to similar fact rule, the Commission believed that overall it worked fairly well and needed only a clearer statutory formula to clarify the difficult borderline between similar fact evidence and background or explanatory evidence. However, the 1898 Act was viewed as being entirely out of date, and was in need of being repealed and reworked to enable defendants to challenge more effectively the central features of the case against them, without making their previous convictions or bad character admissible.

---

[691] [1970] AC 304.

[692] See eg *Murdoch and Taylor* [1965] AC 574.

[693] This was also the case under as under section 1(3)(b). But see *R v Randall* [2004] 1 WLR 56. The House of Lords held that where two defendants are jointly charged with a crime, and each blames the other for its commission, thus permitting both to cross-examine the other as to his previous convictions under section 1(3)(c) of the 1898 Act, one accused may rely on the criminal propensity of the other. Furthermore, the trial judge was not required to direct the jury that the bad character revealed went only to the credibility of the other accused.

[694] Law Commission, *Evidence of Character in Criminal Proceedings*, Report No 273 (2001: London, HMSO).

While broadly accepting the Law Commission's recommendations, the government issued a White Paper, *Justice for All*,[695] which outlined its legislative proposals. It was clear that the government intended to go further and admit the defendant's bad character and previous convictions in a greater range of circumstances than the previous regime had permitted, and which the Law Commission had proposed. The White Paper's proposals were expanded upon in the Criminal Justice Act 2003 (sections 98 to 113), which now govern the admissibility of evidence of the bad character of a defendant and non-defendant. The adduction of the bad character of a witness or victim (dealt with in section 100 of the 2003 Act) is considered in Chapter 5.[696] Here we are concerned only with the admissibility of evidence relating to the character of the accused.

WHAT CONSTITUTES 'BAD CHARACTER'?

Section 98 of the 2003 Act defines 'bad character' as 'evidence of, or a disposition toward misconduct'. The term 'misconduct' is subject to further definition in section 112, where it is labelled 'the commission of an offence or other reprehensible behaviour'. It will be apparent that this description was intended to be a broad, and encapsulates any evidence that shows that a person has committed an offence or has acted in a reprehensible way, as well as evidence from which such conduct may be inferred. Even if past criminal charges are relatively minor in nature, they will still constitute 'misconduct' under section 112.[697] Likewise, such evidence may include previous convictions; charges being tried concurrently; evidence relating to offences for which a person has been charged, but where prosecution opts not to proceed; and charges of which for the defendant has been acquitted at a subsequent trial.[698]

On a literal reading, and possibly contrary to the intention of the drafters, the phrase 'other reprehensible conduct' is potentially wide enough to cover a broad range of conduct, including that which is not criminal.[699] However, some of the early decisions on this suggest that the courts are reluctant to interpret the provision in such a broad manner. In *R v Renda*,[700] an absolute discharge following a finding that the defendant was unfit to plead was held not to constitute 'misconduct' for the purposes of the Act. In the view of Judge LJ, the term 'reprehensible' 'carries with it some element of culpability or blameworthiness'.[701] In the consolidated appeals reported as *R v Weir*,[702] the Court of Appeal had to determine whether two separate instances of behaviour amount to

---

[695] Home Office, *Justice for All*, Cmnd 5563 (2002: London, Home Office).

[696] See above, Ch 5, pp 142–45.

[697] Furthermore, section 108 CJA 2003 repeals the previous prohibition on the use in evidence of offences committed by the defendant while a child, but in order for these to be admitted, both the offence for which the defendant is being tried and the offence for which the defendant was convicted must be indictable, and the court should be satisfied that the interests of justice require the evidence to be admissible. A similar approach is taken on 'spent convictions' under the Rehabilitation of Offenders Act 1974. Though admissible in criminal proceedings, *Practice Direction (Criminal:Consolidated)* [2002] 3 All ER 904 recommends that advocates should not refer to a spent conviction when such reference can reasonably be avoided. However, where the prosecution do wish to adduce such evidence, leave should be obtained and the judge will should then exercise his discretion to ensure that there is no unfairness to the defendant.

[698] See *R v Z (Prior Acquittal)* [2000] 2 AC 483, discussed below.

[699] See further Munday, R. 'What Constitutes "Other Reprehensible Behaviour" under the Bad Character Provisions of the Criminal Justice Act 2003?' [2004] Crim LR 533.

[700] [2006] 1 Cr App R 380.

[701] At [24].

[702] [2006] 1 WLR 1885.

'bad character' for the purposes of section 98. In *Manister*, where the accused was charged with indecent assault on a 13-year-old girl, the fact that he had a previous relationship with a 16-year-old girl was deemed inadmissible. So too was a comment that he had made to the 15-year-old sister of that girl, where he allegedly asked her 'Why do you think I am still single? If only you were a bit older and I a bit younger'. Both of these comments were deemed by the Court of Appeal to fall outside the scope of section 98. Strictly speaking, there was nothing per se reprehensible about a relationship between a 34-year-old man and a young woman above the age of consent. Some additional feature would be required to make such conduct reprehensible, such as evidence of grooming her as a minor or disapproval by the girl's parents. As regards his comment to the girl's sister, this was 'unattractive', but could not be said to be reprehensible.

In *Osbourne*,[703] the Court of Appeal rejected the proposition that shouting at one's partner in the presence of a child, whilst 'not to be commended', fell short of the threshold of 'reprehensible'. By contrast however, the Court of Appeal took a much dimmer view of violent images and rap lyrics found in the possession of the accused in *Saleem*.[704] Both the images and the lyrics made specific reference to the defendant's plan to commit violent acts on his seventeenth birthday (the day on which he was allegedly party to a violent assault) were held to be admissible.

In the light of these decisions, we are still in the dark somewhat as to when non-criminal conduct might be considered reprehensible enough to fall within the ambit of the legislation. Indeed, some of the decisions discussed above might legitimately be questioned. It seems particularly odd, for example, that a clear expression of sexual attraction by a 34-year-old man to a 15-year-old girl was not considered to be sufficiently reprehensible, whereas lyrics to a rap tune composed by a teenager were. As the law currently stands, no clear principle or test has emerged as to when previous behaviour might cross the threshold. Some measure of clarity on this point is urgently required, and hopefully the issue will be addressed by the House of Lords in the not too distant future.

Previous acquittals and allegations

The inclusion of acquittals within the ambit of bad character evidence reflects the previous law and preserves the decision of the House of Lords in *R v Z*. There, the House of Lords held that there was no special rule that required the exclusion of evidence that a person had been involved in earlier offences, even if he had been acquitted of those crimes at a previous trial. Z was charged with a single count of rape committed in 1998. The prosecution sought leave to adduce evidence of four previous incidents involving Z and four different women who complained of rape in 1984, 1985, 1989 and 1993. Z was tried on a charge of rape in respect of each of these incidents. In each case, it was admitted that intercourse had taken place and the central issue was whether the complainant consented. Only in one case was Z convicted; in the other three he was acquitted.

The trial judge accepted the Crown's case that the four incidents involved circumstances sufficiently similar to those of the present case for them to have been admissible under the principles established in *DPP v Boardman* and *DPP v P*. However, the judge held that the fact of the prior acquittals in respect of three of the complainants meant that the Crown could not adduce evidence involving those incidents as similar fact evidence in respect of

[703]*Osbourne* [2007] Crim LR 712.
[704][2007] EWCA Crim 1923.

the present charge of rape. Standing by itself, one conviction did not present a sufficiently cogent picture of similar incidents to be admissible.

The Crown's appeal was rejected by the Court of Appeal, but it referred the case to the House of Lords, certifying that a question of general public importance was involved in their decision, namely:

> Other than in cases of *autrefois acquit*, (a) is evidence admissible on behalf of the Crown in a trial of offence A which also proves guilt in respect of one or more prior incident (B, C and D) in respect of each of which the defendant has been tried and acquitted; and (b) is evidence so admissible if its nature and purpose is to show guilt in respect of offence A on the basis that offence A was not an isolated offence, but one in a series of similar incidents (including those in respect of which the defendant was tried and convicted)?

The House of Lords found in favour of the Crown. Lord Hutton, giving a speech with which all their Lordships agreed, came to the following conclusions:

- The principle of double jeopardy operated to cause a criminal court in the exercise of its discretion to stop a prosecution where the defendant was being prosecuted on the same or substantially the same facts as had given rise to an earlier prosecution that had resulted in his acquittal or conviction.

- Provided that a defendant was not placed in double jeopardy in that way, evidence that was relevant on a subsequent prosecution was not inadmissible because it showed or tended to show that the defendant was, in fact, guilty of an offence of which he had earlier been acquitted.

- It followed that a distinction should not be drawn between evidence that showed guilt of a previous offence of which the defendant had been acquitted and evidence that tended to show guilt of such an offence or that appeared to relate to one distinct issue rather than the issue of guilt of such an offence.

In this instance, the defendant was not placed in double jeopardy because the facts giving rise to the present prosecution were different from those that had given rise to the earlier prosecution. The evidence of the earlier complainants was accepted to be relevant and to come within the ambit of the similar fact rule, and therefore it was not inadmissible because it showed that the defendant was, in fact, guilty of the offences of which he had earlier been acquitted. The admissibility of previous acquittals would be subject to the judge's discretion to exclude them after weighing the evidence's prejudicial effect against its probative value.

Under the 2003 Act, Z is still good law, and furthermore, it may apply to convictions in respect of any offence. Thus, if there were a series of robberies, and the defendant was acquitted of involvement in them, evidence tending to show that he had committed those earlier robberies could be given in a later case involving a similar charge. This may be particularly likely if such evidence showed that if the previous incidents took place in similar circumstances to those in the case at hand.

In *R v Smith (David)*,[705] the Crown successfully relied on the decision in Z to argue for the admissibility of previous allegations which had never come to court. At his original trial for nine different counts of rape and other sexual offences, the judge stayed proceedings in relation to three of the charges as the police had previously told the accused that no further action would be taken. However, the prosecution then succeeded in obtaining leave to admit the evidence as tending to show the defendant's propensity to commit the kinds of offences charged. The Court of Appeal rejected the appellant's contention that the

---

[705]This was one of the consolidated appeals reported as *R v Edwards* [2006] 1 WLR 1524.

evidence had been improperly admitted. In the view of the Court, there was no difference in principle between evidence on which a defendant had previously been acquitted and evidence relating to allegations that had never been tried. The Court proceeded to state that, as a general rule, all evidence that is relevant to the question whether the accused is guilty or innocent of the offence charged will be admissible under the bad character provisions of the 2003 Act.[706]

The provision would thus be potentially broad enough to cover the previous history of Ian Huntley, who was convicted in December 2003 of the infamous murder of Holly Wells and Jessica Chapman in Soham two years previously. Between 1995 and 1999, Huntley had been investigated for four alleged rapes, four cases of sex with under-age girls and one indecent assault on an 11-year-old girl. A charge was preferred in respect of only one of these allegations, but the Crown Prosecution Service discontinued the prosecution because there was no reasonable prospect of conviction. No charges were brought in respect of the other allegations and no record was kept of them. However, even if records had been kept, the allegations would have remained unproven and Huntley's record would have remained unblemished.

'Evidence of the facts of the offence charged'

Section 98 does not affect the admissibility of evidence of the facts arising from the offence in question, or those facts that are closely related to it in terms of time, place or circumstances. These fall outside the definition of bad character provided in section 98. Thus, if the defendant were charged with burglary, the prosecution evidence of the facts of the offence, including any witnesses to the crime, and any forensic evidence gathered, would be admissible outside the terms of these provisions.

It is also important to bear in mind that many offences will inherently contain elements of certain other offences. For example, a person committing robbery may have a weapon in his possession; or a burglar may commit criminal damage in the course of the burglary. These will all be accepted by the courts as facts which are directly relevant to the charges at hand. Evidence that the defendant had tried to intimidate prosecution witnesses would also be admissible as evidence of misconduct in connection with (as appropriate) the investigation or the prosecution of the offence, as would allegations by the defendant that the evidence had been planted. Nevertheless, it is important to draw the distinction between these types of facts and facts which relate to another episode entirely. Thus, for example, evidence that the defendant had committed a burglary on another occasion, or that a witness had previously lied on oath, would not be evidence to do with the facts of the offence or its investigation or prosecution, and would therefore fall within the scope of section 98.

CONDITIONS FOR ADMISSIBILITY

Section 101(1)(a) to (g) of the 2003 Act set out seven circumstances in which the prosecution, or in certain cases a co-defendant, can adduce evidence of bad character. These are

(a) where all the parties agree to the evidence being admissible;

(b) where the evidence is adduced by the defendant himself, or is given in answer to a question asked by him in cross-examination and intended to elicit it;

---

[706] cf R v Bovell; Dowds [2005] 2 Cr App R 401.

(c) where it is important explanatory evidence;

(d) where it is relevant to an important matter in issue between the defendant and the prosecution;

(e) where it has substantial probative value in relation to an important matter in issue between the defendant and a co-defendant;

(f) where it is evidence to correct a false impression given by the defendant; or

(g) where the defendant has made an attack on another person's character.

Each head of admissibility is then expanded upon by a number of sections which provide additional definitional material.[707] It should also be noted that two of these heads of admissibility, subsections 101(1)(d) and 101(1)(g), are subject to a judicial discretion to refuse to admit the evidence if, on application by the defendant, the trial judge is of the opinion that it would have such an adverse effect on the fairness of the proceedings that it ought not to be admitted.

Although evidence admissible under section 101 of the 2003 Act will primarily go to the credit of the defendant and allow his or her character to be known by the jury, there is no strict rule (as there was in the 1898 legislation) that prevents the jury taking the character of the accused into account when adjudicating the issue of guilt. This was the core issue that confronted the Court of Appeal in one of the most important cases to date on the new character provisions, *R v Campbell*.[708] The defendant had been convicted of false imprisonment and assault occasioning actual bodily harm. At trial, the prosecution applied under section 101(1)(d) of the Act to adduce evidence of two previous convictions that the defendant had for violence against women. Permission was granted on the grounds that the convictions showed a propensity to commit acts similar to those which were the subject of the current charge. The judge proceeded to explain the relevance of these convictions to the jury, in line with the Judicial Studies Board's specimen directions. He also told them that the convictions were not only relevant to the accused's propensity to commit acts of violence towards women, but also to the question as to whether the defendant had told the truth to the court.

The defendant was convicted, and argued on appeal that the jury should not have been told that his previous convictions were relevant to his propensity to tell the truth. Applying the earlier decision of *R v Highton*,[709] the Court dismissed this argument and stated that once evidence of bad character was introduced, it was for the jury to determine in what respect it was relevant. In the view of the Court, it was unhelpful for the judge to draw a distinction between propensity to commit the type of offence charge and matters pertaining to credibility. As a matter of common sense, where the jury learnt that a defendant had shown a propensity to commit criminal acts, it may in turn conclude that he was less likely to be telling the truth whilst testifying:

> The summing up that assists the jury with the relevance of bad character evidence will accord with common sense and assist them to avoid prejudice that is at odds with this .... It is open to the jury to attach significance to it in any respect in which it is relevant. To direct them only to have regard to it for some purposes and to disregard its relevance in other respects would be to revert to the unsatisfactory practices that prevailed under the old law ...[710]

---

[707] CJA 2003, sections 102–6. See discussion below.
[708] [2007] 1 WLR 2798.
[709] [2005] 1 WLR 3572.
[710] At [24–25].

> In considering the inference to be drawn from bad character the courts have in the past drawn a distinction between propensity to offend and credibility. This distinction is usually unrealistic. If the jury learn that a defendant has shown a propensity to commit criminal acts they may well at one and the same time conclude that it is more likely that he is guilty and that he is less likely to be telling the truth when he says that he is not.[711]

However, it was underlined that the question as to whether a defendant had a *propensity* for being untruthful would not normally be capable of being described as 'an important matter in issue', unless dishonesty was actually element of the offence in question. Even when such circumstances did arise, the propensity to tell lies was only likely to be relevant if the lying was done in the context of committing criminal offences. In the rare case where propensity to be untruthful was an important issue, the judge should always warn the jury that a propensity for untruthfulness would not, of itself, go very far to show that the accused had committed the offences charged.

Gateways (a) and (b)

The first two gateways under the legislation are probably the least contentious and are fairly self-explanatory. Under both of these provisions, the defence must be content to have the evidence adduced before the court. In practice, they will rarely adopt such tactics unless they form part of the overall strategy to reveal previous convictions or other character traits. There are a number of potential scenarios where this may be desirable. Defence counsel may, for example, want to launch an attack on the character of prosecution witnesses. In all probability, the trial judge would then allow evidence of the defendant's bad character to be introduced under section 101(1)(g).[712]

Alternatively, such a ploy may be adopted where the defendant is charged with an offence involving violence, but has convictions only for non-violent offences. For example, Ralph is charged with armed robbery, but his previous convictions are for shoplifting and theft from cars. Those previous convictions might well be disclosed to the jury in an effort to persuade them that the defendant is a small-time criminal and not into major league crime involving violence of the kind charged. In *R v Shaw*,[713] the accused pleaded self-defence to a charge of assaulting police officers. In order to support this defence, he sought to adduce evidence of his bad relationship with the police, including an arrest for murder, in order to show his state of mind as being more likely to imagine he was under threat from police officers. The Court of Appeal held that the bad character of the defendant was properly admitted on behalf of the defendant for that purpose. Once bad character evidence is properly revealed to the jury the prosecution can cross-examine the defendant in details on the matters raised, though the trial judge should prevent counsel from dwelling on the evidence too much, lest the jury be given the impression that it is of greater importance than is the case. Cross-examination may also follow bad character evidence revealed by the defendant inadvertently or by other witnesses, provided such evidence is properly adduced.

In *Jones v DPP*,[714] the accused had been arrested following the rape of a Girl Guide and the murder of a second girl just one month later. He was first tried for the rape

---

[711] At [28].
[712] See below, pp 194–96.
[713] [2003] Crim LR 278.
[714] [1962] AC 655.

and was convicted. He was then tried for the murder of the second girl. The circumstances of the murder resembled those of the rape in many respects, but the prosecution made no attempt to admit them as similar fact evidence to avoid putting the victim through the ordeal of giving evidence again. When giving evidence at his murder trial, Jones attempted to explain a false alibi he had given to the police on being questioned by stating that he had been 'in trouble with the police' on a previous occasion. He then put forward a new alibi at trial, in which he said he had been with a prostitute in London at the time. He gave an account of his return home and an account of a conversation with his wife, in which he assured her that his late return home had nothing to do with the crime which had been reported in the newspapers. The prosecution were then given leave to cross-examine him about a previous occasion on which he had claimed to have had exactly the same conversation with his wife, again after supposedly visiting a prostitute in London. Counsel did not indicate what that previous occasion was, but it must have been obvious to the jury, given the notoriety of the case, that it was the occasion on which he had been charged with the rape of the Girl Guide. The cross-examination was directed at discrediting the new alibi given by Jones, and placed an emphasis on how unlikely it was that Jones and his wife should repeat an earlier conversation word for word.

The appeal against conviction, which argued that leave should not have been given to cross-examine, went to the House of Lords. Their Lordships interpreted the words of section 1(3) of the 1898 Act, which prohibited questions 'tending to show that he has committed or been convicted of or been charged with any offence', as meaning 'tending to show the jury for the first time matters which had not been already disclosed to them'. Since Jones himself had revealed the facts upon which the cross-examination was based, the cross-examination was properly allowed.

In the earlier case of *R v Chitson*,[715] the defendant was convicted of unlawful sexual intercourse with an under-age girl. The girl was allowed to give evidence that the defendant had boasted to her of his sexual relationship with another girl. The Court of Appeal held that he was properly cross-examined about these claims on the basis that, if they were true, it would strongly corroborate the young girl's evidence that he had had sexual intercourse with her.[716] The Court of Appeal's decision that it was admissible under section 1(2) of the 1898 Act was disapproved of by the House of Lords in *Jones*, but the basis for this distinction is not particularly clear, given that it would appear to be caught by the principle enunciated by their Lordships in that very case: namely that the statement was already before the court, and therefore the prohibition in section 1(3) did not apply. However, section 99 of the CJA abolishes the common law rules governing the admissibility of evidence of bad character, and the prosecution must seek leave to admit the evidence of bad character under section 101.[717] The *Jones* case is likely to fall under section 101(1)(b), but if *Chitson* were tried under the new rules, the previous conviction for under-age sexual intercourse might not be admissible under the provision given that the defendant did not directly adduce the evidence. Nevertheless, it might still be admissible under section 101(1)(d) as relevant to an important matter in issue between the defendant and the prosecution since it includes the question whether the defendant has a propensity to commit the kind of offence charged.[718]

---

[715] [1909] 2 KB 945.

[716] In *Chitson*, the defendant's statement made to the girl was properly admitted as an exception to the rule against hearsay.

[717] In the event that the prosecution fail to seek leave, the trial judge nevertheless retains a discretion to admit such evidence – see *Lawson* [2007] 1 WLR 1191.

[718] See below, pp 184–88.

Gateway (c) – important explanatory evidence

For evidence to be admissible as 'important explanatory evidence', it must be such that, without it, the factfinder would find it impossible or difficult to understand other evidence in the case.[719] If, therefore, the facts or account to which the bad character evidence relates are largely understandable without this additional explanation, the evidence should not be admitted. The explanation must also give the court some substantial assistance in understanding the case as a whole. In other words, it will not be enough for the evidence to assist the court to understand some trivial piece of evidence.

At common law, explanatory (or background) evidence was always admissible as an exception to the rules that excluded evidence of bad character. In the Australian case of *O'Leary v R*,[720] a number of men employed at a timber camp went on a drunken rampage for several hours, during which time several serious assaults were committed. After the rampage one of the men, who had been seriously assaulted, was found dying. At the trial for murder it was held that the episode should be treated as one event, which included the other assaults that had occurred:

> The evidence disclosed that, under the influence of the beer and wine [the prisoner] had drunk and continued to drink, he engaged in repeated acts of violence which might be regarded as amounting to a connected course of conduct. Without evidence of what, during that time, was done by those men who took any significant part in the matter and especially evidence of the behaviour of the prisoner, the transactions of which the alleged murder formed an integral part could not be truly understood and isolated from it, could only be presented as an unreal and not very intelligible event. The prisoner's generally violent and hostile conduct might well serve to explain his mind and attitude and, therefore, to implicate him in the resulting homicide.[721]

The difficulty in providing the essential background information is contained in the phrase 'to implicate him in the resulting homicide'. As in *O'Leary* itself, it could include evidence of other offences committed by the defendant, or evidence of other misconduct on his part. In *R v Sidhu*,[722] the defendant was charged with conspiracy to possess explosives in England. It was held that the trial judge had rightly admitted a video tape, which appeared to show the defendant leading a band of armed rebels in Pakistan. Although the evidence suggested to the jury that the defendant had been involved in other criminal activities, it was justified as being necessary to explain the background to the defendant's activities in England and the motives for his activities.

Similar reasoning was applied in *R v Sawoniuk*,[723] where the accused was charged with the murder of Jews during the Nazi occupation of Belorussia in 1942. Evidence was admitted that during that period the accused had been a member of a group of police officers who had carried out search and kill operations for Jewish survivors of an earlier massacre. In this case, background evidence was necessary to enable the jury properly to understand the circumstances which prevailed such a long time ago in a foreign country. The Court recognised that it would have been highly unlikely that any of the jurors had an understanding of the particular atmosphere in which ethnically based war crimes were committed, and noted that criminal charges cannot fairly be judged in a factual vacuum.

---

[719] Criminal Justice Act 2003, section 102.
[720] (1946) 73 CLR 566.
[721] *Ibid.*, per Dixon J, at 577.
[722] (1994) 98 Cr App R 59.
[723] [2000] 2 Cr App R 220.

Evidence describing context and circumstances in which the offences were said to have been committed was deemed to be necessary.

In *R v M (T)*,[724] the defendant had been charged with raping his sister. The Court of Appeal held that a long history of sexual and physical abuse within the household was rightly admitted as essential background evidence to explain why the victim had not turned to her parents for help when her brother allegedly raped her. The evidence was that daughters and sons were raped and buggered by the father, and the sons were forced to watch him abuse their sisters. In one particular instance, M was forced to watch the abuse and later made to copy what his father had done. By the time he had reached the age of 16, he was abusing his 10-year-old sister on a regular basis. Without this evidence, the Court felt the jury would have received incomplete and incomprehensible account. However, it was solely for this purpose that the evidence was admitted – explanatory evidence may not be used by the jury as evidence of propensity tending to show guilt.

Although some critics fear that the use of explanatory evidence is sometimes used as a backdoor means of admitting evidence of the defendant's bad character, the courts have put in place very stringent guidelines as to when precisely such evidence can be used, and how it ought to be evaluated by the jury. Certainly, in the cases above it can be clearly seen how the facts in question may have appeared incomplete or incomprehensible without such evidence being given. However, by the same token, one can readily see that such evidence may be a useful tool in the prosecutor's war chest in proving the guilt of the defendant.

Gateway (d) – relevance to an important matter in issue between prosecution and defendant

This subsection roughly equates with the similar fact principle applied at common law, and is the primary gateway under the bad character evidence admitted under the Act. Such evidence will be admissible if it is relevant to an important matter in issue between the defendant and the prosecution. Section 103(1) states that for the purposes of section 101(1)(d), matters in issue between the defendant and the prosecution include the question 'whether the defendant has a propensity to commit offences of the kind charged, except where his having such a propensity makes it no more likely that he is guilty of the offence'. Section 103(2) provides that such a propensity can be established by evidence that the defendant has been convicted of offences of the same description, or of the same category. The 'description' of an offence simply relates to its given name within the criminal law – i.e. theft, burglary, driving whilst disqualified, handling stolen goods, etc. The 'category' in which a particular offence falls will be prescribed by the Secretary of State.[725]

On that basis, it can be assumed that the scope of 'propensity' under the 2003 Act is considerably wider than what it had been under the similar fact rule at common law. However, a number of caveats apply to this observation. First, section 103(3) provides that evidence of a conviction of the same description or category is not to be admitted

---

[725]Criminal Justice Act 2003, section 103(4)(b). At the time of writing, two such orders are in place: one categorising offences related to 'theft'; another related to 'sexual offences involving persons under the age of 16' – see Criminal Justice Act 2003 (Categories of Offences) Order 2004.

'if the court is satisfied, by reason of the length of time since the conviction or for any other reason, that it would be unjust for it to apply in his case'. The judge must therefore approach each case on its own facts, and consider carefully the precise nature of the previous offences, any underlying reasons for the offender's behaviour, and the time that has since elapsed.

Second, the discretion in section 101(3) also applies to this gateway: the court may exclude the evidence if it appears that its admissibility would have such an adverse effect on the fairness of the proceedings that the court ought not to admit it. Here the judge may pay particular attention to the seriousness of the previous offence(s). The more serious they are, the more weight the jury may attach to them. As suggested above, this is not necessarily 'unfair' to the accused, but it does mean that the judge should consider carefully the potential consequences of allowing the prosecution to use such evidence.

Third, it should be borne in mind that evidence of a propensity to act in a particular way is not admissible if 'the existence of such a propensity makes it no more likely that the defendant is guilty of the offence charged'.[726] It follows that the trial judge must determine that the particular propensity evidence is sufficiently relevant to make it more likely that the defendant is guilty of the offence charged. Finally, it should also be underlined that section 103(2) states that showing an offence falls within the same category or description is only one means of illustrating propensity; it may be proved in any other way. This could potentially include someone with a history of being subject to previous criminal investigations in similar offences where charges were never brought or were later dropped. This information may still be regarded by the court as carrying some form of probative value.

Unfortunately, there is still relatively little guidance from the courts on how these various provisions will dovetail with each other in practice. The leading case to date is that of *R v Hanson*,[727] where the Court of Appeal stated that essentially there are three questions to be considered:

- Did the history of his convictions establish a propensity to commit offences of the kind charged?

- Did that propensity make it more likely that the defendant had committed the offence charged?

- Was it just to rely on the convictions of the same description or category; and, in any event, would the proceedings be unfair if they were admitted?

Therefore, such evidence might be relevant to a number of issues in the case. For example, it might assist the prosecution to prove the defendant's guilt by establishing his involvement or state of mind, or by rebutting a defence or explanation of his conduct. Previous convictions for offences which are of the same description or category as those charged are admissible to prove a propensity to commit that kind of offence, or to be untruthful when either of these matters is in issue. Notwithstanding this, the Court of Appeal did issue a warning that there should not be a presumption of admissibility merely because a particular offence falls within the same category or description. In highlighting the broad nature of the 'theft' category of offences, noting that it encapsulated both handling stolen goods and aggravated vehicle taking,[728] the Court stated that these offences were significantly

---

[726]Criminal Justice Act 2003, section 103(1).
[727][2005] 1 WLR 3169.
[728]*Ibid.*, 3176.

different from each other and, furthermore, neither would show a propensity to burgle or steal on the part of the defendant.

In determining probative value, the judge should assess each case on its own facts, carefully examining the degree of similarity between the offences in question before arriving at a decision. Furthermore, as the Court of Appeal observed in *R v Edwards*,[729] the direction given to the jury on how to treat such evidence is of the utmost importance. The Court of Appeal underlined that judges should take care to direct the jury carefully about the degree of weight they should place on previous offences. In particular, judges should issue a clear warning to the jury against placing undue emphasis on previous convictions, and should remind them that, by themselves, they cannot prove guilt. In addition, the judge should explain precisely the purpose of the evidence and the ways in which it is relevant to their decision.

Propensity to be untruthful

Propensity to commit the offence in question is only one ground on which evidence may be admitted under section 101(1)(d). Section 103(1)(b) provides that evidence relating to whether the defendant has a propensity to be untruthful can also be admitted. However, such evidence will not be relevant to the question of guilt, and can only be used by the jury in determining whether or not the accused is to be regarded as a credible witness.[730] This provision is directed primarily to cover evidence such as a conviction for perjury or offences involving dishonest deception (for example, obtaining property or a pecuniary advantage by deception).

It is not, however, intended that a conviction for any criminal offence should be admissible by virtue of this provision, only those which show a propensity to be untruthful where it is suggested that the defendant's case is untruthful in one particular respect. As the Court of Appeal noted in *Hanson*, a propensity to untruthfulness is not the same as a propensity to dishonesty.[731] In practice, this provision is likely to be relied on most frequently where the defendant and the prosecution are agreed on the facts of the alleged offence and the question is whether all the elements of the offence have been made out. For example, Joe is charged with burglary and theft of a CD player from his neighbour's house. Joe admits that he entered the property and took the CD player, but claims that it belongs to him. The only issue in the case is whether the property alleged to have been stolen 'belonged to another' as required by the definition of 'theft' in the Theft Act 1968. Here, evidence that Joe has been untruthful in his claims could well be supported were the prosecution to adduce evidence of a previous conviction for perjury.

Other matters in issue between the prosecution and defence

It should be underlined that propensity to commit the kind of offence charged, and propensity to be untruthful are only two examples of common issues that may be contested between the parties. The application of gateway (d) is not, however, limited to question of propensity. Evidence which does not establish propensity under section 103 (1) (a) or (b) may still be admissible to prove any other fact in issue. For example, in *R v Tirnaveanu*,[732]

---

[729] [2006] 1 WLR 1524.
[730] *R v Highton* [2006] 1 Cr App R 7.
[731] At 3173.
[732] [2007] 1 WLR 3049.

the defendant was charged with a number of offences in relation to people trafficking. It was alleged by the Crown that he had posed as a solicitor in order to dishonestly obtain money from illegal immigrants from Romania by offering them forged entry documents. At trial he denied the offences, contending that another person had stolen his identity and had framed him for the alleged acts. The prosecution were then granted leave to introduce evidence to show that the defendant had, in the past, entered into a number dealings with other illegal entrants. This evidence was accepted by the Court of Appeal as being relevant to an important matter in issue between the defendant and the prosecution, namely whether it was the defendant who committed the offences and not some other person.

Section 101(1)(d) in operation: some practice scenarios

Although there has been no shortage of reported case law relating to gateway (d) since the CJA took effect, it may still be useful to pause to consider how section 101(1)(d) might be applied in practice through contemplating a number of fictional scenarios. Consider the following:

Michael's case

Michael is charged with obtaining property by deception having sold a necklace, which he said he had inherited from his grandmother. He falsely represented to the buyer that it was a diamond necklace when in fact it was glass. His defence is that he honestly believed it was a diamond necklace, and the issue before the court is whether he genuinely held that belief.

Six months previously, Michael had been arrested and charged with a similar offence in which he sold a glass necklace inherited from a relative, which he had also represented as a diamond necklace. He was acquitted, with the jury having accepted his defence that he honestly believed that it was made from diamonds. The similarity of the offences and the fact that Michael had made the same false representation previously suggest that he now knows the difference between diamonds and glass, and this would be admissible to prove that, contrary to his defence, he knew the necklace was glass. The previous acquittal is thus relevant to an important matter in issue between the defendant and the prosecution, and is admissible under section 101(1)(d), subject to the exercise of the discretion in section 101(3).

Olivia's case

Olivia has two previous convictions, one for obtaining property by deception and one for obtaining a pecuniary advantage by deception. In the first instance, she had used a cheque drawn on a closed account to obtain goods, and later claimed she did not know the account had been closed. In the second case, she used a credit card to purchase goods after being told by the credit card company that she had exceeded her limit and was not to use the card. Here the convictions are relevant to the issue of whether the defendant was dishonest, and where she has a propensity to commit the kind of offence charged.[733] The convictions are for offences of the same description (the offence of dishonestly obtaining property by

---

[733]Criminal Justice Act 2003, section 103(1)(a).

deception) and thus would be admissible under section 101(1)(d) to establish the propensity to commit an offence of the kind charged.

Norman's case

Norman is charged with rape, during which the victim was threatened with a knife. The victim's description of her assailant fitted that of the accused. Norman denied being in the area, and claimed to be away on holiday at the time. However, Norman was arrested the day after the rape while trying to sell stolen goods at a car boot sale. It transpired that some of these items had been stolen from a car parked near the scene of the rape, which had been broken into shortly before the incident took place.

Norman was convicted of the offence of theft from the vehicle, and has previous convictions for violence involving the use of a knife and a number of convictions for theft from cars. Unusually for a rape case, the issue here is whether the defendant was the rapist, or whether, as he states, he was elsewhere at the time. Norman's previous convictions would be admissible under section 101(1)(d), the issue being not whether he has a propensity to commit an offence of rape but whether he has a propensity to be untruthful. The possession of the stolen items and his convictions for theft from the car put him at the scene of the rape and rebut his story that he was elsewhere at the time, and his propensity to violence using a knife assists in identifying him as the rapist.

Barrington's case (revisited)

An example of bad character which fell short of criminal conduct is to be found in the case of *R v Barrington*.[734] Barrington was convicted of indecently assaulting three young girls. They gave evidence to the effect that they had been invited into his house on separate occasions to baby-sit, and were shown pornographic pictures and persuaded to pose nude. At that point, it was alleged that the accused touched the girls inappropriately. Barrington's defence was that the girls were lying and had got together to concoct the charges. Three other young girls were permitted to give evidence of being induced to enter Barrington's house to baby-sit, and were subsequently shown pornographic pictures and invited to pose nude. All three had refused and no offence was committed against them. The Court of Appeal noted:

> That they did not include evidence of the commission of offences similar to those with which the appellant was charged does not mean that they are not logically probative in determining the guilt of the appellant. Indeed we are of the opinion that taken as a whole they are inexplicable on the basis of coincidence and that they are of positive probative value in assisting to determine the truth of the charges against the appellant, in that they tended to show that he was guilty of the offences with which he was charged.[735]

How, then, would the provisions of the 2003 Act apply to Barrington's scenario if it were to come before the courts today? The issue between the defendant and the prosecution would be whether the defendant had indecently assaulted the young girls, or whether they had concocted a false story. Here, although the conduct is not criminal, it may well be viewed as some form of misconduct or reprehensible behaviour under section 112 given that it seems relatively close to an attempt at indecent assault. If the defendant had previous convictions for indecent assault, those convictions would also be admissible under section 101(1)(d),

---

[734](1981) 72 Cr App R 280.
[735]*Ibid.*, at 290.

since the issue between the defendant and the prosecution would include the question whether he has a propensity to commit the kind of offence charged.

Hardik's case

Hardik is charged with conspiracy to defraud Customs and Excise by smuggling cigarettes and selling them without paying duty. He denies knowing or being involved with the men alleged to be his co-conspirators. He has a conviction for affray, in which three of the four co-conspirators were involved and were also convicted. That conviction would be admissible to prove that the defendant knew the co-conspirators – an important matter in issue between the defendant and the prosecution. Section 103(1)(b) makes it clear that the matters in issue include the question whether the defendant has a propensity to be untruthful. The prosecution will suggest that the defendant's case is untruthful, and his conviction for affray, which involved three of his co-conspirators, is admissible to prove that Hardik has a propensity to be untruthful.

Dan's case

Dan is charged with causing grievous bodily harm. Following an incident during a local football match, the match referee sent him off for punching an opponent. The following day the defendant approached the referee in his local pub and, after verbally berating him, struck the referee with a beer glass, fracturing his cheekbone. Dan has a number of previous convictions for assault, ranging from common assault to assault occasioning actual bodily harm. In addition, he has been sent off in football matches for violent conduct on seven previous occasions. Dan is pleading not guilty, and claims that the incident was accidental. He claims he was gesticulating and forgot he had the glass in his hand.

The issue between the defendant and the prosecution is whether the defendant intended to cause the referee serious bodily harm, or whether it was, as the defendant alleges, an accident. The convictions for violence would be admissible under section 101(1)(d). Convictions for assaults ranging from common assault to assault occasioning actual bodily harm may not be of the same description as defined by section 103(4) (since the statement of the offence in the indictment would be different), but there can be little doubt that they will be of the same category.[736] The previous convictions will therefore be admissible to show a propensity to commit offences of the kind charged.

As noted above, the history of violence need not involve criminal convictions and can include the defendant's disciplinary record. At common law the disciplinary record of a rugby player, accused of assaulting an opponent during a match, was admitted in the case of R v Marsh.[737] Although the appellant had no previous convictions, the Court of Appeal held he was properly cross-examined on his disciplinary record, which included being sent off a number of times. Thus, in Dan's case, since his own disciplinary record shows a propensity to violence, it will also be admissible under this head.[738]

---

[736] However, at the time of writing the Secretary of State has not made an order prescribing such offences.
[737] [1994] Crim LR 52.
[738] Similarly, in many cases of domestic violence, the police may have attended the home following a complaint from a wife that her husband had assaulted her. A relatively commonplace scenario may be that the wife is taken to hospital for treatment and the husband is arrested. Next day the wife withdraws her complaint and no prosecution follows. That history of violence, together with any witness accounts of the husband assaulting the wife in the past, will be admissible if the husband is tried for causing grievous bodily harm to his wife and, possibly, on a charge of causing grievous bodily harm to anyone else.

The distinction between section 101(1)(c) and under section 101(1)(d)

There is often a fine line between important explanatory evidence, admitted under gateway (c), and evidence of a propensity, admitted under gateway (d). Explanatory evidence is intended to enable the court and jury better to understand the evidence and the case as a whole. Unlike evidence admitted under section 101(1)(d), it is not intended to demonstrate a propensity to commit the kind of offence charged, although it is questionable whether juries are capable of using such evidence only for the intended purpose.

The difficulty is illustrated by the decision in *R v Dolan*,[739] where the defendant was charged with the murder of his 3½-month-old son by shaking him to death. Evidence of the defendant's tendency to lose his temper with inanimate objects and react violently toward them was wrongly admitted as what we now call important explanatory evidence because it did not show a tendency to lose his temper with human beings. As such it served no useful function, and diverted the jury from the real and important issue before them. It would seem to follow that had there been evidence of the defendant's tendency to lose his temper with human beings, and of his violent reaction towards them, that would have been admissible as important explanatory evidence.

However, had the defendant's loss of temper resulted in violence towards persons, it might well be admissible under gateway (d) in terms of the current law. Suppose the facts of *Dolan* were slightly different. The defendant has been charged with the murder of his young child by shaking him to death. There is evidence that he is quick to lose his temper when criticised or on the losing side of an argument. In addition, he has a number of convictions for assault occasioning actual bodily harm, and there is a history of violence towards his wife, which has resulted in the police and paramedics being called to the property on various occasions.

If the defendant pleads not guilty to the murder charge and claims the death was accidental, such evidence of bad character would appear to be admissible under section 101(1)(d) as relevant to an important matter in issue between the defendant and the prosecution, the issue being accident or deliberate assault. That issue would include, as section 103(1)(a) makes clear, the question whether the defendant has a propensity to commit an offence of the kind charged. His tendency to lose his temper without provocation, his convictions for assault and his violence towards his wife combine to suggest that the accused has a propensity to commit the kind of offence charged (murder is basically a serious assault resulting in death). As such, the evidence of bad character is likely to be admitted under section 101(1)(d) and is unlikely to be excluded under section 101(3). If the evidence was to be admitted as important explanatory evidence under gateway (c), the emphasis would have to be on the explanatory nature of the evidence (i.e., the circumstances of the accused's home life), rather than its tendency to suggest a propensity to commit the kind of crime charged.

Co-accused taking advantage of bad character evidence

Section 103(6) makes it clear that only prosecution evidence is admissible under section 101(1)(d). Therefore D1 cannot rely on this section to adduce evidence of the bad character of D2. Instead, D1 must rely on section 101(1)(e), discussed further in the chapter. However, once the evidence has been admitted, there is no reason why D1 cannot take advantage

---

[739] [2003] 1 Cr App R 18.

of the prosecution's use of such evidence and cross-examine D2 on the issues it raises. At common law, where evidence of the propensity of a co-accused to commit the kind of offence was relevant to a fact in issue between the prosecution and a co-accused, the trial judge was required to direct the jury that they were to ignore that evidence in considering the case against another co-accused. However, in *R v Randall*,[740] Lord Steyn stated:

> For the avoidance of doubt I would further add that in my view where evidence of the propensity of a co-accused is relevant to a fact in issue between the Crown and the other accused it is not necessary for the trial judge to direct the jury to ignore that evidence in considering the case against the co-accused. Justice does not require such a direction to be given. Moreover, such a direction would needlessly perplex a jury.[741]

Supposing Jackie and Ted are charged with robbery at a local off-licence. Ted denies that he was involved in the robbery, and claims that Jackie was acting on his own. The prosecution apply successfully for leave to introduce Jackie's previous convictions for robbery, in order to prove a propensity to commit offences of this type. The jury, when considering Ted's liability, can take account of the fact that Jackie has previous convictions for robbery, which might be instrumental in persuading them that Ted was not involved.

Gateway (e) – Substantial probative value in relation to an important matter in issue between defendant and co-defendant

The question as to what constitutes an 'important matter in issue' between co-defendants will differ according to the circumstances of the case. As in the scenario described above, often it will simply boil down to which one of the accused committed the offence charged. This scenario arose in the recent House of Lords case of *Randall*, where Randall and Glean were jointly charged with murder. Each raised a 'cut-throat defence', claiming that the other had killed the deceased. Each had given evidence of his own bad character during his evidence-in-chief. While Randall had minor convictions for driving offences and disorderly behaviour, Glean had convictions for theft and nine separate convictions for burglary, the most recent of which involved burglary of a dwelling house by an armed gang who threatened the owner with hammers and screwdrivers.

At the time of the murder, Glean was on the run from the police following another robbery, committed by a gang armed with knives. One of the robbers held a knife to the victim's throat and Glean admitted threatening a witness, saying 'If they get me for this I will get you'. Counsel for each defendant told the jury that the propensity of the other accused to use violence was relevant to the likelihood of that accused having attacked the deceased. However, the trial judge directed the jury that the previous convictions were relevant only to the credibility of each defendant and were irrelevant to the likelihood of his having attacked the deceased. Randall was convicted of manslaughter and Glean was acquitted. Randall appealed, arguing that evidence of Glean's bad character was relevant to the issue of who, as between Randall and Glean, was more likely to have inflicted serious violence on the deceased.

The Court of Appeal agreed that evidence of propensity was relevant to guilt, not just credibility, and ordered that Randall be retried. However, the Court certified a question of law for the House of Lords as follows: 'Where two accused are jointly charged with

---

[740] [2003] 2 Cr App R 442.
[741] *Ibid.*, 451.

a crime, and each blames the other for its commission, may one accused rely on the criminal propensity of the other?' Their Lordships unanimously answered the question in the affirmative, and cited with approval the dictum of Kennedy LJ in the Court of Appeal:

> [I]n the particular circumstances of the present case, where there was a cut throat defence, the antecedent history of Glean was relevant not only in relation to the truthfulness of Glean's evidence but also because of the imbalance between that history and the antecedents of Randall … the evidence tended to show that the version put forward by one co-accused was more probable than that put forward by the other'.[742]

Although this case was heard before the 2003 Act came into force, there is little doubt that the previous convictions of Glean and Randall could be admitted under section 101(1)(e), the important matter in issue between them being which of them was more likely to have been responsible for the death of the deceased. Glean's propensity to commit crimes that involved violence would make it more likely that he killed the deceased.[743] Randall could, as he did in the above case, adduce his own bad character under section 101(1)(b) with a view to demonstrating the lack of a propensity to violence. If Glean had convictions for offences of the same description or of the same category, the prosecution could adduce them under section 101(1)(d), but offences of burglary, or aggravated burglary and robbery, are not of the same description or category as murder, which was not committed in the course of either of those offences.

Section 104 also limits the admissibility of evidence of the defendant's propensity to be untruthful to circumstances in which the defendant has undermined his co-defendant's evidence. Under section 1(3)(c) of the Criminal Evidence Act 1898, a co-defendant was permitted to cross-examine another defendant on his previous convictions or bad character when that defendant gave evidence against the co-defendant. This was interpreted as evidence that directly supported the prosecution case against the co-defendant, or indirectly undermined the co-defendant's defence. Section 101(1)(e) and section 104 replace that provision. These sections relate to evidence that is relevant to an issue between the defendant and a co-defendant. Section 104(1), whilst covering evidence which is relevant to the question whether the defendant has a propensity to untruthful, states that such evidence is only admissible if 'the nature and conduct of his defence is such as to undermine the co-defendant's defence'.

In *R v Varley*,[744] the Court of Appeal gave the following guidance as to the meaning of 'evidence against a co-defendant' under the 1898 Act:

(1) If it is established that a person jointly charged has given evidence against a co-defendant that defendant has a right to cross-examine the other as to previous convictions and the trial judge has no discretion to refuse an application.

(2) Such evidence may be given either in chief or during cross-examination.

(3) It has to be objectively decided whether the evidence either supports the prosecution case in a material respect or undermines the defence of the co-accused. A hostile intent is irrelevant.

(4) If consideration has to be given to the undermining of the other's defence care must be taken to see that the evidence clearly undermines the defence. Inconvenience to or inconsistency with the other's defence is not of itself sufficient.

---

[742][2003] 2 Cr App R 442, 451.
[743]See also *Price* [2005] Crim LR 304.
[744][1982] 2 All ER 519.

(5) Mere denial of participation in a joint venture is not of itself sufficient to rank as evidence against a co-defendant. For the [provision] to apply such denial must lead to the conclusion that if the witness did not participate then it must have been the other who did.

(6) Where the one defendant asserts or in due course would assert one view of the joint venture which is directly contradicted by the other such contradiction may be evidence against the co-defendant.[745]

Under section 101(1)(e), the courts are likely to take a similar view of the meaning of the words 'the nature and conduct of his defence is such as to undermine the co-defendant's defence'. However, the 1898 Act allowed cross-examination on any aspect of the co-defendant's bad character only if the co-defendant had given evidence against the other co-defendant. Under the 2003 Act, the requirement that the co-defendant undermines the defence of the other co-defendant is confined to the situation in which a co-defendant seeks to adduce evidence of the other defendant's propensity to be untruthful. Other evidence that is of substantial probative value in relation to an important matter in issue between the defendants is admissible whether or not the nature or conduct of the other's defence is such as to undermine the co-defendant's defence.

Evidence of a propensity to be untruthful may include offences of dishonesty and convictions for perjury which suggest that the defendant is not a credible witness. However, as the Law Commission envisaged, it is not confined to such convictions:

D1 (who has previous convictions for robbery) and D2 are jointly charged with robbery. D1's defence is that D2 did it on her own. In order to get D1's criminal record admitted under the co-defendant exception on the basis that D1 has undermined D2's case, D2 must show that his convictions show that he is likely to lie on oath. What is in issue is D1's propensity to tell the truth not his propensity to rob.[746]

The Law Commission accepted that such evidence is less likely to be admitted as being relevant to credibility than under the then existing law, and recognised that previous convictions for robbery will be more directly relevant to the issue of who committed the robbery. In such circumstances the prosecution will seek to adduce those convictions under section 101(1)(d). However, if the trial judge were to exclude those convictions under section 101(3), D2 in the above scenario could seek to adduce them under section 101(1)(e). The discretion to exclude does not apply to section 101(1)(e), but D2 must demonstrate that the convictions are of substantial probative value in relation to an important issue between himself and D1.

'Important issue' vs. 'substantial probative value'

Under section 101(1)(e), evidence is admissible only if it has substantial probative value in relation to an important issue between a defendant and co-defendant. The two conditions, 'substantial probative value' and 'an important issue', make it clear that evidence that has marginal or trivial value will not be admissible; neither will it be admissible if the issue to which it relates is marginal or trivial in the case as a whole. Under the 1898 Act, a denial of guilt by one defendant was not evidence against the other unless the circumstances were such that in denying guilt the defendant was inevitably accusing the other.

---

[745]See also *R v Davis* [1975] 1 All ER 233; *R v Crawford* [1998] 1 Cr App R 338.
[746]Law Commission, op cit n 694, [14.49].

For example, in *R v Davis*,[747] the circumstances were such that a stolen necklace could only have been taken by the defendant or his co-accused. The defendant's denial that he had taken the necklace was then inevitably evidence against the co-accused. Such circumstances are rare, and an ordinary denial of guilt was not evidence against the other defendant and would not raise an issue between the defendants under this head.

In *R v Bruce*,[748] Bruce, M and another were charged with robbery. The prosecution case was that they had frightened a passenger in a train into giving them money. M gave evidence that there had been a prior agreement to commit a robbery, but claimed he played no part in the offence. Bruce denied that there had been any such plan. The trial judge ruled that this claim constituted evidence against his co-defendants, who were then permitted to cross-examine Bruce on his past record. However, this decision was reversed by the Court of Appeal. Although Bruce had contradicted part of M's evidence, he had not specifically challenged M's statement that he took no part in the robbery. Indeed, Bruce's evidence did more to contradict the prosecution case, and gave M an additional line of defence. In the view of the Court, if a defendant contradicts his co-defendants, but in doing so gives the co-defendant a better defence, it ought not to be viewed as evidence against the co-defendant. This is also likely to be the position under the 2003 Act.

At common law, and under the 1898 Act, the courts had no discretion to exclude defence evidence. Their task was confined to ensuring the defence evidence was relevant and, in the context of the 1898 Act, that the defendant had 'given evidence against a co-defendant'. Similarly under the new scheme, the discretion under section 101(3) is confined to gateways (d) and (g). Therefore, under section 101(1)(e), the task of the trial judge is confined to determining whether the evidence has substantial probative value in relation to an important issue in the case.[749]

Gateway (f) – Evidence to correct a false impression

For section 101(1)(f) to apply, the defendant must have been responsible for an assertion that gives a false or misleading impression about his or her character. This might be done expressly, for example by claiming to be of good character when this is not the case, or impliedly, through conduct in court, or through appearance or dress.[750]

The provision largely reflects the old law contained in section 1(3) of the Criminal Evidence Act 1898, which permitted the prosecution to cross-examine a defendant about his previous convictions or bad character if 'he has personally or by his advocate asked questions of the witnesses for the prosecution with a view to establishing his own good character or has given evidence of his good character'. Although the courts have never devised a definitive test, the cases under the 1898 Act suggest that an accused gives evidence of his good character if he gives evidence that he has previously handed lost property back to its owner;[751] gives evidence that he is a religious man who has attended

---

[747](1974) 60 Cr App R 157.
[748][1975] 1 WLR 1252.
[749]See further *R v Lawson* [2007] 1 WLR 1191. Each accused alleged that the other was lying, but counsel for D1 cross-examined D2 about a previous conviction for assault without giving notice to the court. The appeal on this ground was, however, dismissed, since the judge had the power to dispense with notice requirements under r 35.5 CPR 2005.
[750]Criminal Justice Act 2003, section 105(4)–(5).
[751]*R v Samuel* (1956) 40 Cr App R 8. The charge here was theft.

church services for years;[752] asserts that for the past four years he has been carrying on an honest living;[753] or asserts that he is a married man, with a family and in regular work.[754] Such cases are likely to continue to be seen as examples of a direct assertion of good character which, if true, may be rebutted by evidence admissible under gateway (f) of the 2003 Act.[755]

By contrast however, giving evidence of general relations with customers with a view to negating a charge of fraud was not found to be an attempt to assert good character,[756] and neither was the wearing of a regimental blazer in court.[757] Furthermore, it is perhaps obvious to state that a mere attempt to assert innocence or repudiate guilt could not constitute evidence of good character. Otherwise, it would be impossible for any defendant to mount a successful defence without risking losing his or her shield.[758]

It is likely to be those cases which involve an implied assertion of good character that will trouble the appellate courts most frequently in the years to come. Indeed, it was recognised by the Criminal Law Revision Committee back in 1971 that such implications are necessarily subjective, but are not always clear cut.[759] One example the Committee cited was drawn from a case tried at the Old Bailey in 1968. One of two men charged with conspiracy to rob (both of whom had long criminal records) went into the witness box wearing a dark suit and looking every inch the respectable businessman. Asked by his counsel when and where he met his co-defendant, he replied: 'About eighteen months ago at my golf club. I was looking for a game and the secretary introduced us'. The Committee had no doubt that this was an imputation of good character, as was the suggestion in another case that the defendant, who lived on crime, was negotiating the purchase of a substantial property. However, it is questionable whether the same conclusions would be drawn in the twenty-first century. The Committee appeared to assume that golf clubs only admit persons of good character as members. This might have been the case in the 1960s, but in the modern era membership of a golf club, or even the purchase of a substantial property, are unlikely, per se, to be indicative of good character in the minds of the general public.

The *Notes of Guidance* to the 2003 Act suggest, as an example of asserting good character by dress or conduct, a defendant wearing a clerical collar to which he was not entitled. Such extreme examples are likely to be rare, but this comes fairly close to the manner in which the accused presented himself in Z.[760] In a television dramatisation of the trial,[761] the defendant stood in the dock dressed in a dark suit, white shirt and tie, clutching a Bible with both hands as though in prayer. That might now be seen as asserting a false good character, given that he had a conviction for rape and had been acquitted of rape a number of times.

---

[752] *R v Ferguson* (1909) 2 Cr App R 250.

[753] *R v Baker* (1912) 7 Cr App R 252.

[754] *R v Coulman* (1927) 20 Cr App R 106. The charge here concerned indecency with young boys – the stable family relationship suggested he was unlikely to have committed such an offence.

[755] In *Renda*, however, the Court seemingly disapproved of citing pre-2003 Act cases, and stated that they are merely 'factual examples of occasions when it was decided that an individual defendant had put his character in issue (at 2952).

[756] *R v Ellis* [1910] 2 KB 746.

[757] *R v Hamilton* [1969] Crim LR 486. This case might now be decided differently given that section 105(5) makes it clear that 'conduct' in section 105(4) includes appearance or dress. It would, of course, be only a *false* impression if the defendant is not *entitled* to wear that regimental blazer.

[758] *R v Rouse* [1904] 1 KB 184.

[759] Criminal Law Revision Committee, op cit n 671, [135 et seq].

[760] See above, pp 174–76.

[761] 'Dispatches', *Still Getting Away with Rape*. Channel 4, 16 March 2000.

The circumstances were somewhat similar in *R v Robinson*.[762] The defendant, a rather difficult witness, gave evidence at his trial for theft holding a small Bible in his hand whilst gesticulating, so that it could be clearly seen by the jury. The trial judge said that this was a cynical and manipulative action calculated to make the jury think he was a religious person and likely to tell the truth, and accepted the prosecution's argument that he had put his character in issue. However, the Court of Appeal disagreed, and held that he did not put his character in issue by taking the oath, or by reminding the jury of the oath he had sworn on the Bible. Ultimately, there was no evidence that the impression he gave of himself was false, so the conviction was unsafe and a retrial was ordered. There is nothing within section 105(4) that would suggest the court would arrive at a different conclusion under the new law.

Section 105(2) sets out the circumstances in which a defendant is to be treated as being responsible for an assertion. These will usually occur through the defendant making the assertion himself whilst giving evidence. A relatively straightforward example can be found in *R v Renda*, which was decided under the 2003 Act. Here, the defendant claimed to have suffered a head injury whilst serving with the armed forces, and also stated he was employed as a security guard at the time of the alleged offence. This information was false, and the prosecution were thus entitled to introduce evidence of his previous involvement in a serious assault.

Alternatively, the defendant may now make such an assertion whilst being questioned under caution or being charged with the offence. This circumstance represents a change to the previous law, which took the view that any assertion had to be made by the defendant in evidence. Thus in *R v Holman*,[763] the accused was charged with stealing two necklaces which were found in his possession. He told the police he had found them in the garden of a house when he went to recover a car, and intended to telephone the police and tell them. It was held that he had given evidence of his good character and the prosecution were allowed to cross-examine him under section 1(3)(b) of the 1898 Act. The Court of Appeal held that the judge should not have allowed counsel to do so since the accused did not state this in direct testimony to the court.

Under the 2003 Act, that is no longer the position. If the defendant makes any assertion whilst being questioned under caution before charge, or on being charged with the offence, and that statement is then admitted in evidence, he will now be seen as being responsible for it.[764] Furthermore, the defendant is also seen as being responsible for assertions made by defence witnesses; those made by any other witness in response to questions by the defendant which were intended (or likely to) elicit them; and out-of-court assertions made by anybody if adduced in evidence by the defendant.

Correcting the false impression

In correcting the impression, the prosecution may introduce evidence of the defendant's misconduct that has a probative value in correcting it.[765] Exactly what evidence is required in order to do this will turn on the facts of each specific case and, in particular, the nature of the misleading impression that has been given. Evidence is admissible under section 105(6)

---

[762] [2001] Crim LR 478.
[763] (1992) *The Times*, 9 September.
[764] Criminal Justice Act 2003, section 105(2)(b)(i)–(ii).
[765] Note that only the prosecution may correct a false impression under section 105(7). A co-defendant is not able to do so.

only if it goes no further than is necessary to correct the false impression. This reverses the common law rule that character was indivisible.[766] Thus where a defendant is charged with theft, and asserts his reputation for honesty, convictions for offences of dishonesty will be admissible to correct that false impression, but a conviction for a sexual offence would be excluded. If, however, the defendant gives the impression, either verbally in evidence or by his conduct and dress, that he is an upstanding citizen, convictions for any and all offences would be admissible as necessary to correct that false impression.

As a final point in relation to gateway (f), it is worth noting that a defendant may withdraw or disassociate himself from a false or misleading impression by correcting the impression himself, through his or her own testimony, or through cross-examination of witnesses.[767] Evidence to correct the false impression will not then be admissible. However, the Court of Appeal was keen to stress in *Renda* that, for the shield to be restored, the defendant's renunciation of his or her claims must be unequivocal:

> There is a significant difference between the defendant who makes a specific and positive decision to correct a false impression for which he is responsible, or to dissociate himself from false impressions conveyed by the assertions of others, and the defendant who in the process of cross-examination is obliged to concede that he has been misleading the jury. A concession extracted in cross-examination that the defendant was not telling the truth in part of his examination-in-chief will not normally amount to a withdrawal or dissociation from the original assertion for the purposes of section 105(3).[768]

Given that the defendant can prevent bad character evidence being admitted by such withdrawal or disassociation, the opportunity to apply under section 101(3) to have such evidence excluded through the judicial discretion does not apply to this subsection.

Gateway (g) – Attacks on another person's character

Under the eighth and final gateway, a defendant's own bad character will become admissible when there has been an attack on another person's character. This is deemed to occur where the accused gives evidence that a particular individual committed an offence (either the one charged, or a different one), or has behaved or is disposed to behave in a reprehensible way.[769] This is a continuation of the 'tit-for-tat' principle which applied under section 1(3)(b) of the Criminal Evidence Act 1898. However, the nature of the provision in the new legislation is significantly wider, since there is no longer any requirement that the rule will only be triggered where the character of a prosecution witness or the prosecutor is attacked. There is now no such limitation, with section 101(1)(g) simply referring to 'another person'. One can understand why an attack on the character of someone involved in the trial should result in the defendant's bad character being put before the court or jury: in determining whether a witness or the defendant is to be believed, it is only right that the character of the person who has attacked the credibility of the witness or deceased victim be known so that his credibility can be properly judged. However, by the same token, casting the net so widely under the new law seems somewhat unnecessary. Suppose, for example, the defendant alleges that his brother, who is not a witness in the trial, committed the crime.

---

[766]This position has been confirmed by the Court of Appeal in *R v Somanathan* [2006] 1 WLR 1885. For an example of the operation of the former common law rule, see *R v Winfield* (1939) 27 Cr App R 139,
[767]Criminal Justice Act 2003, section 105(3).
[768]*Renda*, 2952.
[769]CJA 2003, section 106(1)(a), section 106(2).

It is not entirely clear why gateway (g) should apply in these circumstances. If the accused has a propensity to be untruthful, evidence to show that characteristic is admissible under section 101(1)(d). Adducing previous convictions on a 'tit-for-tat' basis here would make little sense, and would arguably be grossly unfair to the accused.

The definition of 'attacking another persons's character' for the purposes of gateway 'g' is similar to the generic definition of 'bad character' in section 98, but includes evidence relating to the facts of the offence charged and its investigation and prosecution. Thus, a defendant would be attacking a prosecution witness if he claimed that he or she was lying whilst giving evidence, or was in some way biased or had been motivated by animosity to give false evidence. Indeed, the provision will apply to any evidence whatsoever of previous misconduct that has been introduced to undermine the witness's credibility. The defence will also be regarded as having attacked another person's character where questions are put to opposing witnesses that are likely to elicit evidence of this sort, or if the defendant makes an allegation of this nature when questioned under caution or on being charged with the offence.[770] Unlike section 101(1)(f), where the character attack occurs, there is no provision to allow the defendant to withdraw or disassociate himself from the attack.

It might be asked whether it matters if such an attack or imputation is true or false. Under the 1898 Act, the veracity of such an attack did not affect the loss of the shield. In *R v Bishop*,[771] it was said that 'an imputation on character covers charges of faults or vices whether reputed or real'.[772] Similarly, in *R v Wainwright*,[773] the court rejected the submission that there can only be an imputation if the facts are disputed. It would seem to follow that the attack on another person's character, or an imputation about the other person, need not be untrue for the purposes of gateway (g).

Many cases under the 1898 Act arose from claims by the defence that a prosecution witness had fabricated a confession or obtained it through duress. Not all such claims were false, particularly before PACE took effect. In practice, this meant that corrupt police officers were essentially able to use the 1898 Act as a shield for their misconduct. The introduction of tape-recording of interviews, and now video-recording, has largely brought an end to such allegations. However, it is still not unusual for police officers and other law enforcement officials to have their characters attacked. It could be alleged, for example, that evidence was obtained through an illegal search, or that real evidence had been tampered with. All such attacks will fall within the ambit of section 101(1)(g). However, an assertion of innocence or emphatic denial of guilt will not trigger the provision, providing it does not constitute a direct attack on a prosecution witness. As the facts of *Bishop* demonstrate there is a thin line between an emphatic denial of guilt and attacks on the veracity of the prosecutor or his witnesses. The outright denial of having given a confession, or disclaiming knowledge of an article found during a search by police, is one thing; but to claim that the police concocted the confession or planted the evidence is another. Whether such evidence constitutes a mere denial of guilt or an attack on the character of an opposing witness will turn on the facts of each case.

The discretion to exclude evidence of bad character under section 101(3) applies to section 101(1)(g). At common law, the purpose of the discretion was to prevent an overly

---

[770]Section 106(1). Providing the statement is then admitted in evidence – this may occur, for example, where a police officer gives evidence of an interview with the defendant or of his response on being charged.
[771][1975] QB 274.
[772]*Ibid*., 282.
[773][1998] Crim LR 665.

harsh application of section 1((3)(b) of the 1898 Act. In *R v Burke*,[774] the Court of Appeal accepted that 'cases must occur in which it would be unjust to admit evidence of character gravely prejudicial to the accused, even though there may be some tenuous grounds for holding it technically admissible'.[775] Nonetheless it concluded that:

> In the ordinary and normal case the trial judge may feel that if the credit of the prosecutor or his witnesses has been attacked, it is only fair that the jury should have before them the material on which they can form their judgement whether the accused person is any more worthy to be believed than those he has attacked. It is obviously unfair that the jury should be left in the dark about an accused person's character if the conduct of his defence has attacked the character of the prosecutor or the witnesses for the prosecution within the meaning of section 1(3)(b) of the Act of 1898.[776]

The same approach is likely to be taken under the 2003 Act, as the Court of Appeal has already declared that the old case law relating to the 1898 Act should still apply.[777] The discretion could be used to limit the application of the subsection in cases where the accused had attacked the character of a person not involved in the trial. Though technically admissible, such evidence might be seen as having such an adverse effect on the fairness of the trial that it ought not to be admitted. However, if the defendant makes a deliberate attack on a prosecution witness, the judge is likely to share the opinion of the Court of Appeal in *Burke* that it is 'obviously unfair that the jury should be left in the dark about [the] accused person's character'.

COLLUSION AND CONTAMINATION

Trials involving multiple victims

As indicated above, many cases involving similar fact evidence at common law were cases in which the defendant was charged with the commission of the same type of crime against several victims. In such a case, several counts (charges) are joined in the same indictment and all are tried together rather than several separate trials. The normal rule applying to such trials was that the jury must consider the evidence on each count separately, and in determining the defendant's guilt on one count, they were not permitted to take into account the evidence on the other counts. The similar fact principle operated to override this rule and permit the evidence of each of the other victims to be cross-admissible, and to be possibly taken into account by the jury when considering the evidence on a charge against another victim. The practical effect was that each victim became a witness for the other victims, greatly increasing the likelihood of conviction on all charges.

The exclusion from the definition of 'bad character' of 'evidence of the facts of the offence charged' would seem at first sight to put trials involving multiple victims outside the framework of the new law. However, section 112(2) of the 2003 Act provides that 'where a defendant is charged with two or more offences in the same criminal proceedings, this Chapter ... has effect as if each offence were charged in separate proceedings; and references to the offence with which the defendant is charged are to be read accordingly'.

---

[774] (1986) 82 Cr App R 156.
[775] *Ibid.*, 161.
[776] *Ibid.*
[777] *Hanson*, 3173. This is not, however, the case with gateway (f). See further *Renda*.

The effect of this subsection is that in trials in which the defendant is charged with a number of offences in the same indictment, the evidence of the alleged facts of each individual offence, together with evidence of misconduct in connection with the investigation or prosecution of that offence, is admissible without seeking leave under section 101. However, if the prosecution want the jury, when considering the guilt of the defendant on one count, to take into consideration the evidence of the witnesses and victims of other counts, leave must first be sought.

The intention is that this part of the Act will provide a new basis for the admissibility of previous convictions and other misconduct. Accordingly, section 99 abolishes the common law rules governing the admissibility of such evidence. Statutes dealing with admissibility are also repealed,[778] although this abolition does not extend to the rule that allows a person's bad character to be proved by his reputation. At common law, it was held in *R v Rowton*,[779] that character evidence should be confined to reputation in the community. 'Reputation' referred to the accused's reputed disposition or propensity to act, think or feel in a given way, as opposed to his actual disposition or propensity to act, think or feel in a given way. Evidence of opinion, or of particular acts or other examples of conduct, should not be given, but the decision in *Rowton* (though never overruled) was often ignored in practice and, as an indulgence to the accused, such evidence was frequently admitted. This common law rule is preserved as a category of admissible hearsay in section 118(2).[780]

The risk of collusion or contamination

Where the accused faces a trial involving more than one victim, it is not uncommon for the defence to allege that the victims have collaborated in concocting a joint story, thereby destroying its corroborative value. Such allegations were commonplace in cases involving multiple victims of sexual abuse, particularly when the victims were known to each other. Police and prosecutors are well aware of the possibility of collusion in such cases and would rarely prosecute if there was a likelihood of contamination. Witnesses who have yet to give evidence are not allowed in the court while others give evidence, but they often sit together outside the courtroom, and there have been cases in which a witness who has given evidence has been seen talking to a witness who has yet to do so. It follows that while such collusion or contamination is rare, it is not entirely unknown.

The leading case prior to the 2003 Act was that of *R v H*,[781] where the House of Lords held that the admissibility of similar fact evidence should be approached on the basis that the evidence is true. There, the defendant was charged with a number of sexual offences against his adopted daughter and stepdaughter between 1987 and 1989. At the defendant's trial, the judge directed the jury that they had to consider whether the girls had colluded and invented a false story against their father, and whether they, as the defence claimed, might have fantasised about the assaults. He further directed that it was for the prosecution to satisfy the jury that the girls were in fact telling the truth, and that the evidence of one girl could support the evidence of the other only if the jury were sure that the girls had not collaborated to concoct a false story.

---

[778]Criminal Justice Act 2003, sch 37.
[779](1865) Le & Ca 520 CCR.
[780]See Ch 7 below, p 231.
[781][1995] 2 AC 596.

The defendant was convicted and appealed, contending that the judge had misdirected the jury on the risk of collusion. The House of Lords dismissed the appeal and advocated a two-stage approach where the question of witness collusion arose. First, the judge should consider whether the similar fact evidence, if true, was so probative of the crime of which the defendant was accused that it ought to be admitted notwithstanding the prejudicial effect of disclosing that the defendant had committed other crimes. If the evidence was admitted, it was then for the jury to determine its credibility as a question of fact. The judge should direct them that they could not properly rely on the evidence as corroboration unless they were satisfied that it was reliable and true and not tainted by collusion or other defects. Only when it was obvious that no reasonable jury could accept the evidence as free from collusion or contamination should the judge direct the jury that they should not rely on the evidence at all.

Section 107 of the CJA 2003 now deals with the circumstances where bad character evidence has been admitted, but it later emerges that the evidence is contaminated through collusion of prosecution witnesses. It is still for the jury to decide whether or not to believe evidence and decide on the weight to be placed on it, but an additional duty is conferred on the judge to stop the case if the contamination is such that, considering the importance of the evidence to the case, a conviction would be unsafe. Having stopped the case, the judge may then consider that there is still sufficient uncontaminated evidence against the defendant to merit his retrial, or may consider that the prosecution case has been so weakened that the defendant should be acquitted.[782]

The provision has featured in two recent cases before the Court of Appeal. In the first, R v Chopra,[783] a dentist appealed against his conviction of indecently touching two teenage patients. He had been acquitted of indecently touching a third. Each of the three complainants alleged that C had squeezed her breast during an examination. The girls did not know each other, and the incidents allegedly took place over a 10-year period. As such, the trial judge ruled that the all the evidence should be cross-admissible. The defendant was convicted, and argued on appeal that the judge should have directed the jury that an acquittal on the counts relating to one complainant would undermine the likelihood that the complainants of the other girls were more likely to be true. The appeal was, however, dismissed, with the Court stressing that the critical question for the judge was whether or not the evidence of one complainant was relevant as going, or being capable of going, to establish propensity to commit offences of the kind charged. In this case, there was sufficient similarity between the allegations to make them cross-admissible, and the fact that three girls were making the same allegation made it more likely to be true than if only one of them had made it.

Chopra was considered some months later by the Court of Appeal in R v Lamb.[784] The defendant had been convicted of sexual activity as an abuse of his position of trust with two 17-year-old students at the school where he taught. The girls had alleged that the accused made sexual advances towards them at two separate leavers' balls. A key

---

[782]Section 107(1) provides for the judge to take either of these courses. If, however, an acquittal is ordered then the defendant is also to be acquitted of any other offence for which he could have been convicted, if the judge is satisfied that the contamination would affect a conviction for that offence in the same way (section 107(2)). Section 107(3) extends the duty to the situation where a jury is determining, under the Criminal Procedure (Insanity) Act 1964, whether a person, who is deemed unfit to plead, did the act or omission charged. Section 107(4) makes it clear that section 107(3) does not affect any existing court powers in relation to ordering an acquittal of discharging a jury.

[783][2007] 1 Cr App R 16.

[784][2007] EWCA Crim 1766.

difference between this case, and that of *Chopra*, was that the two complainants here admitted they had discussed their experiences, and one prompted the other to make her complaint. While stopping short of alleging that the girls had maliciously concocted their stories, the appellant alleged that each account had been subject to some degree of 'innocent contamination', which should have been explained to the jury. In this case, the appeal was allowed.

In the view of the Court of Appeal, the trial judge had materially misdirected the jury. Although he had explained that they should consider the potential for false fabrication, this was not appropriate in the case at hand. Instead, he should have directed them as to the possibility of innocent contamination, as there was some evidence that the girls may have either consciously or unconsciously influenced each other's account. Therefore, not only was the necessary point not made, but the wrong point was emphasised.

In summary then, section 107 requires that the trial judge must not only be alert to the possibility of collusion, but should also actively consider the form and extent of such collusion. If he suspects that collusion has taken place and that cross-admissibility is central to the case, the trial should be halted. Otherwise, the direction to the jury should contain some form of warning about the risk of possible contamination of the evidence.

EVIDENCE OF GOOD CHARACTER

Where defendants are of good character,[785] the common law has traditionally allowed them to put their character in issue. Ironically, even before defendants were competent to testify in their own defence, the courts recognised the desirability of informing the jury that the accused had a clean slate.[786] The Criminal Justice Act 2003 has not altered the common law rules, and if the defendant places his or her character in issue, such evidence will be deemed relevant to both credibility and guilt.[787]

The leading case is that of *R v Vye*,[788] which places an obligation on the judge to issue a specific two-limb direction to the jury where the defendant is of good character. Where the defendant testifies directly of his own good character, or calls witnesses to that effect, he or she is entitled to the 'first limb' direction. This will mean that the judge must instruct the jury that they are to accept the defendant's good character when assessing the credibility of his or testimony. All accused persons of good character are entitled to the 'second limb' of the direction. This is an instruction to the jury that they ought to consider the defendant's good character when determining whether he had a disposition to committing the offence in question. However, before giving this limb of the direction, some representation from the defence will usually be necessary, and the judge must be sure that there is relevant information that can be properly and safely be relied upon.[789]

Such a direction is mandatory in all cases, and failure to give it is likely to amount to a material irregularity which will normally constitute good grounds for an appeal.[790] However, a specific form of words need not be used, and the judge should feel free to tailor a

---

[785]i.e. he has no criminal record, nor has he been involved in any form of misconduct covered by CJA, section 98.

[786]See eg *R v Stannard* (1837) 7 C & P 673.

[787]*R v Aziz* [1996] AC 41.

[788][1993] 1 WLR 471.

[789]*Thompson v R* [1998] AC 811.

[790]*R v Fulcher* [1995] 2 Cr App R 251.

direction to the specific circumstances of each case.[791] The issuing of such a direction usually poses few problems where defendants have no previous criminal convictions. However, the situation becomes more complex where a defendant has a few convictions for minor offences in the distant past, or where there is evidence to suggest involvement in some form of criminality, despite the absence of formal convictions.

It was the view of the Court of Appeal in *Nye*[792] that good character directions in cases where the defendant had spent convictions were contrary to both the language and spirit of the law. This advice appeared to be heeded in *Bailey*,[793] where a defendant with four spent convictions, the most recent of which was 25 years old, was refused leave to present himself as a person of good character. More recently however, the courts have been more generous to the accused. For example, in *R v Timson and Hales*,[794] the Court of Appeal held that the trial judge should have given a good character direction in favour of the appellant, despite a conviction five years previously for drunk driving. Whilst in *Aziz* the House of Lords suggested that it would be an 'insult to common sense' to give the direction where it would be clearly misleading, it was unfortunate that their Lordships did not take the opportunity to clarify the precise circumstances when a direction was required. This task was left to the Court of Appeal in *R v Gray*,[795] which set out seven key guidelines:

(i) The primary rule is that a person of previous good character must be given a full direction covering both credibility and propensity. Where there are no further facts to complicate the position, such a direction is mandatory and should be unqualified.

(ii) If a defendant has a previous conviction which, either because of its age or its nature, may entitle him to be treated as of effective good character, the trial judge has a discretion so to treat him, and if he does so the defendant is entitled to a *Vye* direction … but

(iii) Where the previous conviction can only be regarded as irrelevant or of no significance in relation to the offence charged, that discretion ought to be exercised in favour of treating the defendant as of good character … In such a case the defendant is again entitled to a *Vye* direction …

(iv) Where a defendant of previous good character … has been shown at trial, whether by admission or otherwise, to be guilty of criminal conduct, the *prima facie* rule of practice is to deal with this by qualifying a *Vye* direction rather than by withholding it … but

(v) In such a case, there remains a narrowly circumscribed residual discretion to withhold a good character direction in whole, or presumably in part, where it would make no sense, or would be meaningless or absurd or an insult to common sense, to do otherwise …

(vi) Approved examples of the exercise of such a residual discretion are not common … Lord Steyn in *Aziz* appears to have considered that a person of previous good character who is shown beyond doubt to have been guilty of serious criminal behaviour similar to the offence charged would forfeit his right to any direction … On the other hand Lord Taylor CJ's manslaughter/murder example in *Vye* … shows that even in the context of serious crime it may be crucial that a critical intent separates the admitted criminality from that charged.

[791] *Vye*, at 477.
[792] (1982) 75 Cr App R 247.
[793] [1989] Crim LR 723.
[794] [1993] Crim LR 58.
[795] [2004] 2 Cr App R 30.

(vii) A direction should never be misleading. Where therefore a defendant has withheld something of his record so that otherwise a trial judge is not in a position to refer to it, the defendant may forfeit the more ample, if qualified, direction which the judge might have been able to give.[796]

These principles should thus be seen as a valuable guide where aspects of the defendant's past appear somewhat murky. However, in *R v Payton*[797] it was stated that they should not be taken as prescribing precisely what a judge must do; it was vital that each case turned on its own facts, and the overriding duty of the judge was to ensure fairness to the parties. In short, the trial judge will have discretion as to the nature and form of any direction that is given. However, it may be prudent to assume that there is a need for some form of qualified or diluted version of the *Vye* direction where the defendant's previous record is minor in nature and has no real bearing on the question of guilt.

KEY LEARNING POINTS

- Prior to the 2003 Act, evidence of the accused's bad character could only be admitted under the similar fact rule at common law, or under the Criminal Evidence Act 1898.

- This regime has now been abandoned as replaced by the provisions contained in sections 98–113 of the Criminal Justice Act 2003.

- Evidence of bad character will only be admissible if it falls under one of the eight 'gateways' in section 101.

- Where it is clear that evidence has been contaminated, the judge must stop the case if the contamination is such that, considering the importance of the evidence to the case, a conviction would be unsafe.

- Where the defendant has no previous record of misconduct, the judge is under an obligation to issue a *Vye* direction.

? QUESTIONS

1. Consider whether the bad character of the defendant is admissible at his trial in the following alternative circumstances:
    (a) Mandy is charged with theft from the person. It is alleged that she stole a handbag from a woman after showing her a purse and asking if it was hers. When the woman took her handbag out from her shopping bag to check, Mandy snatched it and ran off. Mandy has two previous convictions for theft from the person using the same trick.
    (b) Gerry is charged with causing grievous bodily harm to Julian, with whom he had an altercation after allegedly being "cut up" on a slip-road. Julian, who sustained bruises and a broken shoulder, says Gerry punched him and he fell to the ground breaking his shoulder. Gerry claims that Julian,

Continued

---

[796] *Ibid.*, [57].
[797] [2006] Crim LR 997.

?   *QUESTIONS (Continued)*

who had stopped at the roadside, fell while trying to avoid an HGV that overtook as he was climbing out of his car. Gerry has three previous convictions for assault, one of which followed a road rage incident.

(c)   Eric is charged with causing actual bodily harm to Victor. In his evidence Eric says that he was walking in the park when a young girl complained to him that Victor had made indecent suggestions to her. Eric claims that he then challenged Victor, who responded with violence. In his evidence, Victor said that he went to the park with his children. While in the play area other children told him that Eric, who had been hanging around, had asked several of them if they wanted to come with him to feed the ducks. When Victor approached Eric to ask him about this, Eric punched him a number of times. Eric has two previous convictions for indecently assaulting young girls and is on the Sex Offenders Register.

(d)   Les is charged with assault occasioning actual bodily harm on Leeroy. The arresting officer gave evidence that, on being charged, Les said, 'Well, he's gay, and he told me he wanted to take me into the toilets for some fun, so I thumped him'. Les has two convictions for burglary, three for taking a motor vehicle without consent and one for indecent assault on a female.

(e)   (i)   Mervyn is charged with indecent assault. In his evidence-in-chief he told the jury that he was a respected member of the community, he regularly attended church and he had been a verger. There is evidence that he had attended church regularly and had been a verger until December 2002. However, following an investigation by the Church authorities into allegations that he had touched choirboys inappropriately in the vestry, he had been required to resign from his position as verger and he no longer attended church.

(ii)   Two of Mervyn's alleged victims, Marcus and Maurice, are friends with Mervyn's 12-year-old son, Alan. The defence alleges that the two boys have known each other all their lives and concocted their stories together as revenge against Mervyn because he had banned them from seeing his son.

2.   'Evidence of the accused's previous misconduct can be highly prejudicial to the case of the defence and should only be admissible in the most exceptional of circumstances. The current rules, contained in the Criminal Justice Act 2003, too readily allow for such evidence to be admitted'.

Critically evaluate the above statement.

SUGGESTED FURTHER READING

Law Commission, *Evidence in Criminal Proceedings: Previous Misconduct of a Defendant*, Report No 273 (2001: London, Law Commission).

Lloyd Bostock, S 'The effects on juries of hearing about the defendant's previous criminal record: a simulation study' [2000] Crim LR 734.

Munday, R 'What constitutes a good character?' [1997] Crim LR 247.

Munday, R 'What constitutes "other reprehensible behaviour" under the bad character provisions of the Criminal Justice Act 2003?' [2005] Crim LR 24.

Munday, R 'Cut-throat defences and the "propensity to be untruthful" under section 104 of the Criminal Justice Act 2003' [2005] Crim LR 625.

Spencer, J R *Evidence of Bad Character* (2006: Oxford, Hart).

Waterman, A and Dempster, T 'Bad Character: feeling our way one year on' [2006] Crim LR 614.

CHAPTER 7

HEARSAY EVIDENCE

INTRODUCTION

Hearsay may be defined as any oral or written statement, made by a person other than the maker, which is offered in evidence to prove the truth of the matter asserted. Put more simply, it is evidence that aims to establish the existence of a fact not through the witness's first-hand knowledge, but through what a third party has stated out of court. The rule against the admissibility of hearsay evidence has traditionally been regarded as one of the defining features of the Anglo-American trial. Until recently, such statements, whether in oral or written form, were inadmissible at common law unless they fell within a common law or statutory exception.

Various rationales have been cited for the rule.[798] The most common justification, however, tends to centre around concerns over the potential unreliability of such evidence. Just as in the game of 'Chinese Whispers', it is clear how a statement can become increasingly distorted or misconceived as it passes along the chain of communication. A second reason for excluding hearsay, which is arguably of equal importance, is that the adversarial system places a high value on oral evidence given on oath before a jury. In theory at least, this enables the trier of fact to observe the demeanour of the witness and evaluate the strength of the evidence under cross-examination. The hearsay rule was thus a necessary corollary of the adversarial paradigm: admitting such evidence would have undermined basic tenets of the system.[799]

Over the course of the twentieth century, the hearsay rule was stringently enforced. Judges had no discretion to admit hearsay evidence, even where the evidence was seemingly extremely reliable. As illustrated below, this resulted in a number of manifest injustices, to both the prosecution and the defence. Gradually, the courts, and later Parliament, sought to counteract these effects by crafting a large number of exceptions; and on occasions courts simply sidestepped the rules by interpreting what was quite plainly hearsay as real evidence. By the end of the twentieth century, the parameters of the hearsay rule had become so uncertain, and its rationale so dubitable, that the common law regime was abandoned and replaced with a new statutory scheme contained in the Criminal Justice Act 2003.

EVOLUTION OF THE MODERN LAW

What is hearsay?

In *Subramaniam v Public Prosecutor*,[800] it was stated that:

> Evidence of a statement made to a witness by a person who is not himself called as a witness may or may not be hearsay. It is hearsay and inadmissible when the object of the evidence is

---

[798]See generally Choo, A. *Hearsay and Confrontation in Criminal Trials* (1996: Oxford, Oxford University Press), Ch 1.
[799]See comments of Lord Normand in *Teper v R* [1952] AC 480, at 486.
[800][1956] 1 WLR 965.

to establish the truth of what is contained in the statement. It is not hearsay and is admissible when it is proposed to establish by evidence, not the truth of the statement, but the fact that it was made.[801]

It follows from the above statement that in order to identify a statement as hearsay, the purpose for which such evidence adduced has to be ascertained. This is not always a straightforward task, and, as indicated above, there are many cases in which the courts treated real evidence as hearsay when it was not, and vice versa. Thus, in *Woodhouse v Hall*,[802] the defendants were charged with managing a brothel at premises described as a sauna and massage parlour. Magistrates refused to allow police officers who had posed as customers to give evidence of conversations between them and the masseuses, giving details of the availability and cost of sexual services, stating that the conversations were hearsay. The Divisional Court allowed the prosecution appeal against this refusal. Donaldson LJ had some sympathy with the magistrates, whom he thought had been misled by *Subramaniam*, but he stated that there was no question of the hearsay rule applying to these conversations. The relevant issue here was not the content of the statements, but the fact that offers of sexual services were actually made.

Similarly, in *Roberts v DPP*,[803] the question arose as to whether certain documents were hearsay. The accused was charged with assisting in the management of a brothel and running an unlicensed massage parlour. He had been seen entering the premises, and a search of the office of the company of which he was the managing director revealed a number of documents relating to the company's ownership of the premises used as a brothel, including a telephone account for the premises in the accused's name; documents relating to goods and services supplied to the premises; and adverts placed for the premises, invoiced to the company. A search of the accused's home revealed other documents relating to the premises, including a gas bill. He was convicted and appealed, arguing that these documents should not have been admitted. Dismissing the appeal, the Court accepted that the documents were not admissible to show the truth of their contents but were admissible as circumstantial or 'real' evidence, to which the hearsay rule did not apply. The prosecution did not seek to rely on the truth of the contents of the documents but on the fact that they were in the accused's possession, from which the inference could be drawn that he was involved in the management of the premises. His knowledge that the premises were being used as a brothel was an easy inference to draw from the fact that he had visited the premises, plus the letter requesting adverts in a magazine. There was therefore ample evidence to convict.

Direct and indirect hearsay

Hearsay may be direct (or first-hand), or indirect (second-hand or multiple hearsay). For example, Alex sees a robbery taking place; he notes the registration number of the getaway car and the physical features of one of the robbers who removed his mask. He immediately makes a statement to the police in which he states what he saw, but dies before the case is brought to trial. In such circumstances, the prosecution may seek to rely on the statement Alex made to the police before his death. However, since the purpose of adducing the statement would be to prove the truth of the facts asserted (i.e. the identity of a particular person/vehicle), then this would constitute hearsay evidence. Moreover, it

---

[801] *Ibid.*, at 970.
[802] (1980) 72 Cr App R 39.
[803] [1994] Crim LR 926.

would be classed as direct or first-hand hearsay, because the witness perceived the events directly before communicating them to the police. In these circumstances, this statement would have been inadmissible at common law unless it fell within one of the established exceptions to the rule of exclusion.

Now imagine a slightly different set of facts. What if Alex had seen the above events unfold, but decided not to report it to the police at all? Instead, he told his friend Bryan what he had seen. Unable to convince Alex to go to the police, Bryan relays the account to DC Rollins. Now when the case comes to trial, not only is Alex dead, but Bryan has emigrated and cannot be traced. If the prosecution now wish to seek to rely on Bryan's statement, by calling DC Rollins as a witness, his evidence will be second-hand or multiple hearsay, since it has passed through one further conduit before reaching the court. Traditionally, multiple hearsay has been seen as the least reliable form of hearsay given the possibility of distortion, which increases as the chain of communication grows longer. For that reason, multiple hearsay was generally inadmissible at common law. As we shall see further, however, there are certain circumstances where it may well be admissible under the new statutory arrangements.[804]

Reliable evidence excluded

One of the problems of the common law regime was that it was extremely rigid, and operated to exclude evidence no matter how reliable. In *Myers v DPP*,[805] the prosecution wished to adduce microfilm records from a car manufacturer, showing the different vehicle identification numbers (VINs) that had been assigned to the stolen cars at the time of manufacture in the factory. The purpose of adducing this evidence was to show that the numbers corresponded with those of certain stolen vehicles that had been seized. The manufacturer operated a system under which the VIN passed through several operators in the production line before being recorded in a log. It was, however, impossible to determine who those persons were. The House of Lords, while accepting that the evidence of the VIN was reliable and recommending major statutory change to the law, upheld the decision of the trial judge to refuse to admit the evidence because it was hearsay.[806]

Myers was not the only cases that resulted in an obvious injustice. In *Sparks v R*,[807] the defendant, who was white, was convicted of indecently assaulting a three-year-old girl. Since the child was not competent to give evidence, the trial judge ruled that a statement by the girl that her assailant was 'a coloured boy' was inadmissible hearsay. The Privy Council upheld this ruling, despite it served to show that the accused was innocent. Similarly, in

---

[804]Multiple hearsay was also inadmissible under section 23 of the Criminal Justice Act 1988 if contained in a document. However, it is relatively commonplace in business, and section 24 of the 1988 Act (and now section 117 of the Criminal Justice Act 2003) allowed such a statement in a document to be admitted provided that the statement was created or received by a person in the course of a trade, business, profession, etc, and the information contained in the statement was received by each person in the chain of communication in the course of a trade, business, profession, etc. Under the 2003 Act, multiple hearsay remains inadmissible if it is in oral form but is now subject to discretionary admissibility under section 114(1)(d) (see pp 240–42 below).

[805][1965] AC 1001.

[806]It was not until the enactment of section 68 of the Police and Criminal Evidence Act 1984 (later replaced by section 24 of the Criminal Justice Act 1988, and now covered by section 117 of the Criminal Justice Act 2003) that such evidence became admissible as a statutory exception to the hearsay rule.

[807][1964] AC 964.

R v Thompson,[808] the accused was charged with using an instrument to procure an abortion. The woman died before trial from an unrelated cause. The trial judge ruled that two statements from the woman – the first, made before the operation by the defendant, that she intended to operate on herself, and the second, made after the operation, that she had in fact done so – were inadmissible hearsay. The Court of Appeal upheld this ruling as correct.

The esoteric nature of the rule against hearsay and its potential inconvenience to the criminal justice system was again illustrated in *R v Hussain*,[809] where the accused was convicted of the murder of his sister-in-law. It was alleged that he drove over her several times, killing her. Four men, including the defendant, were regular drivers of the car that killed her. A witness, X, identified the accused as the driver at the time and as a person he had seen driving the car previously. He knew him as H, because the deceased had told him that the person he recognised as H was her brother-in-law. H's appeal against conviction was allowed on the basis that X's evidence was hearsay and should not have been admitted. The Crown was seeking to rely on X's evidence to prove two facts: (i) X recognised the man he had previously seen; and (ii) the man X had previously seen was H. The only basis on which they could establish the second fact was by relying on the hearsay statement of the deceased. The Court of Appeal expressed some sympathy with the trial judge in that this ought to be a matter of weight rather than admissibility, but it was not for the court to seek to legislate in relation to the long-established hearsay rule, to which the present situation was not an exception. A retrial was ordered, at which H pleaded guilty to manslaughter.

Avoiding the rule

It should be underlined that the courts will not always deem that a statement constitutes hearsay. For example, if the purpose of the evidence is to establish the state of mind of the maker of a statement, then the rule will not apply. In *Ratten v R*,[810] the defendant was convicted of murdering his wife by shooting her. His defence was that the gun had gone off accidentally while he was cleaning it. The time of death was put at between 1.12 and 1.20 pm. A telephonist was permitted to give evidence that at 1.15 pm she had received a telephone call from Ratten's house made by a sobbing and hysterical woman, who had said, 'Get me the police please'. The Privy Council held that this was correctly admitted. Holding that there was no element of hearsay, the Board held that the evidence was relevant, first, to show that, contrary to Ratten's evidence denying that his wife had made the call, the call had been made; and, second, to show the state of mind of the wife as being fearful at an existing or pending emergency, which was capable of rebutting the accused's defence that the shooting was an accident.[811]

In a similar vein, statements are also admissible to prove the state of mind of the witness who heard the statement. In *Subramaniam*, the accused had been charged with unlawful possession of ammunition. He ran the defence of duress, alleging that he had been threatened by a terrorist organisation. Although the trial judge excluded the evidence

---

[808] [1912] 3 KB 19.

[809] [1998] Crim LR 820.

[810] [1972] AC 378.

[811] Note, however, that the House of Lords in *R v Kearley* [1992] 2 All ER 345 took the view that the evidence of the telephonist was hearsay, but that it was admissible as an exception to the rule as being part of the *res gestae*. Evidence of the state of mind of a person is admissible as an exception to the rule against hearsay under the *res gestae* principle, discussed at pp 232–38 below.

of the threats as hearsay, the conviction was quashed on appeal. In the view of the Court of Appeal, the central issue was whether the defendant held a genuine belief that he would be killed if he refused to follow the orders of the terrorist group. Since there was no other way to establish this belief, other than admitting evidence that threatening words were actually spoken, the statement should have been admitted. As the decisions in *Ratten* and *Subramaniam* demonstrate, the Courts concern themselves primarily with the *effect* of the statement, rather than the truth of its actual contents. If a statement is tendered for any purpose other than proving the truth of its contents, it is should thus be regarded as direct evidence.

However, sometimes it can be difficult to draw such a stark dividing line. In *R v Blastland*,[812] the defence sought to draw a distinction between the use of a statement to prove the truth of its contents, and its use to prove a state of knowledge of particular facts. Here, the accused was convicted of the buggery and murder of a 12-year-old boy. He gave evidence that he had attempted to bugger the boy but stopped when the boy said it was too painful. Shortly afterwards he had seen M nearby and, afraid that he had been seen trying to commit a serious offence, he had run off and gone home. He sought to adduce evidence from a number of witnesses that M had, before the death of the boy had been made public, told them that the boy had been murdered. M had also confessed to the police that he had killed the boy, but later withdrew that statement, so the defendant applied to call M and treat him as a hostile witness. Both applications were refused and the accused was convicted on both counts. His appeals to the Court of Appeal and to the House of Lords were both dismissed, both courts holding that the evidence had been correctly excluded. Lord Bridge pointed out that to admit statements of a third party, not called as a witness, confessing to the crime for which the defendant was being tried, would be to create a significant and (many may think) a dangerous new exception to the hearsay rule.

Hearsay 'fiddles'

The cases discussed thus far indicate that the hearsay rule can mean that cogent and reliable evidence may be excluded. Whilst, over the years, the courts and Parliament developed exceptions to the rule, judges and counsel often sought ways to sidestep it altogether. Hearsay 'fiddles' arise when the court deems that evidence which is plainly hearsay is not, in order to avoid an inconvenient result. Using somewhat creative judicial reasoning, the courts have displayed a willingness to admit clearly reliable and relevant evidence when there is no hearsay exception which fits the circumstances.

In *Glinski v McIver*,[813] Lord Devlin roundly condemned the practice of attempting to evade the rule by disguising the nature of the evidence being adduced. He was particularly scathing about the common device which involves counsel attempting to avoid the rule by enticing the content of the statement from the witness through a series of carefully thought-out 'yes' or 'no' questions. For example:

Counsel: Did you go to see Peter?

Witness: Yes.

Counsel: Do not tell us what he said, but as a result of what Peter told you, did you do something?'

---

[812][1986] AC 41.
[813][1962] AC 726.

Witness: Yes.

Counsel: What did you do?

Such questioning thinly disguises the fact that the witness is responding to what a third party said, but by the letter of the law, such a practice is just as inadmissible as repeating what the third party actually said. This is illustrated by the case of *R v Saunders*,[814] where the prosecution sought to prove that the defendant, charged with obtaining by deception, had not carried on a genuine business. Counsel asked a witness whether he had made any enquiries as to whether any trade had been done by the defendant. The witness replied that he had made the enquiries. Counsel then asked whether, as a result of those enquiries, he had found that any trade had been done, to which the witness had replied that he had not. The Court of Appeal quashed the conviction because the line of questioning was intended to circumvent the hearsay rule.

There was an even more blatant attempt at evasion of the rule in *Jones v Metcalfe*,[815] an eyewitness to a road accident memorised the number of the lorry he thought responsible, and later dictated it to a police officer. The officer made a note of it, but the witness did not verify the note as correct. At trial the witness could not remember the number and, because he had not verified the note made by the officer, he was not permitted to refresh his memory from that note. However, another officer (not the one to whom the witness had dictated the note) was allowed to give evidence that he had interviewed the accused and had put the allegation to him that he was responsible for the accident. Quashing the conviction, Diplock LJ pointed out that although the inference that the appellant was the driver of the lorry at the time of the accident was irresistible as a matter of common sense, what the witness had said to the police was inadmissible hearsay and the inference was based on that evidence.

Likewise, courts have also strained the concept of 'real' evidence to cover what really ought to have been considered hearsay. This has been a particularly common ploy where strict application of the rule would have resulted in the exclusion of highly cogent evidence. An example can be found in *R v Rice*.[816] Part of the prosecution case on a charge of conspiracy was that Rice had taken a flight to Manchester on a particular date, in the company of a co-accused, H, who had already given evidence to this effect. To rebut Rice's denial of this, the prosecution produced an airline ticket to Manchester on the date in question in the names of Rice and another co-accused, M. Rice denied all knowledge of the ticket, but it was nonetheless admitted in evidence and shown to the jury as an exhibit. On appeal, it was argued that the ticket should not have been admitted. Since it was tendered by the prosecution to show that Rice had flown to Manchester on the date in question with a co-accused, it was plainly hearsay and should have been excluded. The Court of Appeal rejected that argument, holding that the ticket was relevant and admissible circumstantial evidence from which the jury would be entitled to draw the inference that Rice had taken the flight. Such reasoning was certainly guileful on the part of the Court: an inference can be drawn only if one assumes that the statement on the ticket is true; so it follows that the purpose of adducing the ticket was to prove the truth of the facts asserted and thus the ticket should really have fallen under the reach of the hearsay rule. Such reasoning was similarly adopted in *R v Lilley*,[817] where the Court of Appeal held that a notebook bearing

---

[814][1968] 1 QB 490.
[815][1967] 1 WLR 1286.
[816][1963] 1 QB 857.
[817][2003] All ER (D) 143.

the inscription 'Sharon's notebook', containing practice signatures, was not hearsay when used to connect section with a conspiracy to obtain benefits using stolen benefit books.

In *R v Shone*,[818] it was established that hearsay statements can be used to prove the non-existence of a fact, providing an officer in charge of the records comes to testify as to the non-existence of a particular fact. Here, a stock clerk and a sales manager gave evidence to the effect that workers in a firm would have made an entry on record cards if certain items had been disposed of lawfully. However, since there were no such entries, the jury were deemed free to draw the inference that the items in question must therefore have been stolen. In the view of the court, it seems that if an inference was drawn from what a document said, the document was hearsay; but if an inference was drawn from what it did not say (or from the fact that no document existed), then this was a form of direct evidence.

THE EROSION OF THE RULE

As the above cases demonstrate, courts were becoming increasingly frustrated with the operation of the rule against hearsay in the second half of the last century. There was an increasing willingness among judiciary in the lower courts to allow hearsay evidence to slip through the net, and a corresponding reluctance of the appellate courts to interfere with these decisions. The enactment of sections 23 to 30 of the Criminal Justice Act 1988 made most hearsay statements in documentary form admissible, subject to certain conditions and judicial discretion.[819] Thus, the airline ticket in *Rice* would have been admissible under section 24 of the 1988 Act, and would still be admissible today under section 117 of the 2003 Act without the need for the court to try to justify it as a form of real evidence. By the end of the century, exceptions to the rule had been created either by common law or by statute in the following areas:

- Admissions and confessions of parties and their agents.
- Statements by deceased persons:
   - declarations against interest;
   - declarations in the course of duty;
   - declarations as to public interests;
   - dying declarations (in the case of homicide);
   - declarations as to pedigree;
   - declarations by testators as to their wills;
   - testimony given in a previous trial.

---

[818] (1983) 76 Cr App R 72.

[819] The written statement was admissible if the maker of the statement was unable to give oral evidence because he was dead, mentally or physically unable to give oral evidence, out of the country or who was in fear. In addition, business documents not made for the purposes of criminal proceedings were admissible without proof that the maker was unavailable for one of the above reasons. Admissibility was subject to judicial discretion, but that discretion was seen as being overly concerned with whether admitting the document would be unfair to the defendant, who could not cross-examine on it, and failed to take account of the interests of the prosecution. There were also wide powers under the Criminal Procedure and Investigations Act 1996 to admit at trial depositions taken by magistrates from witnesses at committal proceedings or statements admitted at such proceedings. They were inadmissible if either party to the trial objected, but the objection could be overridden if the court considered it to be in the interests of justice to do so. There was, however, no guidance as to how this wide discretion should be exercised.

- Reputations of family traditions:
  - of bad character (reputations only);
  - of pedigree;
  - of the existence of a marriage;
  - of the existence or non-existence of any public or general rights;
  - to identify any person or object.
- Public documents.
- Statements admitted as part of the *res gestae* (see below).
- Statements made by a party to a common enterprise, admitted against another party to the enterprise as evidence of any matter stated.

Reform of the rule

By the beginning of the 1990s, the law on hearsay in criminal cases had become 'exceptionally complex and difficult to interpret'.[820] In recommending major reform, the Royal Commission on Criminal Justice concluded that:

> In general, the fact that a statement is hearsay should mean that the court places less weight on it, but not that it should be inadmissible in the first place. We believe that the probative value of relevant evidence should in principle be decided by the jury for themselves, and we therefore recommend that hearsay evidence should be admitted to a greater extent than at present.[821]

At the suggestion of the Royal Commission, the Law Commission considered this area of law and made recommendations in its report on *Evidence in Criminal Proceedings: Hearsay and Related Topics*.[822] These recommendations, along with those contained in Sir Robin Auld's *Review of the Criminal Courts*,[823] formed the basis of legislative reform proposals which the government first outlined in the White Paper, *Justice for All*:[824]

> Another area ripe for change is the principle that evidence must be given by witnesses in person to the court. This is based on the idea that seeing and hearing the evidence of a witness in the witness box is the best means of getting at the truth. Whilst reported evidence or 'hearsay', is generally less satisfactory than first hand, there may be some cases where this is not so and others where it is all that is available and should therefore be considered by the court. The strict application of the rules also means that the previous statements of witnesses are not admissible as evidence even on long forgotten issues of detail, and that video recorded evidence is only admissible in a limited range of specified cases.
>
> We believe that the right approach is that, if there is a good reason for the original maker not being able to give the evidence personally (for example, through illness or death) or where

---

[820] Royal Commission on Criminal Justice (1993) *Report* (Cmnd 2263) (London: HMSO), Ch 8, [26].
[821] *Ibid*.
[822] Law Commission *Report* No 245 (1997: London, Law Commission).
[823] Sir Robin Auld took the view that the Law Commission had not gone far enough in its proposed relaxation of the rule. He proposed the strict rule against the admission of hearsay evidence in criminal proceedings should be abandoned. Instead, a more flexible approach should be adopted where evidence was admitted on a much more widespread basis, and trust was placed in fact-finders to evaluate the weight of such evidence fairly. Auld, Sir Robin *Review of the Criminal Courts of England and Wales*, Cmnd 9376 (2002: London, HMSO), [95]–[104].
[824] Home Office, *Justice for All*, Cmnd 5563 (2002: London, Home Office).

records have been properly compiled by businesses, then the evidence should automatically go in, rather than its admissibility being judged. Judges should also have a discretion to decide that other evidence of this sort can be given. This is close to the approach developed in civil proceedings.

We believe it is important to ensure that when witnesses are testifying, rules of evidence do not artificially prevent the true and full story from being presented to the court. Justice is not served if important information is excluded for no good reason. Therefore we propose to legislate to make it easier for witnesses to give their evidence by making their previous and original statements, often made at the time or shortly after the incident, more widely admissible at trial and allowing witnesses to refer to them when they give their evidence in court. We also propose to extend the scope for witnesses to give evidence on tape or by TV link.[825]

On the basis of this proposal, the government introduced a new Criminal Justice Bill into Parliament which would radically overhaul the existing scheme by substituting the old common law rules with a new statutory framework.

THE CRIMINAL JUSTICE ACT 2003

The reforms were enacted in Pt 11 of the Criminal Justice Act 2003. With the exception of eight of the common law exceptions to the rule against hearsay which are preserved, the common law rules governing the admissibility of hearsay evidence are entirely abolished. Sections 23 to 30 of the Criminal Justice Act 1988, which made much documentary evidence admissible subject to judicial discretion, are repealed and replaced with similar, but improved, statutory provisions. Section 114 of the 2003 Act makes clear that there is still a general rule that excludes hearsay evidence. However, such a statement may be admissible, providing that it comes under one of the heads set out in section 114(1)(a)–(d):

(a) it is admissible under any statutory provision (including the 2003 Act itself);

(b) it is admissible under a common law rule preserved by the 2003 Act;

(c) the parties agree that it should be admitted; or

(d) the court gives leave to admit the statement.

For the most part, these headings are fairly self-explanatory, and the circumstances within the Act under which hearsay can be admitted are considered in depth further.[826] However, it may be useful at this juncture to flag up the importance of circumstance (d). Effectively, this confers an inclusionary discretion on the court to admit *any* hearsay evidence, even if its admissibility is not expressly provided for elsewhere within the statute. However, before the court can grant leave to admit such a statement under section 114(1)(d), it must be satisfied that, despite the difficulties there may be in challenging the statement, it would not be contrary to the interests of justice to admit the evidence. The intention, therefore, is that the court should be able to admit an out-of-court statement which does

---

[825] *Ibid.,* [4.60–62].

[826] Note also that section 114(3) provides that out-of-court statements may still be excluded even if they fulfil the requirements of the 2003 Act. For example, confessions must meet the additional requirements of sections 76, 76A and 78 of the Police and Criminal Evidence Act 1984 (see Ch 8). If the out-of-court statement includes evidence of the bad character of a witness or defendant, the statement must also satisfy the requirements of sections 100 or 101 of the CJA 2003, and may be excluded under section 101(3) of the Act (see Chs 5 and 6).

not fall within any of the other categories of admissibility, but only where such evidence is cogent and reliable. The discretion extends to multiple hearsay (where the statement passes through more than one person before it is recorded) as well as first-hand hearsay (where a statement is made by a person who directly perceived the facts of which the evidence is being given).

Section 114(2) sets out a number of factors that the court must consider when deciding whether to grant leave under the discretion in section 114(1)(d):

(a) how much probative value the statement has (assuming it to be true) in relation to a matter in issue in the proceedings, or how valuable it is for the understanding of other evidence in the case;

(b) what other evidence has been, or can be, given on the matter or evidence mentioned in paragraph (a);

(c) how important the matter or evidence mentioned in paragraph (a) is in the context of the case as a whole;

(d) the circumstances in which the statement was made;

(e) how reliable the maker of the statement appears to be;

(f) how reliable the evidence of the making of the statement appears to be;

(g) whether oral evidence of the matter stated can be given and, if not, why it cannot;

(h) the amount of difficulty involved in challenging the statement;

(i) the extent to which that difficulty would be likely to prejudice the party facing it.

This list is not intended to be exhaustive,[827] but aims to focus attention on whether the circumstances surrounding the making of the statement indicate whether it can be treated as reliable enough to enable it to be considered by the trier of fact, despite the fact that it will not be subject to cross-examination. In *R v Taylor*,[828] the Court of Appeal made clear that, in determining weighing up the above factors, a judge is not under an obligation to reach a specific conclusion on each one. He or she must simply bear them in mind in determining whether it would be in the interests of justice to admit the evidence.

The creation of an inclusionary discretion by the 2003 Act is one of the most radical and contentious of the evidence-based reforms introduced by the legislation. The main reason why is it so controversial is that it is worded in an extremely broad fashion; aside from the factors set out in section 114(2), the discretion is unfettered. This has given rise to a fear that, if current trends away from the principle of orality should continue in years to come,[829] the general rule of exclusion could eventually give way to a presumption of inclusivity, unless it would be manifestly unfair to use the evidence in question. Some commentators have gone so far as to suggest that there are circumstances where use of the mechanism could potentially conflict with the defendant's right to a fair trial under Article 6 of the European Convention on Human Rights.[830] These arguments will be examined in greater depth towards the end of this chapter.

In addition to the new inclusionary discretion, it can be noted that the Act also provides for an exclusionary discretion. Thus, even if a hearsay statement is admissible under section 114, the court may then refuse to admit it under section 126, which allows trial judges to exclude superfluous out-of-court statements if the court is satisfied that the value of

---

[827] *R v M* [2007] All ER (D) 21.
[828] [2006] 2 Cr App R 14.
[829] See Ch 1, pp 20–23.
[830] See e.g. McGowan, L. 'Hearsay Evidence: *R v Al-Khawaja*' (2006) 70 J Crim L 401.

the evidence is outweighed by the undue waste of time which its admission may cause. Furthermore, section 126(2) preserves both the existing common law power for the court to exclude evidence where its prejudicial effect outweighs its probative value, and the discretion contained in section 78 of the Police and Criminal Evidence Act 1984 regarding the exclusion of evidence which would have such an adverse effect on the fairness of the trial that it ought not to be admitted. While both of these devices are commonly used to exclude improperly obtained evidence,[831] the Criminal Justice Act 2003 clearly envisages that they may also be used to exclude hearsay evidence where it would result in unfairness to the accused.

Implied assertions and direct evidence

Section 115 of the 2003 Act is concerned with the distinction between assertions and direct evidence, and seeks to resolve the difficulties created by certain common law decisions. There are two basic ways of proving a fact in issue. First, it may be proved by proving some other fact which renders it more likely to be true; the other fact is directly probative of the fact to be proved. Second, it may be proved by a person's assertion that it is true. The hearsay rule applied only to the latter form of proof.

An assertion can consist of words, or conduct or both. Nonetheless, merely because a person's words or conduct are relied upon as evidence of a fact, it does not follow that they constitute an assertion of that fact. For example, a person's words may betray guilty knowledge without amounting to a confession of that person's guilt. Often, it will be apparent when a person's words or conduct are adduced as proof of a fact on the basis that they are directly probative of it, but as illustrated below, this will not always be clear to the court. In *Wright v Tatham*,[832] the issue was whether letters in which the writers appeared to assume the sanity of their intended recipient could be admitted as evidence of his sanity. It was held that the letters were hearsay since they were not directly probative of the facts to be proved, but only an assertion of it. The decision was explained by the example of a sea captain who boards his ship and sets sail, from which a court might be tempted to infer that the ship was seaworthy. It was said that the hearsay rule would apply to such conduct, and evidence of it would be inadmissible. In the more recent case of *R v Harry*,[833] the accused and his flatmate P were charged with possession of a controlled drug with intent to supply. The accused's defence was that P was the sole supplier. He sought to prove this by calling police officers to give evidence that while they were at the flat after arresting Harry and P, the police officers had answered a number of telephone calls from persons who could not be traced, but who had asked for P and enquired whether P had drugs for sale. The trial judge refused to allow evidence of the content of the calls to go before the jury because it was hearsay, on the ground that the callers impliedly alleged P to be the supplier. Harry was convicted and P acquitted. The Court of Appeal upheld the judge's ruling, while recognising that Harry felt a justifiable grievance.

That decision was approved of by a bare majority of the House of Lords in *R v Kearley*.[834] The issue here was whether, on a charge of possessing drugs with intent to supply,

---

[831] See Ch 9.
[832] (1837) 7 Ad & E 313.
[833] (1988) 86 Cr App R 105.
[834] [1992] 2 AC 228.

a prosecutor could rely on evidence by the police that, on a search of D's property, they had taken a number of telephone calls (and received seven callers at the door) asking for the defendant and whether he had any drugs for sale. A majority held that the hearsay rule applied where it was sought to draw an inference of a fact from words or conduct which were intended to be assertive of some other fact, or not intended to be assertive at all. As evidence of the fact that the defendant dealt in drugs, the callers' words were hearsay; and, being unable to find any applicable exception to the rule, the majority of the House held them inadmissible.

Lord Browne-Wilkinson and Lord Griffiths dissented on the basis that while a single call asking for P and requesting drugs would be of little probative value and would cause great prejudice to P's case if the jury drew the wrong inference; they saw no reason why the evidence of multiple calls should not be admitted. Lord Browne-Wilkinson thought that *Harry* had been wrongly decided; the words 'Can I have some drugs?' were not, in his view, a statement making an assertion, but a fact, and therefore a form of direct evidence. In both cases, the property in question was being used to supply drugs, and the only issue was the identity of the supplier. Since the words of the callers were clearly directed at P, they constituted direct evidence that P was supplying drugs. Lord Browne-Wilkinson thought that the inference to be drawn by the jury was not from the *words* used by the callers but from the *fact* that there were callers who were seeking to acquire drugs.

Evidence of the kind that was excluded in *Wright* and *Kearley* was commonly referred to as an 'implied assertion', and came to vex both criminal lawyers and academics alike for some time. Section 115(3) seeks to resolve these difficulties by giving effect to the Law Commission's recommendation that a person's words or conduct should not be caught by the hearsay rule unless the purpose, or one of the purposes, of that person appears to cause the hearer to believe that the matter stated is true, or to act on the basis that it is true. Thus the evidence of police officers in *Kearley* that they received 17 calls from persons asking for drugs would not be a matter to which the 2003 Act applies unless it could be shown that the purpose, or one of the purposes, of the callers was to cause the police officers to believe that K was a drug dealer. Section 115 thus effectively constitutes a statutory reversal of *Kearley*. The Court of Appeal recently confirmed this was the case in *R v Singh*,[835] where the appellant unsuccessfully tried to argue that telephone numbers saved in the memory of his mobile phone should be inadmissible since they gave rise to an implied assertion. Likewise, in *R v N*,[836] it was held that a private diary of a rape victim fell outside the scope of the hearsay rule as it was not intended that it would be read by anyone else.

Machine-generated statements

Section 115(3)(b) of the 2003 Act preserves the common law position whereby statements which are not based on human input fall outside the ambit of the hearsay rule. Providing the machine computes the information automatically and without human input, it will not be considered hearsay, but will qualify as direct evidence. The hearsay rule does not therefore apply to tapes, films or photographs which record disputed incidents actually taking place, or to documents produced by machine which automatically recorded an

---

[835] [2006] 1 WLR 1564.
[836] [2006] EWCA Crim 3309.

event or circumstances. Thus surveillance cameras in stores or streets,[837] as well as devices used to analyse specimens of breath or blood,[838] are seen as direct evidence and not hearsay. In *Spiby*,[839] an automatic computer log of telephone calls made from a hotel bedroom was viewed as real evidence, as was a computer log of mobile phone calls in *R v Robson, Mitchell and Richards*.[840]

By contrast, in *R v Wood*,[841] the prosecution sought to prove that metal found in the possession of the accused was of the same type as a stolen consignment, by adducing evidence of tests. The results of these tests had been produced by a computer, but the information had been fed into the computer by chemists. This scenario was therefore distinct from the cases discussed above, since the computer analysis had been dependent upon human input. In this particular case, it was admissible only because the chemists themselves were able to give oral evidence of the results.[842] However, had they been unable to do so, the computer analysis would not have been excluded under the hearsay rule. Thus, to qualify as real evidence, the computer must merely be used as a calculator or collator of information.[843]

Photofit identification

Witnesses to a crime are often asked to provide a description of the criminal. This used to be done by a sketch artist, who drew a likeness of the person based on the description given. In modern times, computer-generated images have largely replaced the artist, but the process and underlying principles remain the same. Typically, the witness describes the person's features, and the computer operator will then select the facial characteristics most closely fitting the description. At common law, sketches and photofits were held to fall outside the scope of the hearsay rule, since they had effectively been made by the witness who merely directed the hand of the artist or the person compiling the photofit.[844] A literal reading of section 115(2) appears to contradict the idea that such evidence is direct evidence, in defining a statement as inclusive of 'a representation made in a sketch, photofit or other pictorial form'. Since sketches, photofits and computer-generated images are all intended to cause another person to believe that they accurately depict the characteristics of the suspect, it appears to fall within the section 115(3), and the hearsay rule will thus apply. Moreover, such evidence is not covered by any of the common law exceptions preserved by section 118, and since section 118(2) abolishes all other common law rules governing

---

[837]See e.g. *Taylor v Chief Constable of Cheshire* [1987] 1 All ER 225; *Attorney-General's Reference (No 2 of 2002)* [2003] Crim LR 192.

[838]*Castle v Cross* [1984] 1 WLR 1372.

[839]*R v Spiby* (1990) 91 Cr App R 186.

[840][1991] Crim LR 362.

[841](1982) 76 Cr App R 23.

[842]In this respect, it is also worth noting that section 129 is relevant. It provides that where a statement generated by a machine is based on information relayed to the machine by a human, the output of the device will be admissible only where it is proved that the information was accurate. S 129(2) preserves the common law presumption that a mechanical device has been properly set or calibrated.

[843]See also *R (O) v Coventry Magistrates Court* (2003) *The Times*, 22 April, where the Queen's Bench Divisional Court held that a computer printout recording successful and unsuccessful attempts to enter a website was admissible as real evidence, applying *Spiby* and the above line of cases. The case involved attempts to download child pornography from an American company. The printout in question was obtained from the database of the company running the website, and contained a breakdown of the defendant's successful and unsuccessful attempts to access the website, and charges made to his credit card.

[844]See further *Smith (Percy)* [1976] Crim LR 511; *Okorodu* [1982] Crim LR 747; *Cook* [1987] QB 417.

the admissibility of hearsay evidence, it would appear that photofits and sketches are now to be considered as hearsay for the purposes of the 2003 Act.

However, it may be recalled from the discussion in Chapter 5 that section 120 of the Act will provide an alternative avenue under which such evidence may be admitted. It provides that a previous statement of a witness may be admissible under certain conditions. Section 120(4) provides as follows:

> A previous statement by the witness is admissible as evidence of any matter stated of which oral evidence by him would be admissible, if
>
> (a) any of the following three conditions is satisfied, and
>
> (b) while giving evidence the witness indicates that to the best of his belief he made the statement, and that to the best of his belief it states the truth.

The first condition, as laid down in section 120(5), is that the statement identifies a person, an object or a place.[845] The photofit statement (and section 115(2) makes it clear that it is a statement) identifying the person seen by the witness is a previous statement made by the witness which satisfies the terms of section 120(4) and meets this condition in section 120(5). Subject to the specific facts in each case, a photofit or computer-generated image is also capable of meeting the other two conditions referred to in section 120(4). The second condition, contained in section 120(6), is that the statement was made by the witness when the matters stated were fresh in his memory but he does not remember them, and cannot reasonably be expected to remember them well enough to give oral evidence of them in the proceedings. The third condition, in section 120(7), lays down six separate stipulations that must be satisfied before the evidence is admitted.[846] Although at common law such evidence could only be admitted as evidence of consistency, under section 120, it is admissible as evidence of the truth of the matters stated. Section 120 is dealt with in Chapter 5, and will not be subject to any further discussion here.

Section 116 – Where the witness is unavailable

Section 116 of the 2003 Act replaces sections 23–26 of the Criminal Justice Act 1988, and is primarily concerned with statements made by persons who would have been witnesses in criminal cases but are unable to attend court. The provisions apply to any first-hand hearsay statement, in either oral or in a documentary form. By contrast, section 117, considered further in the chapter, is concerned with statements made by persons in the course of a trade or business, and concerns only written statements. Thus where a statement in a document

---

[845]Subject to the specific facts in each case, a photofit or computer generated image is also capable of meeting the other two conditions referred to in section 120(4). The second condition is that the statement was made by the witness when the matters stated were fresh in his memory but he does not remember them, and cannot reasonably be expected to remember them, well enough to give oral evidence of them in the proceedings. The third condition is that (a) the witness claims to be a person against whom an offence has been committed; (b) the offence is one to which the proceedings relate; (c) the statement consists of a complaint made by the witness; (d) the complaint was made as soon as could reasonably be expected after the alleged conduct, (e) the complaint was not made as a result of a threat or a promise, and (f) before the statement is adduced the witness gives oral evidence in connection with its subject matter. See further Ch 5, pp 126–27.
[846]These are: (a) that the witness claims to be a person against whom an offence has been committed; (b) the offence is one to which the proceedings relate; (c) the statement consists of a complaint made by the witness; (d) the complaint was made as soon as could reasonably be expected after the alleged conduct, (e) the complaint was not made as a result of a threat or a promise, and (f) before the statement is adduced the witness gives oral evidence in connection with its subject matter.

is involved, the statement may be admissible under both sections 116 and 117, but where the statement was prepared for the purposes of criminal proceedings (usually a witness statement) there will seldom be any advantage in arguing for admission under section 117. Where the statement was made orally, it may be admitted only under section 116 or under one of the exceptions preserved by section 118 (see below). In practice, circumstances will dictate which head of admissibility can be best argued.

A statement made out of court may be admissible under section 116 (subject to the additional conditions to be considered further in the chapter) if the person who made the statement: (a) is dead; (b) is physically or mentally ill; (c) is outside the United Kingdom; (d) cannot be found despite taking reasonably practicable steps; (e) does not give oral evidence through fear. Each of these heads of admissibility will be examined below. However, before proceeding, it is important to note that two further conditions must be satisfied before evidence can be admitted in any of these circumstances.

Section 116(1)(a) requires that oral evidence given in the proceedings by the person who made the statement would be admissible as evidence of that matter. It follows that, before admitting any hearsay statement under this section, the court must ask whether the original maker of the statement would have been able to give oral evidence if he or she had been available to do so. There are three main reasons why such oral evidence might not be admissible. First, like all forms of evidence, the matter contained in the statement may not be relevant to any issue in the case. Second, the person who made the statement may not have been a competent witness, by reason of age or cognitive capability.[847] Thirdly, the matters stated may be excluded by an exclusionary evidential rule. They may, for example, contain evidence of bad character, or the matters themselves may constitute hearsay. While first-hand hearsay is admissible under section 116, but multiple hearsay is not.[848] Thus, if Doris was stabbed when she answered her door, and staggered to her neighbour, Bill, to tell him that Ivanna had stabbed her, the unavailability of Doris to testify will permit Bill to give evidence of what she told him under section 116.[849] However, if Bill is also unavailable, the cumulative use of the hearsay statement will not permit B's statement to be admitted to the court by anyone else under section 116.

The second condition, under section 116(1)(b), requires that the person who made the statement is identified to the satisfaction of the court. This will enable the opposing party to challenge the absent witness's credibility under section 124, which allows the opposing party to put before the jury any evidence relevant to the credibility of that witness which counsel could have used as part of any cross-examination had the witness testified in person.[850]

Providing these two conditions in section 116(1) are met, the party adducing the hearsay evidence must then show the court that one of the circumstances within section 116(2) are satisfied.

---

[847]It will be recalled that section 53 of the Youth Justice and Criminal Evidence Act 1999 states that a person is not competent to give evidence in criminal proceedings if it appears to the court that he is not a person who is able to understand questions put to him as a witness and give answers to them which can be understood. This position is confirmed by section 123 CJA 2003.

[848]See further below, pp 240–42.

[849]These circumstances also fall within the common law exception to the hearsay rule known as *res gestae* (preserved by section 118(1),(4)(a) and discussed at pp 232–38 below).

[850]The section provides a replacement for the provision in section 28(2) of and Sch 2 to the CJA 1988. One presumes that the absent witness will be protected against the admission of bad character evidence to the same extent as a witness who gives oral evidence in person. See further the discussion in Ch 4, pp 142–45, dealing with a non-defendant's bad character.

Where the relevant person is dead

Section 116(2)(a) stipulates that a hearsay statement may be admitted if the relevant person is dead. This head is largely self-explanatory, although a death certificate will generally be necessary as proof.[851]

Relevant person is physically or mentally ill

Section 116(2)(b) applies where the relevant person is unfit to be a witness because of his physical or mental condition. Medical evidence will be necessary to prove the unfitness to attend by reason of physical or mental condition, and this may also be in documentary form if such evidence is uncontested. However, in *R v Elliott and others*,[852] where the prosecution sought to rely on a written statement rather than his oral testimony on the ground that the witness was unfit through illness, it was held that the defence should ordinarily be given an opportunity to cross-examine the relevant doctor who was providing support for the application. In a disputed case it would not be sufficient for the prosecution merely to provide a written statement recording the doctor's views.

A physical disability will not affect the competence of the witness but a mental condition may do so, depending on its severity and whether that condition was present before the statement was made. In *R v Setz-Dempsey*,[853] an important identification witness was mentally unfit to give evidence at the time of trial and his written statement was admitted under section 23 of the Criminal Justice Act 1988. Allowing the appeal, the Court of Appeal held that the trial judge should not have admitted the written statement. He had failed to take into account the effect of medical evidence about the witness's state of mind on the quality of the identification evidence, and the unfairness to the defendant in being unable to cross-examine the witness. This suggests that the witness was mentally incapable when the identification and subsequent statement were made. If so, the witness was not competent to give evidence and would not have satisfied the requirements of section 23, and neither would he/she now satisfy the condition in section 116(2)(b).

Relevant person is outside the United Kingdom

Section 116(2)(c) deals with the scenario where the relevant person is outside the United Kingdom and it is not reasonably practicable to secure his attendance. It is worded in almost exactly the same terms as the previous provision under the 1988 Act.[854] These provisions were considered in *R v Case*.[855] Here, the defendant was charged with theft, having allegedly taken a purse from S's handbag. S was a Portuguese tourist, holidaying at the time with her friend, G. The defendant's defence was that S and G were either mistaken or lying, and that he was put under pressure to admit the offence whilst in custody to secure the release of his companion. The prosecution sought leave to admit in evidence the statements of the two tourists. G had given a Portuguese address, but she had made no mention of where she normally lived, nor of the length of time she had been in Britain or

---

[851] Note that a death certificate itself is admissible as a public document (a common law exception to the hearsay rule preserved by section 118(1)(b)).

[852] (2003) *The Times*, 15 May.

[853] (1994) 98 Cr App R 23.

[854] See section 23(1)(b)(i)-(ii) CJA 1988.

[855] [1991] Crim LR 192.

how long she intended to stay. S's statement was similarly vague, and she made it clear that she was living temporarily in a hotel. That was the only evidence that the witnesses were outside the UK, and there was no evidence that any attempt had been made to find out if either was willing to attend court. The trial judge inferred from the statements that they would be unwilling to attend and that it would not be reasonably practicable to secure their attendance given the expense involved. He therefore admitted the statements, and the defendant was convicted.

However, in quashing his conviction, the Court of Appeal found that there was no evidence before the court that the witnesses were outside the country. Even if it had been permissible to look at the contents of the statements, in the circumstances of this case, there was still insufficient evidence. While the word 'reasonably' implied that financial implications could be considered, there was no evidence whatsoever as to whether it was practicable for them to attend court on the day. Given that the criminal standard of proof had to be satisfied, there was no evidence upon which the trial judge could have been satisfied that the conditions had been made out. This amounted to a material irregularity requiring the quashing of the conviction.[856]

It should normally be possible for a party to prove the existence of a condition under section 116(2) by another document admissible under section 116 or 117. In *R v Castillo*,[857] the Court of Appeal, applying the 1988 Act, held that it was permissible to prove that a witness was unable to attend by using a statement of another person admitted under section 23 of the Act. That case involved the importation of cocaine from Venezuela and the prosecution sought to admit the statement of M, an airline official, about tickets from a destination in Venezuela which had been issued to Castillo. At the *voir dire*, evidence was given about enquiries made of one Tyler, the drugs liaison officer in Venezuela, as to the ability of M to attend. The judge ruled that it was not reasonably practicable for Tyler to attend and admitted his statement under section 23(2)(b). He also ruled that having admitted Tyler's statement, it revealed that attendance was not practicable, so that M's statement was also admissible.

It was argued on appeal that it was not open to the trial judge to apply section 23 twice, first as to the statement of M and, second, as to the statement of Tyler. Section 23, it was argued, applied to first-hand hearsay, and this was, in fact, multiple hearsay. This argument was rejected. In the view of the court, there was no reason why the inability of M to attend should not be proved by the statement of Tyler, whose own inability to attend had already been proved and whose statement had been admitted in evidence under section 23(2)(b). The Court also pointed out that, although it might well be *possible* for a witness to attend, this did not necessary mean that it was 'reasonably practicable' to do so. In order to determine this question, the court had to consider a number of facts. First, it had to question the importance of the evidence the witness could give and whether or not it was prejudicial, and how prejudicial, to the accused if he did not attend. In this case, the evidence of Tyler was concerned only with what M had told him, and it was M's evidence with which the court was concerned. Second, there were considerations of expense and inconvenience in securing attendance. That should not be a major consideration, but in this case it would be a matter of considerable expense for Tyler to travel from Venezuela simply to give evidence which could not seriously be challenged in cross-examination. Third, the judge had to consider reasons

---

[856]Even if the lesser burden of proof is applied to section 116, it is suggested that there would still be insufficient evidence to satisfy the trial judge that the condition had been satisfied.
[857][1996] Crim LR 193.

put forward as to why it was not reasonably practicable for the witness to attend. Those were findings of fact with which their Lordships would not lightly interfere, and they had not been persuaded in this case that the judge's ruling was wrong. It is likely that the courts would take a similar approach if the above facts were to re-occur under the 2003 Act.

It should thus be underlined that what is deemed to be 'reasonably practical' does not necessary equate to what is physically possible. In *R v Maloney*,[858] the trial judge admitted the written statements of two Greek cadets after hearing that they were either at sea, or on leave in Cyprus. The Court of Appeal held that there was evidence from which the judge could find that it was not reasonably practicable to secure their attendance. Whilst the term 'practicable' must be construed in the light of the normal steps which would be taken to arrange the attendance of a witness at trial, the phrase 'reasonably practicable' involved a further qualification of the duty, to secure attendance by taking the reasonable steps which a party would normally take to secure a witness's attendance having regard to the means and resources available to the parties.

This was obviously a consideration of the court in *R v Jiminez-Paez*.[859] Here, the appellant was arrested at Heathrow en route from Colombia, where she lived, to Italy. Customs officers found 564 grammes of cocaine, with a street value of £50,000, secreted on her person. At her trial she admitted that she was involved in smuggling, but said that she thought she was smuggling emeralds, which she had illegally exported from Colombia before. She sought to introduce in evidence a letter from the Colombian Embassy's adviser in charge of consular affairs. The letter stated that there was a black market in emeralds in Colombia and that they were frequently illegally exported, and one method of concealment was the type used in the appellant's case. The defence sought to rely on a provision similar to section 116(2)(c), arguing that the consular official, who had diplomatic immunity and was therefore immune from process, was effectively outside the United Kingdom, despite the fact that she was physically present but unwilling to give evidence. Not surprisingly, the trial judge rejected the argument and excluded the letter as hearsay. The Court of Appeal held that he was right to do so. The defence contention would not give effect to the two distinct requirements that the person was outside the UK and that it was not reasonably practicable to secure his attendance. Had the letter been sent from an official in Colombia, it would have satisfied the subsection and would thus be admissible under section 116(2)(c).

Relevant person cannot be found

Under section 116(2)(d), a statement may be admissible where the relevant person cannot be found although such steps as it is reasonably practicable to take have been taken. The above discussion of 'reasonably practicable' applies with equal measure to this provision. It is not uncommon for witnesses to leave the area without informing the police or lawyers in order to avoid having to give evidence, and, on occasions, a witness will be kept out of the way by persons acting for the defendant. The question of what steps are 'reasonably practicable' to take to find such witnesses will depend on the individual circumstances of each case, and it will be for the party seeking to have the statement admitted to satisfy the court that they have taken all such steps as are reasonable in the particular circumstances.

---

[858][1994] Crim LR 525.
[859][1993] Crim LR 596.

Relevant person is in fear

Section 116(2)(e) may apply where a person is reluctant to give evidence oral evidence through fear. For the purposes of this provision, 'fear' is to be widely construed and (for example) includes fear of the death or injury of another person or of financial loss,[860] although the court may only give leave to admit evidence under this head if it considers that the statement ought to be admitted in the interests of justice, having regard to a range of factors set out in section 116(4).[861] The provision replaces section 23 of the CJA 1988, which gave the trial judge discretion to allow a written statement to be used where a witness would 'not give oral evidence through fear'. Use of the section was, however, confined to written statements that the prosecution sought to rely on. Moreover, such statements had to be made to the police or other investigatory authority. The new provision under section 116(2)(e) is broader, insofar as it apples to both written or oral statements, and is available to defence and prosecution witnesses.

The case law stemming from section 23 CJA 1988 addressed a number of key issues relating to fearful witnesses which will no doubt continue to guide the courts in their application of the new law. For example, in *R v Acton Justices, ex p McMullen*,[862] the Divisional Court rejected the argument that the fear of the witness had to be based on reasonable grounds. Dismissing the appeal, the Court stated that it was 'not helpful in the context to speak of the objective or subjective approach. It would be sufficient that the court, on the evidence, was sure that the witness was in fear, as a consequence of the material offence or of something said or done subsequently in relation to it and the possibility of the witness testifying as to it'.[863]

Like its predecessor, section 116(2)(e) thus requires a causal connection between the fear of the witness and the prospect of giving of evidence.[864] However, the fact that the average witness would not be in fear, or that the fear of the witness in question is wholly unreasonable, is irrelevant. The fact that the witness is timid or vulnerable because of age or other factor is relevant, but the test can still not be said to be subjective in nature. It is simply that it is easier to prove that such witnesses are in fear as a result of the crime or the possibility of testifying as to it. It should nonetheless be underlined that the provision is not limited to protecting those witnesses traditionally viewed as being at heightened risk of reprisals, such as those testifying in cases involving terrorism or organised crime. It is perfectly conceivable that the measure could also protect the young, the elderly or infirm who have been psychologically damaged by the crime and fearful of giving evidence in open court in front of their assailants.

The wording of section 23(3) of the 1988 Act, 'does not give evidence through fear', raised the question whether the provision would apply where a witness came to court, took the oath and started to give evidence but refused to continue, or simply took the oath and then declined to give any evidence at all. It was argued in *ex p McMullen* that the wording of the subsection meant that it did not apply when a witness who had started to give evidence stopped through fear. As soon as the witness uttered one word of testimony,

---

[860] Whether financial loss would have sufficed for the purposes of the 1988 Act was never raised, but one can readily see that the threat to fire bomb a witness's business or home could be as effective as, if not more effective than, a threat to his person. Precisely how much financial or proprietary loss will be sufficient to satisfy the section 116(2)(e) and justify the admission of a hearsay statement remains to be seen.

[861] See below, pp 225–27.

[862] (1991) 92 Cr App R 98.

[863] *Ibid.*, at 105.

[864] See also *Neill v North Antrim Magistrates' Court* (1993) 97 Cr App R 121.

the section ceased to apply. The Court, however, rejected this argument, holding that the better interpretation of the section was that the witness 'should not have given evidence of any significant relevance to the case'. The wording of section 116(2)(e), 'does not give (or does not continue to give) oral evidence', ensures that the wide interpretation placed on the wording of the old statute continues to apply.

A further issue which vexed the courts was how, precisely, the extent of the fear was to be ascertained. Few, if any, witnesses are likely to relish the prospect of giving evidence under adversarial circumstances. Therefore the vast majority, to some extent, are likely to be fearful about testifying. Clearly the legislation was not designed to cover all witnesses: something over and above the baseline apprehension that affects most witnesses is clearly required. The most straightforward manner in which the judge can assess the degree of fear is through questioning the witness in person, whilst observing his or her demeanour. In *R v Ashford and Tenterden Justices, ex p Hilden*,[865] the accused was committed for trial on a charge of causing grievous bodily harm to his girlfriend, after the magistrates allowed a written statement of the girlfriend to be admitted under section 23 of the 1988 Act. The girlfriend had managed to get as far as taking the oath, but then simply said she could not remember anything or had no comment to make when questioned. The prosecution thus applied to the magistrate to have the statement admitted under section 23, since the witness was clearly in fear. The magistrate noted that it was obvious from the girl's conduct in the witness box that she was in a genuine state of fear, and accordingly admitted the statement. The Divisional Court refused D's application for judicial review on the basis that the magistrate had satisfied herself from the demeanour of the witness and her responses that the witness was refusing to give evidence through fear.

Similarly, in *R v Greer*,[866] there had been a serious assault by three men on C and G, both employees in a kebab shop. The sole issue in the case was identification. The Crown sought leave to admit statements of three witnesses, C, D, and G, under section 23 of the 1988 Act on the basis that they were afraid to give live evidence. The recorder dismissed the application in respect of D since he had no opportunity to assess his state of mind. However, since C and G were both present in court and explained, without being sworn, why they could not give evidence, their statements under section 23 were admitted. On appeal it was argued that since C and G had been able to come to court to explain their fear to the judge, section 23 should not apply. Dismissing this contention, the Court of Appeal held there was no reason, either as a matter of practice or on the wording of the statute, why the recorder should not hear from the persons concerned of their actual fear. C and G were not giving evidence as they had not been sworn as witnesses; they had come to court to explain to the judge why they were reluctant to do so. Indeed, this was a helpful and sensible course of action since it allowed the court to determine the matter before the time came for the witnesses to give evidence.

Indeed, a major difficulty faces the court if the witness is unable or unwilling to personally satisfy the judge of his or her state of mind. In *Neill v North Antrim Magistrates' Court*,[867] police officers recounted what the two witnesses, who did not give evidence through fear, had told their mother. This was clearly hearsay, being a third-hand account of the witnesses' apprehension. Since there was no other evidence given of their fear, the House of Lords held that the statements should not have been admitted. However, Lord Mustill, delivering a speech with which all of their Lordships agreed, pointed out that the

---

[865] (1993) 96 Crim App R 92.
[866] [1998] Crim LR 572.
[867] (1993) 97 Cr App R 121.

police officers could have given evidence of what the witnesses had said about their fear, since it had been long established that a declaration as to a contemporaneous state of mind constitutes an exception to the hearsay rule. It was emphasised that the evidence must *not* be that the witnesses were afraid (that is an inference for the court to draw), but that the witnesses *said* they were afraid and that their demeanour was consistent with what they had said.

Once the court has established that the witness is genuinely in a state of fear, it must then determine whether that the statement ought to be admitted in the interests of justice. Under section 116(4), the court should take a range of factors into account in making this assessment:

(a) the statement's contents;

(b) any risk that its admission or exclusion would result in unfairness to any party to the proceedings (and in particular to how difficult it will be to challenge the statement if the relevant person does not give oral evidence);

(c) whether, in appropriate cases, a special measures direction could be made under section 19 of the Youth Justice and Criminal Evidence Act 1999; and

(d) any other relevant circumstances.

It will be noted that section 116(4) applies only to section 116(2)(e), the statement of a fearful witness: this test is not applied to any of the other heads under section 116. It is particularly noteworthy that section 116(4)(b) refers to any risk that the admission or exclusion of the statement will result in unfairness to *any* party to the proceedings; this is a clear departure from the criteria contained in the CJA 1988 which referred only to any unfairness towards the defendant.

In the leading case under the 1988 Act, *R v Cole*,[868] the defendant was convicted of an assault on a security guard. The prosecution applied for the statement of a deceased witness to be admitted under section 23. The defence, who disputed the circumstances of the assault as described in the witness's statement, resisted the application. The trial judge ruled that in relation to section 26(b)(ii), which referred to the possibility of 'controverting' the statement noted that the defendant might, if he chose, controvert the statement by his own evidence or that of other witnesses.[869] On appeal, it was contended that the trial judge had erred on this point, since this effectively placed an improper pressure on the defence to call witnesses. The trial judge, it was argued, should have had particular regard to the words 'any risk' of unfairness arising, particularly given the importance of that specific statement to the outcome of the proceedings.

Dismissing the appeal, the Court of Appeal noted that the court was not required to disregard the likelihood of the possibility of controverting the statement by the evidence of the accused or of witnesses called on his behalf. The overall purpose of the statutory provisions was to widen the power of the court to admit documentary hearsay evidence, while ensuring that the accused received a fair trial. In determining the issue of fairness, a balance had to be struck between the interests of the public in enabling the prosecution case to be properly presented, and the interests of a particular defendant in not being put in a disadvantageous position. The matters to which the court must have regard included any risk of unfairness, having regard to the possibility of controverting the statement.

---

[868] [1990] 1 WLR 866.
[869] 'To controvert' simply means 'to challenge'. Thus section 116(4)(b) of the 2003 Act refers to inability to 'challenge' the statement.

However, there was no reason to imply any such restriction upon the plain meaning of the words as counsel for the appellant had suggested. If Parliament had intended the question to be considered on such a narrow basis, express words would have been used to that effect.

If this decision is followed under the 2003 Act, the courts will seek to achieve a balance between the contents of the statement and the risk of unfairness to any party from any inability to cross-examine. To this end, the quality of the evidence in the statement will be the crucial factor: the higher the quality, the less risk there will be of any resulting unfairness. The degree of quality will also impact on the question whether it is in the interests of justice to admit the statement: the higher the quality, the more probative the statement will be to the issues in the case, and the interests of justice would demand that such evidence be admitted. It will be noted that in *Cole* the Court of Appeal approved the warning given to the jury by the trial judge that the hearsay statement had not been subjected to cross-examination. This was seen as a counterbalance to any possible unfairness, and such a warning became normal practice in all cases where such a statement was admitted. This is now seen as a standard requirement, and will continue to apply where statements are admitted under section 116 of the 2003 Act.

A further matter for the judge to consider under section 116(4) is the potential availability of a special measures direction for the fearful witness. Section 17 of the Youth Justice and Criminal Evidence Act 1999 provides that witnesses in fear or distress are eligible for special measures, providing such measures would improve the quality of their evidence.[870] The potential use of such measures will naturally be preferable to admitting a hearsay statement, since the opposing party is then able to test the evidence through cross-examination. This point was emphasised in *R v H and others*,[871] where the Court of Appeal stressed that before the judge could be satisfied that a witness did not give oral evidence through fear, the court should be informed of any, and if so what efforts had been made to persuade the witness to attend or to alleviate his fears, by, for example, an offer of witness protection, or of screens at court. If that was not practical, the Court recommended that the prosecution should interview any witness asserting fear on a video link, or indeed to have a tape recording of the actual conversation, in order for the judge fully to appreciate that proper efforts had been made to secure his or her attendance. Such information would allow the court to assess as the level of the determination of the witness not to give evidence, and the reasons on which it was founded.

However, the Court of Appeal in *R v Davies*[872] stated that the decision in *H* did not represent the law contained in the CJA 2003. Here, the defendant was convicted of causing actual bodily harm and possession of an offensive weapon. Three complainants had made written representations to the judge that they were frightened of the accused and did not wish to give evidence in court. Thus written statements were read, pursuant to section 116(2)(e). The appellant argued that there had been insufficient evidence of their fear, and the trial judge had failed to take proper steps to assess the basis for the complainants' assertions. This contention was rejected:

> In our judgment, the judge was perfectly entitled to reach a conclusion as to the genuineness of the witnesses' fears on the basis of the evidence to which we have referred. It must always

---

[870]See Ch 2, pp 33–47.
[871](2001) *The Times*, 6 July.
[872][2007] 2 All ER 1070.

be recalled that fear is to be widely construed … and that it was the purpose of this part of the 2003 Act to alter that which had previously been the law under section 23 of the Criminal Justice Act 1988. The law previously referred to, particularly in *R v H*, is no longer that which should guide the courts under the new regime. Indeed, courts are ill-advised to seek to test the basis of fear by calling witnesses before them, since that may undermine the very thing that section 116 was designed to avoid.

Of course, judges must be astute not to skew a fair trial by a too ready acceptance of assertions of fear since it is all too easy for witnesses to avoid the inconvenience and anxiety of a trial by saying they do not want to come. But having said that, in the instant case there was ample evidence to justify the course that the judge took. In those circumstances, there is no basis for the suggestion that he was wrong to do so. Normally a judge will have a much better feel of the truth or otherwise of the assertions of fear than this court could ever do, but we accept that the judge made his ruling at the outset and in those circumstances based it purely upon the written assertions of the witnesses. Had we thought he was plainly wrong, then there would have been merit in this appeal, but, on the contrary, we take the view that he was right.[873]

Where the accused is responsible for any of the conditions in section 116(2)

Section 116(5) of the Act provides that the hearsay statement will be rendered inadmissible if a party, or any person acting on his or her behalf, causes the original maker of the statement to be unavailable. Thus, for example, if the defendant has an alibi witness whom he thinks will not stand up to cross-examination, he may encourage him to be absent, maybe by offering him a holiday, or demanding that he stays out of the way during the trial. The subsection applies to both the prosecution and defence, and it will be for the party opposing the admission of the statement to satisfy the court that the other side is responsible for the operation of the particular condition.

Similarly, it would be difficult for a defendant to argue against the admission of the statement of a witness who is physically unable to attend if he had been shown to be responsible for an attack on the witness, who was subsequently unable to attend the trial. In *R v Moore*,[874] the appellant challenged his conviction on the ground that the trial judge had erred in admitting the statement of an 82-year-old woman who was not fit to attend court. The witness had let a garage to the defendant, in which he stored his car. He then alleged the vehicle had been stolen in order to claim on his insurance. The trial took place five years after the committal because the defendant had absconded. He argued that the statement of the elderly woman was crucial and was the foundation of the prosecution case. Therefore, the only way to challenge it was for the defendant to give evidence, and it was unfair to force him to give evidence in this way. Applying *Cole* and dismissing the appeal, the Court of Appeal noted that the more important the evidence, the greater the damage it may do to the defendant. However, there was no general principle that it would be unfair and contrary to the interests of justice to admit a statement if the only way of controverting the statement is for the defendant to testify in person. In this particular case, the court paid particular attention to the fact that the defendant had evaded trial for so long that the prosecution's elderly witness was no longer fit to give evidence. As was stated in *Cole*, fairness required a balance between the prosecution and the defence, and the prosecution should not be put in a disadvantageous position by the

---

[873] *Ibid.*, [14]–[15].
[874] [1992] Crim LR 882.

illness of a witness, especially where the defendant's conduct contributed to this state of affairs.

Section 117 – Use of business and other documents

Section 117 of the 2003 Act replaces sections 24 and 25 of the CJA 1988, and provides for the admissibility of documentary hearsay created or received in the course of trade, business or a profession, subject to certain conditions. Section 24 of the 1988 Act was worded in similar terms, and it was broadly accepted that statements in business documents were likely to be reliable and less susceptible to challenge by cross-examination. It must be emphasised that while section 116 is concerned with both oral and written statements, section 117 is concerned only with written statements. It will be apparent from the discussion below that there will be circumstances in which a statement in a document will be admissible under either section 116 or section 117. However, all statements admitted under section 116 must satisfy one of the conditions in section 116(2). Under section 117, the document will have had to have been created or received in the course of business.[875]

Section 117(1) refers to 'a statement contained in a document' and section 117(2)(b) refers to 'information contained in the statement'. Before proceeding further however, it may also be useful to clarify what precisely the three key terms used in these provisions – 'document', 'statement' and 'information' – actually mean. As defined by section 134(1), a 'document' means 'anything in which information of any description is recorded', and is therefore merely a container for a statement which has been reduced to writing or another form.[876] It may therefore apply to tape recordings or any other form of recording, including data entered on a computer.[877] The Court of Appeal in *R v Carrington*[878] held that a document may contain more than one statement, and this is impliedly accepted by section 117(2)(a), which refers to 'the document or part containing the statement'. Every statement contains 'information', and in this context the supplier of that information must have had, or be reasonably supposed to have had, personal knowledge of the matters in question. For the purposes of section 117(5), the supplier of the information is thus deemed to be the 'relevant person'.

The conditions of admissibility

Documents created or received in the course of a trade, business, profession, etc. are admissible under section 117(1) if three conditions are satisfied:

(a) oral evidence given in the proceedings would be admissible as evidence of any matter stated;

(b) the requirements of section 117(2) are satisfied; and

---

[875] In practice there will rarely any advantage to be gained in using section 117 rather than section 116. The rare occasion when it might be advantageous to use section 117 is when a party seeks to rely on section 117(5)(b) (see p 230 below).

[876] As noted above, 'statement' is widely defined by section 115(2) as 'any representation of fact or opinion made by a person by whatever means; and it includes a representation made in a sketch, photofit or other pictorial form'.

[877] See e.g. *Wellington v DPP* [2007] EWHC 1061 (Admin), where it was held that a record in the police national computer that a person had used a particular alias may be admitted under section 117.

[878] [1994] Crim LR 438.

(c) the requirements of section 117(5) are satisfied, in a case where section 117(4) requires them to be.

The condition contained in section 117(1)(a) is the equivalent criterion as that laid down by section 116(1)(a).[879] The court must ask whether oral evidence of the information within the statement would otherwise be admissible (i.e. it would be relevant, and would not be subject to any other exclusionary rule).

In addition, section 117(1)(b), requires the statement must satisfy three further conditions laid down in section 117(2):

(a) the document was created or received by a person in the course of a trade, business, profession or other occupation, or by the holder of a paid or unpaid office; and

(b) the person who supplied the information in the statement (the relevant person) had or may reasonably be supposed to have had personal knowledge of the matters dealt with in the statement; and

(c) each person through whom the information was supplied received the information in the course of a trade, business or profession, or as the holder of a paid or unpaid office.

While section 117(2)(a) requires that the document was created or received by a person in the course of a trade, business, profession, etc. the particular industry in question need not have any connection with the statement in the document, nor with the maker of that statement or the supplier of the information. For example, assume that a robbery occurs in a grocery shop, which is witnessed by Andrea, the shop assistant. She tells the driver of a delivery truck what she saw, and the driver writes it down. The driver then passes the statement, now contained in documentary form, to a police officer. In the meantime, Andrea has left the area and cannot be found. However, the prosecution will be able to rely on section 117 in seeking to admit the documentary statement in evidence. Since Andrea, the person who supplied the information, had personal knowledge of the matters contained in the statement, and it was created by the truck driver in the course of business, and received by the police officer in the course of business, it should be prima facie admissible. However, had she simply given the details to her next door neighbour, section 117 would not apply as the customer would not have created the document in the course of business.[880]

These facts were not entirely dissimilar to those of *Maher v DPP*, one of the first cases to be decided on the new provisions. The accused had collided with the vehicle and driven off. His actions were observed by a passer-by, who recorded his registration on a slip of paper and left it under the windscreen wiper of the damaged vehicle. The injured party subsequently contacted the police, who took a note of the registration and subsequently arrested and charged the defendant. The Divisional Court held that the trial judge had improperly admitted the evidence under section 117, since the owner of the damaged vehicle had not received the information in the course of business.[881]

---

[879]See above, p 219.

[880]In this scenario section 117(4) requires that the additional requirements of section 117(5) must be satisfied (see further). Thus, one of the conditions in section 116(2) must be satisfied, which it will be in this instance since A cannot be found. Therefore, though the statement *may* be admitted under section 117, there is no advantage in seeking to admit it under that section given that section 116 applies.

[881]However, the Court declined to quash the conviction on the basis that it would have been admissible in the interests of justice under section 114(1)(d). It can also be noted that such a statement would not have been admissible under section 116, since subsection (1)(b) would not be satisfied: the person making the statement would not have been identified to the court's satisfaction. [2006] EWHC 1271 (Admin).

Even if the evidence *Maher* had been received by third party in the course of business (for example, if the passer-by had left the note at the front desk of a police station), a further hurdle would have been overcome before the prosecution could rely on the evidence in court. As with Andrea in the fictional scenario above, the passer-by in *Maher* clearly prepared the note of the registration in order that the injured party could contact the police. This will therefore amount to a statement prepared for the purposes of contemplated criminal proceedings, and thus the requirements of section 117(5) must also be satisfied. The statement must either satisfy one of the five conditions in section 116(2), or, alternatively, the additional condition set out in section 117(5)(b); where 'the relevant person cannot reasonably be expected to have any recollection of the matters dealt with in the statement'.

The facts of *R v Carrington*[882] provide an example of the circumstances in which this latter provision might apply. The accused attempted to use a stolen credit card in a supermarket. The cashier called a supervisor, B, who called another supervisor, S, who was about to go off duty. B told the customer that she was going to check on the card. At that point, the defendant left the store and was spotted by S, as she walked to her car. She noticed that he was driving a white Peugeot car, which left the car park at high speed. S made a note on a magazine of the make of the car, the registration number and a brief description of the man. She went back into the store and, using the internal telephone, passed the description of the man and the car to B, who subsequently noted it on her memo pad. S then went home without checking that the memo was correct, and did not keep the magazine.

At trial, the memo written by B was admitted as a business document under what would now be section 117 (formerly section 24 of the Criminal Justice Act 1988). Dismissing the appellant's arguments that the memo should not have been admitted, the Court of Appeal held that the key issue was whether the requirements of section 24(4)(iii) (now section 117(5)(b)) were satisfied. In these particular circumstances, S could not reasonably be expected, having regard to the time which had elapsed and to all the circumstances, to have any recollection of the matters dealt within the statement. The parties had been incorrect to agree amongst themselves that B was the maker of the statement in the memo. Although B recorded the statement, the supplier of the information was S. She could remember passing on the information about the man and the car and giving the registration number, but could not recall the registration number when giving evidence in court. The fact that S was available to give direct evidence, and did give direct evidence, was the basis of the defence objection to the admissibility of the memo under section 24. In other words, the argument being put forward here by the appellant was essentially that if a person was present and did give evidence, he or she should not fall within section 24. Rejecting that predication, the Court held that a document consists of a number of statements, therefore parts of the document may be admissible as independent statements notwithstanding that the maker has a clear recollection of some parts of the document. The prosecution were therefore entitled to treat the part of memo which contained the registration number of the car as an independent statement for the purposes of section 24.

Were the facts of *Carrington* to arise under the current law, the outcome would be the same. It will be noted that B received the information during the course of her trade, and the statement in the document was created by her from information supplied by her supervisor S, who clearly had personal knowledge of the matters therein. In this case the statement was prepared for the purposes of a criminal investigation, therefore section 117(4)

---

[882] [1994] Crim LR 438.

requires that a condition in section 116(2), or the additional condition in section 117(5), be satisfied. Since S was present and able to give evidence, none of the conditions in section 116(2) could be satisfied. However, section 117(5)(b) would apply. However, it is worth noting that, in these circumstances, the legislation provides for an additional safeguard. The judge could still potentially refuse to admit the evidence under subsections (6) and (7), if he or she is not satisfied as to its reliability given its contents, the source of the information contained in it, or the way in which, or the circumstances in which, the information or document itself was supplied or received.

Where the creator and recipient of the document are the same person

Section 117(3) allows for the possibility that persons mentioned in section 117(2)(a) and (b) may, in some cases, be the same person. It would not be an infrequent occurrence in the course of business for an individual to put information that has come to light into written form for a formal record. In such circumstances, that person will be both the creator of the document and the supplier of the information it contains. If, for sake of argument, that same person then posted the document addressed to himself/herself, the creator and maker of the document would, in due course, also become the recipient of the document.

Section 118 – Preservation of common law exceptions

It will be recalled that the common law originally developed a number of exceptions to mitigate the harsh operation of the rule against hearsay in practice. Section 118 preserves some of the categories of hearsay evidence that were admissible at common law. Some of these exceptions, concerning certain forms of documentary evidence, such as public documents,[883] works of reference,[884] maps and plans are now of less importance, and their admissibility is largely accepted without contention. Further exceptions apply in relation to matters concerning reputation or family tradition. However, this form of evidence is now extremely rare in practice, and, as such, their scope will not be considered any further here.

Several of the common law exceptions do, however, continue to play a prominent role in contemporary practice. Foremost amongst these are confessions, which continue to be viewed as an exception to the hearsay rule by virtue of section 118(1) 5. These are considered in the next chapter. Likewise, experts are frequently permitted to cite out-of-court evidence in support of their opinions. This, too, is a preserved common law exception to the rule against hearsay,[885] and we consider this issue in greater depth in Chapter 10. For the purposes of this chapter, we will focus on the most part on the scope of the *res gestae* exception, although brief comment will also be made on the use of hearsay in respect of common enterprises. Before proceeding, however, it should be borne in mind that all common law exceptions were decided on a case-by-case basis and, inevitably, some are more developed than others. For that reason, some of the common law exceptions continue to be uncertain in their scope and still require some further clarification by the appellate courts.

---

[883] eg entries on Register of Births, Marriages and Deaths, Land Registry, Company Registry, etc.
[884] This category includes any relevant published work dealing with any matter of a public nature.
[885] Criminal Justice Act 2003, section 118(1) 8.

Res gestae

This exception, preserved by section 118(1) 4, is in fact an umbrella term which encapsulates a number of distinct, albeit similar, exceptions. The expression *res gestae* is a corruption of a longer Latin phrase meaning 'part of a story'. The basis of this exception is that the human conduct consists of words and actions, and often the actions cannot be understood without the words. Looking at actions in isolation may serve to decontextualise events and thereby give a false impression. By contrast, taking account of both actions and words should, in theory at least, give us a clearer picture of what happened in the past, and why. To that end, we may have a better prospect of uncovering the truth about past events. It should be pointed out that, because section 116 of the 2003 Act provides for the admissibility of a statement where a witness is unavailable, it will not be uncommon for there to be a considerable degree of overlap in the types of situations where both section 116 and 118 may apply. In particular, reliance may be placed on either section where, as will often be the case, the maker of the statement is dead or otherwise unavailable. In practice however, it will generally be more straightforward for a party wishing to adduce a hearsay statement to rely on section 116, although section 118 remains a viable alternative in certain circumstances.

Under section 118(1) 4, there are three forms of statements that are considered to form part of the *res gestae*:

(a) statements made by a person so emotionally overpowered by an event that the possibility of concoction or distortion can be disregarded;

(b) statements accompanied by an act that explain the act of the maker;

(c) statements of a person's own contemporaneous state of mind.

Section 118(1) 4(a) – Statements made by a person so emotionally overpowered ...

This head constitutes the most common application of the *res gestae* principle. American lawyers sometimes describe it as the 'excited utterance rule', since the statement must be made spontaneously and contemporaneously with the events subject of the trial. This will usually occur in a scenario involving a serious and violent offence, since it will depend upon an instinctive and spontaneous reaction on the part of the maker of the statement. The exception has been traditionally justified on the basis that a sudden and emotional reaction to an unusual event will effectively rule out the possibility of fabrication or concoction by the maker. A good example can be found in *R v Fowkes*.[886] Here, a witness to a murder was heard to shout, 'There's Butcher!' (the name by which the defendant was known), just as a face appeared at the window from which the fatal shot had been fired. The policeman who had heard this exclamation was allowed to relay it to the court in evidence. A further example can be found in the case of *Ratten*, where the Privy Council held that if, contrary to their decision, the telephone call from the victim had been hearsay rather than evidence of state of mind, it would have nonetheless fallen under the *res gestae* exception.[887]

The requirement that the statement be made contemporaneously with the relevant act does not mean that the statement and act must exactly coincide in point of time. At one time the common law did require exact contemporaneity. In *R v Bedingfield*,[888] the victim

---

[886] (1856) *The Times*, 8 March.
[887] See p 208.
[888] (1879) 14 Cox CC 341.

staggered out of a room in which she had been with the accused, with her throat cut. Pointing to the wound, she said to her aunt, 'Oh dear Aunt, see what Harry has done to me!' This was excluded because '[i]t was not part of anything done, nor something said while something was being done, but something said after something was done'.[889] However, this decision no longer represents the law.

The leading case is now *R v Andrews*.[890] The accused was charged with murder. Immediately after a savage knife attack, the victim staggered downstairs to the flat of a neighbour, seeking assistance. Shortly afterwards the police arrived, and the victim made a statement identifying the accused as one of his assailants. He died some two months later of his injuries. The police officers were allowed to give evidence of what the victim told them as part of the *res gestae*. The House of Lords held that this evidence had been properly admitted as evidence of the truth of the facts asserted. Lord Ackner, with whom all of their Lordships agreed, summarised the relevant principles to be applied when admitting evidence under the *res gestae* doctrine, as follows:

(1) The primary question which the judge must ask himself is: can the possibility of concoction or distortion be disregarded?

(2) To answer that question the judge must first consider the circumstances in which the particular statement was made, in order to satisfy himself that the event was so unusual or startling or dramatic as to dominate the thoughts of the victim, so that his utterance was an instinctive reaction to that event, thus giving no real opportunity for reasoned reflection. In such a situation the judge would be entitled to conclude that the involvement or pressure of the event would exclude the possibility of concoction or distortion, providing that the statement was made in conditions of approximate but not exact contemporaneity.

(3) In order for the statement to be sufficiently 'spontaneous' it must be so closely associated with the event which has excited the statement that it can fairly be stated that the mind of the declarant was still dominated by the event. Thus the judge must be satisfied that the event which provided the trigger mechanism for the statement was still operative. The fact that the statement was made in response to a question is but one factor to consider under this heading.

(4) Quite apart from the time factor, there may be special features in the case, which relate to the possibility of concoction or distortion. In the instant appeal the defence relied on evidence to support the contention that the deceased had a purpose of his own to fabricate or concoct, namely a malice ... The judge must be satisfied that the circumstances were such that, having regard to the special feature of malice, there was no possibility of a concoction or distortion to the advantage of the maker or the disadvantage of the accused.

(5) As to the possibility of error in the facts narrated in the statement, if only the ordinary fallibility of human recollection is relied on, this goes to the weight to be attached to and not the admissibility of the statement and is therefore a matter for the jury. However, here again there may be special features that may give rise to the possibility of error. In the instant case there was evidence that the deceased had drunk to excess. Another example would be where the identification was made in circumstances of particular difficulty or where the declarant suffered from defective eyesight. In such

---

[889]The trial judge contrasted this with a cry such as 'Don't Harry!' uttered while the act was done which, if heard by the aunt, would have been admissible.
[890][1987] AC 281.

circumstances the trial judge must consider whether he can exclude the possibility of error.[891]

Thus, while *approximate* contemporaneity is required, the emphasis is on the reliability of the statement. The shorter the time gap between the event and the statement, and the more dramatic and unusual the event is, the less likely it will be that the court will find the statement to have been concocted or distorted. In *Andrews* itself, the relevant time gap was some 15 minutes. It was, however, emphasised that the *res gestae* doctrine should not be used to avoid calling witnesses who can give direct evidence of the matter.[892] In *Tobi v Nicholas*,[893] the accused was convicted of failing to stop after an accident. The evidence was that the accused's car had collided with a coach and had failed to stop. Some 20 minutes after the accident a police officer went to a house where the damaged car was parked, and there heard the coach driver identify the accused as the driver of the car which had collided with him. The officer was allowed to give evidence of this oral identification, the court ruling that it was admissible under the *res gestae* doctrine. The conviction was quashed on the ground that the coach driver was available, but had simply not been called to give evidence. It was also said that, in this particular case, the event in question was not *so* dramatic as to have dominated the mind of the maker of the statement. This, together with the fact that the statement was made some 20 minutes after the event, did not rule out the possibility of error or concoction. It should be underlined, however, that this decision should not be read as authority that states that a time lapse of 20 minutes is the upper limit of approximate contemporaneity. Had the event been more dramatic or unusual, the mind of the maker might still have been dominated by it. However, a minor road accident will generally not fall into this sort of category.

In *R v Carnall*,[894] the accused was charged with the murder of V. Two witnesses had seen V in the street outside their house. He was bleeding and asking for help. He claimed he had been attacked with knives and a baseball bat, and it had taken him about an hour to crawl from his home to the house. The witnesses asked him who had attacked him, and he subsequently named the defendant. At hospital, before V died, he gave a statement to a police officer, again naming V as the attacker. The trial judge admitted both the statement to the witnesses and that given to the police officer as part of the *res gestae*. On appeal it was argued that he had been wrong to do so. It was alleged that the time which had elapsed between the attack and the making of the statements (over an hour between the attack and the first statement and nearer two hours in respect of the second statement), coupled with the fact that the statements had been made only in response to questions meant that it was not sufficiently contemporaneous. Moreover, the appellant also contended that the statement was inherently unreliable, since the victim had lost a lot of blood, which could have resulted in a confused state of mind.

Dismissing the appeal, it was held that the crucial question was whether there was any real possibility of concoction or distortion, or whether the judge felt confident that that the thoughts of the maker of the statements were at the time so dominated by what had happened that what the speaker said could be regarded as unaffected by any ex post facto reasoning or fabrication. In answering this question, the trial judge had taken account of the appalling nature of the attack itself; the horrific injuries that were inflicted; the pain that the victim was undergoing; and the obsession he had at the time with getting help and

---

891 *Ibid.*, at 300–301.
892 See also *Edwards and Osakwe v DPP* [1992] Crim LR 576.
893 [1987] Crim LR 774.
894 [1995] Crim LR 944.

trying to stay alive. The time factor was not conclusive. As to the question of the loss of blood, the judge had rightly taken the view that this was merely speculative on the part of the appellant. Thus, the central issue for the court was not a question of a lapse of time, but whether there was a real possibility of concoction or distortion as a *result* of the lapse of time or any other proven factor.

In *R v Newport*,[895] the facts were similar to those in *Ratten*. The defendant's wife left the house after an argument, pursued by N wielding a bread knife. The victim was subsequently stabbed, and later died of her wounds. The prosecution case was that the accused deliberately stabbed her to death. He denied this, and claimed the death was an accident. Evidence was admitted of a telephone call made by the wife to a friend on the evening of her death. The friend said that the deceased was in an agitated and frightened state, and had asked if she could come to her friend's house if she had to flee in a hurry. This evidence was admitted as part of the *res gestae* and the accused was convicted.[896] The Court of Appeal found that the evidence of the telephone call had been admitted on the basis that it had been made immediately before the wife left the house, when in fact it had been made 20 minutes earlier. In view of that, it was held that the evidence was not a spontaneous and unconsidered reaction to an immediate impending emergency and should not have been admitted. However, on taking into account the weight of the other evidence before the jury, the conviction was not considered unsafe.

As these cases make clear, the admissibility of spontaneous exclamations as *res gestae* is governed by the test laid down in *Andrews*. There is no longer a strict requirement of contemporaneity between the event and the exclamation. What is essential is that the trial judge is satisfied that the 'possibility of concoction or distortion can be disregarded', which involves considering whether the event was so unusual or startling or dramatic as to dominate the thoughts of the declarant.

In *Attorney-General's Reference (No 1 of 2003)*,[897] the defendant was charged with causing grievous bodily harm to his mother. Prosecuting counsel told the court that he thought the accused's mother might not give reliable evidence, and sought the court's permission to call a number of witnesses who heard her shouting and identifying the accused as her attacker. The trial judge refused to admit this evidence as *res gestae*, since the victim was prepared to testify. The Court of Appeal held that there was no rider to the *res gestae* exception to the effect that the rule was not applicable where better evidence was available. Nonetheless, while the prosecution had not sought to disadvantage the defence by not calling the victim, it was fundamentally unfair to the accused not to call her and rely instead on *res gestae* evidence.[898]

While most statements admitted under the *res gestae* principle are made by victims who are not able to give evidence, the rule applies to statements made by the accused as well. Where those statements are inculpatory in nature, they will be admissible as a confession. However, the *res gestae* principle could apply to statements not amounting to an admission.

---

[895] [1998] Crim LR 581.

[896] The relevance of this evidence lies in the deceased's agitated and frightened state and the claim that she might need to flee her husband. Since he claimed the death was an accident, evidence that the wife was in fear and preparing to flee contradicted this and was clearly relevant.

[897] [2003] Crim LR 547.

[898] However, had the prosecution not called the victim, the Court noted that the trial judge could have excluded the *res gestae* evidence under section 78 of the Police and Criminal Evidence Act 1984 as being in breach of the fair trial provisions of Article 6(1) of the European Convention on Human Rights. One way around this kind of problem might have been to call the victim and, if she did not give the expected evidence, to call the other witnesses, whose evidence would then be admissible under the *res gestae* exception.

In *R v Glover*,[899] the accused assaulted another man and was forcibly restrained by other persons present. He shouted, 'I am David Glover', and then made threats to shoot the man and his family. There was a possibility that the man was not David Glover but, having considered that possibility and discounted it, the judge admitted evidence from witnesses who were present at the scene. If we return briefly to the facts of *Bedingfield*, had the accused been heard to say, 'I'm Harry Bedingfield and I've come for you', that would have been admissible as part of the *res gestae*.

Section 118(1) 4(b) – Statements that accompany and explain acts of the maker

In order to be admissible under this head, a statement must relate to, accompany and explain the act, which must itself be relevant and must be made contemporaneously. A simple example is that of a person who runs off on the approach of a police officer. In isolation it looks like a guilty act; however, if it is accompanied by the words, 'Sorry, I must run, the last bus leaves in two minutes', it takes on a different meaning. Most examples of this exception are to be found in the civil law. Thus in order to prove that money was a gift, a witness would be allowed to say in evidence that she heard the claimant say, on handing over money, 'This is for your birthday'. However, the principle was applied within a criminal context in *R v McCay*.[900] Here, a witness, who had viewed a pre-trial identification parade through a one-way glass screen, said to the police officer, 'It's number 8'. However, he could not remember which number he had said when he came to give evidence at trial. The police officer was permitted to give evidence that the witness had said 'It's number 8', because those words were deemed to accompany and explain a relevant act.[901]

Section 118(1) 4(c) – Statements of the maker's own contemporaneous state of mind

Statements by a person which constitute evidence of his or her physical or mental state are admissible on the basis that only that person knows how he or she feels, and there would be no way of proving such emotions unless that statement were admissible. The rule regarding contemporaneity is more flexible in this area. It may, for example, include a statement about the person's physical or mental condition at some earlier point in time. Statements have been admitted on matters such as a person's political opinion, marital affection, the dislike of a child and, more recently, to prove (for the purposes of what is now section 116(2)(e)) that a witness who will not give evidence was in fear. It also seems that this head will cover statement of intentions, and that such a statement is admissible to support an inference that the intention referred to existed at a time prior to or after that statement had been made. However, where the statement expresses an intention to do

---

[899] [1991] Crim LR 48.
[900] [1990] 1 WLR 645.
[901] The same means could have been used in *R v Osbourne and Virtue* [1973] QB 678. An eyewitness had identified Osbourne at an identification parade, but at trial claimed that 'she did not remember that she had picked out anyone on the last parade'. The prosecution had to call a police inspector to confirm the positive identification. The Court of Appeal upheld the trial judge's decision to admit the evidence, although it preferred a somewhat doubtful application of the *res gestae* principle as the basis of its decision. The decision compares unfavourably with that in *Kearley*, where the House of Lords stated that telephone calls and words of the personal callers could have fallen within the *res gestae* exception if the offence was seen as continuing during the time the officers were in the flat: thus the words of the callers who have had effectively accompanied the continuing act of the defendant. Unfortunately, however, that possibility was not considered by the court.

an act, the authorities conflict as to whether it can be relied upon to prove that the act in question was actually committed.

In *R v Buckley*,[902] the defendant was charged with the murder of a police officer. A statement made by the deceased officer to a senior officer, that he intended to watch the accused's movements on the night he was killed, was admitted to prove the accused had committed the offence. More recently, in *R v Moghal*,[903] the accused, who was charged with aiding and abetting a murder, alleged that his mistress, S, (who had already been tried and acquitted) had committed the murder alone. The Court of Appeal expressed the opinion that a tape-recorded statement made some six months before V's death, in which S was heard to say that she intended to kill V, should have been admissible in evidence. This decision was, however, doubted in *R v Blastland*,[904] where the House of Lords questioned whether it was really relevant to the issue as to whether Moghal aided and abetted S. Had S said that she planned to kill V alone, then it would clearly have been relevant in that it would have tended to suggest that D had no part in the murder. Indeed, in *R v Wainwright*,[905] a statement by the murder victim that she was going to the accused's premises was held to be inadmissible because it was only a statement of intention, which she might or might not have carried out. Similarly in *R v Thompson*,[906] the statement by a woman that she intended to abort herself, and the statement after her miscarriage that she had caused it herself, were both held to be inadmissible hearsay on a charge against the accused of using an instrument to procure an abortion. The difference may lie in the fact that the police officer in *Buckley* was seen to be more reliable than the murder victim in *Wainwright* and the woman whose pregnancy had been terminated in *Thompson*. Had any of these statements been in documentary form, they might now be admissible under section 116 of the Criminal Justice Act 2003.

The most recent case on this particularly form of *res gestae* is *R v Gilfoyle*.[907] The defendant had been convicted of the murder of his wife, who had been found hanging from a beam in the garage of her house. There was a note in her handwriting, in which she said she was going to take her own life. At first, her death was thought to have been suicide. However, sometime later, a friend of the deceased made a statement to the police in which she said that the deceased had told her that her husband, who was an auxiliary nurse, was doing a project on suicide at work. He had asked his wife to help him out by writing examples of suicide notes. Two other friends made similar statements to the police. Although these three statements had been ruled inadmissible by the trial judge, the defendant was convicted. The Court of Appeal ruled that all three statements ought to have been admitted. The statements attributed to the deceased by her three friends threw light on her state of mind, which was one of the principal issues in the case. Accordingly, their Lordships were satisfied that the statements should have been used to show that the deceased was not in a suicidal frame of mind when she wrote the notes, instead believing that she was assisting the appellant in a project.[908]

---

[902] (1873) 13 Cox CC 293.

[903] (1977) 65 Cr App R 56.

[904] [1986] AC 41. See also *R v Callender* [1998] Crim LR 337.

[905] (1875) 13 Cox CC 171.

[906] [1912] 3 KB 19.

[907] [1996] 3 All ER 883.

[908] In a second appeal in *R v Gilfoyle* [2001] 2 Cr App R 5, the Court of Appeal rejected evidence of what was described as a 'psychological autopsy' of the deceased's wife in order to show that she was, in fact, suicidal. See further Ch 10, p 318.

As a final point, it is worth noting that evidence of the telephone call made by the deceased in *Newport* should also have been admissible under this head.[909] Here, the deceased's husband claimed that the stabbing was an accident, but the wife's telephone call to a friend suggested an ongoing argument, which had made her so agitated and frightened that she was contemplating almost immediate flight from the matrimonial home. Evidence of this state of mind was then clearly relevant to rebut the defence of accident.

Section 118(1) 7 – Statements made by a party to a common enterprise

Where two or more persons conspire to commit an offence, an out-of-court statement of one may be admissible in evidence against the other, and also against the maker of the statement.[910] If the statement contains facts upon which the prosecution propose to rely, those facts are admissible as an exception to the rule against hearsay. However, a condition of admissibility is that the statement must have been made in pursuance of the conspiracy subject of the charge. Where there is more than one conspiracy charged, as where A is alleged to have conspired with B and B is alleged to have conspired with C, a statement made by A in pursuance of his conspiracy with B is not admissible in relation to the alleged conspiracy between B and C.

The leading case in this area is *R v Blake and Tye*.[911] The defendants were convicted of fraudulent conspiracy to evade payment of customs duties. The prosecution case was that Blake, a customs official, and Tye, an agent for an importer, falsified documents, by declaring a smaller amount of goods than was actually imported to avoid paying duty. The conspiracy was largely proved by entries in a book kept by Tye, which showed the true quantity of goods imported. It was held that these entries were properly proved against both conspirators, being statements made in pursuance of the conspiracy. However, entries on cheque book stubs by Tye, recording the division of spoils between Tye and Blake, were not admissible, because they were made after the offence had been completed. They could not therefore have been made in pursuance of the conspiracy.

The decision regarding the cheque stubs in the above case may be compared with that in *R v Davenport*.[912] Here, a document dealing with the proposed division of the proceeds from the alleged conspiracy was held to be admissible against all the parties concerned, on the basis that it was compiled before the conspiracy was complete and was made in pursuance of it. In *R v Jenkins and Starling*,[913] the defendants, directors of a company, were charged with conspiracy to defraud a local authority by falsely claiming a refund of business rates. It was alleged that they had conspired either with a council employee, or with an employee of a computer servicing company. At the trial, Exhibit 1 was a document bearing the word 'refund request' with the word 'overpayment' endorsed on it. The signatories of the document were not called as witnesses. On appeal, the prosecution conceded that the document was hearsay, but argued that it was admissible as a document made in pursuance of a conspiracy. The Court of Appeal disagreed. Allowing the appeal, it was held that, in order for such evidence to be admissible, there had to be an assertion by the signatory

---

[909] See, p 235.
[910] For a recent example, see *R v Platten* [2006] Crim LR 920.
[911] (1844) 6 QB 126.
[912] [1996] 1 Cr App R 221.
[913] [2003] Crim LR 107.

that he knew the contents to be true. Additionally, there was no evidence as to when the document had been prepared. If prepared after the refund had been received, it was not made *in pursuance* of the conspiracy, since by then the fraud would have had already been completed.

The principle that a statement made by a party to a common enterprise is admissible against the maker and the other participants is not confined to those offences that involve a conspiracy. In *R v Gray*,[914] the Court of Appeal approved and adopted the dictum of Dixon CJ in the Australian case of *Tripodi v R*,[915] to the effect that the rule also applied to substantive offences committed by two or more persons with a common purpose. The Court attempted to define the application of the rule on the basis of a statement found in *Phipson on Evidence*:

> Where two [or more] persons engage in a common enterprise, the acts and declarations of one in pursuance of that common enterprise are admissible against the other(s). The principle applies to the commission, by one or more people acting in concert, of a substantive offence or series of offences, but is limited to evidence which shows the involvement of each of the defendants in the commission of the offence or offences.[916]

As with conspiracies, the acts or declarations must be made in pursuance of the common enterprise, so that statements made after the completion of the enterprise are admissible only against the maker.[917]

Hearsay and previous inconsistent statements

Section 119(1) of the Criminal Justice Act 2003 clarifies the relationship between hearsay evidence and previous statements. This provides that once it has been proved that a witness has made a previous inconsistent statement, such a statement is not only evidence which undermines the witness's credibility, but, in contrast to the previous law, can also be used as evidence of the truth of its contents.[918] Section 119(2) provides:

> If in criminal proceedings evidence of an inconsistent statement by any person is given under section 124(2)(c) (to attack the credibility of the person), the statement is admissible as evidence of any matter stated in it of which oral evidence by the witness would be admissible.

The provision envisages the following type of situation. Amanda makes a statement to the police that she saw Thelma 'outside the jewellers at midday on Monday'. Amanda is unavailable to testify at trial, but her statement is admitted under section 116. Evidence may then be introduced to attack the credibility of Amanda, including the fact that she made another statement inconsistent with this account (for example, if Amanda had earlier told Mark that she did not see Thelma at all on Monday).[919] In these circumstances, section 119(2) provides that if there is such an inconsistent statement, it goes not only to the credibility of

---

[914] [1995] 2 Cr App R 100.

[915] (1961) 104 CLR 1.

[916] 14th ed, (1990: London, Sweet and Maxwell), [25–10].

[917] Some writers argue that statements by the parties to common enterprises involving substantive offences are admissible under other exceptions either as part of the *res gestae*, or as informal admissions. *Cross and Tapper on Evidence* classify them as 'admissions by agents', while *Andrews and Hirst on Criminal Evidence* see them as a species of *res gestae*.

[918] See Ch 5, pp 141–42.

[919] Criminal Justice Act 2003, section 124(2)(c).

A, but also is admissible as to the truth of its contents (i.e. that Amanda did not, in fact, see Thelma on Monday).

Multiple hearsay

As noted earlier in this chapter, 'multiple hearsay' arises where information passes through more than one person before it is recorded. Traditionally, the law of evidence has been extremely restrictive in its approach to admitting such evidence, since it is seen as highly unreliable. Under the 2003 Act, different rules apply to multiple hearsay, depending on the form and context in which it is used at trial. Section 121 provides:

> (1) A hearsay statement is not admissible to prove the fact that an earlier hearsay statement was made unless—
>
> (a) either of the statements is admissible under section 117, 119 or 120,
>
> (b) all parties to the proceedings so agree, or
>
> (c) the court is satisfied that the value of the evidence in question, taking into account how reliable the statements appear to be, is so high that the interests of justice require the later statement to be admissible for that purpose.
>
> (2) In this section 'hearsay statement' means a statement, not made in oral evidence, that is relied upon as evidence of the matter stated in it.

It will be apparent from the above excerpt that multiple hearsay will not be admissible for the purposes of section 116. This provision is based on the recommendation of the Law Commission, which noted:

> Suppose, for example, that A said that event x had occurred, and that A knew this because B had seen it happen and had told A about it immediately afterwards, in such circumstances that A could have given oral evidence of B's statement under the res gestae rule. But A is dead. Should A's statement be admissible as evidence of x?
>
> The statement is multiple hearsay, since A has no personal knowledge of the fact stated. The unavailability exception should not apply because A had no such knowledge, A would have been unable to give oral evidence of that fact. But in this case A could have given such evidence – by virtue not of personal knowledge, but of the res gestae exception. The question is: should it be sufficient for the purposes of the unavailability exception that the declarant could have given oral evidence of the fact stated, even if that evidence would have been (admissible) hearsay? Or should it be necessary that the declarant could have given oral evidence without resort to a hearsay exception?
>
> We have concluded that the answer should depend on which hearsay exception would have rendered A's oral evidence admissible – in other words, how B's statement (the statement on which the statement of the unavailable declarant A is based) itself comes to be admissible. If B gives evidence then the fact that B is available for cross-examination is in our view sufficient to compensate for the fact that A's statement is multiple hearsay. And if B's statement is admissible on the ground that it was made in a business document, we think the presumed reliability of such documents is again sufficient to outweigh the drawbacks of multiple hearsay.
>
> If, however, B's statement is only admissible on the basis that B is unavailable to testify, or under one of the common law exceptions (such as res gestae) that we recommend should be preserved (section 118), we think it would be going too far to permit B's statement to be proved by another hearsay statement merely because the maker of that other statement is unavailable to testify. Our reasons are essentially those that we have given for excluding multiple hearsay in general from the unavailability

exception – namely that with each additional step in the chain, the risk of error or fabrication increases.[920]

The scope of section 121 was the subject of the appeal in *R v Xhabri*.[921] The accused here was charged with kidnapping a Latvian woman, and subjecting her to rape and forced prostitution. One of the statements on which the prosecution proposed to rely was the testimony of a police officer, who had spoken to two unidentified men who had come to the police station to report that a woman had told them that she was being held at a particular address against her will. Since the men did not have personal knowledge of this, the only way it could be admitted in evidence was if it complied with one of the three requirements set down in section 121(1). In this particular case, since the victim had already given evidence of what she had told the two men, section 120(7) applied.[922] The statement was thus admissible under section 121(1)(a). However, the Court of Appeal pointed out that, even if it had not been admissible by virtue of section 120, this was the type of case where it would have been appropriate for the court to exercise its discretion and admit the evidence in the interests of justice under section 121(1)(c). This provision allows the court to admit multiple hearsay if it is highly reliable and the interests of justice require that it be admitted, and is similar to the generic discretion contained in section 114(1)(d). Although there is no formal requirement under section 121 to consider the factors contained in section 114(2), the Divisional Court stated in *Maher v DPP*[923] that these same factors should be taken into account where the court was considering whether to exercise its discretion under section 121(1)(c) to admit multiple hearsay.[924]

Whilst multiple hearsay is inadmissible under section 116, it may be adduced under section 117, subject to certain conditions. The rationale for the differentiation according to the form of the hearsay statement is based on the assumption that, since the chain of communication will be contained within a business context, the risks of distortion or fabrication are considerably reduced. Furthermore, section 117 contains a further safeguard, in that the court may give a direction under section 117(6) that the statement is not admissible if it believes the statement is unreliable.

Suppose, then, an assembly worker on a production line allocates a specific number to a cylinder block. He tells his foreman, who tells the line manager, who tells the records clerk, who enters the information onto a computer. The document (i.e. the data file or printout) was created in the course of a business by the clerk from information originally supplied by the assembly worker. Thus section 117(2)(c) is satisfied and the evidence would be admissible. The 'relevant person' in this chain of communication is the assembly worker, who allocated the number to the cylinder block, and who passed the information to the foreman. Under the previous legislation there was some confusion as to who actually constituted the 'maker' of the statement, but this was resolved *R v Deroda*,[925] where it was made clear that the maker was the person who first compiled the statement as a representation of fact. Thus where A passes information to B, who passes it to C, who writes it down or otherwise records it, A will be regarded as the relevant person for the purposes of these sections.

---

[920] Law Commission, op cit n 822, [8.19–22].

[921] [2006] 1 Cr App 26.

[922] i.e. her statement related to a previous complaint about the offence charged. See further Ch 5, p 127.

[923] (2006) 1 70 JP 441.

[924] Alternatively, the court may choose to admit the statement directly under section 114(1)(d) without relying on section 121 at all.

[925] [2000] 1 Cr App R 41.

However, it is worth bearing in mind that section 123(2) provides that a statement may not be admitted under section 117 if any person who supplied or received the information, or created or received the document, did not have the required capability or, where that person cannot be identified, cannot reasonably be assumed to have had the required capability to testify. It follows that, if anyone who supplied or received the information that is the subject of an application under section 117 was not capable of 'understanding questions put to him about the matters stated, and giving answers to such questions which can be understood',[926] the information cannot be admitted.

HEARSAY AND HUMAN RIGHTS

As indicated above, one of the greatest concerns about the use of hearsay evidence generally is that it denies the opposing party the opportunity to cross-examine the maker of the statement. Potentially, the use of such evidence may violate Article 6(3)(d) of the European Convention on Human Rights (the right to examine opposing witnesses). While the scope of this right is clearly not absolute,[927] there have been instances where hearsay evidence has been found to fall foul of the provision.[928]

Even in the years before the provisions of the 2003 legislation took effect, there was an upsurge in academic concern, both in the United Kingdom and farther afield, that there was an increasing array of circumstances in which the use of hearsay evidence may interfere with the fair trial rights of the accused.[929] Increasingly, such arguments were also being recited in the higher courts.[930] In *R v M (KJ)*,[931] the accused was charged with murder but was found unfit to plead. Subsequently, a hearing was convened to determine whether he had committed the acts alleged by the prosecution. The statement of the sole prosecution witness was admitted under section 23 of the 1988 Act, as the court had found him to be in fear of giving evidence in person. M appealed, arguing that the statement should not have been admitted and that its admission was incompatible with Article 6(3)(d). In support of this contention, counsel relied upon the decision of the European Court of Human Rights in *Luca v Italy*,[932] where the Court stated that Article 6 was likely to be breached where a conviction was based solely or to a decisive extent on untested statements made out of court. Dismissing this argument, the Court of Appeal stated this rule had to be subject to certain exceptions, since a blanket exclusion of such evidence would simply encourage witness intimidation and operate to prevent convictions in cases involving serious and organised crime. Thus, where the witness gave evidence that he would not give live testimony because threats had been made, and the judge drew the inference that the threats were made by or at the instigation of the accused or with his approval, a hearsay statement could normally be admitted without infringing Convention rights.

---

[926]Criminal Justice Act 2003, section 123(3).

[927]See Ch 2, pp 48–49.

[928]See e.g. *Kostovski v Netherlands* (1990) 12 EHRR 434, *Windisch v Austria* (1991) 13 EHRR 281; *Van Mechelen v Netherlands* (1998) 25 EHRR 647; *PS v Germany* (2003) 36 EHRR 61.

[929]See e.g. Osborne, C. 'Hearsay and the European Court of Human Rights' [1993] Crim LR 255; O'Brian, W Jr, 'The Right of Confrontation: US and European Perspectives' (2005) 121 *Law Quarterly Review* 481; Prithipaul, R. 'Observations on the Current Status of the Hearsay Rule' (1996) 39 *Criminal Law Quarterly* 84;

[930]See e.g. *R v Gokal* [1997] 2 Cr App R 266; *R v Thomas* [1998] Crim LR 887; *R v Radak* [1999] 1 Cr App R 187.

[931][2003] 2 Cr App R 21.

[932](2001) 36 EHRR 807.

Notwithstanding the decision in *M*, the English courts have been careful to warn that the problem of witness intimidation should not be used as a smokescreen for prosecutors to prioritise hearsay statements over live evidence. This note of caution was first sounded by the Court of Appeal in *R v Arnold*,[933] and later endorsed in *R v Sellick*.[934] In the latter case, the accused was charged with a murder that had allegedly stemmed from a botched drug deal in the criminal underworld. Strong evidence was presented that associates of the accused had attempted to intimidate two key prosecution witnesses, and so the prosecution sought to adduce their evidence in hearsay form. The defendant was subsequently convicted, and appealed, contending that his right to cross-examine opposing witnesses under Article 6(3)(d) of the Convention had been breached. Following a thorough survey of the Strasbourg case law, the Court of Appeal put forward four main propositions:

(i) The admissibility of evidence is primarily for the national law;

(ii) Evidence must normally be produced at a public hearing and as a general rule Article 6(1) and (3)(d) require a defendant to be given a proper and adequate opportunity to challenge and question witnesses;

(iii) It is not necessarily incompatible with Article 6(1) and (3)(d) for depositions to be read and that can be so even if there has been no opportunity to question the witness at any stage of the proceedings. Article 6(3)(d) is simply an illustration of matters to be taken into account in considering whether a fair trial has been held. The reasons for the court holding it necessary that statements should be read and the procedures to counterbalance any handicap to the defence will all be relevant to the issue, whether, where statements have been read, the trial was fair.

(iv) The quality of the evidence and its inherent reliability, plus the degree of caution exercised in relation to reliance on it, will also be relevant to the question whether the trial was fair.[935]

Adopting this framework of analysis, the court noted the high degree of probability that the witnesses had been intimidated by the defendant in the instant case, but warned that section 116(2)(e) should not be viewed by the prosecution as an open door through which hearsay evidence could automatically be admitted in every case where a witness was on fear. In each instance, the court should care to balance the potential merits and risks of admitting such evidence. Crucial to the final decision will be the extent to which counterbalancing measures are in place for the accused. In this particular case, it was observed that the evidence of both witnesses was credible, and the defence had been able to challenge their credibility. Moreover, the trial judge had given a clear warning to the jury about the potential shortcomings of hearsay evidence compared to live evidence. Since the defendant was the author of his own inability to examine the witnesses in question, the statement was rightfully admitted.[936]

As contended in Chapter 2, there is no right of 'confrontation' either at common law or under the European Convention on Human Rights.[937] Witnesses do, however, have a prima facie right to cross-examine witnesses, which should not be dispensed with lightly. In summary then, the key requirement under both the Convention jurisprudence and that

---

[933] [2005] Crim LR 56.
[934] [2005] 1 WLR 3257.
[935] *Ibid.*, [50].
[936] *Sellick* was followed in *Campbell and others* [2005] EWCA Crim 2078.
[937] See Ch 2, pp 48–49.

of the English courts seems to be that the defence must be given sufficient opportunity to challenge the evidence of such witnesses. It is not necessary for a face-to-face encounter to take place as part of a public trial; the benchmark in all cases is whether the fairness of the trial requires some form of cross-examination to take place. It follows that courts should strive to achieve a balance between the contents of the statement and the risk of unfairness to any party from the inability to cross-examine if the statement is admitted or excluded.[938] Providing this approach is followed in future years, courts will still have an opportunity to hear the evidence of some of the most vulnerable witnesses in many cases concerning society's most serious offences.

KEY LEARNING POINTS

- Hearsay evidence is only admissible under one of the four circumstances outlined in section 114(1) Criminal Justice Act 2003.
- Statements of absent witnesses may be admitted under section 116, subject to certain conditions.
- Statements contained in a document created in the course of business, trade or any profession may be admissible under section 117.
- Several common law categories of admissibility are preserved under section 118. The most important of these is the *res gestae* rule.
- Multiple hearsay is not admissible under section 116, but may be admissible under section 117. It may also be admitted at the discretion of the court under section 121(1)(c) or section 114(1)(d).
- Some commentators fear that hearsay evidence is now too readily admitted in English criminal trials. However, convictions based on hearsay evidence will not normally contravene the defendant's fair trial rights, particularly in cases where the witness is fearful of intimidation.

?   **QUESTIONS**

1. Albert was killed in a brutal attack as he left a London nightclub. He was stabbed and kicked by two men and died of his injuries two days later. Duncan Davies and Eric Evans are charged with his murder. Consider whether the following statements can be admitted at their trial:
   (a) Albert's girlfriend, Mattie, who had attended the nightclub with him, told the police that just before leaving the club on the night of his death, Albert told her he had been threatened by Davies and Evans and said he was going to leave to avoid any trouble.

Continued

---

[938] In conducting this exercise, the quality of the evidence in the statement will be the crucial factor. The higher the quality of the evidence in the statement the less risk there will be of unfairness to any party resulting from the inability to cross-examine. The degree of quality will also impact on the question whether it is in the interests of justice to admit the statement: the higher the quality the more important the statement will be to the issues in the case and the interests of justice would demand that such evidence be admitted.

(b) Albert was unconscious when the ambulance arrived but revived briefly on his way to the hospital. He told Kelly, the paramedic attending him, 'It was Davies and Evans. Make sure they don't get away with it.'

(c) Stanley, the barman at the nightclub, made a statement to the police on the night of the assault in which he said that he was taking a cigarette break outside the main entrance when he saw Davies and Evans, who were frequent visitors to the club and were well known to him, leave the club and pass between them what appeared to be a knife. The barman has since emigrated from England to Australia and in response to a request from the prosecution that he should return to give evidence wrote that he had no intention of doing so.

(d) The defence have notified the prosecution that Davies and Evans had an alibi for the night of the assault. They claim to have written statements from James and Paul Murray, who both claim they were at home playing cards with Davies and Evans at the time of the attack. Police officers have tried to contact both men but were unable to find them. The defence solicitor states that a week before trial, she received a telephone call from James Murray in which he said the police were looking for him and his brother and they were too scared to give evidence. There is no evidence of any efforts by the defence to find the two witnesses.

2. Akram, Boris and Chardonnay are charged with conspiracy to evade the duty on cigarettes and tobacco. Police and Customs officers raided a warehouse, and found several thousand packs of cigarettes and tobacco on which duty had not been paid. All three defendants deny involvement in the conspiracy and each denies knowing the other alleged conspirators. Consider the following pieces of evidence which the prosecution wish to adduce at their trial and indicate whether they are likely to be admissible in evidence:

(a) A container of cigarettes and tobacco had been taken from a bonded warehouse by two men claiming to represent the exporting agency. One had driven a tractor to which the container had been attached; the other drove a white car that followed the container. Michael, a customs officer leaving the warehouse having completed his shift, saw the container leaving and, being suspicious of the direction taken, rang Chris, his supervisor, and gave him the registration number of the white vehicle that proved to be owned by Akram. The supervisor made a note of the number on a memo pad and attached it to his statement. Michael made no note of the number and cannot remember it.

(b) The owners of the warehouse had leased the premises to a private company known as Enterprize North on the basis that gas, electricity and water supplies would be arranged and paid for by Enterprize North. Following a search of Boris's home, police found letters addressed to Enterprize North acknowledging the request for the supply of gas, electricity and water to the warehouse and bills for their supply.

Continued

(c) Telephone bills were obtained from a mobile telephone company that were automatically produced by a computer. These showed regular calls made to and from mobile telephones owned by the three defendants to each other over a period of two years.

(d) Following the arrest of Chardonnay, a police officer conducting a search of her property received five telephone calls from persons asking for her and requesting further supplies of cigarettes. The prosecution wish to call the officer to give evidence of receiving the calls in order to prove the involvement of Chardonnay in the unlawful supply of cigarettes.

SUGGESTED FURTHER READING

Birch, D 'Hearsay – same old story, same old song?' [2004] Crim LR 556.
Callen, C 'Interdisciplinary and comparative perspectives on hearsay and confrontation' in P Roberts and M Redmayne (eds), *Innovations in Evidence and Proof* (2007: Oxford, Hart).
Choo, A *Hearsay and confrontation in criminal trials* (1996: Oxford, Oxford University Press).
Law Commission, *Evidence in Criminal Proceedings: Hearsay and Related Topics*, Law Commission Report No 245 (2001: London, Law Commission).
Pattenden, R 'Conceptual versus pragmatic approaches to hearsay' (1993) 56 MLR 138.
Spencer, J *Hearsay evidence in criminal proceedings* (2008: Oxford, Hart).
Taylor, G 'Two English hearsay heresies' (2005) 9(2) *International Journal of Evidence & Proof* 110.

CHAPTER 8

CONFESSIONS

INTRODUCTION

One of the key factors that may influence the outcome of the trial is the manner in which the accused has responded to police questions. The interrogation of suspects remains one of the primary investigative techniques for the police, and the most desirable outcome in virtually every interview will be an incriminating statement from the suspect under questioning. If the prosecution have such an admission to rely upon at trial, their task in proving the accused's guilt beyond reasonable doubt is likely to be considerably more straightforward.

The use of confessions in court in this manner prima facie constitutes an infringement of the rule against hearsay. However, a confession is admissible at common law as evidence of the truth of its contents on the basis that a person is likely to be telling the truth when he says something against his own interest.[939] During the 1990s, false or unreliable confessions were the source of several high profile miscarriages of justice.[940] This led to calls in some quarters to impose corroboration requirements, to make it impossible for a defendant to be convicted solely on the basis of his or her confession. Although the Royal Commission on Criminal Justice rejected this option,[941] in practice there have been sufficient examples to caution courts against the ready acceptance of confessional evidence alone, and to remind the police and Crown Prosecution Service of the desirability of supporting evidence.[942]

The modern test for the admissibility of a confession is contained in sections 76 and 76A of the Police and Criminal Evidence Act (PACE) 1984.[943] Section 76(1) provides that a confession made by an accused person is admissible insofar as it is relevant to any matter in issue in the proceedings and is not excluded by the court in pursuance of that section. Subject to its passing the relevance threshold, a confession may be used as evidence of any issue, including any matter favourable to its maker.

Section 76(2) provides that the prosecution can be required to prove, beyond reasonable doubt, that the confession that they propose to introduce in evidence was not obtained by oppression (section 76(2)(a)) or in circumstances of unreliability (section 76(2)(b)). Section 76A makes similar provisions for the admissibility of a confession made by an accused person on behalf of a co-accused,[944] though a co-accused need only prove on

---

[939]Confessions are also known as 'informal admissions' in contrast to a statement made while by the accused whilst giving evidence or in more formal circumstances under section 10 of the Criminal Justice Act 1925.

[940]See further Gudjonsson, G 'Unreliable Confessions and Miscarriages of Justice in Britain' (2002) 4 *International Journal of Police Science and Management* 332. The cases of the Guildford Four and Judith Ward are perhaps the most notorious in respect of the emphasis placed on confessions by the prosecution at trial.

[941]Royal Commission on Criminal Justice (1993) *Report* (Cmnd 2263) (London: HMSO), [13.10]. See further Pattenden, R 'Should Confessions be Corroborated?' (1991) 107 LQR 317.

[942]Principle (b) of the *Principles of Investigative Interviewing* encourages police to seek supportive evidence, and stresses that the courts look for it in respect of mentally disordered defendants.

[943]Before PACE 1984 came into force, a trial judge who found that a confession had been obtained by oppression or as a result of threats or inducements from a person in authority which rendered it involuntary, would exclude it as a matter of law (*Ibrahim v R* [1914] AC 599). There was also a discretion to exclude a confession obtained in breach of the Judges' Rules, the precursor of what is now Code C.

[944]Inserted by CJA 2003, section 128.

the balance of probabilities that the confession was not obtained by oppression or in circumstances of unreliability. Even if the prosecution successfully clears these hurdles, section 78 provides for a broad judicial discretion to exclude prosecution evidence if it would have such an adverse effect on the fairness of the proceedings that it ought not to be admitted. These provisions are examined below in some detail. First, however, we turn to the question of how the law of evidence defines a 'confession'.

WHAT CONSTITUTES A CONFESSION?

Section 82(1) of the Police and Criminal Evidence Act 1984 defines a 'confession' as 'any statement wholly or partly adverse to the person who made it, whether made to a person in authority or not and whether made in words or otherwise'. A confession may thus be made orally, in writing, by conduct or in any other way that information may be communicated. Thus if the defendant, by words or conduct, indicates that he accepts an accusation made by the victim of a crime, or by someone else who is on an equal footing, then to the extent that he has accepted it, the statement becomes his own.[945] The re-enactment of a crime by an accused that is video-taped by the police is clearly a confession within section 82(1) insofar as it is adverse to him. For example, he may demonstrate how he picked a lock, or how he stabbed a victim.[946]

The definition will encompass any informal admission made out of court, and it is immaterial to whom the confession is made. Although the great majority of confessions are made to the police or other investigative bodies such as HM Revenue and Customs, this is not a requirement of the legislation. Under section 82(1), a confession made to anyone such as a spouse, friend, social worker or police is subject to the same test of admissibility under section 76. In *Rumping v DPP*,[947] a letter written by the defendant to his wife was held to constitute a confession, and the same reasoning would apply to a letter of apology written by the defendant to the alleged victim.

A further example can be found in a report that appeared in *The Times* several years ago.[948] A murder suspect in Portugal, Sid Ahmed Rezala, was said to have confessed to a journalist that he took part in the killing of three girls in France, including the British student, Isabel Peake. That statement, though made to a journalist in the context of an interview, would be a confession for the purposes of section 82(1).[949] The same edition of *The Times* reported the conviction for murder by an American court of a mother and son, despite the fact that the prosecution failed to find the body. The son had kept detailed notes of the plot to kill the victim, a Manhattan socialite, in order to gain control of her $7 million town house using forged documents. These notes were admitted as confession evidence in that trial, and would also constitute a confession for the purposes section 82(1).

Similarly, in the trial of four youths for the murder of Damilola Taylor in March 2002, the prosecution adduced evidence of confessions made to other inmates at a detention centre in the presence of a member of staff. In that case, these confessions were challenged under section 76(2)(b) as being unreliable, but were nevertheless admitted. However, in

---

[945] *R v Christie* [1914] AC 545.
[946] *Li Shu-Ling v R* [1989] AC 270.
[947] [1964] AC 814.
[948] *The Times*, 20 May 2000.
[949] If introduced in evidence in an English criminal trial, the admissibility of this statement may well be the subject of a challenge under section 76(2)(b) of the 1984 Act since Rezala had been paid for his story.

Benedetto v The Queen; Labrador v The Queen,[950] the Privy Council warned that juries must be cautious before accepting a cell confession allegedly made by the accused to a fellow prisoner, particularly if he or she is on remand. Such prisoners might well have something to gain from assisting the prosecution and their evidence was inherently unreliable.

In *R v Ellaray*,[951] the defendant was convicted of rape solely on the basis of admissions made to a probation officer preparing a pre-sentence report. The appellant alleged the judge was wrong to admit the statements, given the nature of the relationship between an offender and his probation officer. The Court of Appeal held that before proceeding in a case such as this, the prosecution should carefully consider whether it was right to rely upon evidence provided by conversations between a probation officer and an offender, and should rely upon it only if it was in the public interest to do so. The court should bear in mind the contrast between an interview involving the police and the offender, and an interview between a probation officer and the offender. A number of key differences should be taken into account: there was a need for frankness between the offender and the probation officer; there might not be a reliable record of what was said; and the offender had not been cautioned and was not legally represented. Section 78 of PACE 1984 was available to ensure no unfairness occurred,[952] but in the instant case such factors were taken into account and the appeal was dismissed.

Content of the confession

The content of a confession can take various forms. The confession may constitute a full, signed admission of guilt, or it may simply constitute one potentially incriminating comment that the suspect has inadvertently made under the pressure of interrogation. By confining the definition of 'confession' to 'adverse' statements, section 82(1) does not cover exculpatory statements, but it will cover so-called 'mixed statements' – those that contain both incriminatory and exculpatory elements. For example, the statement, 'Yes, I drove the getaway car but I had no idea they [the others implicated] were going to do a robbery' is a confession insofar as its maker admits being the driver of the getaway car. By the same token, it is also exculpatory as the maker states he had no idea he was involved in a robbery. In order to avoid potential unfairness to the accused, the whole statement should be admitted in evidence.[953] However, the evidential value of self-serving extracts from a confession may be slight and the judge may well comment on their lack of weight.

Statements that are overly vague will not be considered as confessions,[954] and similarly those which are wholly exculpatory, such as 'I had nothing to do with it', are not covered by section 82(1). Such a statement may be admissible to show the suspect's reaction when accused of the offence and arrested, but should not be treated as confession evidence for the purposes of PACE. This principle has recently been confirmed by the House of Lords in *R v Hasan*.[955] Hasan was convicted of aggravated burglary, which he admitted subject to the defence of duress. At trial, the prosecution were permitted to cross-examine him and call rebuttal evidence concerning a confidential 'off the record' conversation with the police which took place after the suspect had been charged. Although the conversation was

---

[950][2003] 1 WLR 1545
[951][2003] 2 Cr App R 11.
[952]See pp 275–83 below.
[953]*R v Sharp* [1988] 1 All ER 65.
[954]See e.g. *R v Schofield* (1917) 12 Cr App R 191, where the defendant exclaimed 'just my luck!'
[955][2005] 2 WLR 709.

entirely exculpatory, the appellant argued that it should have been treated as a 'confession' since the prosecution had used it against him at trial to show that it was inconsistent with his testimony in some material respects.

The Court of Appeal agreed that the conversation should not have been admitted. Statements made by Hasan during that conversation later transpired to be adverse to him within the meaning of section 82(1), and thus constituted a confession for the purposes of section 76(2). Since the original conversation took place in circumstances that might have made the confession unreliable, the prosecution should have been obliged to prove that it did not. However, this decision was subsequently reversed by the House of Lords. In the view of Lord Steyn, the conversation was not adverse to the accused at the time it took place. Thus it was entirely exculpatory, and could not qualify as a confession for the purposes of section 82(1).

THE PRINCIPLE OF EXCLUSION

Section 76(1) of PACE provides that:

> In any proceedings a confession made by an accused person may be given in evidence against him in so far as it is relevant to any matter in issue in the proceedings and is not excluded by the court in pursuance of this section.

Breaches of PACE 1984 and Code of Practice C, which govern the detention and questioning of suspects, and Code of Practice E, which requires the tape-recording and/or the video-taping of interviews with suspects, tend to be the grounds on which the defence will most commonly seek the exclusion of a confession. The custody record, which is created in respect of every person arrested and taken to a police station, details every action in respect of the suspect. This record, together with the tape-recording and/or the video-recording of interviews with the suspect, may provide the defence with evidence of any violation, which they can then use to put the prosecution to proof that section 76 or section 78 of the 1984 Act have not been breached.

Any breach of procedure outside the police station may also be grounds for excluding a confession. In these circumstances, there are two overriding principles that must be applied. First, as soon as a police officer has grounds to suspect that a person has committed an offence and wishes to question him, a caution must be given in the following terms:

> You do not have to say anything. But it may harm your defence if you fail to mention when questioned something which you later rely on in court. Anything you do say may be given in evidence.

Second, an interview with a suspect should normally take place in a police station soon after arrest, where the suspect will have all the protections of the 1984 Act and Codes of Practice (particularly Codes C and E), which include access to legal advice and an audio or video recording of the interview.[956]

The importance of these two principles stems from the fact that an arrest (and caution) should only take place where the officer has 'reasonable grounds to suspect' involvement in an offence.[957] It follows that the on-street questioning which precedes an arrest should only be of the kind which provides the reasonable grounds for arrest. The questioning

---

[956]See further Ch 9, p 290–95.
[957]PACE, section 24(6).

should cease once the arrest takes place, and any further interrogation should take place at the police station in accordance with Codes of Practice C and E. As we shall see further, any deliberate attempt to circumvent the protections provided by the Act and Codes is likely to be met by exclusion of any evidence obtained in this way. However, it should be underlined that the courts will not necessarily automatically exclude anything said by the suspect outside the interview room, so anything that the defendant may have said spontaneously following his arrest may still be given in evidence if it is not ruled out by section 76.

The scope of section 76(2)

Section 76(2) provides:[958]

> If, in any proceedings where the prosecution proposes to give in evidence a confession made by an accused person, it is represented to the court that the confession was or may have been obtained—
>
> (a) by oppression of the person who made it; or
>
> (b) in consequence of anything said or done which was likely in the circumstances existing at the time, to render unreliable any confession which might have been made by him in consequence thereof,
>
> the court shall not allow the confession to be given in evidence except insofar as the prosecution proves to the court beyond reasonable doubt that the confession (notwithstanding that it may be true) was not obtained as aforesaid.

There are thus two grounds in section 76 under which a confession may be excluded: oppression and unreliability. The onus lies on the defence to 'represent' to the court that either one of these grounds applies. The defence will usually intimate their intention to challenge the admissibility of the confession before counsel for the prosecution makes his opening address; the prosecution will then make no reference to it at this stage.[959] It is then for the court to determine the question of admissibility within a *voir dire*.[960]

The *voir dire*

The *voir dire* can take two main forms. Sometimes this will take place before the trial proper, but more often the jury will be sent out at the point where the prosecution intend to call the police officer(s) to whom the confession was made. It is for the prosecution to prove beyond reasonable doubt that the confession was not obtained in breach of the legislation. If counsel fails to discharge this burden, the trial judge must exclude the evidence, and has no discretion in this matter. However, as a starting point in the *voir dire*, the defence

---

[958]Section 76A(2) is identical, except for the reference in the first line to 'a co-accused' rather than the prosecution and the final clause, which read as follows: 'The court shall not allow the confession to be given in evidence for the co-accused except insofar as it is proved to the court on the balance of probabilities that the confession (notwithstanding that it may be true) was not so obtained'. It follows from the lower standard of proof that a confession that is ruled inadmissible for the prosecution could be admitted for a co-defendant.

[959]Depending on the importance of the confession to the case, the issue of its admissibility may be decided before the prosecution give any evidence at all. Indeed, if a confession is central to the prosecution case but is excluded, the trial judge may then withdraw the case from the jury and direct an acquittal.

[960]*R v Millard* [1987] Crim LR 196. See Ch 1, pp 4–5.

will need to produce some prima facie evidence to suggest that the confession was or may have been so obtained. This evidence may appear on the face of the custody record, which should reveal any prolonged periods of questioning or lack of entitlements under PACE 1984 or Codes of Practice. Alternatively, violations may be apparent from the recording of the interview. Often, the judge will seek evidence from the police officers or other law enforcement officials who conducted the interview.

The defendant may also testify, but cannot be compelled to do so.[961] In practice, however, there will be many cases in which the accused must testify if he or she is to stand any chance of getting the confession excluded. In the *voir dire*, the sole issue for the court is the admissibility of the confession. It may be declared inadmissible even if it is true, since the section is concerned only with the question whether it was obtained by oppression or in circumstances of unreliability. This is understandable where oppression has been applied, but arguably less so when the issue is the reliability of the confession. The question of whether or not a confession is likely to be true is perhaps the best measure of its reliability, but the truth is not in issue within the *voir dire*. Evidence led, or cross-examination conducted, by the prosecution designed to show that the confession is true will ultimately be irrelevant to the issue of admissibility. Thus in *R v Cox*,[962] the defendant, who was mentally handicapped, was interviewed in the absence of an 'appropriate adult' which constituted a violation of Code C.[963] During the interview he admitted being involved in two burglaries. At the *voir dire*, the defendant gave evidence and admitted his involvement in one of the burglaries, which persuaded the judge that the confession was reliable and should be admitted. The Court of Appeal held that the trial judge had applied the wrong test. The essential question was not whether the confession was true, but whether the breach of the Code was likely in the circumstances to produce an unreliable confession.

The admissibility and relevance of a confession are thus questions of law to be decided by the judge prior to the confession being admitted in evidence. By contrast, the question of how much weight ought to be placed on it is for the jury to decide. Even if the prosecution successfully discharges its burden in the *voir dire* and the confession is admitted, the defence may still raise the issue again in the course of the trial. Counsel would be free to intimate to the jury that the confession was not reliable, despite that question having been already determined for the purposes of admissibility by the trial judge. If is quite possible, for example, for counsel to elicit new information from police officers in conducting a cross-examination that might lead the confession to be viewed in a different light. The jury would then be free to attach little weight to the confession, or to disregard it altogether. Alternatively, the trial judge may choose to revisit his decision to admit the evidence. In these circumstances, section 76 and section 78 of PACE are prospective, and cannot be used to exclude the confession where it has already been admitted in evidence. The judge will, however, be able to apply the common law discretion and instruct the jury that they are to disregard the evidence entirely.[964]

---

[961] *R v Davis* [1990] Crim LR 860.

[962] [1991] Crim LR 276.

[963] An 'appropriate adult' is an independent person who must be present to protect the interests of juveniles and the mentally handicapped as required by Code C, [3.6–3.14].

[964] *Sat-Bhambra* (1988) 88 Cr App R 55. The scope of the common law discretion is discussed in Ch 10, pp 287–88. That discretion is distinct from the discretion contained in section 78 PACE, and is expressly preserved by section 82(3). It should also be noted that, unlike section 76, section 78 and the common law discretion apply only to prosecution evidence.

The confessions of co-defendants

In *R v Beckford*,[965] section 76 was held to apply only to confessions tendered by the prosecution. This was confirmed by the House of Lords in *R v Myers*,[966] where it was held that D1 could make use of a confession made by D2, even if D2's confession was inadmissible against him on behalf of the prosecution having been excluded under section 76. Arguably, this decision was fundamentally unfair to D2, whose confession had been excluded as against the prosecution either because it was obtained by oppression, or because it was potentially unreliable.

This problem was recognised by the government, and section 128 of the Criminal Justice Act 2003 amended the law to prevent any potential unfairness arising by inserting a new section 76A into PACE. As section 76A now makes clear, a confession made by an accused may be admissible on behalf of a co-accused where the provisions of that section are satisfied. If D1 seeks to rely on a confession made by D2, counsel for D1 will have to prove on the balance of probabilities that neither of the grounds within section 76A(2)(a) or (b) applies. It is thus possible that the prosecution may fail to prove beyond reasonable doubt that a confession was not obtained in breach of these provisions, while a co-accused, bearing the lower standard of proof, may well succeed. In these circumstances, the confession may then be relied upon by the co-accused and will be evidence against the defendant who made it. Although the evidence was not adduced by the prosecution, it will nonetheless serve to assist the prosecution in proving their case against that particular defendant. Simultaneously, however, it may also act to undermine the case of the prosecution against the co-accused in whose favour the confession was admitted.

Since an accused is generally neither competent nor compellable for the prosecution, an out-of-court statement by D1 *against* D2 is inadmissible as evidence. However, this is subject to the recent House of Lords decision in *R v Hayter*.[967] Three defendants were charged with murder and jointly indicted as principals in proceedings relating to a contract killing. The first defendant, Bristow, wanted to arrange a contract killing of her husband. The second defendant, Hayter, was the go-between who engaged and paid the third defendant, Ryan, to kill the husband. Bristow's husband was shot in the head at point blank range, dying instantly. The evidence against Ryan, the killer, was solely based on a confession which he allegedly made to his girlfriend. The trial judge directed the jury to consider in logical phases the case against Ryan, the alleged killer, then against Bristow, the woman who allegedly procured the killing, and finally against the middleman, Hayter.

The trial judge directed the jury in clear terms that the confession that Ryan allegedly made to his girlfriend was only evidence against him and not evidence in the separate cases against Bristow and Hayter. In his summing up he also told the jury that they should consider the case against Ryan first. If they found him guilty of murder they could then use that finding of guilt in their consideration of the case against Bristow and Hayter while taking care not to allow anything in the girlfriend's evidence of Ryan's confession to play any part in their consideration of the case against either. The jury found all three guilty and the House of Lords dismissed the appeal, holding that where the prosecution case against D1 is dependent upon the prosecution proving the guilt of D2, and the evidence against D2 consisted solely of his own out-of-court confession, then such

---

[965][1991] Crim LR 833.

[966][1997] 3 WLR 552.

[967][2005] 1 WLR 605. See further McGourlay, C 'Is criminal practice impervious to logic?' (2006) 10 *International Journal of Evidence and Proof* 128.

a confession would be admissible against D1. However, this could only be used insofar as it went to proving the guilt of D2. If D1 then chooses to testify and admits his part in the offence and incriminates his co-defendant, that can then be taken as evidence against D2. Similarly, if D1 ceases to be a defendant, where, for example, the prosecution offers no evidence against D1 or files a *nolle prosequi*, D1 can then give evidence for the prosecution against D2.

CRITERIA FOR ADMISSIBILITY

The prosecution may be required to jump up to three hurdles before a confession can be admitted in evidence. The first is 'oppression' under section 76(2)(a); the second is 'unreliability', under section 76(2)(b). The third hurdle is the general discretion provided for by section 78, where the trial judge must be satisfied that admitting the confession would not have 'such an adverse effect on the fairness of the trial that the court ought not to admit it'. Usually a defendant will allege a breach of section 76(2)(a) and/or (b). Occasionally the defence look solely to section 78. Exceptionally, a defendant might represent that a confession ought to be excluded under all three heads by representing, first, section 76(2)(a), then, if that should fail, allege a violation of section 76(2)(b). As a last resort, they may urge the court to exclude in the interests of a fair trial under section 78. However, the Court of Appeal has held that if the prosecution succeed in discharging the burden under section 76(2)(a) and (b), prima facie there are no grounds for exclusion under section 78.[968]

Oppression

The defence may represent to the court that the confession 'was or may have been obtained ... by oppression of the person who made it'. This reflects the views of the Criminal Law Revision Committee,[969] and those of the Royal Commission on Criminal Procedure,[970] that society's abhorrence of methods of investigation amounting to oppression should be signalled by the automatic exclusion of a confession obtained thereby, even if the confession turns out to be true. It also reflects the pre-PACE position of the common law.[971]

Defining 'oppression'

At common law, the test for the admissibility of a confession was that it was voluntary and not forced from the mind by pressure of threats or inducements.[972] The characteristics of the accused were of particular significance, and it was recognised that conduct which might not have been oppressive in the case of an experienced person (e.g. someone with a criminal record and well used to police interrogatory methods) might well be deemed to be oppressive in the case of an inexperienced young man or woman, or a person who

---

[968]See *Halawa v Federation Against Copyright Theft* [1995] 1 Cr App R 21.
[969]Criminal Law Revision Committee, Eleventh Report, *Evidence (General)*, Cmnd 4999) (1972: London, HMSO).
[970]Royal Commission on Criminal Procedure, *Report* (Cmnd 8092) (1981: London, HMSO).
[971]Oppression was first established as a ground of inadmissibility in *Callis v Gunn* [1964] 1 QB 495. This was then incorporated, but not defined, in the revised Judges' Rules of 1964.
[972]*R v Priestly* (1965) 51 Cr App R 1.

is vulnerable for other reasons. As we shall see below, such characteristics are similarly relevant to the statutory test under PACE.

Section 76(8) offers a non-exhaustive statutory definition of the term. 'Oppression' includes 'torture, inhuman or degrading treatment and the use of threat of violence (whether or not amounting to torture)'. The phrase 'torture or inhuman or degrading treatment' is derived from Article 3 of the European Convention on Human Rights. This is undoubtedly a high threshold: torture is widely recognised in international law as the most severe form of oppression and, according to a resolution of the United Nations in 1975, 'constitutes an aggravated and deliberate form of cruel, inhuman or degrading treatment or punishment'.[973] It suggests a systematic and premeditated course of action rather than a spontaneous act of violence: in the 1984 United Nations Convention against Torture and Other Cruel, Inhuman and Degrading Treatment or Punishment, torture is defined as 'any act by which severe pain or suffering, whether physical or mental, is intentionally inflicted on a person for such purposes as obtaining from him or a third person information or a confession'.[974]

'Inhuman treatment' has been described by the European Commission of Human Rights as covering 'at least such treatment as deliberately causes severe suffering, mental or physical'.[975] In *Ireland v United Kingdom*,[976] the European Court of Human Rights described the interrogation techniques (prolonged wall-standing, hooding, subjection to white noise, deprivation of sleep and rationing of food and drink) employed by British security forces in Northern Ireland as 'degrading', because they were 'such as to arouse in their victims feelings of fear, anguish and inferiority capable of humiliating and debasing them and possibly breaking their physical or moral resistance'.[977]

It is thus clear that psychological, as well as physical, acts are included within the ambit of the statute, and the alleged maltreatment of 'illegal combatants' at Guantanamo Bay and at Abu Ghraib prison, Baghdad, would also fall within the definition of 'inhuman treatment' if not 'torture'. It would clearly constitute 'oppression' under section 76(2)(a), and may explain why the United States was reluctant to allow the British prisoners held at Guantanamo Bay to be repatriated and tried in the United Kingdom. Any confession evidence obtained from these prisoners whilst in custody would almost certainly be excluded by an English court.

The definition of oppression with section 76(8) is not, however, exhaustive, and the drawing of subtle distinctions within the terminology is unnecessary. Indeed, the expansive view of oppression taken by the Court of Appeal in *R v Fulling* has meant that the narrow terms of section 76(8) are virtually redundant.[978] Fulling was convicted of obtaining property by deception. The defendant staged a burglary at her flat along with her boyfriend, and then claimed some £5,000 from an insurance company. In seeking to exclude a confession made after a number of interviews, the defendant claimed that during a break in the final interview, a detective had told her that her boyfriend had been having an affair with a girl called Christine, who had also been arrested and was in the cell next to her. This, she said, caused her distress and, she claimed, amounted to oppression. The police denied telling her this. The trial judge made no finding as to whether she or the

---

[973]GA/RES/3452 (1975).
[974]UN Doc. A/39/51 (1984), Art 1.
[975]*The Greek Case* (1969) 12 *Yearbook* 1, 186.
[976](1978) 2 EHRR 25.
[977]See also *Soering v UK* (1989) 11 EHRR 439.
[978][1987] QB 426.

police were telling the truth, but was prepared to assume for the purpose of argument that the defendant's version was true. Ruling that the confession was admissible, the trial judge remarked:

> Bearing in mind that whatever happens to a person who is arrested and questioned is by its very nature oppressive, I am satisfied that in section 76(2)(a) of the Police and Criminal Evidence Act 1984 the word oppression means something above and beyond that which is inherently oppressive in police custody and must import some impropriety, some oppression actively applied in an improper manner by the police. I do not find that what was done in this case can be so defined and, in those circumstances, I am satisfied that oppression cannot be made out on the evidence I have heard in the context required by the statutory provision.[979]

The Court of Appeal adopted this part of the ruling, and held that 'oppression' in section 76(2)(a) should be given its ordinary dictionary meaning, taking the third definition of that word in the *Oxford English Dictionary*, which runs as follows:

> the exercise of authority or power in a burdensome, harsh, or wrongful manner; unjust or cruel treatment of subjects, inferiors etc; the imposition of unreasonable or unjust burdens.

Such a wide definition more than encapsulates everything within section 76(8) and extends oppression well beyond that partial definition. The Lord Chief Justice also added that the Court found it 'hard to envisage any circumstances in which such oppression would not entail some impropriety on the part of the interrogator'.[980] Furthermore, he implicitly adopted the trial judge's ruling that 'oppression' means something above and beyond that which is inherently oppressive in police custody, and must import some degree of impropriety on the part of the police.

The requirement of impropriety initially focuses the court's attention on what the investigator has done rather than on the effect of his conduct on the suspect. It will be noted that the prosecution must prove beyond reasonable doubt that the suspect was not oppressed. If the court is persuaded that the confession was or *may* have been obtained by oppression of the person who made it, the confession is inadmissible. It follows that there is no need to prove that the suspect was *actually* oppressed. Instead, the prosecution must prove beyond reasonable doubt that he was not oppressed or, if he was, that there was no causal connection between the conduct alleged to have been oppressive and the obtaining of the confession. As noted above, if a co-accused seeks to rely on a confession by another co-accused, he or she must do so on the balance of probabilities.

In order for section 76(2)(a) to be triggered, *Fulling* suggests that there should be some serious impropriety on the part of the police or other investigatory authority. This will often occur within the confines of the police station, but it should be borne in mind that questioning or conduct that occurred at the time of arrest or while the person was being conveyed to a police station may be similarly relevant. In any event, the court will wish to hear an account of the whole proceedings that took place between the police and the accused, before deciding whether there has been oppression. Whilst a breach of the Code of Practice may be seen as wrongful, it is unlikely to amount to oppression unless it amounts to an accumulation of breaches which together form a gross breach.[981] Lesser impropriety is more likely to come within section 76(2)(b). This would usually include the

---

[979] *Fulling*, above, at 429–30.
[980] *Ibid.*, 432.
[981] See *R v Davison* [1988] Crim LR 442.

application of tricks, such as covert tape-recording of a suspect that will not per se amount to oppression.[982]

In *Fulling*, Lord Lane seems to suggest that, 'impropriety' is a synonym for 'wrongful' as used in the definition, but it appears to refer to serious wrongdoing rather than minor breaches of procedure. However, a number of lesser breaches may take a cumulative toll on the suspect, and together may amount to oppression. This was held to be the case in *R v Davison*, which contained a catalogue of improprieties. The defendant was arrested at 6.25 am for handling a stolen ring. At the police station, he agreed to be interviewed in the absence of a solicitor but made no admissions. The judge found that by 11.00 am, the police had no evidence against the defendant and should have released him under section 34 of PACE. In fact, the suspect remained in custody, and an entry in the custody record at 1.15 pm purported to authorise further detention to allow further interviews to take place. That was a breach of section 37 of the Act. By 3.00 pm, the police had learnt that the defendant had provided information to a third party that led to a serious robbery, and then sought the authority of a superintendent to delay access to a solicitor under section 58(8) of PACE 1984.[983] When the defendant did ask to see a solicitor this was denied, and although there were then no grounds in section 58(8) under which delay could be lawfully authorised.

At 4.30 pm a confrontation took place between the defendant and the robbery suspects, followed by a 'conversation' in which the police told the defendant he was being questioned about an armed robbery. He was not, however, arrested for that offence as required by section 31, thus constituting yet another breach of the PACE. Both the confrontation and the conversation were recorded in the police officers' notebooks, but no attempt was made to show the defendant the notes and obtain his confirmation. This was a breach of Code of Practice C. At 5.10 pm, the suspect was interviewed in the absence of a solicitor and made admissions. The trial judge found that the defendant had been unlawfully detained from 11.00 am, and there was a total failure to arrest him for the armed robbery. The police were found to have been exercising their powers in a 'wrongful manner', which was found to amount to oppression under the terms of *Fulling*. The judge therefore excluded all the evidence after the first interview under section 76(2)(a).

The method of questioning

Overly zealous or aggressive questioning of suspect may also amount to oppression as defined in *Fulling*. In *R v Mason*,[984] the defendant was falsely told that forensic evidence had been found linking him to the crime. Although the Court of Appeal felt that this fell short of the dictionary definition of oppression, it did state that was possible to envisage circumstances where such conduct may fall within the remit of section 76(2)(a). For example, if a suspect were falsely told that a parent was close to death, and that he or she should confess to get home, this could amount to oppressive treatment.

Nevertheless, the deliberate abuse of power would seem to be essential, as *Fulling* stipulates that oppression must be 'actively applied'. In *R v Miller*,[985] a paranoid

---

[982]*R v Parker* [1995] Crim LR 233.
[983]See below, pp 278–80.
[984][1987] 3 All ER 481.
[985](1986) 83 Cr App R 192. This decision was, however, based on the law before PACE took effect.

schizophrenic confessed to killing his girlfriend. The confession contained delusions mixed with facts. A psychiatrist testified that the questioning had triggered delusions. The judge's decision that the questioning was not oppressive, as it was not deliberately designed to induce delusions. However, had the police been aware of the defendant's mental state and deliberately set out to induce delusions, that may well have passed the threshold for oppression.

There is, however, no doubt that persistent, heavy-handed or bullying questioning interspersed with misrepresentations could qualify. For example, in *R v Beales*,[986] a confession extracted during a 35-minute interview was excluded because the officer had invented evidence against the defendant and forcefully confronted him with it. In addition, he repeatedly misrepresented the defendant's answers and 'hectored and bullied [him] from first to last'. Similarly, in *R v West*,[987] there was oppression when the interviewing officer interrupted the suspect on a large number of occasions before he had finished his reply, often vigorously and rudely with a raised voice, and used obscenities to indicate that he was lying. It was clear to the court that the officer had made up his mind that the defendant had committed the offence, and would continue to question him until he admitted this. However, the extent of oppression will always be a matter of degree, and it should be borne in mind that the very purpose of police interrogations is to gather further information, which may involve applying pressure to the interviewee. In *R v Emmerson*,[988] a police officer lost his temper, shouted and swore at the suspect, but this was deemed to fall short of the required threshold.

Much more clearly oppressive than any of the above cases was the conduct of the interviewing officers in *R v Paris, Abdullahi and Miller*,[989] often dubbed 'The Cardiff Three'. There, the officers shouted at one suspect and told him what they wanted him to say, despite his denying involvement some 300 times. The suspect was of low intelligence, which made such questioning more obviously oppressive for that particular suspect. As indicated above, it is always going to be a matter of degree whether aggressive and hostile questioning amounts to oppression. It is more likely to do so if the suspect is a weak or vulnerable person, so in that sense there is a subjective element to the test for oppression. Though initially the trial judge is likely to be concerned with the conduct of the police, the characteristics of the person on the receiving end of that conduct are also important, as are the particular circumstances in which the questioning takes place.[990] While, unlike the common law test, the *Fulling* test of oppression excludes the inherent oppression involved in arrest and custody, the characteristics of the suspect can be considered in determining whether a confession was obtained by oppression and in determining the related question of whether the conduct was 'burdensome', 'harsh' or 'cruel' within the definition of oppression. In *Paris, Abdullahi and Miller*, the fact that one of the suspects was below normal intelligence and on the borderline of mental handicap was taken into consideration, though the method of questioning in that case may still have been deemed 'oppressive' for a person of average intelligence. Likewise, in *R v Seelig*,[991] the Court of Appeal held that the trial judge was correct to take into account the fact that the defendant was an experienced and intelligent merchant banker.

---

[986] [1991] Crim LR 118.
[987] Unreported, 2 May 1988.
[988] (1990) 92 Cr App R 284.
[989] (1993) 97 Cr App R 99.
[990] Other factors which the judge may take into account include the weakness of the overall case against the defendant and any initial failure to allow access to a solicitor. See *R v L* [1994] Crim LR 839.
[991] [1991] 4 All ER 429.

In many of the cases discussed above, the availability of a tape-recording will be crucial in helping a court to decide whether the questioning has reached a sufficient degree of impropriety to be described as oppressive. Lord Taylor LCJ was clearly shocked after listening to the tape-recording of the interview with Miller (the third of *The Cardiff Three*), and expressed the view that short of physical violence, it was hard to conceive of a more hostile and intimidating approach by police officers to a suspect. The three defendants were accused of the murder of a prostitute, Lynette White, who was stabbed some 50 times. After a trial in which the prosecution relied on the evidence of two discredited witnesses and admissions made by Miller after exhaustive interviews, all three were convicted. Miller was described by a defence doctor as 'on the borderline of mental handicap' with an IQ of 75, a mental age of 11 and a reading age of 8. The following extract, taken from one of 19 taped interviews totalling 13 hours, and recorded over five days, may provide something of the flavour of the type of questioning the suspect faced. What the extract below cannot convey, however, is that the questioner was shouting in a frustrated manner, thumping the table and spluttering in his indignation so much that he failed to finish sentences:

Miller:	'I wasn't there'.
DC Greenwood:	'How can you ever ...?'
Miller:	'I wasn't there'.
DC Greenwood:	'How you ... I just don't know how you can sit there ...'
Miller:	'I wasn't ...'
DC Greenwood:	'Really don't ...'
Miller:	'I was not there, I was not there'.
DC Greenwood:	'Seeing that girl, your girlfriend, in that room that night like she was ... I don't know how you can sit there and say it'.
Miller:	'I wasn't there'.
DC Greenwood:	'You were there that night'.
Miller:	'I was not there'.
DC Greenwood:	'Together with all the others, you were there that night'.
Miller:	'I was not there. I'll tell you already'.
DC Greenwood:	'And you sit there and say that'.
Miller:	'They can lock me up for 50 billion years, I said I was not there'.
DC Greenwood:	'Cause you don't wanna be there'.
Miller:	'I was not there'.
DC Greenwood:	'You don't wanna be there because if ...'
Miller:	'I was not there'.
DC Greenwood:	'As soon as you say you were there you know you're involved'.
Miller:	'I was not there'.
DC Greenwood:	'You know you were involved in it'.
Miller:	'I was not involved and wasn't there'.
DC Greenwood:	'Yes you were there'.
Miller:	'I was not there'.
DC Greenwood:	'You were there, that's why Leanne is come up now ...'
Miller:	'No'.
DC Greenwood:	'Cause her conscience is ...'
Miller:	'I was not there'.
DC Greenwood:	'She can't sleep at night'.
Miller:	'No. I was not there'.
DC Greenwood:	'To say you were not there that night ...'
Miller:	'I was not there'.
DC Greenwood:	'Looking over her body seeing what she was like ...'

Miller:	'I was not there'.
DC Greenwood:	'With her head like she had and you have got the audacity to sit there and say nothing at all about it'.
Miller:	'I was not there'.
DC Greenwood:	'You know damn well you were there'.
Miller:	'I was not there'.

Having heard the entire tape, the Court had no doubt that this constituted oppression within the meaning of section 76(2). The convictions were quashed, and a damning judgement was delivered by Lord Taylor CJ.[992] One of the factors that concerned him most was that a solicitor was present for the vast majority of the interviews but had failed to intervene. The solicitor's failure to protect his client was subject to particularly heavy criticism, which was instrumental in leading to a change in the training and authorisation of solicitors who attend police stations. The police were also prompted to retrain their officers in interrogation (interviewing) techniques so that this kind of questioning is unlikely to be repeated. For that reason, where the defence seek to exclude a confession on the grounds of aggressive questioning alone, they may be more likely to be successfully in arguing their case under the 'unreliability' head in section 76(2)(b).

The requirement for a causal link

As a final point in relation to oppression, it is necessary that a causal link be established between the oppressive conduct and the suspect's confession. If the defendant confesses before being subjected to oppressive treatment, section 76(2)(a) does not apply. More realistically, there may be occasions when the police have used oppression but the accused confesses for other reasons unconnected with it, for example after a night in a cell, following oppressive treatment, when he or she decides to get the 'matter off his chest' or simply wants to be released from custody. In practice, the defence will in all probability raise the issue of oppression, in which case it will be extremely difficult for the prosecution to rebut the alleged causal connection between the police conduct and the confession. Indeed, the night in the cell may be seen as an opportunity for the oppressive treatment to take effect by giving the accused time to think over the options.

While some form of causal link must be established, the oppressive conduct in question need not emanate from the police. For example, assume that the defendant, a suspected paedophile, is severely beaten by enraged neighbours, and confesses to police who arrive on the scene that he has committed a number of serious sexual offences against children. Although the police have done nothing improper within this scenario, the members of the public have committed an assault against the defendant. In these circumstances, the defence would be entitled to represent that his only reason for confessing was to appease his attackers. The prosecution would thus be put to proof on the issue.

---

[992]*The Times*, 5 July 2003 reported the conviction of one Jeffrey Gafoor for the murder of Lynette White. After the conviction, South Wales police announced that they would hold another inquiry, overseen by the independent Police Complaints Commission. In May 2005, this investigation into the original conviction of the 'Cardiff Three' resulted in five retired police officers finally being arrested on suspicion of false imprisonment, conspiracy to pervert the course of justice and misconduct in public office after an investigation into this conviction (*The Times*, 19 May 2005.)

It is, of course, possible that the defendant will make a second confession which is not induced by the oppression, but that will be a question of fact for the court to determine. It may be legitimately determined that a period in custody away from the threats of others may break the chain of causation, in which case the court would find that the subsequent confession was not tainted by the oppressive conduct of those who attacked the accused.

If, however, the police are responsible for the oppressive conduct within custody, it will be much more difficult for the court to find that the chain of causation has been broken. If, for example, a confession has been elicited through oppression in one interview, all subsequent interviews will be deemed to be tainted by the original oppressive conduct. Thus if the suspect repeats a confession on a number of occasions, the general rule states that each confession will be deemed to be inadmissible.[993] If that were not the case, PACE and the Codes of Conduct could be endlessly flouted until a confession was obtained, providing at least one interview was conducted properly.

It is, however, a question of fact and degree in each case as to whether a later unobjectionable interview should be excluded. Much will depend upon the objections raised to the earlier interview, and whether those objections were of a fundamental and continuing nature. Occasionally it may be possible for the Crown to prove that there is no link at all between interviews. This might occur where, for example, the defendant confesses subsequent to oppressive conduct. He is released on bail, but several days later he returns to the station with his lawyer and confesses again.[994] In such a case, the chain of causation may well be broken. In *R v Conway*,[995] the defendant alleged that during a visit to his cell by a police officer, he had been promised that if he admitted the offence he could go home to his sick mother. There was no record of the visit in the custody record, no caution was given and no note of the conversation was made. The defendant then confessed in an interview some 20 minutes later. The prosecution did not seek to rely on the interview in the cell, but the defence sought to exclude the later interview upon which the prosecution did rely. The trial judge's decision that there was no oppression or unreliability was overturned on appeal. The cell interview would have been excluded as unreliable, and there was nothing in the intervening 20 minutes to suggest that the effect of the earlier breaches had ceased to have any effect on the defendant.

Similarly, in *R v Neil*,[996] police took a witness statement from the defendant in which he admitted giving a knife to the man who stabbed the deceased before driving him from the murder scene. Immediately afterwards, Neill was arrested, cautioned and kept in custody overnight before being interviewed as a suspect when he made the same admission. The original witness statement was excluded under section 78, but the second interview was admitted. The Court of Appeal reversed this decision, and stated that the defendant had no opportunity to seek legal advice before being interviewed as a suspect, and may well have felt bound by the admissions in the earlier statement.

Other factors may come into play that would make it difficult in practice to rectify breaches in a later interview. In *R v Wood*,[997] the defendant, who was of limited mental capacity, was charged with manslaughter of a child by striking him a heavy blow. During an interview with no solicitor, no caution and no contemporaneous record, he admitted striking the boy on the day before his death. In a second, properly conducted interview

---

[993] *R v Blake* [1991] Crim LR 119; *R v Ismail* [1990] Crim LR 109.
[994] *R v Gillard and Barrett* [1991] Crim LR 280.
[995] [1994] Crim LR 838.
[996] [1994] Crim LR 441.
[997] [1994] Crim LR 222.

he repeated this admission. The medical evidence, however, suggested that the blow that killed the boy had been delivered on the day of his death, not on the previous day. This in itself suggested that the defendant's confession was unreliable, and in the absence of a record of the earlier interview, it was impossible for the prosecution to prove that the second interview was not tainted by the first.

Unreliability

Section 76(2)(b) of PACE 1984 stipulates that a confession will be inadmissible if it:

> was or may have been obtained ... in consequence of anything said or done which was likely, in the circumstances existing at the time, to render unreliable any confession which might be made [by the person] in consequence thereof.

As with section 76(2)(a), once it is represented that the confession was or may have been given in circumstances of unreliability, the burden passes to the prosecution to prove beyond reasonable doubt that it was not so obtained. While the trial judge must initially determine the question of unreliability, if the confession is admitted, the jury will also do so in reaching their verdict. In order to avoid potential embarrassment to the jury who may, in effect, overrule the trial judge by reaching a different conclusion, the judge will be primarily concerned with the factors that led the suspect to confess as opposed to the *content* of the incriminating statement.

In order to determine the ambit of section 76(2)(b), close attention should be paid to the precise wording of the legislation. As a starting point, it can be noted that the phrase 'anything said or done' is potentially very broad in scope, and will certainly encompass conduct which amounts to oppression under section 76(2)(a). It will, however, stretch well beyond these circumstances, and may include threats, inducements or some form of promise. Everything said or done before, and during, the period of detention must be considered, and the court will seek to gain an insight of the whole picture surrounding the incriminating statement rather than focusing on selective parts of it. In *R v Barry*,[998] the defendant was interviewed over two days. On the first day he was told that it would be 'beneficial' for him to assist the police to recover certain property. On the second day, he was interviewed and confessed. The judge's conclusion that the statement on the first day had no effect on the confession made on the second day was rejected by the Court of Appeal. The court stipulated that judges should follow a three-stage test to determine whether a confession should be excluded on grounds on unreliability:

(a) The first step is to identify what was said or done and this should include everything said or done.

(b) The next step is to decide whether what was said or done was likely to render a confession unreliable; all the circumstances should be taken into account. The test is hypothetical.

(c) Finally, the judge should ask whether the prosecution had proved beyond reasonable doubt that the confession had not been made as a result of what was said or done.

In the context of this case, the promise of some benefit on the first day was 'something said' which had to be taken into account. It was likely to render any confession made

---

[998] (1992) 95 Cr App R 384.

unreliable, and the fact that the defendant had some time to think about it made it more likely that he would be influenced by it. This is not to say that something 'said or done' cannot be rendered ineffective by time; much depends on what was said or done and the particular circumstances. A connection, or causal link, must be established between what was 'said or done' and the obtaining of the confession; any delay in time may weaken that connection.

Something 'said or done' can also embrace conduct that is directed towards a person other than the suspect. Notable examples include a promise to take another offence into consideration at the trial rather than prosecute him separately for that offence;[999] a threat to, or promise not to, prosecute the accused's spouse or mistress or other close relation;[1000] and a threat to prosecute the defendant on a charge unrelated to the one under investigation.[1001] Other possible circumstances would include threats to have children put into care, or to report the suspect's or a related person's activities to the Inland Revenue or Benefits Agency. While such actions in themselves are not illegal, and may even be appropriate courses of action in certain circumstances, they should not be used as means to induce the suspect to confess.

The courts have established that things 'said or done' by the accused must arise from external factors which exert some form of pressure on the accused to confess. Thus, the court will not consider the motives of the person making the confession as 'something said or done'; neither, it seems, will it consider self-inflicted drug addiction, which could prompt the defendant to agree to anything in order to be released from custody to feed an addiction. In *R v Goldenberg*,[1002] a heroin addict was convicted on a charge of conspiracy to provide diamorphine. Following a search of the defendant's premises, where heroin and some £1,600 in cash were found, he was arrested and remanded in custody. Five days later the defendant requested another interview and confessed. According to the defence, his motive in doing so was to obtain credit for helping the police and which would increase his prospects of obtaining bail. Subsequently, he would be able to satisfy his craving for a 'fix'.

On appeal, Goldenberg contended that these circumstances fell within section 76(2)(b), and served to render his confession unreliable. The Court of Appeal rejected this argument:

> In our judgment the words 'said or done' in section 76(2)(b) of the 1984 Act do not extend so as to include anything said or done by the person making the confession. It is clear from the wording of the section and the use of the words 'in consequence' that a causal link must be shown between what was said and the subsequent confession. In our view it necessarily follows that 'anything said or done' is limited to something external to the person making the confession and to something which is likely to have an influence on him.

The Court was thus concerned more with the motives of a suspect for making a confession, rather than the condition of the suspect who was suffering the immediate effects of withdrawal. However, in *R v Crampton*,[1003] the Court was faced with a defendant, who was a drug addict more immediately affected by withdrawal symptoms, and

---

[999] *R v Northam* (1968) 52 Cr App R 97.

[1000] *R v Middleton* [1974] 2 All ER 1190. However, it should be underlined that the more remote the relationship, the less likely it is that there will be a causal connection between the threat/promise and the making of the confession.

[1001] *Commissioners of Customs and Excise v Harz and Power* [1967] 1 AC 760.

[1002] (1989) 88 Cr App R 285.

[1003] (1991) 92 Cr App R 369.

who, it was alleged, was prepared to say anything in order to get out of the police
station and 'get a hit'. The defendant was convicted of conspiracy to supply heroin.
The police were aware that he was an addict and postponed interviewing him until
the day after his arrest. Having rejected the offer of a solicitor and confirmed that he
was feeling well enough to be questioned, the suspect made a number of incriminating
remarks under interrogation. Afterwards however, he complained that he was suffering
withdrawal symptoms. A doctor was called, and deemed the defendant to be lucid despite
showing some symptoms. Some time later, a second doctor examined the suspect, who
noted that withdrawal symptoms were subjective, appearing eight to 16 hours after
the last dose, and potentially worsening for up to 24 hours. However, in his opinion,
at all times sufferer would be lucid with no mental confusion, though there was a
possibility that he may attempt to manipulate or lie to the police in order to obtain more
drugs.

In the *voir dire*, the defence argued that the confession should be excluded as unreliable
under section 76(2)(b) or as unfair under section 78, relying on the fact that the defendant
had been interviewed while suffering from withdrawal symptoms. However, the judge
admitted the confession and the defendant was convicted. On appeal, counsel for the
defence sought to distinguish *Goldenberg* on the basis that in this case the police decided
when the interview should be conducted and it was not at the request of the appellant. The
Court of Appeal doubted that the mere holding of an interview at a time when the appellant
was experiencing symptoms of withdrawal from heroin addiction was something 'said or
done' within section 76(2)(b), but was prepared to assume that it was for the purposes of
the appeal. The reason for the Court's doubt was that section 76(2)(b) is concerned with
the nature and quality of the words spoken, or things 'said or done, which are likely, in the
circumstances existing at the time, to render the confession unreliable in the sense that it
is not true'. The Court went on to uphold the decision of the trial judge that the confession
had been correctly admitted:

> It is plain that the experienced officers, who dealt with drug addicts, considered that he was fit
> to be interviewed. More important, perhaps, Dr Koppel [the first doctor to see the defendant]
> said that when he saw the appellant he considered he was then fit to be interviewed. It follows
> a fortiori that the appellant would have been fit at the time of his interview which occurred
> earlier ... In our judgement, the position is this. Whether or not someone who is a drug addict
> is fit to be interviewed, in the sense that his answers can be relied upon as being truthful, is
> a matter for judgement of those present at the time.[1004]

The Court also referred to the provisions of Code C, which stipulates the need to call
a doctor if the police are in any doubt as to whether or not the defendant is well enough to
be interviewed:[1005]

> If the police had summoned Dr Koppell, and he had seen the appellant before the
> interview, the doctor would have certified that he was fit to be interviewed. That is
> the evidence that he effectively gave and the evidence which the trial judge accepted.
> It is then for the judge at the trial within a trial to decide whether the assessment of
> those present at the time was correct. The mere fact that someone is withdrawing, and
> may have a motive for making a confession, does not mean the confession is necessarily
> unreliable.[1006]

[1004] *Ibid.*, 372.
[1005] Code C, Notes 9A-9C.
[1006] *Ibid.*, 374.

The Court then proceeded to cite with approval the observations of the Lord Chief Justice in *Rennie*:[1007]

> Very few confessions are inspired solely by remorse. Often the motives of an accused are mixed and include a hope that an early admission may lead to an earlier release or a lighter sentence. If it were the law that the mere presence of such a motive, even if prompted by something said or done by a person in authority, led inexorably to the exclusion of a confession, nearly every confession would be rendered inadmissible. This is not the law. In some cases the hope may be self-generated. If so, it is irrelevant, even if it provides the dominant motive for making the confession. In such a case the confession will not have been obtained by anything said or done by a person in authority. More commonly the presence of such a hope will, in part at least, owe its origin to something said or done by such a person. There can be few prisoners who are being firmly but fairly questioned in a police station to whom it does not occur that they might be able to bring both their interrogation and their detention to an earlier end by confession.

The decision in *Crampton* does not exclude the possibility that the fact that the defendant is withdrawing can be a circumstance within section 76(2)(b) which could render any confession made in consequence unreliable. The important question is whether the confession was made in consequence of the withdrawal symptoms. As should be apparent from the discussion below, the test is to be applied objectively. It is not a question of what the police *believe* to be the facts, but what the facts actually are (or would have been) as ascertained by a doctor who examines the suspect.

In *R v Everett*,[1008] the defendant, aged 42, had a mental age of 8 and an IQ of 61 when he pleaded guilty to indecent assault. He lived with a family who had known him for some years, and was left alone with a 5-year-old boy and a 6-year-old girl. The mother returned to find that the boy's tracksuit bottoms were pulled down and his underpants crumpled. She told the police, describing the defendant as slightly mentally defective and slow in speech. He was arrested, and on the way to the police station he told police that he had touched the boy and had then touched himself. The police, however, failed to appreciate that he had a mental disability, and subsequently interviewed him on tape in the absence of an appropriate adult or solicitor. In the course of this interview the defendant admitted indecently touching the boy, and the tape of the interview was the only evidence at his trial. Had the police been aware of the fact the suspect was mentally subnormal, they would have been obliged by the Code of Practice to call an appropriate adult to look after his interests while at the police station and while being interviewed. In spite of this, the trial judge decided to admit the interview tapes. However, the Court of Appeal quashed the conviction on the grounds that the judge had paid insufficient attention to the 'circumstances existing at the time', which obviously included the mental condition of a suspect. Even if the police were unaware of the suspect's disability, the test was essentially objective and the medical evidence adduced at the *voir dire* should have meant that confession was excluded.

Thus, while a self-infliction addiction to narcotics will normally mean that a case falls outside the scope of section 74(2)(b), there is no doubt that the mental condition of the suspect is a relevant circumstance to be taken into account. Indeed, in *R v Walker*,[1009] the Court of Appeal had to consider the case of the suspect with a personality disorder and a drug habit. The defendant, a prostitute, was convicted of robbery. It was alleged that she

---

[1007] (1982) 74 Cr App R 207, 212.
[1008] [1988] Crim LR 826.
[1009] [1998] Crim LR 211.

took the car keys from a man and demanded money for their return, whilst showing the man a knife concealed in her waistband. At the police station following her arrest, she was seen by a police doctor. She told him she was a heroin addict and was taking methadone, which she was duly prescribed. In a interview, she denied having a knife, but admitted that she had tried to frighten the victim into giving her money.

The defence sought to exclude the confession, alleging that the defendant had smuggled crack cocaine into the police station and was under its influence when she was interviewed. Psychiatric evidence was also called to the effect that the defendant suffered from a severe personality disorder. Having listened to the tapes of the interview, the psychiatrist expressed the opinion that the suspect's condition might render her admissions unreliable. In particular, the suspect would have been prone to embellishing her account without understanding the implications, and this effect was likely to be exacerbated if she was a user of crack cocaine. For their part, the prosecution claimed that her condition remained the same throughout the suspect's time in custody, and rebuked the suggestion that her personality disorder would have rendered the interview unreliable. On that ground, the judge refused to exclude the confession and stated that he disbelieved the defendant's evidence that she had smoked crack cocaine in the police station.

On appeal it was argued, first, that the trial judge had adopted the wrong approach to section 76(2)(b); and, second, that there was new evidence from the duty solicitor that the defendant had smoked crack cocaine earlier in the day. Allowing the appeal, the Court of Appeal noted that the evidence of the psychiatrist was uncontradicted. In his analysis of the evidence, the trial judge appeared to limit the question of whether the defendant's personality disorder was such as to render the confession unreliable, by reference to previously decided cases of what he termed 'mental impairment' or of 'impairment of intelligence or social functioning'. This was the wrong approach to section 76(2)(b), and there was no requirement for any wrongdoing by the police. The defendant's mental condition was one of the circumstances to be taken into account (*Everett*), and nothing in that case limited or defined the particular form of mental or psychological condition or disorder upon which the defendant could rely to show that he confession was unreliable: any mental or personality abnormalities may be of relevance.

Having come to that conclusion, it was not necessary to rule on the new evidence, although the Court had considerable reservations as to whether there had been a reasonable explanation for not adducing the evidence at trial. Had it been available to the judge, it would have been influential on his decision on the factual issue of whether or not she took the drug. However, that issue was not central to the evidence of the psychiatrist, which was principally concerned with the pre-existing disorder.

It is unfortunate that the Court did not consider the effect of the new evidence, which might have led to a clarification of the question whether, and if so in what circumstances, self administration of drugs and/or the symptoms of withdrawal can be a relevant consideration. *Goldenberg* was not considered in *Walker*. Therefore *Goldenberg* remains authority for the proposition that 'anything said or done' in section 76(2)(b) does 'not extend so as to include anything said or done by the person making the confession', but rather these words are 'limited to something external to the person making the confession' and to something that is likely to have some role in inducing the confession.

While *Goldenberg* was not directly concerned with a suspect under the influence of drugs or suffering withdrawal symptoms, there is no doubt that the taking of a narcotic substance and its subsequent effect does constitute 'something done' by the person making the confession and is not to be regarded as something external. There is some dispute among the medical fraternity as to whether withdrawal from drugs has any effect on cognitive function. In *Crampton*, one doctor said withdrawal did not affect intelligence, while the other stated that the sufferer would be lucid with no mental confusion but may be manipulative and prepared to lie in order to get more drugs. *Crampton* appears to assume that interviewing a heroin addict in withdrawal can be something 'said or done which was likely in the circumstances existing at the time' to render the suspect's confession unreliable. If the doctor's evidence had been that the defendant was a heroin addict in withdrawal and that those symptoms could influence him in such a way that any confession would be unreliable, there seems little doubt that it would fall within the scope of section 76(2)(b).

In her commentary on the decision in *Walker*, Professor Birch notes:

> In order to give effect to the purpose of the subsection, which (as the present case acknowledges) is not to attach penalties to police misconduct at interview, but rather to prevent reliance on potentially unreliable material, the better approach would be to include the drugged (or drug-dependent) state of D as potentially relevant 'circumstances', and to concede that even the perfectly ordinary interviewing of somebody in such a state might be 'something said or done' which is conducive to the making of an unreliable confession. This seems to be the approach taken in the present case (though without consideration of the effect of *Goldenberg*) and it would seem, with respect, to be right.[1010]

In a Home Office survey published in 1998,[1011] 61% of arrestees had taken at least one illegal drug: 46% tested positive for cannabis; 18% for opiates/heroin; and 10% for cocaine/crack. Nearly half the arrestees across all five areas said their drug use was connected with their offending. Therefore, given that the number of people arrested whilst on drugs is so high, there may be an element of policy behind the decision to exclude confessions since the suspect's impaired state of mind is self-induced. However, if the medical evidence is correct in stating that the intelligence of drug-dependent suspects is not affected by withdrawal, then it is arguable that the drug-dependent suspect is in no different position from the suspect who is desperate to get bail for other, equally compelling reasons. Where a suspect confesses in the self-generated hope of some benefit, then the confession should not be excluded under section 76(2)(b). Moreover, where a defendant confesses in the hope or belief that he will get bail, but without any threat, encouragement or inducement on the part of the police, this will also fall outside the remit of the statute.

There may be other conditions which, perhaps coupled with impaired intelligence, might constitute a 'circumstance' which could result in an unreliable confession. In *R v McGovern*,[1012] a woman aged 19, six months pregnant and with a mental age of 10, was arrested on a charge of murder. She was interviewed twice. On the first occasion, she was improperly denied access to a solicitor, and confessed under questioning. She was then interviewed for a second time with a solicitor present, when she again incriminated herself. The Court of Appeal held that the confessions in both interviews were inadmissible because the first interview had tainted the second. However, the absence of legal counsel by itself was not the sole ground on which the evidence was excluded: this factor interacted with the fact she was young, pregnant and was mentally subnormal. Together, the combined effect of these elements meant that the confession was unreliable.

[1010] [1998] Crim LR 211.
[1011] Bennett, T *Drugs and Crime: The Results of Research on Drug Testing*, Home Office Research Study No 183 (1998: London, Home Office).
[1012] (1991) 92 Cr App R 228.

Something 'said or done' need not emanate from the police

The most obvious external event that might constitute something 'said or done' is the conduct of the police. However, this need not necessarily be the case. In *R v Harvey*,[1013] the defendant confessed to a murder. The previous day, she had had heard that her lover had confessed to the same offence. The defendant was mentally subnormal, and two psychiatrists had suggested that she might have confessed in a childlike attempt to protect her lover. Though the police had acted properly throughout, the prosecution were unable to prove beyond reasonable doubt that hearing her lover confess did not cause her to confess. On these grounds, the confession was considered to be unreliable.

In *R v Wahab*,[1014] the accused was arrested for conspiracy to supply drugs together with members of his family. He was interviewed in the presence of his solicitor, and after the third interview, he asked his solicitor to approach the police to see whether the members of his family who were also in custody would be released if he confessed. The solicitor did so, but the police made it clear that no such guarantee could be given. The solicitor then told his client that if he confessed police would look at the whole picture and, if the evidence against his family was 'borderline', they would be released. The suspect confessed to playing the role of a 'middleman' shortly afterwards. At his trial, the accused challenged the admissibility of the confession on the basis that he had been incompetently advised by his solicitor. He called another solicitor to show that the conduct of the first solicitor had fallen below the proper standard of professional competence. However, this evidence was rejected by the trial judge, who admitted the confession.

Dismissing Wahab's appeal, the Court of Appeal noted that advice properly given by a solicitor did not normally provide a basis for exclusion of a subsequent confession under section 76(2)(b). Although one of the duties of a legal adviser was to give the client realistic advice, that emphatically did not mean the advice had to be directed to 'getting the client off' or simply making life difficult for the prosecution. In the instant case, the cross-examination of the second solicitor was not relevant to the reliability of Wahab's confession. Applying *Goldenberg*, the Court held that conduct of the solicitor did not ultimately influence Wahab's decision to confess.

Other forms of conduct that are 'external' to the police may include a threat by a parent to a child that the latter had better tell the truth or she/he will be beaten; a promise by an employer to an employee that if she/he admits the misconduct she/he will not be dismissed; or a threat by a headteacher to a pupil that unless the latter tells the truth to a police officer, he or she will be disciplined. However, by the same token it should be emphasised that there must be a causal connection between what was said or done and the obtaining of the confession. It may be that, in many such cases, the prosecution would be able to prove that there was no such connection, particularly where the police are aware of what was said or done, and have taken steps to ensure that the suspect is no longer influenced by it when interviewed.

Improper conduct by the police

Just as in *Fulling* it was held that the inherent oppression involved in arrest and custody is not enough to trigger section 76(2)(a), for the purposes of section 76(2)(b), it is clear that the phrase 'anything said or done' implies something out of the ordinary, beyond

---

[1013][1988] Crim LR 241.
[1014][2003] 1 Cr App R 15.

the proper exercise of normal police powers and procedures. However, in contrast to oppression under section 76(2)(a), no impropriety on the part of the police is required under section 76(2)(b).[1015] This is clearly the correct approach, since the section 76(2)(b) focuses on the likely reliability of the confession and not the propriety of police conduct per se. The fact that 'something said or done' includes almost anything external to the suspect, and does not require any impropriety on the part of the police, may, however, encourage the defence to raise the issue of unreliability in many more circumstances than were possible in the pre-PACE era under the common law. Certainly there is a narrow dividing line that separates legitimate police responses from illegitimate ones. Difficulties arise, for example, in relation to how the police ought to respond to questions from the suspect concerning the prospect of bail or the nature of any charges that might be brought.[1016]

Code of Practice C seeks to sidestep these issues by providing that the police should give 'proper and warranted' responses to these sorts of questions.[1017] Notwithstanding this provision, it still remains within the power of the court to decide whether a proper response to a suspect's question was likely to induce an unreliable confession. In practice however, it is unlikely that the courts will find that a proper response could be used as the basis for exclusion. As the case law discussed above illustrates, it may often be the case that the suspect is merely seeking support for his own motives for confessing, having recognised that a confession will bring an end to the interrogation and to his release on bail. Nonetheless, a police officer would still be well advised to think twice before responding to a suspect's questions lest the answer be seen as improper and an inducement to confess. This danger was seemingly ignored by the interviewing officer in *R v Howden-Simpson*,[1018] who promised the defendant that he would be charged with only two offences if he confessed, but many more if he failed to do so. This evidence was excluded, though the court relied on section 78, rather than section 76(2)(b). The latter provision is really the appropriate tool for excluding this type of evidence since the conduct of the police clearly impacted upon the reliability of the admission. Indeed, the behaviour of the interviewing officer in this case is precisely the type of inducement with which section 76(2)(b) was intended to address. In relying on section 78 in such cases, the Court risks excluding inadmissible evidence on a purely discretionary basis which should automatically be excluded under section 76.[1019]

Even in relation to more serious breaches of the Codes of Practice, the courts have demonstrated a preference for section 78 above section 76. For example, in *R v Sparks*,[1020] a failure to caution and to record the interview were breaches of Code C, but were held not to be likely per se to affect reliability. Instead, the court held that they should have been excluded under section 78. Similarly, the latter provision is favoured in cases involving the improper denial of access to legal advice.[1021] To some extent, this is understandable, since failure to allow access to a solicitor will not necessarily lead to unreliability. However, in order to gauge whether or not unreliability has resulted, the court should first take into account a range of factors, including the seriousness of the offence under investigation. Undoubtedly, the protective presence of a solicitor will be seen as even more necessary in where the suspect is being questioned about serious offences. Moreover, if the suspect is

---

[1015]See *R v Harvey* (above) and *R v Morse* [1991] Crim LR 195.
[1016]See respectively *R v Barry* (1992) 95 Cr App R 384; *R v Phillips* (1988) 86 Cr App R 18.
[1017]PACE Code of Practice C, [11.5].
[1018][1991] Crim LR 49.
[1019]See comments of Ralph Gibson LJ in *Halawa v Federation Against Copyright Theft* [1995] 1 Cr App R 21, 33.
[1020][1991] Crim LR 128.
[1021]See below, pp 278–80.

vulnerable, a juvenile or mentally disordered, or as in *McGovern*, young, of low intelligence and pregnant, it may do so and almost certainly will do so, especially if coupled with a failure to provide an appropriate adult.[1022] Indeed, if such an adult is not present, this in itself may amount to grounds for exclusion.[1023]

The provisions within Code C that concern the accurate keeping of records in connection with the interview are designed to protect the accused against abuse by 'verballing', which refers to the act of attributing words to the suspect which he or she never said, or taking them out of context to attribute to them a different meaning.[1024] If the police failed to record the interview,[1025] or to show it to the suspect for approval, and the suspect later disagrees with the officer's recollection of the record, this will effectively amount to an allegation that the police have fabricated or misrepresented the confession. The failure to record, coming after the confession was made, in itself may not be regarded as 'something said or done' within section 76(2)(b), but the alleged fabrication or doctoring of the confession would certainly qualify. Crucially, a failure to record deprives the prosecution of evidence which might be used to rebut the allegation. In practice, this may mean that the prosecutor may find it difficult to convince the trial judge that the burden of proof has been successfully discharged.

Following an amendment to Code F in June 2002, many police interviews must now be video-recorded. This adds an additional protective dimension for the suspect and, indeed, for the police officers conducting the interview. It is not unusual for the defendant to allege that physical intimidation took place, and this could potentially be evidenced by recordings of shouting or screaming. The advent of video-recording means that the court will now have an opportunity to view, quite literally, the whole picture of what took place. This should, in theory, avoid words or noises on the audio recording being taken out of context.

The method of questioning

The tape-recording or video-recording of interviews has meant that police officers must now take considerable care to ensure that the method of questioning does not fall foul of section 76. For this reason, cases that are likely to cross the 'oppression' threshold of section 76(2)(a), such as *Paris, Abdullahi and Miller*, are very rare in practice.

However, there is no doubt that the 'unreliability' head under section 76(2)(b) clearly encompasses a much wider range of conduct. Such conduct may well lack the gravity of oppression, but it may still have an effect on the particular suspect that might induce an unreliable confession. Therefore, in practice, the defence will often plead both limbs of section 76. This may encourage a court to decide that even if section 76(2)(a) does not apply, the lower threshold of section 76(2)(b) might nonetheless be crossed. In *R v Beales*,[1026] for example, the suspect was subjected to a course of aggressive and persistent questioning, which included a number of misrepresentations by the officer. Although this conduct

---

[1022] PACE Code of Practice C, [11.15]; see *R v Moss* (1990) 91 Cr App R 371.

[1023] *DPP v Blake* (1989) 89 Cr App R 179; *R v Cox* [1991] Crim LR 276. See also *R v Morse* [1991] Crim LR 195, where the 'appropriate adult' himself was incompetent.

[1024] The requirement to tape record interviews reduces the importance of the Code C requirement that written records of the interview be kept. That provision was directed at the pre-tape recording era when the requirement was that the interview be recorded in writing, read to and signed by the suspect.

[1025] e.g. *R v Waters* [1989] Crim LR 62; *Doolan* [1988] Crim LR 447.

[1026] [1991] Crim LR 118.

was found to fall short of 'oppression', it was enough to suggest a state of confusion or hopelessness on the part of the suspect to such an extent that it might have resulted in an unreliable admission.

The question thus arises as to how far section 76(2)(b) extends. The key issue will often be the extent of the causal connection between the conduct in question and the circumstances in which the confession was made. In practice, this requires that the court look carefully at the circumstances of the detention, and take into account the characteristics of the particular suspect. If the judge, putting himself or herself in the position of the suspect, decides that any confession made in those circumstances is likely to be unreliable, it is then for the prosecution to prove the converse beyond reasonable doubt.

Clearly the method of questioning may produce an unreliable confession in that the suspect may speak for a variety of motives other than that of telling the truth. As some of the cases discussed have illustrated, the suspect may want to protect someone; may be keen to leave the police station and is prepared to say anything, in the hope of retracting it later; may be suggestible and anxious to appease the interrogator; may be induced by threats or promises; or may become confused and mistakenly make an incriminating statement.

In *Fulling*, the Lord Chief Justice decided that the following definition of oppression, laid down in *R v Priestly*,[1027] was insufficient for section 76(2)(a) but suggested that it may include the type of conduct captured section 76(2)(b):

> [Q]uestioning which by its nature, duration or other attendant circumstances (including the fact of custody) excites hope (such as the hope of release) or fears, or so affects the mind of the subject that his will crumbles and he speaks when otherwise he would have stayed silent.[1028]

Of course, this definition places the court (and initially the prosecution) in a very difficult position in trying to fathom the defendant's motives for speaking. It is easier if the defendant falls within a group identified by PACE 1984 and the Code as 'vulnerable' (e.g. juveniles, the mentally handicapped). Such persons may be suggestible or readily manipulated, with the consequence that certain styles of questioning are likely to produce unreliable confessions. In these types of cases, the prosecution can face an uphill task. Thus, in *R v Delaney*,[1029] the interviewing officer had throughout suggested to the defendant that he really needed psychiatric help, and that if he owned up, people would help him. The officer played down the significance of the criminal offence and falsely aroused the defendant's hopes of treatment. As the Lord Chief Justice put it, 'he might, by the same token, be encouraging a false confession'.[1030] In less extreme circumstances, such as those present in *Harvey*, the evidence of psychiatrists or psychologists as to the likely effect of police conduct on the defendant could readily sow sufficient seeds to raise a reasonable doubt.

As regards 'non-vulnerable' suspects, the court must consider all the circumstances of the interrogation and what was said by the police, or any other relevant person. Such a person may include a parent, friend, or a co-accused; even a solicitor who suggests that the accused pleads guilty in order to obtain a lesser sentence could potentially fall within section 76(2)(b). In addition, the court should take into account the likely effect of what was said on the mind of the accused, taking into account his or her personal

---

[1027] (1965) 51 Cr App R 1.
[1028] *Fulling*, at 430. Cited with approval in *Prager* [1972] 1 All ER 1114.
[1029] (1989) 88 Cr App R 338.
[1030] *Ibid.*, at 344.

characteristics. However, the task of reconstructing the picture of what actually took place at the police station will not necessarily be a straightforward task, since the judge will be required to place himself or herself in the suspect's shoes at the time of the interrogation. Few judges are likely to have gained personal experience of the pressures that a police interrogation might engender.[1031]

Section 76(2)(b) may also be triggered where police tricks or misrepresentations are practised on the suspect in the course of questioning. The difficulty here, however, is that deceptions which suggest that there is conclusive evidence of guilt may lead to a reliable confession, rather than an unreliable one. For example, in *R v Blake*, the confession was ruled out as unreliable after the defendant was falsely told that his voice has been recognised on a tape. However, this decision can be contrasted with in *Mason*, where the defendant was falsely told that his fingerprints had been found on a part of a bottle used as a petrol bomb. Here section 76(2)(b) was not argued, presumably because in the circumstance the confession was, in fact, reliable. Instead, the defence invoked section 78 on the basis that the deceit practised on the solicitor led him to advise his client on the basis of false facts.

Facts discovered subsequent to an excluded confession

Section 76(4)–(6) deals with the conundrum that arises in relation to evidence discovered as a consequence of an excluded confession.[1032] By way of example, let us assume Beverly has been charged with theft. Under questioning, she is subjected to a hostile and aggressive interrogation, and there is also evidence to suggest that she was threatened with physical violence if she failed to confess. She eventually does so, and tells the police where they can find a quantity of designer handbags that she had stolen. Although her confession is subsequently excluded at the *voir dire*, police have uncovered the handbags exactly where Beverly had told them they would be. Can then the prosecution (a) produce the goods at the Beverly's trial, and (b) link their discovery to what she had told the police? The Criminal Law Revision Committee had unanimously recommended an affirmative answer to (a) and, by a majority, to (b).[1033] However, the 1984 Act opted for a halfway house. On the one hand, the prosecution can use in evidence 'any facts discovered as a result of the confession' even if the confession is itself inadmissible.[1034] On the other hand, proof that those facts were discovered as a result of a wholly or partly inadmissible confession is not admissible, unless the accused himself gives evidence that they were so discovered.[1035]

The policy underlying this rule is that it is unfair for the inadmissibility of a confession to be negated by the admissibility of the 'fruits of the crime', unless the accused so chooses. Such an approach seems wholly justifiable where confessions are obtained by oppression. However, it appears somewhat illogical where a finding of unreliability is involved. If we recall the above scenario involving Beverly, the discovery of the stolen goods at the place

---

[1031] See the observation of the Lord Chief Justice in *Rennie* (above); see also *Goldenberg* and *Crampton*.

[1032] It should be highlighted that the principles contained subsections (4) and (5) are applicable only to a confession excluded under section 76. There is no equivalent provision in section 78.

[1033] Criminal Law Revision Committee, Eleventh Report, *Evidence (General)*, Cmnd 4999) (1972: London, HMSO).

[1034] PACE 1984, section 76 (4)(a).

[1035] PACE 1984, section 76 (5)–(6). This places the old common law rule in *R v Berriman* (1854) 6 Cox CC 388 upon a statutory footing.

where she said they would be seems to indicate that the confession was reliable in the first instance. Nonetheless, the law states that the prosecution can produce the stolen goods at trial, but cannot show that they were discovered as a result of the defendant's confession. The difficulty thus arises for the prosecution when a link to the defendant can only be established by specific reference to the confession. So, for example, if Beverly had told the police they were concealed in a ditch on a country lane, it may be impossible to connect the goods to her in any way. If, however, such stolen goods could be linked to her without the aid of the confession (e.g. they were found on her premises, or there was forensic evidence connecting her to the goods), there is no difficulty for the prosecution given that no reference to the confession need be made.

It should also be underlined that, where only a part of a confession is excluded, evidence found as a result of the admissible part may still be relied upon.[1036] It is perfectly possible, for example, for the court to exclude only one interview if the suspect has confessed on a number of different occasions. Moreover, those parts of a confession which are relevant as showing that the accused 'speaks, writes or expresses himself in a particular way' are still admissible for that purpose.[1037] The object of this exception is illustrated by *R v Voisin*,[1038] where the body of a murder victim had been found alongside a piece of paper bearing the words 'Bladie Belgiam'. The accused was asked by the police to write the words 'Bloody Belgian' and he happily wrote 'Bladie Belgiam'. This evidence was held to be admissible, and would now be admissible under section 76(4)(b), even if the confession itself fell within section 76(2)(a) or (b).

This rule was applied in a more recent context in the unreported case of *R v Nottle*.[1039] Here, the defendant had been charged with criminal damage to a vehicle. It was alleged that he scratched an obscene message onto the paintwork, referring to the owner of the car, whose name was 'Justin' as 'Jutin'. The suspect was then asked by the police to write the same phrase, which he did, and wrote 'Jutin' instead of 'Justin'. In this particular case, this was held to constitute a confession that was not found to be unreliable. However, had there been some incidence of oppression or something said or done to make that statement unreliable, the prosecution could still use it in evidence as a sample of handwriting to identify the characteristics mentioned in section 76(4)(b). Likewise, where the defendant is charged with kidnapping and the victim states that the kidnapper spoke with a local accent and stammered, the non-incriminating parts of the defendant's excluded tape-recorded confession can be used for voice comparison.[1040]

Confessions by the mentally handicapped

Section 77 of the PACE 1984 provides:

> Where at such a trial (on indictment)—
>
> (a) the case against the accused depends wholly or substantially on a confession made by him; and

---

[1036]PACE 1984, section 76(6)(b).

[1037]PACE 1984, section 76(4)(b).

[1038][1918] 1 KB 531.

[1039][2004] EWCA Crim 599.

[1040]See *R v Robb* (1991) 93 Cr App R 161. See further *R v Deenick* [1992] Crim LR 578 for the admissibility of voice recognition evidence by a non-expert such as a police or customs officer.

(b) the court is satisfied;

    (i) that he is mentally handicapped; and

    (ii) that the confession was not made in the presence of an independent person,

the court shall warn the jury that there is a special need for caution before convicting the accused in reliance on that confession.

In addition, Code C provides that no interview with a juvenile, mentally disordered, or mentally handicapped person should take place unless an 'appropriate adult' is present.[1041] In respect of juveniles, the 'appropriate adult' may be a parent, friend or anyone else deemed appropriate. However, in other cases, the 'appropriate adult' referred to in section 77 must be independent of the person to whom the confession is made. Thus he or she may not be a friend or relative; the 'independent person' must be entirely non-aligned with the police, the solicitor and the mentally disordered/handicapped suspect.[1042]

The function of the 'appropriate person' is to advise the vulnerable suspect, to see whether or not the interview is being conducted fairly and properly, and to facilitate communication between the suspect and police.[1043] On that basis, any confession made in the absence of an independent person is likely to fall foul of section 76(2)(b) and should be excluded as unreliable. As such, section 77 should apply only in exceptional circumstances. For example, in *R v Moss*,[1044] a mentally disordered person was interviewed nine times over a long period before confessing. The trial judge admitted the confession and gave a section 77 warning, but the Court of Appeal thought it should have been automatically excluded under section 76(2)(b). The Court further suggested that the section was directed at two types of cases: first those where the interview had been in the emergency circumstances envisaged in paragraph 11.1 of Code C; and second where the interview was in breach of the Code requirements but consisted of not more than one interview, conducted over a short period of time. The second set of circumstances envisaged by the court may be doubted as there is no reason why an appropriate adult should not be in attendance, however short the interview. It is, nonetheless, sometimes difficult for the police to determine that a suspect is mentally disordered/handicapped, but the test is objective. However, it matters not what the police think (if indeed they gave the issue any thought); what is important is any information that has subsequently been ascertained from medical experts.[1045]

In *R v McKenzie*,[1046] a defendant with a personality disorder was convicted of two offences of manslaughter and two of arson. The prosecution case on the manslaughter charge depended almost entirely on his unsupported confession while the arson charges were supported by other evidence. Quashing the convictions for manslaughter, the Court of Appeal held where the defendant suffers from a 'significant degree' of mental illness and the case against him depends wholly upon confessions which are 'unconvincing to the point where a jury properly directed could not convict upon them', then the trial judge (assuming he/she has not already excluded the confessions) should withdraw the case from the jury. In this case, the confessions were particularly unconvincing since they lacked the incriminating details which would have made them reliable, and because the defendant

---

[1041] PACE Code of Practice C, [11.15].
[1042] *R v Bailey* [1995] Crim LR 723.
[1043] PACE Code of Practice C, [11.16].
[1044] (1990) 91 Cr App R 371.
[1045] See *Everett*, above.
[1046] (1993) 92 Cr App R 369.

had confessed to twelve other killings which no one believed he had committed. There was also the possibility that the defendant had confessed to ensure that he stayed in the secure hospital where he was detained.[1047]

In *R v Law-Thompson*,[1048] the suspect suffered from Asperger's Syndrome. It was characterised by marked obsessionality, extreme rigidity of thought, and strict adherence to rules and rituals. One manifestation in this particular case was that the suspect thought his mother was evil. One morning he attacked his mother with a meat cleaver shouting, 'I'm going to kill you'. He was restrained and the police were called. On being asked what the cleaver was for, the accused replied, 'It's my duty to kill her'. On being arrested and cautioned he then told the police, 'I won't harm you. I only intend to kill my mother'. At the police station a psychiatrist found him fit to be interviewed, and the police had arranged for an appropriate adult to be present. However, a social worker advised that it was not necessary, and consequently the suspect was then interviewed in the presence of a solicitor, but without an appropriate adult. In the interview, he again made it clear that his intention had been to kill his mother and he would try again given the opportunity.

At trial, the remark made to the police before caution was excluded, although the interview itself was admissible. A psychiatrist stated that, although the defendant had a personality disorder, he was not mentally ill. He understood the nature and quality of his action, but did not comprehend that they were wrong. However, the defendant refused to plead insanity and was duly convicted of attempted murder. He then appealed, one ground being the absence of an appropriate adult (independent person) at the interview which, according to the defence, rendered the interview inadmissible.

Dismissing the appeal, the Court of Appeal held that it was not easy to apply section 76(2) to these facts, since there was nothing to suggest that the confession was obtained *in consequence* of the absence of an appropriate adult, or that such absence rendered the confession unreliable. The focus was then on section 78 which gave the judge a discretion to exclude which was at least as wide as that at common law. In support of exclusion, defence counsel argued that the prosecution were in breach of Article 6 of the European Convention on Human Rights. While accepting that the trial judge would have been entitled to consider Article 6 had his attention been drawn to it, the Court said that his focus had to be on section 76 and section 78. Even if there had been a breach of Article 6, it did not lead to the conclusion that evidence thus obtained must be excluded. Section 77 was not argued in this case, presumably because the case did not depend wholly or substantially on his confession. Had this been the case, it would have been highly improbable that the prosecution would have proceeded relying solely on a confession obtained in the circumstances envisaged by section 77.[1049]

Section 78: discretionary exclusion

Section 78 of PACE provides for any evidence to be excluded if it appears to the court that 'having regard to all the circumstances, including the circumstances in which the evidence was obtained, the admission of the evidence would have such an adverse effect on the fairness of the proceedings that the court ought not to admit it'.

[1047]See also *Wood*, above.
[1048][1997] Crim LR 674.
[1049]See also *R v Campbell* [1995] 1 Cr App R 522.

Although use of the provision is sometimes simply labelled 'unfairness' as a form of academic shorthand, the section actually requires more than this. An adverse effect will not be enough; the word 'such' imports a degree of adverse effect over and above the baseline of 'adverse effect'. As Spencer argues, a fair trial does not mean a trial which is free from all possible detriment or disadvantage to the accused.[1050] Thus, in exercising its discretion under section 78, the question as to whether a particular method or technique used to gather evidence will amount to unfairness should always be considered as a matter of extent and degree.[1051]

It should be noted, however, that unlike the exclusionary rules contained in section 76(2), the concept of burden of proof has no part to play under section 78. In *R (Saifi) v Governor of Brixton Prison*,[1052] the Divisional Court noted that the situation where a judge is considering whether or not to exercise his discretion under the section, the process is distinct from any other decision-making aspect of the trial proper. The judge must be satisfied, after hearing evidence from both sides, that a decision to admit the evidence would have such an adverse effect on the fairness of the trial that it ought not to be admitted. The decision to exclude is thus a question to be determined by the court and does not require 'proof' by either side, although the defence should normally first present an argument that the evidence ought not to be admitted.[1053]

It should be emphasised that this section confers a discretion on the court; it does not impose a duty. Since section 78 took effect, trial judges at first instance have traditionally enjoyed a considerable degree of latitude in determining in what circumstances evidence should be excluded. Provided the judge interprets the 1984 Act and the Codes correctly, and professes to consider all the circumstances of the case, he or she will be final arbiter as to when the evidence in question should be excluded. The prospects of a successful appeal on the grounds that the discretion was improperly exercised are slight.[1054] In *R v Dures and others*,[1055] the trial judge's refusal to exclude evidence of interviews held in the cell, which were neither contemporaneously recorded nor confirmed and signed by the second appellant, was upheld on the basis that it was not a decision which no reasonable judge could have reached. The standard is thus effectively that of *Wednesbury* unreasonableness.[1056]

The broad nature of the discretion also means that it should not be fettered by the erection of rules, since each decision rests on its own particular facts.[1057] If an appellate court concludes that the discretion has been wrongly exercised (or not exercised at all), it may be able to put itself in the position of the trial judge and consider if or how the discretion should have been exercised.[1058] Nonetheless, the general unwillingness of the appellate courts to uphold appeals based on section 78 has not held defence counsel back

---

[1050] Spencer, JR 'Orality and the Evidence of Absent Witnesses' [1994] Crim LR 628.

[1051] The relevant confession has usually been made to the police but this is not essential. Section 78 can be used to exclude a confession made to others (e.g. a doctor as in *R v McDonald* [1991] Crim LR 144; or a probation officer as in *R v Ellaray* [2003] 2 Cr App R 11).

[1052] [2000] 1 WLR 1134.

[1053] *R v Raphaie* [1996] Crim LR 812.

[1054] *R v O'Leary* (1988) 87 Cr App R 387.

[1055] [1997] 2 Cr App R 247.

[1056] As outlined by Lord Taylor CJ in *R v Quinn* [1995] 1 Cr App R 480, 487: 'Before this Court could reach the conclusion that the judge was wrong [to exercise his discretion under section 78 as he did] we would have to be satisfied that no reasonable judge, having heard the evidence that this learned judge did, could have reached the conclusion that he did'.

[1057] *R v Canale* [1990] 2 All ER 187; *R v Gillard and Barrett* [1991] Crim LR 280.

[1058] *R v Mason* (above).

from using it as a ground of appeal across a wide range of circumstances, albeit with varying degrees of success.

The terse terms of section 78 give little help as to the proper interpretation of the section and the courts have displayed a range of approaches. Three general points can be made. First, the section is to be construed widely.[1059] Second, the test is fairness of the proceedings, not fairness to the defence. In other words, fairness to the prosecution and to the court (that it be able to hear all the relevant evidence) must also be considered.[1060] Third, as Auld J remarked in *R v Jelen and Katz*:[1061]

> The circumstances of each case are almost always different, and judges may well take different views in the proper exercise of their discretion even where the circumstances are similar. This is not an apt field for hard case law and well founded distinctions between cases.[1062]

In *R v Oliphant*,[1063] the Court of Appeal further emphasised the need to consider the facts of each case against the statutory language of PACE 1984 when it stated, *per curiam* that '[i]t is important, in deciding admissibility of evidence under PACE, not to be diverted by other decisions of the court, often on different facts, from considering the statutory language'.[1064]

Section 78 and confession evidence

It was initially thought that, in light of the relatively stringent exclusionary requirement contained in section 76(2), section 78 might not apply to confessions. This was not, however, a view that was shared by the courts, and as such it is difficult to draw a neat dividing line between case law that is strictly relevant to confession evidence, and that which is relevant to the application of section 78 in respect of more general issues arising from improper police conduct. In the discussion that follows, we have sought to highlight some of the key features of the provision insofar as it may apply to confession evidence. However, this discussion should not be read in isolation from that which follows in the next chapter. In order to understand how section 78 operates in practice, it is vital both aspects of the discussion are taken into account.

One of the first cases in which the Court of Appeal applied section 78 to confession evidence was that of *Mason*. The Court made it clear that the word 'evidence' in section 78 included a confession and held that the trial judge had wrongly exercised his discretion under section 78 by failing to take account of the deceit practised on the appellant and his solicitor. Despite failing to explain *how* that deceit had an adverse effect on the fairness of the trial, the Court made it clear that the conviction should nonetheless be quashed:

> It is obvious from the undisputed evidence that the police practised a deceit not only on the appellant, which is bad enough, but also on his solicitor, whose duty it was to advise him. In effect, they hoodwinked both solicitor and client. That was a most reprehensible thing to do. It is not however because we regard as misbehaviour of a serious kind conduct of that nature that we have come to the decision soon to be made plain. This is not the place to discipline the

[1059] *R v Keenan* [1990] 2 QB 54.
[1060] *DPP v Marshall* [1988] 3 All ER 683; *R v Quinn* [1990] Crim LR 581.
[1061] (1990) 90 Cr App R 456.
[1062] *Ibid.*, 465. Approved in *R v Roberts* [1997] 1 Cr App R 217.
[1063] [1992] Crim LR 40.
[1064] *Ibid.*, 41.

police. That has been made clear here on a number of previous occasions. We are concerned with the application of the proper law. The law is, as I have already said, that a trial judge has a discretion to be exercised of course upon right principles to reject admissible evidence in the interests of a defendant having a fair trial. The judge in the present case appreciated that ... So the only question to be answered by this Court is whether, having regard to the way the police behaved, the judge exercised that discretion correctly. In our judgement he did not.[1065]

Although one may take issue with the court's view that it had no role to play in disciplining the police,[1066] the use of section 78 can be justified in these circumstances on the basis that the provision of false information led the defendant's solicitor to misadvise him. This effectively amounted to a denial of the defendant's fundamental right to legal advice based on the true facts.

Improper denial of access to legal advice

The case law on section 78 abounds with many examples of improper denial of access to legal advice. Section 58 of PACE confers all suspects with the right to consult a solicitor in the police station, both before and during the interview. This right was significantly bolstered by the decision of the Court of Appeal in *R v Samuel*,[1067] where the accused had been charged with burglary. At first, the suspect denied any involvement. He was then interviewed again, and denied access to a solicitor. On this occasion, he confessed to robbery. The Court of Appeal held that refusal of access to a solicitor after the first charge constituted a breach of section 58 of PACE. Noting that it was 'one of the most important and fundamental rights of the citizen', it was held that the judge should have at least considered the question as to whether the confession ought to be excluded under section 78. Since he had failed to do so, the conviction for robbery was unsafe and was quashed. It is, however, somewhat lamentable that the Court of Appeal chose to overlook entirely the question of reliability of the confession, turning immediately to section 78 and ignoring section 76(2)(b). As suggested in the previous section, the courts have largely continued this approach, with the result that permitting access to a solicitor is seldom considered to lead to unreliability where the suspect is an adult and not vulnerable for any reason.[1068]

The decisions in both *Mason* and *Samuel* serve to emphasise that denial of legal advice per se is not enough. It must also be shown that the denial produced an adverse effect. To some extent, the complexity of the offence under investigation may increase the need for legal advice and exacerbate the potential adverse effect stemming from its improper denial.[1069] However, much will depend upon the individual character and experiences of the accused. This latter point was addressed in *Alladice*,[1070] where the confession was admitted, notwithstanding the wrongful denial of access to a solicitor. The Court of Appeal noted that the defendant, having been regularly accustomed to police interviews, was already aware of his rights. Therefore the solicitor's presence would not have made a difference, and there was no unfairness to the proceedings. Similarly, in *R v Chahal*,[1071] the

---

[1065] *Mason*, at 484.
[1066] See further Ch 9, below, pp 291–92.
[1067] [1988] QB 615.
[1068] See above, p 269.
[1069] See *R v Guest* (1988) (Unreported, 20 January).
[1070] (1988) 87 Cr App R 380.
[1071] [1992] Crim LR 124.

defendant said he did not want a solicitor and later confirmed this. However, unknown to Chahal, his family had instructed a solicitor who attended but was refused access by the police on the grounds that the defendant did not want a solicitor. His appeal against conviction was dismissed. The defendant was a capable and mature businessman, who knew the consequences of his initial decision to refuse legal advice. As such, he had suffered no prejudice.

As *Alladice* and *Chahal* illustrate, suspects who are familiar with the criminal justice system, or those who are considered capable of handling police interrogation effectively themselves, will not generally be prejudiced to any great extent by the absence of a legal representative.[1072] However, the courts have tended to take a much dimmer view of the improper denial of legal advice to vulnerable suspects. In *R v Franklin*,[1073] the defendant, a young unemployed man, initially said he did not want a solicitor. Ten minutes later he asked that his father be informed of his arrest, so he could obtain a solicitor for him. However, the suspect nonetheless agreed to be interviewed without a solicitor present, and made admissions. In the meantime, the defendant's father had instructed a solicitor, who attended at the police station but was told that the defendant would not be informed because he did not want legal advice.[1074] Two further interviews followed at which the defendant was reminded of his right to legal advice, but was not told that a solicitor had attended. The trial judge admitted the evidence of all four interviews believing he was bound by *Chahal*.

The Court of Appeal disagreed, and noted there were significant differences between the two cases. In *Chahal* the solicitor had merely telephoned, and, furthermore, the suspect was a mature businessman. In this case the solicitor actually attended and the defendant was a young unemployed man who had never been in a police station before. The trial judge had therefore exercised his discretion wrongly. However, the case against the defendant was overwhelming, and notwithstanding the error, the appeal was dismissed.[1075] Likewise, in *R v Sanusi*,[1076] it was held that a confession made by a foreign suspect with no understanding of the English legal system should have been excluded under section 78, because he was wrongly denied access to a solicitor. Arguably, however, the absence of a solicitor in both *Franklin* and *Sanusi* may well have produced *unreliable* confessions which should, accordingly, have been dealt with under section 76(2)(b) as opposed to section 78.[1077] These decisions again highlight the judicial tendency to ignore section 76 altogether, which means that, in practice, judges are exercising a discretion to exclude evidence which should really be automatically inadmissible.

The potential for inferences to be drawn from silence under the Criminal Justice and Public Order Act 1994 also increases the need for legal advice in the police station, and

---

[1072]See also *R v Dunford* (1990) 91 Cr App Rep 150, where the improper denial of legal advice was balanced by the defendant 's knowledge of his rights and ability to cope on his own.

[1073][1994] *The Times*, 16 June.

[1074]See now PACE Code of Practice C [6.15], which requires that the defendant be informed that the solicitor has attended.

[1075]Other cases in which denial of access to legal advice led to exclusion of the confession include *R v Vernon* [1988] Crim LR 445, where the defendant was not told of the duty solicitor scheme or that a solicitor was on the way; *R v Absolam* [1989] Cr App R 332, where the defendant was not told of his right to legal advice and proceeded to make damaging admissions, and, to similar effect, *R v Williams* [1989] Crim LR 66; *R v Beycan* (below), where D was wrongfully denied a solicitor being told 'we usually interview without a solicitor' (this decision seems particularly unfair since the suspect was a foreigner with poor English and therefore vulnerable).

[1076][1992] Crim LR 43.

[1077]See also *R v Beycan* [1990] Crim LR 185.

increases the likelihood of an adverse effect to result from its improper denial. Even the Alladices of this world may not fully appreciate the potential effect of remaining silent under police interrogation. As noted in Chapter 4, the Youth Justice and Criminal Evidence Act 1999 has amended the Criminal Justice and Public Order Act 1994 so that inferences cannot be drawn under those sections unless the defendant has had access to a solicitor.[1078] This statutory intervention, together with the decision in *Samuel*, mean that any decision to deny a suspect immediate access to a solicitor will only be lawful in the most exceptional of circumstances.

Other breaches of PACE

In relation to other violations of PACE or the Codes of Practice, each case will turn on its own particular facts, with particular emphasis being placed on the nature and extent of the breach. If the procedure is regarded by the court as an important one, it does not matter whether lack of adherence to it was wilful or inadvertent; the degree of adverse effect on the proceedings is the key issue which the court will need to determine.[1079]

The case of *R v Canale*[1080] offers some guidance as to when a failure to record interviews at the police station might give rise to exclusion. Here, the defendant was suspected of assisting in a robbery. He allegedly confessed in two interviews, although no recording of these confessions was made, nor was any reason given for a failure to record. In two subsequent interviews, the defendant repeated the admissions, which were then contemporaneously recorded. At trial, the judge admitted the evidence of the four interviews. D appealed, contending that the first two interviews should not have been admitted since he had been tricked and induced into making the confessions. Allowing his appeal and quashing his conviction, the Court of Appeal stated that the lack of a contemporaneous note of the initial interviews meant that the judge was deprived in the *voir dire* of the very evidence which enabled him to decide whether the admissions were admissible. The contemporaneous notes of the subsequent interviews did not cure the initial breaches of Code C, since their admissibility depended on whether the admissions on the unrecorded interviews were properly obtained. Importantly, it was also noted that since the police officers had flagrantly and deliberately breached Code C, the judge should have exercised his discretion to exclude the evidence.

By contrast, in *R v Dunn*,[1081] the accused was charged with aggravated burglary. Following an interview in a police station, there was a conversation during the signing of the interview notes, and in the presence of the solicitor's clerk, when D allegedly confessed to the offence. The conversation was not recorded contemporaneously and no note of it was ever shown to the appellant. The defendant and the solicitor's clerk denied that any such conversation took place. Dismissing the appeal, the Court of Appeal held that although there were clear breaches of Code C, this was counterbalanced by the presence of the defendant's legal adviser during the interview. Likewise, in *R v Matthews*,[1082] the defendant's alleged admissions were noted after the interview ended but the note was not subsequently shown to her. Here, the Court of Appeal accepted that there had been a

---

[1078] YJCEA 1999, section 58. See further Ch 4, pp 105–08.
[1079] *R v Kerawalla* (1991) Crim LR 252. See further Ch 9, p 294.
[1080] [1990] 2 All ER 187.
[1081] (1990) 91 Cr App R 237.
[1082] [1990] Crim LR 190.

clear breach of the Code C but did not disturb the trial judge's refusal to use section 78, apparently on the basis that he had considered all the circumstances and his discretion could not be challenged.[1083]

Since the advent of tape- and video-recording of interviews under Code E, the failure to record interviews in police stations is rare, with much of the relevant case law predating PACE. Nowadays, any failure to record will usually relate to statements made outside the interview room. In *R v Maloney and Doherty*,[1084] interviews outside and inside the station were not contemporaneously recorded, notes of the interviews were not shown to the suspects and, although they could not read, no lawyer or third party was made available to assist them. It was held that these should have been excluded. In *RSPCA v Eager*,[1085] the accused was interviewed in her home by RSPCA inspectors who drew up their record of the interview in their car at a later point in time, giving D no opportunity to verify it. Again, the Court held this should have been ruled out. By contrast, in *R v Courtney*,[1086] customs officers intercepted parcels of herbal cannabis and one posed as a postman to deliver them to the defendant's address. A note of the defendant's comments on the doorstep was made but was not shown to the defendant. In this instance, the breach was not significant or substantial, and the note was admitted.

Exclusion under section 78 is more likely if the breach is flagrant;[1087] or wilful;[1088] or in bad faith.[1089] Ultimately, however, the key question for the trial judge is when the breach is so substantial that it interferes with the fairness of proceedings. In the case of *Walsh*,[1090] the denial of legal advice, omitting to note the reason for not recording an interview contemporaneously, and failure to show the defendant the record of interview were regarded as significant and substantial breaches which were not cured by good faith. This case has become a standard reference point for cases involving breach of PACE 1984 and the Codes, particularly those involving wrongful exclusion of a solicitor, but, as Woolf LJ pointed out in *Oliphant*, the words 'significant' and 'substantial' are not terms of art but are simply offered as guides to ruling out of consideration those merely technical breaches which have no adverse consequences. In *R v Quinn*,[1091] it was further suggested that any act that was deliberate would automatically render proceedings unfair. Since this particular case concerned the inadvertent breaches of Code C on the conduct of an identity parade, it was held the judge had been correct not to exclude the evidence.

The presence of other evidence against the defendant should not affect the decision regarding unfairness.[1092] However, where there is enough other evidence to convict the defendant, the court might be more easily persuaded to exclude the peripheral and disputed evidence whilst still allowing the rest to go before the jury.[1093] By contrast, the absence

---

[1083]See also *Gill* [2004] 1 WLR 469.

[1084][1988] Crim LR 523.

[1085][1995] Crim LR 59.

[1086][1995] Crim LR 63.

[1087]In *R v Canale* [1990] 2 All ER 187, the Lord Chief Justice found a cynical disregard of the rules governing the contemporaneous recording of interviews.

[1088]*R v Nagah* (1991) 92 Cr App R 344 where, although the defendant agreed to an identification parade, he was released so that a street identification could more easily be made.

[1089]See the remarks by Lord Lane CJ in *R v Alladice* (1988) 87 Cr App R 380 that a court might find it easier to employ section 78 if bad faith on the part of the police is proved.

[1090](1990) 91 Cr App R 161.

[1091][1990] Crim LR 581.

[1092]That aspect is the preserve of section 2(1) of the Criminal Appeals Act 1968, the proviso to which can counterbalance any refusal to exclude evidence under section 78 – see further *Walsh*.

[1093]*Waters* (above); *Keenan* (above).

of other evidence, apart from the disputed area, could be crucial to the fairness of the trial. For example, in *R v Cochrane*,[1094] the interviews were the only evidence against the defendant and, since section 58 had been transgressed, it would have been unfair to use them. A further problem is that such other evidence that does exist may even be linked to and be tainted by the improper conduct. In *Beycan* it was held that once admissions at the station had been excluded under section 78, it was unfair to admit statements made in the car en route there. Indeed, as with section 76, an earlier improper interview may affect a subsequent one conducted properly to such an extent that the exclusion of all the interview evidence is warranted. As in *Canale*, this may be because the impropriety still influences the later interview, or because the court is determined not to let the police flagrantly flout the rules and then 'get away with it' by sticking to them on subsequent occasions.[1095]

Section 78 and the right to silence

One of the seminal cases concerning breach of the Codes of Practice is that of *Keenan*,[1096] where the defendant was charged with possessing an offensive weapon. He challenged the admissibility of statements made in the course of interviews with the police, alleging that no proper record had been kept in contravention of paragraphs 11 and 12 of the Code of Practice. Although the trial judge acknowledged the police had breached the Code, he refused to rule the evidence out, and said that the defendant could counteract the effect of the breaches by testifying himself in court. Having opted to exercise his right to silence, the accused was convicted and appealed. Quashing the conviction, the Court of Appeal held that the function of Codes of Practice was to provide safeguards against the police inaccurately recording or inventing words, and to make it difficult for unfounded allegations to be made against the police. It was stressed that, as in the instant case, where there had been 'significant and substantial' breaches of these provisions, evidence should 'frequently' be excluded.[1097] Furthermore, it was stressed that it could not be assumed that any unfairness to the defendant could be remedied by his testimony at court, since the defendant was entitled to rely on his right to silence. The evidence should therefore have been excluded.

In *R v Roberts*,[1098] the accused was arrested on suspicion of robbery of a building society and two banks. Roberts was interviewed over a number of days and although he remained silent was nevertheless charged with two of the robberies. C was arrested on suspicion of involvement in one of the robberies with Roberts. He was also interviewed a number of times and implicated himself in a number of offences including conspiracy to rob, supplying drugs, large scale shoplifting and escaping from police custody, but he denied involvement in the robbery for which he had been arrested.

When visited by a police officer in his cell, and without prompting, C asked to move in with Roberts so that he could get Roberts to admit the robbery. This, he said, would clear him of any involvement. A note was made of this conversation but, in breach of Code C, it

---

[1094][1988] Crim LR 449.

[1095]See *Canale*. However, the court, in exercising its discretion may find that the later interview is not so tainted, and can simply refuse to exercise its discretion to exclude. See *R v Gillard and Barrett* (1991) 92 Cr App R 61. The distinction between this case and *Canale* is narrow and seems to depend on the degree of flagrancy of the misconduct.

[1096][1990] 2 QB 54.

[1097]*Ibid.*, 69.

[1098][1997] 1 Cr App R 217.

was not read to or signed by C. Both men were duly placed in a cell together, and a listening device was covertly installed. In a recorded conversation, C was heard pressing Roberts to clear him of the robbery, and Roberts also admitted participating in two further robberies after being questioned about them by C. Evidence of the conversations was admitted at his trial and Roberts was convicted of all of the offences which he had admitted to in the recorded conversation.

On appeal, Roberts claimed there had been a material irregularity in the trial insofar as the judge had wrongly permitted the prosecution to adduce evidence of the covert tape recordings of the conversation in the police cell where C, a police stooge, was placed to obtain admissions from Roberts in breach of the Code of Practice. No solicitor was present and he alleged that he had been deceived into believing his conversation was in private. However, dismissing the appeal, the Court of Appeal held that it was not part of the purpose of the Code of Practice to protect an accused in relation to breaches of the Code in respect of another suspect. Accordingly, since there had been no causal link between the breaches of the Code and the appellant's subsequent spontaneous admissions, the judge was right to regard those breaches as insignificant in relation to the appellant. Furthermore, each case of this kind was to be decided on its own facts and it was inappropriate to draw a distinction between mere eavesdropping and putting a person in the cell with the suspect. The true test was whether the conduct of the police, either wittingly or unwittingly, led to unfairness or injustice, and in the instant case the trial judge's application of this test could not be faulted.

Unfortunately, the precise basis on which discretion is exercised is not always so clearly articulated. Indeed, sometimes the courts, despite what was said in *Walsh*, proceed almost automatically to apply section 78 where improprieties have been established without first considering the statutory language.[1099] Thus, it is difficult to elicit any overriding principles. The best that can be done is to survey the existing cases and try to gauge the types of factors that are likely to warrant exclusion and those which are not. Clearly, some forms of breaches are more likely to result in exclusion than others.

KEY LEARNING POINTS

- Confession evidence may be excluded on three grounds: oppression, unreliability, or through the exercise of judicial discretion.
- If there is serious impropriety in the criminal process which may amount to oppression, section 76(2)(a) should be relied upon in the first instance.
- If the impropriety amounts to something said or done (or not done) which was likely in the circumstances to lead to an unreliable confession, section 76(2)(b) should be relied upon. This is likely to envelope conduct that falls short of the threshold for section 76(2)(a).
- If either of these circumstances applies, the court must exclude the evidence.
- Facts obtained as a result of a confession are admissible, providing no connection is made in court with the suspect having confessed.
- Where section 76(2) does not apply, the defence may ask the court to use its discretion to exclude the evidence under section 78.

[1099] See further *R v Hughes* [1988] Crim LR 519.

- The exercise of the exclusionary discretion under section 78 is a matter for the trial judge. Generally, breaches of PACE will have to be 'significant and substantial' before they are likely to give rise to exclusion.

? **QUESTIONS**

Consider whether the trial judge should exclude the following confessions:

1. Aron is a mature businessman, a director of a number of companies and former mayor. He was arrested on a charge of corruption at 6.30 am on Monday in the presence of his wife and taken to a police station. He was refused access to a solicitor by a superintendent who stated that in reliance on section 58(8)(b) of the Police and Criminal Evidence Act 1984, he had reasonable grounds to believe that others suspected of involvement in the offence and not yet arrested would be alerted. He was interviewed three times. During the course of these interviews he made it clear that he knew his rights and refused to answer a number of questions. However, during the third interview he admitted that he had corruptly received money from a number of contractors in return for ensuring that council contracts went to them.

2. Ben is a heroin addict who was arrested for burglary. The police realised he was a drug addict and made no attempt to interview him until 18 hours after his arrival at the police station. Before being interviewed he was asked if he wanted to see a solicitor. He said he did not and signed the custody record to that effect. Ben made no complaint during the 18 hours of detention, and told the police he felt able to answer questions. He was subsequently interviewed by two police officers, having again refused a solicitor. During the interview he admitted involvement in a number of burglaries, which, he said, he did to get money to feed his habit. After the interview he complained that he was suffering withdrawal symptoms. A doctor then attended him, and, on finding a high pulse rate, prescribed medication. However, he expressed the opinion that Ben was otherwise fit to be detained. Ben now says the confession was false. He was suffering from withdrawal symptoms and was prepared to say anything in order to get out and obtain a 'fix'.

3. Julie is a 21-year-old medical student. During her training on a hospital ward, a young boy died after his oxygen equipment had been tampered with and a tube detached. Police arrested Julie on suspicion of murder. She was detained for a total period of 49 hours. Owing to an administrative error, the last thirteen hours were not properly authorised in accordance with PACE and the Code of Practice. Julie was interviewed in the presence of a solicitor six times, for periods of two hours over two days. On the tape recording of the interview the interviewing officer can be heard repeatedly telling Julie in an aggressive voice that she killed the boy. Despite Julie's denial, the officer repeated the accusation some thirty times over the six interviews. Towards the end of the fifth interview a police officer showed Julie a picture of the little boy taken during the post-mortem and told her to take it to her cell and

? QUESTIONS (Continued)

reflect on what she had done. During the final interview the interviewing officer could be heard shouting at Julie and demanding that she tell the truth. Julie then made a series of statements in which she accepted responsibility for the boy's death. Julie's solicitor said nothing during the interviews.

4. Ahmed and his girlfriend were arrested on suspicion of making a fraudulent claim on their insurance in respect of an alleged burglary of their flat. Ahmed refused a solicitor and signed the custody record to that effect. During a taped interview, Ahmed asked the interviewing officer what was likely to happen to his girlfriend. The officer told him that she would be interviewed and, if found to be involved, she would be charged. Ahmed then made a confession in which he said he was totally to blame and that the girlfriend was not involved.

Would your answer to (4) above differ, if the interviewing officer told Ahmed that if he admitted the offence, his girlfriend would not be prosecuted?

SUGGESTED FURTHER READING

Hartshorne, J 'Defensive use of a co-accused's confession and the Criminal Justice Act 2003' (2004) 8(3) *International Journal of Evidence & Proof* 165.

Hirst, M 'Confessions as proof of innocence' (1998) 57 *Cambridge Law Journal* 146.

Kassin, S M 'The psychology of confession evidence (1997) 52 *American Psychologist* 221.

Mirfield, P *Silence, confessions and improperly obtained evidence* (1997, Oxford: Oxford University Press).

Munday, R 'Adverse denial and purposive confession' [2003] Crim LR 850.

CHAPTER 9

IMPROPERLY OBTAINED EVIDENCE

INTRODUCTION

Aside from confessions, convictions based on other forms of evidence obtained by allegedly illegal or unfair means are regularly challenged in the appellate courts. Such evidence may take a variety of forms, but commonly falls into three main areas: cases dealing with failure to abide by the protocols laid down by PACE and the Codes of Practice; cases involving covert surveillance; and cases involving tricks or so-called 'entrapment' evidence.

At common law such evidence has traditionally been admissible, although the courts have expressly disapproved of such practices. In *Brannan v Peek*,[1100] Lord Goddard CJ described an attempt by undercover police officers to uncover unlicensed gambling establishments by involving themselves in illegal betting rings as 'wholly wrong'.[1101] Although courts had the discretion to exclude evidence that was obtained unfairly or as a result of the actions of an *agent provocateur*, it is only in more recent times that statutory intervention has begun to regulate such evidence in a closer manner than has previously been the case. Indeed, it now appears that the police and CPS need to exercise considerably more caution in basing prosecutions around evidence that might be regarded as suspect. As Dennis suggests, there are two main reasons why the use of such evidence should concern us.[1102] First, it impacts upon procedural fairness. Arguably, it is inherently unfair to make use of evidence that was not obtained according to the law. Second, it impacts upon the accuracy of the verdict. If, for example, improperly obtained evidence is both highly cogent and highly relevant to the charge, it must be questioned whether it should nevertheless be excluded on the grounds that it would be unfair to the defence.

EXCLUSION AT COMMON LAW

Unlike many other jurisdictions, there is neither any defence of entrapment in English law, nor any rule that evidence that has not been obtained in accordance with the law cannot be used in court. In other words, the question as to how evidence was obtained will not affect its admissibility; courts have never seen it as their function to police the police or the CPS. In the words of Crompton J: 'It matters not how you get it, if you steal it even, it would be admissible in evidence'.[1103]

This position has been largely reflected in the evolution of the case law during the last century. Despite the appellate courts having indicated that judges had a general discretion to exclude evidence obtained unfairly,[1104] it was rarely resorted to by counsel, and it was even rarer for the failure to use that discretion to result in a successful appeal.[1105]

[1100] [1948] 1 KB 68.

[1101] *Ibid.*, 72.

[1102] Dennis, I *The Law of Evidence* (2007: London, Sweet and Maxwell), p 294.

[1103] *R v Leatham* (1861) 8 Cox CC 498, 501.

[1104] See e.g. *Kuruma v R* [1955] AC 197; *King v R* [1969] 1 AC 304; *Jeffrey v Black* [1978] QB 298. Interestingly, however, civil courts have no such discretion: *Helliwell v Piggott-Sims* [1980] FSR 582.

[1105] A rare exception was *R v Payne* [1963] 1 WLR 637, a drink driving case where the court excluded the evidence of a doctor since the driver had been told that the doctor would only examine him to ascertain whether he was suffering from any illness or disability.

The leading case on the scope of the common law discretion is that of *Sang*.[1106] Here, a currency counterfeiter had arranged a meeting with someone claiming to be interested in forged banknotes, only to discover that the person in question was an undercover police officer. Having failed to persuade the trial judge that the evidence should have been excluded, the defendant pleaded guilty, but duly appealed contending that the judge should have exercised his discretion to disallow the evidence since the offence was instigated by an *agent provocateur*. His appeal was rejected first by the Court of Appeal, and then by the House of Lords. Their Lordships accepted that a judge in a criminal trial has a general discretion to refuse to admit evidence where its probable prejudicial effect so outweighed its probative value as to make its admission unfair to the accused, but ruled that the evidence must in some way impact upon the fairness of proceedings. As Lord Diplock famously surmised:

> save with regard to admissions and confessions and generally with regard to evidence obtained from the accused after the commission of the offence, [the judge] has no discretion to refuse to admit relevant admissible evidence on the ground that it was obtained by improper or unfair means. The court is not concerned with how the evidence was obtained.[1107]

Thus, according to Lord Diplock, the potential scope of any such discretion is extremely limited, and it cannot be used merely to reprimand the police or any other investigatory authority for reprehensible conduct. Only in instances that were already well defined by the law (including evidence of similar facts, previous convictions and breaches of the Judges' Rules), should a judge exclude evidence that was otherwise relevant. Whilst Viscount Dilhorne largely concurred with Lord Diplock's speech, a slightly less restrictive view was expounded by the other Law Lords. In the views of Lords Fraser, Salmon and Scarman, it was incorrect to limit judicial discretion to pre-defined areas since the overall duty of the trial judge was to ensure that both sides receive a fair trial. Despite the lack of unanimity in their analyses, it was clear that all their Lordships agreed that there was no defence of entrapment in English law. However, little guidance was provided in the speeches as to the circumstances in which judges could feel free to rule out evidence on the grounds that its probative value was outweighed by its prejudicial effect. Indeed, the subsequent decisions in *Trump*[1108] and *Fox*[1109] did little to clarify the scope of the common law discretion.

EXCLUSION UNDER PACE

It was thus clear that the common law discretion to exclude evidence was very restrictive in scope. It was concerned not with how the evidence was obtained but with the effect of the evidence on the fairness of the trial. In practice however, the effect of the decision in *Sang* was to be short-lived. Parliament's enactment of section 78 of PACE was much more certain terms the nature of the judicial discretion to exclude evidence.[1110] As noted in the previous chapter, under this provision a court may exclude the evidence if it appears that 'having regard to all the circumstances, including the circumstances in which the evidence was obtained, the admission of the evidence would have such an adverse effect on the fairness of the proceedings that the court ought not to admit it'.

[1106][1980] AC 402.
[1107]*Ibid.*, 437.
[1108](1980) 70 Cr App R 300.
[1109](1986) 82 Cr App R 295.
[1110]It should be stressed, however, that PACE expressly preserved the common law discretion under section 82(3).

It may prima facie appear that the statutory provision simply codifies the position of the common law. Certainly, as the Court of Appeal noted in *Christou*,[1111] the standard of unfairness is essentially the same. However, the common law discretion to exclude evidence applied only to prosecution evidence and was concerned not with how the evidence was obtained but with the effect of the evidence on the fairness of the trial. Section 78 now provides a broad discretion to exclude any evidence, including confessional evidence obtained in a manner which, while not rendering it unreliable, would have an adverse effect on the fairness of the trial if admitted.[1112] It is broader than the common law discretion for a number of reasons. First, it can take into account the manner in which the evidence was obtained in determining its effect on the fairness of the trial. Thus, unlike the common law discretion, it may cover instances of entrapment by *agents provocateurs*.[1113] Second, it applies not only to confessions and evidence obtained after the commission of the offence, but it can cover *any* form of evidence on which the prosecution proposes to rely. This may include hearsay and bad character, notwithstanding other statutory provisions that may prima facie appear to allow their admission. However, both the statutory and the common law discretions are concerned with the effect the evidence has on the fairness of the trial. As recognized by the Court of Appeal in *Smurthwaite and Gill*,[1114] the statutory provision did not change the rule of substantive law that entrapment does not per se afford a defence to a criminal charge.

In the light of the strong similarities between the two forms of discretion, it might be asked whether there is any role left for the common law discretion in contemporary criminal practice. Arguably, the drafters of PACE envisaged that there would: section 82(3) preserves any power of a court to exclude evidence. One use was suggested in *R v Sat-Bhambra*.[1115] Like the use of section 76 in relation to confession evidence, section 78 is incapable of applying retrospectively. In this case, the defendant's confession had been admitted following a *voir dire*, but later, on hearing further medical evidence, the judge changed his mind. In these circumstances, it was recognised here that the common law discretion allows the court to remedy earlier unfairness to the accused by excluding a previously admitted confession. The common law discretion thus remains as a separate head for excluding evidence, but in almost all cases where evidence could properly be excluded at common law it can be excluded under section 78 before it is actually admitted.[1116]

It may also be the case that where the improperly obtained evidence, other than confession evidence, would not be excluded at common law it will not be excluded either under section 78. This was the case in *R v Stewart*,[1117] where it was argued that evidence of tampering with an electricity meter should be excluded under section 78 because of breaches of section 16 PACE and Code B concerning entry to the premises. In dismissing the appeal, the Court of Appeal found it unnecessary to decide whether PACE 1984 or the Code applied, or even whether the entry was unlawful. In the view of the Court, there was simply no unfairness in admitting the evidence which was there for all to see whether the entry was effected properly or not. This is consistent with the common law's approach to the exclusion of real evidence. There is no question of unreliability, the evidence speaks for

---

[1111] [1992] 2 QB 979.

[1112] *Mason* [1987] 3 All ER 481.

[1113] See below, pp 302–07.

[1114] [1994] 1 ALL ER 898.

[1115] (1988) 88 Cr App R 55.

[1116] See further comments of Lord Lane CJ in *Delaney*, and those of May LJ in *O'Leary*. See also *Matto v Wolverhampton Crown Court* (1987) RTR 337.

[1117] [1995] Crim LR 500.

itself and whilst admitting it may operate unfortunately for the accused, it does not operate unfairly.

The discretion to hold a *voir dire*

When section 78 is raised, the court has a discretion as to whether to hold a *voir dire*,[1118] although it remains unclear precisely how it should exercise that discretion. In *R v Keenan*,[1119] Hodgson J offered the following guidance:

- Sometimes, evidence of police irregularity is plain for all to see (e.g., on the custody record, officers' notebooks, or through witness statements).
- Where there is prima facie evidence of irregularity, this must be justified by evidence from the prosecution. An order refusing access to a solicitor can only be justified by compelling evidence from the senior police officer who made the order.
- In some (albeit rare) cases, the defence will need to adduce evidence from the accused himself or herself to support the case for exclusion.

Hodgson J also acknowledged the problem that, in many cases when the application to exclude is made at an early stage, the judge is unlikely to know the defendant's line of defence. Effectively, this means that the judge is ill-equipped to determine the potential degree of adverse effect, since he or she will only have access to a limited version of the facts. This observation highlights the underlying problem with the Court of Appeal decision in *R v Bailey*,[1120] where it was stated that all the circumstances of the case should be taken into account, including the amount of other evidence against the accused and the characteristics of the accused. The provisions of the Criminal Procedure and Investigations Act 1996, which require that the defence provide the prosecution with a statement setting out the general nature of their defence, operate to overcome this difficulty to some extent, but, in the absence of a closer understanding of the case, the question of adverse effect may have to be resolved on a fairly minimalist evidential basis. The alternative is to require more from the defence at the *voir dire*. Indeed, if the defence case is thin, the onus then lies on the defence to establish the alleged adverse effect.[1121]

Breaches of PACE and the codes of practice

The most common trigger for the application of section 78 is where the defence can show that there has been a breach of PACE 1984 or the Codes of Practice. The Codes of Practice, introduced subsequent to section 66 of PACE, stipulate the parameters under which the police must conduct themselves in the investigation of crime. In *Jelen and Katz*,[1122] it was emphasised that the overriding purpose of the codes was 'the protection of those who are vulnerable because they are in the custody of the police'.[1123] Observations of a similar effect were made in *Elson*.[1124] There is now a total of eight separate codes annexed to

---

[1118] *Carlisle v DPP* (Unreported, 9 November 1987).
[1119] [1990] 2 QB 54.
[1120] [1995] 2 Cr App R 262.
[1121] See the commentary to *Rajakuruna* [1991] Crim LR 407.
[1122] (1990) 90 Cr App R 456.
[1123] *Ibid.*, per Auld J, 464.
[1124] (1994) *The Times*, 30 June.

the Act.[1125] Although the Codes are not legally binding in themselves, compliance with them is obviously expected in order to safeguard the civil liberties of the suspect and ensure the moral integrity of the criminal process. On the other hand, it can be contended that occasional misconduct, particularly if unintentional or if it is of little consequence, should not undermine the strong public interest in the prosecution process. Certainly, such arguments seem stronger in cases involving serious crime where public policy dictates that the protection of the public should not be jeopardised by single instances of human error.

In practice, most police officers involved in the interrogation of suspects are highly trained and intentional illegality is thus exceedingly rare. However, inadvertent mistakes are still made in the application of the Codes of Practice, and the appellate courts have had to face calls for the use of section 78 to exclude evidence in such circumstances. It has nevertheless been clearly established that not every breach of correct procedures will be greeted with exclusion of evidence. Thus in *R v Walsh*,[1126] it was said that a breach of Code C meant that, prima facie at least, the standards of fairness set by Parliament have not been met and any evidence admitted in such circumstances must have an adverse effect on the fairness of the trial. However, it was underlined that this did not mean that exclusion should be automatic:

> The task of the court is not merely to consider whether there would be an adverse effect on the fairness of the proceedings, but such an adverse effect that justice requires the evidence to be excluded.[1127]

Certainly, the courts have remained loyal to their historical reluctance to use the exclusionary discretion as a sword to discipline the police.[1128] However, it is suggested that such reasoning is disingenuous for, no matter how the court expresses it, an inevitable consequence of exclusion of evidence is that the police are disciplined by the collapse of a prosecution. Hodgson J, it is submitted, came closer to the mark in *Samuel* when he described police disciplinary procedures as 'a much less secure method of ensuring compliance' with PACE 1984 than sections 76 and 78.[1129] Thus, in practice, the courts are increasingly prepared to use the discretionary exclusion where the police have acted in bad faith. In *Matto v Wolverhampton Crown Court*,[1130] for example, it was held that evidence of the defendant's blood alcohol level should have been ruled out after police conducted a breath test on the accused's driveway, despite his protests that they were on private property. Section 78 has also been used to condemn the tactics and content of police questioning. In fact this was the concern of the first leading case on the section, *R v Mason*.[1131] It will be recalled from the previous chapter that the Court of Appeal was enraged that the defendant's solicitor had been hoodwinked, thereby affecting the advice he gave his client. On that basis, section 78 was used to exclude the defendant's confession.

[1125]The Codes were substantially revised following a Home Office review in 2004. Code A deals with stop and search powers; Code B deals with the searching of premises and seizure of property; Code C concerns the detention, treatment and questioning of suspects; Code D lays down requirements regarding identification and accurate record-keeping; Code E refers to the tape recording of interviews; Code F concerns audio-visual recording; Code G (introduced January 2006) concerns statutory powers of arrest; and Code H (introduced in July 2006) concerns the detention of terrorism suspects.

[1126](1990) 91 Cr App R 161.

[1127]See also *Keenan* (above); *R v Delaney* (1988) 88 Cr App R 338; *R v Waters* [1989] Crim LR 62).

[1128]See e.g. *Delaney* (above); *Mason* (above); and *R v Fennelley* [1989] Crim LR 142.

[1129][1988] QB 615, 628. See also the trenchant criticism of police conduct by Lord Lane CJ in *R v Canale* [1990] 2 All ER 187 and more recently of officers of Customs and Excise whose disregard of Code C caused the Court in *R v Weerdesteyn* [1995] 1 Cr App R 405 caused some concern.

[1130][1987] RTR 337.

[1131]See discussion above, Ch 8, pp 277–78.

It is thus evident that the courts do see themselves as exercising *some* function in using the provision to discipline or punish the police. That may be no bad thing, but an honest acceptance of that principle would assist in understanding the application of the section. In theory at least, the question whether or not evidence should be excluded will be determined by looking to the extent of any departure from the standards contained within PACE and the impact this has upon the fairness of proceedings as a whole. This means that some degree of uncertainty as to the consequences of a breach is likely to arise when the requirements laid down in the Codes are not followed.

Many cases arising under section 78 involve confession evidence. These were considered in the previous chapter, but it should be borne in mind that there is a considerable degree of overlap between the principles that apply in cases concerning confession evidence, and those which do not. In the discussion below, we have attempted, where possible, to avoid repeating what has already been discussed in the previous chapter. However, in some cases, it will be necessary to refer back to some of case law that has already been covered.

Irrespective of whether a confession is involved, it will be recalled that courts tend to take a particularly dim view of those cases where a suspect was improperly denied access to legal advice.[1132] In *Walsh*, for example, there were a multitude of violations of PACE, including improper denial of access to legal advice under section 58. In addition, the police had failed to note the interview contemporaneously, had failed to keep a record of the reasons for not recording the interview, and failed to give the suspect an opportunity to read and sign the interview record that they later compiled. In the *voir dire* at first instance the judge accepted that none of the officers had acted in bad faith, and held that access to a solicitor would have made no difference. Thus he refused to rule any of the evidence out under section 78. Allowing the appeal, it was held that this series of breaches were indeed 'significant and substantial' and failed to measure up to the benchmark of fairness set down by Parliament in passing the legislation. The appeal was allowed.[1133]

Likewise, the absence of a caution is often considered a sufficiently serious breach of Code C that may lead to exclusion. In *R v Sparks*,[1134] the failure of the police to issue a caution, and to record the interview, was regarded as a substantial breach of Code C and warranted exclusion of the conversation under section 78. The Court of Appeal also found a substantial breach in *R v Saunders*,[1135] where the key component of a caution (that the defendant need not say anything) was omitted. On the other hand, failure to tell or remind the defendant that he is a volunteer and is free to leave is not necessarily a substantial breach,[1136] particularly where the defendant ought to have known that he was a suspect in an investigation.[1137] Indeed, there are many provisions in the Code that are generally considered to be of lesser importance, including stipulations on the precise timing to provide meals or drinks, record the times of when interviews commenced and finished, and the mandatory eight hour period of continuous rest. A failure to abide rigidly with these requirements did not weigh particularly heavy in the view of the court in *R v Deacon*,[1138] and the courts have frequently remarked that not every breach of the Code that will lead

---

[1132]See Ch 8, pp 278–80.
[1133]cf *R v Williams* [1989] Crim LR 66.
[1134][1991] Crim LR 128.
[1135][1988] Crim LR 521
[1136]See PACE Code of Practice C, [10.2].
[1137]*R v Rajakuruna* [1991] Crim LR 460.
[1138][1987] Crim LR 404.

to automatic exclusion under section 78. As suggested in *Walsh*, and in many subsequent cases, the breaches must be significant and substantial to justify exclusion. Those provisions that are mandatory are more likely to be so than those which are directory.[1139] Also, there may be an accumulation of minor breaches of procedure which together justify the exercise of the section 78 discretion.[1140]

It will be recalled from the previous chapter that, in *Keenan*,[1141] the Court of Appeal stated that the primary function of Codes of Practice was to provide safeguards for the accused against the abuse of police power. Thus, where breaches of the Codes were 'significant and substantial', the evidence should 'frequently' be excluded.[1142] However, the decision in *Keenan* was distinguished in *Sanghera*.[1143] The defendant, a postmaster, appealed against his conviction for theft on the ground that evidence obtained as a result of a police search should have been ruled out since he had failed to give the necessary consent required by Code B. Although the Court of Appeal acknowledged that the search was unlawful, evidence found as a result of that search was not unreliable. However, the Court differentiated the nature of the breaches that occurred here from those that arose in *Keenan*: they were fundamentally different and less serious in nature. Each case should turn on its own particular facts to determine whether the fairness of the trial had been adversely affected. In this particular instance, there was nothing to suggest that the necessary consent under Code B would not have been granted had it been requested by the police. It was held that the judge had been correct to admit the evidence.

Thus considerable care needs to be taken in generalising about the nature of the case law relating to breaches of the Codes of Practice. One of the key factors will certainly be the particular type of PACE procedure that has been breached. It should be noted that 'the mere fact that there has been a breach of the Codes of Practice does not of itself mean that evidence has to be rejected'.[1144] A link between the breach and fairness to the proceedings must be established.[1145] If the PACE procedure is an important safeguard for the suspect, an adverse effect on the fairness of the proceedings is inevitable and that effect is likely to be so adverse that justice demands the exclusion of any evidence thus obtained. In this context, most important are the provisions designed to prevent 'verballing' of the suspect; that is, concocting admissions through unfair means.[1146] Transgression of these standards often leads to exclusion under section 78 because it is unfair to deprive the defendant of his rights; it is unfair to the court since it is deprived of a more accurate record of an interview; and dangerous to the overall integrity of the criminal process since it would essentially allow the prosecution to win by foul play.

Thus even where the police do not explicitly intend to violate the Codes of Conduct, their actions may still result in the evidence being excluded. In *Nathaniel*,[1147] N, who had been convicted of rape, appealed on the ground that DNA evidence presented at his trial should have been excluded. This evidence was obtained primarily from a blood sample he had given four years previously, whilst under investigation for two other rape offences. He had agreed to give these samples only after assurances were given by police that

---

[1139] *R v Grier* (1989) LAG April, 14.
[1140] See e.g. *R v Moss* (1990) 91 Cr App R 371.
[1141] [1990] 2 QB 54.
[1142] *Ibid.*, 69.
[1143] [2001] 1 Cr App R 299.
[1144] *Delaney* (above), at 341 *per* Lord Lane CJ.
[1145] *R v Hughes* [1988] Crim LR 519; *R v Dunford* (1990) 91 Cr App R 150.
[1146] See e.g. *Keenan* (above).
[1147] [1995] 2 Cr App R 565.

the sample would be destroyed if he was acquitted of those crimes (in accordance with section 64 PACE). Owing to an administrative error, this was not done, and the samples relating to the previous offences were used to connect N with the offence in question. Allowing his appeal, the Court held that since the police had both misled N as to the use of the samples, and had failed to comply with their statutory obligation to destroy them, it would have been proper to exclude them under section 78 of the 1984 Act.

However, many other cases suggest that mistaken conduct on the part of the police carried out in good faith may tilt against the use of section 78, or at very least be a neutral factor in the equation. Examples include: *R v Clarke*,[1148] where the officers did not realise that the defendant was deaf, but the breach of what is now Code C, paragraph 13.5 could still be considered; *R v Younis*,[1149] where the suspect 'volunteered' most of the remarks in the police car and there was no evidence of deliberate police prompting; and *R v Kerawalla*,[1150] where the absence of bad faith was considered to be one of a number of relevant factors that could be taken into account. However, it should be borne in mind that, unlike section 76(2)(a), impropriety is not essential for the section 78 discretion to be exercised,[1151] and good faith will not serve to remedy a significant or substantial breach of PACE procedures.

Section 78 may also be used to exclude real evidence, although the courts seem reluctant to apply it in this fashion. The only recorded case in which real evidence has been excluded is *R v Fennelly*,[1152] which concerned a failure to comply with the stop and search requirements of PACE 1984. A quantity of heroin was seized from the underpants of the defendant, but this evidence was excluded on the basis that, in the view of the court, it would have been unfair to admit it. The decision was, however, doubted in the case of *R v Khan, Sakkaravej and Pamarapa*.[1153] Pamarapa, a Thai diplomat, was convicted of importing around £5 million of drugs into the United Kingdom. He was met at Heathrow by Sakkaravej. Pamarapa was wearing his diplomatic identity card, but was nonetheless arrested. His suitcase had already been searched in the hold of the aircraft and on arrest his hand luggage was searched. The prosecution case was that Khan's father had organised the importation and Khan had overseen it because his father was terminally ill. The Thai government waived Pamarapa's diplomatic immunity. At the trial it was argued that the search of Pamarapa's suitcase was in breach of Article 36(2) of the Vienna Convention on Diplomatic Relations 1961, which is given the force of law in the UK by the Diplomatic Privileges Act 1964. Under the Convention the search should have taken place in Pamarapa's presence and then only if the customs/police had serious grounds to believe it contained prohibited goods, which, it was argued, they did not have. It was also argued that the arrest was unlawful and the subsequent search of his bag also unlawful. The trial judge refused to exclude the evidence of the search under section 78 or at common law. He found that there were grounds to believe the bags contained drugs, the only illegality was the absence of Pamarapa when the search took place. The Convention provided a right to search, which implied a right to detain, and therefore there was no unlawful arrest. Even if the second search was unlawful, there would be no unfairness in admitting it.

The Court of Appeal, dismissing the appellant's arguments, upheld the trial judge's exercise of his discretion. If the second search had been illegal, the trial judge had a

---

[1148] [1989] Crim LR 892.
[1149] [1990] Crim LR 425.
[1150] (1991) Crim LR 252.
[1151] *R v O'Leary* (1988) 87 Cr App R 387; *Samuel* (above).
[1152] [1989] Crim LR 142.
[1153] [1997] Crim LR 508.

discretion, not an obligation, to exclude it. Whilst acknowledging that section 78 had enlarged the judge's discretion to exclude evidence obtained by unfair means, it remained the effect on the fairness of the trial which was relevant, and only if this was subject to interference should the court conclude that the evidence should not be admitted. The trial judge correctly found that the first search did not taint the second, but even if there had been some lingering illegality, or further illegality in respect of Pamarapa's arrest, it had no effect on the quality of the evidence, or the fairness of admitting it.

Covert surveillance

A second major area where section 78 is often invoked concerns eavesdropping or covert electronic bugging. A number of cases have come before the Court of Appeal in recent years concerning covert surveillance both in custodial and non-custodial settings. Where the surveillance takes place in custody, it seems unlikely the courts will be keen to exclude the evidence. In *Bailey and Smith*,[1154] two suspects charged with robbery chose to remain silent when questioned by police. Unknown to the men, their cell had been bugged, and incriminating evidence was recorded. Dismissing their appeal, it was held that the police were under no duty to protect prisoners from making incriminating statements to one another, even in circumstances where they had exercised their right to silence.

Similarly, in *R v Loveridge and others*,[1155] three defendants were convicted of robbery after the prosecution had relied on a covert video recording of them waiting in the holding area of a magistrates' court. An expert witness compared the video-recording with film taken by a surveillance camera at the scene of the robbery, and concluded that the defendants were those depicted in the surveillance camera. The trial judge accepted that the recording contravened section 41 of the Criminal Justice Act 1925, which makes filming in the precincts of a court unlawful. However, while not approving or encouraging the tactics adopted by the police, the judge determined that the admissibility of the video film would not have an adverse effect on the fairness of the trial.

The Court of Appeal agreed. It was accepted that filming in the court was unlawful being a breach of section 41 of the 1925 Act, and that there may also have been a breach of the Codes of Practice or Article 8 of the European Convention. However, so far as the outcome of the appeal was concerned, such breaches were only relevant if they interfered with the right of the defendants to a fair hearing. Satisfied that the fairness of the hearing had not been subject to interference, the Court of Appeal ruled that the judge had been entitled to admit the evidence. Collectively, the evidence of the involvement of each of the defendants was overwhelming. The trial was fair and the convictions were not in any way unsafe.

However, bugging a meeting between solicitor and client, which is legally privileged, is considered much more reprehensible. As stated by Lord Taylor in *R v Derby Magistrates' Court, ex p B*,[1156] '[l]egal privilege is … much more than an ordinary rule of evidence … [i]t is a fundamental condition on which the administration of justice rests'.[1157] The Court of Appeal confirmed this principle in *R v Grant*,[1158] and the common law largely mirrors the

---

[1154](1993) 97 Cr App R 365.
[1155](2001) *The Times*, 3 May.
[1156][1996] AC 487, 507.
[1157] *Ibid.*, 507.
[1158](2005), *The Times*, 12 May.

jurisprudence of the European Court of Human Rights.[1159] Thus a breach of Article 5 of
the European Convention on Human Rights can be found even if it cannot be proved that
the accused did not have a fair trial as long as it is shown that there was an infringement of
the right to confidential legal advice. In *R v Sutherland and others*,[1160] Mr Justice Newman
held that the prosecution of five men for murder could not proceed owing to an abuse
of process. Police in Grantham, Lincolnshire, who suspected the defendants had been
involved in a murder, were granted permission under the Regulation of Investigatory
Powers Act 2000 to place listening devices in the cells and communal areas at two police
stations.[1161] In the event, a listening device was also placed in the exercise area and
conversations between the defendants and their solicitors were also recorded in breach
of the defendants' right to legal privilege. The prosecution did not seek to use these
conversations in evidence, and therefore section 78 could not be relied upon. However,
although the police denied listening to the taped conversations between lawyer and client
or making any use of them, the trial judge did not accept this. He held that knowledge
of the conversations must have informed their decisions and their use of the privileged
conversations prejudiced the defendants and amounted to an abuse of process. The trial
judge concluded that 'in this case justice had been affronted in a grave way' and said he
was satisfied that there could be no fair trial into all the issues to which the trial gave rise.

Outside of custodial settings, eavesdropping on suspects is becoming increasingly
commonplace as technology advances and bugging devices become smaller. In *R v Chalkley
and Jeffries*,[1162] the prosecution sought to rely on covertly obtained tape-recordings of
conversations between the defendants, charged with conspiracy to rob. In order to obtain
the recordings, police arrested Chalkley and his partner on unrelated charges and, in their
absence, entered their house and planted a listening device. The defence, contending that
it would be fundamentally unfair to admit the recordings, argued that they should be
excluded using section 78. The trial judge concluded that he was obliged to conduct a
balancing exercise between the interests of justice, the effective prosecution of offences,
and the wider public interest in discouraging the abuse of police power. He concluded
that, in this particular case, the balance lay with the effective prosecution of offences and
admitted the evidence. The defendants then changed their plea to guilty.

On appeal, the primary question was whether in these circumstances the Court of
Appeal had the power to quash a conviction following a guilty plea. The Court concluded
that it did not, and whilst that was enough to determine the outcome of the appeal, the
Court went on to consider the arguments put forward in relation to section 78. It concluded
that there was no basis for the defence submission that admission of the taped conversations
would have such an adverse effect on the fairness of the proceedings that they ought to
have been excluded. Accordingly, the appeals were dismissed on that ground as well.
In doing so, the Court of Appeal disapproved of the way in which the trial judge came
to the same conclusion using a balancing exercise drawn from case law concerning the
abuse of process, and made further observations on the scope and effect of section 78. In
particular, the court noted that the reference in the provision to 'the circumstances in which
the evidence was obtained' was not intended to widen the common law rule stated by Lord
Diplock in *Sang* to the effect that the judge has 'no discretion to refuse to admit relevant and

---

[1159]See *Lanz v Austria* (App No 24430/94, 31 January 2002); *S v Switzerland* (1992) 14 EHRR 670; *Niemitz v
Germany* (1992) 16 EHRR 97; *Brennan v UK* (2002) 34 EHRR 18.
[1160]Unreported, 29 January 2002.
[1161]See discussion below at pp 300–01 on the Regulation of Investigatory Powers Act 2000.
[1162][1998] 2 All ER 155.

otherwise admissible evidence solely on the ground that it was obtained by improper or unfair means'.[1163] The quality and reliability of the evidence had to be considered; therefore the trial judge had been wrong to apply the balancing process applicable to abuse of process cases in relation to section 78. The appellant took his case to the European Court of Human Rights claiming a breach of Article 6(1), but the Court found that proper procedure had been followed and it had not been unfair to admit the surveillance evidence.[1164]

The decision in *Chalkley and Jeffries* was applied in *R v Hardy and another*.[1165] Undercover officers answered an advertisement by BH and subsequently met with him, and then proceeded to record conversations concerning the smuggling of cannabis. One of the officers then drove BH's lorry to the Netherlands and collected a consignment of cannabis, which was then swapped for dummy packages, before delivery to BH. BH and others were then arrested and charged with conspiracy to supply cannabis. At the trial the defence sought disclosure of the authority for surveillance. The judge refused because the surveillance was clearly properly authorised and therefore of no help to the defence. However, the prosecution did disclose the authorities in reduced form. The defence submission, that the tape-recording was an interception of communications which was neither in conformity with the Regulation of Investigatory Powers Act 2000 nor with the ECHR, was rejected by the trial judge. Hardy's appeal against conviction was dismissed. The Court of Appeal noted that tape-recording was not an interception of communications, but was essentially the same as a face-to-face recording. It had been properly authorised and properly admitted.

It is impossible, however, to ignore the human rights dimension of cases involving covert surveillance. Article 8 of the European Convention seeks to protect privacy and the right to a family life. Although a right to privacy never evolved under the common law, the desirability of such a concept has received a considerable degree of attention in recent years, particularly in the post-Human Rights Act era. With respect to covert surveillance, the leading case is *R v Khan*,[1166] which was heard by the House of Lords before the Human Rights Bill was even drafted. Police were suspicious of the behaviour of the appellant, who had recently arrived in the UK from Pakistan. Covert listening devices were placed at the home of a third party, a suspected drug dealer, which recorded K making a number of incriminatory statements concerning the supply of heroin. K was convicted of being knowingly concerned in the importation of a Class A controlled drug, and appealed alleging that the evidence obtained by the listening device should have been excluded under section 78.

The defence contention was that a private conversation in a private house was analogous to a private telephone call, the interception of which is governed by the Interception of Communications Act 1986 and the decision of the European Court of Human Rights in *Malone v United Kingdom*.[1167] Section 9 of the 1986 Act forbade the use in evidence of material used by the interception of communications and a similar restriction should be applied to materials obtained by aural surveillance devices. Lord Nolan, delivering the decision of the House of Lords, rejected this argument because it required the formulation of two new principles: (a) that the appellant enjoyed a right of privacy in respect of the taped conversation; and (b) that evidence of a conversation obtained in breach of that right was inadmissible. There was no such right of privacy in English law, and even if there

[1163]See also *Khan*, discussed in depth below.
[1164]*Chalkey v UK* [2003] Crim LR 51.
[1165][2003] 1 Cr App R 30.
[1166][1997] AC 558.
[1167](1984) 7 EHRR 14.

were, evidence obtained improperly or even unlawfully, remained admissible, subject to the trial judge's power to exclude it at his discretion.

Turning to the issue of whether the judge should have exercised his discretion to exclude the evidence in the exercise of his common law discretion or under section 78, Lord Nolan stated the only relevant element of the common law discretion was that part which authorised the judge 'to exclude evidence if it is necessary in order to secure a fair trial for the accused'.[1168] It was unnecessary to consider the common law position separately from that under section 78, since both are concerned with securing a fair trial. In response, the civil liberties group, Liberty, contended that if the evidence had been obtained in breach of the European Convention (which under Article 8 does include a right to privacy) then that should be regarded as grounds for excluding what was otherwise admissible evidence.

In Lord Nolan's view, while the principles reflected in the European Convention could hardly be irrelevant to the exercise of the section 78 power under English law, there was nothing unlawful about a breach of privacy (note that the case was decided well before the Human Rights Act took effect). The appellant's case rested wholly upon the lack of statutory authorisation for that particular breach of privacy (it then being authorised under administrative guidelines laid down by the Secretary of State) and the consequent infringement of Article 8. In these circumstances the appellant could no more succeed on this second issue than he could on the first. Even if the evidence had been obtained in breach of Article 8 or, for that matter, in breach of the law of a foreign country, that fact would be of no greater significance per se than if it constituted a breach of English law. Upon the facts of the instant case, their Lordships considered that the judge was fully entitled to hold that the circumstances in which the relevant evidence was obtained, even if they constituted a breach of Article 8, were not such as to require the exclusion of the evidence. Lord Nolan went on to say that it would be a strange reflection of our law if a man who had admitted his participation in the illegal importation of a large quantity of heroin should have his conviction set aside on the ground that his privacy had been invaded. This was a serious criminal offence, and the police had acted within Home Office protocols, notwithstanding the absence of any statutory regulation. While the American exclusionary principle does permit the guilty man to go free if his privacy or other rights are infringed, the English common law principle, and the statutory power under section 78, do not. The appeal was dismissed.

Though unsuccessful in the domestic courts, Khan took his case to Strasbourg and was successful in alleging a breach of Article 8.[1169] The Strasbourg Court found that since domestic law did not regulate the use of covert listening devices at the time of the applicant's conviction, the actions of the police did constitute a violation of Article 8. The Court went on to state that not only should some form of regulation have been in place, but that 'the law must be sufficiently clear in its terms to give individuals an adequate indication as to the circumstances in which and the conditions on which public authorities are entitled to resort to such covert measures'.[1170] Importantly, however, the failure of the judge at first instance to exclude the evidence was found not to constitute a violation of Article 6. The discretionary mechanism to exclude evidence if it would lead to substantive unfairness (section 78) was sufficient to protect the applicant's right to a fair trial.

As the decision in *Khan* suggests, Article 8 is not an absolute right. Violations of the right can be justified by signatory states, providing it is shown that such an interference 'is in

---

[1168] *Ibid.*, 578, citing Lord Griffiths in *Scott v The Queen* [1989] AC 1242, 1256.
[1169] *Khan v United Kingdom* App No 35394/97, 12 May 2000.
[1170] *Ibid.*, at [26].

accordance with the law and is necessary in a democratic society in the interests of national security, public safety or the economic well-being of the country, for the prevention of disorder or crime, for the protection of health or morals, or for the protection of the rights and freedoms of others'.[1171] However, any state seeking to rely on Article 8(2) as a defence must first illustrate that the interference is prescribed in law: this was not the case either in *Khan* or in the earlier case of *Malone*. Even if such a law does exist, the state must then show that is proportionate for the purposes of achieving one of the objectives in Article 8(2). This was a hurdle that Germany failed to overcome in *Klass v Germany*.[1172] The law in question permitted the police to intercept mail in certain circumstances. The court found that this situation constituted a 'menace of surveillance' for all citizens who made use of the postal service. This was a 'menace' that violated the freedom of communication between individuals, and constituted a breach of Convention requirements. The Court noted that:

> Powers of secret surveillance of citizens, characterizing as they do the police state, are tolerable under the Convention only in so far as strictly necessary for safeguarding the democratic institutions.[1173]

There has, however, been relatively little discussion of the suspect's right to privacy in a police station, even by the Strasbourg Court. It did, however, arise in the case of *PG and JH v United Kingdom*,[1174] where the use of covert listening devices in a police station was held to violate Article 8. Here, B was suspected of preparing for a robbery, and authorisation was then given for listening devices to be placed in his flat. However, after B and others discovered the bugs, they left the flat and the police began to think that the robbery had been called off. Several days later, B and others were arrested in a stolen car containing two black balaclavas, five black plastic cable ties, two pairs of leather gloves and two army rucksacks. In order to obtain speech samples to compare with the tapes from the flat, police were granted authorisation to use covert listening devices in the cells and on the police officers who were to be present when B and others were charged. Evidence derived from the listening devices was admitted at their trial for conspiracy to rob. They were convicted and their appeal was rejected.

The Strasbourg Court, applying its own decision in *Khan v UK*, held that the use of a covert listening device in B's flat was not in accordance with the law existing at the time as there was no statutory provision for surveillance. Similarly, the Court held that there was a breach of Article 8 in respect of the use of covert surveillance devices in the police station. However, no breach was found in respect of Article 6, the right to a fair trial. The taped evidence was not the only evidence against B and the others. There was ample opportunity to challenge both the authenticity and the use of the recordings. Even though the domestic courts had declined to exclude the evidence, the Court further considered that there was no unfairness in leaving it to the jury, on the basis of a thorough summing up by the trial judge, to decide where the weight of the evidence lay. The defence claim that the use of voice samples to compare with other recordings was a breach of their right not to incriminate themselves was rejected by the Court which saw these as akin to the use of blood or other samples used in forensic analysis to which that right did not apply. This decision is consistent with those considered above where the fact that the evidence was obtained unlawfully does not necessarily mean that admitting it will have such an adverse effect on the fairness of the trial that it ought not to be admitted.

[1171] Art 8(2).
[1172] (1978) 2 EHRR 214.
[1173] *Ibid.*, [3f].
[1174] App No 44787/98, 25 September 2001.

The interaction between Articles 6, 8 and section 78 of PACE was considered again in *Allan v United Kingdom*.[1175] The applicant, who had been arrested for robbery, contended that his Article 8 rights had been infringed when police tapped his cell and the prison visiting area in order to obtain evidence that he had been responsible for a murder. Following his arrest, Allan chose to remain silent, but the prosecution relied upon three statements he had made to his cellmate; to his friend who had visited him; and to another police informant briefly placed in the cell alongside him. His application to the European Court of Human Rights rested on the argument that the judge should have ruled out the statements as they were unfairly obtained and infringed his right to privacy. The government accepted, on the basis of *Khan*, that the lack of any regulatory regime did mean that Article 8 had indeed been infringed. However, they contested the allegation that use of the evidence interfered with the fairness of proceedings, contrary to Article 6. In relation to the first two statements, made to his cellmate and to his visiting friend, the Court held that there was nothing inherently contrary to Article 6 in the way in which the evidence was used. The judge had taken a decision to admit them at the *voir dire*, and taking into account all relevant factors, had concluded that the evidence was reliable and its use would not result in an unfair trial. However, the Court came to a different conclusion in relation to the evidence obtained by the police informer. Inculpatory statements made by the applicants were not made voluntarily, but instead had been induced by persistent questioning by the informer. As such, these statements were unreliable and thus affected the fairness of the trial.

In summary then, from the perspective of European human rights law, covert surveillance of any type is likely to fall foul of Article 8 if it is not regulated by legislation. Where some form of regulation is in place, each alleged interference must be considered on the particular facts and circumstances of each case, taking into account the clarity of the relevant law, the basis for surveillance and whether the actions of the state can be regarded as proportionate. That use of surveillance is an interference with rights protected by Article 8 of the European Convention on Human Rights and is prima facie a violation of those rights unless the interference is in accordance with the law, is in pursuit of one or more of the legitimate aims established by Article 8(2) and is 'necessary in a democratic society'.

In response to these decisions, the use of electronic surveillance is now much more closely regulated in the United Kingdom. The Police Act 1997 stipulates that the use of covert listening devices by the police in private places, such as homes, offices and hotel bedrooms first requires prior authorisation by a Commissioner, unless the need for surveillance is urgent, in which case a Commissioner must be informed as soon as practicable. Forms of surveillance not covered by the Police Act are mostly regulated by the Regulation of Investigatory Powers Act 2000 (RIPA), which covers 'directed surveillance', 'intrusive surveillance' and the use of covert human intelligence sources.

'Directed surveillance' is a type of covert surveillance where police, intelligence agencies and other public authorities observe an individual in public and record their actions. It is not intrusive, and is undertaken for the purposes of a specific investigation in such a manner as is likely to result in the obtaining of private information about a person, (whether or not specifically identified for the purpose of the investigation or operation).[1176]

[1175] (2002) 36 EHRR 12.

[1176] RIPA 2000, section 26(2). Directed surveillance can be ordered by a superintendent, or, if a superintendent is not available, an inspector. Authorised surveillance must be proportionate to what is sought to be achieved by carrying it out, and must meet one of the grounds set out in section 3. These are (a) the interests of

'Intrusive surveillance' would include surveillance by an individual or device on residential premises or in a private vehicle (i.e. from an observation point), but observing activity elsewhere would be classed as directed surveillance.[1177] The main issue is that the surveillance is carried out in relation to anything taking place on any residential premises or in a private vehicle and involves the presence of an individual on residential premises or in a private vehicle etc. This is considerably more contentious than directed surveillance, since it involves interference with privacy, and a potential prima facie breach of Article 8 of the Convention. If any public authority wishes to engage in intrusive surveillance, authorisation must be sought by either the Secretary of State or a senior authorising officer.[1178] Permission may be granted providing the surveillance is considered proportionate,[1179] and if such action is necessary:

(a) in the interests of national security;

(b) for the purpose of preventing or detecting serious crime; or

(c) in the interests of the economic well-being of the United Kingdom.[1180]

In addition to authorisation by the authorising officer, the grant (or renewal) of an authorisation for intrusive surveillance must be approved by a Surveillance Commissioner unless the case is one of urgency.[1181]

The conduct of covert human intelligence sources is also dealt with in the legislation. Under section 26(8), a person is considered a covert human intelligence source under section 26(8) of the Act if he or she:

(a) establishes or maintains a personal or other relationship with another person for the covert purpose of facilitating the doing of anything falling within paragraph (b) or (c) below;

(b) covertly uses such a relationship to obtain information or to provide access to any information to another person; or

(c) covertly discloses information obtained by the use of such a relationship or as a consequence of the existence of such a relationship.

Covert human intelligence sources would therefore include informants, whistleblowers or undercover police officers. Examples would be placing a police informer in a cell, as in *Allan v UK*, or the use of officers as part of an operation to apprehend those dealing in drugs or stolen goods, as in *Looseley* or *Christou* (see further in the chapter). An authorisation to use a covert human intelligence source must be made on the same grounds as for directed surveillance set out above. It must therefore be proportionate and, in addition, meet one of the statutory criteria stipulated in section 29(3).

---

national security; (b) for the purpose of preventing or detecting crime or of preventing disorder; (c) in the interests of the economic well-being of the United Kingdom; (d) in the interests of public safety; (e) for the purpose of protecting public health; (f) for the purpose of assessing or collecting any tax, duty, levy or other imposition, contribution or charge payable to a government department; or (g) for any purpose (not falling within paragraphs (a) to (f)) which is specified for the purposes of this subsection by an order made by the Secretary of State. The authorisation must be granted by the Chief Constable where the likely consequence of the directed surveillance would be for any person to acquire knowledge of confidential material.

[1177] RIPA 2000, section 26(3).
[1178] In the case of the police, this will usually be a Chief Constable.
[1179] RIPA 2000, section 32(3).
[1180] RIPA 2000, section 32(3).
[1181] RIPA 2000, section 35.

Undercover operations and entrapment

Operations involving covert 'human intelligence sources' have traditionally been referred to in straightforward layman's terms as 'undercover' or 'sting' operations. *R v Christou*[1182] is a classic case. A jewellery shop, 'Stardust Jewellers', was set up in London, staffed by undercover officers who made it known that they would be prepared to deal in stolen property. All the transactions were recorded by covert video cameras and sound equipment, and sellers were asked to sign receipts for the money that they had received. The defendants, who had sold stolen items to the shop on a number of occasions, were convicted of burglary and handling stolen goods. They appealed, alleging that the evidence of the undercover operation should have been excluded either at common law or under section 78.

The Court of Appeal agreed with the decision at first instance to admit the evidence. Although the police had practised a form of trickery, they had not acted as *agents provocateurs* in the sense that they did not encourage the commission of a crime that had not already taken place. In the words of Lord Taylor, 'the trick was not applied to the appellants; they voluntarily applied themselves to the trick'.[1183] The trial judge, by considering the operation as a whole, had exercised his discretion correctly. Code C of the Codes of Practice was primarily devised to protect potentially vulnerable parties from the abuse or pressure from police officers under questioning, and did not apply in these circumstances, where the suspects were not aware of the true identity of the police officers. As such, they interacted in equal terms. By way of a caveat, it was added that it would be wrong for police to use such an undercover operation simply to evade the Code of Practice's provisions and evidence obtained in that way should normally be excluded. Observations were also made on the nature of the bases for exclusion under common law and the 1984 Act. Both thresholds were essentially the same; it would be illogical to have differing standards in place.

The *Christou* test, which seemed to hinge upon whether or not the defendants had voluntarily applied themselves to the trick, was applied in three subsequent Court of Appeal decisions which followed shortly afterwards. In the first of those decisions, *Bryce*,[1184] it was held that evidence of the conversations between the appellant and an undercover police officer should have been excluded because these conversations went directly to the crucial issue of guilty knowledge, they were hotly disputed, and, in contrast to *Christou*, there was no contemporary record of them. As noted in the previous chapter however, a preferable avenue for their exclusion should have been section 76(2)(b), since the decision seemed to be based more on concerns about the reliability of the statements rather than the potential impact upon the fairness of the proceedings.

In the second case, *MacLean and Kosten*,[1185] D was found to be carrying cannabis through customs concealed in a car. Anxious to catch the importer as well as the courier, a story was concocted whereby the courier was said to be in hospital following a road accident. Subsequently, and according to plan, the importer arranged to recover the car in order to obtain his order of cannabis. He appealed against conviction on the grounds that the evidence should have been excluded since it had been unfairly obtained through trickery. Dismissing the appeal, it was held that there had been nothing unfair about the means

---

[1182] [1992] 2 QB 979.
[1183] *Ibid.*, 989.
[1184] [1992] 4 All ER 567.
[1185] [1993] Crim LR 687.

adopted to make D incriminate himself since he had already committed the crime in question.

The third case to follow on the heels of *Christou* concerned the more contentious circumstances that arose in *Williams and O'Hare*.[1186] The defendants were charged with interfering with a motor vehicle with intent to commit theft. Police had left an unlocked and unattended van in a busy high street where there had been a high rate of vehicle crime. Imitation cigarette cartons were visible through its rear window. The appellants were observed walking around the van and removing cartons from it. Following conviction, it was contended that the evidence against them should have been excluded by the trial judge under section 78 PACE on the ground of entrapment. Dismissing the appeal, the Court found in favour of the Crown. Applying *Christou*, the Court underlined that they did not act as *agents provocateurs* because they made no communication with the defendants and did not set out to catch any particular thieves when they placed the van. Central to their decision was the fact that the appellants committed the crime 'voluntarily, of their own free will'.[1187] They had, according to Farquharson LJ , committed the act as a result of their inherent 'criminal instincts' rather than as a result of the actions of the police.[1188] As Geoffrey Robertson contends,[1189] the proper application of the *Christou* test is highly questionable, since there was no basis (as there was in *Christou*) for suspecting that they would have committed the act in question had the sting operation not been put in place. While the court highlighted the absence of any verbal act of incitement or encouragement, no explanation was given as to why the physical act of tempting persons to commit a crime is fundamentally different from the verbal one. As Robertson notes:

> This decision appears to allow section 78 to operate in cases where the incitement to crime comes from the mouth of an *agent provocateur* but not where the temptation, however hard to resist, results from a carefully laid trap which contains its own lure. The distinction is artificial, but it has permitted police to take 'crime initiatives' which initiate crime, yet which are described as 'entirely legitimate enterprise'.[1190]

Following these cases, it appeared questionable as to whether circumstances of entrapment would ever give rise to an obligation to exclude evidence.[1191] In *Smurthwaite and Gill* however,[1192] the Court of Appeal made clear that it could do so, subject to the application of a number of factors by the trial judge in the exercise of his section 78 discretion. Both appellants (in two separate cases) were convicted of soliciting a contract killer to murder their spouses. In each case the police sent undercover officers to pose as contract killers and recorded the conversations. Arguing that the police should be considered to be acting as *agents provocateurs*, they contended on appeal that all the covert recording should have been excluded. In an echo of the House of Lords decision in *Sang*, the Court of Appeal repeated that the fact that the evidence was obtained by entrapment, or by *agent provocateur* or by a trick did not place the judge under an obligation to exclude it. Such actions were not, however, entirely irrelevant; but

---

[1186] (1994) 98 Cr App R 209.

[1187] *Ibid.*, 213.

[1188] *Ibid.*, 215.

[1189] Robertson, G 'Entrapment evidence: manna from heaven, or fruit of the poisoned tree?' [1994] Crim LR 805.

[1190] *Ibid.*, at 811.

[1191] This was the view of Stocker LJ in *Harwood* [1989] Crim LR 285, who stated that section 78 could not be used as a basis for exclusion in entrapment cases.

[1192] [1994] 1 All ER 898.

any decision to exclude evidence on that basis must be taken through the application of the statutory test. In deciding whether such actions might have an adverse effect on the fairness of proceedings, Lord Taylor proceeded to list a number of 'relevant factors' which should be taken into account by the trial judge in arriving at his decision. These were:

> Was the officer acting as an agent provocateur in the sense that he was enticing the defendant to commit an offence he would not have otherwise committed? What was the nature of any entrapment? Does the evidence consist of admission to a completed offence or does it consist of the actual commission of an offence? How active or passive was the offficer's role in obtaining the evidence? Is there an unassailable record of what occurred or is it strongly corroborated? Further consideration for the judge in deciding whether to admit an undercover officer's evidence is if he has abused his role as a police officer to ask questions and if they are in accordance with the codes.[1193]

The Court of Appeal thus departed from *Sang* in acknowledging that entrapment may give rise to procedural unfairness that might warrant exclusion. The Court suggested a series of guidelines as to when section 78 might come into play, but the decision stopped short of offering any solid, guiding principle that would add any element of predictability as to how entrapment evidence would be treated at first instance.

Entrapment may not only produce circumstances that require the exclusion of evidence under section 78, but may also lead the court to stay a prosecution on grounds of abuse of process. Such a scenario arose in *R v Latif and Shahzad*,[1194] which concerned a plan to import heroin from Pakistan. The plan was partly instigated and organised by a police informer along with offers from Customs and Excise. Despite acknowledging that the offence would probably never have been committed but for the role played by the authorities, the House of Lords acknowledged that the case posed something of a conundrum. If, on the one hand, prosecutions were always to be stayed in such circumstances, this would have an inevitable knock-on effect on the protection of the public. If, on the other hand, courts refused blankly to stay proceedings, then that would undermine public confidence in the criminal justice system. It was thus required to chart a middle course between these two extreme options. The proper approach advocated by their Lordships comprised a two-pronged test. First, it should be asked whether the conduct in question rendered a fair trial impossible. If the answer was 'yes', it would be appropriate to stay proceedings at that point. If the answer was 'no', the second limb of the test asked whether, despite a fair trial being possible, proceedings should be nonetheless stayed on the grounds of 'an affront to the public conscience'. Applying this test to the scenario before the Court, their Lordships held that the judge had rightfully declined to stay proceedings. He had properly taken into account all the relevant considerations, including the fact that Shazad was a major importer in the heroin trade and had initially proposed the operation.

In the aftermath of the decision, judges at first instance were thus left with a choice on what to do in cases where an unfair trial might be the result of entrapment by the authorities. They could either exclude the evidence under section 78 PACE where the evidence-gathering adversely affected the fairness of the case, or stay proceedings for abuse of process by executive authorities. Furthermore, courts faced an additional challenge in that

---

[1193] *Ibid.*, at 903.
[1194] [1996] 1 WLR 104.

the Human Rights Act was shortly to enter in force. Increasingly, therefore, jurisprudence from Strasbourg on the matter had to be taken into account.

The leading Strasbourg case was that of *Texiera de Castro v Portugal*.[1195] The case concerned an offer to purchase drugs made by undercover police operators to a suspected dealer. The applicant, who was previously unknown to the police, had been introduced to the officers by a third party. Unaware of the identity of the undercover officers, the applicant was offered cash in the back of a car in exchange for a quantity of heroin. After he had obtained it for them, he was arrested and convicted on the basis of the undercover operation.

The applicant contended that he had not had a fair trial, since he had been incited to commit the offence by the plain-clothes officers. He maintained that he had no previous convictions and would never have committed the offence had it not been for the intervention of the police as *agents provocateurs*. In addition, he argued that the police officers had acted on their own initiative, without any supervision by the courts, and without any preliminary investigation. The Court agreed that there had been a violation of his fair trial rights. The key basis for the decision was the fact that the officers had taken on an active role in procuring the offence. A distinction was made with those cases where the police attempted to purchase drugs from known suppliers, which would not ordinarily amount to a breach of Article 6.

The impact of the decision on domestic law was considered in *Nottingham City Council v Amin*,[1196] which provides a useful illustration of the distinction between *causing* the commission of the offence and providing an *opportunity* for its commission. The defendant had been charged with running a taxi within an area where it was not licensed to ply for hire. The taxi was hailed by two plain clothes officers, who duly paid their fare before charging the driver with plying for hire without a licence. At first instance, the magistrate excluded the evidence on the ground that the police had acted as *agents provocateurs*, and accepted the argument of the accused that he would not have committed the offence in question but for the actions of the officers. Reversing the decision of the magistrate, and distinguishing the case from *Teixera*, the Divisional Court found that there had been no incitement or pressure placed on the defendant to commit the offence. As Lord Bingham of Cornhill CJ observed:

> On the one hand it has been recognised as deeply offensive to ordinary notions of fairness if a defendant were to be convicted and punished for committing a crime which he only committed because he had been incited, instigated, persuaded, pressurised or wheedled into committing it by a law enforcement officer. On the other hand it has been recognised that law enforcement agencies have a general duty to the public to enforce the law and it has been regarded as unobjectionable if a law enforcement officer gives a defendant an opportunity to break the law, of which the defendant freely takes advantage, in circumstances where it appears that the defendant would have behaved in the same way if the opportunity had been offered by anyone else.[1197]

For Lord Bingham, the fact that this particular fare involved two undercover police officers did not provide a basis for abuse of process, since they had acted as ordinary members of the public. They did not wave £50 notes or pretend to be in distress, and this suggested that the defendant would have provided a fare for anyone else who flagged him down.

[1195](1998) 28 EHRR 101.
[1196][2001] 1 WLR 1071.
[1197]*Ibid.*, 1076–1077.

Each case must turn on its own facts, and crucial to this decision was the fact that the police did not take on any active role in applying pressure.

The leading case on entrapment is now *R v Looseley; AG's Reference (No 3 of 2000)*.[1198] This joined case brings together many of the different strands of the above cases, and provides a relative degree of clarity on the position of entrapment in domestic law post-HRA. Looseley, a known heroin dealer, contended that he had been lured into supplying drugs by an undercover police officer. In the second case, the defendant, G, had been acquitted, following the trial judge's decision to stay proceedings for abuse of process. The facts here were somewhat different. The Prosecution contended that undercover officers supplied the defendant with contraband cigarettes, and one then asked the defendant whether he could 'sort out any brown'. The defendant, it seems, took some persuading, and told the officers that he 'wasn't really into heroin'. He eventually obtained it from another source, and duly supplied it, but in the police interview he told them that he had 'nothing at all' to do with heroin, and only agreed to supply it as a favour after the two men had approached him offering cheap cigarettes.

The House of Lords acknowledged the absence of any doctrine of entrapment in English law, but also stated that proceedings should be stayed where the actions of the police were so seriously improper as to bring the administration of justice into disrepute. To that end, a useful guide was to consider whether the police 'did no more than present the defendant with an unexceptional opportunity to commit a crime'.[1199] In the view of Lord Nicholls, four factors ought to be taken into account in deciding whether conduct should be classified as "seriously improper":

> *The nature of the offence.* The use of proactive techniques is more needed and, hence, more appropriate, in some circumstances than others. The secrecy and difficulty of detection, and the manner in which the particular criminal activity is carried on, are relevant considerations.
> *The reason for the particular police operation.* It goes without saying that the police must act in good faith and not, for example, as part of a malicious vendetta against an individual or group of individuals. Having reasonable grounds for suspicion is one way good faith may be established, but having grounds for suspicion of a particular individual is not always essential. Sometimes suspicion may be centred on a certain place, such as a particular public house. Sometimes random testing may be the only practicable way of policing a particular trading activity.

> *The nature and extent of police participation in the crime.* The greater the inducement held out by the police, and the more forceful or persistent the police overtures, the more readily may a court conclude that the police overstepped the boundary: their conduct might well have brought about the commission of a crime by a person who would normally avoid crime of that kind. In assessing the weight to be attached to the police inducement, regard is to be had to the defendant's circumstances, including his vulnerability. This is not because the standards of acceptable behaviour are variable. Rather, this is a recognition that what may be a significant inducement to one person may not be so to another. For the police to behave as would an ordinary customer of a trade, whether lawful or unlawful, being carried on by the defendant will not normally be regarded as objectionable.

> *The defendant's criminal record.* The defendant's criminal record is unlikely to be relevant unless it can be linked to other factors grounding reasonable suspicion that the defendant is currently engaged in criminal activity...[1200]

[1198] [2001] 1 WLR 2060.
[1199] *Ibid.*, 2069.
[1200] *Ibid.*, 2070.

As a general principle, it would be acceptable for police officers to provide a person with an unexceptional opportunity to commit an offence crime and, if they proceeded to do so freely, then there were no grounds for exclusion of evidence or abuse of process. However, if a person committed an offence where they would not have ordinarily done so, following some form of inducement or allurement, this would serve to undermine the need for the police to carry out their work in good faith. This position was in line with the decision of the European Court of Human Rights in *Teixeira* and, where a violation had resulted, the appropriate remedy was a stay of proceedings under the abuse of process doctrine. In relation to the two cases before the court, it was acceptable in Looseley's case for an officer to pose as an addict looking for drugs, since he was a known dealer. By contrast, in relation to the other case, the officers had overstepped the boundary since they had incited and encouraged G to commit an uncharacteristic offence. Their actions were so seriously improper as to bring the administration of justice into disrepute, and thus the proceedings had been properly stayed. The abuse of process doctrine, rather than section 78, was the appropriate remedy in this type of situation. The latter provision was directed 'primarily at matters going to fairness in the actual conduct of the trial; for instance, the reliability of the evidence and the defendant's ability to test its reliability'.[1201] However, even if the threshold for abuse of process is not met, it would seemingly remain open for the evidence to be excluded under section 78'.

The decision in *Looseley* was applied in the unreported case of *Moon*.[1202] Following considerable persuasion by an undercover policewoman, the accused had supplied her with a small quantity of heroin which she obtained from a dealer. While she pleaded guilty to an offence of possession, she contested the charge of supply on the ground that she had been entrapped. The judge refused her application to stay the prosecution because, although procedural errors were made, the undercover operation was found to be largely bona fide since, in his opinion, the defendant would have committed the offence even if the errors had not been made. However, the appellant's conviction was quashed on appeal. Whilst agreeing that the undercover police operation had been bona fide, there was no evidence that she would have been prepared to supply any would-be purchaser. Moon had no predisposition to deal and had no previous history of dealing. Furthermore, it was the police officer who made the first approach. Taking these factors into account, the Court concluded that the appellant had been lured into committing the offence, and, following *Looseley*, the proceedings should have been stayed.

Certainly, in the light of *Looseley*, a considerable degree of clarity has been shed on the law. In determining whether proceedings should be stayed on grounds of entrapment, each case will continue to turn on its own facts. However, it is now clear that a defendant who commits an offence that he or she would not have otherwise committed as a consequence of the actions of the authorities should normally have proceedings stayed. In those cases where conduct does not meet this threshold, section 78 remains available, though in such circumstances the courts are more concerned with the reliability of any statements made than the conduct of the police. However, there continues to be some degree of uncertainty as to when precisely actions of the police that fall short of the *Looseley* requirements may give rise to the adverse effect required for section 78 to be invoked.

[1201] *Ibid.*, 2066.
[1202] [2004] EWCA Crim 2872.

KEY LEARNING POINTS

- Improperly obtained evidence (other than confessions) may or may not be admissible in English law.
- The judge will have a discretion both at common law and statute as to whether the evidence should be admitted.
- For both forms of discretion, the key test will be whether the actions of the police have resulted in unfairness at the trial.
- Breaches of PACE and the Codes of Codes may have this effect if they are 'significant and substantial'.
- Covert surveillance will not normally be grounds for exclusion, although it should be properly authorised under the Police Act 1997 or RIPA 2000.
- There is no defence of entrapment in English law. However, where the actions of the police are so seriously improper as to bring the administration of justice into disrepute, proceedings should be stayed.

? QUESTIONS

(1) In *Sang* [1980] AC 402, Lord Diplock stated that a trial judge 'has no discretion to refuse to admit relevant admissible evidence on the ground that it was obtained by improper or unfair means' (at 437). Is this still an accurate summary of the law?

(2) Critically evaluate how serious violations of PACE and the Codes of Practice have to be before evidence will be ruled out under section 78.

(3) Police suspect that Joe and Dave are dealing in cannabis. Having kept them under close surveillance, two officers break into the flat one night after seeing the two men leaving. Without the appropriate authorisation, they install covert listening devices in the kitchen. Over the next two weeks, a number of incriminating statements are transmitted by the devices, but police fear they still do not have enough evidence to charge them.

Consequently, Jemima, an undercover officer is sent to a local pub where the two men have allegedly dealt cannabis on previous occasions. She approaches them in the car park, and asks whether they could supply her with some heroin. Joe tells her he 'doesn't do hard stuff', but Jemima says that if he could get hold of a large quantity for her, she would 'make it worth his while' and would pay 'through the roof'. A week later, the two men meet Jemima and supply her with the requested amount of heroin. Both men are arrested and prosecuted.

The prosecution now seek to use both the recordings transmitted by the listening devices and the heroin offered to Jemima as evidence against Joe and Dave.

Advise Joe and Dave.

SUGGESTED FURTHER READING

Ashworth, A 'Redrawing the boundaries of entrapment' [2002] Crim LR 161.

Choo, A and Nash, S section 'Improperly obtained evidence in the Commonwealth: lessons for England and Wales?' (2007) 11(2) *International Journal of Evidence and Proof* 75.

Ormerod, D 'ECHR and the exclusion of evidence: trial remedies for Article 8 breaches?' [2003] Crim LR 61

Ormerod, D and Birch, D 'The evolution of the discretionary exclusion of evidence'. [2004] Crim LR 767.

Ormerod, D and Roberts, P 'The trouble with Teixeira: Developing a principled approach to entrapment' (2002) 6(1) *International Journal of Evidence and Proof* 38.

Squires, D 'The problem with entrapment' 26(2) *Oxford Journal of Legal Studies* 351.

CHAPTER 10

OPINION EVIDENCE

INTRODUCTION

At the time of writing, the role played by opinion evidence in criminal trials is the source of considerable consternation. 'Opinion' has been defined by the Australian courts as 'an inference drawn or to be drawn from observed and communicable data,'[1203] and this definition, though seemingly broad, would appear to be widely accepted. As a general rule, evidence of opinion is inadmissible in criminal trials since it is the opinion of the jurors, and not the witnesses, which will determine the question of guilt. As this chapter demonstrates, it can, however, be difficult to draw a neat dividing line between what constitutes fact, and what constitutes opinion. After all, we are all accustomed to expressing opinions regularly in both our professional and personal lives. Each of us will hold an opinion about what is moral or immoral, what fashion we like, what music we like, and so on. Similarly, the general practitioner may well form an opinion about what is wrong with his patient on the grounds of what is said in his surgery and the barrister will form an opinion about the client's chances of success when he receives instructions from a solicitor. Of course, such opinions may be correct, or incorrect: a specialist consultation may reveal the general practitioner was wrong in his original diagnosis, and the barrister could eventually find the judge takes a rather different view of the strength of a particular case.

In terms of expressing an opinion in court, the law of evidence has developed two different sets of rules for experts and lay witnesses. Before proceeding to examine these in depth, it may be worth underlining why, rather suddenly, the use of opinion evidence has provoked such public debate. The current controversy has been largely triggered by a number of high profile miscarriages of justice which came to light in the early part of this decade. The first of these concerned a former solicitor, Sally Clark, who was convicted of murdering her two young children in November 1999. Both infants were found dead in their cots in 1996 and 1997, having seemingly suffered cot deaths. Evidence against her was largely circumstantial, although the prosecution sought to rely on the expert opinion of paediatrician Professor Sir Roy Meadow. Sir Roy stated his opinion that one cot death was a tragedy, two were suspicious, and three were murder, unless proven otherwise. More controversially, he proceeded to state that there was a 1:73 million chance that two children in the same family would die of cot death. This was despite the fact that the expert had no specialist knowledge of statistics. The jury convicted Ms Clark, but the conviction was quashed by the Court of Appeal in January 2003 on grounds that Sir Roy's presentation of the statistics and interpretation of them was misleading.[1204]

Sally Clark's appeal was followed shortly afterwards by that of Angela Cannings.[1205] Like Ms Clark, she had been convicted the previous year of murdering two infant children who had apparently suffered cot deaths. Again, the prosecution relied upon the evidence of Sir Roy Meadow. Once more, the appeal succeeded. Not long afterwards, a third high profile case with very similar facts, involving Donna Anthony, was again the subject of a

---

[1203] *All-State Life Insurance Co Ltd v Australian and New Zealand Bank Group Ltd (No 36)* (1996) 136 ALR 627, 629.
[1204] [2003] 2 FCR 447.
[1205] [2004] 1 WLR 2607.

successful appeal.[1206] Together, these cases provoked a backlash in the press, and resulted in a review of 297 other cases where convictions had been based on expert witness opinion. In February 2006, the Attorney-General announced that three of these cases should be reconsidered by the courts, but that the majority did not give cause for concern.[1207]

The recent media coverage of these miscarriages of justice has prompted increased discussion among lawyers and expert witnesses themselves as to how the opinion of experts should be presented in court and the weight that ought to be attached to it. Traditionally, a desire to uphold maximum freedom of proof by the parties has meant that both policy-makers and the courts have been reluctant to become overly involved in regulating what expert witnesses say. According to adversarial theory, if one party calls an expert who presents unreliable data or questionable evidence, the other party should be able to rebut it with expert evidence of their own. However, as the above-noted series of miscarriages have underlined, unfettered freedom of proof may no longer be quintessentially a 'good thing' if it results in innocent defendants being convicted in court.[1208]

It is against this backdrop that we proceed to discuss how the law of evidence deals with witnesses who wish to express an opinion in court. The vast majority of witnesses who testify are not considered 'experts' of any sort, but instead are regarded as witnesses to the fact. Their primary purpose will be to relate to the trier of fact what they did, saw or heard at a particular point in time. We shall begin by examining the rules concerning the opinions of non-expert witnesses, before proceeding to consider the rules regulating the opinions of experts later in the chapter.

NON-EXPERT WITNESSES

As a general rule, the role of a non-expert witness will be to provide evidence of what they perceived, which will be used by the prosecution or defence to either prove or disprove a particular fact in issue. This position is a natural corollary of the rule against hearsay, and it follows that witnesses are not permitted to express opinions about subjects that fall outside what they did, saw, or heard, etc. Opinion evidence will include drawing inferences from facts and forming value judgements.[1209] It would therefore be wrong for a witness to say 'I saw Tina there that evening, she's definitely guilty', or 'It couldn't have been Adam, he would never have done something like this'. Such statements are regarded as extraneous, and may act to confuse or prejudice the jury. This is known as the 'ultimate issue' rule, and is discussed in greater depth below in the context of expert witnesses.

However, if the opinion of the witness is so closely interlinked with other aspects of their testimony, the courts have recognised an exception to the rule and will usually permit opinion evidence where it cannot be neatly severed from events about which the witness is testifying. By way of example, imagine a robbery trial in which Mary alleges she was attacked on the street on the way home from the cinema. The attacker threatened her with a knife and stole her handbag. The defendant, James, claims he is the victim of mistaken identification and was at home alone on the evening in question. Mary will give evidence to the court as to where she was on the night in question, at what time she left the cinema, where she was going, etc. These are all facts, which Mary should be able to recollect from

---

[1206] [2005] EWCA Crim 952.
[1207] See *The Daily Telegraph*, 22 December 2004.
[1208] See further Wilson, A 'Expert Witness in the Dock' (2005) *J Crim L* 330.
[1209] Dennis, I *The Law of Evidence* (2007: London, Sweet and Maxwell), p 846.

her memory. In addition, she will typically be asked by prosecuting counsel to describe her attacker. She may reply that he was male, tall, lean, fair-haired and aged around 20 years old. James is in fact 23 years old, of medium height and build, and has blonde hair. Mary's opinion thus differs slightly from James's actual physical appearance. However, this does not necessarily mean that she is lying, or, indeed, that James was not her attacker. Her opinion simply represents what she perceived on the night in question. In particular, her perception of James as tall may be explained by the fact that she herself is small, and was comparing his height with her own. Likewise, the different hair tone could be explained by lighting conditions. Ultimately, it is for the jury to infer from her testimony whether James was, in fact, the assailant.

In this sense, the line between fact and opinion is not as clear-cut as it may prima facie appear. Ultimately, the accuracy of everything that a witness experiences first hand, and later relays to the court is dependent upon three key variables: perception, memory and recall. Even where a witness states something as simple as 'I saw Joe at the restaurant', he is relying upon his ability to correctly identify Joe as the person he believed that he saw.[1210] He is also depending upon his memory of what he perceived at the time, and upon his ability to retrieve the necessary details from his memory in order to articulate them to the court. It would be nonsensical to exclude identification evidence on the basis that it was only an opinion, as it may be particularly cogent and may carry a lot of weight in the eyes of the jury. At the end of the day, there may be no other form in which such evidence could be put before the court. As the Law Reform Committee noted:

> Unless opinions, estimates and inferences which men make in the daily lives reach without conscious ratiocination as a result of what they perceive with their physical senses were treated in the law of evidence as if they were statements of fact, the witnesses could find themselves unable to communicate to the judge an accurate impression of the events they were seeking to describe.[1211]

Another example of this blurred boundary between fact and opinion frequently arises in relation to the complainant's evidence in sex trials. As we saw in Chapter 4, a rape trial may frequently boil down to a battle of credibility between the defendant and the complainant as to whether the latter was consenting. Thus the defendant is entitled to express to the court his opinion that the victim was consenting. Indeed, without this information, he would be unable to establish his defence. In the same way, a complainant would be entitled to tell the court that it was clear to her that the accused knew that she was not consenting at the time of the intercourse. For that reason, the courts readily accept that witnesses may give evidence relatively freely about what they perceived and in what circumstances, even though some aspect of subjective interpretation in relation to perception or memory will naturally arise. It is therefore commonplace for witnesses to express opinions about appearance (such as age, hair/skin colour), the position or speed of vehicles, visibility, weather and related matters.

On occasions, witnesses may also give opinions *about* those matters which they have directly perceived. In *R v Davies*,[1212] the accused was tried for driving whilst unfit. There, the witness's opinion that the defendant was drunk was held to be admissible since the witness had spoken to the accused moments after he had collided with a stationary vehicle. However, it would have been wrong for him to proceed to give evidence that the accused

---

[1210]See discussion in Ch 1, pp 18–20, on identification evidence.
[1211]Law Reform Committee, *Evidence of Opinion and Expert Evidence*, Cmnd 4489 (1970: London, HMSO).
[1212][1962] 1 WLR 1111.

was unfit to drive, simply because he was a driver himself. Similarly, in *R v Tagg*,[1213] a passenger on board an aircraft was permitted to give evidence that the defendant appeared to have consumed excess alcohol. However, it should be underlined that witnesses in both these cases would have been expected to substantiate *why* they believed the defendants to be drunk. They may, for example, have referred to the defendants' unstable stance, slurred speech, smelly breath, etc. There are clear policy reasons as to why this should be so. Drunkenness in charge of a vehicle or on board an aircraft poses a significant risk to public safety, but, in the absence of a formal breath analysis, the chances of a successful prosecution are slim. Thus the opinion of the witness may provide the prosecution with a crucial additional string in their bow to corroborate any other evidence. For the same reason, section 89(2) of the Road Traffic Regulation Act 1984 allows witnesses to estimate the speed of a vehicle.[1214] Evidently, speed cameras cannot be everywhere all of the time, and if a victim happens to be injured or killed on the road due to excess speed, it may be difficult to establish this in the absence of concrete information from a speed camera. Thus, a witness's views about how fast a vehicle was travelling could serve to corroborate forensic evidence, such as tyre marks, and thus contribute towards the prosecution case against the suspect.

In certain circumstances, the courts have also permitted lay witnesses to give evidence of the mental state of another person. For example, in *Wright v Tatham*,[1215] a testator had left a substantial estate to his steward. The will was contested by Tatham, who would have stood to inherit the property upon intestacy. He alleged that the will should be regarded as invalid, given that the testator was insane. Counsel for Wright introduced letters to show that, in the opinion of the letter writer, their intended recipient (the testator) was sane. Applying this to the context of a criminal hearing, it follows that witnesses may express an opinion about the mental state of another person, providing they do not stray into territory that would require medical expertise. Take, for example, the following scenario. Billy is charged with murder, but his defence counsel alleges he was suffering from diminished responsibility at the material time. Billy's father Geoff testifies that his son seemed to be 'miserable, withdrawn and depressed' for a period of weeks before the alleged murder. This is merely an observation of a father about the mental state of his son, and may or may not constitute a correct assessment of Billy's state of mind. The jury may well choose to place a considerable degree of weight on this evidence if the father and son had a reasonably close relationship, but they could not infer from Geoff's testimony that Billy suffered from an abnormality of mind at the time of the attack. Instead, if the defence wish to establish that Billy was suffering from a recognised medical condition, they will need to call an expert, most probably a psychiatrist. While the opinions of a lay witness may give the factfinder a useful insight into the mental state of an individual, they must not stray into an area of expertise that is outside their knowledge or experience.

EXPERT EVIDENCE

In every trial on indictment, the jury will always be the ultimate adjudicator of questions of fact and it is self-evident that they will not be expected to be experts in all matters

---

[1213] [2002] 1 Cr App R 22.

[1214] However, the legislation also provides that a defendant cannot be convicted for speeding solely on the testimony of one particular witness.

[1215] (1838) 4 Bing NC 489. See above, Ch 7, p 215.

that they may be asked to decide upon. Moreover neither the judge nor the advocates may be competent to explain complex or technical issues to them. In the above scenario, for example, presumably none of them could have provided a diagnosis that Billy was suffering from an abnormality of mind. For that reason, the law of evidence has created an exception to the general principle that opinion evidence should not be admissible in criminal proceedings. Where real evidence is adduced that falls outside the ordinary knowledge or understanding of the court, experts may give their professional opinion and explain it, where it would otherwise be difficult for the jury to comprehend.

Traditionally, expert opinion evidence has predominantly fallen within well-established academic sciences, most commonly medicine and its allied forensic branches. There was traditionally widespread acceptance that members of professional bodies who held relevant qualifications would qualify to act as expert witnesses where their opinion was needed. Throughout the twentieth century, science and technology both rapidly advanced, and so too did the tendency of lawyers to rely on the testimony of experts to establish their cases. In particular, our understanding of forensics and DNA is constantly evolving, and what may be considered a standard methodology or finding today, may become debunked or superseded tomorrow. Thus, where either party in the trial wishes to rely on some form of real evidence that falls within such fields, it would be prudent for them to ensure that their expert's knowledge is up-to-date and that he or she is well respected within their field.

The evidence of pathologists, fingerprint experts, psychiatrists, ballistic experts and graphologists now plays a key role in case construction for both the defence and prosecution. It has also become increasingly commonplace to call experts from outside the traditional 'academic' sciences. It is no longer unusual for experts in engineering, computing and communications systems to give evidence. Likewise, in cases involving fraud, experts in business transactions, banking or accounting may testify. Dennis cites several examples where experts with more bizarre interests were called, including *Browning*[1216] (involving a specialist in identifying different models of the Renault 25), and *R v Cooper*[1217] (involving a zoologist specialising in the social behaviour of bottle-nosed dolphins). Certainly, so broad is the range of issues on which experts might potentially testify, that it would be impossible to devise any sort of exhaustive list that would cover them all.[1218]

However, as the range of fields of research continues to expand, and as the use of expert witnesses becomes ever more commonplace, questions are rightly being asked about when it is necessary to have an 'expert' give a view to the court. Where a party intends to rely on expert evidence, the trial judge will need to decide two matters. First, he or she must determine whether expert opinion is necessary; and second, he or she will need to determine whether the witness is adequately qualified to be regarded as an 'expert' before the court.

When is expert opinion necessary?

Not everything will be regarded as suitable for expert comment, and the general rule states that expert opinion will not be regarded as necessary where the matter in question does not

---

[1216] (1991) 94 Cr App R 109.

[1217] (1991) *The Times*, 13 December.

[1218] The UK Register of Expert Witnesses has currently over 17,000 entries in its subject list.

call for specific expertise. For example, in *R v Anderson*,[1219] the Court refused to admit expert evidence on the question whether certain articles in a satirical magazine were 'obscene' for the purposes of the Obscene Publications Act 1959; that was regarded as a question of fact for the jury to determine and it was not considered necessary for an expert to assist them in this task.[1220] By contrast, a different approach to an obscenity charge was taken in *DPP v A and BC Chewing Gum*.[1221] Here, the defendants had been charged with distributing obscene battle cards contrary to section 2(1) of the 1959 Act. The Divisional Court held that the magistrate had improperly refused the prosecution the opportunity to call an expert to testify about the likely impact of the cards upon the minds of children. Since the jury was composed of adults, it was felt that an expert was needed to help them determine how such cards might affect a child as young as five.

These two decisions reflect the general rule as laid down in *Turner*:[1222] if a particular issue does not require specialist knowledge, an expert should not be called and the matter should be left entirely to the jury. It should be noted, however, that the decision as to whether or not a matter requires expert comment will ultimately lie with the trial judge. There is thus no guarantee that what the judge determines to be a matter of common sense will not need clarification in the eyes of the jury. The particular facts of *Turner* provide a useful example. Here, D was charged with the murder of his girlfriend, and had admitted hitting her over the head with a hammer. However, the defendant raised the defence of provocation, and claimed that he lost his self-control after his girlfriend had admitted a string of affairs. The trial judge refused to grant leave for the defence to call a psychiatrist, who was prepared to testify that D suffered an immediate and explosive outburst of rage at the time of the attack. In the judge's view, the question as to whether or not D had lost his self-control was a question of fact for the jury, and should not be the subject of expert comment. Dismissing the appeal, the Court of Appeal found that the expert evidence need not have been admitted as, through their own experience of human nature and behaviour, the jurors were in a position to determine for themselves whether or not D had been so affected by the events in question so as to lose his self-control. In summary then, the fundamental principle is that the purpose of expert evidence is to provide the Court with information which is outside the experience and knowledge of a judge and jury. Where a particular matter falls within the knowledge and experience of the jury, or where it concerns an issue of human nature and behaviour within the limits of normality, expert evidence will not be admissible.

The application of Turner *to mental states*

Interestingly, had the accused in *Turner* pleaded insanity or diminished responsibility, expert evidence would have been invariably permitted.[1223] This underlines the fine line courts will have to draw in relation to mental states. Unless the accused is suffering from a recognised medical condition which impacts upon his or her state of mind, expert evidence will not usually be allowed. Thus, in *Hegarty*,[1224] the Court of Appeal stated that questions

---

[1219][1972] 1 QB 304.
[1220]See also *Stamford* [1972] 2 QB 391.
[1221][1968] 1 QB 159.
[1222][1975] 1 All ER 70.
[1223]See *R v Holmes* [1953] I WLR 686 and *R v Bailey* [1977] 66 Cr App R 31 respectively. Likewise, a defence of automatism will usually be deemed to fall outside the jury's normal experience, and experts may also testify in this regard: *Smith* [1979] 1 WLR 1445.
[1224][1994] Crim LR 353.

of emotional instability were not suitable for expert comment. Such a scenario also arose in *R v Toner*,[1225] where the Court of Appeal held that the defence had been wrongly prevented from asking a medical witness about the extent to which hypoglycaemia could impact upon the accused's ability to form specific intent. Similarly, in *R v Huckerby*,[1226] it was held that the jury were entitled to hear expert evidence concerning the impact of post-traumatic stress disorder.

Occasionally, expert evidence may also be used as part of the defence's case to have a confession excluded on grounds of unreliability.[1227] In *Ward*,[1228] it was held that expert testimony was admissible to show that the confession was unreliable as a result of a severe personality disorder. However, such evidence will not be admissible in cases where the accused was merely unstable or emotionally disturbed at the time of the confession; unless he or she suffers from a mental illness or is below the 'normal' intelligence threshold.[1229]

The courts are equally unwilling to admit expert evidence concerning the formation of intention or mens rea generally. In *Chard*[1230] the court determined that the expert opinion on such matters fell outside the scope of the *Turner* criteria. Here, the appellant had been convicted of murder, but appealed on the grounds that the trial judge had refused to allow a prison doctor to give evidence that, in the light of his personality, the accused could not have formed the requisite mens rea for murder. However, the Court of Appeal held that the trial judge was correct in refusing to allow expert opinion on this matter. Such evidence should only be admissible where D had an underlying medical condition which could interfere with his cognitive ability to form intention to kill or cause GBH. In a similar vein, in *R v Weightman*,[1231] a psychiatrist's evidence concerning the impact of stress upon the defendant was deemed inadmissible, and in *R v Browning* a psychologist was not permitted to testify as to the likely extent of memory loss in a normal witness.[1232] Even where the accused may have aspects of his personality which may be said to be abnormal, this will not justify admission where he is within the normal IQ range and is not suffering from a recognised medical condition.[1233] Yet this stipulation can prove contentious, as the case of *Masih*[1234] illustrates. Here, D was charged with rape, and one of the defendants alleged that he was forced to commit the crime by his co-accused. D had an IQ of 72, and wished to call a psychiatrist to testify that he was immature and easily led. In these circumstances, the Court of Appeal again rejected the need for expert testimony. Although D had a low IQ, it was still within the 'normal' range and thus medical evidence was unnecessary. Had the defendant scored below 70, he would have been classed as 'mentally defective' and expert evidence to this effect would have been admissible. Although the logic for this position is that the jury will be less able to comprehend the actions of someone whose mental state is not 'normal', such an artificial cut-off point raises the question as to whether justice can really be administered where the hands of the court are tied in such a rigid fashion.

[1225] (1991) 93 Cr App R 382.
[1226] Unreported, [2004] EWCA Crim 3251.
[1227] See Ch 8, pp 262–72.
[1228] [1993] 2 All ER 577. See further below, p 326.
[1229] *Smith* [2003] EWCA Crime 927.
[1230] [1971] 56 Cr App R 268.
[1231] (1991) 92 Cr App R 291.
[1232] [1995] Crim LR 227.
[1233] *R v Wood* [1990] Crim LR 264.
[1234] [1986] Crim LR 395.

Just as experts cannot usually comment on the state of mind of an accused, neither should they comment on the state of mind of a victim. In *Gilfoyle*,[1235] a woman's body was found hanging in a garage. The prosecution alleged she had been murdered by her husband, whereas the defence contended that the victim had committed suicide. They wished to call a forensic psychologist, who would review the life of the deceased and her medical records, and ultimately corroborate the defence's case that she was likely to have taken her own life. The evidence was excluded on the basis of *Turner* by the trial judge. This decision was subsequently upheld by the Court of Appeal on the grounds that an expert was no better placed to determine 'levels of happiness or unhappiness' than a lay person. The Court cited two main reasons why his evidence should not be put before the court:

> First... he had never previously embarked on the task which he set himself in this case. Secondly, his reports identify no criteria by reference to which the court could test the quality of his opinion, there is no database comparing real and questionable studies and there is no substantial body of academic writing approving his methodology.[1236]

Although the courts have generally remained loyal to the rule on *Turner*, there are a few cases that sit somewhat uncomfortably alongside it. In *Lowery v R*,[1237] two co-defendants ran a cut-throat defence, each alleging that the other was to blame for the murder of an adolescent girl. One of the accused, K, successfully applied to the court to have a forensic psychologist testify to the fact that he was immature, vulnerable, easily led and that he tended to be dominated by his co-accused, L, who had a much more dominant and aggressive character. In addition, the psychologist stated that L had a much more callous and impulsive personality and was not capable of relating well to others. In the view of the Privy Council, this evidence was admissible since it would have been unfair to K to have excluded it, since it tended to show his innocence. Where a party seeks to establish that a defendant is prone to certain forms of behaviour, but is not necessarily mentally defective, *Lowery* seems to indicate that expert evidence may be admissible depending on the particular circumstances of the case.

Although *Lowery* remains good law, there can be no doubting that it is something of an anathema to the line taken in the other decisions discussed above. In *Turner* itself, the Court of Appeal suggested that the decision in *Lowery* was based on its own particular facts, and did not have any wider application. This line was followed in *Rimmer*,[1238] where an accused attempted to show it was more likely to be his co-accused who killed the victim as he had a history of mental illness. Here, the Court of Appeal upheld the decision of the trial judge. However, the House of Lords decision in *R v Randall*[1239] suggests that *Lowery* should be viewed as constituting a categorical exception to *Turner*. In *Randall* two co-defendants, R and G, had been jointly charged with murder. As in *Lowery*, each defendant ran a cut-throat defence, and alleged that the other inflicted the fatal blows. Whilst both co-accused had previous convictions, G had a considerably more serious record, which included convictions for violent burglary and robbery. The judge had directed the jury that the evidence undermining G's character was only relevant to the issue of credibility, and did

---

[1235] [2001] Cr App R 5.

[1236] *Ibid.*, [25]. See further *The Times*, 25 February 2008. One of the experts who prepared an initial report for the CPS (but was refused permission to testify for the prosecution at trial) has since changed his mind in light of new research and is now convinced that the suicide note was genuine. His revised report is likely to form the basis of a fresh submission to the Criminal Cases Review Commission.

[1237] [1974] AC 85.

[1238] [1983] Crim LR 250.

[1239] [2004] 1 WLR 56.

not have any bearing on whether G actually committed the offence. Subsequently, R was convicted of manslaughter and G was acquitted. R appealed, arguing that the evidence concerning G's propensity to use and threaten violence was not relevant to the issue of whether R had inflicted the fatal blows. The House of Lords proceeded to state that the propensity to violence of a co-accused may be relevant to the issues between the Crown and the accused tendering such evidence. As such, this would appear to imply that expert evidence to this effect would be admissible.

On the basis of *Randall*, it would thus seem that where D1 wishes to call an expert to testify against D2, even where both defendants are within the 'normal' psychological range, this will be regarded as relevant and admissible evidence insofar as it relates to character or psychological profiles. Admittedly, however, the House of Lords did not go so far as to state this and, as a result, some degree of legal uncertainty continues. Certainly, there seems to be little logical basis for one co-defendant to be able to call an expert against another, but the prosecution cannot call one in a trial against a single defendant. This anomaly, we assume, will have to be dealt with by the higher courts in due course.

All these decisions illustrate the relatively high level of faith that is placed both in juries to arrive at factual judgements, and in the ability of judges to make a determination whether something is or is not viable for expert comment. While the overall trend seems to indicate a marked reluctance to call experts too readily, there is a danger that the lack of clear guidance as to when experts should be called could result in inconsistent decisions. In questionable contrast to the line of authorities discussed above, in *Emery*[1240] the Court of Appeal seemed quite happy to allow an expert to opine on degrees of happiness or unhappiness in admitting the testimony of a counsellor that the accused had been helpless and unable to protect her child from paternal abuse. In *Humphreys*,[1241] the accused ran the defence of provocation, and was able to call upon a psychiatrist to testify to the fact that she was a compulsive attention seeker and was prone to sudden and irrational behaviour. Indeed, there are some cases where the appellate courts have criticised one of the parties for failing to produce expert witnesses. One such example was *Toohey v MPC*,[1242] where the Court of Appeal underlined that an expert should have been allowed to explain to the jury that alcohol may exacerbate hysteria, since the victim of an offence was more prone to hysteria than other people.

Determining the competency of experts

The increasingly diverse range of matters which lend themselves to expert testimony highlights the fact that the courts must take steps to ensure that all who purport to be experts have a sufficient level of competency in their fields. In the traditional sciences, such as medicine, membership of a professional body such as the Royal College of Physicians, would generally suffice. However, as fields of research become simultaneously broader and deeper, it becomes apparent that given individuals have a limited degree of expertise, even within their own particular field. The degree of knowledge and understanding any given person has will vary tremendously. For example, a recent medical graduate may well know more about coronary heart disease than the average lay person, but will know less than a junior doctor with two years' experience, and presumably will be much less well-informed than a clinical professor of coronary medicine. Yet that same professor of medicine, owing

---

[1240] (1993) 14 Cr App R (S) 394.
[1241] [1954] All ER 1008.
[1242] [1965] AC 595.

to the specialist nature of his work, may know no more than the medical graduate about
the most effective drugs that may be used to treat kidney disease, or the latest innovations
in chemotherapy treatment. By contrast, only a century ago, medicine, engineering and
other scientific disciplines were considerably less specialised. Experts called to court may
have had a broader knowledge base than their peers, although obviously the depth of that
knowledge was considerably less given the rapid advances made in science and technology
in the past few decades.

Unlike most other witnesses who testify, experts will not have perceived any of the
contested events at first hand. Many of their opinions about the case will be based primarily
on speculation about certain hypotheses that will be put to them by counsel. Given that
the jury may well attach significant weight to the evidence presented by someone who is a
highly educated and respected professional, it is vital for the integrity of the criminal trial
that those who are called to give evidence are qualified to do so. As Bingham LJ stated in
R v Robb:[1243]

> We are alive to the risk that if, in a criminal case, the Crown are permitted to call an expert
> witness of some, but tenuous, qualifications the burden of proof may imperceptibly shift and
> a burden be cast on the defendant to rebut a case which should never have been before a
> jury at all. A defendant cannot be fairly asked to meet evidence of opinion given by a quack,
> a charlatan or an enthusiastic amateur.[1244]

On occasions, legislation will lay down specific stipulations as to qualifications that a
particular expert should hold. For example, legislation provides that a jury should not
acquit on grounds of insanity or arrive at a finding of unfitness to plead unless evidence
to this effect is provided by two or more medical experts who have been approved by the
Secretary of State.[1245] For the most part however, competency in a particular field will be
a question for the judge to determine within a *voir dire*. It will be for the party calling the
witness to establish, on the balance of probabilities, that the witness is competent to give
an expert opinion to the court.

The competency of the expert, Professor Sir Roy Meadow, was one of the key points
of contention to arise from the *Sally Clark* case (see above). Whilst Sir Roy was a highly
renowned paediatrician, he was neither trained in, nor had he any expertise in, statistics.
The odds that he presented to the court of 1:73 million of two cot deaths within the same
family were found by the Court of Appeal to be extremely dubious, as Sir Roy had not taken
into account other relevant variables such as sleep patterns, genetic determinations, type of
bedding and general living conditions. In the view of the Court, the prosecution's reliance
on this evidence had contravened the core rule that an expert should not give evidence on
any matter outside their own field of expertise.

Arguably, the fault for this miscarriage of justice lay not with Sir Roy, or even the
prosecution, but with the trial judge. It is, after all, the responsibility of the trial judge to
ensure that an expert witness is adequately qualified and to determine what information
the factfinder should take into account. However, case law suggests that the judicial
intervention on this point is relatively inconsistent, and there is certainly no blanket test of
expert competence that can be applied as to what precisely an expert is or is not qualified to

---

[1243](1991) 93 Cr App R 161.

[1244]*Ibid.*, 166.

[1245]One of whom should be approved by the Secretary of State as having special experience in the diagnosis
or treatment of mental disorders. Regarding unfitness to plead, see section 1(1) Criminal Procedure (Insanity
and Fitness to Plead) Act 1991. Regarding fitness to stand trial, see section 4 Criminal Procedure (Insanity)
Act 1964.

say. Certainly, professional qualifications may be a good indicator of expertise, but, as the *Clark* case illustrates, even well-established experts with numerous qualifications can still make mistakes. Thus while judges should rightly attach a considerable degree of weight to the qualifications of a witness, they should not be the ultimate determinant. Indeed, in many cases, they have not even been a prerequisite. In *Silverlock*,[1246] the court accepted the expert evidence of a solicitor who undertook the study of handwriting as a hobby in his spare time; and in *Ajami v Controller of Customs*,[1247] an experienced Nigerian bank official was permitted to give evidence of banking law in Nigeria, even though he had no legal qualifications. Sometimes resorting to experts who hold no formal qualifications reflects the fact that experts in these fields are difficult to find. For example, in *Hodges*,[1248] a police officer gave expert testimony as to the market for heroin dealing in a particular vicinity, and in *Dallagher*,[1249] expert evidence was given by a Dutch police officer who had worked with ear prints for over 10 years, even though he had no forensic qualifications. His evidence was accepted alongside that of a leading professor of forensic medicine, and it was acknowledged that was a new and emerging field of forensics with little consensus in the scientific community. However, the Court of Appeal seemed to analyse 'expertise' as something of a spectrum in stating that both scientific and non-scientific testimony should be subject to the 'ordinary tests of relevance and reliability'. In doing so, the Court seemed to overlook the fact that forensic science, by its very nature, demands to be subjected to a specialist and scientific standard, rather than that used by the courts to receive non-specialist evidence.[1250]

The courts have now accepted that the difficulty in finding suitably qualified experts in new or emerging fields means that, on occasions, the court may have to forego the desirability of formal qualifications and rely on experience or personal knowledge instead. In *R v Clare and Peach*,[1251] a police officer had undertaken a prolonged study of a poor quality video-recording in order to gauge what precisely was happening in the footage. Although he had no personal qualifications in reading such footage or facial mapping (see below), the court held that his experience in watching the video some 40 times in slow motion had qualified him to make expert comment.

Of course, acquisition of a skill through experience will depend very much on the nature of the particular field. We can safely assume that the police officer in *Clare and Peach* could not have acquired through experience a skill such as forensic pathology, consulting engineering or psychiatry. Since these established fields of expertise are all subject to regulation by professional bodies, there is usually little problem in finding someone who is well qualified to comment on a particular matter. Indeed, the Council for the Registration of Forensic Practitioners has maintained a database of competent practitioners in 13 specified fields, and plans are currently under consideration for a similar registration scheme for forensic psychologists.[1252] However, this is not the case with all disciplines, and indeed there is some controversy as to whether the skills of some of the experts who testify have any scientific basis at all.

[1246][1894] 2 QB 766.

[1247][1954] 1 WLR 1405.

[1248][2003] 2 Cr App R 15.

[1249][2003] 1 Cr App R 195.

[1250]See further O'Brian, W 'Scrutiny of Expert Evidence: Recent Decisions Highlight the Tensions' (2003) 7 E & P 172.

[1251][1995] 2 Cr App R 333.

[1252]See Department of Health, *Applied Psychology, Enhancing Public Protection* (2005: London, Department of Health).

In *R v Luttrell*,[1253] the prosecution were attempting to show that the defendant was involved in a criminal conspiracy with several others. As part of the case against him, they sought to call a lip-reading expert, H, who had analysed CCTV footage of a conversation between the men. The ability to lip-read from televised evidence was such a specialised area that, at the time of the trial, there were apparently only four other people in the United Kingdom who would have been considered to have had the necessary expertise to testify in court. Before the Court of Appeal, the appellant argued that lip reading evidence from video footage had never been shown to be reliable, and should therefore have been inadmissible. This argument was, however, rejected by the Court. Lip reading itself was a well-recognised skill and lip reading from video footage was merely a further application of that skill, notwithstanding that it may increase the difficulty of the task. Noting that it was 'entirely appropriate' for the level of expertise to be challenged in court in order to establish the credibility of the expert, the Court stated that trawling through the track record of the witness should not be repeated at subsequent trials. In an ironic twist, at another trial shortly afterwards, the defence was able to illustrate significant cracks in H's CV. Shortly afterwards, the CPS announced that they were reviewing all files where H had been involved and would not be calling her again.[1254]

Lip-reading is just one field of expertise that has been regarded with some degree of suspicion; other relatively novel and narrow fields within the realm of science and medicine have been similarly questioned. These have included the existence of Gulf War Syndrome and Battered Women Syndrome. Particular concern seems to focus on the use of voice identification techniques, and facial mapping evidence, both of which are becoming increasingly commonplace in criminal trials.

The leading case regarding voice identification is that of *R v Robb*.[1255] Here, a highly trained and experienced voice identification expert gave evidence, even though he relied on a particular methodology that was accepted by many of his peers to be unreliable since it did not adopt acoustic analysis. Moreover, the expert had produced no empirical findings that were capable of lending weight to the reliability of his method. Despite the appellant arguing his evidence should be regarded as unreliable, the Court of Appeal found that just because he held a minority viewpoint in his field, it would be wrong of the courts to exclude his evidence on that basis. Ultimately, it was for the judge to determine whether the expert had sufficient expertise, and it was sufficient that he had directed the jury that the opinion of the expert was not binding upon them. In the opinion of the judge, the expert was an experienced academic who had completed a doctorate and published widely in the area. On that basis, the expert was qualified to testify. This decision, however, remains the source of some consternation, particularly given the fact that the judge had not explained to the jury the fact that they ought to pay attention to the fact that the expert held a minority academic opinion.[1256]

So-called 'facial mapping' has also attracted considerable debate in recent years.[1257] Facial mapping basically involves comparing two images of the accused. Generally one of these images will have been retrieved from the crime scene, most commonly using CCTV

[1253][2004] 2 Cr App R 31.

[1254]See further Jackson, S. 'Read my Lips' 154 *New Law Journal* 1146.

[1255]See p 320 above.

[1256]cf *R v O'Doherty* [2003] 1 Cr App R 77, where the Northern Ireland Court of Appeal rejected voice identification evidence where acoustic analysis had not been adopted. See further Ormerod, D 'Sounding out expert voice identification' [2002] Crim LR 771.

[1257]See generally Costigan, R 'Identification from CCTV: the risk of injustice' [2007] Crim LR 591.

or video stills. The appellant in *R v Stockwell*[1258] had been convicted of a bank robbery. Since the robber was disguised, the prosecution sought to identify him through the testimony of an expert in facial mapping. The Court of Appeal rejected the appellant's contention that there was no need for expert evidence on such a matter, and stated that the expert's evidence could provide the jury with a useful basis on which to conduct their fact-finding exercise.

In *R v Clarke*,[1259] another case involving a bank robbery, the appellant argued that the technique of facial mapping was so novel that it was fundamentally unfair to allow an expert to testify at trial against the accused. It was suggested that evidence obtained in such a way should have been excluded under section 78 of the Police and Criminal Evidence Act 1984. Rejecting this argument, the Court held that the technique of facial mapping was a form of real evidence, to which no different rules applied. However, if such evidence was not sufficiently intelligible to a jury, then an expert's opinion could be called upon in order to assist the jury in their interpretation of the real evidence. The probative value of such evidence depended on the reliability of the scientific technique, which was a matter of fact, and had been fully explored in the *voir dire*. The trial judge had been fully justified in admitting the evidence. The Court added that it would be slow to prevent experts from testifying in novel fields, since new techniques were constantly developing in relation to criminal investigations:

> There are no closed categories where such evidence may be placed before a jury. It would be entirely wrong to deny to the law of evidence the advantages to be gained from new techniques and new advances in science.[1260]

The case of *R v Hookway* required more careful consideration.[1261] Unlike *Stockwell* and *Clarke*, the case against the accused was based on facial mapping alone. Since there was no corroborating evidence linking the defendant to the crime scene, the appellant argued that his conviction should not have been based solely on the opinion of the expert. This contention was rejected by the Court, who noted that the images were of exceptionally high quality and, as such, the evidence was highly probative. However, this decision underlines the fact that the cogency of the evidence will always be a matter of degree. Had the video stills in this case been taken from a greater distance, or under poorer light, it may well have been determined that the evidence of the expert in itself would not have been a sound basis for the conviction.

Limitations on expert evidence

The freedom of the expert to testify is not unfettered. Experts must confine their comments to matters that fall within their area of competence. They may outline the results of research conducted by themselves or their peers, or present an overview of the current state of knowledge. They should, however, be prepared to corroborate their evidence if challenged by citing other admissible evidence. It is therefore not unusual for experts to refer to their own works, experiments, scientific data, and publications, but they may also cite other authorities and works within their field. Under cross-examination, the

---

[1258] [1993] 97 Cr App R 260.
[1259] [1995] 99 2 Cr App R 425.
[1260] *Ibid.*, 430.
[1261] [1999] Crim LR 750.

expert should also be prepared to be asked about the significance of any contradictory studies.

In defending their opinion, experts are not curtailed by the hearsay rule to the same extent as non-expert witnesses. For example, a pathologist may wish to rely on primary facts discovered by a member of his or her staff during an investigation. Strictly speaking, if the individual pathologist did not uncover those facts, he or she should not testify about them, since to do so would infringe the hearsay rule. However, under section 127 of the Criminal Justice Act 2003, it is permissible for experts to give an opinion based on any primary facts where the investigation was carried out by an assistant.[1262] Experts may also wish to explain the basis of their opinion through citing findings or studies by others in their field. They may legitimately refer to such works as the basis of a particular opinion, and there is no requirement that any direct evidence be submitted to the court. Ultimately, it would be impractical for every witness to be able to account for and defend the findings of every piece of information they have ever absorbed, and it would be equally unrealistic to call other experts to verify that studies of theirs which may have been referred to were accurate and relied upon in the correct context. In *R v Abadom*,[1263] the expert testified concerning the refractive index of a piece of glass found in the shoe of the defendant, who was charged with robbery. The expert proceeded to state that as the refractive index in question would be found in only 4 per cent of all glass, the piece found in the shoe was highly likely to have come from the window of the premises, since it had the same refractive index. The appellant argued that the expert had no personal knowledge of the analysis on which these statistics were based since, by his own admission, he had relied on unpublished statistics provided to him by the Home Office. The Court of Appeal rejected this contention, and stated that part of the reason for calling experts in the first place was their knowledge of, and ability to, interpret unpublished data. Provided the expert had acknowledged the source as the basis for his findings, such evidence was admissible. Ultimately, if the source on which the expert is relying appears to the court to be especially weak or overly speculative, there is nothing to prevent the judge excluding it under section 78 of PACE or at common law.[1264]

Traditionally, a further limitation on the expert's role was the operation of the 'ultimate issue rule' at common law. This prevented experts (and indeed all witnesses) from commenting on anything that was properly to be determined by the jury. For example, if an expert were explaining to the court that the fingerprints on a murder weapon matched a sample that the accused had provided to the police, the common law originally stated that he or she should not proceed to comment that D fired the weapon to kill V. The rationale behind this position was to prevent the lay jury being swayed by the reasoning process of someone who was likely to be highly educated and well-renowned within a specialism. Over the years, however, the ultimate issue rule has largely fallen into disuse, and experts may now express an opinion on those issues which do ultimately fall to the jury for determination. As Parker CJ remarked in *DPP v A & BC Chewing Gum*:[1265]

> Those who practise in the criminal courts see every day cases of experts being called on the question of diminished responsibility, and although technically the final question 'Do you

---

[1262]Provided that the information supplied by the assistant related to matters which the assistant had, or might reasonably be supposed to have had, personal knowledge. The court may decline, however, to admit such information where it would be contrary to the interests of justice under subs (4).
[1263][1983] 1 All ER 364.
[1264]Dennis, op cit n 1210, p 871.
[1265][1968] 1 QB 159.

think he was suffering from diminished responsibility?' is strictly inadmissible, it is allowed time and again without objection.[1266]

As the above dictum suggests, in practice it is now commonplace for experts to express opinions on what technically should be matters for the jury. Arguably however, this may be no bad thing, given that their specialist qualifications may mean that they are better placed to express such an opinion than lay witnesses. However, it remains the case that judges should intervene where the expert comments on an ultimate issue that is unrelated to his field of expertise. In *R v Doheny and Adams*,[1267] the Court of Appeal reprimanded a scientist giving an opinion as to the probability of a random match between DNA found at the crime scene, and that gathered from a sample provided by the defendant. While it was legitimate for the expert to explain the match between the DNA samples, he or she should not go so far so as to give an opinion on the chances of the defendant having left a stain at the crime scene as he was not qualified to do so. Furthermore, even where the expert does confine his comments to the scope of his field, the judge should issue a warning to the jury that it is not bound to adopt the opinion presented by the expert.[1268] The jury are thus free to reject expert evidence as they see fit, and where they choose to do so this will not generally give rise to a ground for appeal. In *Lanfear*[1269] the Court of Appeal declined to quash the applicant's conviction for murder despite strong medical evidence at the trial that he was insane at the time of the killing. However, at the same time, the appellate courts may quash a conviction where they feel that the jury has gone as far so as to act contrary to the weight of the evidence. The murder conviction in *R v Bailey* was quashed in these circumstances, since the prosecution had failed to rebut evidence adduced by a defence expert suggesting the accused suffered from diminished responsibility.

Contesting expert evidence

One of the most frequent criticisms of the adversarial system is that, since parties are in charge of the evidence they present, they will actively seek out an expert whose evidence is likely to favour their case. There have certainly been a number of notorious cases where the expert's evidence has fallen well short of being objective, and in North America it is not uncommon for parties to vet dozens of potential experts in order to find the one that will paint their case in the most favourable light. However, the idea that experts can simply be paid a fee to say what the advocate desires is probably still some way off the mark in England. Although the principle of free proof dictates that experts will generally support the case of the party that calls them, it should be underlined that an expert's primary duty is towards the court.[1270] In addition to giving an objective account of the evidence, the expert is under an obligation to inform the court if he or she did not have the necessary level of expertise within a particular area or if there is insufficient evidence on which to express an opinion.[1271] If an expert fails to understand this duty to the court, then he or she should be debarred from giving evidence.[1272]

[1266] *Ibid.*, at 164.
[1267] [1997] 1 Cr App R 369.
[1268] *R v Stockwell* (1993) 97 Cr App R 260. See further Jackson, J 'The Ultimate Issue Rule: One Rule Too Many' [1984] Crim LR 75.
[1269] [1968] 2 QB 77
[1270] *National Justice Compania Naviera v Prudential Assurance Co Ltd* [1995] I Lloyd's Rep 455.
[1271] *Ibid.*
[1272] *Stevens v Gullis* [2000] 1 All ER 527.

Furthermore, if, in the course of investigations, an expert should come across evidence that would tend to contradict or cast doubt upon his original opinion, he is under an obligation to inform the solicitor who has instructed him. This was another problem that arose in the Sally Clark case; a pathologist had failed to disclose that, in one of the two deceased children, a form of potentially lethal bacteria had been isolated during a post-mortem examination. Indeed, on occasions, the desire of experts to assist the prosecutor instructing them has caused them to depart from objectivity and be selective in their investigations, the results that are disclosed, or what they may say in court. The most notorious case where this occurred was that of Judith Ward,[1273] who had been convicted for the murder of 12 people aboard a military coach in 1974. Having spent 18 years in prison, her conviction was quashed by the Court of Appeal in 1992 who felt that three government scientists had put objectivity to one side in an effort to help the police secure a conviction. In the view of the Court:

> [We] have identified the cause of the injustice done to the appellant on the scientific side of the case as stemming from the fact that three senior forensic scientists at RARDE regarded their task as being to help the police. They became partisan. It is the clear duty of government forensic scientists to assist in a neutral and impartial way in criminal investigations. They must act in the cause of justice. That duty should be spelt out to all engaged or to be engaged in forensic services in the clearest terms.[1274]

Such cases underline the fact that, just because an expert is highly trained and well renowned in a particular field, that does not necessarily mean that the evidence that eventually comes before the trier of fact will be accurate. Furthermore, even if experts do testify faithfully to the best of their ability, their opinion may not be shared by others within the scientific community.

In such cases, there is a clear risk that unless the defence are able to counter prosecution evidence with expertise of their own, the weight placed on expert evidence by the jury may result in a de facto reversal of the burden of proof. After all, it is ultimately for them to determine whether or not to accept the opinion presented by the expert. They are not under any obligation to do so,[1275] but by the same token, they should not be instructed that they may ignore such evidence if they so choose.[1276] From the point of view of a lay juror, the fact-finding task may be complicated by the fact that there may exist a grey area between what constitutes an ascertainable forensic 'fact' and what amounts to a well-informed, though entirely subjective opinion. Certainly, the trial judge will bear a considerable burden in formulating a correct direction that instructs the jury in an appropriate and objective fashion.

There are no easy solutions to the difficulties relating to expert evidence. Certainly the courts seem reluctant to move on the issue, bar offering some generic guidance on the contents of experts' reports.[1277] It seems any reform will be dependent upon the action of government. In his Review of the Criminal Courts of England and Wales, Lord Justice Auld recommended the establishment of a new governing body to oversee standards and maintain a register of experts from all disciplines. Inclusion of an individual's name on the register would serve as an indicator of competence, thereby sidestepping the need for

---

[1273] *R v Ward* [1993] 2 All ER 577.
[1274] *Ibid.*, 628.
[1275] *R v Stockwell* (1993) 97 Cr App R 260.
[1276] *Anderson v R* [1972] AC 100.
[1277] See comments of Gage LJ in *R v Lorraine Harris & Others* [2006] 1 Cr App R 5.

lengthy adversarial argument as to whether a particular expert was credible or not.[1278] At the time of writing, several organisations maintain databases or registers of experts, who have been vetted with varying degrees of rigour. These include the Society of Expert Witnesses, the Academy of Experts, the Expert Witness Institute, the Law Society, the UK Register of Expert Witnesses and the Council for the Regulation of Forensic Practitioners.[1279] In spite of the growing number of such bodies, inclusion of a name on their lists cannot be taken to be an absolute assurance of reliability. In the same way, there may be many other competent professionals who, for one reason or another, are not included on any such registers.

As an alternative to a unified or court-approved register, other jurisdictions have attempted to overcome some of the problems discussed above in more radical ways including:

- The introduction of legislation which would regulate more closely expert accreditation in some of the more contentious fields of science to have emerged in recent years. However, this may be seen as tying the hands of trial judges, and could prove overly limiting.

- The accreditation of a small pool of experts as 'court approved'. Such a move would avoid lengthy courtroom battles about the credibility of witnesses, but the vetting procedure could prove costly and complex. Furthermore, there is a risk that experts who subscribe to minority views on unpopular theories would never be heard by juries. Issues would also arise as to how such experts should be selected and whether the prosecution or defence could object to their evidence.

- A single expert or a small conference of experts could be summoned to a pre-trial conference to devise a report on any contentious issues. This option could also prove costly, but the main problem would be that counsel would not have the opportunity to cross-examine the experts in court. This is the system followed in most inquisitorial jurisdictions, although the parties normally have the power to call their own expert evidence if so desired.

- A similar proposal would involve the use of a court-appointed expert at the application of either party. This is currently the approach adopted in civil proceedings.[1280]

- Both the prosecution and defence could be obliged to agree on a single expert who would conduct investigations and testify at trial. Such an approach would sit very uneasily within the adversarial paradigm as it would interfere with the principle of free proof. Furthermore, it may arguably interfere with a defendant's right to be able to effectively challenge all evidence adduced against him.

- A 'general acceptance' test could be adopted. This approach was followed by the US courts until the Federal Rules of Evidence were introduced in 1972. In order to be admitted, expert evidence had to have been 'sufficiently established to have gained general acceptance in the field where it belongs'.[1281] Again, however, such an approach is open to the objection that it would exclude minority viewpoints, which may be perfectly valid.

[1278] Auld, Sir Robin *Review of the Criminal Courts of England and Wales*, Cmnd 9376 (2002: London, HMSO), [129]–[151].

[1279] The latter receives a subsidy from the Home Office.

[1280] Civil Procedure Rules, r 35.10.

[1281] *Frye v United States* (1923) 293 F 1013. The strict test itself now applied is slightly different, and can be found is Rule 702.

- The current approach in the USA gives the courts greater discretion through following a 'checklist' of points in order to ensure the expert is competent in his field.[1282]

Many of these options, however, would be likely to face stiff opposition by lawyers, policymakers, or experts themselves, who are handsomely remunerated for their time. As technology and forensic science continue to advance into new fields, expert evidence seems set to become an evermore familiar aspect of the adversarial trial.

KEY LEARNING POINTS

- The general rule is that opinion evidence is inadmissible in court.
- For lay witnesses, opinion evidence may be admitted by eyewitnesses where it is difficult to separate it from the facts.
- A further exception applies to expert witnesses, who may give opinions provided (a) it is beyond the ordinary knowledge of the jury and (b) they are adequately qualified to do so.
- Expert opinion regarding mental states is not usually admissible, unless the subject suffers from a medical condition which affects his or her mental state, or is classed as being mentally sub-normal.
- Expert evidence remains contentious following a number of high profile miscarriages of justice. Particularly polemical is the role of experts in new or emerging fields of science and medicine.

? | QUESTIONS

1. 'The general rule is that expert evidence of a psychologist or psychiatrist is inadmissible where the defendant is a normal person'
    To what extent does the above statement accurately reflect English law?

2. Graeme is called to testify against Hugh, who is on trial for causing death by dangerous driving. Graeme was at the pub with Hugh on the evening in question. They had several pints of beer together, followed by some whisky. As they left the pub, Hugh appeared unstable on his feet and fell over twice. Graeme advised Hugh that he was very drunk and should not drive home, but Hugh ignored this advice and proceeded to get into his car before driving off. Will Graeme be able to tell the court that Hugh was unfit to drive?

3. Molly has recently been diagnosed with depression. She finds it difficult to concentrate and is easily agitated. She has recently been charged with the murder of her friend, Alisa, and wishes to run the defence of diminished responsibility. Will the defence be able to call an expert to testify in connection with these matters?

Continued

[1282]See *Daubert v Merrell Dow Pharmaceuticals* 113 S Ct 2786 (1993). These are: whether a theory or technique is scientific knowledge that will assist the trier of fact and whether it can be (and has been) tested; whether the theory or technique has been subjected to peer review and publication; the known or potential rate of error; and whether or not there is widespread acceptance of a particular technique.

> ? **QUESTIONS** *(Continued)*
>
> 4. Andrew and Zack are charged with inflicting GBH on George contrary to section 18 of the Offences Against the Person Act 1861. Andrew alleges he kept watch while Zack beat George with a cricket bat in a nearby alleyway. Zack claims he kept watch while Andrew attacked George. Andrew's counsel wishes to call a forensic psychologist to testify that Zack was more likely than Andrew to have carried out the attack since he has an aggressive personality and is prone to violent outbursts. Will he be allowed to do this?

SUGGESTED FURTHER READING

Alldridge, P 'Forensic science and expert evidence' (1994) 21 *Journal of Law and Society* 136.

Costigan, R 'Identification from CCTV: the risk of injustice' [2007] Crim LR 591.

Milroy, C 'Medical experts and the criminal courts' (2003) 326 *British Medical Journal* 294.

Ormerod, D 'Sounding out expert voice identification' [2002] Crim LR 771.

Ormerod, D 'Psychological autopsies: Legal implications and admissibility' (2001) 5 *International Journal of Evidence and Proof* 1.

Redmayne, M *Expert evidence and criminal justice* (2001, Oxford: Oxford University Press).

Roberts, P and Willmore, C (1993) *The role of forensic science evidence in criminal proceedings*, RCCJ Research Study No 11 (London, HMSO).

INDEX